MULTIMEDIA BASICS

Suzanne Weixel
Jennifer Fulton
Karl Barksdale
Cheryl Morse
Bryan Morse

THOMSON

COURSE TECHNOLOGY

Australia • Canada • Mexico • Singapore • Spain • United Kingdom • United States

Multimedia BASICS

By Suzanne Weixel, Jennifer Fulton, Karl Barksdale,
Cheryl Morse, and Bryan Morse

Senior Vice President
Chris Elkhill

Managing Editor
Chris Katsaropoulos

Senior Product Manager
Dave Lafferty

Product Manager
Robert Gaggin

Product Marketing Manager
Kim Ryttel

Associate Product Manager
Jodi Dreissig

Development Editor
Custom Editorial Productions Inc.

Production Editor
Anne Chimenti, Custom Editorial
Productions Inc.

Compositor
GEX Publishing Services

Disclaimer
Course Technology reserves the right to revise this publication and make changes from time to time in its content without notice.

Microsoft and the Office logo are either registered trademarks or trademarks of the Microsoft Corporation in the United States and/or other countries. Course Technology/Thomson Learning is an independent entity from Microsoft Corporation and not affiliated with Microsoft Corporation in any manner. Macromedia is a registered trademark of Macromedia, Inc. Adobe is a trademark of Adobe Systems Incorporated.

ISBN 0-619-05533-2 (hard cover)
ISBN 0-619-05535-9 (soft cover)

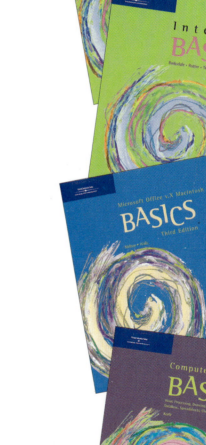

How to Use This Book

What makes a good computer instructional text? Sound pedagogy and the most current, complete materials. Not only will you find an inviting layout, but also many features to enhance learning.

Objectives— Objectives are listed at the beginning of each lesson, along with a suggested time for completion of the lesson. This allows you to look ahead to what you will be learning and to pace your work.

Step-by-Step Exercises—Preceded by a short topic discussion, these exercises are the "hands-on practice" part of the lesson. Simply follow the steps, either using a data file or creating a file from scratch. Each lesson is a series of these step-by-step exercises.

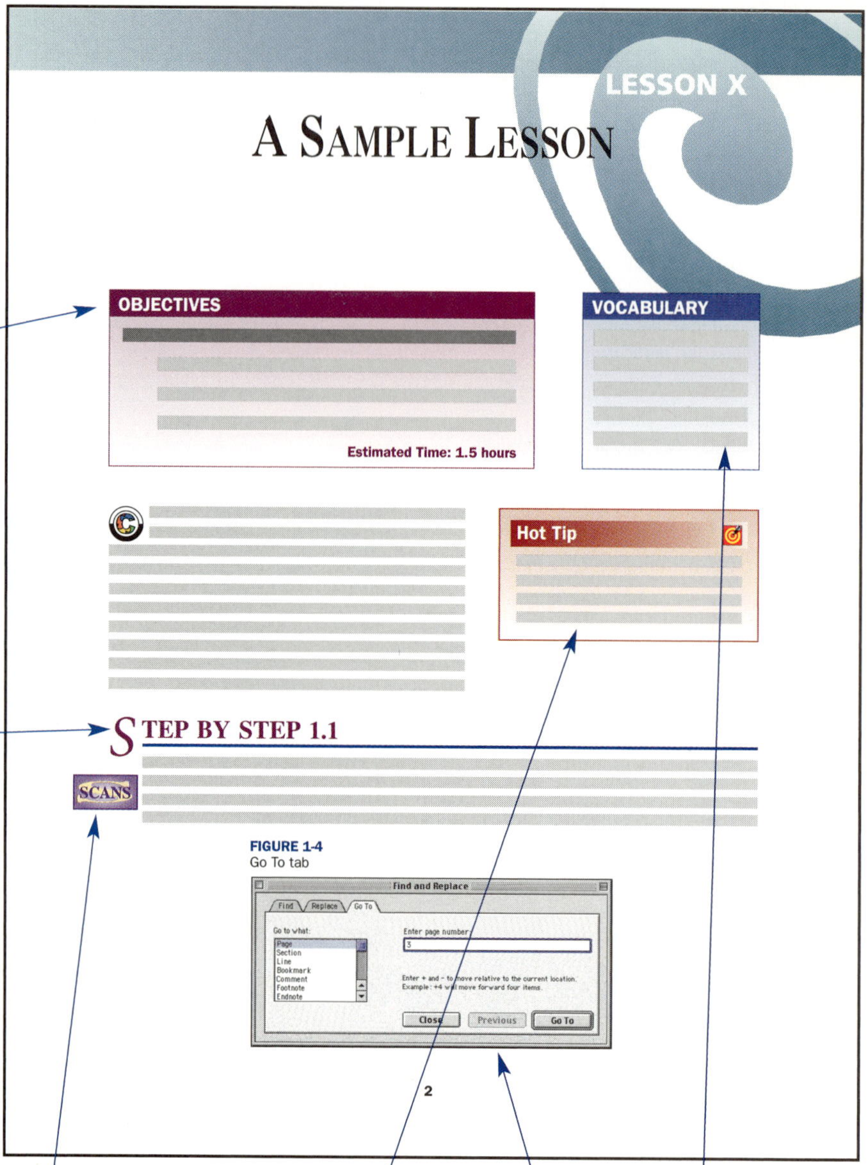

A SAMPLE LESSON

LESSON X

OBJECTIVES

Estimated Time: 1.5 hours

VOCABULARY

Hot Tip

STEP BY STEP 1.1

SCANS

FIGURE 1-4
Go To tab

Find and Replace

SCANS—(Secretary's Commission on Achieving Necessary Skills)—The U.S. Department of Labor has identified the school-to-careers competencies.

Marginal Boxes— These boxes provide additional information, such as Hot Tips, fun facts (Did You Know?), Computer Concepts, Internet Web sites, Extra Challenges activities, and Teamwork ideas.

Vocabulary—Terms identified in boldface throughout the lesson and summarized at the end.

Enhanced Screen Shots—Screen shots now come to life on each page with color and depth.

How to Use This Book

Summary—At the end of each lesson, you will find a summary to prepare you to complete the end-of-lesson activities.

Vocabulary/Review Questions—Review material at the end of each lesson and each unit enables you to prepare for assessment of the content presented.

Lesson Projects—End-of-lesson hands-on application of what has been learned in the lesson allows you to actually apply the techniques covered.

Critical Thinking Activities—Each lesson gives you an opportunity to apply creative analysis and use various resources to solve problems.

End-of-Unit Projects—End-of-unit hands-on application of concepts learned in the unit provides opportunity for a comprehensive review.

Simulation—Realistic simulation jobs are provided at the end of each unit, reinforcing the material covered in the unit.

Lesson X   Intro Excel   3

SUMMARY

VOCABULARY*Review*

REVIEW*Questions*

PROJECTS

CRITICAL*Thinking*

PROJECTS

SIMULATION

PREFACE

In today's fast-paced, media-driven business environment, it is essential to understand how to take a multimedia approach to capture an audience and deliver a message. Whether it involves presenting a slide show to a prospective client or developing a Web page for a non-profit organization, success depends on being able to create a product that effectively incorporates graphics, animation, video, text, and sound.

Multimedia BASICS takes a generic, non-software–specific approach to learning the most popular multimedia tools. This text covers the following applications: Macromedia Fireworks MX, Macromedia Flash MX, Adobe Premiere, Microsoft PowerPoint 2002, Microsoft Publisher 2002, Adobe PageMaker 7, Macromedia Dreamweaver MX, and Microsoft FrontPage 2002. You may also find it helpful with other programs.

By completing the lessons and activities in this book, you'll learn to use multimedia in a variety of applications. Topics include individual and integrated coverage of graphics, animation, video, presentation systems, desktop publishing, and Web page development. *Multimedia BASICS* is divided into units and lessons. You will learn a concept and then apply it through hands-on step-by-step activities. The book will take you through each step in a logical, easy-to-follow manner.

In the *Graphics* unit, we'll introduce you to the fundamentals of creating and editing graphics images. You'll learn to work with both bitmap and vector graphics to develop eye-catching pictures that can be used in print, on the Web, in animations and video, and in presentations. Lessons incorporate the basic principles of design and color while covering techniques that even artistically challenged learners can use to create exciting and informative computer graphics. Concepts in this unit are illustrated using screen captures from Macromedia Fireworks MX.

In the *Animation and Video* unit, graphics and video clips come to life on your computer screen. You'll learn the basics of generating frame-by-frame, motion, and path animations as well as how to create, import, and edit video files. In addition, you'll explore the fundamentals of sound and find out how to optimize files for different uses. Lessons cover the basics of both computer animation and video, as well as how to incorporate the files in presentations and Web pages. Concepts in this unit are illustrated using screen captures from Macromedia Flash MX and Adobe Premiere.

In the *Presentation Systems* unit, you'll learn how to design and create slide shows and computer-generated presentations. Lessons cover all aspects of presentation development, including planning, topic management, and the generation of support materials, as well as the technical details of creating, organizing, and formatting content. You learn how graphics and animation, special effects, and color affect the quality and impact of a presentation. Finally, you learn different methods for displaying a presentation, including presentation conferences, slide shows, and Web site access. Concepts in this unit are illustrated using screen captures from Microsoft PowerPoint 2002.

In the *Desktop Publishing* unit, printed materials take center stage. Before you even start using a software program, you'll learn the importance of identifying an audience and selecting the right materials. You'll find out how to plan and schedule a publication from start to finish, including how to select a publication type and printing method, and even how to stay within a budget. Lessons cover such topics as creating a publication from scratch, using a design template, working with type, selecting and applying colors and special effects, and incorporating graphics. You'll also learn how to use the principles of design to organize content on a page so that it is both appealing to look at and easy to read. Concepts in this unit are illustrated using screen captures from Microsoft Publisher 2002.

In the *Web Site Development* unit, you'll learn how to design and create Web pages and link them into a Web site. Lessons cover the importance of page layout and design in capturing a visitor's attention and delivering a message, as well as how to use color, text, graphics, and animations to enhance a page. Other topics include how to incorporate navigation tools, when and how to make use of sound, and methods for previewing and testing a page prior to publication. Concepts in this unit are illustrated using screen captures from Macromedia Dreamweaver MX.

The book culminates with the *Integrated Projects*, which include exercises and activities that combine aspects from all five units to challenge the learner and reinforce the covered skills. For example, you'll have the opportunity to practice developing graphics for print and then using them in a publication, or importing a graphic image into an animation, then using the animation in a presentation. For those who need a refresher on Windows, Appendix A covers Windows basics such as working with folders, launching a program, and installing hardware and software.

Acknowledgments

We would like to express our appreciation to the many individuals who have contributed to the completion of this book. Putting this book together has been a pleasant experience due largely to the good work of the people whose names appear here.

- Robert Gaggin, Product Manager, Course Technology
- Dave Lafferty, Senior Product Manager, Course Technology
- Jodi Dreissig, Associate Product Manager, Course Technology
- Chris Katsaropoulos, Managing Editor, Course Technology
- Betsy Newberry and Anne Chimenti of Custom Editorial Productions Inc., with writing and editing contributions from Cat Skintik
- Reviewer Donna Occhifinto
- GEX Publishing Services

About the Authors

Suzanne Weixel is a self-employed writer and editor specializing in the technology industry. Her experience with computers began in 1974 when she learned to play football on the Dartmouth Time-Sharing terminal her brother installed in a spare bedroom. She graduated from Dartmouth College in 1981 with a degree in art history and currently lives in Marlborough, MA, with her husband, Rick, their sons Nathaniel and Evan, and their dog, a Samoyed named Cirrus.

Jennifer Fulton, iVillage's former "computer coach," is an experienced computer consultant and trainer with more than 20 years in the business. Jennifer is a best-selling author of more than 100 computer books written for both the education and retail markets.

Karl Barksdale has authored a number of textbooks on a variety of computer subjects. Karl has trained thousands of students and teachers across the country. He teaches middle school business classes and authors textbooks from his home in Springville, UT.

Bryan Morse is an Associate Professor of Computer Science at Brigham Young University where he teaches courses in Digital Signal and Image Processing, Computer Vision, Computer Graphics, and Programming Languages. Outside the classroom, his research interests range from interactive photo-editing tools to medical imaging. Dr. Morse holds a Ph.D. in Computer Science from the University of North Carolina at Chapel Hill. He has also worked for IBM, has been a visiting researcher at the National Library of Medicine, and has served as a consultant for a number of computer software companies. He lives in Provo, UT with his wife, Cheryl, and their four children.

Cheryl L. Morse is an instructional technologist for the Center for Instructional Design at Brigham Young University. She graduated from BYU with a bachelor of science in elementary education and special education in 1988. She is a contributing author of *Corporate View: Management and Human Resources*, published by South-Western Educational Publishing. Cheryl has been involved in teaching speech-recognition workshops for SpeakingSolutions, Inc. Before coming to Brigham Young University, she was a senior project manager for Course Technology/Thomson Learning. Cheryl is an avid runner completing three marathons with plans to run a fourth in October 2003. She lives in Provo, UT with her husband, Bryan, and their four children.

GUIDE FOR USING THIS BOOK

Please read this Guide before starting work. The time you spend now will save you much more time later and will make your learning faster, easier, and more pleasant.

Conventions

The different type styles used in this book have special meanings. They will save you time because you will soon automatically recognize from the type style the nature of the text you are reading and what you will do.

ITEM	TYPE STYLE	EXAMPLE
Text you will key	**Bold**	Key **Don't litter** rapidly.
Individual keys you will press	**Bold**	Press **Enter** to insert a blank line.
Web addresses that you might visit	*Italics*	More information about this book is available at *www.course.com*.
Web addresses that you should key	**Bold**	Start your browser and go to **www.course.com**.
Glossary terms in book	***Bold and italics***	The ***menu bar*** contains menu titles.
Words on screen	*Italics*	Click before the word *pencil*.
Menus and commands	**Bold**	Choose **Open** from the **File** menu.
Options/features with long names	*Italics*	Select **Normal** from the *Style for following paragraph* text box.

Review Pack and Instructor Resources CD-ROMs

The *Review Pack* CD-ROM contains all the data files needed to complete the exercises in the text. Data files for the *Graphics* unit are in Macromedia Fireworks format, or formats supported by Fireworks. Data files for the *Animation and Video* unit are in Macromedia Flash and Adobe Premiere formats, or formats supported by those two programs. Data files for the *Presentation Systems* unit are in PowerPoint format. For the *Desktop Publishing* unit, data files in Microsoft Publisher 2002 and Adobe PageMaker 7.0 formats are provided. And, for the *Web Site Development* unit, data files consist of graphics in .gif format and a spreadsheet, in Microsoft Excel format, which can be placed in Web pages developed in either Macromedia Dreamweaver or Microsoft FrontPage.

The *Instructor Resources* CD-ROM contains a wealth of instructional material you can use to prepare for teaching this course. The CD-ROM stores the following information:

- Data and solution files. Data and solution files for the *Graphics* unit are in Macromedia Fireworks format, or formats supported by Fireworks. Data and solution files for the *Animation and Video* unit are in Macromedia Flash and Adobe Premiere formats, or formats supported by those two programs. Data and solution files for the *Presentation Systems* unit are in PowerPoint format. For the *Desktop Publishing* unit, data and solution files in Microsoft Publisher 2002 and Adobe PageMaker 7.0 formats are provided. And, for the *Web Site Development* unit, data files consist of graphics in .gif format and a spreadsheet, in Microsoft Excel format, which can be placed in Web pages developed in either Macromedia Dreamweaver or Microsoft FrontPage; the solution files can be opened in either Dreamweaver or FrontPage.

- ExamView® tests for each lesson. ExamView is a powerful testing software package that allows instructors to create and administer printed, computer (LAN-based), and Internet exams. ExamView includes hundreds of questions that correspond to the topics covered in this text, enabling learners to generate detailed study guides that include page references for further review. The computer-based and Internet testing components allow learners to take exams at their computers, and also save the instructor time by grading each exam automatically.

- Electronic *Instructor Manual* that includes lecture notes for each lesson, lesson plans, Quick Quizzes, and troubleshooting tips.

- Answers to the lesson and unit review questions, and suggested/sample solutions for Step-by-Step exercises, end-of-lesson activities, and Unit Review projects.

- Copies of the figures that appear in the text, which can be used to prepare transparencies.

- Suggested schedules for teaching the lessons in this course.

- Additional instructional information about individual learning strategies, portfolios, and career planning, and a sample Internet contract.

- PowerPoint presentations that illustrate objectives for each lesson in the text.

SCANS

The Secretary's Commission on Achieving Necessary Skills (SCANS) from the U.S. Department of Labor was asked to examine the demands of the workplace and whether new learners are capable of meeting those demands. Specifically, the Commission was directed to advise the Secretary on the level of skills required to enter employment.

SCANS workplace competencies and foundation skills have been integrated into *Multimedia BASICS*. The workplace competencies are identified as 1) ability to use resources, 2) interpersonal skills, 3) ability to work with information, 4) understanding of systems, and 5) knowledge and understanding of technology. The foundation skills are identified as 1) basic communication skills, 2) thinking skills, and 3) personal qualities.

Exercises in which learners must use a number of these SCANS competencies and foundation skills are marked in the text with the SCANS icon.

System Requirements

The concepts and exercises in this book are designed to be compatible with many different software programs, including, but not limited to, the following:

- *Graphics* unit: Macromedia Fireworks MX

- *Animation and Video* unit: Macromedia Flash MX, Adobe Premiere 6.5

- *Presentation Systems* unit: Microsoft PowerPoint 2002

- *Desktop Publishing* unit: Microsoft Publisher 2002, Adobe PageMaker 7.0

- *Web Site Development* unit: Macromedia Dreamweaver MX, Microsoft FrontPage 2002

Computer systems that support these programs include PCs running Microsoft Windows. In order to complete some of the Step-by-Step activities and projects in this book, you should have access to the Internet via a modem or a direct connection.

TABLE OF CONTENTS

GRAPHICS UNIT

ANIMATION AND VIDEO UNIT

PRESENTATION SYSTEMS UNIT

DESKTOP PUBLISHING UNIT

WEB SITE DEVELOPMENT UNIT

GRAPHICS

Unit

🕐 **Estimated Time for Unit: 9.0 hours**

CREATING GRAPHICS

OBJECTIVES

Upon completion of this lesson, you should be able to:

- Understand Vector and Bitmap graphics.
- Create, save, and close a graphics file.
- Open an existing graphics file.
- Use drawing tools.
- Select stroke and fill options.
- Change the view.
- Modify the drawing area.
- Print an image.

Estimated Time: 2 hours

VOCABULARY

Active

Bitmap

Default

Drawing area

Fill

Graphics

Hexadecimal code

Layer

Objects

Pan

Panels

Pixels

Points

Resolution

Selection handles

Stroke

Toggle

Vector

View

Zoom

G*raphics* are building blocks for developing exciting and informative multimedia documents, presentations, and publications. They are the images you use to enhance the work you do on your computer, and include drawings, photographs, cartoons, charts, and maps. A newsletter that includes pictures is more inviting to a reader. Inserting a chart into a slide show makes the content easier for viewers to understand. A Web page that includes an animated drawing is more likely to hold a visitor's attention.

Graphics programs provide the tools you need to create, edit, and manipulate images on your computer. There are many different types of graphics programs available. Some programs, such as Adobe Illustrator and Macromedia Freehand, are designed specifically for creating graphics that can be printed, while other programs, such as Adobe Photoshop and Macromedia Fireworks, are designed for creating graphics that can be printed or displayed electronically in a file or on a Web page. There are programs intended for home use and programs designed for professionals. Some graphics programs are available only as part of other programs. These usually do not have as many features as the stand-alone programs. For example, Microsoft Office comes with drawing and picture editing tools. In this book, you will learn how to use a full-featured graphics program to create and modify original artwork as well as to work with existing images of all different types.

The first step in mastering the use of graphics is to learn how to create drawings. In this lesson, you will learn how to use a graphics program to draw basic shapes, to save the drawings in a graphics file, and to print the file.

Understand Vector and Bitmap Graphics

You'll find that there are two basic types of graphics used in computer applications: *bitmap* and *vector*. Vector graphics consist of lines and curves—called vector paths—that are defined by mathematical objects called vectors. Shapes you draw using computer programs are vector graphics. Vectors use geometric characteristics such as size, position, and shape, as well as color, to describe graphics. To edit a vector image, you change the individual vectors. For example, you change the diameter of a circle, or the position of a curve. Bitmaps, which are sometimes called raster images, use colored dots—called *pixels*—arranged in a grid to define an image. Each pixel has a specific location and color that, when combined with the other pixels, create the image. To edit a bitmap, you have to edit the color and/or position of the individual dots.

Vector files are usually smaller than bitmap files because they consist of a series of mathematical formulas rather than many pixels, so they are easier to store and incorporate in other applications. The images also retain their original definition and perspective when resized, so they can be displayed at different resolutions without losing quality. This is useful if you need to show the same image on different monitors, such as when different users access the same Web page. Bitmaps tend to lose definition as they are resized, because the individual dots become visible. Usually, photographs and clip art graphics are bitmaps. Figure 1-1 shows the difference between a vector circle (on the left) and a bitmap circle (on the right) that have been magnified 600%. The edges of the bitmap are rough because you can see the individual pixels at this magnification.

FIGURE 1-1
Vector graphics retain their quality when enlarged, while bitmaps do not

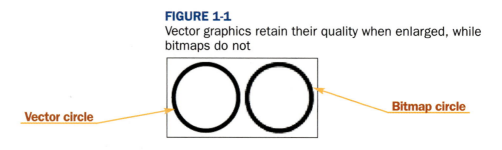

Vector circle   Bitmap circle

Full-featured graphics programs such as Adobe Photoshop and Macromedia Fireworks can be used to create and edit both vector drawings and bitmaps for use on Web pages and in presentations as well as in printed documents. Programs such as Adobe Illustrator and Macromedia Freehand are designed specifically for drawing and editing vector images. Vector graphics programs do not have tools for editing bitmap images, and programs designed for working with bitmaps have few tools for working with vectors. If you are using a vector graphics-only program, or a bitmap graphics only program, you may find as you work through the lessons in this book that some of the features are not available in your program.

Create, Save, and Close a Graphics File

Before you can begin working with graphics, you must learn how to create and save a graphics file. Some graphics programs start with a new blank file already open. In that case, you can simply begin using the available tools to create a picture. Some graphics programs start without a file open. You can open an existing file or create a new one. In any case, you can create a new file without closing and restarting the graphics program. Once you create the file, you must save it so you have it available for use in the future.

Create a Graphics File

To create a new graphics file, use the New command on the File menu or click the New button on the main or standard toolbar. Some programs automatically create the file using the *default* size, color, and *resolution* settings for the *drawing area*, but other programs display a dialog box where you can select the settings you want to use. Default settings are the standard options already selected in the program. Resolution is the quality or sharpness of an image, usually measured in *pixels* per inch or per centimeter. Pixels—short for *picture elements*—are dots used to define some images on a computer screen. The drawing area is the area within the document window where you draw and edit the image. Some programs call this area the *canvas* or the *stage*. You may change the settings when you first create the file or at any time in the future.

When you select the New command, the program creates a new blank file similar to Figure 1-2. In addition to the standard screen elements such as a document window, menu bar, toolbars, and scroll bars, most graphics programs include a drawing area, a collection of drawing tools, and panels or palettes where you can select options. The appearance of the screen depends on the program you are using as well as the default options set for your computer, so don't worry if your screen doesn't look exactly the same as the one in the illustration.

FIGURE 1-2
Typical graphics program window

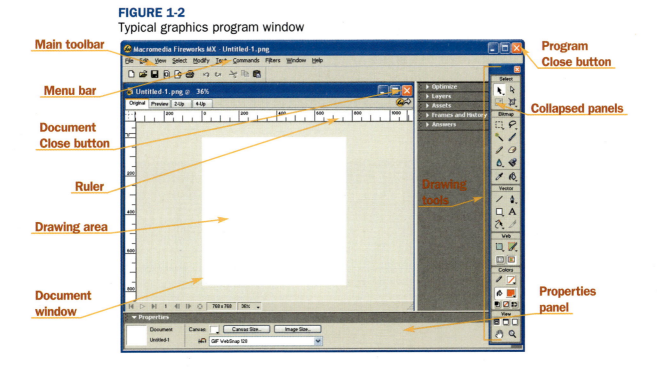

New files usually have a generic name such as Untitled or New File, and are numbered consecutively. So, the first file you create is Untitled1, the second is Untitled2, and so on. You customize the name of the file when you save it. Most graphics programs let you have more than one file open at a time, although only one can be *active*. The active file is the one in which you are currently working.

S TEP-BY-STEP 1.1

1. Launch your graphics program.

2. Click **File** on the menu bar, and then click **New**. This command may open a new file or a New Document dialog box.

3. Click the **OK** button in the dialog box to create a file with the default drawing area settings.

4. Leave the new file open to use in the next exercise.

> **Note** ☑️
>
> Don't worry if there is no New Document dialog box, or if the dialog box has a different name. You may be using a graphics program different from the one used to illustrate this book. Your program version or operating system may also affect the contents of the dialog box.

Save a Graphics File

Use the Save As command on the File menu to save a graphics file for the first time. When you save a file for the first time, you give it a name and select a storage location. You should use filenames that help to identify the file contents, and, of course, you must follow standard filename rules. That means you cannot use the following characters in the filename: /, \, >, <, *, ?, ", !, :, ;.

By default, most programs will save a new graphics file in the My Pictures folder on your local hard disk, or in the same folder where you most recently saved a file. However, you can select a different location. You can save a file on a local hard disk, on a network drive, or on removable media, such as a 3½-inch disk or a CD-R.

Different programs save in different file formats. Table 1-1 lists some common graphics file formats. You'll learn more about working with different file formats in Lesson 2.

TABLE 1-1
Common graphics file formats

GRAPHICS FILE FORMAT	FILE EXTENSION	DESCRIPTION
Portable Network Graphic	.png	This format is often used for graphics on the World Wide Web. It can support up to 32-bit color as well as effects such as transparency. It is the native file format for Macromedia's Fireworks MX graphics program.
Joint Photographic Experts Group	.jpg or .jpeg	This format is used for photographs and other high-color images. It supports millions of colors and can be compressed. It does not support transparency.

TABLE 1-1 Continued
Common graphics file formats

GRAPHICS FILE FORMAT	FILE EXTENSION	DESCRIPTION
Graphics Interchange Format	.gif	GIF files are popular for use on the World Wide Web. They can contain up to 256 colors. They are used for cartoons, logos, graphics with transparent areas, and animations.
Bitmap	.bmp	BMP is the Microsoft graphics file format and is used frequently for bitmap images.
Wireless Bitmap	.wbmp	The Wireless Bitmap format is used for displayed images on Wireless Application Protocol (WAP) pages on mobile devices such as personal digital assistants (PDAs). It uses a 1-bit format, so it can display only two colors—black and white.
Tagged Image File Format	.tif or .tiff	TIFF files are used for storing bitmap images. This format is commonly used in desktop publishing and other multimedia applications.
PICT	.pict	PICT is the file format used by programs that run on Apple Macintosh computers.
Photoshop	.psd	PSD is the file format used by the Adobe Photoshop graphics program.

STEP-BY-STEP 1.2

1. Click **File** on the menu bar, and then click **Save As**. The Save As dialog box opens, as shown in Figure 1-3.

FIGURE 1-3
Save As dialog box

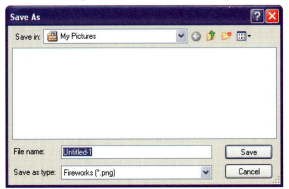

2. In the **File name** box, with the default name already selected, key **Drawing**. This will be the name of the new file.

STEP-BY-STEP 1.2 Continued

3. From the **Save in** list, select the location where you want to store the file.

4. Click the **Save** button in the dialog box. The file is saved with the new name in the selected storage location.

5. Leave the **Drawing** file open to use in the next exercise.

Once you have saved a file for the first time, you can use the Save As command to save the file with a new name or in a new location. The original file will remain unchanged.

Close a Graphics File

When you have finished using a graphics file, you should close it. You can close a file by using the Close command on the File menu, or by clicking the Document Close button on the document's title bar. After you close a file, the graphics program remains open so that you can continue using it.

If you have not saved the file before issuing a close command, the program displays a dialog box asking if you want to save. Click the Yes button to save the changes and close the file. Click the No button to close the file without saving the changes. Click the Cancel button to close the dialog box and continue working in the file. If you close the file without saving, all changes that you made since the last time you saved the file will be lost.

STEP-BY-STEP 1.3

1. Click **File** on the menu bar, and then click **Close**. The empty drawing closes.

2. Leave your graphics program open to use in the next exercise.

> **Note**
>
> You can close the program and all open files at the same time if you are finished using the program. Use the Exit command on the File menu or click the Program Close button. If you haven't saved an open file, the program prompts you to save before closing.

Open an Existing Graphics File

To work again with a file you have closed, you must open it in your graphics program. You can use the Open button on the main or standard toolbar or the Open command from the File menu to display the Open dialog box. By default, the Open dialog box displays the files in the My Pictures folder. Or the dialog box may display the location from which you last opened a file. You can use the Open dialog box to locate and select the file you want to open.

STEP-BY-STEP 1.4

1. Click **File** on the menu bar, and then click **Open**. The Open dialog box displays the list of files in the folder, as shown in Figure 1-4. (Don't worry if your Open dialog box does not look exactly the same as the one in the figure. Your program may be set to display the filenames differently.)

FIGURE 1-4
Open dialog box

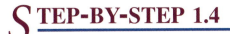

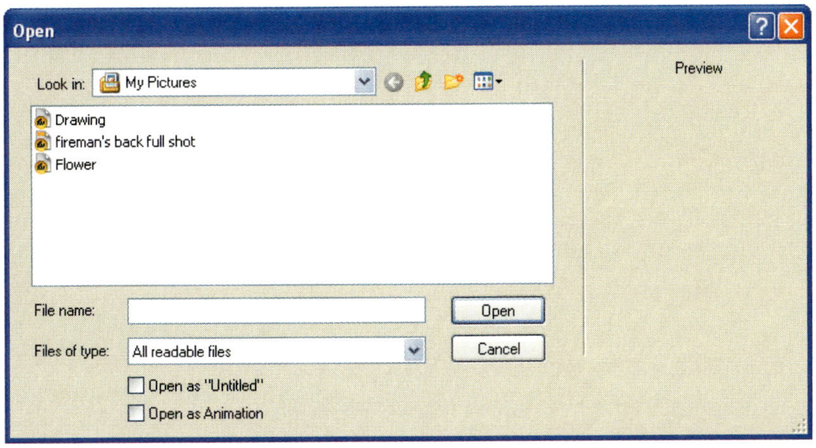

2. If the Drawing file is not listed in the dialog box, click the **Look in** list drop-down arrow and then select the location where the file is stored.

3. In the list of files, click **Drawing**.

4. Click the **Open** button in the dialog box. The file opens in the program window.

5. Leave the **Drawing** file open to use in the next exercise.

Did You Know?

Some programs also have a command for opening recently used files. In some cases, the most recently used files are listed at the bottom of the File menu, so you can just click the File menu and then click the name of the file you want to open. In other programs, the recently used files are listed on a submenu. If that is the case, you must open the File menu, click the Open Recent command to display the submenu, and then click the name of the file you want to open.

Use Drawing Tools

To create a vector drawing in a graphics program, you use drawing tools to insert ***objects*** in the document window. In general, an object is any element, such as a shape or a line. The drawing tools are a collection of buttons from which you select the specific type and style of object you want to create. Although some tools vary from program to program, most programs offer a set of tools for drawing basic shapes such as rectangles, ovals, and lines; for drawing freehand objects; and for creating different polygons. Some programs also have options for modifying the way a tool works, such as adding rounded corners to a rectangle, and for changing or reshaping an object that has already been drawn.

Tools are usually available on a toolbar, in a toolbox, or in a tools panel along the edge of the program window, and are often grouped according to function. For example, one group may be for drawing basic shapes, another may be for modifying existing shapes, and another may be for selecting existing shapes.

To use a drawing tool, click on it to select it. The mouse pointer changes to a crosshair. Hold down the mouse button and drag in the document window to create the shape. The shape is inserted in the drawing using the current *stroke* and *fill* settings. The stroke is the line used to draw a shape, and the fill is the area inside a shape. You learn about changing the stroke and fill settings later in this lesson. In addition, small rectangles called *selection handles* are displayed around the shape. These handles indicate that the shape is selected, and you can drag one to resize the shape.

In many programs, some tools in the toolbox display a small triangle or drop-down arrow. This means that the tool that is currently displayed is only one of a set of related tools. For example, if the Rectangle tool has the drop-down arrow, it probably hides a set of basic shapes, such as the Ellipse tool, the Rounded Rectangle tool, and the Polygon tool. To see the entire set, position the mouse pointer on the tool, then press and hold the mouse button to open the hidden toolbar (you can release the button once the toolbar is displayed). Click a tool to select it, or press Esc to close the toolbar. Figure 1-5 shows the Basic Shapes toolbar.

Hot Tip 🎯

Hold down the Shift key while dragging in order to constrain the shape. For example, use it with the Ellipse or Oval tool to draw a perfect circle. Use it with the Rectangle tool to draw a perfect square. Use it with the Line tool to draw lines at 45-degree angles.

Note ☑

In some programs, such as Adobe Photoshop, shapes have no stroke and are filled with the foreground color by default. Strokes are applied as an effect or style to enhance the shape.

FIGURE 1-5
Basic Shapes toolbar

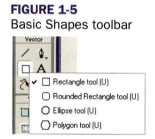

By default in most programs, shapes are placed on the same *layer* in the image. A layer is a transparent plane used to separate objects in a file. In some programs, such as Adobe Photoshop, new shapes are placed on separate shape layers. To select an object, you must first select its layer in the Layers panel.

Table 1-2 describes some of the common graphics drawing tools. Keep in mind, however, that not all programs have the same tools, or use the same names for tools. You may have to experiment or consult your program's Help information to find the specific purpose of each tool.

TABLE 1-2
Common drawing tools

ICON	TOOL NAME	DESCRIPTION
/	Line tool	Use to draw straight lines
○	Ellipse or Oval tool	Use to draw ovals and circles
□	Rectangle tool	Use to draw rectangles and squares
○	Rounded Rectangle tool	Use to draw rectangles and squares with rounded corners
○	Polygon tool	Use to draw multisided shapes such as stars or octagons
✎	Pencil tool	Use to draw freehand as if using a pencil
✒	Pen tool	Use to draw precise lines and curves by plotting and connecting points
✦	Brush tool	Use to draw as if using a paintbrush
▱	Eraser tool	Use to remove objects or parts of objects from a drawing
A	Text tool	Use to insert text in a drawing
▶	Pointer, or Selection, tool	Use to select objects in a drawing

STEP-BY-STEP 1.5

1. In the **Drawing** file, click the **Ellipse** tool. (You may need to use the hidden toolbars to locate the Ellipse tool.)

2. Position the mouse pointer in the upper-middle part of the drawing area. Don't worry about placing the pointer in a precise spot. Just estimate the correct location.

Did You Know?

You can identify tools using ScreenTips. Rest your mouse pointer on a tool button to display the tool's name.

STEP-BY-STEP 1.5 Continued

3. Hold down the mouse button and drag down and to the right to draw the shape, as shown in Figure 1-6. Release the mouse button when you are finished.

FIGURE 1-6
Draw an oval

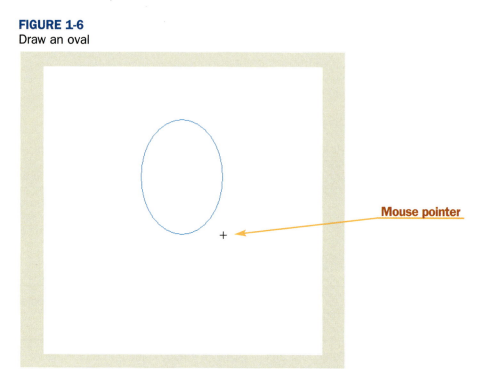

Mouse pointer

4. Click the **Line** tool. Some programs have different types of lines, such as curves and freeforms. Select the tool for drawing straight lines.

5. Move the mouse pointer to the left edge of the drawing area, below the ellipse.

6. Click and drag to the right across the drawing area to create a horizontal line, as shown in Figure 1-7. (Press and hold **Shift** while you drag to create a perfectly horizontal line.) Release the mouse button when you are finished. Don't worry if the color or stroke of the shapes in your drawing are different from those in the figure.

FIGURE 1-7
Drawing with Oval and Line tools

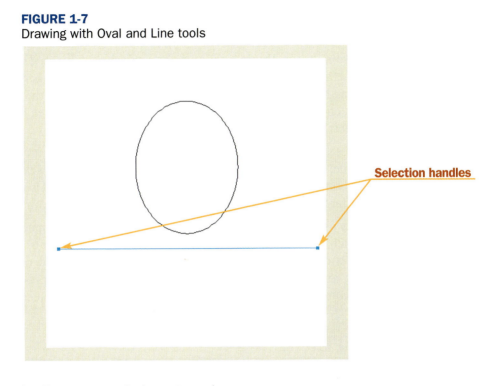

Selection handles

7. Leave the **Drawing** file open to use in the next exercise.

Save Changes to a File

You can quickly save changes to a file by clicking the Save button on the main or standard toolbar, or by using the Save command on the File menu. Saving changes ensures that you don't lose your work if there's a problem with your computer or the software.

Did You Know?

You can draw outside the boundaries of the drawing area. Objects drawn outside the drawing area are saved with the file but do not print. Use this "scratch area" to practice techniques or store objects for future use.

Important

You should get in the habit of saving your files frequently. Until you save, your work is at risk of being lost if there is a mechanical problem with the computer or a power failure. To keep your work safe, you must save it.

STEP-BY-STEP 1.6

1. Click **File** on the menu bar, and then click **Save**. The changes are saved.

2. Leave the **Drawing** file open to use in the next exercise.

Select Vector Objects in a Drawing

To make changes to a vector object, you must first select the object. The easiest way to select an object is to use a selection tool. The tool usually looks like a black pointing arrow, and has a name such as Pointer, Path Selection, or Selection. To select the object, click the selection tool and then click the object. (If the object is on a different layer, click once to select the layer, then again to select the object.)

When an object is selected, selection handles are displayed around its edges. To select more than one object at a time, select the first object, press and hold Shift, and select another object. Or, just drag the selection pointer around all the objects you want to select. (Usually, you cannot select multiple objects on different layers.) To cancel a selection, click a blank area of the drawing.

Graphics programs usually have other selection tools designed for specific purposes, such as the Marquee tool, which is used for selecting bitmaps, the Subselection or Direct Selection tool, which is used for selecting a single object that is part of a group; and the Select Behind tool, which is used to select an object that has another object overlapping it. Some programs have a Select menu that lists commands specific to selecting and deselecting objects.

STEP-BY-STEP 1.7

1. In the **Drawing** file, click the selection tool for your program. This makes the tool active so you can use it to select objects.

2. Click the ellipse shape in the drawing. The ellipse is selected, as indicated by the selection handles displayed around its edges.

3. Click the horizontal line. Now the line is selected, and the ellipse is not.

4. Press and hold **Shift** and then click the ellipse. Both objects are selected.

5. Click a blank part of the drawing area. The objects are deselected.

6. Leave the **Drawing** file open to use in the next exercise.

> **Hot Tip**
>
> To delete an object from a drawing, click it to select it, and then press Delete.

> **Extra for Experts**
>
> Some programs have a History panel that lists recently performed actions. You can undo and redo a series of actions using the History panel. To open the History panel, click Window on the menu bar and then click History. Drag the Undo marker up the list to undo actions or down the list to redo actions.

Use Undo and Redo

If you are unhappy with the results of your drawing efforts, you can use the Undo command to reverse your most recent action, or, in some programs, a series of actions. You can use the Redo command to reverse the results of an Undo action. Both Undo and Redo are available as commands on the Edit menu, or as buttons on the main or standard toolbar. (You may notice that the command name changes, depending on the action to Undo or Redo.) The first time you use the command, the most recent action is reversed. Repeat the command to reverse the action prior to that, and so on.

STEP-BY-STEP 1.8

1. In the **Drawing** file, click the **Rectangle** tool in the toolbox. You may find this tool on a toolbar hidden beneath another basic shapes tool.

2. Position the mouse pointer in the lower-left part of the drawing area, and then drag up and to the right to draw a rectangle. Release the mouse button when you are finished.

3. Click the **Rounded Rectangle** tool in the toolbar. (You may find this tool on a toolbar hidden beneath another basic shapes tool.)

4. Position the mouse pointer in the lower-right part of the drawing area, and then drag up and to the left to draw a rectangle with rounded corners. Release the mouse button when you are finished.

5. Click **Edit** on the menu bar, and then click **Undo**. (It may be Undo Rectangle tool, or it may be just Undo.) The most recent action—drawing the rounded rectangle—is reversed. Notice that the rectangle is removed from the drawing.

6. Click **Edit** on the menu bar, and then click **Undo** again. The next most recent action—drawing the first rectangle—is reversed. It too is removed from the drawing.

7. Click **Edit** on the menu bar, and then click **Redo**. The Redo command reverses the most recent Undo action. In this case, it replaces the first rectangle.

8. Save changes and leave the **Drawing** file open to use in the next exercise.

Select Stroke and Fill Options

As mentioned earlier, when you draw a shape, it uses the current stroke and fill settings, or attributes. The options available for modifying stroke and fill depend on the graphics program you are using. Typically, you can change the thickness, style, and color of a stroke, and you can change the color or pattern of a fill.

Stroke thickness, which is sometimes called weight or tip size, is usually measured in *points*. There are 72 points in an inch. Some programs let you select the size from a menu or change the current value using a slider or increment arrows. The higher the point value, the heavier the stroke.

Stroke style may be specified by type, category, or effect. For example, you may be able to choose a solid line, a dotted line, or a stroke that looks as if it were created using a heavy watercolor brush, a graphite pencil, or a textured airbrush. See Figure 1-8 for examples. Changes to stroke style and weight can modify the impact of an object by softening its edges or adding emphasis.

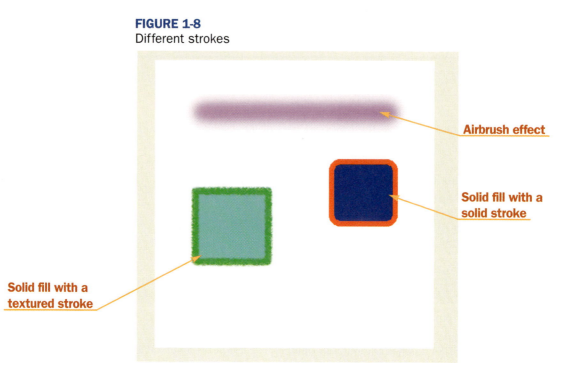

Airbrush effect

Solid fill with a
solid stroke

Solid fill with a
textured stroke

In most programs, you can access stroke and fill options from the toolbox, from menu commands, or from dialog boxes. Some programs have *panels*, which are elements similar to dialog boxes that you can keep open on your screen while you work. You might have Stroke and Fill panels, or you might find these options in the Properties panel. To draw a new object using specific stroke and fill options, select the options before you draw. You can also change the options for existing objects by selecting the object and then selecting the stroke or fill options you want to apply.

Extra for Experts

Many graphics programs provide advanced options for controlling the appearance of strokes and fills. For example, you may be able to change the edges of a line, set the size of the point used to draw a line, adjust the percentage of texture applied to a fill, and even set a position for a stroke in relation to a vector path.

To select a stroke color, you usually need to select a stroke color tool on the toolbar, the toolbox, or in a panel and then choose the desired color from a color palette. Most color palettes are a series of colored boxes that may be called *swatches*. You click the swatch containing the color you want to use. Some also have color bars in a particular color scheme, as well as No Color options, buttons for accessing additional options, and a text box where you can type the *hexadecimal code* for a particular color, as shown in Figure 1-9. Hexadecimal codes are standard alphanumeric values used to identify colors based on their components of red, green, and blue. Lesson 5 includes more information about working with color. After you select a stroke color, it becomes the default color, so all new objects you draw display that stroke color.

FIGURE 1-9
Color palette

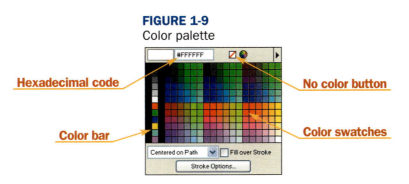

Hexadecimal code

No color button

Color bar

Color swatches

An object's fill can also be modified by style or color. Most graphics programs offer many fill options, such as solids, textures, blurs, gradients, patterns, and so on. You can also apply a fill color from a color palette in the same way you apply a stroke color. Select the fill color tool on the toolbar and then select the desired fill from the color palette.

S TEP-BY-STEP 1.9

1. In the **Drawing** file, click the tool for drawing straight lines in the toolbox.

2. Click the tool for selecting the stroke color. A color palette may open.

3. Click a magenta (dark pink) swatch on the color palette (such as hexadecimal FF00FF). The color palette may close after you select the color.

4. Change the stroke weight or size to **16** by selecting this value from a list or keying the value in the appropriate box. (The option name varies depending on your program. You might have a Line Size box, a Tip Size box, a Stroke Weight box, or some other variation that indicates the option to change the stroke weight. The option might be in the Stroke or Properties panel, in a dialog box that you access using menu commands, or from the Stroke Color palette.)

5. Change the stroke to a basic, solid, soft rounded style. If your program does not offer a basic, soft rounded style, select something similar.

> **Extra for Experts**
>
> In some programs, when you open the color palette the mouse pointer changes to an eyedropper. You can use the eyedropper to pick up any color currently displayed on your screen—even colors that are outside the color palette! For example, click the taskbar or click a color already in the drawing. Any color you click with the eyedropper becomes the current stroke color.

STEP-BY-STEP 1.9 Continued

6. Position the mouse pointer on the left side of the drawing area above the ellipse, press and hold **Shift**, and then click and drag across to the right to draw a straight horizontal line. Release the mouse button when you are finished.

7. Click the selection tool in the toolbox.

8. Select the ellipse in the drawing area so you can change the stroke or fill.

9. Click the tool in the toolbox that selects the fill, and then click a dark blue box (such as hexadecimal code 0000FF) in the color palette. The fill in the ellipse changes to blue. The drawing should look similar to Figure 1-10.

FIGURE 1-10
Drawing with modified stroke and fill

10. Save changes and leave the **Drawing** file open to use in the next exercise.

Change the View

While you are working in your graphics program, you may want to change the *view* to get a different look at your drawing. The view is the way your file is displayed on the screen. Most graphics programs let you display your drawing in different view modes such as normal or standard, full screen, or preview, as well as enable you to *zoom* or *pan* on the drawing area. Zooming adjusts the size of the drawing on the screen by a percentage of its actual size, while panning scrolls the drawing area up, down, left, and right in the document window.

Did You Know?

Most programs have a tool in the toolbox that you can click to revert to the default stroke and fill colors. The default fill is usually white and the default stroke is usually black.

You can also choose to show or hide the elements you need to accomplish a specific task. Most graphics programs have a toolbox, menu bar, toolbars, and panels, as well as a grid and rulers, which can help you align and position objects in the drawing area. Some also have properties boxes and help panes. When everything is displayed, as in Figure 1-11, there's not much room on the screen for the drawing!

FIGURE 1-11
Drawing in Normal mode, with many screen elements displayed

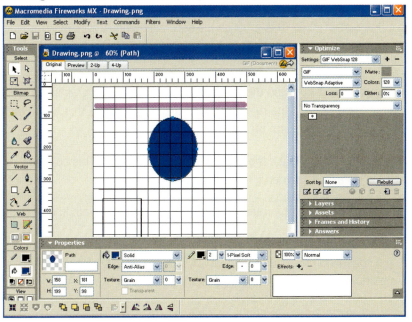

Most of the commands that you use to change the view and display screen elements are located on the View menu. Other commands may be on a different menu, such as the Window menu, or available as buttons on a toolbar. You'll notice that many commands that control the way a program is displayed are *toggles*, which means they are either on or off. Each time you select the command, it switches from on to off, or off to on. When a command is on, it usually has a check mark beside it on the menu.

Keep in mind that the command names and locations depend on the specific graphics program you are using. For example, one program may have toolbar buttons for changing the view mode, while another may have only menu commands. Likewise, one program may have a Full Screen mode option for displaying only the drawing area with no other screen elements, while another program may offer a Full Screen with Menus command that displays the menu bar as well as the drawing area.

STEP-BY-STEP 1.10

1. In the **Drawing** file, change to Full Screen with Menus mode. You may do this by clicking a tool in the toolbox or a command on the View menu. This expands the area of the document window by hiding the program and document title bars. It leaves the menu bar displayed, so you can still use it to access commands. If your program does not have a Full Screen with Menus mode, just change to Full Screen mode in step 2.

> **Hot Tip**
>
> In some programs, you can toggle through the different screen modes simply by pressing F on the keyboard.

2. Change to Full Screen mode. This expands the document window even more by hiding the menu bar, too.

3. Click the tool or command that restores the standard or default view.

4. Choose the command to toggle the rulers off or on. In most programs you will find the Rulers command on the **View** menu. If the rulers were not displayed before, this action toggles them on; if they were displayed, it toggles them off.

5. Choose the command to toggle the drawing area grid off or on. This command is also usually on the View menu or on a Grid submenu.

6. Repeat steps 4 and 5 until the rulers and the grid are not displayed. In other words, toggle the rulers and grid off.

7. Choose the command to toggle the toolbox or Tools panel off or on. This command is usually on the Windows menu, but it may be on the View menu.

8. Practice toggling different elements on and off to change the view. For example, show and hide the toolbars, and explore the different panels available in your program. When you are finished, be sure that the toolbox and the main, or standard, toolbar are displayed in Standard mode.

9. Save changes and leave the **Drawing** file open to use in the next exercise.

> **Hot Tip**
>
> In most programs, elements such as panels have handles you can use to drag the item to a different location on the screen. For example, you can move the toolbox to the bottom of the screen or drag a panel closer to the drawing area. Some panels have arrows you can use to expand or collapse the element. This is useful if you want to keep the element displayed, but need to shrink it temporarily so you can see more of a drawing.

Change the Zoom

When you need to get a closer look at a drawing, zoom in. As mentioned earlier, zooming increases or decreases the magnification of the drawing on your screen by a percentage of its original size. For example, zoom in to 200% to display the drawing at twice its actual size, or zoom out to 50% to display it at half its actual size. Zooming in gives you a closer look and makes it easier to see and work with a particular area, while zooming out makes the drawing look smaller and gives you an overall view of its entire composition.

In most programs, you can use commands on the View menu to zoom in, zoom out, or select a magnification percentage from a list. You can also simply click the Zoom tool and then click in the drawing area. Some programs have both a Zoom In tool and a Zoom Out tool, while other programs have only a single Zoom tool that zooms in by default. In that case, to zoom out, click the Zoom tool, press Alt, and then click the drawing area. Your graphics program may offer other options for zooming. For example, some programs have options to automatically adjust the zoom so all objects fit in the document window or only the selection fits in the document window, and some programs have a Zoom box on the Status bar you can click to select from a list of magnification percentages.

Extra for Experts

Most programs have shortcuts you can use to quickly adjust the zoom. For example, double-click the Zoom tool to restore 100% magnification, or double-click the Hand tool to fit all objects in the window.

STEP-BY-STEP 1.11

1. In the **Drawing** file, click **View** on the menu bar, and then click the command to zoom in. The magnification is increased and you get a closer look at the drawing.

2. Click **View** on the menu bar, and then click the command to zoom out. The magnification is decreased, giving you a wider view of the drawing.

3. Click the tool for zooming in in the toolbox, and then click on the magenta horizontal line in the drawing area. The display zooms in on the line.

4. Click the tool for zooming out in the toolbox, and click on the magenta line again. The display zooms out. (If your program has only one Zoom tool, click it and press and hold **Alt** while you click in the drawing area.) Now, try zooming to a specific magnification.

5. Locate and click the Magnification menu in your program window. It may be on the status bar, at the bottom of the drawing area, or on the View menu.

STEP-BY-STEP 1.11 Continued

6. On the Magnification menu, click **200%**. The drawing is displayed at twice its actual size. Depending on the size of your monitor, and the other elements that you have displayed, you probably can see only a small portion of the drawing, as shown in Figure 1-12.

FIGURE 1-12
Drawing magnified to 200%

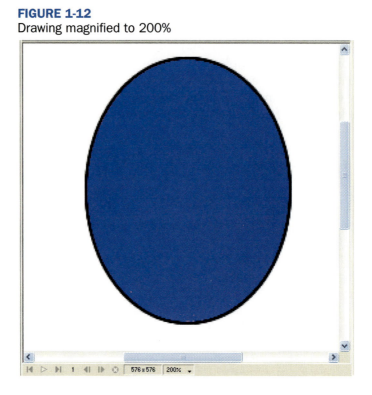

7. Save changes and leave the **Drawing** file open to use in the next exercise.

Pan around a Drawing

Pan in the document window to shift the display so you can see a different part of the drawing area. Panning is particularly useful in large drawings or when you are zoomed in to a high magnification. In both circumstances, panning lets you scroll to move the parts of a drawing that were outside the document window into the document window. In most programs, you can pan by using the scroll bars to shift the display up, down, left, or right. Some programs have a tool for panning, called the Hand tool. You use it to drag the drawing area around within the document window.

S TEP-BY-STEP 1.12

1. In the **Drawing** file, click the **Hand** tool in the toolbox. Notice that the mouse pointer changes to resemble a hand. If your program doesn't have a Hand tool, use the scroll bars to complete the steps in this exercise.

2. Position the mouse pointer over the ellipse in the document window, and then drag the object down and to the left. The display pans to reveal the upper-right section of the drawing area, including the magenta line. Notice that the zoom magnification remains the same—200%.

STEP-BY-STEP 1.12 Continued

3. Drag the ellipse up and to the right. This pans to show the lower-left section of the drawing area, including the horizontal line and the rectangle. Release the mouse button when you are finished panning.

4. Adjust the zoom so all objects fit in the drawing area.

5. Leave the **Drawing** file open to use in the next exercise. (You do not need to save because you did not make any changes to the file.)

Modify the Drawing Area

As mentioned earlier, the drawing area—or canvas—is created using default settings for size, resolution, and background color when you create a new file. You can select different settings when you first create the file, or you can change settings at any time. Usually, the size is set in pixels, but you can use inches or centimeters (or another measurement system your program offers), if you prefer. Note that changing the size of the drawing area does not change the size of the existing drawing. This means that reducing the size of the drawing area may crop off part of the drawing, while enlarging the drawing area may leave too much blank space around the drawing.

Depending on your graphics program, you may be able to change all of the drawing area settings in a single dialog box, or you may need to use different dialog boxes for each setting. Commands for changing drawing area settings are usually found on the File or Modify menu, or in the Properties panel or dialog box.

> **Hot Tip**
>
> You can change the height and/or width of an image to make it larger or smaller. Look for the Image Size command to open a dialog box on the Modify menu or in a panel such as Info or Properties.

> **Hot Tip**
>
> In addition to changing the size of the drawing area, some programs have options for changing its color, which is like changing the background color for the entire image, and for trimming it, which is like cutting off its edges.

STEP-BY-STEP 1.13

1. In the **Drawing** file, locate and select the command for changing the size of the drawing area. For example, click Modify on the menu bar, click Canvas, and then click Canvas Size, or click File, and then click Document Setup. The Canvas Size (or similar) dialog box is displayed.

2. Click the drop-down arrow in the width unit of measure box and click **Inches**. You should change the unit of measure before you set the new size.

3. Click the **Width** box and key **8**. (You may need to select the current value before keying to replace it with the new value.) This sets the width of the drawing area to 8 inches.

SUMMARY

In this lesson, you learned:

■ You can create new graphics files or open existing graphics files.

■ When you save a new file, you give it a name and a storage location. You should save frequently to avoid losing work.

■ You can draw basic shapes such as ovals, rectangles, and lines using the drawing tools.

■ You can change the color or style of strokes and fills in selected shapes or before you draw a new shape.

■ You can use different view modes to change the way a file is displayed.

■ You can toggle elements on or off depending on whether you want them displayed on the screen.

■ You can zoom in on an object to get a closer look, zoom out to get an overall look at the entire drawing, or pan to shift the display to show areas outside the document window.

■ You can modify the size, color, and resolution settings of the drawing area when you first create a new file or at any time.

■ You can print an image to see how it will look on paper.

VOCABULARY *Review*

Define the following terms:

Active	Layer	Selection handles
Bitmap	Objects	Stroke
Default	Pan	Toggle
Drawing area	Panels	Vector
Fill	Pixels	View
Graphics	Points	Zoom
Hexadecimal code	Resolution	

REVIEW *Questions*

TRUE / FALSE

Circle T if the statement is true or F if the statement is false.

T   F   1. Some graphics programs start with a new blank file already open.

T   F   2. Use the Save As command to quickly save changes to a file.

T   F   3. Shapes are drawn using the current stroke and fill settings.

T   F   4. The pointer tool is used to select objects in a drawing.

T   F   5. Undo can reverse only the most recent action.

T   F   6. Vector graphics files are usually smaller than bitmap graphics files.

T   F   7. Stroke thickness is usually measured in points.

T   F   8. You can select only one drawing object at a time.

T   F   9. Zoom out to get a closer look at a particular part of an image.

T   F 10. You must always specify settings in a Print dialog box before printing a file.

WRITTEN QUESTIONS

Write a brief answer to the following questions.

1. What are some of the common drawing tools?

2. What action might cause a bitmap image to lose definition?

3. What shape might the mouse pointer take when you open a color palette?

4. How can you tell if a screen element is toggled on?

5. If you want to display a drawing at 500 times its actual size, what should the zoom magnification be set to?

FILL IN THE BLANK

Complete the following sentences by writing the correct word or words in the blanks provided.

1. Some programs refer to the drawing area as the _____ or stage.

2. Although more than one file may be open at the same time, only one can be _____.

3. Use the _____ drawing tool to draw a multisided shape.

4. Hold down the _____ key when using the Ellipse tool in order to draw a perfect circle.

5. The small rectangles around the edge of a shape indicate that the shape is _____.

6. If you are unhappy with the results of your drawing, click the _____ button.

7. _____ graphics use pixels to define an image.

8. _____ in the document window to shift the display so you can see a different part of the drawing area.

9. Commands for showing and hiding panels are usually found on the _____ menu.

10. If you know it, you can type the _____ code for a particular color into the color palette text box in order to select that color.

PROJECTS

PROJECT 1-1

1. Create a new graphics file using the default drawing area settings.

2. Save the document as **Face**.

3. Use the drawing tools to draw a face with the following stroke and fill settings:
   A. Use the **Ellipse** tool with a 3-point black stroke and a white fill for the head.
   B. Use the **Polygon** tool with a 3-point black stroke for the eyes.
   C. Use the **Line** tool with a 2-point black stroke for the nose.
   D. Use a freeform or vector path tool with a 2-point red stroke to draw a mouth.
   E. Fill the eyes with brown.
   F. Use a freeform or vector path tool with an airbrush-type stroke in brown to draw hair.

4. Print one copy of the file.

5. Save and close the **Face** file, but leave your graphics program open to use in Project 1-2.

PROJECT 1-2

1. Open **GR Project 1-2** from the data files.

2. Save the file as **Revised Face**.

3. Zoom in on the right eye.

4. Select the right eye and change the fill color of the right eye to green.

5. Pan over to the left eye.

6. Change the fill color of the left eye to yellow.

7. Zoom out so you can see the entire drawing.

8. Delete the nose.

9. Undo the deletion.

10. Print one copy of the file.

11. Save and close the **Revised Face** file, but leave your graphics program open to use in Project 1-3.

PROJECT 1-3

1. Open **GR Project 1-3** from the data files.

2. Save the file as **Flower**.

3. Select all of the petals and change the fill to light green.

4. Change the color of the fill in the ellipse at the center of the flower to pale pink.

5. Increase the size of the drawing area to 7.5 inches by 7.5 inches.

6. Print one copy of the file.

7. Save and close the **Flower** file. Close your graphics program.

WEB PROJECT

Since primitive humans first drew pictures on the walls of caves, people have been using graphics to communicate and to express themselves creatively. Choose a time period in history and use the Internet to research graphics in that period. For example, you may choose the Renaissance and research how the artist Michelangelo painted the Sistine Chapel, or you may explore how Native Americans used pictures to tell stories as well as for decoration, or you may want to look into the impact digital graphics have had on modern society.

Use the information you gather in your research to write a report or essay that you can share with the class. Illustrate the report with an image that might have been created by people living during the period of your research.

TEAMWORK PROJECT

As a group, compile a list of the different types of graphics programs that are available, including information about the features of each program, the system requirements, and the price. You may want to record the information in a database program or a spreadsheet. You can find the information on the Internet, in a software magazine, or by visiting or contacting a store that sells software. Once you compile the information, rate the programs in terms of value.

Consider such factors as the cost as well as the number of features, the types of files you can create, whether you would need to purchase additional hardware to use the program, and whether the program is easily available in stores or on the Internet. When you are finished, share the results with your classmates.

CRITICAL*Thinking*

SCANS **ACTIVITY 1-1**

Use your graphics program to create a drawing that you might use as part of a logo for a business. For example, a realtor might use a drawing of a house, a day-care provider might use a drawing of building blocks, and a landscaper might use a drawing of trees or flowers. Try to use as many drawing tools as you can, as well as different stroke and fill options. When you are finished, save the file, print it, and share it with your classmates.

IMPORTING AND EXPORTING GRAPHICS

OBJECTIVES

Upon completion of this lesson, you should be able to:

- Scan images.
- Acquire images from a digital camera.
- Import files.
- Open different file formats.
- Acquire clip art.
- Optimize and export images.

Estimated Time: 1.5 hours

VOCABULARY

Clip art

Color depth

Color palette

Compatible

Device driver

Dithering

Download

Export

File format

Import

Key term

Loss

Native file format

Optimize

Scanner

Search site

Smoothing

TWAIN

Websafe colors

Wizard

Y ou can acquire graphics files in a number of ways without having to draw original artwork. You can use *clip art* files, which are images already saved in a graphics file format. You can scan printed material, capture original photographs with a digital camera, or even draw on a graphics tablet. You can insert the images into other documents or files, or *import* them for use in your graphics program. Importing makes a file available for editing. For example, you can import a photograph from a digital camera and then crop it, add vector shapes, and insert text, or you can download a clip art drawing from the Internet and change its background color.

Before you can use any hardware device to acquire pictures, the device must be correctly attached to your computer—or your computer network—and installed. Attaching the device usually means physically connecting the cables from the device to your computer, although some devices, such as internal modems, connect to slots inside the computer itself. Some other devices might involve optical or other wireless connections.

Installing the device also means installing the software that comes with the device and making sure the *device driver* works. The device driver is a software program that enables your computer to communicate with the hardware device. The driver usually comes on

Note ☑

You must consider a number of things when you import graphics images, including the quality of the image, its composition, and its subject content. If the image needs modification, make sure you can make the necessary changes using the tools you have available. Otherwise, you may want to look for a different image.

a CD with the device, or you can download it from the manufacturer's Web site. Your operating system may include drivers for common devices. When you set up and install new hardware, make sure you read and follow all instructions, or consult a professional.

Once you finish editing your graphics files, you can *export* them for use in other programs. Exporting stores the file so that it can be opened and used by other types of computer programs. That way, you can easily use the graphics to illustrate Web pages, presentations, or other documents. In this lesson, you will learn how to acquire graphics from different sources and how to import and export graphics using your graphics program.

> **Note** ☑️
>
> Most images that you acquire will be bitmaps, not vectors. Some graphics programs, including Macromedia Freehand and Adobe Illustrator, do not offer features for editing bitmaps. However, you can import and open bitmaps in all graphics programs. You learn more about working with bitmaps in Lesson 3.

Scan Images

When you have a printed image that you want to convert into a graphics file, use a *scanner*. A scanner is a hardware device that uses light to capture a digital version of a picture, which is then stored as a graphics file on your computer. Like any hardware device, the scanner must be correctly connected and installed on your computer in order to work.

Most scanners come with software that lets you select where you want to store the imported images and also determines the file format. However, because so many programs support scanning and **TWAIN**, which is the software language that is used to control scanners, you can probably import the image directly into the program of your choice. For example, you can scan an image into your graphics program so you can edit it, or you can scan an image into your desktop publishing program so you can include it in a publication.

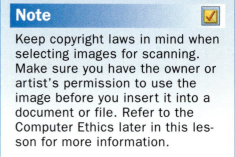

> **Note** ☑️
>
> Keep copyright laws in mind when selecting images for scanning. Make sure you have the owner or artist's permission to use the image before you insert it into a document or file. Refer to the Computer Ethics later in this lesson for more information.

Scan an Image into Your Graphics Program

To scan an image directly into your graphics program, place the printed picture in the scanner and click the Scan command. The location of the Scan command depends on your program. Look for it on the File menu or the Insert menu if there is one. In some programs, a submenu offers you a choice of scanning the image or selecting the specific scanning device you want to use. In most cases, you then select options in a Scan dialog box. The options offered depend on the type of scanner

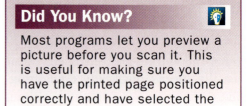

> **Did You Know?** 💡
>
> Most programs let you preview a picture before you scan it. This is useful for making sure you have the printed page positioned correctly and have selected the options you need.

you are using and your graphics program, but usually include settings for scanning in color, black and white, or grayscale, as well as for scanning text. When the scan is complete, the image is displayed as a new, unnamed file in the program window.

STEP-BY-STEP 2.1

1. Make sure your scanner is correctly installed for use with your computer.

2. Launch your graphics program.

3. Insert a printed picture into the scanner. Make sure it is correctly positioned on the glass, and close the scanner cover.

4. Click **File** on the menu bar, and then click **Scan**. If the Scan command is not on the File menu, look for it on the other main menus. If you still don't see it, your program may use the Import command instead, or the command may be located on a submenu. For example, you may have to click Insert on the menu bar, click Picture, and then click Scan, or you may have to click File on the menu bar, click Import, and then click From Scanner.

> **Note** ☑
>
> If your graphics program does not have a Scan command, it may not support acquiring an image directly from a scanner. In that case, you might have to use a different program to scan the image, as described in the next exercise.

5. Click the **TWAIN Acquire** command on the submenu and then click the name of the specific scanning device you want to use, if necessary. Again, the specific command depends on the program you are using. It may simply say TWAIN or TWAIN_32, or there may not be a submenu at all. A Scan dialog box may display on your screen, as shown in Figure 2-1. If the Scan dialog box on your computer is different from the one in Figure 2-1, you are probably using a different graphics program, a different scanner, or both. However, the basic options should be similar.

FIGURE 2-1
Typical Scan dialog box

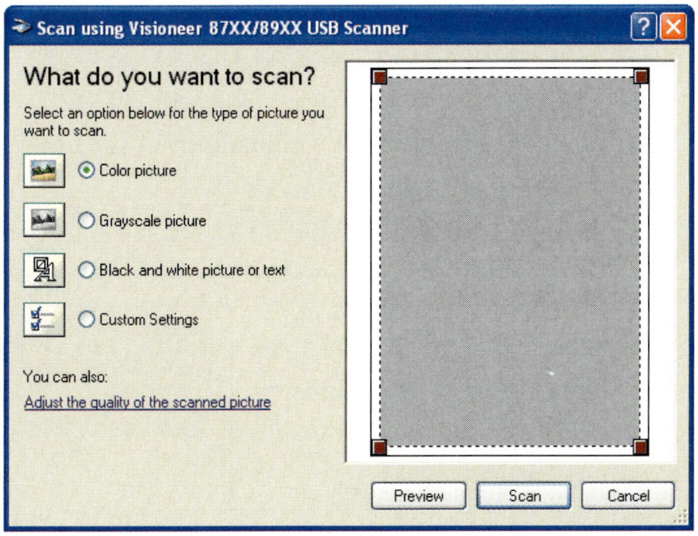

STEP-BY-STEP 2.1 Continued

6. Click the options you want to use, and then click the **Scan** button in the dialog box. The scanner acquires the image and displays it in the drawing area, as shown in Figure 2-2.

FIGURE 2-2
Scanned image in the drawing area

7. Save the new image file as **Scanpic**, and close the file. Leave your graphics program open to use in the next exercise.

Scan an Image into a Document File

The steps for scanning directly into a document vary depending on the program you are using. In most cases, however, you select the Scan command from the Insert menu.

STEP-BY-STEP 2.2

1. Launch the program you are using to create the document. For example, if you are creating a slide show with Microsoft PowerPoint, launch Microsoft PowerPoint.

2. Save the document with an appropriate name.

3. Position the insertion point where you want to insert the scanned image.

4. Click **Insert** on the menu bar, and then click **Picture**. In most cases, a submenu displays.

> **Did You Know?**
>
> If you have a graphics tablet, you can use it to draw or trace artwork or other images into a graphics file. A graphics tablet is a hardware device that lets you use a pen-like instrument called a stylus to write or draw on a flat surface. The input is digitized and saved in graphics file format.

STEP-BY-STEP 2.2 Continued

5. Click **From Scanner** on the submenu. A Scan dialog box may open so you can select the options you want to use.

6. Select options, and then click the **Insert** button. The image is scanned and then inserted in the file at the insertion point location.

7. Save changes to the file and close it, as well as the program you were using.

Acquire Images from a Digital Camera

Digital cameras make it easy to take original photographs that you can transfer as files to your computer. Once you acquire the pictures, you can edit them or use them as is. The steps for acquiring pictures from a camera depend on the type of camera and the software you use. In most cases, the photographs are stored as files in the camera's internal memory or on a storage device attached to the camera, such as a disk, memory stick, or memory card. Usually, cameras store pictures in JPEG format, but some high-end cameras use TIFF. JPEG compresses the pictures, so they take up less space on the storage device than TIFF files, but some quality may be lost in the compression process.

Digital cameras have many of the same features as 35 millimeter "point and shoot" cameras, including zoom, auto-focus, and automatic flash. Digital camera resolutions range from 640×480 pixels to upwards of 1600×1200 pixels. You can get lenses you must focus manually, lenses that support digital zoom, and even cameras that let you use the lenses from your standard 35 mm camera. Of course, the more features a digital camera supports, the more the camera costs. Other considerations include the type of interface used to connect the camera to the computer and the format used to store the pictures. Most digital cameras come with cables for connecting to USB, serial, or other external ports on your computer. In some cases—as with Flash cards—you may be able to insert the camera's storage device directly into a memory slot in the computer.

Most cameras come with software that automatically transfers the picture files from the camera to your computer. You can also acquire images from a digital camera by copying the files to your hard drive. When a digital camera is correctly connected to a computer, most operating systems read the camera as just another disk drive. That makes it easy to use the Copy and Paste commands to transfer the files from the camera to your hard disk. Then, you can use the Open command in your graphics program to open the file. This is convenient if you know you want to use the image as it is, without making changes to it in your graphics program.

STEP-BY-STEP 2.3

1. Make sure your camera is correctly installed for use with your computer.

2. Open the **My Computer** window from the desktop. My Computer displays the storage devices installed on your computer system, including the camera, as shown in Figure 2-3.

FIGURE 2-3
Digital camera listed as a storage device in My Computer

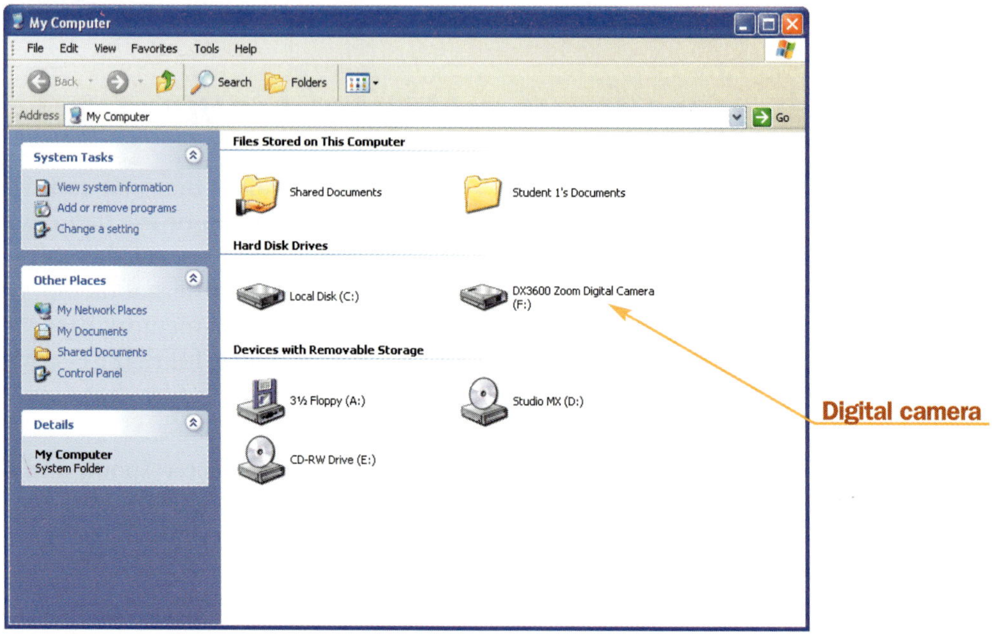

3. Double-click the icon representing the camera. A window displaying the contents of the camera opens. If necessary, double-click the specific location where the files are stored, such as internal memory or a storage device.

4. Click the file you want to copy to select it.

5. Click **Edit** on the window's menu bar, and then click **Copy**.

6. Open the **My Documents** window, or the window that contains the folder where you want to store the image file.

> **Hot Tip**
>
> To select more than one file at a time, press and hold Ctrl and click the additional files.

7. Click the **My Pictures** folder icon, or the icon representing the folder where you want to store the image file.

8. Click the **Edit** menu on the window's menu bar, and then click **Paste**. Your operating system copies the image file into the selected folder.

9. Close all open windows.

Import Files

Most graphics programs let you import files from any storage device attached to your computer, including hard drives, network drives, removable drives, and connected devices such as digital cameras. To import files, you usually create a new blank file, select a command such as Import or Place from the File menu, then define the area in the new file where you want the imported data displayed. In this exercise, you import a file from a digital camera. The steps will be similar for importing from any storage device.

STEP-BY-STEP 2.4

1. Make sure your camera is correctly installed for use with your computer.

2. Launch your graphics program.

3. Create a new, blank, graphics file using the default drawing area settings. Most programs require that you import an image into an existing file.

4. Click **File** on the menu bar, and then click a command such as **Import**. A dialog box similar to the one shown in Figure 2-4 opens.

FIGURE 2-4
Import dialog box

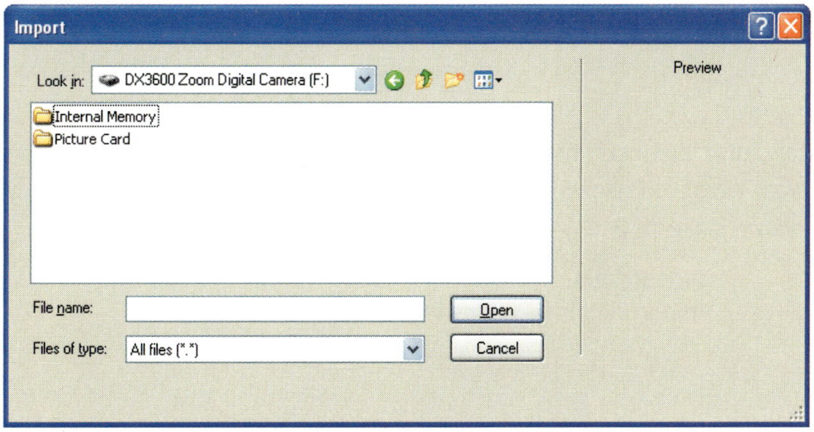

5. In the **Look in** list, open the location representing your digital camera's storage media, or any location where the file to import is stored.

STEP-BY-STEP 2.4 Continued

6. Click the name of the file you want to import, and then click the command to import the file, usually **Open**. Your program may automatically import the picture and display it in the drawing area, or the insertion pointer may be displayed in an otherwise blank drawing area as shown in Figure 2-5. If so, you must define the area where you want the image displayed.

FIGURE 2-5
Drag insertion pointer to define import area

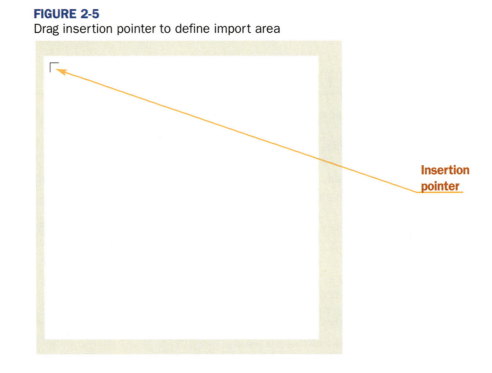

Insertion
pointer

7. If necessary, drag the insertion pointer from the upper-left corner to the lower-right corner of the drawing area. When you release the mouse button, the imported image is displayed in the drawing area, as shown in Figure 2-6.

FIGURE 2-6
Imported image in drawing area

STEP-BY-STEP 2.4 Continued

8. Save the file as **Camerapic**, and close it. Leave your graphics program open to use in the next exercise.

Open Different File Formats

Most graphics programs are associated with a default *file format*, or file type. The file format is the way the data in a file is stored. For example, Macromedia's Fireworks uses Portable Network Graphics (.png) as its default file format (Common graphics file formats are listed in Table 1-1 in Lesson 1.) Sometimes, the default file format for a particular program is called the *native file format*.

Most programs also let you open files that have been saved in a *compatible* file format. A compatible format is one that a program can open, read, and save, even if it is not the default. Sometimes compatible files are referred to simply as readable files.

You can easily open compatible files in your graphics program using the Open command. In the Open dialog box, click the Files of type list to display compatible file types. Most graphics programs list many different types of graphics files, as well as options for displaying all compatible files or all files, whether they are compatible or not. The list usually includes the name of the file format, as well as the file extensions associated with that format. After you have selected the desired file type, you can locate and open the file you need.

Once the file is open in your graphics program, you can save it in your graphics program's native file format. That way, you save edits and modifications while leaving the original file unchanged.

> ### Did You Know?
> Some programs make it easy to view stored images using a Filmstrip or Slide Show view. In Filmstrip view, thumbnail-sized pictures display across the bottom of the window, with a preview of the selected picture in the center of the window. In Slide Show view, pictures fill the entire display screen and may advance automatically at timed intervals.

> ### Note
> If you try to open a noncompatible file, your program will not know how to read and display the data. As a result, your program will display a warning message instead of opening the file. You can try opening the file in its original program and saving it in a format that is compatible with your program.

STEP-BY-STEP 2.5

1. Launch your graphics program if it is not already open.

2. Click **File** on the menu bar, and then click **Open**.

3. Use the **Look in** list to navigate to the data files folder.

STEP-BY-STEP 2.5 Continued

4. Click the drop-down arrow in the **Files of type** box. This displays a list of compatible file types, similar to the one shown in Figure 2-7.

5. Click **BMP**. The Files of type list closes and only files in BMP—bitmap—format are displayed in the Open dialog box.

6. Click the **Files of type** drop-down arrow again, and then click **GIF**. Now, only Graphics Interchange Format files are displayed.

7. Click the GIF-formatted file named **GR Step 2-5**, and then click the **Open** button in the dialog box. The file opens in your graphics program, as shown in Figure 2-8.

FIGURE 2-8
GIF file open in graphics program window

8. Click **File** on the menu bar, and then click **Save As**. The Save As dialog box opens so you can save the file in your program's native file format.

STEP-BY-STEP 2.5 Continued

9. Key the filename **Tracks** in the **File name** box. If necessary, select your program's default file format from the **Files of type** or **Format** list.

10. Select the location where you want to save the file from the **Save in** list, and then click the **Save** button.

11. Close the **Tracks** file as well as your graphics program. You do not need it in the next exercise.

Acquire Clip Art

Many programs come with clip art collections, or you can buy clip art on a disk or CD. You can also download some clip art from the Internet. If you want to edit or modify a clip art image, you can open the file in your graphics program. If you want to use the image as is, simply insert it directly into the file of your choice. For example, you can insert clip art into a report, Web page, or presentation file.

> **Did You Know?**
>
> Not all clip art files are graphics. Some are animations, movies, or sounds that you can use to enhance your documents.

Insert Clip Art into a Document File

The steps for inserting clip art into a document vary depending on the program you are using. In most cases, however, you select the Clip Art command from the Insert menu. A dialog box, panel, or separate program window opens to provide access to the program's clip art files. You may select a category to see the pictures stored for that category, or search for specific subjects using a search box. Some programs allow you to choose what type of pictures to find, such

---

Computer Ethics

COPYRIGHT LAWS

Although many sources allow you to download or scan images for your personal use, in other cases acquiring images without permission is illegal. Copyright laws protect artists and photographers just as they protect authors. In addition, even original photographs may cause problems if they include other people or other people's property in the picture without their permission. You may need to have people who appear in your photographs sign a "release," allowing you to use the picture, particularly if it will appear in a publication or on a Web site. For images from other sources, sometimes you can obtain permission to use them by writing or e-mailing the owner. In some cases, you may be asked to pay a fee. Even when you obtain permission, you should always cite the source of the image. You can do this by adding a caption to the image or by creating a list of sources similar to a bibliography. You should include the name of the artist, the title of the image, the source where you obtained the image, the copyright date, which is the date the image was originally published, and the date you downloaded or acquired the image.

as photographs or drawn clip art pictures. You may need to scroll through pictures to find one you want. Click on a picture to select it and then select the command to insert it into the current document. Some programs have an option for inserting the picture file. That is useful if you know the filename and storage location for the clip art image.

STEP-BY-STEP 2.6

1. Launch the program you are using to create the document. For example, if you are creating a newsletter with Microsoft Publisher, launch Microsoft Publisher.

2. Create a new blank document and save the document with an appropriate name.

3. Position the insertion point where you want to insert the image.

4. Click **Insert** on the menu bar, and then click **Picture**. In most cases, a submenu opens.

5. Click **Clip Art** on the submenu to display the dialog box or panel that gives you access to clip art images.

6. Select a category to see the pictures stored in that category, or type a word or phrase that describes the subject of pictures you want to find in a search box.

7. Click the image you want, and then, if necessary, click the **Insert** button. The image is inserted in the file at the insertion point location.

8. Save changes to the file and close it, as well as the program you were using.

Hot Tip

One of the easiest ways to insert a clip art picture is to use the Clipboard. Right-click the image and click Copy, then right-click the file where you want to insert the image and click Paste.

Download Images from the Internet

You can find many Web sites that provide free clip art for all occasions. You simply visit the site, locate the image you want, and then *download* it. Downloading copies the file from the Web site to your computer.

To find a list of clip art sites, use your favorite *search site* and search for the *key term* "clip art." A search site is a Web site that helps you locate a Web page even if you don't know the page's address. A key term is a word or phrase that you believe identifies the Web site. After you search for a key term, the search site lists Web addresses of sites that match your term. Click on the Web address or the site name to jump directly to that site.

Net Tip

It is important to know the source of any file you download from the Internet. Some files may be copyrighted material that you need permission to use, while some files may have viruses that could infect your computer and other computers on the same network.

If you know the address of a site, you can also key the address directly in your browser's Address bar. Then press Enter or click a button such as Go to jump to that site.

Although some clip art sites ask you to register by entering your name and e-mail address, many sites do not. You can simply download any file you want to use. Some sites have download procedures for copying clip art files to your hard disk, or you can use your browser's Save As command to save the image as a graphics file on your computer.

You must have access to the Internet in order to locate and download clip art files. That means your computer must be connected to the Internet and you must have an account with an Internet Service Provider (ISP).

S TEP-BY-STEP 2.7

1. Sign in to your Internet Service Provider (ISP) account and launch your Internet browser.

2. Go to your favorite search site, or key **www.google.com** in your browser's Address bar and press **Enter** or click the **Go** button.

3. Key **clip art** in the search box and then press **Enter**, or click the **Search** button. A list of clip art sites is displayed on your screen. You should be able to tell from the descriptions whether these sites charge a fee for using the clip art images or provide free access.

4. Click the link to the Clip-Art.com Web site. (You may have to scroll down to find this link.) If the site is not listed on your search results page, key **www.clip-art.com** in your browser's Address bar and press **Enter** or click the **Go** button.

5. If necessary, click the **CLIP-ART.COM** tab at the top of the home page to open the Clip-art.com page.

6. Click the **Free Images** link to the left of the Next button. A page listing categories of images opens, similar to the one in Figure 2-9.

FIGURE 2-9
Free clip art Web site

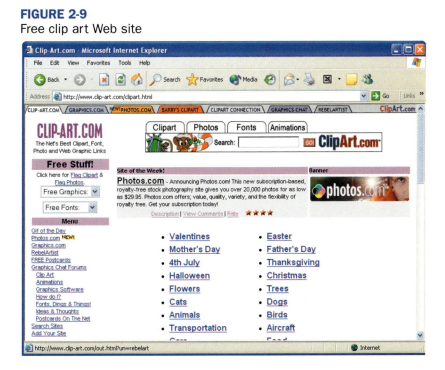

7. Click the **Flowers** link.

STEP-BY-STEP 2.7 Continued

8. Right-click the picture on the right side of the first row, and then click **Save Picture As** on the short-cut menu. The Save Picture dialog box opens, as shown in Figure 2-10. Don't worry if the dialog box on your computer looks different from the one in the illustration.

FIGURE 2-10
Save Picture dialog box

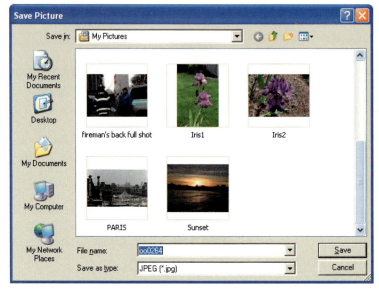

9. Key the filename **Bouquet.jpg**. (You must key the file extension to save the picture properly.)

10. Click the **Save as type** drop-down arrow and then click **JPEG (*.jpg)**. If JPEG is already selected, you can skip this step.

11. From the **Save in** list, select the location where you want to save the file, and then click the **Save** button in the Save Picture dialog box. The file is saved in JPEG file format.

12. Log off from the Internet, and close your browser.

Note ☑

The graphics file format types available depend on the picture you are trying to download.

Did You Know?

You can usually use your Web browser's Save As command to save any picture displayed on any Web site as a file on your computer. Of course, remember that you may need permission to use the picture in your documents and files.

Open Clip Art in Your Graphics Program

Use the Open command on the File menu to open a clip art image in your graphics program. The steps are the same as for opening any compatible file type. You can save the file in your program's native file format, and then make changes if you want.

S TEP-BY-STEP 2.8

1. Launch your graphics program.

2. Click **File** on the menu bar, and then click **Open**. The Open dialog box displays. Depending on your graphics program, the Open dialog box may list all graphics files or only those in the native file format.

3. If necessary, navigate to the location where you stored the **Bouquet.jpg** file that you downloaded from the Internet in the previous exercise.

4. Click the drop-down arrow in the **Files of type** box to display the list of compatible file types.

5. Click **JPEG**, the file type you used to save the file you downloaded from the Internet in the previous exercise. Now, the Open dialog box displays only JPEG files.

6. Click the **Bouquet.jpg** file to select it, and then click the **Open** button. The file opens in your graphics program window, as shown in Figure 2-11.

FIGURE 2-11
Downloaded picture open in graphics program

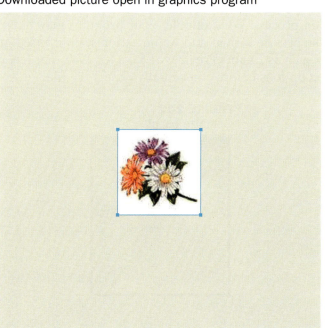

7. Click **File** on the menu bar, and then click **Save As**. The Save As dialog box opens, and you can save the file in your program's native file format.

8. Key the filename **Bouquet2** in the **File name** box.

9. If necessary, select your program's native file format from the **Files of type** or **Format** list, select the location where you want to save the file from the **Save in** list, and then click the **Save** button.

10. Leave the **Bouquet2** file open to use in the next exercise.

Optimize and Export Images

When you want to convert a file to a different file format, you use the Export command. Exporting converts a copy of the file to a different format, while leaving the original file intact. There are many reasons to export files to a different format. For example, if you plan to insert the file on a Web page, you want to use a small file that is supported by most Web browsers, such as GIF. If an image has solid colors, or very few colors, GIF is also appropriate. If you plan to insert the file in a newsletter that will be printed, you want to use a file type such as TIFF, which reproduces well on paper. Color photos usually are best saved as JPEG, but some grayscale and black and white photos can be saved as GIF without loss of quality. Refer to Lesson 1, Table 1-1, for a description of common graphics file formats.

Before you export a graphic, you should *optimize* it for the export file format. Optimizing involves selecting options for the best combination of file size and quality, depending on the export format you select. The methds for optimizing and exporting files vary greatly depending on your graphics program. Usually, you can export a file quickly without setting optimization options by clicking File on the menu bar, clicking Export or Save As, selecting the export file type, and then saving the file. In some programs, you may be able to select from a list of preset optimization options for different file types, or to select a file type and then select specific settings in a dialog box or panel similar to the one in Figure 2-12. Some programs let you combine the export and optimization process. For example, your program may have an Eport Wizard that automatically selects the best fle format and optimization setting based on how you plan to use the image, or a feature such as Export Preview or Save for Web that lets you preview the effects of selected optimization options before you actually export the file.

FIGURE 2-12
Optimize panel

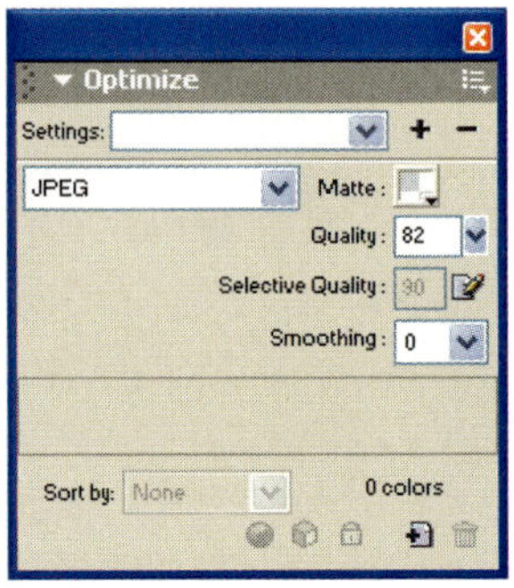

About Optimizing a File

In general, the goal of optimizing is to keep the file size as small as possible, while maintaining the highest possible quality. The optimization options vary, however, depending on the export file type.

If you are working with 8-bit graphics file formats such as GIF, TIFF, BMP, PICT, or PNG, the optimization options include *color palette*, color depth, dither, and loss settings. A color palette is a set of up to 256 colors that may be used in a file. Most programs have a number of built-in palettes suitable for different types

> **Note** ☑
>
> In some programs, you can only optimize files for specific purposes, such as for use on the World Wide Web. In those programs, you access optimization options by clicking File on the menu bar and then clicking a command such as Save for Web.

of files, and you may be able to customize the palettes, import palettes from other programs, or create your own palettes.

Table 2-1 describes some common color palettes. Note that some palettes use *websafe colors*, which are colors that are displayed the same way in all Web browsers. Although many browsers display more colors than are included in websafe palettes, many designers prefer to use a websafe palette to ensure that all visitors to a Web page see the same colors in images.

TABLE 2-1
Common color palettes

PALETTE NAME	DESCRIPTION
Adaptive	A custom palette that includes the actual colors that are in the file. Usually produces a high-quality image. An adaptive palette is a good choice for preserving colors if you convert a file to GIF.
WebSnap Adaptive	An adaptive palette that converts actual colors to websafe colors.
Web 216	A palette of 216 websafe colors. These colors look the same regardless of computer platform.
Exact	A palette that contains the exact colors used in the image. It can contain no more than 256 colors and automatically converts to an adaptive palette when more than 256 colors are present.
System	Palettes of 256 colors that are defined by the current computer system.
Grayscale	A palette of up to 256 shades of gray. If you select this palette, the image is converted to grayscale.
Black & White	A two-color palette consisting of black and white.
Uniform	A palette based on the RGB (red, green, blue) color system.
Custom	A palette that has been modified or imported from another source.

Color depth refers to the number of colors in an image or on a screen. The depth of an image is usually measured by the number of colors in the image. The depth of a screen is usually measured in bits per pixel. The higher the color depth in an image, the larger the file size is, but the better the quality as well. If you reduce the color depth in order to reduce the file size, the image will probably lose quality.

Dithering is a process a program uses to approximate colors that are not part of its color palette. That means that the colors displayed may be similar to those in the original image, but not exactly the same. Dithering usually increases file size, but it can come in handy in certain situations. For example, use dithering to offset the way some monitors display gradients as separate bands of color instead of as a gradual change.

The *loss* setting is used to control compression. Increase the loss setting to allow more compression, which results in a smaller file but lower quality.

If you select the JPEG file type, you should set the quality and *smoothing* options. Smoothing is the degree of sharpness in edges. When you increase the smoothing setting, you decrease the sharpness, which results in a smaller file, but a less focused image. When you compress a JPEG file, some quality is lost. Set the quality percentage higher to maintain quality and minimize compression.

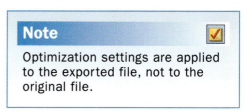

Note

Optimization settings are applied to the exported file, not to the original file.

Preview and Export a File

Although you can follow some basic rules in order to optimize your files, you must also use some trial and error. Most graphics programs provide preview features you can use to determine whether the settings you select compromise the quality of the image. In addition, the programs usually tell you the file size, and some even give you an estimate of the download time, which is important if you plan to use the image on a Web page.

When you select the preview feature, your graphics program may automatically suggest a format for exporting the image. If you are happy with the settings, you can export the image. You can also try different file formats, and then change the settings to achieve the results you want. If your program has a split screen preview feature, you can even compare the same file with different settings. This method gives you a great deal of control over the results of the export process.

STEP-BY-STEP 2.9

1. In the **Bouquet2** file, click **File** on the menu bar, and then click a command such as **Export Preview** or **Save for Web**. The file is displayed in a Preview window similar to the one shown in Figure 2-13. Notice the information at the top of the window: file size, download time, and file type.

FIGURE 2-13
Preview window

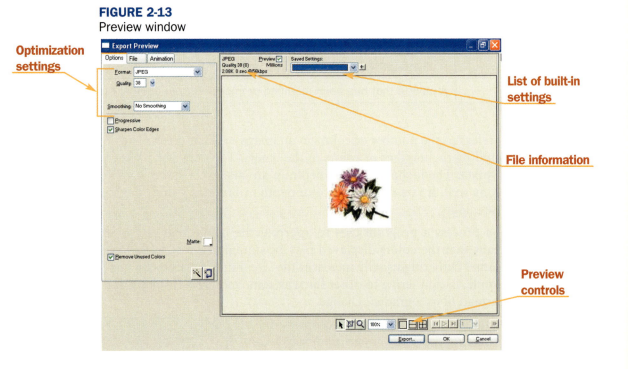

Optimization settings

List of built-in settings

File information

Preview controls

STEP-BY-STEP 2.9 Continued

2. Click the list of saved or built-in settings and select **GIF Adaptive 256**, or another GIF format that uses the Adaptive palette, if this format is not already selected.

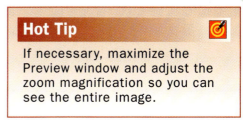

Hot Tip

If necessary, maximize the Preview window and adjust the zoom magnification so you can see the entire image.

3. Click the list of file formats and select **TIFF 8** (or PNG 8 if TIFF is not available). The file size increases slightly.

4. Click the option to allow dithering. The file size increases again.

5. If your program has a split screen preview mode, click the button to display two preview windows.

6. Click the image on the bottom half (or left) of the window to select it, then click the list of built-in settings for the bottom image and select **JPEG - Smaller File** (or **JPEG low**). In Figure 2-14, you can see that while the file is much smaller than the TIFF file, the image is less well defined.

FIGURE 2-14
Preview of both JPEG and TIFF files

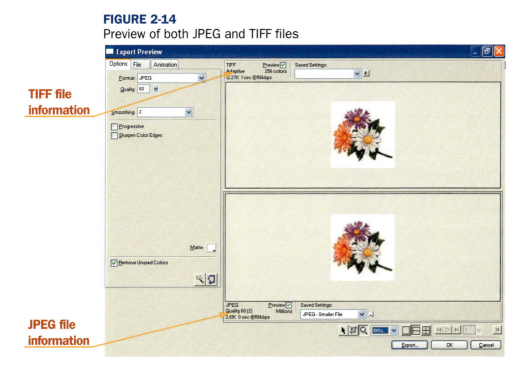

7. Click the list of built-in settings for the bottom image again and select **GIF Adaptive**, or another GIF format that uses the Adaptive palette. The quality improves and the file size and download time change as well.

8. Deselect the option to allow dithering.

9. Click the **Loss** box and key the value **25** or select 25 from the drop-down list. The quality does not change much, but the file size decreases.

STEP-BY-STEP 2.9 Continued

10. Click the **Export** or **Save** button in the dialog box. Another dialog box may open, as shown in Figure 2-15. This dialog box allows you to key a filename and select a storage location for the new file.

FIGURE 2-15
Export dialog box

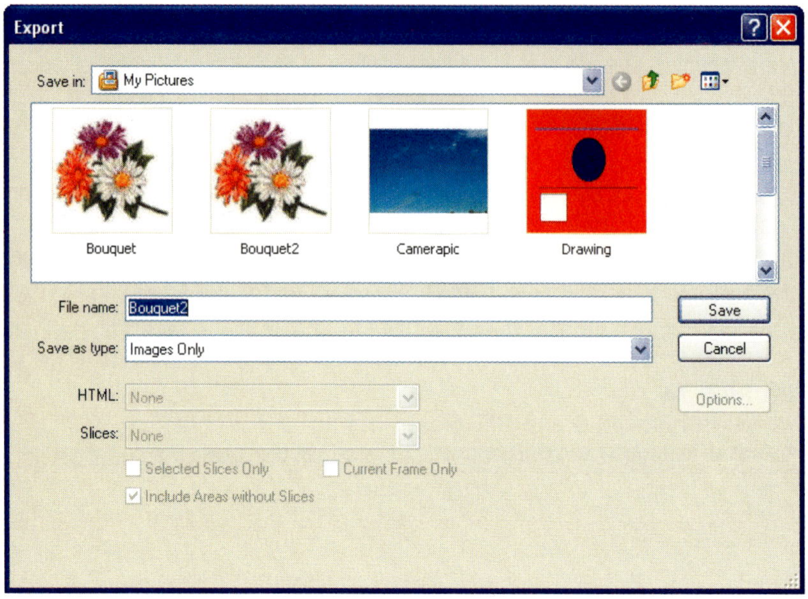

11. Key the filename **Bouquet3** in the **File name** box.

12. From the **Save in** list, select the location where you want to store the exported file, and then click the **Save** button. The file is exported to the specified location and saved with the new name in the new format. The **Bouquet2** file remains open in your graphics program.

13. Leave the **Bouquet2** file open to use in the next exercise.

Export a File without Optimizing

In most programs, you can export a file without selecting optimization settings, or by accepting default settings, by using the Export command or the Save As command. This is a good method to use if you know the program you want to export the file to, but are not sure how to set the specific file formatting options.

STEP-BY-STEP 2.10

1. In the **Bouquet2** file, click **File** on the menu bar, and then click **Export** or **Save As**. The Export dialog box opens.

2. Key the filename **Bouquet4** in the **File name** box.

STEP-BY-STEP 2.10 Continued

3. Click the **Save as type** drop-down arrow and select **Photoshop PSD**. (If you are using Photoshop as your graphics program, select a different file type, such as PNG.)

4. From the **Save in** list, select the location where you want to store the exported file, and then click the **Save** button. The **Bouquet4** file is exported as a Photoshop file while **Bouquet2** remains open in your graphics program.

5. Leave the **Bouquet2** file open to use in the next exercise.

Use an Export Wizard

Not all graphics programs offer an Export Wizard, but if yours does, you may find it a quick and easy way to export files. A *wizard* is a series of pages or dialog boxes that step you through a process that may otherwise be confusing or complicated. An Export Wizard provides prompts that help you select the appropriate file type based on the image quality and file size you need.

STEP-BY-STEP 2.11

1. In the **Bouquet2** file, click **File** on the menu bar, and then click **Export Wizard**. The first page of the Export Wizard is displayed on your screen, as shown in Figure 2-16. The default option is to use the Wizard to select a file format. There may be other options available, as well. If your program does not offer an Export Wizard, click **Export** or **Save As** on the **File** menu and then go to step 6.

FIGURE 2-16
First page of Export Wizard

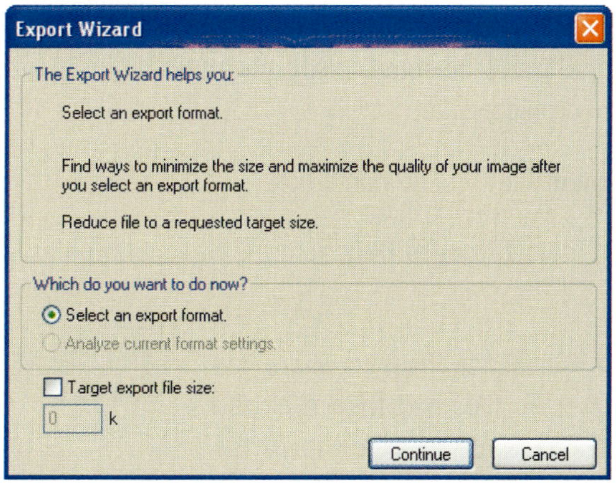

2. Click the **Continue** button. The second page of the Export Wizard opens. This page lists destination options, including a Web page, a desktop publishing program, and an image-editing program. You should select the option that best describes how you plan to use the exported image.

3. Click the option button for **A desktop publishing application**, and then click the **Continue** button. The Format Selected page of the Wizard is displayed on your screen. Because you specified the option for *A desktop publishing application*, the Wizard recommends using TIFF format.

STEP-BY-STEP 2.11 Continued

4. Click the **Exit** button. The Wizard closes and the Export Preview dialog box opens, as shown in Figure 2-17. The options in the Export Preview dialog box depend on the selected file format. In this case, because the TIFF format is selected, there are no additional options.

FIGURE 2-17
Export Preview dialog box with TIFF format selected

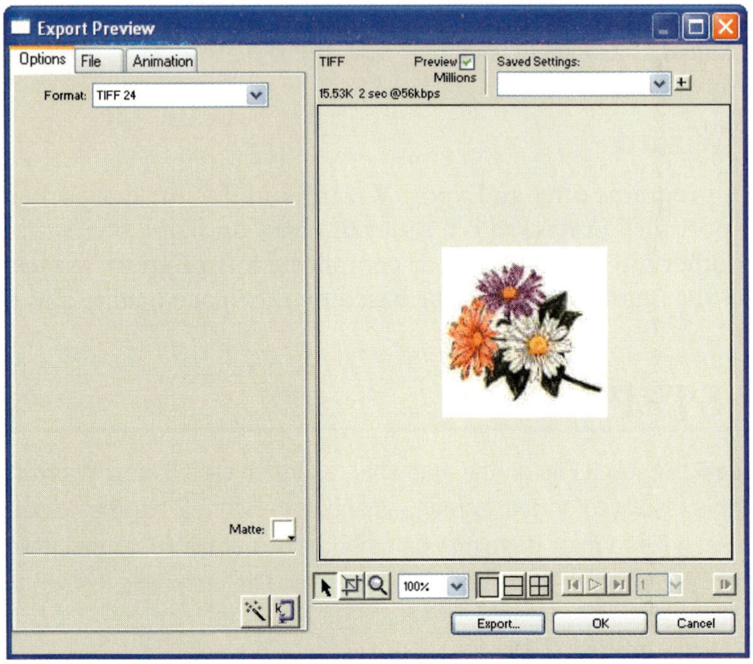

5. Click the **Export** button. The Export dialog box is displayed on your screen, with the options you used previously to export the image selected. If you have not used the wizard, select the **TIFF** file type from the **Save as type** drop-down list.

6. Key the filename **Bouquet5** in the **File name** box.

7. If you used the wizard, select **Images Only** from the **Save as type** list. If you did not use the wizard, select TIFF.

8. From the **Save in** list, select the location where you want to store the exported file, and then click the **Save** button. The **Bouquet5** file is exported to the specified location in the TIFF format. The **Bouquet2** file remains open in your graphics program.

9. Close the **Bouquet2** file as well as your graphics program.

> **Note**
>
> As you may have noticed, you now have five copies of the same image, each in a different file format. Because each file is in a different format and is associated with a different file extension, you did not *have* to change the filename. However, having multiple files with the same name, even if they are in different formats, can get confusing.

SUMMARY

In this lesson, you learned:

■ You can import graphics images from a variety of sources, including scanners, digital cameras, and the Internet.

■ In order to import graphics using a hardware device, you must make sure the device is correctly attached and installed to work with your computer.

■ You can scan images directly into a graphics program or into a document file.

■ You can use your operating system to copy files from a digital camera to your computer.

■ Most graphics programs can import pictures directly from a digital camera.

■ Graphics programs can open compatible files.

■ Many Web sites let you download clip art for free.

■ You can insert clip art pictures into document files, or you can open them in your graphics program for editing.

■ You can export files from your graphics program so you can use them in other programs.

■ When you export a file, you have the opportunity to optimize the file by selecting options for the export file format.

VOCABULARY *Review*

Define the following terms:

Clip art	Export	Scanner
Color depth	File format	Search site
Color palette	Import	Smoothing
Compatible	Key term	TWAIN
Device driver	Loss	Websafe colors
Dithering	Native file format	Wizard
Download	Optimize	

REVIEW *Questions*

TRUE / FALSE

Circle T if the statement is true or F if the statement is false.

T   F   **1.** The only way to acquire a graphics image is to draw it yourself.

T   F   **2.** A scanner uses light to capture a digital version of a printed picture.

T   F   **3.** TWIX is the software language used to control scanners.

T   F   **4.** Most computers can read a digital camera just like another disk drive if it is attached correctly to the computer.

T   F   **5.** Most graphics programs can open only files saved in their native file format.

T   F   **6.** Before you can insert clip art into a document, you must open it in your graphics program.

T   F   **7.** Use the Save Picture As command to download clip art.

T   F   **8.** When you export a file to a different format, it overwrites the original file.

T   F   **9.** When you use a wizard to export a file, you do not have the opportunity to optimize settings.

T   F   **10.** Dithering usually increases file size.

WRITTEN QUESTIONS

Write a brief answer to the following questions.

1. What are some of the different hardware devices you can use to acquire graphics images?

2. What are some reasons for exporting a file from your graphics program?

3. How might you find clip art pictures on the Internet?

4. Why might you want to scan a picture into your graphics program instead of directly into a document file?

5. What operating system commands can you use to transfer files from a digital camera to your computer?

FILL IN THE BLANK

Complete the following sentences by writing the correct word or words in the blanks provided.

1. If a program supports the _____ software language, you can use it to import pictures from a scanner.

2. To open a file in a different program, _____ it from your graphics program.

3. If a digital camera is correctly attached to your computer, you'll see it listed as a storage device in the _____ window.

4. The default file format for a particular program may be referred to as the _____ file format.

5. A(n) _____ format is one that a program can open, read, and save, even if it is not the default.

6. A(n) _____ helps you locate a Web page, even if you don't know the page's address.

7. Use your browser's _____ command to save a clip art image on the Web as a graphics file on your computer.

8. In order to download clip art, your computer must be connected to the Internet and you must have a(n) _____ with an Internet Service Provider (ISP).

9. If a graphics file retains its resolution no matter what type of screen it is displayed on, it is suitable for use on a(n) _____ .

10. A(n) _____ is a series of pages or dialog boxes that step you through a process that might otherwise be confusing or complicated.

PROJECTS

PROJECT 2-1

1. Using a pen and piece of paper, draw a map from your house to your school. Think about how the page will fit in the scanner before beginning.

2. Scan the map into your graphics program, making sure it is correctly positioned.

3. Save the file as **Map**.

4. Zoom in on your house, and then use the drawing tools to draw a 2-point red oval with no fill around it.

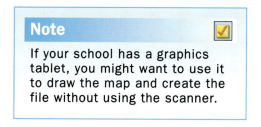

> **Note** ☑
>
> If your school has a graphics tablet, you might want to use it to draw the map and create the file without using the scanner.

5. Pan to the school, and then use the drawing tools to draw a 2-point red oval with no fill around it.

6. Print one copy of the file.

7. Save and close the **Map** file, but leave your graphics program open to use in Project 2-2.

PROJECT 2-2

1. Using a digital camera, take a picture of someone in your class.

2. In your graphics program, create a new graphics file using the default drawing area settings.

3. Import the picture from the camera into the graphics file.

4. Save the file as **Photo**.

5. Using the drawing tools, draw a 10-point white rectangle with no fill around the head of the person in the photo.

6. Export the file in TIFF format and save it as **Modified Photo**.

7. Close the **Photo** file without saving changes.

8. Open the **Modified Photo** file in your graphics program. Notice that it includes the rectangle shape.

9. Print one copy of the file.

10. Close the **Modified Photo** file without saving changes, but leave your graphics program open to use in Project 2-3.

PROJECT 2-3

1. Using your graphics program, open **GR Project 2-3.bmp** from the data files or use the Internet to locate and download a clip art image of an American flag.

2. Save the file as **Flag** in your program's native file format.

3. Increase the size of the drawing area to at least 5 inches by 5 inches.

4. Use the drawing tools to draw a polygon around the clip art image using no fill and a blue, 8-point, soft-rounded basic line (or formats available in your program). If possible, pick up the blue color from the clip art image.

5. Export the file in GIF Adaptive 256 format with the name **Revised Flag**.

6. Close the **Flag** file without saving changes.

7. Open the **Revised Flag** file in your graphics program. Notice that it includes the polygon shape.

8. Print one copy of the file.

9. Close the **Revised Flag** file without saving changes, and then close your graphics program.

WEB PROJECT

Use the Internet to compare features and prices of digital cameras, scanners, and graphics tablets. Which features do the more expensive devices offer that the low-end models do not? Which features do you think are the most important, and which do you think you could do without? Which device do you think represents the best value? Write a brief report using a word processing program, a text editor, or paper and a pen, explaining which device you would purchase and why.

TEAMWORK PROJECT

Discuss with your classmates the qualities to look for when you evaluate a graphics image you might want to import and use. Think about the fundamental concepts of graphic design, including composition and lighting, as well as how to identify the point of interest and the attributes that determine prominence and support the subject. If possible, gather different images to compare and contrast. Discuss the rules of composition, including the rule of thirds and the golden section/rectangle. Consider harmony and balance in the images, as well as discord and drama. You can research these topics on the Internet or in graphics design books and magazines that you have in the classroom or in your library. If possible, have different groups explore these ideas in relation to different types of graphics, such as Web pages, presentations, brochures, posters, book jackets, stationery, and even billboards. Present the results to the rest of your class.

CRITICAL *Thinking*

ACTIVITY 2-1

Import a picture into your graphics program using any of the methods discussed in this lesson. You might use clip art, a scanned image, a digital photo, or even a picture you draw using a graphics tablet. Save the picture in your program's native file format, and try printing it. Then, export the picture so you can open it in a different program, or insert it into a word processing document.

MODIFYING GRAPHICS

OBJECTIVES

Upon completion of this lesson, you should be able to:

- Work with bitmap images.
- Reshape vector paths.
- Position and align objects.
- Group and stack objects.
- Scale objects.
- Skew and distort objects.
- Rotate and flip objects.
- Copy objects.
- Crop an image.

Estimated Time: 2 hours

VOCABULARY

Align

Bounding box

Clipboard

Coordinates

Crop

Distort

Distribute

Flip

Group

Rotate

Scale

Skew

Stack

Transform

Modify graphics in order to improve, enhance, and correct images. You can modify original artwork that you create using the drawing tools in your graphics program, or you can modify images that you import from other sources. You can modify portions of an image or the entire image in order to achieve the desired results.

Even people who lack innate artistic talent can create wonderful graphics by making use of pattern, color, texture, and spatial relationships within an image. When you modify an image, you should keep in mind the basic principles of design in order to create an image that conveys the appropriate message, fits the purpose for which you are using it, and is pleasing to look at. These principles include *proportion*, which describes the size and location of one object in relation to other objects in the image; *balance*, which refers to the visual weight of objects and the way they are arranged; and *contrast*, which refers to the juxtaposition of different elements in order to create visual interest. You should also consider using *variety* to create visual interest by incorporating different elements in an image and *emphasis*, which is used to highlight or focus attention on a particular aspect of an image. In this lesson, you learn how to use your graphics program to modify bitmap and vector graphics.

Work with Bitmap Images

When you click a bitmap object using a selection tool, the entire object is selected just like a vector object. Most programs display a ***bounding box*** to indicate an object is selected. A bounding box is a rectangular shape with selection handles displayed around the object. Once the object is selected, you can make basic changes, such as moving it or resizing it. However, since a bitmap is made of dots—or pixels—you can make some changes to the image by changing the dots themselves. For example, you can change the colors of bitmaps by changing the colors of the dots. You can even erase the dots to remove parts of the image.

> **Note** ☑
>
> Vector illustration programs, such as Macromedia Freehand or Adobe Illustrator, do not include the bitmap editing tools discussed in this lesson. If possible, use a program such as Macromedia Fireworks or Adobe Photoshop, which provides tools for working with both bitmaps and vectors, or a program such as Paint, which is a Microsoft Windows accessory program that allows basic bitmap editing.

Some programs designate certain tools specifically for creating and modifying bitmap images. For example, you may use the Brush or Pencil tool to paint bitmaps, the Marquee or Lasso tool to select pixels in a bitmap image, and the Brush or the Paint Bucket to change the color of selected pixels.

Most graphics programs offer additional tools you can use to make subtle changes or add effects to bitmaps. For example, you might be able to smudge the color or make the image look out of focus. Table 3-1 describes some common tools used for working with bitmaps. Keep in mind that different programs may have different names for the tools, but in most cases the function is the same.

TABLE 3-1
Tools used to work with bitmaps

ICON	TOOL NAME	DESCRIPTION
	Marquee	Use the Marquee to select a rectangular area in a bitmap.
	Oval Marquee	Use the Oval Marquee to select an oval area in a bitmap.
	Lasso	Use the Lasso to select a freeform area.
	Polygon Lasso	Use the Polygon Lasso to select a straight-sided freeform area.
	Magic Wand	Use the Magic Wand to select pixels based on color.
	Brush	Use the Brush tool to create a new bitmap object, or to apply the current stroke style and color to selected pixels in a bitmap.
	Pencil	Use the Pencil tool to draw a new bitmap object.
	Paint Bucket	Use the Paint Bucket tool to fill selected areas with color.
	Eraser	Use the Eraser to remove pixels from a bitmap image.

Vector illustration programs, such as Macromedia Freehand and Adobe Illustrator, do not support editing bitmap images. Therefore, in those programs the tools described in this table are used to create and modify vector graphics. You can usually open bitmaps and make basic changes such as resizing in vector programs, but you must use a program such as Macromedia Fireworks or Adobe Photoshop to access full-featured bitmap editing tools.

Select Pixels Using a Marquee

When you want to work with just a portion of a bitmap object, you use either the Marquee tool or the Lasso tool to drag an outline around the area you want to select. The Marquee tool lets you select a regular-shaped area. The Lasso tool lets you select a freeform area.

When you release the mouse button after using either of these tools, a dashed line defines the area, and all the pixels in that area are selected. In some programs, the line flashes so that it is clearly visible in the image. Once an area is selected, you use other tools to modify it. To cancel a selection, simply click anywhere outside the selection, or use the Deselect command, which you will usually find on a menu. You can move a selection marquee by dragging it or by pressing the arrow keys on your keyboard, and you can add to the selected area by holding down Shift and using any bitmap selection tool to define another area overlapping the first. When you release the mouse button, the overlapping areas combine into one.

> **Note** ☑
>
> Although in some graphics programs you actually have to change to bitmap mode in order to use the bitmap tools, most programs that support both types of graphics let you work with either bitmap or vector tools interchangeably.

> **Hot Tip** ◎
>
> As with other selection tools, you can select more than one area—overlapping or not—by selecting one, pressing and holding Shift, then selecting others.

Some programs offer variations of these tools for selecting special shapes. An Oval Marquee tool, for example, selects an oval area. A Polygon Lasso tool lets you draw a straight-sided polygon to define a selection. To use the Polygon Lasso, you click at each point where you want a side of the shape to begin or end, then double-click to complete the shape. Many programs also let you select pixels in a bitmap based on color by using the Magic Wand tool and setting the tolerance level property. The lower the tolerance level, the more closely matched adjacent colors must be to be included in the selection. For example, if you select the Magic Wand tool and set the tolerance level to 0, when you click a pixel only adjacent colors that are exactly the same tone are selected. If you set the tolerance level to 50 or higher, you can select a wider range of tones.

S TEP-BY-STEP 3.1

1. Launch your graphics program, and open **GR Step 3-1** from the data files.

2. Save the file as **Coffee**.

3. Zoom in to 100% magnification, or even larger if necessary. When selecting pixels, zooming in on the image makes it easier to select the area you want.

> **Note** ☑
>
> If you find you cannot edit the file, you are probably using a vector graphics only program. Try using a program that provides tools for editing bitmap graphics.

STEP-BY-STEP 3.1 Continued

4. Click the **Marquee** tool in the toolbox, and then click and drag a rectangle around the cup, excluding the steam from the selection. The dashed line indicates the selected area, which includes the cup and some of the background, as shown in Figure 3-1.

FIGURE 3-1
Use Marquee tool to select rectangular area of pixels

Selection marquee

5. Click outside the selection to deselect the area, and then click the **Lasso** tool in the toolbox.

STEP-BY-STEP 3.1 Continued

6. Position the tip of the **Lasso** pointer along the edge of the saucer. Click and drag along the outline of the saucer to select it, as shown in Figure 3-2. Try to stay as close as possible to the outline of the saucer. (If your graphics program has a Polygon Lasso or a Magic Wand tool, try using it instead of the Lasso tool to select the saucer.)

FIGURE 3-2
Use Lasso tool to select freeform area of pixels

Lasso pointer

Selection marquee

7. Leave the **Coffee** file open to use in the next exercise.

Use the Brush, Pencil, and Eraser

Use the Pencil tool to draw freeform lines in a bitmap image using the current stroke color. Use the Brush tool to apply the current stroke style and color to selected pixels in a bitmap image. The Eraser tool lets you erase pixels from a bitmap image. Simply drag the eraser across the area you want to remove. If no area is selected, you can use the brush, pencil, and eraser anywhere in the drawing area. However, if an area is selected, these tools will affect only pixels within the selection.

STEP-BY-STEP 3.2

1. In the **Coffee** file, with the saucer still selected, click the **Brush** tool in the toolbox. You will use the brush to change the color of the selected area.

2. Click the stroke color palette and select red (such as hexadecimal code FF0000), and then set the stroke style to a 10-point soft line.

3. Drag the mouse pointer across the selected area to change its pixels to red. Notice that only the pixels within the area are modified. If you drag outside the selection, no change is made.

STEP-BY-STEP 3.2 Continued

4. Click the **Marquee** tool in the toolbox, and click anywhere outside the selected area to deselect it.

5. Click the **Pencil** tool in the toolbox, and then change the stroke to black. Drag the mouse pointer along the middle of the line of steam. This colors a black line of pixels as you drag.

6. Click the **Marquee** tool again, and select the entire area in the image above the cup, including the background and the line of steam. You may select part of the drawing area, too.

7. Click the **Eraser** tool in the toolbox, and then drag within the selected area. As you drag the tool, you erase the pixels, revealing the drawing area behind the image. When you have erased everything in the selected area, the image should look similar to Figure 3-3.

FIGURE 3-3
Modified bitmap file

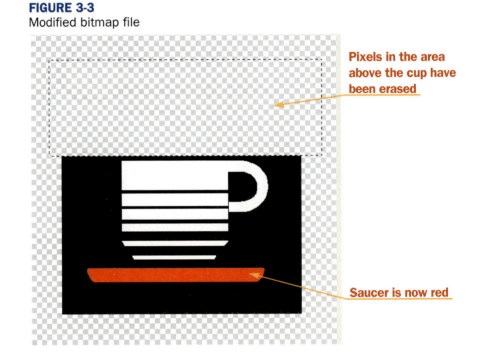

Pixels in the area above the cup have been erased

Saucer is now red

8. Click the **Marquee** tool and click anywhere outside the selection.

9. Save changes and leave the **Coffee** file open to use in the next exercise.

Use the Paint Bucket

The Paint Bucket tool applies the current fill color to pixels within a set color tolerance range. As for the Magic Wand tool, the lower the tolerance level, the more closely matched adjacent colors must be to be affected. The default tolerance setting is 255—the highest setting—allowing the change to affect a wide range of pixels.

Extra for Experts

Some graphics programs also have a Gradient tool that you can use to fill an area with a gradient color. Gradient color shades gradually from a dark hue to a light hue. You can use the Paint Bucket and Gradient tools to fill vector shapes as well as bitmaps.

S TEP-BY-STEP 3.3

1. In the **Coffee** file, click the **Paint Bucket** tool in the toolbox.

2. Select a blue fill such as hexadecimal code 0000FF.

3. Position the **Paint Bucket** mouse pointer so that the tip of the paint pouring out of the bucket is touching anywhere within the red saucer area, and then click the mouse button. The fill in the saucer area changes to blue.

4. Move the mouse pointer so it touches the cup handle, and click the mouse button. Since no area is selected, the cup handle and the top part of the cup, which are the same color and so fall within the same color tolerance range, are filled, as shown in Figure 3-4.

FIGURE 3-4
Use Paint Bucket to fill shapes with color

5. Click **Edit** on the menu bar, and then click **Undo**. This reverses the previous action to remove the fill. Now, select and fill the handle only.

6. Click the **Marquee** tool, and select a rectangular area around the cup handle. You can include part of the background in the selection because it is a different color.

7. Click the **Paint Bucket** tool, and then click the cup handle. Only the white pixels of the cup handle within the selected rectangle are filled.

8. Click the **Marquee** tool and click anywhere outside the selection to deselect it. Now, change the fill color of the background.

STEP-BY-STEP 3.3 Continued

9. Select a lighter color blue from the fill color palette, such as hexadecimal code 0099FF, click the Paint Bucket tool, and then click anywhere on the black background. The current fill color is applied to the background, as shown in Figure 3-5.

FIGURE 3-5
Fill a background in a bitmap image

10. Save changes and close the **Coffee** file. Leave your graphics program open to use in the next exercise.

> **Hot Tip**
>
> Remember, you can use the Eyedropper tool to make any color displayed on screen the current stroke or fill color. Simply click the palette you want to change, click the Eyedropper tool, and then click the color you want to pick up.

Reshape Vector Paths

Vector graphics are defined by points, which are positioned along the lines and curves that comprise the shape. You can change the shape by moving the points. Simply select the object with the Subselection tool, and then drag any point to a new location. In most programs, you can add, delete, and move points as well.

The tools for shaping vector paths vary, depending on your program. For example, some graphics programs have a Redraw Path tool that you use to extend or redraw existing vector paths. Select the tool, and then position the mouse pointer over the path to change. When the mouse pointer changes to the Redraw Path pointer, drag to extend or redraw the existing path.

A few programs offer tools that let you change the shape of a vector regardless of where the points are located. Points are moved, removed, or added as necessary. Select an object, and then select the Freeform tool. The mouse pointer changes to indicate the current action. Position the pointer on the selected path to pull or near the path to push. The path is modified based on the current size of the pointer, which you can change in the Properties panel or dialog box.

The Reshape Area tool lets you move all selected paths within an area defined by a circle attached to the pointer. Select the path and then select the Reshape area tool. Position the pointer over the selected path. When you drag, the portion of the path that falls within the pointer's circle moves. The portion outside the circle remains unchanged. As with the Freeform tool, change the size of the pointer in the Properties panel or dialog box.

Not all programs have the specific tools named in the following exercise. Experiment with the tools you have available in order to achieve the result shown in Figure 3-6.

> **Note** ☑
>
> Your program may display a message telling you that a selected shape must be ungrouped before you can edit its points. Click OK to continue.

STEP-BY-STEP 3.4

1. Open **GR Step 3-4** from the data files.

2. Save the file as **Head**.

3. Select the oval that makes the head and then select the **Freeform** tool.

4. Move the pointer so it is directly over the middle handle on the left side of the shape, and then drag it in about 0.25 inch. When you release the mouse button, the path is reshaped.

5. Move the pointer so it is directly over the middle handle on the right side of the shape, and then drag it in about 0.25 inch. Again, when you release the mouse button, the path is reshaped.

6. Click the **Subselection** tool in the toolbox, and then click the diagonal line that defines the length of the nose. Notice that the vector points that make the shape are displayed instead of selection handles.

7. Drag the top point up until it is even with the top of the eyes. When you release the mouse button, the path is redrawn.

8. Select the line that defines the mouth, and then select the **Reshape Area** tool. Change the size property to **50**.

9. Position the mouse pointer over the middle of the selected line, then press the mouse button. A circle appears around the mouse pointer, indicating the area that will be redrawn.

STEP-BY-STEP 3.4 Continued

10. Drag the mouse pointer down about 0.25 inch to change the line of the mouth into a smile. The image should look similar to the one in Figure 3-6.

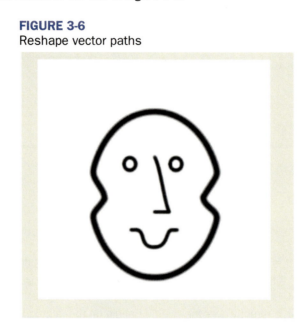

11. Save changes and close the **Head** file. Leave your graphics program open to use in the next exercise.

Position and Align Objects

When you create a graphics image, arrangement of the objects in the drawing area is important. The way you position objects in the foreground, middle distance, and background of an image can focus a viewer's attention on a particular part of the image, as well as give the image depth, perspective, and visual appeal. (Some programs have a Move tool specifically for this purpose.) When combined with different-sized objects, position can even give an image a three-dimensional effect.

You do not have to place each object in the perfect spot when you first create an image, because you can easily reposition objects after drawing them. The easiest way to position an object is to select it and then drag it to a new location. You can usually also use the arrow keys on the keyboard to move an object in small increments, such as 1 point for each press of the key. You may find the grid and rulers helpful for positioning objects. With the grid displayed, you can easily see whether objects are even or offset horizontally and vertically, and how much *white space*—the area between objects—there is.

In some programs, if you want to position the object in a precise location, you can set horizontal (X) and vertical (Y) *coordinates*. The coordinates are specific points laid out in an invisible grid in the drawing area. The grid starts in the top left corner, with coordinates of 0, 0. As you move an object to the right, the X coordinate increases. As you move down, the Y coordinate increases. You can view and/or control object coordinates using a panel or palette such as Info, shown in Figure 3-7, or Transform. By default, the top left corner of the object is located at the coordinates displayed in the panel. You enter the coordinates based on the current unit of measure. By default, most programs use pixels, but you can usually change to inches or centimeters. The command for changing the unit of measure varies, depending on your program. It may be on the Options drop-down menu in the Info panel or in the Preferences dialog box. (To open the Options drop-down menu in a panel, click the Options menu button in the upper-right corner.)

FIGURE 3-7
Info panel

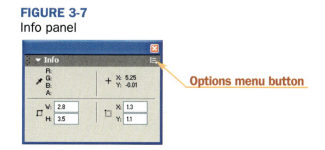

Options menu button

You can also usually *align* and *distribute* objects in an image. When the snap to grid option is toggled on, the objects automatically align with the nearest gridline. You can also align an object to adjust its position horizontally and vertically relative to the top, bottom, left, and right of the drawing area or to the currently selected area. Distributing objects adjusts the space between them. Alignment and distribution options are usually available on a panel or palette, as shown in Figure 3-8.

FIGURE 3-8
Align panel

S TEP-BY-STEP 3.5

1. Open **GR Step 3-5** from the data files.

2. Save the file as **Daisies**. This file contains three objects that are not positioned in an appealing way.

3. Select the large flower with the orange petals.

4. Move the selection pointer over the object, and then drag the object so the bottom of its stem is positioned near the bottom center of the drawing area. Release the mouse button when the object is in the correct location. Now, try moving one of the flowers by entering X and Y coordinates.

STEP-BY-STEP 3.5 Continued

5. Select the smaller blue flower on the left.

6. Open the panel or dialog box that contains the coordinate settings.

7. Click in the **X** box and key **25** using pixels as the unit of measure. Click in the **Y** box and key **320**, and then press **Enter**. The selected flower moves to the specified coordinates. Now, position the third flower by using the Align options.

8. Select the third flower. Open the panel, menu, or dialog box that contains the alignment options.

9. Select the option to align the object with the drawing area, and then select the option that aligns the option to the right edge. The flower moves to align with the right edge of the drawing area.

10. Select the option that aligns the selected object with the bottom edge. The flower moves to align with the bottom edge of the drawing area. The file should look similar to Figure 3-9. (If necessary, drag the flowers into position as shown.) Finally, put the finishing touches on the positions of the three objects by distributing them horizontally. (If a distribution option is not available in your program, skip to step 13.)

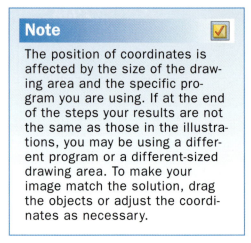

Hot Tip

If the bottom part of the panel is not displayed, simply drag the bottom border down.

Note

The position of coordinates is affected by the size of the drawing area and the specific program you are using. If at the end of the steps your results are not the same as those in the illustrations, you may be using a different program or a different-sized drawing area. To make your image match the solution, drag the objects or adjust the coordinates as necessary.

FIGURE 3-9
Objects aligned in the drawing area

STEP-BY-STEP 3.5 Continued

11. With the third flower still selected, press and hold **Shift**, click the large flower, and then click the small flower on the left. All three objects are now selected.

12. In the Align panel, click the tool that distributes the selected objects horizontally by center. The objects shift slightly so they are evenly distributed.

13. Save changes and leave the **Daisies** file open to use in the next exercise.

Group and Stack Objects

As you have learned, you can select more than one item at a time so that you can modify all objects at one time. In some programs, you can also *group* multiple objects. Grouped objects can be selected and modified as one unit. For example, if you create a group of three rectangles, you can change the fill color of all three objects at once. Group objects when you want the items to remain as one. That way, you don't have to worry about selecting all items each time you want to make changes.

To create a group, simply select the objects you want to include and then click the Group command on a menu such as Modify. Selection handles surround the entire group, rather than the individual objects in the group. Use the Ungroup command on the same menu to turn off grouping so you can work with the individual objects again.

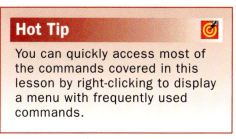

Hot Tip

You can quickly access most of the commands covered in this lesson by right-clicking to display a menu with frequently used commands.

Most graphics programs also provide a tool with a name such as Subselection or Group Selection that allows you to select one or more items in a group without ungrouping all objects. You can then easily edit a portion of the group.

As you draw objects, they **stack** in the drawing area, even if they do not actually overlap each other. The first object you create is at the bottom or back of the stack, and the last object you create is at the top or front of the stack. You will sometimes need to rearrange the stacking order of objects to make sure that an object displays properly or to create overlapping effects.

To rearrange the stacking order, select the object you need to change and then click the Arrange command on a menu such as Modify. Most programs give you four options for adjusting stacking order: Send to Back, Send Backward, Bring Forward, and Bring to Front. Send to Back moves an object behind all other objects, while Bring to Front positions an object in front of all other objects. Send Backward and Bring Forward move objects forward or backward one position at a time.

Extra for Experts

Do not confuse the stacking order with layers. Some programs have a Layers feature you can use to separate an image into individual transparent planes. Layers are used for creating complex images, animations, and certain special effects.

S TEP-BY-STEP 3.6

1. In the **Daisies** file, select all three flowers if they are not already selected.

2. Select the command to group the objects. The three objects are now grouped together to make up a single object. Notice that the selection handles are displayed on the corners of the entire group, as shown in Figure 3-10. Changes that you make now will affect the entire group. Try changing the alignment.

FIGURE 3-10
Three objects are part of a single group

3. If the Align panel is not open, open it. Make sure the option to align objects to the drawing area is selected, and then click the tool that aligns the selected object at the top edge. The entire group moves up to the top of the drawing area. Now, ungroup the objects so you can change the stacking order.

4. Select the command to ungroup the objects. The three objects are ungrouped, although all three remain selected.

5. Click anywhere outside the selected objects to deselect them, and then select the small flower on the left.

6. Set the X coordinate for the selected object to **130** pixels and set the Y coordinate to **125** pixels or drag the flower so that its stem and a few petals overlap the large flower.

7. Select the small flower on the right. Set the X coordinate to **260** and the Y coordinate to **75**, or drag the flower so that it overlaps the large flower.

8. With the flower on the right still selected, click the **Arrange** command, and then click **Send to Back** on the submenu. The selected flower moves behind the other objects.

STEP-BY-STEP 3.6 Continued

9. Select the large flower. Click the **Arrange** command, and then click **Bring to Front** on the submenu. The large flower moves in front of the other objects. The image should look similar to Figure 3-11.

FIGURE 3-11
Modified image includes stacked objects

10. Save changes, and leave the **Daisies** file open to use in the next exercise.

Scale Objects

When you want to resize an object to make it larger or smaller, you can *scale* the object. To scale means simply to change an object's size.

Some programs allow you to simply drag a selection handle to scale an object. Other programs offer a Scale tool or Scale command for this purpose. When you select the Scale tool, *transform* handles may be displayed around the selected object. Transform is a term used to describe changes to the characteristics of an object or selection. You drag the transform handles to change the height, the width, or both dimensions at once. Most programs also allow you to scale an object precisely by specifying height and width in a panel or dialog box. Most programs also allow you to scale an object precisely by specifying height and width in a panel or dialog box using pixels, inches, or centimeters as the unit or measure.

STEP-BY-STEP 3.7

1. In the **Daisies** file, select the large middle flower if it is not already selected.

2. Click the **Scale** tool in the toolbox. A bounding box with transform handles may display around the object, as shown in Figure 3-12.

FIGURE 3-12
Object selected for scaling

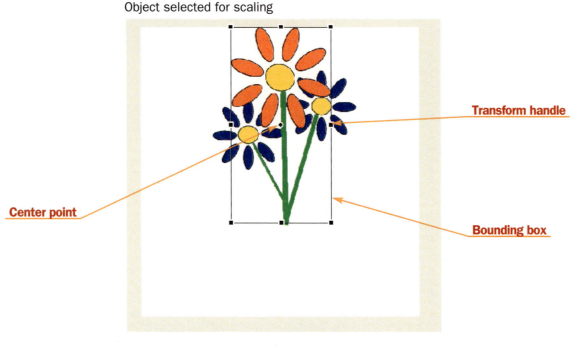

Transform handle

Center point

Bounding box

3. Position the mouse pointer over the bottom center transform handle. When the pointer is positioned correctly, it looks like a vertical double-headed arrow with a horizontal line in the middle.

STEP-BY-STEP 3.7 Continued

4. Drag the handle down to the bottom of the drawing area. When you release the mouse button, the object is resized, as shown in Figure 3-13. Notice that since you changed the height but not the width, the flower looks distorted and out of proportion.

FIGURE 3-13
Height of the object has been increased

5. Select the flower on the left.

6. Click the **Scale** tool in the toolbox to display the transform handles around the selected flower. Position the mouse pointer over the handle in the top left corner and then drag up and to the left to the top of the drawing area. When you release the mouse button, the object is resized. This time, you changed both the height and width so the flower does not look distorted. Now group the objects and scale the entire group at the same time.

> **Hot Tip**
>
> Press and hold Shift while you drag a corner handle to maintain the original proportions of an object while scaling.

7. Use the selection tool in the toolbox to drag a rectangle around all three flowers in the image. This selects the flowers so you can group them. When selecting stacked objects, it may be easier to drag the selection tool around the objects to select than to click each object.

8. Select the command to group the objects. This time, set precise dimensions for scaling the entire group.

STEP-BY-STEP 3.7 Continued

9. In the panel or dialog box that allows you to specify an object's size, select to use pixels as the unit of measure, then click in the **Width** box and key **250**, click in the **Height** box and key **300**, and then press **Enter**. The object is scaled to the specified dimensions, as shown in Figure 3-14.

FIGURE 3-14
Scaled group

10. Save changes and close the **Daisies** file. Leave your graphics program open to use in the next exercise.

Skew and Distort Objects

Sometimes you might want objects in an image to look distorted or slanted. You can *skew* an object to slant it along its horizontal or vertical axis. Most graphics programs supply a Skew tool or Skew command that you can use to display transform handles. Drag a center side handle to skew the object vertically, or drag a center top or bottom handle to skew the object horizontally. Drag a corner handle to skew it both vertically and horizontally at the same time, and to achieve perspective in the image.

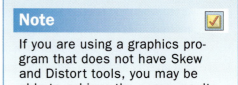

> **Note** ☑
>
> If you are using a graphics program that does not have Skew and Distort tools, you may be able to achieve the same results simply by moving the vector points as described earlier in this lesson. Ask your instructor for information on how to proceed.

When you *distort* an object, you change its height and/or width without maintaining the original proportions. Click the Distort tool or select the Distort command to display transform handles, then use the handles to move the sides or corners of the object to change its size and proportions. Use distorting to achieve a three-dimensional effect.

S TEP-BY-STEP 3.8

1. Open **GR Step 3-8** from the data files.

2. Save the file as **Road**.

3. Select the object, and then click the **Skew** tool in the toolbox or select the **Skew** command. (You may find the Skew tool on a hidden toolbar beneath a tool such as the Scale tool.) The transform handles display around the object.

4. Move the mouse pointer so it is touching the bottom left handle, then drag the handle out to the lower left corner of the drawing area. In most programs both the left and right lower corners of the object move, as shown in Figure 3-15. (If both handles do not move in the program you are using, repeat the step to drag the right handle to the lower-right corner.) Release the mouse button to complete the transformation.

FIGURE 3-15
Skewing an object

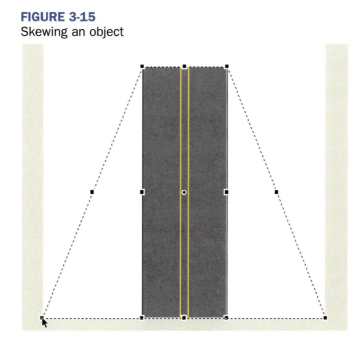

STEP-BY-STEP 3.8 Continued

5. Move the mouse pointer so it is touching the top left handle, then drag the handle in so that it is just to the left of the center handle. If both handles do not move, repeat the step to drag the right corner to the center. The image should look similar to Figure 3-16. Notice how skewing the object has made it look as if it is a road disappearing into the distance. Now, use the Distort tool to add a three-dimensional effect to the image.

FIGURE 3-16
Skewed object

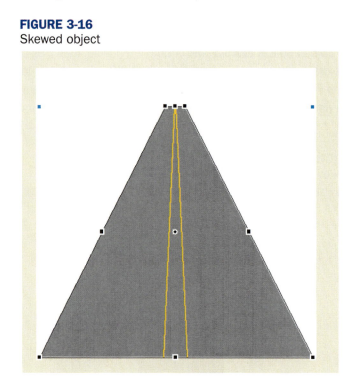

6. Click the **Distort** tool in the toolbox or select the **Distort** command, then drag the bottom center handle to the right. Release the mouse button when the handle you are dragging is positioned in the lower right corner of the drawing area. Don't worry about the part of the object that is hidden from view outside the drawing area.

7. Drag the top center handle toward the upper-left corner of the drawing area. Release the mouse button or press **Enter** to complete the transformation. When you deselect the object, the image should look similar to Figure 3-17.

STEP-BY-STEP 3.8 Continued

FIGURE 3-17
Modified image has depth and perspective

8. Save changes and close the **Road** file. Leave your graphics program open to use in the next exercise.

Rotate and Flip Objects

Two other methods of transforming an object are rotating and flipping. When you *rotate* an object, it pivots around an axis of rotation, sometimes called the point of origin. To rotate an object, select any transformation tool or the Rotate command and then move the mouse pointer near the object outside the bounding box. When the pointer changes to a rotation pointer, drag in any direction to rotate the object. Alternatively, some programs have a Rotate tool. Click the tool, and then drag a corner handle to rotate the object. Some programs also have menu commands that let you rotate by 180 degrees, or by 90-degree increments, and some programs let you enter a specific value for the rotation.

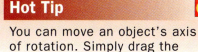

Hot Tip

You can move an object's axis of rotation. Simply drag the point to a new location.

You can *flip* an object horizontally or vertically to reverse the image from left to right or top to bottom. Most programs have Flip Horizontal and Flip Vertical commands, but some programs use a Reflect tool for flipping. When you use a Reflect tool you set a specific axis across which to flip the object. The default axis is 90 degrees, which flips the object to create a mirror image.

STEP-BY-STEP 3.9

1. Open **GR Step 3-9** from the data files.

2. Save the file as **Daisies2**. This file is similar to the Daisies file you worked with in previous exercises, but it has only two flower objects.

3. Select the larger flower on the left.

4. Click the **Scale** tool or select the **Rotate** Command to display transformation handles. Your program might have a Rotate tool that displays rotation handles

5. Move the mouse pointer to an area outside the edge of the object until it changes to the rotation pointer. If your program has rotation handles, move the mouse pointer to touch a rotation handle. Drag counterclockwise—to the left—until the top right transformation handle is positioned straight up, as shown in Figure 3-18. Release the mouse button to complete the rotation.

FIGURE 3-18
Drag selected object to rotate it around its axis

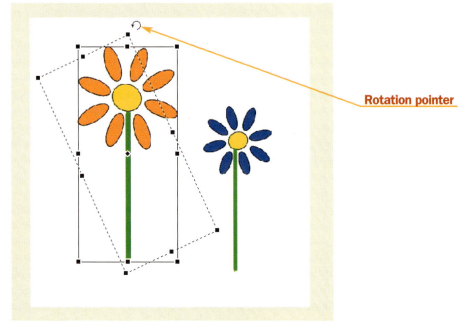

Rotation pointer

6. Select the smaller flower on the right.

7. Click the **Scale** tool if necessary, or select the **Rotate** command and then move the mouse pointer outside the edge of the object to display the rotation pointer. This time, drag clockwise—to the right—until the top left transformation handle is positioned straight up. Release the mouse button.

Extra for Experts

If you want to rotate the object in 15-degree increments, hold down Shift while you drag.

STEP-BY-STEP 3.9 Continued

8. With the small flower still selected, click the command to flip the object horizontally. It should look similar to Figure 3-19.

FIGURE 3-19
Smaller flower has been flipped

9. Select the larger flower and then click the command to flip the object horizontally.

STEP-BY-STEP 3.9 Continued

10. Set the X coordinate for the larger flower to **240** and the Y coordinate to **45**, then set the X coordinate for the smaller flower to **90** and the Y coordinate to **125**. The image should look similar to the one in Figure 3-20. (You may need to adjust coordinates or drag the objects to match this figure.)

FIGURE 3-20
Flowers have been rotated, flipped, and positioned

11. Save changes and leave the **Daisies2** file open to use in the next exercise.

Copy Objects

When you want to duplicate a vector object or a complete bitmap object, you can use commands such as Copy and Paste or Duplicate. In some programs, the Copy and Paste commands create a new object directly on top of the original object, while in other programs the pasted object appears in the center of the drawing area. The Duplicate command creates a new object overlapping the original object. No matter what means you use to copy an object, you can move the copy to any location in the drawing area.

There are variations of the Copy, Cut, and Paste commands in most programs. For example, Paste Special lets you paste an item with a link to the original object. Some graphics programs have Paste in Front or Paste in Back commands. These commands paste the copied object directly on top of or behind the original object. Other variations include Paste as Mask, Paste Inside, and Paste Attributes, which lets you copy just the formatting from one object to another.

> **Note** ☑
>
> The Copy, Cut, and Paste commands are used in all Windows programs to copy and move text as well as objects from one location to another. The item that is cut or copied is placed on the **Clipboard**, a temporary storage area in your computer's memory. When you select the Paste command, the item is inserted at the current location.

In programs that support bitmap editing, you can also use the Copy and Paste commands to create a bitmap object from selected pixels. Simply select the pixel area, click Copy on the Edit menu, and then click Paste on the Edit menu. The selected area becomes an object that you can select and modify as a complete unit. Most programs also have tools for duplicating an area of selected pixels without creating an object. Duplicating pixels is a great way to touch up photographs because you replace the pixels you don't like with copies of pixels you do like.

STEP-BY-STEP 3.10

1. In the **Daisies2** file, select the smaller flower on the left.

2. Click **Edit** on the menu bar, and then click **Copy**. The object is copied to the Clipboard.

3. Click **Edit** on the menu bar, and then click **Paste**. A copy of the object is pasted into the graphics file. Don't worry if nothing seems to have happened! The new object may be positioned directly over the original object.

4. With the new object selected, click the command to flip the object horizontally. Drag the flipped object to the right so the bottom of its stem aligns with the bottoms of the other two stems. It will appear to be lying almost on top of the larger flower. Now, duplicate the larger flower.

5. Select the larger flower.

6. Click **Edit** on the menu bar, and then click **Duplicate**. A duplicate of the object is inserted overlapping the original. The duplicate object is selected.

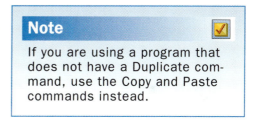

Note ☑

If you are using a program that does not have a Duplicate command, use the Copy and Paste commands instead.

7. Click the command to flip the object left to right. The duplicate of the large flower is flipped horizontally. Drag the flower to the left so the bottom of its stem aligns with the bottoms of the other stems.

8. Select the command to send the selected object to the back of the stacking order, if necessary. Now, try copying more than one object at a time. (If you cannot group the objects in your program, copy and transform each one individually.)

9. With the duplicate large flower still selected, press and hold **Shift** and click the small flower overlapping it. Now, both flowers on the left are selected. You could group the two together, but since you don't plan on modifying them as a unit all the time, you can just work with the two selected objects.

10. Click **Edit** on the menu bar, and then click **Duplicate**. Duplicates of both objects are created, overlapping the originals. Both new duplicates are selected.

STEP-BY-STEP 3.10 Continued

11. Rotate the objects until they appear about vertical. Then, drag the objects to the right so the bottoms of the stems are all aligned. Click the selection tool to remove the transformation handles. The image should look similar to Figure 3-21.

FIGURE 3-21
Image includes multiple copies of the original two objects

12. Save changes and close the **Daisies2** file. Leave your graphics program open to use in the next exercise.

Crop an Image

When you want to remove portions of an image, you *crop* it. Cropping cuts out the portions of a file that you don't want. To crop an image in most graphics program, you use the Crop tool to define a rectangular bounding box in the image. Double-clicking in the box, or pressing Enter, retains the content inside the rectangle while removing the content outside the rectangle. The drawing area is resized to fit the area within the box. In some programs, you can specify dimensions for the area you want to crop in a dialog box or panel.

Did You Know?

You can use the Copy, Cut, and Paste commands to copy or move an object from one graphics file to another. You can even move the object to a file created with a different program. Just copy or cut the object to the Clipboard, position the insertion point in the file where you want to paste the object, and click the Paste command.

Hot Tip

Some programs have commands for cropping or trimming the drawing area itself. Use such a command to automatically delete extra space around the image.

S TEP-BY-STEP 3.11

1. Open **GR Step 3-11** from the data files.

2. Save the file as **Planes**.

3. Click the **Crop** tool in the toolbox, move the mouse pointer to the top right corner of the image, and then drag down and to the right to draw a rectangle that includes the full width of the image, but excludes the telephone wires, as shown in Figure 3-22.

FIGURE 3-22
Drag to define the area to crop

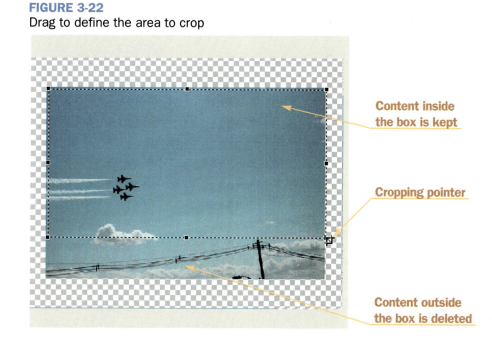

Content inside the box is kept

Cropping pointer

Content outside the box is deleted

4. Release the mouse button when you have completed the rectangle. You can drag the handles on the bounding box to adjust the size of the crop area if necessary.

5. When you are satisfied with the area you have defined for cropping, double-click within the bounding box, or press **Enter**. The image is cropped, and the drawing area is resized.

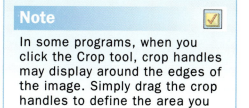

Note ☑

In some programs, when you click the Crop tool, crop handles may display around the edges of the image. Simply drag the crop handles to define the area you want to crop.

STEP-BY-STEP 3.11 Continued

6. Click **View** on the menu bar, and then click **Fit All** to increase the magnification. The image should look similar to Figure 3-23.

FIGURE 3-23
Cropped image does not include the telephone wires

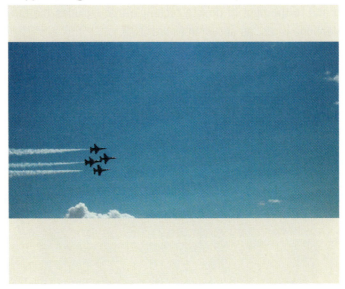

7. Save changes and close the **Planes** file. Close your graphics program.

> **Extra for Experts**
>
> In a file that contains multiple objects, you can crop a single bitmap object, or selected pixels in the bitmap, while leaving the other objects in the drawing area intact. Simply select the object or pixels you want to crop, then click Crop Selected Bitmap on the Edit menu. Adjust the bounding box as desired, and then double-click within the bounding box to complete the procedure.

SUMMARY

In this lesson, you learned:

- Some programs have graphics tools designed specifically for working with bitmap images.
- You can select and modify areas of pixels in a bitmap image.
- There are tools you can use to reshape vector paths.
- You can move objects around in an image.
- Most graphics programs have tools for aligning and distributing objects in an image.

- You can group multiple objects together so that you can modify them as one unit.
- Objects stack from back to front as you create them in a drawing; you can rearrange stacking order to change the way objects overlap.
- There are many ways to transform an object, including scaling, skewing, distorting, flipping, and rotating.
- You can create exact duplicates of vector and bitmap objects.
- Cropping lets you remove parts of an image you don't want.

VOCABULARY *Review*

Define the following terms:

Align	Distort	Rotate
Bounding box	Distribute	Scale
Clipboard	Flip	Skew
Coordinates	Group	Stack
Crop		Transform

REVIEW *Questions*

TRUE / FALSE

Circle T if the statement is true or F if the statement is false.

T   F   **1.** Use the Lasso tool to draw freeform vector paths.

T   F   **2.** Use the Paint Bucket tool to copy pixels.

T   F   **3.** The easiest way to position an object is to select it and then drag it to a new location.

T   F   **4.** The X coordinate sets the vertical position of an object.

T   F   **5.** Once you group objects, you cannot edit them individually.

T   F   **6.** Bring an object to the front if you want it stacked on top of all the other objects in the image.

T   F   **7.** If you change the height of an object without changing its width, you lose its original proportions.

T   F   **8.** Skew an object to change its height and width proportionally.

T   F   **9.** When you use the Duplicate command, the new object overlaps the original object.

T   F   **10.** When you crop an image, the drawing area is resized to fit the remaining content.

WRITTEN QUESTIONS

Write a brief answer to the following questions.

1. How is modifying bitmap images different from modifying vector images?

2. Why might you want to use the Lasso tool instead of the Marquee tool to select pixels?

3. What effect can you achieve by skewing an object along both its horizontal and vertical axes?

4. What's the difference between aligning objects and distributing objects?

5. What is one reason for using the X and Y coordinates to position an object instead of just dragging it?

FILL IN THE BLANK

Complete the following sentences by writing the correct word or words in the blanks provided.

1. One way to duplicate a complete bitmap object is to use the _____ and _____ commands.

2. To reverse an image, _____ it.

3. The area between objects is called _____.

4. When you _____ an object, you change its height and/or width without maintaining the original proportions.

5. Drag a(n) _____ handle to skew an object horizontally and vertically at the same time.

6. Use the Subselection tool to move vector _____.

7. To make sure an object is stacked behind all other objects in the image, use the _____ command.

8. To position an object along the bottom of the drawing area, you should _____ it with the bottom edge.

9. Use the _____ tool to apply the current stroke style and color to selected pixels in a bitmap image.

10. When you select pixels with the Marquee tool or the Lasso, a(n) _____ dashed line defines the selected area.

PROJECTS

PROJECT 3-1

1. Open **GR Project 3-1** from the data files.

2. Save the file as **Leaves**.

3. Use the **Marquee** tool to select the leaf on the right.

4. Flip the selection vertically.

5. Use the **Marquee** tool to select the small, green leaf on the left.

6. Use the **Paint Bucket** tool to change the main color of this leaf from green to yellow.

7. Use the **Lasso** tool to select the leaf in the center.

8. Use the **Paint Bucket** tool to change the main color of this leaf from brown to brick red.

9. Use the **Paint Bucket** tool to change the background color from black to the same color as the veins in the large leaf on the right:
   A. Make sure nothing is selected in the image.
   B. Click the **Paint Bucket** tool.
   C. Open the fill color palette, and then click the mouse pointer (it is shaped like an eye-dropper) on the veins in the large leaf. This picks up the color and makes it current.
   D. Click anywhere in the background.

10. Print one copy of the file.

11. Save and close the **Leaves** file, but leave your graphics program open to use in Project 3-2.

PROJECT 3-2

1. Open **GR Project 3-2** from the data files.

2. Save the file as **Dog**.

3. Crop the photo so that only the dog remains.

4. Resize the drawing area to 7 inches by 7 inches.

5. Select the image object, open the **Align** panel, and select the options for aligning with the top left corner of the drawing area.

6. Use the **Copy** and **Paste** commands to create three copies of the object, and align one in each corner of the drawing area:
   A. With the object selected, copy and paste the object.
   B. Align the object with the top right corner.
   C. Paste the object again, and then align the object with the bottom right corner.
   D. Paste the object again, and then align the object with the bottom left corner.

7. Paste the object one more time. This time, scale the object to 295 pixels wide by 455 pixels high, and align it in the center both horizontally and vertically.

8. Set the stacking order so the four smaller objects are in front of the larger object.

9. Use the **Marquee** tool to select the entire drawing area, and then fill the selection with a red color that you pick up from the flowers on the bush in the background of the image:
   A. Click the **Paint Bucket** tool.
   B. Open the fill color palette, and then move the mouse pointer (it is shaped like an eye-dropper) over the flowers in the background until the red color you want to use is displayed in the fill color palette. Click the mouse pointer to pick up the color and make it current.
   C. Click anywhere in the selection.

10. If necessary, change the stacking order of the selected area to send it to the back, behind the images of the dog.

11. Print one copy of the file.

12. Save and close the **Dog** file, but leave your graphics program open to use in Project 3-3.

SCANS PROJECT 3-3

1. Create a new file in your graphics program and save it as **House**.

2. Use the drawing tools to draw a picture that includes a house, a street, and at least one tree.

3. Use the skills you have learned in this lesson to integrate the objects together into a unified image. For example, define the foreground, middle ground, and background of the image by scaling and positioning objects appropriately. Stack, skew, and distort objects in order to create depth and perspective. Use fill and stroke properties to define shapes.

4. When you are satisfied with the drawing, save the file.

5. Print one copy of the file.

6. Save and close the **House** file, but leave your graphics program open to use in Project 3-4.

PROJECT 3-4

1. Open **GR Project 3-4** from the data files.

2. Save the file as **Arrow**.

3. Display the grid.

4. Select the triangle with the **Subselection** tool to show the vector points.

5. Drag the point at the tip of the lower left of the triangle diagonally down and to the left to the corner of the next grid line.

6. Drag the point at the tip of the lower right of the triangle diagonally up and to the right to the corner of the next grid line.

7. Select the **Freeform** tool and change the size to **75**.

8. Position the pointer inside the triangle. Create a semicircular bulge pushing out in the middle of the line on the right side of the triangle by using the Freeform pointer to push the middle of the line up and to the right.

9. Use the same tool to create a semicircular bulge pushing in at the middle of the other two lines.

10. Print one copy of the file.

11. Save and close the **Arrow** file, and close your graphics program.

WEB PROJECT

M.C. Escher was an artist known for his use of perspective and proportion to achieve optical illusions in his images. Use the Internet to research Escher and to locate some of his artwork that you can download. Write an essay explaining how Escher uses the basic principles of design, and why his images are so unique. Can you identify tools available in your graphics program such as duplicating and flipping that could help you achieve Escher-like images? Try your hand at creating such an image, then print it, and share it with your classmates.

TEAMWORK PROJECT

Discuss with your classmates the basic principles of design and how you can use them to achieve different effects in an image. Gather together some pictures such as posters, book covers, and magazine illustrations. Have each person in the team look for a specific design principle, such as proportion, balance, and contrast. Determine whether or not the artist made use of variety and emphasis. Discuss whether you think the image works, or if it could be improved by applying a transformation, such as changing the scale or the color. Rank the images on how many principles of design each one uses, and then share your results with the class.

CRITICAL*Thinking*

ACTIVITY 3-1

Look up a definition of the word *perspective* in a standard dictionary and in an art dictionary. Look at different images to determine how the artist uses perspective. When you believe you have an understanding of how perspective can enhance an image, create a new file and use basic shapes to draw an image that uses perspective. It may be realistic, abstract, or stylized. Make use of the drawing and editing tools for both vectors and bitmaps to transform and modify the shapes in your drawing. Use color, alignment and positioning as well as distortion and skewing. When you are finished, save the file, print it, and share it with your classmates.

ADDING TEXT TO GRAPHICS

OBJECTIVES

Upon completion of this lesson, you should be able to:

- Create a text object.
- Check spelling.
- Apply character formatting.
- Set text direction and alignment.
- Apply fills and strokes to text.
- Import text.
- Transform a text block.
- Convert text to vector graphics.

Estimated Time: 1.5 hours

VOCABULARY

Baseline

Expandable text block

Fixed-width text block

Font

Font size

Font style

Insertion point

Justified

Kerning

Leading

Orientation

Text block

Text flow

Wrap

Text may be incorporated in a graphics file as shapes that make up part of the image itself or more traditionally, as words in captions, headlines, titles and so on. For example, you may want to use the letter *M* as the focal point for a logo for a gift shop named Marigolds, or you may want to include the shop's address and store hours in an image to be used as a print advertisement.

Most graphics programs include tools for entering and editing text in much the same way as in a word processing or desktop publishing program. You can change character formatting, adjust spacing and alignment, and even check your spelling for errors. You can also convert text characters into shapes that you can modify using the tools you use to modify other vector objects. By combining the features of desktop publishing with graphics effects such as fills, strokes, and transformations, you can create exciting text objects that enhance your images and provide useful information. In this lesson, you learn how to create and modify text objects in a graphics file.

Create a Text Object

To enter text in a graphics file, you use a tool with a name such as Text or Type to create a *text block*, and then key the text using your computer keyboard. An *insertion point* within the block indicates where characters appear when keyed. The text is entered using the current formatting options set in your program, including the fill color, which determines the text color.

A selected text block has a bounding box and handles, similar to other selected objects in a graphics file. As you will learn, you can resize, move, duplicate, and otherwise modify a text block using many of the same commands you use to modify other graphics objects.

Most graphics programs let you create either a fixed-width text block of a certain size or an expandable text block with a size determined by the number of characters it contains. After you key text in a text block, you can edit it just as in a word processing program.

Create a Fixed-Width Text Block

In a *fixed-width text block*, you specify the block size before you begin keying the text. As you key text, it *wraps* within the block, which means that when text reaches the end of one line within the block, it moves automatically to the beginning of the next line. You can resize the block, if necessary, to adjust how the text fits in the block or how the block fits into the image as a whole. To create a fixed-width text block, select the text tool and then drag the pointer to define the size of the block.

STEP-BY-STEP 4.1

1. Launch your graphics program and open **GR Step 4-1** from the data files.

2. Save the file as **Beans**.

3. Set the fill color to black if necessary. Text color is determined by the current fill color.

> **Note** ☑
>
> You may find it helpful to display the ruler.

4. Click the text tool in the toolbox, and then drag in the lower-left corner of the drawing area to draw a fixed-width text block that is approximately 120 pixels wide by 50 pixels high. If the unit of measure in your graphics program is set to inches, the block should be about 1.25 inches wide by 0.5 inches high. Notice that when you release the mouse pointer, a bounding box defines the area of the text block and an insertion point is flashing in the block. Text will be inserted to the left of the insertion point.

5. If necessary, change the font to Arial, the font size to 12, and the alignment to left. Deselect all font styles, such as bold and italics. (You learn more about text formatting options later in this lesson.)

STEP-BY-STEP 4.1 Continued

6. Using your keyboard, key the text **Beans and Beyond 622 Elm Street Sudbury, MA 01776**. Do not press Enter to start new lines in the address—the text should wrap within the text block. It should look similar to the text block in Figure 4-1. However, if the text does not wrap into three lines as shown in the figure, you can drag the right selection handle out to increase the block width.

Did You Know?

You can set a precise size for the text block by entering specific dimensions the same way you enter dimensions for other graphics objects. In most graphics programs, that means keying the height and width in the Info panel, Size dialog box, or Properties panel.

FIGURE 4-1
Text wraps within a
fixed-width text block

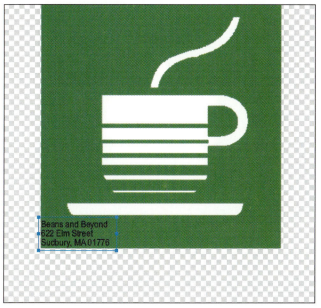

Beans and Beyond
622 Elm Street
Sudbury, MA 01776

7. Click the tool used for selecting objects in the toolbox, and click anywhere outside the text block to deselect the text block.

8. Save changes and leave the **Beans** file open to use in the next exercise.

Note

In some programs, you can tell whether the insertion point is active in a text block by looking for a shape in the upper-right corner of the bounding box in place of a sizing handle. The shape may be a small square (usually in a fixed-width block) or a small circle (in an expandable block). Double-click the shape to switch from one type of block to the other.

Create an Expandable Text Block

Most graphics programs also let you create expandable or auto-sizing text blocks. In an *expandable text block*, text is entered on a single line, which increases in width to accommodate as many characters as you enter. To create an expandable text block, select the text tool, click in the drawing area where you want to position the block, and start keying text.

STEP-BY-STEP 4.2

1. In the Beans file, click the text tool in the toolbox, and then click in the top portion of the cup, midway between the left edge of the cup and the line of steam. Do not hold down the mouse button or drag after clicking. An expandable text block is created at the spot where you clicked, as shown in Figure 4-2.

FIGURE 4-2
Expandable text block

2. Key the text **Beans and Beyond**. Notice that as you type, the text block expands horizontally so that all of the characters are displayed on one line.

STEP-BY-STEP 4.2 Continued

3. Click the pointer or selection tool in the toolbox. The file should look similar to Figure 4-3.

FIGURE 4-3
All text fits on one line in expandable text block

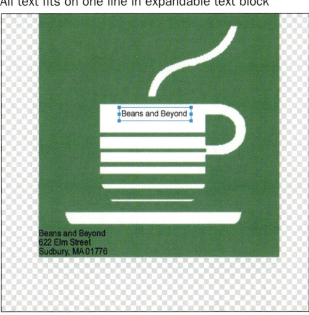

4. Save changes and leave the **Beans** file open to use in the next exercise.

Edit Text

In most graphics programs, you use the same standard text-editing commands as in other programs to move the insertion point within a text block and to make changes to the text. To position the insertion point in the text so you can make changes, double-click where you want to place the insertion point, or click the text tool and then click where you want to position the insertion point. Table 4-1 describes some of the common keystrokes used to work with text.

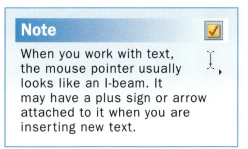

Note

When you work with text, the mouse pointer usually looks like an I-beam. It may have a plus sign or arrow attached to it when you are inserting new text.

TABLE 4-1
Common text-editing keystrokes

PRESS THIS KEY	TO DO THIS
↑	Move insertion point up one line.
↓	Move insertion point down one line.
←	Move insertion point one character to the left.
→	Move insertion point one character to the right.
← BACKSPACE	Delete the character to the left of the insertion point.
DELETE	Delete the character to the right of the insertion point.
↵ ENTER	Start a new paragraph.
INSERT	Toggle between inserting and overwriting characters.

Use the same methods to select a text block that you use to select other graphics objects. To select an entire block, use the pointer or selection tool to click the text block. To select multiple objects, including text blocks, select the first, then press and hold Shift while you select additional objects.

You can use standard text selection methods to select text within the block. For example, with the mouse, click and drag across the text to select, or with the keyboard, position the insertion point at the beginning of the text to select, press and hold Shift, then press arrow keys to define the selection.

S TEP-BY-STEP 4.3

1. In the Beans file, click the selection tool in the toolbox, and then double-click in the fixed-width text block.

2. Use the arrow keys to position the insertion point at the beginning of the word *and* in the first line of text.

3. Press **Delete** three times to delete the word *and*.

4. Key **&** (an ampersand character) to replace the word *and*. (You may need to adjust the width of the text block if the street address number moves back to the first line after you have edited the text.)

5. Click the text tool in the toolbox if necessary, and then click on the word *and* in the expandable text block.

STEP-BY-STEP 4.3 Continued

6. Delete the word *and,* and then replace it with an **&** character. The file should look similar to the one in Figure 4-4.

FIGURE 4-4
Edited text in both text blocks

7. Save changes and leave the **Beans** file open to use in the next exercise.

Check Spelling

There is nothing like a spelling mistake to ruin a perfectly good graphics file. Luckily, many graphics programs include a spell checking feature you can use to make sure all words in your files are spelled correctly. You can check the spelling in one or more selected text blocks, or in an entire file. If no blocks are selected, the spelling checker checks all text in the file. When the checker identifies a misspelled word, it highlights it. You can choose to change the spelling or ignore the error. Some programs have additional options, such as ignoring or fixing all occurrences of the same error, or adding the highlighted word to the spelling checker's dictionary.

Of course, even the best spelling checker won't catch all spelling errors. For example, if you key the word *hole* when you mean to key *whole,* the spelling checker will not identify the mistake. The only way to be certain your text is correct is to proofread it carefully.

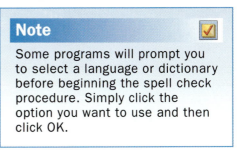

Note

Some programs will prompt you to select a language or dictionary before beginning the spell check procedure. Simply click the option you want to use and then click OK.

STEP-BY-STEP 4.4

1. In the Beans file, click the text tool, and then click in the upper-left corner of the image to create an expandable text block.

2. In the text block, key the following text, including the spelling errors: **Fine Cffee and Tasty Treets from Around the World**.

3. Click the command to start the spelling checker in your program. It may appear on a menu such as Text, Type, or Tools.

4. The spelling checker should highlight the word *Cffee* in the text block and display a dialog box similar to the one in Figure 4-5.

FIGURE 4-5
Check Spelling dialog box

5. Click the correctly spelled word *Coffee* in the dialog box, and then click the **Change** button.

6. The spelling checker should highlight the word *Treets*. Click the correctly spelled word *Treats*, and then click the **Change** button.

7. Close any additional dialog boxes that are displayed to complete the spell check.

8. Save changes and leave the **Beans** file open to use in the next exercise.

Apply Character Formatting

Character formatting determines the appearance and spacing of text characters. Character formatting options in a graphics program are generally similar to those in word processing or desktop publishing programs. For example, you can change the design, size, and style of text, and you can adjust spacing between characters as well as between lines of text.

You can select character formatting options before you key new text, or you can apply formatting to existing text. In most programs, text formatting options are available on a menu such as Format or Text or in a panel with a name such as Character or Text. In some programs, such as Macromedia's Fireworks, you can select text formatting options directly in the text object's Properties panel or dialog box.

To format an entire text block, select the block and then select the formatting options. Alternatively, select just the text you want to format, and then select the formatting options.

Apply Font Formatting

Change the look of text using font formatting. A *font* is the design of a set of characters, including letters, numbers, and symbols. You have three main font formatting options: you can change the font itself, the font size, and the font style.

There are two basic types of fonts: serif fonts and sans serif fonts. *Serif fonts* have short lines and curlicues at the ends of the lines that make up each character. Serif fonts are generally easy to read and so are often used for lengthy paragraphs, reports, or letters. Some common serif fonts include Times New Roman, Garamond, and Century. *Sans serif fonts* have straight lines without serifs and are often used for headlines and titles. Some common sans serif fonts are Arial, Impact, and Tahoma. Other types of fonts include script fonts, which imitate handwriting, and symbol fonts, which include sets of symbols that you can insert as characters into text. Figure 4-6 shows examples of different fonts.

FIGURE 4-6
Sample fonts

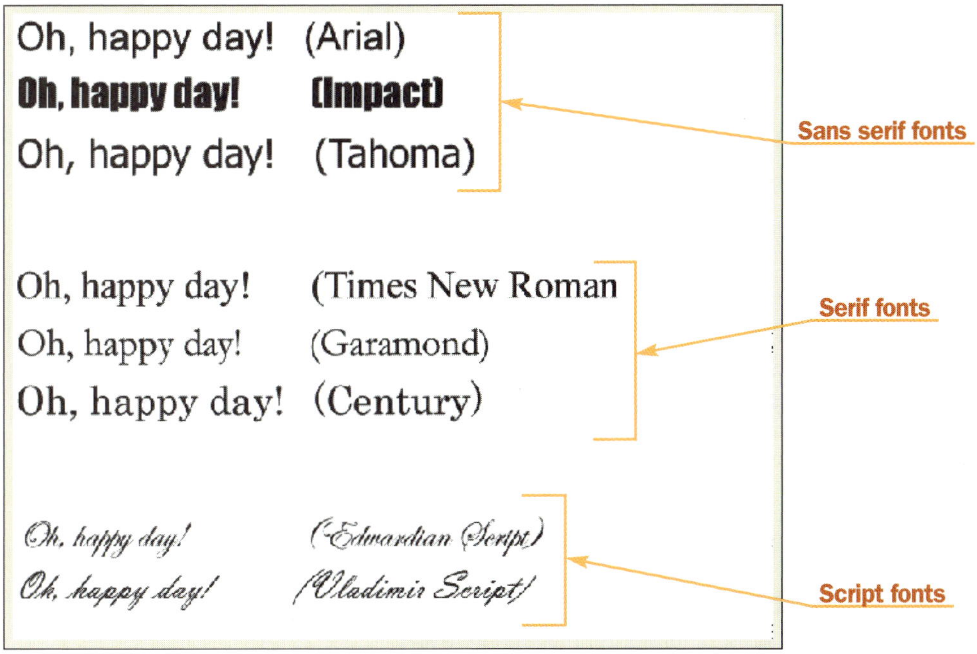

Your graphics program probably comes with some built-in fonts, and you may have other fonts available on your computer as well. You can buy and install font sets you need, or download them from the Internet.

Your graphics program uses a default font, such as Arial, for text objects, or it uses the most recently selected font. To choose a new font, locate your program's font list on a menu or in a panel or palette. In most cases, the fonts are listed in alphabetical order in the font list, and you can sometimes see a preview of a font when you select it in the list.

Text objects also have a *font size* that you can change when formatting text. Font sizes are measured in points according to the height of an uppercase letter in the font set. There are 72 points in an inch. Select a new font size by locating your program's font size list on a menu or panel. You can choose one of the sizes on the list or key a size in the font size box. When changing font size, keep in mind the importance of the text in your image. If you want the text to dominate a large image, use a large font size. If the text has to fit in a small corner of the image, use a small font size.

Font style is the slant and weight of characters in a font set, such as bold and italic. Some programs also offer underlining as a font style. Font styles are used to call attention to the text. Bold is usually used to highlight text and make it stand out, while italic is usually used for subtle emphasis. Some programs allow you to apply font styles to any font, while others may limit the styles that can be applied to specific fonts.

STEP-BY-STEP 4.5

1. In the Beans file, select the expandable text block containing the text *Beans & Beyond*. To format all text in a block, you select the entire block. Remember, when an object is selected, it has a bounding box and selection handles around it.

2. Click the **Font** list, and then click the font named **Impact**. If Impact is not available on your computer system, select a different sans serif font.

3. Select the current value in the **Font Size** list, and then key **16**. Now, the text in the text block is formatted in 16-point Impact.

4. Click the text tool, and then click and drag across the text *Beans & Beyond* in the fixed-width text block in the lower-left corner of the image to select it. To format some text in a block, you select the specific text.

5. Click the **Font** list, and select **Impact**. Then click the **Font Size** list and select **14**. The selected text is formatted in 14-point Impact, while the rest of the text in the text block remains unchanged.

6. Select the expandable text block at the top of the image.

7. Change the font to 16-point Garamond.

8. Apply **bold**, **italic**, and **underline** font styles, if available. You can use buttons or options   **B** *I* <u>U</u>
in a panel or on a menu to apply these styles.

STEP-BY-STEP 4.5 Continued

9. Click anywhere outside the text block. The image should look similar to the one in Figure 4-7.

FIGURE 4-7
Font formatting changes the look of the image

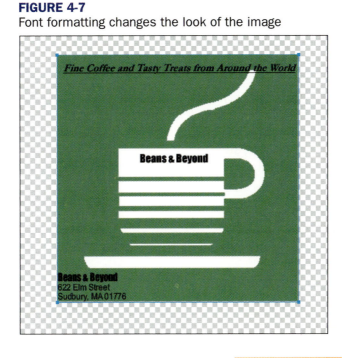

10. Save changes, and leave the **Beans** file open to use in the next exercise.

> **Extra for Experts**
>
> Appropriate use of fonts can make an impact in your graphics files and help define the tone and message you want to convey. Fonts can be elaborate or simple, decorative or plain. It is worth spending some time to select just the right font or combination of fonts to complement your graphics file.

Set Kerning and Leading

Kerning controls the space between pairs of characters. Usually spacing is controlled by the font set, but sometimes when certain characters—such as T and A, or Y and O—are next to each other, you can clearly see uneven spacing. If the spacing within a word is uneven, the reader's eye hesitates, making it harder to read the text. Good kerning spaces characters so that each word is viewed by the reader as a single unit. Pay particular attention to kerning when using large font sizes, in text typed in all uppercase letters, and when using light-colored characters on a darker background. These situations tend to make spacing problems stand out more.

In most programs, you key the kerning setting in a box in the Property panel, the Character panel, or a character formatting dialog box. Kerning is measured as a percentage of the default—or normal—spacing. The normal spacing setting is usually 0. To increase the spacing, increase the kerning setting. To decrease the spacing, decrease the setting. Some graphics programs have an automatic kerning feature you can turn on to automatically adjust the kerning for the best appearance. Turn the automatic kerning feature off if you want to be able to control the kerning manually.

Leading (pronounced to rhyme with *wedding*) is the amount of space between the *baseline*—bottom—of one line of text and the baseline of the next line. Leading is usually determined by the font. For example, if leading is set to 120% of the font size, and the font size is 10 points, the leading is 12 points. In most programs, you key the leading setting in a box in the Property panel, in the Paragraph panel, or in a paragraph formatting dialog box. Leading may be measured in pixels, points, or as a percentage. In most programs, you can select the leading unit you want to use.

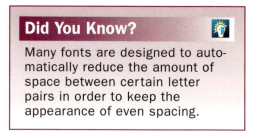

Did You Know?

Many fonts are designed to automatically reduce the amount of space between certain letter pairs in order to keep the appearance of even spacing.

If there is too much or too little space between lines, the reader's eye has trouble following from one line to the next. In general, space between lines should be greater than the space between words, but some situations, such as short lines of text, call for tighter leading. Tighter leading can also help make lines of text fit within a specified area.

STEP-BY-STEP 4.6

1. In the Beans file, select the fixed-width text block in the lower-left corner of the image.

2. Click the **Leading** box, key **90**, and then press **Enter**. This sets the leading to 90%, which should move the lines closer together. Look for the leading box in the Character panel, the Spacing panel, the Properties panel, or in a dialog box with a similar name. If you are unable to set leading to a percent value, you may be able to key or select a value less than the default leading value, such as 12 pt.

3. Notice that the characters *t* and *y* at the end of the word *Tasty* in the expandable text box at the top of the image are so close together that they appear to touch. Click the text tool, and select these two characters. (Your program may require you to click between the characters to change kerning.)

4. Click the **Kerning** box, key **10**, and then press **Enter**. (Or select a value from the kerning box's drop-down list that results in an obvious increase in the space between the characters.) This increases the kerning setting to 10% of normal, which increases the space between the two characters, making the word easier to read.

STEP-BY-STEP 4.6 Continued

5. Click anywhere outside the text block. The image should look similar to the one in Figure 4-8. Don't worry if it appears that the text extends beyond the edge of the image. You adjust the alignment in the next exercise.

FIGURE 4-8
Kerning and leading have been adjusted

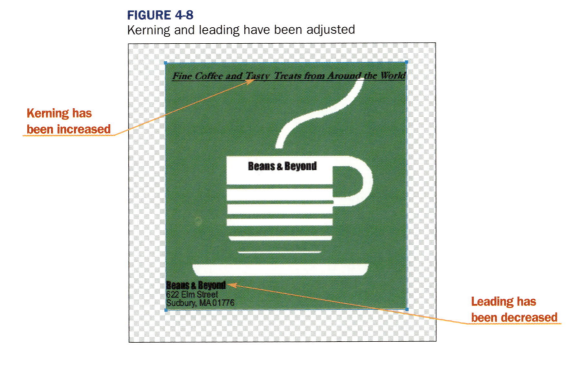

Kerning has been increased

Leading has been decreased

6. Save changes and leave the **Beans** file open to use in the next exercise.

Set Text Direction and Alignment

You can control the position of text within a block using alignment and direction options. Setting alignment and direction can help integrate the text into a graphics image, as well as enhance visual interest. As with character formatting, you can set the alignment and direction options before you key text or for existing text blocks. The commands are usually found on the Text or Format menu or in the Paragraph or Properties panel. You may be able to click a button to apply the option, or you may have to select it from a menu.

In most graphics programs, you set text direction and alignment at the same time. Direction options include both *orientation* and *text flow*. Orientation controls whether the text is displayed horizontally across the width of the block, or vertically from the top to the bottom of the block. Text flow determines whether text can be read from left to right or right to left. It is usually used when you work with languages that flow right to left, such as Arabic or Hebrew.

Alignment controls the position of text in relation to the edges of the text block. Horizontally oriented text can be aligned with either the left or right edge, centered between the left and right edges, or *justified*—which means the space between words is adjusted so that the text aligns with both the left and right edges. Vertically aligned text can be aligned with the top or bottom edge of the text block, centered between the top and bottom edges, or justified between the top and bottom edges. You can also align the text block to the drawing area using tools in a panel such as Align, just as you align other objects. Figure 4-9 shows examples of text formatting with different alignments and orientations.

FIGURE 4-9
Text with different alignments and orientations

Left aligned text in a
text box

Right aligned text in
a text box

Text centered in a
text box

Text justified in a
t e x t   b o x

ot thgir gniwolf txeT
tfel

Vertical Text

v t f l r
e e l e i
r x o f g
t t w t h
i   i   t
c   n t
a   g o
l

l r f t v
e i l e e
f g o x r
t h w t t
   t   i   i
       n   c
       t g a
       o   l

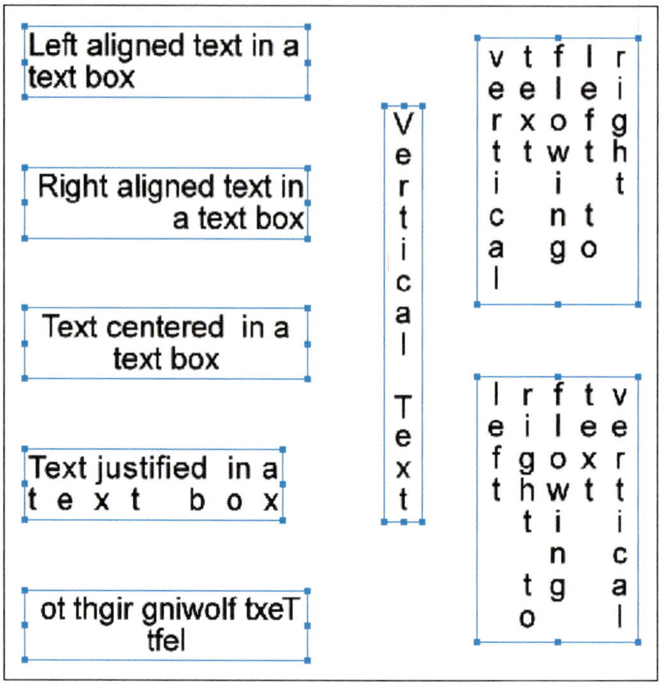

Some programs offer special alignment options such as Stretch alignment or Justify All Lines. Stretch alignment automatically stretches text to fill the width of a text block by adjusting character width. This may make the characters thicker or thinner, but does not change the spacing between them. Justify All Lines justifies every line in a text block, even short lines such as might appear at the end of a paragraph.

S TEP-BY-STEP 4.7

1. In the Beans file, select the fixed-width text block in the lower corner of the image.

2. Click the **right alignment** button. The text aligns to the right of the text block.

3. Drag the text block to the right side of the image.

4. Select the expandable text block at the top of the image.

5. Click the **center alignment** button. Then use the Align panel to center the text block horizontally in relation to the drawing area. Now, the text is centered in the text block, and the text block is centered in the drawing area.

STEP-BY-STEP 4.7 Continued

6. Select the expandable text block in the middle of the image.

7. Change the orientation to vertical, and then drag the text block to position it as shown in Figure 4-10.

FIGURE 4-10
Modify text alignment and direction

8. Save changes and leave the **Beans** file open to use in the next exercise.

> **Note** ☑️
>
> Most graphics programs also allow you to specify how much space to leave before and after a paragraph of text, as well as set an indent for the first line of a paragraph. Some programs may also let you set margins within a text block, adjust the baseline shift to move characters above or below the baseline, and scale the width or height of characters as a percentage of their original size.

Apply Fills and Strokes to Text

Text objects have both a fill and a stroke just like any other drawing object. By default, a text object's stroke is transparent. You can change the color and appearance of text by modifying both fill and stroke options. Stroke options can usually be applied only to an entire text block, but solid fills—as opposed to textured or gradient fills—can be applied to an entire text block or to selected text within a block.

To apply a stroke or fill to text, select the text or the text block, then select the stroke or fill options you want to apply. You can also select the options before you key new text. Besides changing the color of the fill and the stroke, you can often change stroke options such as stroke weight, stroke style, and the position of the stroke relative to the path (outside the path, inside the path, or centered on the path). Depending on your program, the options may be available directly from the toolbox, in panels, or in dialog boxes.

STEP-BY-STEP 4.8

1. In the Beans file, select the text *Beans & Beyond* in the fixed-width text block in the lower-right corner of the image.

2. Click the tool in the toolbox that selects the fill and click the color white. The color of the selected text changes to white.

3. Select the vertically oriented text block.

4. Click the tool that selects the stroke and click the color white. The stroke is applied around the text fill, as shown in Figure 4-11.

FIGURE 4-11
White stroke applied to black text

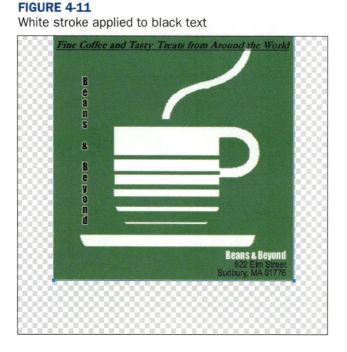

5. Save changes and close the **Beans** file. Leave your graphics program open to use in the next exercise.

Import Text

If the text you want to use in a graphics file is already entered in a different file, you can import it into your graphics program. To import an entire text file into a text block in your graphics file, make the graphics file active and then choose the Import command. Locate and select

> **Note** ☑
>
> If your file does not look the same as the one in the figure, your graphics program may be set to apply the stroke differently. In the figure, the stroke is applied outside the text lines.

the text file and then click the appropriate button in the Import dialog box. You will probably have to change the Files of type list to display all files in order to locate text files in the Import dialog box. You may drag an insertion pointer to define the location and size of the text block you want to create, or just click in the drawing area to insert a default text block. (For more information on importing, refer to Lesson 2.) In most cases, the formatting from the original file will not be imported into the graphics file.

> **Note** ☑️
>
> The type of text files that you can import depends on your graphics program. Some programs may let you import only plain text files while some will let you import Rich Text Format files as well.

S TEP-BY-STEP 4.9

1. Open **GR Step 4-9a** from the data files.

2. Save the file as **Marigold**.

3. Import the text file **GR Step4-9b** into the Marigold graphics file. For example, click File on the menu bar, click Import, change the Files of type list to All Files, then locate and select GR Step4-9b. Drag the insertion pointer to define an import area as wide as the drawing area. The height should adjust automatically. If you don't define an import area, scale the text block to 6 inches by 1.8 inches and align it with the left side of the drawing area.

> **Note** ☑️
>
> If you cannot import the text, open it in Notepad, copy the text, and then paste it in your graphics file. Scale the text block to 6 inches wide by about 1.8 inches high and align it with the left side of the drawing area.

4. Click the **center alignment** button to center the text in the text block.

5. Use the Align panel options to center the entire text block vertically in the drawing area.

> **Did You Know?** 💡
>
> You can also use the Clipboard to copy or move text from a different file into a graphics file. Select the text to copy or move and then click Copy or Cut. In the graphics file, position the insertion point within an existing text block and click Paste. If the insertion point is not in a text block when you click Paste, your graphics program creates a new text block where the text is inserted.

STEP-BY-STEP 4.9 Continued

6. Apply the **bold** font style to all text in the text block and change the fill color to white. At 100% magnification, the file should look similar to the one in Figure 4-12. If necessary, adjust the font size and leading and change to a sans serif font.

FIGURE 4-12
Import text from other files

7. Save changes and leave the **Marigold** file open to use in the next Step-by-Step.

Transform a Text Block

You can transform a text block using the same methods you use to transform other graphics objects. In most programs, that means you can scale, skew, distort, rotate, and flip the entire text block. Transformations on text blocks can create interesting effects, including perspective and depth. Simply select the text block, and then apply the transformation.

STEP-BY-STEP 4.10

1. In the Marigold file, select the text block, click the **Scale** tool, and increase the height of the object to approximately 145 pixels, or 2 inches. Since you are increasing the height without increasing the width, the characters may seem a bit distorted.

STEP-BY-STEP 4.10 Continued

2. Click the tool or menu command that allows you to skew an object, and drag the top right handle down about halfway to the center handle. This creates the appearance of depth; the text seems to be moving into the distance on the right side of the image.

3. Left align the text within the text block.

4. Click the tool in the toolbox that selects the stroke and click a dark gray color. The color is applied around the text, making it stand out more from the background image.

5. Click anywhere outside the text block to deselect it. The image should look similar to Figure 4-13.

FIGURE 4-13
Transform text block to create interesting effects

6. Save changes and close the **Marigold** file. Leave your graphics program open to use in the next exercise.

Convert Text to Vector Graphics

When text is in a text block, you can edit and format the text, and you can transform the entire text block object. If you want to be able to modify and transform the text characters themselves, you can convert the text to vectors. Remember, vector graphics are defined by lines and curves that can be modified in many ways. Converting text to vectors is useful for incorporating the shape of a character into a drawing or larger image. Once the text is converted, you can use all the vector editing tools in your graphics program to modify the shape itself. Keep in mind, however, that you can't edit text that has been converted.

The command to convert text to vector graphics depends on your graphics program. It may be similar to Convert to Paths or Convert to Shape, and it will probably be on the Text menu.

Note

If you convert text to a shape and then change your mind, use the Undo command to revert back to text.

S TEP-BY-STEP 4.11

1. Create a new file in your graphics program. Set the drawing area to 720 pixels by 720 pixels (10 inches by 10 inches) and use the other default drawing area options. Save the file as **Beans2**.

2. Click the text tool, and then set the font to 72-point Times New Roman, left aligned, with a plain font style.

3. Click anywhere in the drawing area, and then key the letter **B**. Change the fill color of the type object to bright blue.

4. Select the text block, and then click the command to convert the text block to a vector shape. The bounding box is replaced by selection handles.

5. Click the **Scale** tool, then size the shape to approximately 95 pixels by 95 pixels (1.3 inches by 1.3 inches), rotate it about 40 degrees to the left, then drag it into the upper-left corner of the drawing area. The file should look similar to Figure 4-14.

FIGURE 4-14
Letter B as a vector shape

STEP-BY-STEP 4.11 Continued

6. Use the text tool to key the letter **E** using the same font settings as for the letter *B*. Change the fill color to red.

7. Convert the *E* to a vector shape, then click the **Scale** tool and size the shape to approximately 72 pixels by 72 pixels (1 inch by 1 inch). Rotate the shape about −40 degrees to the right, then position it to the right and slightly below the letter *B*.

> **Note** ☑
>
> Your program may automatically adjust the dimensions of the character shape slightly to maintain proportion.

8. Repeat the process to insert an **A** with a green fill, convert it to a vector, scale it to approximately 72 pixels by 72 pixels (1 inch by 1 inch), and rotate it −40 degrees to the left. Position the shape to the right and slightly above the letter *E*.

9. Repeat the process again to insert an **N** with an orange fill, convert it to a vector, scale it to approximately 90 pixels by 90 pixels (1.25 by 1.25), and rotate it −40 degrees to the right. Position the shape to the right and slightly below the letter *A*.

10. Repeat the process one more time to insert an **S** with a purple fill, convert it to a vector, scale it to approximately 72 pixels by 72 pixels (1 inch by 1 inch). Instead of rotating this shape, flip it horizontally so that it appears to be written backwards. Position it to the right and slightly above the letter *N*.

11. Select all of the shapes in the file and group them together. Then use the Align panel to center the group horizontally in the drawing area. When you deselect the group, the file should look similar to Figure 4-15. If necessary, ungroup the objects and adjust the position and rotation of the shapes.

FIGURE 4-15
Modified shapes combine to spell a word

12. Save changes and close the **Beans2** file. Close your graphics program.

SUMMARY

In this lesson, you learned:

- You can create text block objects in a graphics file to hold regular text characters.
- There are two types of text blocks: expandable and fixed-width.
- You can enter and edit text using basic word processing commands.
- Many graphics programs have spelling checkers that you can use to locate and correct spelling errors.
- You can apply font formatting to text in a text block.
- Adjusting kerning and leading settings can make text easier to read and help fit it within a defined space.
- Changing text alignment and orientation can help integrate text into a graphics image.
- Fill color determines the text color, but you can also apply stroke color and effects to text.
- You can import text from another file into your graphics file.
- You can transform text by skewing, distorting, rotating, or flipping it.
- You can convert text objects to vector graphics to make possible other modifications to the object.

VOCABULARY *Review*

Define the following terms:

Baseline	Font style	Orientation
Expandable text block	Insertion point	Text block
Fixed-width text block	Justified	Text flow
Font	Kerning	Wrap
Font size	Leading	

REVIEW *Questions*

TRUE / FALSE

Circle T if the statement is true or F if the statement is false.

T   F   **1.** Font sizes are measured in points.

T   F   **2.** All text within a text block must be formatted in the same font.

T   F   **3.** A good spelling checker will catch all spelling errors so you don't have to proofread.

T F 4. Press Enter to toggle between inserting and overwriting characters.

T F 5. In an expandable text block, text is entered on a single line.

T F 6. In a fixed-width text block, text wraps to fit within the size of the block.

T F 7. Leading is always measured in pixels.

T F 8. Text flow determines whether text can be read from left to right or right to left.

T F 9. Text color is determined by the current stroke setting.

T F 10. Usually, existing formatting is lost when you import text into a graphics file.

WRITTEN QUESTIONS

Write a brief answer to the following questions.

1. What types of transformations can you perform on text blocks?

2. What is a drawback of converting text to vector shapes?

3. What is the difference between an expandable text block and a fixed-width text block?

4. What are some spelling mistakes that a spelling checker won't catch?

5. What are the different types of alignment?

FILL IN THE BLANK

Complete the following sentences by writing the correct word or words in the blanks provided.

1. _____ controls whether the text is displayed horizontally across the width of the block or vertically from the top to the bottom of the block.

2. Leading is the amount of space between the _____ of lines of text.

3. The spacing between certain pairs of characters is controlled by _____.

4. Press _____ to remove the character to the left of the insertion point.

5. The mouse pointer usually resembles a(n) _____ when you are entering or editing text.

6. If you use a(n) _____ fill, you can apply it to selected text within a block.

7. _____ controls the position of text in relation to the edges of the text block.

8. There are _____ points in an inch.

9. The font _____ is the slant and weight of the characters in a font.

10. A(n) _____ within a text block indicates where characters that you type will be placed.

PROJECTS

PROJECT 4-1

1. Create a new graphics file using the default drawing area size and save the file as **Intro**.

2. Draw a square 433 pixels by 433 pixels (6 inches by 6 inches) with no stroke and a light gray fill (hexadecimal code CCCCCC).

3. Create a fixed-width text block that is approximately as wide as the drawing area and 2 inches high.

4. Select a sans serif font such as Arial, set the font size to 42 points, and set the font style to bold. If necessary, set the fill color to black so the text color will be black.

5. Type the following text:

   Once upon a time in a small cottage at the edge of a dark forest, a little girl lived with her grandmother ...

6. Check the spelling in the text block and correct errors as necessary.

7. If possible, stretch align the text to fill the width of the block.

8. Skew and distort the text block so that it appears to be receding into the distance:
   A. Select the **Skew** tool.
   B. Drag a top corner handle in toward the center handle.
   C. Select the **Distort** tool.
   D. Drag the top center handle up to the top of the drawing area.

9. Center the text block in relation to the drawing area horizontally and vertically.

10. Print one copy of the file.

11. Save and close the **Intro** file, but leave your graphics program open to use in Project 4-2.

PROJECT 4-2

1. Open **GR Project 4-2** from the data files.

2. Save the file as **Dog2**.

3. Set the fill color to the rust used as a background in the image, and then create a text block and key the character **D** in a sans serif font such as Comic Sans MS.

4. Convert the text to a vector shape, and resize it to about 75 pixels square.

5. Move the shape over the body of one of the small corner pictures.

6. Duplicate the shape three times, and position each one over another of the small corner pictures, so that all four have *D*s on them.

7. Create a new text block and key the word **DOG** in the same font, set to 42 points.

8. Apply a black stroke around the text. If you want, modify the stroke style to change the appearance of the text. For example, select a style such as a dark felt tip, or a graphite pencil.

9. Change the orientation of the text block containing the word DOG to vertical, so the text reads from top to bottom.

10. Drag the text block to position it over the body of the large, central picture.

11. Print one copy of the file.

12. Save and close the **Dog2** file, but leave your graphics program open to use in Project 4-3.

PROJECT 4-3

1. Open **GR Project 4-3a** from the data files.

2. Save the file as **Fall**.

3. Import the file **GR Project 4-3b** into the **Fall** file.

4. Format the text as follows:
    A. Select a 12-point serif font such as Sylfaen.
    B. Apply a golden fill color (such as FFCC00).
    C. Apply a black stroke.
    D. Center the text in the text block.
    E. Align the text block to the bottom of the drawing area, centered horizontally.

5. Create a new text block at the top of the image and key the text **Haiku** in a 36-point sans serif font, such as Tahoma. Center the text horizontally within the block.

6. Format the text in the reverse colors that you used for the imported text (gold stroke, black fill).

7. Center the text block horizontally, and align it with the top of the drawing area.

8. Print one copy of the file.

9. Save and close the **Fall** file, and close your graphics program.

SCANS **WEB PROJECT**

For a report about ancient Egypt, you need information about hieroglyphics, the characters the Egyptians used for writing. You also want to include hieroglyphics in your report. Use the Internet to see if you can find general information about hieroglyphics as well as an actual hieroglyphics font set. Once you locate the font set, find out whether you can download it for free or if there is a charge.

SCANS **TEAMWORK PROJECT**

Discuss with your classmates different logos used by professional sports teams or companies. Think of a few logos that incorporate text, and consider the qualities that make them memorable. For example, the color and font of the Coca-Cola logo are easy to identify.

Together with your teammates, think of a club or team at your school or a business in your community that could use a logo, and then use your graphics program to design one that uses both shapes and text. Make use of the skills you have learned in this lesson as well as in previous lessons. Select font formatting that suits the logo, including a font set and font size. Select stroke and fill settings that make the object easy to read and identify. Layer basic shapes behind the text to create a background, and convert text characters into vectors so you can position and transform them independently. When you are finished, print the logo and compare it to the images created by other teams.

CRITICAL *Thinking*

ACTIVITY 4-1

Use your graphics program to combine text and graphics to design a monogram for yourself that you could use on stationery or a book plate. If you want to modify the characters independently, type each one in its own text block and then convert them to vector shapes. Use the available tools to modify and transform the text. You can try changing the stacking order to overlap text and shapes, using different stroke and fill options to enhance the text characters, and rotating or flipping the objects to make them more interesting. When you are finished, save the file, print it, and share it with your classmates.

CREATING SPECIAL EFFECTS

VOCABULARY

Bevel

Brightness

CMY

Color system

Contrast

Emboss

Glow

Hue

Mask

Opacity

RGB

Saturation

Shadow

Spot color

Style

Value

You can use different effects to improve your graphics images and to create illusions. Color, for example, can convey a mood, change the perception of space and size, focus attention, add emphasis, and even improve image quality. Shadow effects may make an object appear to have three dimensions; an emboss effect may make an object appear to sink into the drawing area; and a blur effect may make an object appear to be far off in the distance. Most graphics programs include features for creating certain common effects, such as shadows, blurs, and glows. In addition, many effects are achieved by incorporating color and scale. In this lesson, you learn to work with color and to apply special effects to bitmap and vector graphics.

Work with Color

Color affects the way people view an image more than any other graphics effect. Color, also called *hue*, is usually the first thing the viewer sees and responds to. Understanding the way viewers react to color and incorporating standard color techniques in your graphics can help you create appealing and informative images.

You have already learned how to apply color to fills and strokes simply by selecting a swatch from a color palette. Most programs also have tools for creating custom colors. You can create a custom color by selecting a color from a color bar or specifying color values in a color mixer panel, palette, or dialog box.

The color mixer panel or palette allows you to mix custom colors based on the current *color system*. A color system defines standard colors. It may also be called a *color model*. Color systems are available for graphics to be displayed on a computer screen (such as on a Web page) and for printed graphics. A graphics program usually has a default color system that you can change at any time.

Use a Color Bar

A color bar displays a spectrum of colors across a rectangle from left to right. Toward the top of the color bar, colors are lighter because they are mixed with white. Toward the bottom of the bar, colors are darker because they are mixed with black.

You can make any color the current stroke or fill color simply by clicking it on the color bar. If your program has a color bar, it's usually found in a color mixer panel or dialog box similar to the one in Figure 5-1. This may be the same location that displays the current color system and values. If this panel does not appear by default in your program, you can usually activate it from the Window menu.

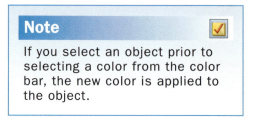

Note

If you select an object prior to selecting a color from the color bar, the new color is applied to the object.

FIGURE 5-1
Color mixer panel

Stroke tool

Fill tool

Values for RGB color system

Color bar

Historically Speaking

For ages, artists and scientists alike have used color wheels to display and classify color. A typical color wheel has 12 gradations of color ranging from red to violet. The primary colors are red, yellow, and blue. Secondary colors are created by combining the primary colors: red mixed with yellow makes orange; yellow mixed with blue makes green; and blue mixed with red makes violet. Intermediate colors are created by combining a primary color with the secondary color adjacent to it on the color wheel. For example, blue-green is an intermediate color. "Cool" colors range from green to violet, while "warm" colors range from red to yellow. Analogous colors are next to each other on the color wheel, while complementary colors are opposite each other.

S TEP-BY-STEP 5.1

1. Launch your graphics program and open **GR Step 5-1** from the data files.

2. Save the file as **Caution**.

3. Open the color mixer panel or dialog box if it is not already open.

4. Click the fill tool. You may click the tool in the color mixer panel or in the toolbox.

5. In the drawing area, select the circle shape surrounding the other shapes.

6. In the color bar, click somewhere in the yellow section. The shape fills with yellow.

7. Select one of the rectangles that represent legs; then press and hold **Shift** and click the other three rectangles and the two circles that represent heads.

> **Note** ☑️
>
> Notice that when you select a color, the color's values are displayed in the current color system boxes.

8. In the color bar, click somewhere in the purple section—the area where the violet blends into the blue. The shapes fill with purple. When you deselect all objects, the image should look similar to the one in Figure 5-2.

FIGURE 5-2
Image with custom fill colors

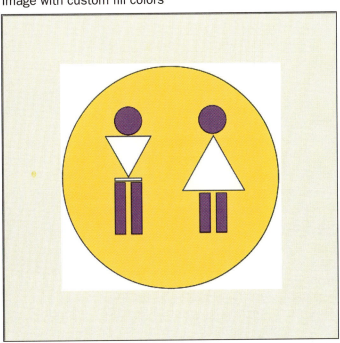

9. Save changes and leave the **Caution** file open to use in the next exercise.

Use a Color System

The two main color systems for use in graphics programs are the RGB model and the CMY (or CMYK) model. Graphics programs may use one of these systems as the default for new drawings, or you may be able to select the system when you start a new drawing. You can change the color system at any time using a menu or pop-up list accessed from the color mixer panel or dialog box.

The *RGB* system creates colors by combining different values of red, green, and blue. These are the basic colors of light in the spectrum we can see. This model mixes colors in the same way that colors of light are mixed. For this reason, the RGB model is most often used when graphics are to be displayed on devices that use light to display colors, such as computer monitors.

The *CMY* (or CMYK) system creates colors by combining percentages of cyan, magenta, and yellow. These colors are the colors of ink—often called *process colors*—used in four-color printing. The CMY system is used most often for drawings that are to be printed, either on a local printer or by a printing press.

The CMY system is called CMYK when black is added to the mix. In theory, combining full percentages of cyan, magenta, and yellow results in black, but for the best-quality output, black is added as a separate color. Having black available also makes it possible to mix more subtle colors.

In four-color printing, all colors are mixed from the four basic process colors. Sometimes, a designer may want to use a specific color of ink rather than have colors created by mixing. The designer can select a *spot color* from a color system such as the Pantone Matching System for a specific color. Use spot colors when it is necessary to have an exact color (such as a client's logo color) or when printing with only one or two colors.

In addition to RGB and CMY, most graphics programs include other color systems such as HSL (Hue, Saturation, Lightness) and Grayscale, which uses percentages of black to create shades of gray. Most programs also include a color system with a name such as Hexadecimal or Web Safe RGB. This color system allows you to key hexadecimal values to mix colors that will display the same way on all computer systems. Use this color system when preparing graphics for Web pages.

To create a color using any color system, insert or adjust values or percentages for each color in the color mixer panel. Some programs allow you to drag sliders to adjust values, or you may need to key values. Units used for values differ by program. For example, RGB values usually range from 0 to 255, but CMY values may use percentages.

One way to find out the value of a color you are using is to select the object that has the color and then look at the values in the color mixer panel or dialog box. In some programs, the color values are listed in the Properties and Info panels as well. If you change the color system while the color is

Extra for Experts

RGB colors are *additive colors*, because if you add full amounts of all three you get white (all colors are reflected). CMY colors are *subtractive colors* because they absorb light. As light passes through a color and is absorbed, that color is subtracted from the reflection that comes back to your eye.

Note

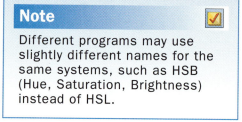

Different programs may use slightly different names for the same systems, such as HSB (Hue, Saturation, Brightness) instead of HSL.

Net Tip

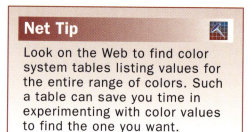

Look on the Web to find color system tables listing values for the entire range of colors. Such a table can save you time in experimenting with color values to find the one you want.

selected, some programs automatically adjust the values for the new system. Figure 5-3 shows the values for navy blue in RGB hexadecimal and in CMY.

FIGURE 5-3
Same color defined with two different color systems:
RGB hexadecimal (left) and CMY (right).

RGB hexadec-imal values

CMY color values

If you create a drawing using the RGB model, you can be fairly certain that your finished drawing will look the same when displayed on your screen, because your monitor uses RGB to display colors. But for a CMY graphic, where the color system used on screen (RGB) is different from the color system used to print (CMY), it can be a bit difficult to make sure that the image will appear on the printed image the same way as it appears on the screen. Some programs have features for converting RGB colors to CMY colors so you can successfully print the image the way you designed it.

Of course, other factors affect the way the colors appear on your computer screen and in print, including the specific printer model, the specific monitor model, the file type, and the software program. You can take steps to ensure that the image people see is as close as possible to the one you created. For example, you can optimize the colors for the export file type. You may also be able to calibrate your monitor and apply color management systems so what you see on your monitor more closely matches the final printed output.

STEP-BY-STEP 5.2

1. In the Caution file, select the triangle that is the female shape's dress (on the right).

2. Switch to the hexadecimal or Web-safe color model. The available color systems may be listed on an options menu available in the color mixer panel or dialog box.

> **Hot Tip**
>
> To open a panel's Options menu, click the drop-down arrow in the panel's upper-right corner. In a dialog box, look for a command or option button.

3. Double-click the **R** box and key **FF**, double-click the **G** box and key **33**, and then double-click the **B** box and key **33**. Press **Enter** to apply the color. FF3333 is the hexadecimal code for an orange-red. Now, try applying a fill using CMY values.

4. Select the triangle that is the male shape's body (on the left), press and hold **Shift**, and then select the rectangle below it.

> **Hot Tip**
>
> You may be able to drag sliders to quickly select these values, or key the value in the first box and then press Tab to move quickly to the next box.

STEP-BY-STEP 5.2 Continued

5. Switch to the CMY or CMYK color model.

6. Double-click the **C** box and key **200**, double-click the **M** box and key **200**, and then double-click the **Y** box and key **0**. If your program has a **K** box, set its value to 0. If your program uses percentages for CMY colors, set C to 80%, M to 20%, and Y (and K) to 0%. Press **Enter** to apply the color. The image should look similar to the one in Figure 5-4.

FIGURE 5-4
Image with additional fill colors

7. Save changes and leave the **Caution** file open to use in the next exercise.

Apply Color Effects

In addition to applying solid colors to fills and strokes, most programs provide options for creating color effects such as *textures*, *gradients*, and *patterns*. Textures can be applied to fills or strokes to make an object look as if it is painted on a textured surface. Patterns are bitmap graphics applied as a fill. Gradients are a type of pattern that blends colors to create different effects. These effects can give objects a three-dimensional look as well as add impact to an image.

Color effects can be selected before you draw new objects, or you can apply them to existing objects. The methods for accessing the color effects options vary depending on the program you are using. In most programs, you can access built-in textures, patterns, and gradient styles from a menu on the Properties panel, from the Stroke or Fill Options dialog box, or from the Filters or Effects menu on your program's main menu bar. Often, you can see a preview of the texture or pattern before you select it. If necessary, consult your program's Help system or ask your instructor for more information on locating the color effects options in your program.

Apply Textures

To apply a texture, select the object you want to format or tool you plan to use to create the object, and then select the texture for either the stroke or fill from a pop-up list or menu. In most programs, the list is similar to the one shown in Figure 5-5. In some programs, you can control the amount of texture applied by setting a percentage. Increase the percentage to make the texture appear heavier; decrease the percentage to make the texture appear lighter.

Hot Tip

Consider the stroke style and weight when you apply a texture. For example, if the stroke is not heavy or thick enough, you may not be able to see the texture, and some stroke styles may interfere with the selected texture.

FIGURE 5-5
List of built-in stroke textures

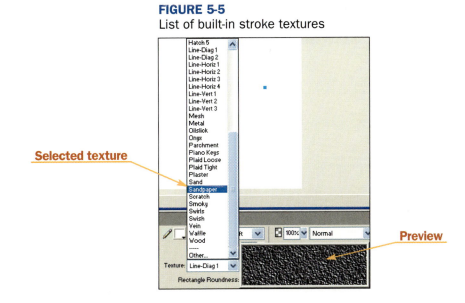

Selected texture

Preview

STEP-BY-STEP 5.3

1. In the Caution file, select all shapes that comprise the bodies except the triangles (select the two heads, the four legs, and the rectangle that is the male's belt).

2. Open the menu listing the available fill textures and select a texture similar to sandpaper.

3. Select the circle shape that makes the background and change the stroke weight to 5.

4. Open the menu listing the available stroke textures and apply a texture similar to mesh. If the option to control the amount of texture is available, set it to **100%**. You may be able to key the percentage in a box or use a slider.

5. Save changes and leave the **Caution** file open to use in the next exercise.

Apply Patterns

In some programs, you may be able to select a pattern directly from a list or pop-up menu, but in most programs, the list of patterns is not available until you select Pattern as the fill type or category. Then, the default pattern or the most recently selected pattern becomes active. It is displayed on the Fill Color tool and is applied to any selected object. Click the Fill Color tool or use the Fill Options dialog box or panel to display a list of built-in patterns, similar to the one shown in Figure 5-6.

> ### Extra for Experts
>
> In some programs you can transform patterns and gradients. Handles are displayed within a selected object filled with a pattern or gradient. Drag the handles to transform the fill.

FIGURE 5-6
List of built-in patterns

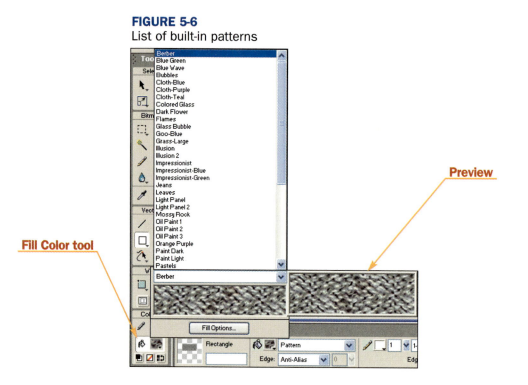

Preview

Fill Color tool

STEP-BY-STEP 5.4

1. In the Caution file, select the two triangles.

2. Open the menu listing the available fill categories and select Pattern. If you are using a program that does not require you to select the category first, skip this step.

3. Open the list of available patterns and select one similar to **Berber**.

4. Save changes and leave the **Caution** file open to use in the next exercise.

Apply Gradients

By default, most gradients blend two colors—the current fill color and black. When you apply a gradient, you usually start by selecting a fill color. Then, you select the gradient pattern type, such as *linear*, which blends the colors horizontally across the object, or *radial*, which blends the colors out from the center of the object, from the Fill category or type list.

When you select a gradient fill, the gradient becomes the active fill and is displayed on the Fill Color tool in the toolbox. If an object is selected, the gradient fill is automatically applied to the selected object. When a gradient fill is selected, any new object you draw has the gradient fill. In some programs, you can apply the fill to an object using a Gradient tool. Click the Gradient tool in the toolbox, and then drag in the object to apply the gradient.

You can edit a gradient by changing the pattern or by changing the colors. In most programs, if you click the Fill Color tool when a gradient fill is active, an Edit Gradient dialog box similar to the one in Figure 5-7 appears in place of the usual swatches palette. To change a color in the gradient, click one of the gradient pointers to select it and then choose a new color. A preview area shows the result. You can also move gradient pointers to adjust the amount of that color in the gradient.

FIGURE 5-7
Options for editing a gradient fill

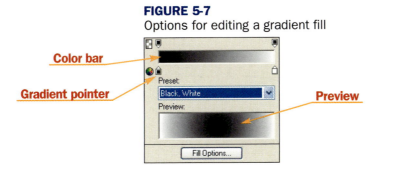

Color bar

Gradient pointer

Preset:
Black, White

Preview:

Preview

Fill Options...

S TEP-BY-STEP 5.5

1. In the Caution file, select the background circle shape.

2. Open the menu listing the available fill categories and select the **Radial** gradient pattern type.

3. Open the dialog box or panel that lists options for editing the gradient colors. For example, click the **Fill Color** tool in the toolbox.

Hot Tip

Some programs have preset gradient color schemes you can select from a drop-down list in the Edit Gradient dialog box.

STEP-BY-STEP 5.5 Continued

4. Change the black used in the gradient to white. For example, click the gradient pointer representing black at one end of the color bar and then click white on the swatches palette. The file should look similar to the one in Figure 5-8.

FIGURE 5-8
File with color effects

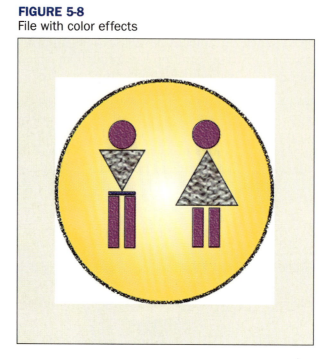

5. Save changes and close the **Caution** file. Leave your graphics program open to use in the next exercise.

Apply Color Correction Effects

Most graphics programs have tools for applying color correction effects to vector obects and bitmap images. For example, you can usually adjust the value, contrast, brightness, saturation, and opacity. *Value*, which is sometimes called lightness, is the range from black to white. Value can be measured by the level of *brightness*. When you increase the brightness, you add white to a hue; when you decrease the brightness you add black. *Contrast* refers to the degree of separation between the values of different parts of an image. You adjust the contrast to change the degree of separation. *Saturation* measures the intensity of color, and *opacity* measures the level of transparency.

> **Note** ☑
>
> Not all graphics programs have the same color controls, or call them by the same names. For example, some programs may use the term *tint* in place of brightness; *transparency* in place of opacity; or *luminosity* in place of lightness. Some vector editing programs may not have color correction effects at all.

You can use color effects in your images to imitate the real effects of light. For example, objects in the distance often appear fuzzy and have a cool tone, such as blue or violet. Objects up close are usually sharp, and have a warm tone, such as red, yellow, or orange. Saturation plays a role in the perception of distance, while brightness affects the perception of size. Closer objects appear highly saturated, while far-off objects appear pale. Objects filled with a bright color, such as yellow, look larger than objects filled with a dark color, such as navy blue—even if the objects are exactly the same size.

You can use these concepts to add dimension to an image and to separate foreground objects from background objects. You can also use them to make it easier for someone with a color deficit condition to see and interpret your images. You can help a person who has trouble seeing and differentiating between colors by increasing the contrast, increasing the lightness differences between foreground and background colors, and by avoiding using colors of similar lightness or saturation next to each other.

The commands for applying color effects are found in different places, depending on the program you are using. Some programs have an Adjust Color menu that you access from the Effects pop-up menu in the Properties panel. Click the Add Effects pop-up menu arrow to open the Effects menu, then click Adjust Color to display a menu of color effects options. In other programs, you may find the color correction options on a submenu such as Adjust, which is accessed from the Image menu; or Colors, which is accessed from the Xtras menu. In any case, you may have to look around a bit, consult your program's Help system, or ask your instructor for more information.

To apply a color correction effect, first select the object to enhance, then select the color effect. Usually, you set the level of the effect by changing the position of a slider in a dialog box, or by entering a specific value.

Set Hue, Saturation, and Lightness

Hue, as mentioned earlier, is another word for color. When you pick a color from a color palette, you pick a hue. You can modify the color by adjusting the saturation, which sets the color intensity, and the lightness, which controls how much light appears to be reflected from a surface. In some programs, you can also modify

> **Hot Tip**
>
> Although you can apply color effects to vectors and to bitmaps, some color effects are particularly suited to bitmaps. For example, adjusting the contrast in a black and white photo can improve the image quality, while adding a sepia tone can make a photo look old. You can combine different color correction effects to achieve different results.

the hue based on the current color system. Many programs group these options together in the same dialog box or panel, as shown in Figure 5-9. In other programs, you may have to set each one individually. By default, these options are set to 0, which is normal, but you can increase or decrease the settings to achieve the effect you want. Most programs provide a preview area so you can view the results of making a change before you actually apply the change.

FIGURE 5-9
Hue/Saturation dialog box

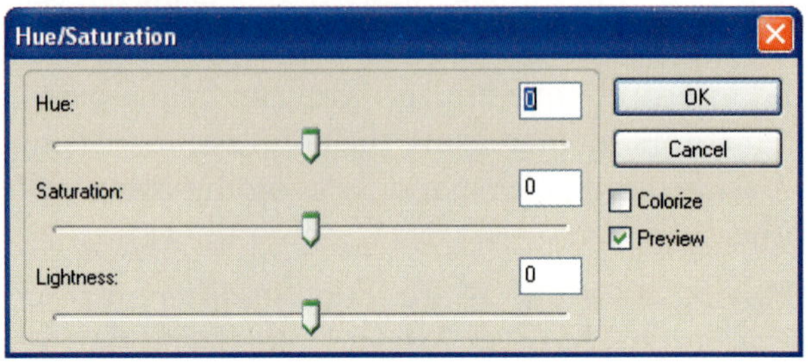

STEP-BY-STEP 5.6

1. Open **GR Step 5-6** from the data files.

2. Save the file as **Dahlia**.

3. Select the petal at the top of the flower.

4. Open the menu that lists color correction options and select the option for adjusting the hue and saturation. If your program has separate dialog boxes for each option, start with Hue.

5. Set the Hue level to **10**. Set the Saturation level to **25**. Set the Lightness level to **30**. You may set the levels by dragging a slider or by keying the value in a box.

> **Note** ☑
>
> Some programs may display a dialog box asking permission to convert the image to a bitmap. Click OK to convert the image and continue.

STEP-BY-STEP 5.6 Continued

6. Click the **OK** button or press **Enter** to apply the effects. Deselect the shape. The image should look similar to the one in Figure 5-10.

FIGURE 5-10
One petal has been modified

7. Select the petal to the left of the one you just modified and set the Hue level to **–10**, the Saturation level to **–25**, and the lightness level to **–30**. Click the **OK** button when you are finished.

8. Select the petal to the left of the one you just modified and set the Hue to **5**, the Saturation to **30**, and the lightness level to **15**. Click the **OK** button when you are finished.

STEP-BY-STEP 5.6 Continued

9. Continue around the flower in a counterclockwise direction, selecting the next petal and setting the values as follows. When you are finished, the image should look similar to the one in Figure 5-11.

	Hue	Saturation	Lightness
Petal 4	–5	–30	–15
Petal 5	5	20	20
Petal 6	15	15	10
Petal 7	–15	–15	–10
Petal 8	5	10	15

FIGURE 5-11
All petals have been modified

10. Save changes and close the **Dahlia** file. Leave your graphics program open to use in the next exercise.

Adjust Brightness and Contrast

You change the brightness and contrast of colors to change how much white or black is added. Increasing the brightness adds white, while decreasing

> **Extra for Experts**
>
> Some programs have a colorize option that you select to add color to a grayscale image or to change an RGB image to a two-tone image.

the brightness adds black. Change the brightness and contrast of an image to correct photographs or other bitmap images that are too dark or too light. You can also use these settings to adjust the color of vector graphics. Most programs combine the Brightness and Contrast settings in the same dialog box, similar to the one in Figure 5-12.

FIGURE 5-12
Brightness/Contrast dialog box

STEP-BY-STEP 5.7

1. Open **GR Step 5-7** from the data files.

2. Save the file as **FDNY**. First improve this image by increasing the brightness to make it appear lighter.

3. Open the menu that lists color correction options and select the option for adjusting the brightness and contrast. If your program has separate options for each, select the option for brightness.

4. Increase the brightness to **30**, and then click the **OK** button to apply the modification. The image should look similar to the one in Figure 5-13. Now adjust the contrast.

FIGURE 5-13
Increasing the brightness adds white to the image

STEP-BY-STEP 5.7 Continued

5. Select the brightness and contrast option again (or just the contrast option) and set the contrast to **5**. The image should look similar to the one in Figure 5-14.

FIGURE 5-14
Increasing the contrast adjusts the shades of gray in relation to each other

6. Save changes and close the **FDNY** file. Leave your graphics program open to use in the next exercise.

Set Opacity

Opacity controls the amount of transparency in a color. It is measured as a percentage, with 100% being completely opaque and 0% being completely transparent. Decreasing the opacity is useful if you want the viewer to be able to see an object that is layered behind another object. Opacity controls may be found on the same menu or in the same dialog box as other color correction options, or it may be an option in the Properties panel.

> **Extra for Experts**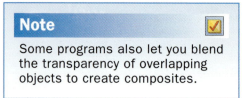
>
> Some programs have built-in commands for quickly applying commonly used effects such as fades, sepia tones, and gray-scales. Look for them on a menu such as Commands.

> **Note** ☑
>
> Some programs also let you blend the transparency of overlapping objects to create composites.

S TEP-BY-STEP 5.8

1. Open **GR Step 5-8** from the data files.

2. Save the file as **Bears**. This file has three stacked objects in it: the yellow circle, which is in the back, then the text object, and then the paw prints on top, which is a bitmap object. Decrease the opacity of the paw prints so the text can be read through them.

3. Select the paw prints.

4. Locate and open the Opacity control and set the opacity level to **80%**. This makes the object 20% transparent, so you can see through it a bit, as shown in Figure 5-15. The result looks as if there are dusty bear tracks across the image.

FIGURE 5-15
Decreasing the opacity makes the object semitransparent

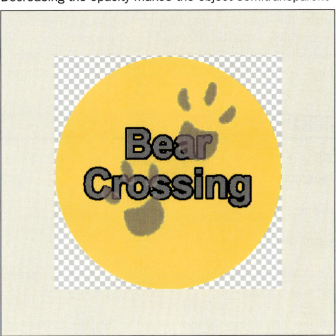

5. Save changes and close the **Bears** file. Leave your graphics program open to use in the next exercise.

Apply Special Effects

Y ou can enhance graphics objects by applying effects such as shadows, glows, bevels, and embossings. Effects can be applied to vector objects, bitmap images, or text objects. Some can be applied to selected pixels in a bitmap as well. In most cases, you can combine effects to achieve different results. For example, you may add both a shadow and a glow to a vector object.

To apply an effect, simply select the object to enhance, and then select the command to apply the effect. As with color correction effects, the location of the commands for applying special effects varies depending on the program you are using. Some may be on the same pop-up Effects menu as are the color correction effects, while some may be on a submenu accessed from the Filter menu. Again, look around to find the options, consult your program's Help system, or ask your instructor for more information.

If settings or options control the way the effect is applied, a dialog box appears and you can make selections. For example, you can adjust the position of a shadow or the shape of a bevel. In addition, some effects are enhanced by hiding—or *knocking out*—the shape itself. Hiding the object that has an emboss effect makes the effect much more dramatic.

Keep in mind that not all programs offer the same effects. For example, your program may have a feature for applying shadows but not glows, or for applying drop shadows but not inner shadows.

Apply Bevels and Embossings

> **Did You Know?**
>
> In some programs, you can use supplemental programs called add-ons or plug-ins to make additional effects available.

Use an *embossed* effect to make an object appear to be pressed into the drawing area. Most programs also let you apply a raised emboss to make an object appear to rise out of the drawing area. *Bevels* also give an object a raised appearance. You can apply an inner bevel, which adds the effect within the edges of the object, or an outer bevel, which adds the effect outside the edges. You can usually adjust the position, sharpness, and width of bevels and embossings. You may also be able to change the bevel shape.

S TEP-BY-STEP 5.9

1. Open **GR Step 5-9** from the data files. This file contains five objects: the monogram group, the text object, two bitmap graphics, and the rectangle background.

2. Save the file as **Card**.

3. Select the monogram object.

4. Open the menu that lists the special effects, select the option for applying an emboss, and then select to apply an inset emboss.

5. Set the width to **5**, and if necessary set the contrast to **75%**, the softness to **2**, and the angle to **135**.

6. If available, click the option to hide or not show the object.

7. Select the bitmap picture of a chair in the lower-left corner.

8. Apply the **Outer Bevel** option from the appropriate menu.

STEP-BY-STEP 5.9 Continued

9. Set the bevel color to dark gray (hexadecimal code 666666); set the bevel width to **5**; set the contrast to **75%**, the softness to **3**, and the angle to **120**. If there is an option for a bevel edge shape, select **Flat**. When you deselect the object, the file should look similar to Figure 5-16.

FIGURE 5-16
Emboss effect draws attention to the monogram,
and bevel makes the picture stand out

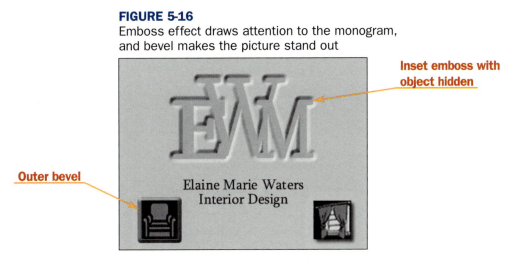

Inset emboss with
object hidden

Outer bevel

Elaine Marie Waters
Interior Design

10. Save changes and leave the **Card** file open to use in the next exercise.

Apply Shadows and Glows

Shadows and *glows* are effects that let you add depth, dimension, and highlights to objects. Drop shadows add a shading along two sides of the outer edge of an object. Inner shadows add the shading inside the edges. Glows apply a halo of color around all edges, and inner glows apply the halo inside the edges. You can usually adjust the position, color, and size of shadows and glows, and you may also be able to adjust other settings such as the sharpness and transparency.

STEP-BY-STEP 5.10

1. In the Card file, select the monogram object.

2. Open the menu that lists special effects options and select to apply a **Glow**.

3. Apply a white glow. If available, set the width to **5**, the opacity to **75%**, the softness to **12**, and the offset to **0**.

4. Select the bitmap image of the chair.

5. Open the menu that lists special effects options and select to apply a **Drop Shadow**.

STEP-BY-STEP 5.10 Continued

6. Position the shadow to the upper-left part of the object by specifying a 120-degree angle. If available, set the distance to **10**, the opacity to **65%**, and the softness to **4**. When you deselect the object, the image should look similar to Figure 5-17.

FIGURE 5-17
Glow effect highlights the monogram and drop shadow highlights the bitmap picture

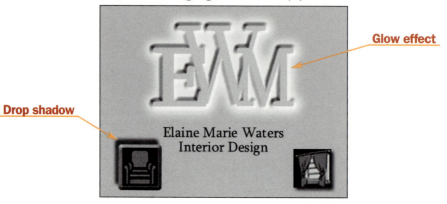

7. Save changes and leave the **Card** file open to use in the next exercise.

Use Sharpen and Blur

Use the sharpen and blur effects to adjust the focus or sharpness of an image. The sharpen effect brings a blurred image into focus, and the blur effect lessens the focus. Most programs offer different levels for each effect, similar to high, medium, and low settings. These effects are most often used on bitmap images, although they can be applied to vector objects and text as well.

Hot Tip

Sometimes the order in which you apply effects makes a difference in the result. For example, if you apply a glow and then apply an emboss, the effect is not the same as first applying an emboss and then applying a glow. Some programs let you reorder effects by changing their position in a list.

STEP-BY-STEP 5.11

1. In the Card file, select the monogram object.

2. Open the menu that lists special effects options and select to apply the lowest level blur effect available.

3. Select the text object.

Extra for Experts

Many programs have Blur and Sharpen tools that you can use to adjust the focus of selected pixels in a bitmap.

STEP-BY-STEP 5.11 Continued

4. Open the menu that lists special effects options and select to apply a middle-level sharpen effect. With all objects deselected, the image should look similar to the one in Figure 5-18.

FIGURE 5-18
Blurring the monogram gives it a softer look, while sharpening the text makes it look crisp and clear

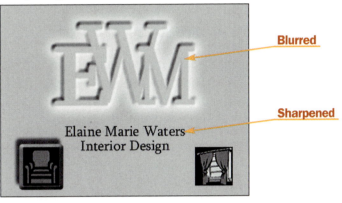

Blurred

Sharpened

5. Save changes and leave the **Card** file open to use in the next exercise.

Save Custom Effects

To achieve a particular effect, you may have to adjust multiple settings and even use multiple effects. Once you have the effect just right, you can save it so the next time you want to use it, you don't have to start from scratch. The method for saving a custom effect varies from program to program, but usually you simply save the applied effects as a *style*, which is a collection of saved formatting settings.

To save formatting settings as a style, you apply the settings to an object and then select the New Style or Save as Style command to open the New Style dialog box. This command is usually available on the special effects menu or in the Styles panel or palette. In the New Style dialog box, you enter a name for the style. You may also be able to select or change the formatting settings. Once you save the style, it is displayed in the Styles panel along with default styles available in your program. To apply the style to other objects, select the object you wish to format and then click the style in the Styles panel.

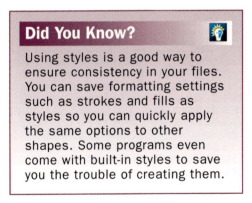

Did You Know?

Using styles is a good way to ensure consistency in your files. You can save formatting settings such as strokes and fills as styles so you can quickly apply the same options to other shapes. Some programs even come with built-in styles to save you the trouble of creating them.

S TEP-BY-STEP 5.12

1. In the Card file, select the bitmap picture of the chair. You will save the effects applied to this object as a style so you can apply them quickly to other objects.

STEP-BY-STEP 5.12 Continued

2. Select the command to create a new style. If necessary, open the Styles panel or dialog box to locate the New Styles button, or select the command from the Options submenu on the special effects pop-up menu. A New Style dialog box displays.

3. Key the name **Shadow Bevel** in the box for the style name, and then click the **OK** button. The style is added to the list of styles.

4. In the **Card** file, select the bitmap picture of a window in the lower-right corner.

5. Open the Styles panel or dialog box if it is not already open, and click the **Shadow Bevel** style in the Styles list. The effects are applied to the selected object, as shown in Figure 5-19.

FIGURE 5-19
Use Styles to apply formatting and effects to objects

Shadow
Bevel style
applied to
the object

Shadow
Bevel style in
Styles panel

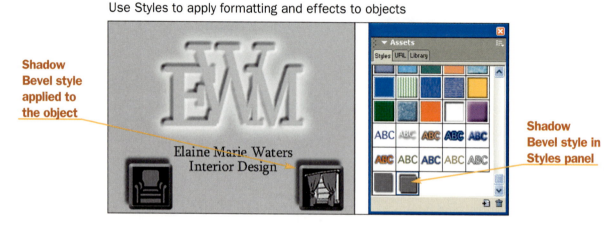

6. Save changes and leave the **Card** file open to use in the next exercise.

Edit and Remove Effects

Edit an effect that has been applied to an object to adjust its settings. For example, you can change the position of a drop shadow, or the shape of a bevel. Most programs have a panel or list that shows effects which have been applied to an object. To edit an effect, select the object and then select the effect in the appropriate panel or list. Depending on your program, you can simply adjust settings to the selected effect, or you may have to click a button or double-click the effect to open a settings panel to edit the effect.

The quickest way to remove an effect is to use the Undo command as soon as you realize you are unhappy with the result. Many programs also have a command for deleting effects. Simply select the effect in the list of effects, and then click the appropriate button or menu command.

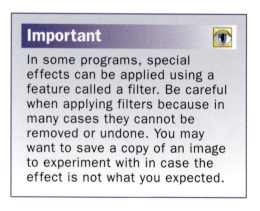

Important

In some programs, special effects can be applied using a feature called a filter. Be careful when applying filters because in many cases they cannot be removed or undone. You may want to save a copy of an image to experiment with in case the effect is not what you expected.

S TEP-BY-STEP 5.13

1. In the **Card** file, select the bitmap picture of a window.

2. Choose to edit the **Drop Shadow** effect.

3. Change the angle from 120 degrees to **60** degrees, or use your program's options to change the location of the drop shadow to the upper-right corner of the object.

4. Choose to edit the **Bevel** effect.

5. Change the angle from 120 degrees to **60** degrees, or use your program's options to move the bevel to the upper-right corner of the object.

6. Select the monogram object.

7. Remove the Blur effect. When all objects are deselected, the image should look similar to the one in Figure 5-20.

FIGURE 5-20
Completed Card file

8. Save changes and close the **Card** file. Leave your graphics program open to use in the next exercise.

Create Masks

The *mask* effect hides or accentuates a specific portion of an image. There are two basic types of masks: vector masks and bitmap masks. The commands for creating masks may be found on a menu such as Modify, Object, or Edit, or in a panel such as the Layers panel. Not all programs offer both types of masks.

Vector Masks

When you create a vector mask, you use a vector graphic to define the shape of the mask. You can use any vector object, such as a rectangle, polygon, or ellipse. Vector masks are also called *clipping masks* in some programs.

To create a vector mask, you first draw the vector object—called the mask object—and position it on top of the object you want to show through the mask. You may then use commands such as Cut and Paste as Mask, Clipping Path, or Paste Inside to create the mask. Only the area within the vector object's path is displayed, while the area outside the path is masked, or hidden.

In some programs, you can adjust properties for the mask to change the way it is displayed. For example, you may be able to show the stroke and fill used to draw the mask object. To show the stroke and fill of the mask object, you must usually select the mask object in a panel such as the Layer panel, and then select an option in a Properties panel to show fill and stroke.

STEP-BY-STEP 5.14

1. Open **GR Step 5-14** from the data files.

2. Save the file as **Jets**.

3. Select the Polygon or Star tool and set the properties to draw a 5-pointed star using 45-degree angles.

4. Center the mouse pointer on the jets in the image, and then drag to draw the star shape. When you release the mouse button, your drawing should look similar to Figure 5-21. If necessary, rotate and move the star so it is in position over the jets.

> **Note** ☑
>
> In this case, it doesn't matter what stroke and fill settings are used to draw the shape. If you plan to display the stroke and fill settings in the mask, you must consider how the settings will look in the finished file.

FIGURE 5-21
Draw the shape to use as a mask

STEP-BY-STEP 5.14 Continued

5. With the star shape selected, select the command to create a vector mask. For example, click the **Edit** menu and click the **Cut** command, then select the image in the file, click the **Edit** menu, and click the **Paste as Mask** command, or click the command in your program that creates a vector mask. The image should look similar to Figure 5-22. All content inside the star shape is revealed, while the content outside the star shape is masked.

FIGURE 5-22
Completed mask

6. Save changes and close the **Jets** file. Leave your graphics program open to use in the next exercise.

Bitmap Masks

Bitmap masks are sometimes called *layer masks* because they overlap and obscure underlying pixels. You can create a bitmap mask using a method similar to creating a vector mask. Simply paste a bitmap object as the mask instead of a vector object.

You can also create an empty mask to either reveal all or hide all the underlying objects. You then use bitmap tools to modify the mask to change the way the underlying object is viewed. For instance, you can use the Paint Bucket tool to add a fill to the mask or even erase parts of the mask to reveal the underlying object.

STEP-BY-STEP 5.15

1. Open **GR Step 5-15** from the data files.

2. Save the file as **Ocean**.

3. Select the image, and then select the command to create an empty mask. For example, click **Modify**, click **Mask**, and then click **Reveal All**. Now, apply a grayscale gradient fill to the mask to make the image look as if the fog is rolling in.

> **Note** ☑
>
> If you create a mask to reveal all, you cannot see it in the file. If you create one to hide all, it displays the current background or drawing area color.

STEP-BY-STEP 5.15 Continued

4. Click the **Gradient** tool in the toolbox. This tool may be on the menu hidden beneath the Paint Bucket tool.

5. Select a black to white linear gradient fill. Depending on your program, you may be able to select the colors directly from the fill color palette, or you may have to use a Gradient dialog box or panel.

6. Drag the Paint Bucket mouse pointer from the upper-left corner of the image diagonally across to the lower-right corner. When you release the mouse button, the gradient is applied. It should look similar to Figure 5-23.

FIGURE 5-23
Bitmap mask

7. Save changes and close the **Ocean** file. Close your graphics program.

SUMMARY

In this lesson, you learned:

- You can mix custom colors using a color bar or by entering color system values.
- You can use color to create illusions of distance, depth, and scale.
- You can use color effects to add texture, patterns, and gradients to fills and strokes.
- Color correction effects make it possible to enhance and improve vector and bitmap images.
- Special effects make it easy to highlight objects as well as add interest and depth to an image.
- You can save special effects as styles to use again.
- If you are unhappy with an effect, you can edit or remove it.
- Masks let you hide or emphasize portions of an image.

VOCABULARY *Review*

Define the following terms:

Bevel	Glow	Saturation
Brightness	Hue	Shadow
CMY	Mask	Spot color
Color system	Opacity	Style
Contrast	RGB	Value
Emboss		

REVIEW *Questions*

TRUE / FALSE

Circle T if the statement is true or F if the statement is false.

T F **1.** Shadows can be applied only around the outer edges of an object.

T F **2.** Opacity controls the amount of transparency in a color.

T F **3.** Saturation is another word for color.

T F **4.** Objects filled with a bright color often look larger than objects filled with a dark color.

T F **5.** CMY is a color system used only for Web graphics.

T F **6.** In most graphics programs, you can apply only one effect to each object.

T F **7.** When you apply a vector mask, the area inside the vector path is displayed and the area outside the path is masked.

T F **8.** Bitmap masks are sometimes called layer masks.

T F **9.** Textures can be applied to strokes but not to fills.

T F **10.** Patterns can be applied to fills but not to strokes.

WRITTEN QUESTIONS

Write a brief answer to the following questions.

1. What are three color effects you can apply to fills, and which one can also be applied to strokes?

2. What are some benefits of creating styles?

3. What is a common reason for adjusting the brightness and contrast of an image?

4. How can you use color to make it easier for someone with a color deficit condition to see and interpret an image?

5. What are the two most common color systems, and what are they typically used for?

FILL IN THE BLANK

Complete the following sentences by writing the correct word or words in the blanks provided.

1. The four colors of ink used in printing are sometimes called _____.

2. Use _____ color when you must match an exact color such as a client's logo.

3. Increasing the brightness adds _____, while decreasing the brightness adds _____.

4. To make a color completely opaque, set the opacity control to _____.

5. Apply a(n) _____ effect to place a halo of color around an object.

6. By default, most gradients blend _____ with the current fill color.

7. Patterns are _____ graphics applied as a fill.

8. Some effects are enhanced by _____ —or knocking out—the shape itself.

9. A(n) _____ gradient blends colors horizontally across an object.

10. _____ measures the intensity of color.

PROJECTS

PROJECT 5-1

1. Launch your graphics program and open **GR Project 5-1** from the data files.

2. Save the file as **Basin**.

3. Select the entire text object and then click the Fill Color button and change the fill color of the text to hexadecimal code 456B59, which is a sea green. You will have to use a color system that accepts hexadecimal values.

4. Apply a raised emboss effect to the text object, setting the width to 10 if the option is available in your program.

5. Select the bitmap image.

6. Change the image to grayscale. You may do this by changing the saturation setting to –100 (as low as possible), or by selecting a command to convert the image to grayscale. (For example, click Commands on the menu bar, click Creative, and then click Convert to Grayscale.)

7. Set the brightness to 5 and the contrast to –10.

8. Print one copy of the image.

9. Save changes and close the **Basin** file, but leave your graphics program open to use in Project 5-2.

PROJECT 5-2

1. Open **GR Project 5-2** from the data files.

2. Save the file as **Masked Flag**.

3. Set the fill color to No Fill and the stroke color to navy blue (hexadecimal code 000080).

4. Use the **Polygon** tool to draw an eight-pointed star with 45-degree angles over the flag.

5. Size and position the star so that the left point is aligned with the left side of the flag; the top point is aligned with the top of the flag; and the bottom point is aligned with the bottom of the flag. The right point probably reaches only about halfway across the width of the flag.

6. Modify the stroke settings to soft-rounded, about 10 pixels thick.

7. Use the star to create a vector mask. (If necessary, cut the shape to the Clipboard and then paste it as a mask.)

8. If possible in your program, select the mask object and choose to show the mask's fill and stroke. (**Hint:** Use the Layers panel to select the mask object, and then find the option for showing the fill and stroke in the Properties panel.)

9. Print one copy of the image.

10. Save changes and close the **Masked Flag** file, but leave your graphics program open to use in Project 5-3.

PROJECT 5-3

1. Open **GR Project 5-3** from the data files.

2. Save the file as **Head2**.

3. Select the modified oval that comprises the outline of the head, and apply a solid brown fill (hexadecimal code 996633).

4. Apply a fill texture similar to piano keys, if available in your program, or select an uneven grid.

5. Apply a stroke texture similar to a tight grid, and set the amount of texture to 100%.

6. Select both eyes and apply a solid dark brown fill (hexadecimal code 660000), and then apply a fill texture similar to a loose grid.

7. Select and group all objects in the image.

8. Select the **Ellipse** tool, set the stroke to a soft-rounded stroke with a weight of 8, and set the fill to a pattern similar to tweed. If tweed is not available in your program, select a geometric pattern that uses brown, black, and white.

9. Draw a circle approximately 4.5 inches in diameter and layer it behind the group.

10. Use the Align panel to center both the circle and the group horizontally and vertically in the drawing area.

11. Print one copy of the image.

12. Save changes and close both the **Head2** file and your graphics program.

WEB PROJECT

Use the Internet to look up color value codes for different color systems. You might try searching for hexadecimal color codes or CMY color codes. Can you find a site that has both? Try entering codes in your graphics program's color mixer to see if the results are what you expect.

TEAMWORK PROJECT

SCANS

Discuss with your classmates the different ways color and effects can be used to enhance graphics used for different purposes. For example, consider how you might change the color and effects you use for the same image on a Web page and in a printed brochure. Then, use your graphics program to design an image that you could use to illustrate a class project. For example, you might design an image of a plant or animal to illustrate a science project, or a scene from a book to illustrate a literature project.

Save two versions of the file—one that you could use on a class Web site and one that you could use on a printed report cover. Change the colors and effects in each file based on its purpose. For example, use the RGB color system for the Web image, and the CMY color system for the printed file. When you are finished, compare the images onscreen and in print.

CRITICAL*Thinking*

ACTIVITY 5-1

Locate a photograph of a scenic view that you can import into your graphics program. For example, take a picture yourself with a digital camera, scan a picture from a book or magazine, or locate a picture on the Internet. You have been asked to prepare the photograph for use in a travel brochure. Examine the picture to determine whether parts of it might benefit from color correction effects. For example, is it too bright or too dark? Could the contrast be improved? Would it look better in black and white or in a sepia tone? Perhaps you should add a bitmap mask to filter the image. Save different versions of the file testing different color correction effects. When you are finished, compare the different files on the computer screen and in print.

GRAPHICS

REVIEW *Questions*

TRUE / FALSE

Circle T if the statement is true or F if the statement is false.

T F   **1.**   In some programs, the drawing area is called the canvas or stage.

T F   **2.**   Dithering lets you remove parts of an image you don't want.

T F   **3.**   You can select and modify pixels in a bitmap image.

T F   **4.**   There are standard tables that list color values for different color systems.

T F   **5.**   You shouldn't rely on a spelling checker to catch every spelling mistake in a file.

T F   **6.**   Most scanners work only with black and white or grayscale images.

T F   **7.**   Text color in a text object is determined by the current stroke color setting.

T F   **8.**   When you increase the brightness of a color, you add black to it.

T F   **9.**   When you optimize an image, you select the best balance of file size and image quality.

T F   **10.**   If a tool displays a drop-down arrow or small rectangle in the lower-right corner, it means you can use it to draw triangles.

3. Create a cube as follows:

   A. Draw a square about 145 pixels by 145 pixels (2.0 inches by 2.0 inches), using a 1-point black, hard line stroke and a rose fill (hexadecimal code FF66CC).

   B. Set the X and Y coordinates for the object to 145 pixels (2.0 inches) to position it approximately 2 inches in from the left edge of the drawing area and 2 inches down from the top edge of the drawing area. You may need to adjust the specified coordinates to position the object correctly in your program.

   C. Zoom in to 200% magnification, and then duplicate the object. Set the X and Y coordinates for the duplicate to 180 pixels (2.5 inches).

   D. Select and duplicate the original object again, leaving it positioned with the X and Y coordinates set to 154 pixels (2.1 inches). Using the **Distort** tool, drag the upper-left corner of the newest square so it aligns with the upper-left corner of the original square. Drag the lower-left corner of the newest square so it aligns with the lower-left corner of the original square. Drag the lower-right corner of the newest square so it aligns with the lower-left corner of the second square. Drag the upper-right corner of the newest square so it aligns with the upper-left corner of the second square. If necessary, fine-tune the alignments to make sure the corners are aligned.

   E. Use the **Line** tool to draw a 1-point black straight line between the upper-right corner of the first square and the upper-right corner of the second square. The result should be an object that gives the illusion of a three-dimensional cube.

4. Select all elements in the drawing, group them, and then create two duplicates. Move the two duplicates so none of the cubes overlap. You may need to zoom out.

5. Change the fill of one of the duplicate cubes to a lighter pink (hexadecimal code FF99CC) and the fill of the other duplicate cube to purple (hexadecimal code CC66CC).

6. Scale the light pink (code FF99CC) cube to about 180 pixels by 180 pixels (2.5 inches by 2.5 inches) and the purple cube to about 105 pixels by 105 pixels (1.5 inches by 1.5 inches).

7. Use the **Brush** tool to fill in the area in the upper-right corner of the original cube, including the vertical stroke of the original square. Use the same fill color as the rest of the cube (code FF66CC). When you are finished, select all components of the cube, and group them.

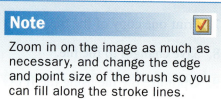

Note ☑

Zoom in on the image as much as necessary, and change the edge and point size of the brush so you can fill along the stroke lines.

8. Repeat step 7 to fill and group the other two cubes. The image should look similar to Figure UR-1.

FIGURE UR-1
Fill and group the cubes

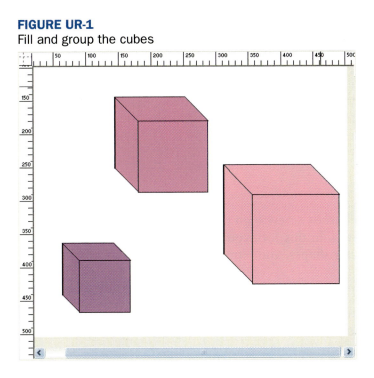

9. Use the text tool to add a text box containing the letter **A** to the front of the purple cube. Use a 32-point serif font such as Times New Roman, in bold black. Size and position the text block to center it on the face of the cube, and then group it with the rest of the cube.

10. Repeat step 9 to add the letter **B** to the rose cube and the letter **C** to the light pink cube. Increase the font size and scale of the text object as necessary to look attractive.

11. Align and arrange the cubes as follows:
    A. Center the C cube horizontally and vertically in the drawing area.
    B. Set the X coordinate for the B cube to approximately 110 (1.5 inches) and the Y coordinate to approximately 250 (3.5 inches). Change the stacking order so the B cube is in front of the C cube.
    C. Set the X coordinate for the A cube to about 235 (3.3 inches) and the Y coordinate to about 325 (4.5 inches). Change the stacking order so the A cube is in the front.

12. Select and group all three cubes.

13. Apply a drop shadow to the group with the angle set to 150 degrees and the width of the shadow set to 25.

14. Print one copy of the file.

15. Save changes to the **Blocks** file, and close your graphics program.

SIMULATION

You are a marketing assistant for Swift River Travel, a travel agency. The company is trying to redefine its image as an adventure tour operator, and you are responsible for designing new graphics for use in printed and electronic media.

Before starting to work in your graphics program, take time to plan the project completely. Working alone or with a partner, review the following steps and then create a schedule for completing the job. Set up a timeline with appropriate milestones. Establish criteria that you believe should be met for each stage of the project, and create a rubric that you can use to gauge your accomplishments.

JOB 1

Swift River Travel needs a new logo to use on business cards, stationery, brochures, advertisements, and Web sites. In this Job, you will use your graphics program to design a logo that incorporates text, vector shapes, and bitmap graphics.

1. Launch your graphics program and open the GIF format image **GR Job 1** from the data files.

2. Use the **Oval Marquee** or **Lasso** tool to select a circular area within the image to the left of the tree. If possible, scale the selection to 180 pixels by 180 pixels (2.5 inches high by 2.5 inches wide), with the river in the center.

3. Cut the selection to the Clipboard and close the **GR Job 1** file without saving changes.

4. Create a new blank file in your graphics program, sizing the drawing area to 7 inches by 7 inches. Use a transparent background and the default resolution.

5. Save the file as **River**.

6. Paste the selection from the Clipboard into the **River** file.

7. Align it in the center of the drawing area horizontally and vertically.

8. Change the color in the image to grayscale (set the Saturation to –100).

9. Use the text tool to key the letter **R** in a 56-point serif font in black. Convert the text to a vector path, scale it to about 35 pixels wide by 45 pixels high (0.5 inches wide by 0.6 inches high), and center it horizontally and vertically in the drawing area.

10. Apply a **Glow** effect to the letter. Set the width of the glow to 1, the blur (or softness) to 4, and the offset to 0. Set the color to blue (hexadecimal code 0066FF).

11. Save the Glow effect as a style named **SRT Glow**.

12. Use the text tool to enter the letter **S** in the same 56-point serif font in black. Convert the text to a vector path, scale it to about 35 pixels wide by 45 pixels high (0.5 inches wide by 0.6 inches high), and position it within the circular picture, diagonally above and to the left of the letter *R*.

13. Repeat step 12 to add the letter **T** to the image, positioning it below and to the right of the letter *R*.

14. Apply the **SRT Glow** effect to both the *T* and the *S*.

15. Select and group all four objects in the image.

16. Apply the **SRT Glow** style to the group. At this point, ask a classmate to review the image onscreen and to offer suggestions for improvement.

17. When you have incorporated suggested changes, optimize the image for export as a **GIF Websnap 128** file, and save the exported file as **River2**.

18. Print the **River** file, and then save it and close it, but leave your graphics program open to use in Job 2.

19. Ask a classmate to review the printed image and to offer comments and suggestions. If necessary, go back to modify the image file to incorporate any suggestions you think will improve the image.

JOB 2

The company president wants new business cards made using the new logo and the new company slogan. In this Job, you will design a prototype for the business card.

Before starting to work in your graphics program, take time to plan the project completely. Working alone or with a partner, review the following steps and then create a schedule for completing the job. Set up a timeline with appropriate milestones. Establish criteria that you believe should be met for each stage of the project, and create a rubric that you can use to gauge your accomplishments.

1. Create a new blank file in your graphics program, sizing the drawing area to 3.5 inches by 2 inches, a standard size for business cards.

2. Save the file as **SRT Card**.

3. Use the **Rectangle** tool to draw a rectangle using no fill and a black 1-point hard line stroke. Size the rectangle about 240 pixels by 130 pixels (3.3 inches wide by 1.8 inches high) and center it horizontally and vertically.

4. Locate and open the GIF file **GR Job 2** from the data files. This is a version of the **River2** file you created in Job 1.

5. Use the **Oval Marquee** or a lasso tool to select the logo in the **GR Job 2** file, and then copy it to the Clipboard. Close the **GR Job 2** file without saving changes.

6. Paste the logo into the **SRT Card** file. Size it to about 90 by 90 pixels (1.3 by 1.3 inches) and position it in the upper left corner of the rectangle.

7. Create a text block in the upper-right corner of the rectangle and key the text **Employee Name** using a 14-point sans serif font, such as Lucida Console, in blue (hexadecimal code 0066FF). Start a new line in the block and key the text **Employee Title** using the same font in 10 points and black.

8. Create another text block at the bottom right of the rectangle. Use the same font in black sized to 8 points, and key the text line by line as follows:

56778 Gulf of Mexico Drive
Longboat Key, Florida 34228
Tel. (941) 555-5555   Fax (941) 555-5556
email employee@swiftriver.net

9. Create a final text block, centered horizontally in the drawing area. Using a serif font such as Book Antiqua in black, sized to 18 points, key **Swift River Travel**. Start a new line, change to 12 points, and key **"Your Key to Adventure"**. If necessary, adjust the position and width of all objects and the size of the logo so that the text doesn't wrap.

10. Select all three text blocks and set the alignment to Right. Then, select each text box individually and adjust the leading to make the text easier to read and attractive. For example, increase the leading in the top and bottom text blocks, and decrease it in the middle.

11. Check the spelling in the file.

12. Select all objects in the file and group them.

13. Print the image. Ask a classmate to review the printed image. If necessary, go back to the file and make changes or improvements.

14. Save changes and close the **SRT Card** file. Leave your graphics program open to use in Job 3.

SCANS JOB 3

Your supervisor has asked you to gather a selection of pictures that might be used to market a bicycle tour in Banff National Park in Alberta, Canada. She needs four pictures, but she has asked you to provide at least eight. They can be photos or drawings, but she wants to see them both on screen and in print, as they will be used for a variety of purposes. In this Job, you research Banff using available resources, including the Internet, books, magazines, and CD-ROMs, to find the pictures. You then optimize the pictures for viewing onscreen and for printing. Before selecting a picture, you should take into consideration its composition and format as well as its content. Think about how the pictures may be used and whether you will need to obtain permission to use them.

First, plan your research by considering accessible sources and the amount of time you have. Decide how to organize the pictures once you locate them, including naming them, storing them, and printing them. Make a schedule to ensure you complete the job on time. Set up a timeline with appropriate milestones. Establish criteria that you believe should be met for each stage of the project, and create a rubric that you can use to gauge your accomplishments.

When you are ready, locate as many pictures as you can on the Internet. You can use a search engine or go directly to a Web site such as canadianrockies.net or banffnationalpark.com. Download the pictures, saving them with unique names such as *Banff1*, *Banff2*, and so on. Record all source information for the downloaded photos in a word processing or text file, or by hand. Include the address of the Web site; the photographer's name, if available; the date of the download; and the date the site was last updated, if available.

Next, try to locate information in a book or magazine. Try looking for pictures in travel magazines, geography books, or an encyclopedia. If you find any pictures, scan them into your graphics programs. Continue the same naming scheme that you used for the downloaded pictures. Record all source information for the pictures, including the publication name, the article name, the artist or photographer, the publisher, the date, and the page number.

Finally, try using a CD-ROM to locate pictures of Banff. You may have access to an encyclopedia on CD, such as Microsoft's Encarta, or you may have a travel or geography CD. If you find any pictures, save them on your computer using the name *Banff* and the next consecutive number. Again, don't forget to record all source information for the pictures.

When you are finished locating at least eight pictures, optimize them for viewing onscreen and for printing. Share them with your classmates and discuss whether they are appropriate for use in a marketing campaign. Select pictures better suited for use on a Web site and those better suited for other media, such as brochures, direct marketing flyers, posters, and presentations.

If possible, store the pictures in a database that you create with a database program or spreadsheet program. You can set up the database to include a preview of the picture or a link to the actual picture file. You can include information such as the source where you located the picture, information about the content of the picture, and how you anticipate using the picture. Write a brief report explaining which pictures you would recommend for each use, and why. If possible, insert the pictures into your report. E-mail the report to your instructor, or to a classmate, asking for an opinion on the selected pictures.

ANIMATION AND VIDEO

Unit

Estimated Time for Unit: 9 hours

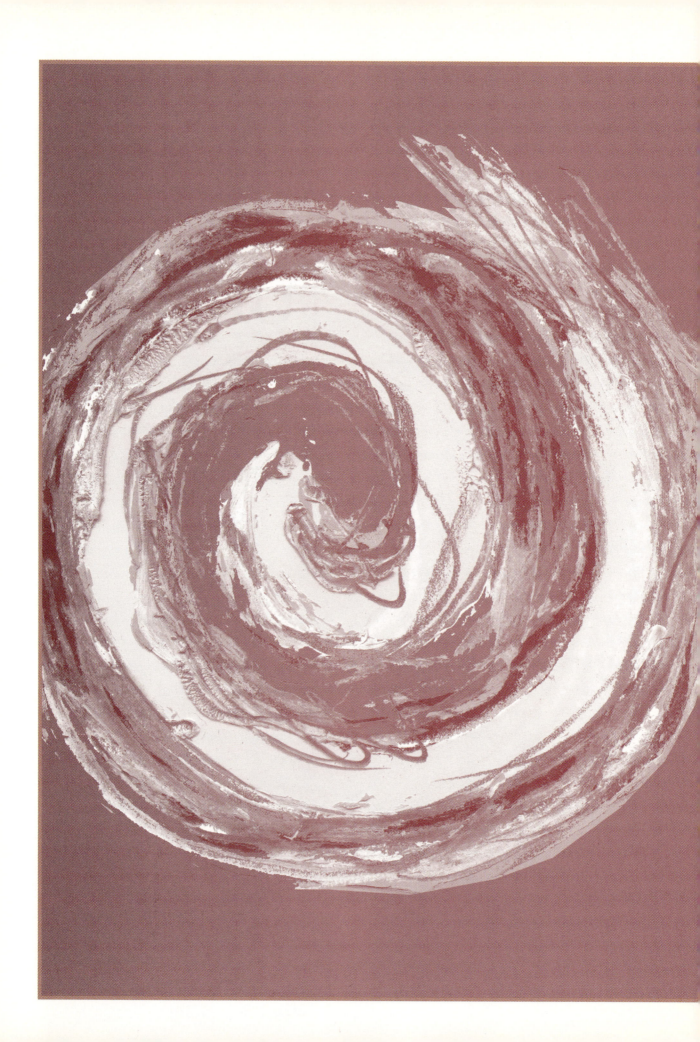

CREATING ANIMATIONS

OBJECTIVES

Upon completion of this lesson, you should be able to:

- Create a new animation file.
- Insert content in frames.
- Add and delete frames and keyframes.
- Create frame-by-frame animation.
- Preview and test an animation.
- Create motion and path animation.
- Use layers.
- Copy and move frames.
- Use the onion skin feature to view multiple frames.

Estimated Time: 1.5 hours

VOCABULARY

Animation

fps

Frame

Keyframe

Layer

Motion path

Movie

Onion skin

Panel

Path animation

Playhead

Project file

Stage

Timeline

Tween

A majority of Web sites today feature animated graphics—that is, graphics with motion. Also called *animations* or *movies*, these graphics take many forms, including moving or blinking logos, flashing advertisements, lively cartoon characters, product demonstrations, or even how-to tutorials. Presentation graphics programs also enable you to use animations to enhance onscreen presentations.

Many graphics programs let you create simple animations such as blinking or spinning logos. Using a more specialized animation program, you can include a variety of objects and different types of motion, sounds, and buttons to build a complex animation. Leading programs for creating animations include Macromedia Flash MX and Adobe LiveMotion. (The figures in this unit show Macromedia Flash MX.) While animation programs differ slightly, most include common elements.

The lessons in this unit present the basic skills for creating an animation. In this lesson, you learn how to create and save an animation file, set options for the file, import graphics for use in the animation, use different methods to control object motion, and preview an animation.

Explore an Animation Program

Before you can create an animation, you must become familiar with the unique features of your animation program. Most animation programs include a *Stage* where you place the content for the animation. The stage is called the *composition* in Adobe LiveMotion. The size and shape of the Stage determines the dimensions of the finished animation. You can import graphics to place on the Stage, or use the animation program's drawing tools to create objects. In addition to the Stage, animation programs include a *Timeline* that holds the *frames* for the animation.

Your animation program offers its own additional tools and features. For example, Flash MX groups its features in *panels* (small floating windows). One key panel, the toolbox, provides tools you can use to draw and format objects in Flash MX. These tools look similar to and are used in much the same way as tools in a graphics program such as Macromedia Fireworks.

> **Note** ☑
>
> You can close or minimize panels if desired to free up more space in the program window for the Stage.

Flash MX also includes a special panel called the Property inspector that appears below the Stage by default. The Property inspector displays settings you can use to alter any object selected on the Stage. Use the Window menu to hide and display the panels you need.

STEP-BY-STEP 1.1

1. Launch your animation application. Your screen looks similar to Figure 1-1. (If a welcome screen displays, close it.)

2. Take some time to review Figure 1-1 to become familiar with the key parts of an animation program's window. As you work through the animation lessons, refer to the figure if you need help remembering the names of the window elements.

FIGURE 1-1
Macromedia Flash MX screen

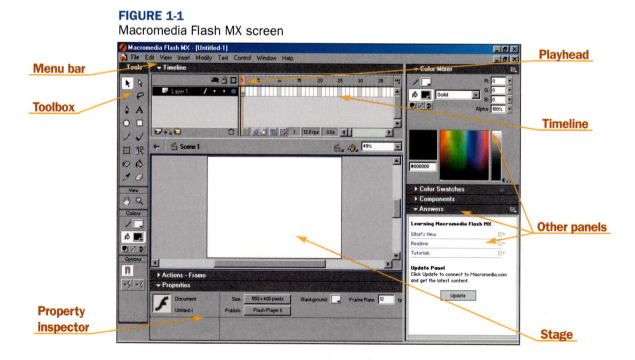

STEP-BY-STEP 1.1 Continued

3. Leave your animation program open to use in the next exercise.

Create a New Animation

When you create an animation, you create a *project file* or work file to hold the animation content. You follow several steps to prepare the file for use. First, you may need to set a size for the stage. Ideally, the stage should be large enough to accommodate the graphics and motion you plan for the animation. You can change the units of measurement for the Stage and even change its background color. After you have set the Stage size, you can adjust a zoom setting to make it easier to work with the Stage.

Save the new project file using the familiar Save As command on the File menu. Your animation program saves the project file in its native file format. In Flash MX, for example, project files use the filename extension *fla*.

STEP-BY-STEP 1.2

1. Click **File** on the menu bar, and then click **New**. The name of the new project file, **[Untitled-2]**, appears in the program window title bar.

2. Open the dialog box for setting the animation properties. For example, in Flash MX, click the **Document properties** button (it has the Stage size on it) in the Property inspector to open the Document Properties dialog box as shown in Figure 1-2.

FIGURE 1-2
Set properties to change the size of the Stage

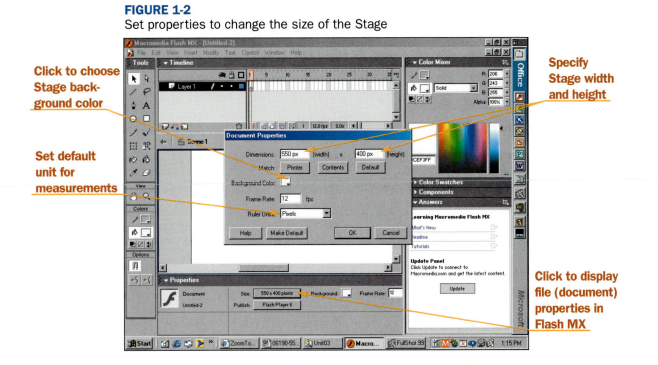

Click to choose Stage background color

Specify Stage width and height

Set default unit for measurements

Click to display file (document) properties in Flash MX

STEP-BY-STEP 1.2 Continued

3. Make sure that measurement units are specified in pixels by checking the appropriate control in the dialog box.

4. Key **100** for the width setting and **100** for the height setting.

5. Click the **OK** button. The Stage appears in its new dimensions.

> **Hot Tip**
>
> In this project, you create an animation that displays four small graphics in succession, so the Stage needs to be only as large as the graphics.

6. Use the scroll bars for the Stage to move it into view, if necessary.

7. Change the zoom for the Stage to **200%** using a command on the **View** menu or a value on a zoom list near the Stage.

8. Click **File** on the menu bar, and then click **Save As** to open the Save As dialog box.

9. From the **Save in** list, select the location where you want to store the file.

10. In the **File name** text box, key **Seasons**.

11. Click the **Save** button in the dialog box.

12. Leave the **Seasons** file open to use in the next exercise.

Insert Content in a Frame

The animation project file initially contains a blank Stage, a single frame, and a single layer. You will learn more about layers later in this lesson. Right now, you have to create and insert content, as well as add layers and frames, to build the animation.

Typically, you add graphics that you've created in another application to build the animation. You import a graphic file into the animation project file using a command such as Import on the File menu. Some programs allow you to import the graphic to a library to make the graphic file easier to use repeatedly.

Another method of adding content to a frame is to use your animation program's toolbox. Use these tools to create shapes, lines, and text objects on the Stage and format them with stroke and fill options just as in a graphics program.

Once you've imported a graphic, you place it on the Stage in the appropriate location. If the graphic is in a library, simply drag it to the Stage. You can rename graphics stored in a library to help you remember their content. Use a command on a menu or shortcut menu to rename a library object.

S TEP-BY-STEP 1.3

1. In the Seasons file, click **File** on the menu bar, and then click **Import to Library** or use your program's Import command. A dialog box opens so that you can select the file to import.

2. Navigate to the data files folder, select **AV Step 1-3**, and click **Open**. To see the file, you may need to click the **Files of type** drop-down list and select the appropriate file format or All Files.

3. If a dialog box prompts you for import settings, choose to import the graphic as a single flattened bitmap, and then click the **OK** button.

4. If the image doesn't appear on the Stage, it has been placed in a library. Choose the command to display the library. In Flash MX, click **Window** on the menu bar, and then click **Library**. The Library panel opens and displays the imported graphic.

5. Place the graphic on the Stage. If the graphic is in a library, drag the graphic from the Library panel to the Stage.

6. Align the edges of the graphic with edges of the Stage as shown in Figure 1-3.

FIGURE 1-3
Import a graphic and then place it on the Stage

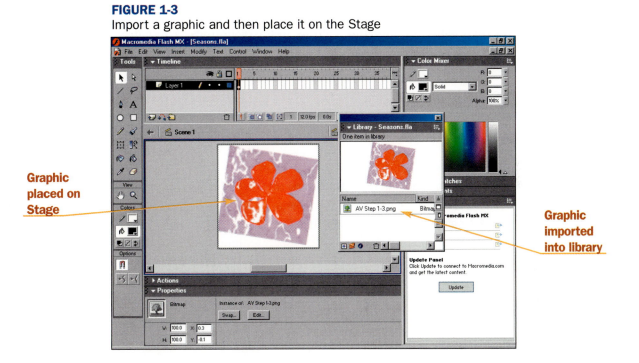

Graphic placed on Stage

Graphic imported into library

7. Rename the graphic in the library as **Spring**. You may be able to right-click the library item and choose the Rename command from the shortcut menu.

8. Save changes and leave the **Seasons** file open to use in the next exercise.

In Macromedia Flash MX, you can convert an imported graphic to a *symbol* to help reduce movie file size. Flash MX stores the symbol file only once in the file even if you use the symbol repeatedly throughout the animation. Use the Convert to Symbol command on the Modify menu to create a symbol. To add a symbol to a frame, drag it from the Library panel just as you would a graphic. You will work with symbols in Lesson 2.

Add and Delete Frames and Keyframes

Cartoons initially were animated by hand. An illustrator drew successive variations of a character on clear acetate *cels*. Each cel showed the character in a slightly different position. When cels were viewed in rapid order, the character then appeared to move. The more cels the artist drew, the longer the animation.

Each frame in your animation is like a single cel. The frame holds the content the movie displays or plays at that point in time. So, to increase the length of your movie, you have to add more frames. If you delete frames, you decrease the animation's length.

Animation programs actually enable you to add two types of frames: regular frames and *keyframes*. Regular frames simply hold content. Keyframes provide greater power. You can use a keyframe to specify a change in the animation, such as a new position for an object.

Add a frame or a keyframe using a command on the Insert menu. Delete frames by first selecting them and then using a command such as Remove Frames. You can delete keyframes using a command such as Clear Keyframe.

STEP-BY-STEP 1.4

1. In the Seasons file, click the **frame 2** position on the Timeline for the first (and only) layer to select frame 2.

2. Click **Insert** on the menu bar, and then click **Frame** or use the command for inserting a frame in your animation program. A small box or marker on the Timeline indicates that you've added the frame.

3. Click the **frame 10** position on the Timeline to select frame 10. This is where you will insert the new keyframe.

4. Click **Insert** on the menu bar, and then click **Keyframe** or use the command for inserting a keyframe in your animation program. Another type of marker on the Timeline indicates that you've added the keyframe.

5. Select frames to delete in the Timeline: drag over the **frame 5** and **frame 6** positions on the Timeline to select frames 5 and 6.

> **Hot Tip**
>
> In Macromedia Flash MX, you can click a frame position on the Timeline and press F5 to add a frame.

> **Hot Tip**
>
> In Macromedia Flash MX, you can click a frame position on the Timeline and press F6 to add a keyframe. In most animation programs, you also can insert a blank keyframe so that you can add completely new content into it.

STEP-BY-STEP 1.4 Continued

6. Click **Insert** on the menu bar, and then click **Remove Frames** or use the command for deleting frames in your animation program. The Timeline shows two fewer frames. See Figure 1-4.

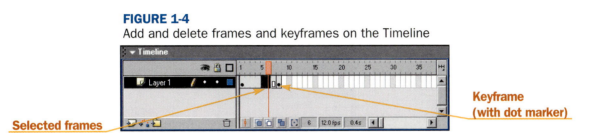

FIGURE 1-4
Add and delete frames and keyframes on the Timeline

Selected frames

Keyframe
(with dot marker)

7. Save changes and leave the **Seasons** file open to use in the next exercise.

Create Frame-by-Frame Animation

At the simplest level, all you need to do to create animation is move one object on one frame to create some movement in your animation. When you play the animation, the object jumps to a new position for that frame, creating the illusion of movement.

When you create your own animations, you'll want to include action in more than one frame. To make the job easier, insert a keyframe at each change in the action. Changing the content in a keyframe changes the content in all regular frames following the keyframe on the timeline until the next keyframe.

If your animation program creates movies at 12 *fps (frames per second)* by default, inserting a keyframe and change every 12 frames results in a change in the action every second. A project with 60 frames results in a 5-second movie.

When you insert a keyframe, you can change its content in a variety of ways. You can add and delete objects, replace one object with another, move objects, resize or rotate objects, and so on. All these actions simulate some kind of motion or action. For example, you may have seen advertisements that flash different messages on the Web. In this case, the animation's creator replaced one image or text object with another at each keyframe.

As you are building your animation, remember to add a keyframe where you want the animation to stop. This keyframe should be placed to allow sufficient viewing time after the final content change. If you insert a new graphic at frame 35, for instance, place the final keyframe at frame 50 to allow for the display of the final graphic.

STEP-BY-STEP 1.5

1. In the Seasons file, clear the keyframe currently in frame 8: select the keyframe, click **Insert** on the menu bar, and then click **Clear Keyframe**, or the command in your program that deletes a keyframe.

2. Import the following graphic files from the data files folder as flattened images to the library: **AV Step 1-5a**, **AV Step 1-5b**, and **AV Step 1-5c**. The files appear in the Library panel.

STEP-BY-STEP 1.5 Continued

3. Rename the **AV Step 1-5a** graphic in the Library panel as **Summer**. Rename **AV Step 1-5b** as **Fall**. Rename **AV Step 1-5c** as **Winter**. Figure 1-5 illustrates the imported images in the Library panel.

FIGURE 1-5
Import and rename graphics
in the Library panel

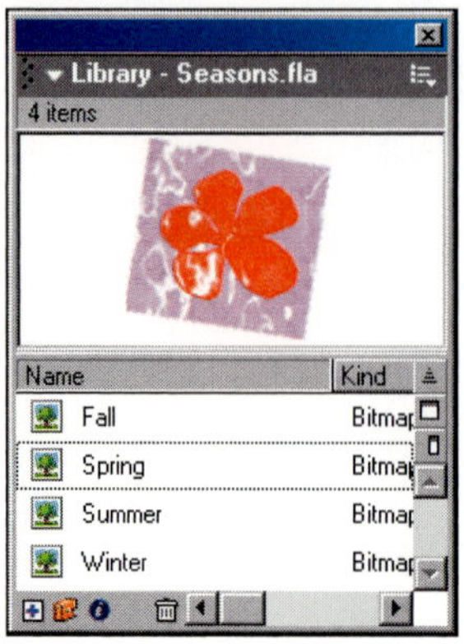

4. Click the **frame 12** position on the Timeline to select frame 12. You will insert a new keyframe in this frame.

5. Click **Insert** on the menu bar, and then click **Keyframe** or use the command for inserting a keyframe in your animation program.

6. Click the **Spring** graphic currently on the Stage to select it, if necessary.

7. Press **Delete** or choose the appropriate command on the **Edit** menu, such as **Delete** or **Clear**, to remove the object.

8. Drag the **Summer** graphic from the Library panel to the Stage for frame 12. Align the graphic's edges with the edges of the Stage.

9. Add additional keyframes at frame 24 and frame 36. In frame 24, delete the Summer graphic and place the **Fall** graphic on the Stage. In frame 36, delete the Fall graphic and place the **Winter** graphic on the Stage.

STEP-BY-STEP 1.5 Continued

10. Add another keyframe at frame 48. This designates the end of the movie. Otherwise, the Winter graphic would appear for a single frame only at the end of the movie. Figure 1-6 illustrates frames 12 through 48 of the finished timeline for your movie.

FIGURE 1-6
Add keyframes to build a movie and designate action changes

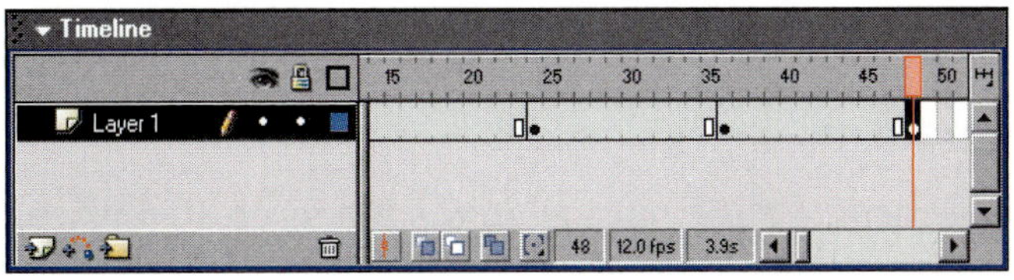

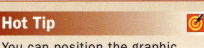

11. Save changes and leave the **Seasons** file open to use in the next exercise.

> **Hot Tip** 🎯
>
> Click on the Timeline between the keyframes to see how your animation program has added the appropriate graphic to the regular frames for you.

Preview an Animation

You can preview an animation at any time during its creation. Leading animation programs offer several ways to preview your final animation. You can drag the *playhead*—the vertical red marker in the Timeline—to see how the animation progresses. (Drag the playhead toward frame 1 to rewind the movie.) You can also use commands on a menu such as Control to play or rewind the movie. By previewing the animation before you publish the final movie, you can identify and eliminate problems.

STEP-BY-STEP 1.6

1. In the Seasons file, drag the playhead to frame 1, if necessary, and observe how the images change as you rewind.

2. Choose the command that starts the preview. In Flash MX, press **Enter**. Or click **Control** on the menu bar, and then click **Play**.

3. If you notice that one of the images jumps in place slightly as it appears, it is not aligned exactly with the Stage. Adjust the position of the graphics if necessary so they change smoothly from one to the next during the movie.

> **Hot Tip** 🎯
>
> You can position the graphic exactly by selecting it and entering values in the X and Y boxes on the Property inspector.

4. Save changes and close the **Seasons** file. Leave your animation program open to use in the next exercise.

Create Motion and Path Animation

Keyframes provide you even greater power when you want to include real action in your animation. You can create a motion *tween* for an object using keyframes. The animation program calculates the proper position for the object in each frame between the keyframes. It's called "tweening" because the program creates the in-be*tween* frames for you.

You can create two different types of movement using tweening: basic motion animation and path animation.

Basic Motion Animation

The first type of movement, a basic motion animation, is created when an object's position is different at the end of the movie from the start of the movie. Place the object in its starting position in the first keyframe. In the last keyframe, move the object to its final position. When you instruct the animation program to create a tween, it creates a straight path between the two positions, and the object moves along that path during the movie.

Animation programs differ greatly in the steps used to create motion. For example, in Adobe LiveMotion, you set keyframes for and animate particular attributes (properties) of each object. In Macromedia Flash FX, you create motion tweens using either a menu command or an option on the Property inspector.

STEP-BY-STEP 1.7

1. Open **AV Step 1-7** from the data files.

2. Save the file as **Brick Path**.

3. Zoom the Stage to **75%**. (You can type this percentage in your program's zoom box if the zoom list does not offer this percentage. In Flash MX, the zoom box is located between the Timeline and the Stage on the right-hand side.)

4. Display the **Library** panel, if necessary.

STEP-BY-STEP 1.7 Continued

5. Drag the **Bricks Logo** graphic from the Library panel and place it near the upper-left corner of the Stage for frame 1, as in Figure 1-7.

FIGURE 1-7
Object in its initial position on the Stage

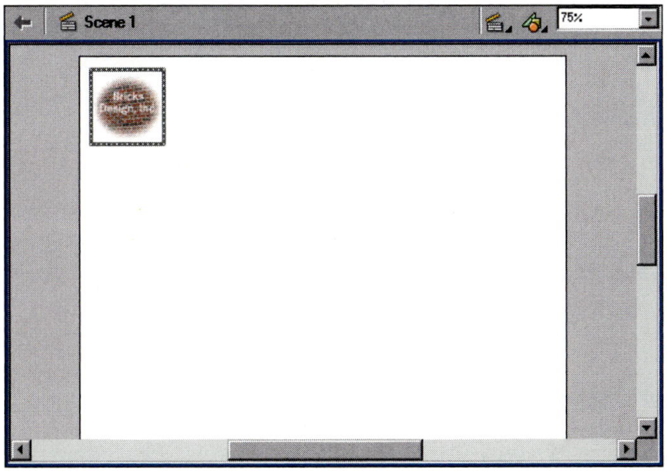

6. Choose the command for creating a motion tween. In Flash MX, click **Insert** on the menu bar, and then click **Create Motion Tween**.

7. Click **frame 15** on the Timeline. You want the motion to start at frame 1 and end at frame 15, so you need to insert a keyframe at frame 15.

8. Click **Insert** on the menu bar, and then click **Keyframe** or use the command for inserting a keyframe in your animation program. You may see a special arrow or marker and color shading on the in-between frames to indicate the tweening.

STEP-BY-STEP 1.7 Continued

9. With frame 15 still selected, drag the logo graphic to a position near the lower-right corner of the Stage. This action specifies the object's ending position for the motion sequence in frames 1 through 15. Your project should now resemble Figure 1-8.

FIGURE 1-8
The object in its end position on the Stage

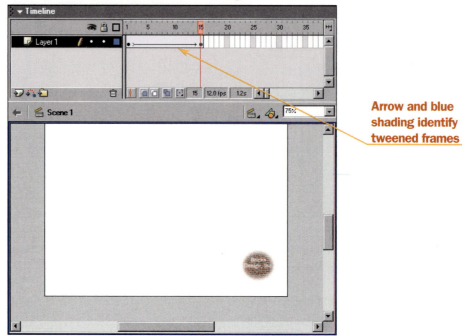

Arrow and blue shading identify tweened frames

10. Play the movie in your animation program to see how the tweening works.

11. Save changes and leave the **Brick Path** file open to use in the next exercise.

Path Animation

If you want your object to follow a more elaborate route, use the second type of movement tweening: *path animation*. When creating a path animation, you draw the route or *motion path* the object should follow. The animation program again calculates the object's proper position along the route for each frame. A motion path can include curves, loops, and angles. You have few limits in determining where you want your objects to travel.

> **Note** ☑
>
> Some animation programs, such as Flash MX, also enable you to create shape tweening. With shape tweening, the animation program calculates the change in an object's shape between keyframes, as well as its position. For example, if you begin an animation with a small logo in the upper-left corner of the Stage and end with a large logo at the bottom-right corner, when tweened the logo both moves across the Stage and becomes larger as it travels.

To create path animation, you must insert a special layer in the animation called a motion guide layer. (You will learn more about layers in the next section.) You draw the path for the animation on this layer. To draw the path, you can use tools such as the Pencil or Pen, or another shape tool.

S TEP-BY-STEP 1.8

1. In the Brick Path file, insert a new keyframe at frame 30. Adding this keyframe extends the movie so you can add the motion path animation in frames 15 through 30.

2. Choose the command for adding a motion path in your animation program. In Flash MX, click **Insert** on the menu bar, and then click **Motion Guide**. A new layer named *Guide: Layer 1* appears above Layer 1 for the motion path.

3. Click **frame 15** on the Guide: Layer 1 layer in the Timeline. Insert a keyframe there. Leave this frame selected for the next step.

4. Choose the command for creating a motion tween. In Flash MX, click **Insert** on the menu bar, and then click **Create Motion Tween**. Leave this frame selected for the next step.

5. Now you need to draw the path itself. Click the **Pencil** tool on the toolbox. Draw on the Stage to create the motion path, beginning at the center of the graphic at the lower-right corner of the stage and ending near the upper-left corner of the stage. You can draw a straight line or a freeform path such as the one shown in Figure 1-9 on the next page. You may want to change the zoom setting so you can see the entire Stage.

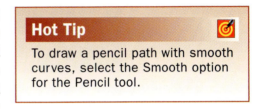

> ### Hot Tip
>
> To draw a pencil path with smooth curves, select the Smooth option for the Pencil tool.

6. Click the **Arrow** or **Selection** tool in your animation program. Choose its **Snap to Objects** setting if necessary. This helps the logo graphic snap to the path you've drawn.

7. Click **frame 15** in the Layer 1 layer, and then click the Bricks Logo graphic. Drag the graphic to position its center point (identified with a special marker) on the starting end of the motion path (if the graphic's center point is not already aligned at the starting point of the guide).

STEP-BY-STEP 1.8 Continued

8. Click **frame 30** in the Layer 1 layer, and then click the Bricks Logo graphic. Drag the graphic to position its center point (identified with a special marker) on the finishing end of the motion path (at the upper-left corner of the Stage). Figure 1-9 shows how your project should look at this point.

FIGURE 1-9
Object at the end of its motion path

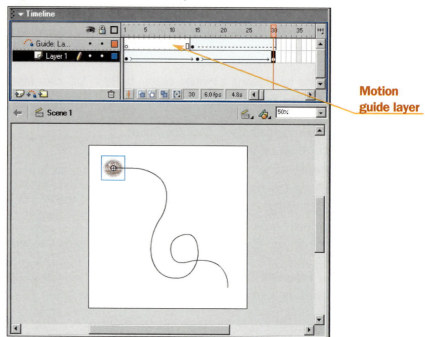

9. Save changes and leave the **Brick Path** file open to use in the next exercise.

> **Note** ✅
>
> Motion animation often requires a great deal of trial and error. To make sure you get it right, preview your work frequently.

Use Layers

Layers enable you to enrich the content of any movie. *Layers* are like transparent sheets stacked on top of each other. Layers appear as part of the Timeline, with a separate row on the Timeline for each layer.

Layers allow you to position objects in front of one another. For example, you can have objects on one or more layers and also use a layer to include a background behind the objects. Placing objects on different layers lets you animate an object on one layer while leaving the other objects static (not moving). You can create simultaneous motion on different layers, such as having an object on one layer follow a motion path while an object on another layer simply changes in color or appearance every several frames or so. Using layers also makes editing easier. You can change the content on one layer without disturbing the work you've done on the other layers in your animation.

Generally, the order of the layers in the Timeline controls which content appears "in front" of the content on other layers. The content of layers higher in the list appears in front of the content on other layers lower in the list. Thus, if you want to create a layer to hold background content, it should be last in the list of layers.

Layers allow you a great degree of flexibility because you can modify them in a number of ways after creating them. You can add and delete layers as needed, hide and redisplay layers, or even lock a layer to prevent further editing. To select a layer to work on, just click the layer name.

S TEP-BY-STEP 1.9

1. In the Brick Path file, click the **Guide: Layer 1** layer for the motion path in the Timeline. The new layer you create will be inserted above this layer.

2. Choose the command or click the button for adding a layer. In Flash MX, click the **Insert Layer** button in the lower-left corner of the Timeline, or click **Insert** on the menu bar and then click **Layer**. The new layer appears in the Timeline. Flash MX names the new layer *Layer 3* by default, as the motion guide layer was the second layer added.

> **Important**
>
> Inserting the new layer below the motion guide layer would cause the new layer to become a guided layer. However, you want the new layer to be a regular layer, so insert it above the motion guide layer.

3. Click **Guide: Layer 1**. Then press and hold **Shift** and click **Layer 1**. Both Guide: Layer 1 and Layer 1 are now selected.

4. Drag the selected layers above Layer 3. This positions Layer 3 at the bottom of the list, so it can hold background content without causing the layer content to follow the motion path. Your Timeline should now resemble Figure 1-10.

FIGURE 1-10
Add and move layers in the Timeline

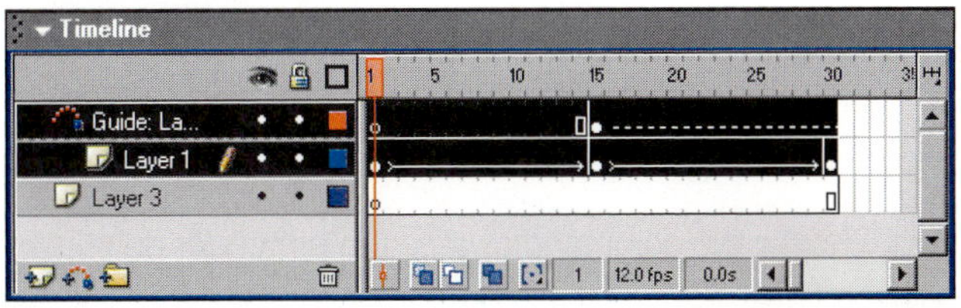

5. Click **frame 1** in Layer 3.

6. Click the **Oval** tool in the toolbox. Specify that the shape will not include a stroke color, and choose a radial gradient as the fill for the object. (In Flash MX, you can find gradients at the bottom of the fill color panel.)

> **Hot Tip**
>
> You can rename any layer. To do so, double-click the layer name, type a new name, and press **Enter**.

7. Open a color mixer panel, if necessary. Specify a radial gradient if you could not do so before. Adjust the gradient colors to use white as the central color and a bright green as the outer color. To adjust gradient colors, click the gradient pointer of the color to adjust and then select a new color.

STEP-BY-STEP 1.9 Continued

8. Click and drag the tool crosshair on the Stage to create an oval or circle for the background. (The object does not have to fill the entire background.)

9. Change the colors used for the gradient fill, turn off stroke color if necessary, and draw several more oval objects on and surrounding the larger, central one. For best results, create all objects in blank areas of the Stage and do not overlap them until you are satisfied with their size and shape.

> **Note** ☑️
>
> Unless you convert drawing objects to *symbols*, you cannot work with them as independent objects. Objects drawn on top of other objects replace the pixels of objects below.

10. To move any object, click the **Arrow** or **Selection** tool, click the object, and drag it to a new position. To adjust the size or shape of any object, click the **Free Transform** or **Transform** tool, click the object, and then drag the handles that appear around the object to adjust its size and shape. When you finish adding and positioning ovals, your project should resemble Figure 1-11.

FIGURE 1-11
Content added to Layer 3

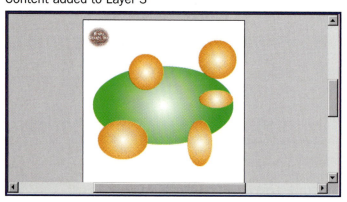

11. Click the dot in the **Lock** column (below the lock icon in Flash MX) on the Layer 3 row or use the technique for locking the layer in your animation program. This prevents further editing on the layer.

12. Now practice adding and deleting a layer. Insert a new layer above Layer 3.

13. With Layer 4 selected, choose the command or click the button for deleting a layer. In Flash MX, you can click the **Delete Layer** button (the trash can icon), or right-click on the layer and click **Delete Layer** in the shortcut menu that appears. The layer disappears from the Timeline.

14. Save changes and leave the **Brick Path** file open to use in the next exercise.

> **Hot Tip** ◎
>
> If you plan to include your animation on a Web page or presentation slide with a colored background, add a matching background in your animation so that it blends seamlessly.

Copy or Move a Frame or Frame Series

Because you may not know exactly what you want from an animation until you see it onscreen, you may need to adjust the order of some frames. Or, you may like a particular animation sequence so well that you decide to copy it to numerous locations in your animation. You may even decide that you need to extend an animation sequence. You can accomplish all these objectives by working with the frames on the Timeline. Table 1-1 lists some of the actions you can perform by working with frames.

TABLE 1-1
Work with frames

TO	DO THIS
Change the duration of an animation sequence	Drag the right keyframe left or right on the Timeline.
Select multiple frames on a layer	Click the first frame, press and hold Shift, and click the next frame.
Select multiple frames on multiple adjacent layers	Click the upper-left frame (on the top layer), press and hold Shift, and click the lower-right frame (on the bottom layer).
Move selected frames	Drag the frames on the Timeline; or click Edit and Cut Frames, click to choose a destination frame on the Timeline, and click Edit and Paste Frames.
Copy selected frames	Press and hold Alt and then drag the frames on the Timeline; or click Edit and Copy Frames, click to choose a destination frame on the Timeline, and click Edit and Paste Frames.
Insert blank frames	Select the frame(s) where you want to insert blanks, and use the command for inserting frames in your animation program.

If you want to move or copy a motion sequence, be sure to select both the first and last keyframes. Pasting the copied or moved sequence overwrites existing content in the destination frames, so insert blank frames first, if needed, to hold the pasted frames.

To move or copy a sequence with a motion path, select the frames on both the motion guide layer and the content layer before moving or copying. When you are inserting or deleting frames on one layer, make sure to adjust the number of frames in other layers as required. Otherwise, the animation may end for one layer but continue for others.

STEP-BY-STEP 1.10

1. In the Brick Path file, zoom the Stage to 50% if necessary. You want to duplicate the motion sequence in this animation, so you must insert frames to hold the duplicate motion sequence and then copy the motion frames.

2. First, select frames so you can insert an exact number of frames in all three layers: click **frame 1** on the layer for the motion path, Guide: Layer 1, in the Timeline. Press and hold **Shift**, then click **frame 16** on Layer 3. This selects frames 1 through 16 on all three layers.

STEP-BY-STEP 1.10 Continued

3. Use the command for inserting new frames. In Flash MX, press **F5**, or click **Insert** on the menu bar and then click **Frame**. New frames appear at the beginning of the animation. Notice that your animation program inserts the same number of frames as the number you selected in the three layers.

4. Move the keyframes from frame 1 to frame 17 on both the Guide: Layer 1 and Layer 1 layers. You can move the frames by dragging them. You now have a series of blank frames where you can paste copied or moved frames without disturbing the frames that follow.

5. Click **frame 31** on the layer for the motion path, Guide: Layer 1, in the Timeline. Press and hold **Shift**, then click **frame 46** on Layer 1. This selects frames 31 through 46, which contain the logo graphic and its motion path for that sequence, on both layers. See Figure 1-12.

FIGURE 1-12
Frames selected on multiple layers

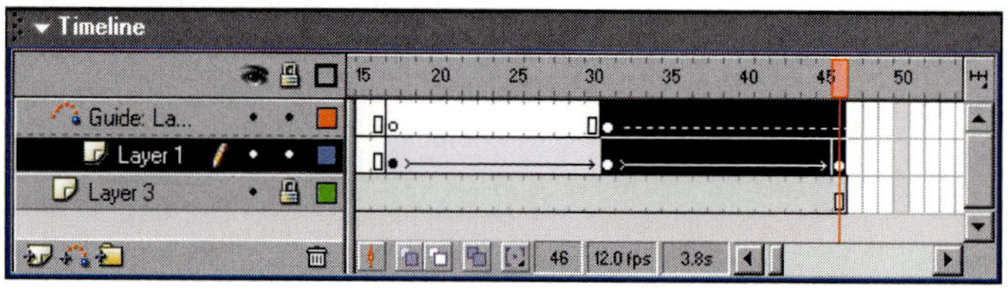

6. Copy the selected frames using the appropriate command in your animation program. In Flash MX, click **Edit** on the menu bar, and then click **Copy Frames**.

7. Click **frame 1** on Guide: Layer 1 in the Timeline. Press and hold **Shift**, then click **frame 16** on Layer 1 to select the new frames 1 through 16 on both layers. This is the destination for the copied frames.

8. Paste the frames using the appropriate command in your animation program. In Flash MX, click **Edit** on the menu bar, and then click **Paste Frames**.

9. Play the animation to see how it now follows the motion path twice.

10. Save changes and leave the **Brick Path** file open to use in the next exercise.

> **Note** ✅
>
> Motion paths do appear in the basic preview. When you preview to a Web format or publish the final movie, the motion paths do not appear.

View Multiple Frames

Most animation programs offer an *onion skin* feature that enables you to view the contents of multiple frames onscreen at once. When you do so, you can check an object's motion and determine whether you may need to make slight changes to the position of an object in a particular frame. In this way, the onion skin functions as a static preview of a portion of your animation.

When active, the onion skin feature displays two markers on the Timeline, a starting marker and an ending marker. Drag these markers to enclose the frames you want to check.

When you use this feature, consider hiding all layers but those holding the motion sequence. You'll be able to see the onion skin objects much more clearly if you do.

STEP-BY-STEP 1.11

1. In the Brick Path file, click the dot in the **Eye** column on the Layer 3 row or use the technique for hiding the layer in your animation program. This hides the display of the background content so you can better see the onion skin content.

2. Click **frame 35** on Layer 1. Choose the command or click the button for displaying onion skins. In Flash MX, you can click the **Onion Skin** button. The onion skin markers display at the top of the Timeline.

3. Drag the left onion skin marker to frame 31 to specify the first frame to display in the onion skin.

4. Drag the right onion skin marker to frame 46 to specify the last frame to display in the onion skin. You may need to move the playhead to adjust the onion skin markers. The onion skin markers show the motion path animation. See Figure 1-13.

FIGURE 1-13
Onion skin shows animation path

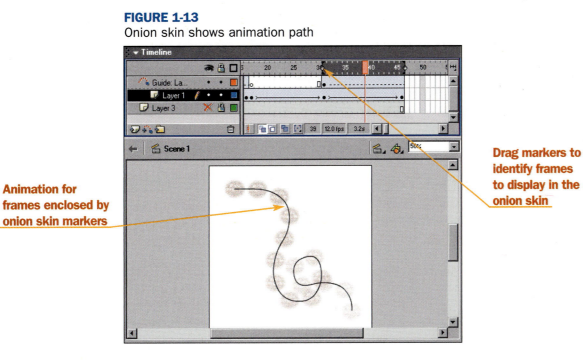

Drag markers to identify frames to display in the onion skin

Animation for frames enclosed by onion skin markers

5. Choose the command or click the button to turn off onion skins. In Flash MX, you can click the **Onion Skin** button again. The Stage now displays the content of the frame currently selected in the Timeline.

6. Click on the **Eye** column (now an X) on the Layer 3 row or use the technique for redisplaying the layer in your animation program. The Layer 3 content reappears on the Stage.

7. Save changes and leave the **Brick Path** file open to use in the next exercise.

Test a Movie

The onion skin feature can really help you fine-tune your animation, but it doesn't offer the excitement of viewing the live motion. You can use a command such as Play to preview animation or test a movie in a window that simulates a Web browser. This allows you to see how your animation may look when viewed on a Web page.

You can find the command to test a movie on the same menu as the command to play the animation. This menu may also offer commands to control how many times the animation plays. A Loop command, for example, prompts the movie to play over and over until you issue a Stop command.

STEP-BY-STEP 1.12

1. Click **frame 1** in Layer 1 in the Timeline.

2. Choose the command that loops the preview. In Flash MX, click **Control** on the menu bar, and then click **Loop Playback** to select it.

3. Play the animation and watch as it loops several times, and then choose the command that stops the preview. In Flash MX, press **Enter**. Or click **Control** on the menu bar, and then click **Stop**.

> **Hot Tip**
>
> To start the preview from a particular frame, click that frame on any layer before previewing.

STEP-BY-STEP 1.12 Continued

4. Choose the command for generating a Web preview of the animation. In Flash MX, press **Ctrl+Enter**; or click **Control** on the menu bar, and then click **Test Movie**. The animation plays in a Web-like window, as shown in Figure 1-14. You can use the commands on the Control menu to start and stop the playback.

> **Note** ☑
>
> Flash MX actually creates a movie file in the Flash format (*.swf* extension) when you perform a Web preview.

FIGURE 1-14
How the animation will look on the Web

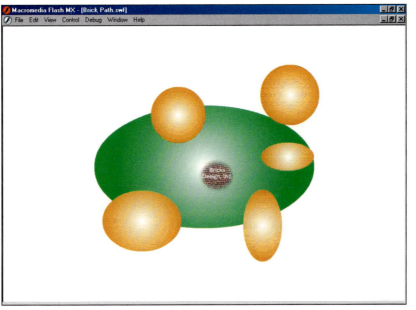

5. Notice that the animation is very quick, so that it is difficult to read the text on the moving object. Click **File** on the menu bar, and then click **Close** or choose the appropriate command for closing the preview in your animation program.

6. Click outside the Stage to deselect any selected objects. Open the dialog box for setting the animation properties, such as the Document Properties dialog box. Change the frame rate to **6** to slow the animation.

7. Test the movie again to see the difference in animation speed.

8. Save and close the **Brick Path** file. Close your animation program.

SUMMARY

In this lesson, you learned:

- When you create a new animation file, you must define the stage size. Specify a stage size that allows for the amount of motion you want to add but also fits on your Web or presentation page.

- Most animation programs require you to import graphics and place them in a library. The library makes it easier to reuse objects. You can also draw objects using tools in the toolbox.

- The Timeline holds frames, each of which represents a single cel or image in the animation.

- To expand the animation, insert additional frames. Use regular frames to hold content. Use keyframes to signal a change, such as a new object or a new position for the object.

- Simply move or replace an object in a keyframe to create a basic animation.

- Use tweening to create motion animations, either from one point to another or along a motion path.

- Add content on multiple layers to animate objects separately and control which objects appear "in front" of the others. The last layer in the list appears farthest back and is thus ideal for background content.

- Drag layers in the Timeline to move them to a new position. You can hide layers and lock layers by clicking the correct column or symbol beside the layer on the Timeline.

- Drag frames in the Timeline to move them to a new position. Use Shift+click to select frames on multiple layers. Drag a keyframe to change the length of an animation sequence.

- Use the Cut Frames, Copy Frames, and Paste Frames commands on the Edit menu to move and copy frames. Because pasted frames cover content in the destination, insert new frames if needed to hold the pasted content.

- Display a static preview of selected frames using the onion skin feature.

- To see a live motion preview, either play the project in your animation program or test the movie in a Web preview.

VOCABULARY *Review*

Define the following terms:

Animation	Motion path	Playhead
fps	Movie	Project file
Frame	Onion skin	Stage
Keyframe	Panel	Timeline
Layer	Path animation	Tween

REVIEW *Questions*

TRUE / FALSE

Circle T if the statement is true or F if the statement is false.

T   F   **1.** You should create a Stage as large as your monitor.

T   F   **2.** A common method of adding content to frames is to import graphics created in another program.

T   F   **3.** Keyframes hold special characters called *controllers*.

T   F   **4.** Insert a keyframe each time you want to change the animation action.

T   F   **5.** It is best to preview an animation only when you have finished creating it.

T   F   **6.** You cannot change the position of frames once you've added them.

T   F   **7.** In basic motion animation, you draw a path for an object to follow.

T   F   **8.** Layers make it easy to position objects in front of one another.

T   F   **9.** Background objects would usually appear in the layer at the top of the layer list.

T   F   **10.** If you intend to copy frames, you should first create blank frames to hold the copied frames.

WRITTEN QUESTIONS

Write a brief answer to the following questions.

1.   What do you add to specify a change such as a new graphic or motion in an animation?

2.   What is the simplest technique for creating movement in an animation?

3.   What do you add to have an object move along a particular route in an animation sequence?

4. What feature enables you to select frames and view a static preview?

5. What can you do to a keyframe to change the length of an animation sequence?

FILL IN THE BLANK

Complete the following sentences by writing the correct word or words in the blanks provided.

1. The _____ holds frames in the animation.

2. The _____ holds imported graphics.

3. Use tools in the _____ to draw or manipulate objects on an animation layer.

4. Drag the _____ to rewind or play a movie in the animation program.

5. To have the animation program calculate movement from one frame to another, create a(n) _____.

6. Insert a(n) _____ layer to create path animation.

7. _____ a layer so that its content does not appear on the Stage.

8. To select multiple layers, click one layer, hold down _____, and click another layer.

9. The _____ feature lets you view the contents of multiple frames at the same time.

10. Use the _____ command to play an animation over and over until you issue a Stop command.

PROJECTS

PROJECT 1-1

You work for a small online retailer. You want to create an animation that alerts viewers to a sale. The Web page where you will place the graphic will have a dark red background. You've previously created some graphics. Now combine them and add the animation.

1. Create a new animation project file.

2. Save the file as **Sale**.

3. Size the Stage at 125 × 125 pixels and add a dark red background color. (Select a background color in the Stage properties dialog box or from a Properties panel.)

4. Zoom the Stage to 200%.

5. Import the **AV Project1-1a** and **AV Project1-1b** files into the library as flattened graphics. Display the Library panel to verify the import. Rename **AV Project1-1a** as **Star** and **AV Project1-1b** as **Text**.

6. Add a new layer above Layer 1.

7. Click **frame 1** of Layer 1. Drag the **Star** graphic from the Library panel to the Stage. Center the graphic on the Stage.

8. Click **frame 1** in Layer 1 and insert a motion tween.

9. Add a keyframe at frame 12 in Layer 1.

10. Click **frame 12** in Layer 1, select the graphic, and rotate it 90 degrees clockwise using the appropriate command or tool in your animation program. (**Hint:** Select the graphic and click the **Free Transform** tool, then use the rotate pointer to rotate the graphic.)

11. On Layer 1, click **frame 24** and insert a keyframe. A motion tween should appear automatically between frames 12 and 24. With frame 24 selected, rotate the graphic another 90 degrees clockwise.

12. Repeat step 11, this time inserting a keyframe in frame 36 and rotating the graphic 90 degrees. Repeat step 11 one more time, inserting a keyframe in frame 48 and rotating the graphic an additional 90 degrees. You have created a "spin" effect for the graphic.

13. Click **frame 1** in Layer 2. Drag the **Text** graphic onto the Stage. Center the graphic on the Stage.

14. Add a keyframe at frame 48 in Layer 2. Preview the motion in your animation program. The star graphic spins while the **Text** graphic remains static. (If you do not see the star spin all the way around, return to each keyframe in Layer 1 and rotate the star to the correct position.)

15. Now you will create a blinking effect for the **Text** graphic on Layer 2. Begin by adding a keyframe at frame 6 in Layer 2.

16. Add another keyframe in frame 13 of Layer 2. Then select frame 6 on Layer 2 and delete the **Text** graphic.

17. Repeat the pattern to add keyframes every six frames on Layer 2 until you reach frame 41, deleting the **Text** graphic from every other 6-frame sequence. (Do *not* delete the final keyframe in frame 48 on Layer 2.)

18. Display the Web preview of your animation. Zoom it to 100% size if necessary. After you view it a few times, stop and close the preview.

19. Save changes and close the **Sale** file, but leave your animation program open to use in Project 1-2.

PROJECT 1-2

You work for a clothing retailer that caters to hip clients. You want to create a fun animation using a retro graphic and motion. You'll be able to use the animation in a variety of ways, so you'll create an attractive gradient background that will work with a variety of page backgrounds. You've previously created a graphic to use in the animation.

1. Create a new animation project file.

2. Save the project file as **Bop**.

3. Size the Stage at 125 × 400 pixels. Leave the background white. This animation will be tall and thin because it could be included in the side pane of a Web page, for example.

4. Zoom the Stage to 75% or a comfortable working size.

5. Import the **AV Project1-2** file into the library as a flattened graphic. Display the Library panel to verify the import. Rename the imported graphic **Flower**.

6. Use the **Rectangle** tool in the toolbox to create a rectangle with a gradient fill and no stroke. Set it up as a linear fill that blends from white to a pale blue. After you draw the rectangle on the Stage, rotate the rectangle so the blue gradient color appears at the bottom. Size the rectangle to cover the Stage.

7. Add two new layers above Layer 1.

8. Click **frame 1** of Layer 2. Drag the **Flower** graphic from the Library panel to the Stage. Position the graphic near the upper-left corner of the Stage.

9. Add a keyframe at frame 36 in both Layer 1 and Layer 2.

10. Insert a motion path layer for Layer 2.

11. Click **frame 1** in Layer 2 and insert a motion tween.

12. Click **frame 1** in the Guide: Layer 2 layer and draw the motion path there. (**Hint:** Keep the motion path within the edges of the Stage and do not include angles, or it won't work.) Create a fun path, as if the object will be falling and arcing from side to side on the Stage.

13. Click **frame 36** in layer 2 and move the **Flower** graphic to the end of the motion path. (**Hint:** Make sure the graphic snaps to the end of the path. If any part of the graphic falls outside the gradient rectangle at the end of the path, redraw the path.)

14. Hide Layer 2 and its motion path layer.

15. Click **frame 1** of Layer 3. Drag the **Flower** graphic from the Library panel to the Stage. Position the graphic near the upper-right corner of the Stage.

16. Add a keyframe at frame 36 in Layer 3.

17. Insert a motion path layer for Layer 3.

18. Click **frame 1** in Layer 3 and insert a motion tween.

19. Click **frame 1** in the Guide: Layer 3 layer and draw the motion path there. Create a path similar to the one you created for the Layer 2 graphic.

20. Click **frame 36** in Layer 3 and move the **Flower** graphic to snap to the end of the motion path.

21. Redisplay Layer 2 and its motion path layer.

22. Preview the animation in your animation program. Fine-tune the motion paths, if desired.

23. Display the Web preview of your animation. Zoom it to 100% size if necessary. After you view it a few times, stop and close the preview.

24. Save changes and close the **Bop** file. Close your animation program.

WEB PROJECT

Visit your favorite Web sites. Identify at least five animations, and write a description of each one. Include in your description your best understanding of how the animations were done.

TEAMWORK PROJECT

Work with a partner to create an animation. Each of you should create at least two graphics using the method of your choice. The final animation should include at least 60 frames. It should include one frame-by-frame animation, one motion animation, and one path animation. Divide the animation into at least three layers, including a layer for background content. E-mail the finished animation project file to your instructor.

CRITICAL *Thinking*

ACTIVITY 1-1

Review your descriptions of the Web animations you identified in the Web Project for this lesson. Think about how you could create an animation similar to each in your animation program. Then, try to recreate at least one of the animations to confirm your thinking.

ENHANCING ANIMATIONS

OBJECTIVES

Upon completion of this lesson, you should be able to:

- Record a sound file.
- Edit a sound file.
- Import a sound into an animation program.
- Add a sound to an animation.
- Add text to an animation.
- Animate text.
- Add button objects to an animation.
- Use action scripts to control an animation.

Estimated Time: 1.5 hours

VOCABULARY

Action

ActionScript

Button

Compression

Interactive

JavaScript

Looping

MP3 file

Rollover

Script

Symbol

Text object

WAV (wave) file

Waveform

In the last lesson, you learned how to add graphic objects to an animation and how to add motion to those objects. In this lesson, you build on that knowledge to enhance your animations with additional elements such as sound, text, buttons, and actions (scripts). These elements not only round out the content of your movie, but also enable you to include more information and interactive controls so the viewer can take charge of movie playback.

Record a Sound File

You have more access to sounds and the ability to record sounds than you might think. Most operating systems include at least a basic utility for recording sound. Many sound cards, particularly top-line models, also include software to enable you to record and manipulate sound files that you can include with an animation or movie. For example, a Creative Soundblaster sound card may include the Creative WaveStudio software for recording and editing WAV sound files.

Most animation and video programs enable you to import sound files in at least two formats: *WAV* (also called wave) and *MP3*. Wave files can have the highest sound quality. However, the higher the quality, the larger the sound file. Larger files take longer to download. To make the files smaller, you can record waves at a lower quality setting. Or, you can use recording or conversion software that uses *compression* and results in a more compact audio file format such as MP3. In theory, the compression process removes frequencies and masked elements that humans can't hear, so to most listeners, MP3 files sound as good as wave files.

You can record or capture sounds from a variety of sources. For example, you can record your voice via a microphone connected to your computer's sound card. Or, you can connect a device such as a CD player, MP3 player, or tape player to the sound card to record CD audio or other pre-recorded material.

Make the Physical Connection

Computers often do not include a microphone and almost never include the type of cable needed for audio recording. You can find basic microphones and audio cables at your local computer store or through online retailers. The microphone and cables you purchase must have the correct type and size of connector to work with the typical sound card. The type of connector on the other end of the cable may need to be different, depending on the *output* or line-out jack available on the device you're using for recording.

Once you have the correct cable, you need to know how to connect it to your computer. Sound cards typically offer three jacks or connections. You can use these connections to plug in speakers, a microphone, and an external audio device such as a CD player.

Make the Recording

Once you've connected the microphone or recording device, you can use your operating system or sound-recording software to make the recording. In Microsoft Windows, use system settings to ensure you've chosen the correct source or *input* (microphone or line-in). Also use the operating system volume controls to adjust the microphone or line-in (sometimes called wave record) volume for recording. Then, you are ready to make the recording. The Step-by-Step below provides an example of recording voice with a basic recorder such as Sound Recorder in Windows.

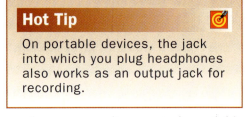

Important

According to copyright law, you can use sounds from CDs or other professional sources only for personal use. If you want to publish a commercial animation on your Web site or create professional presentations and movies, you must use original recordings or obtain permission to use the music from its creator and publisher.

Hot Tip

On portable devices, the jack into which you plug headphones also works as an output jack for recording.

STEP-BY-STEP 2.1

1. Use your operating system controls to make sure the right recording device—the microphone, in this case—is specified as the source and to adjust the volume of that device. For example, in Windows 2000, click **Start**, click **Settings**, and then click **Control Panel**. Click **Sounds and Multimedia** (**Sounds and Audio Devices** in Windows XP) and click the **Audio** tab. Click **Volume** in the Sound Recording section of the dialog box, make the appropriate changes in the Wave In (Recording Control in Windows XP) dialog box (Figure 2-1), and then close all open windows.

> **Note**
>
> Choose CD Audio only to make recordings via your computer's internal CD-ROM drive. Use Line In for an external CD player that you've connected via the line-in jack.

FIGURE 2-1
Choose to record with the microphone

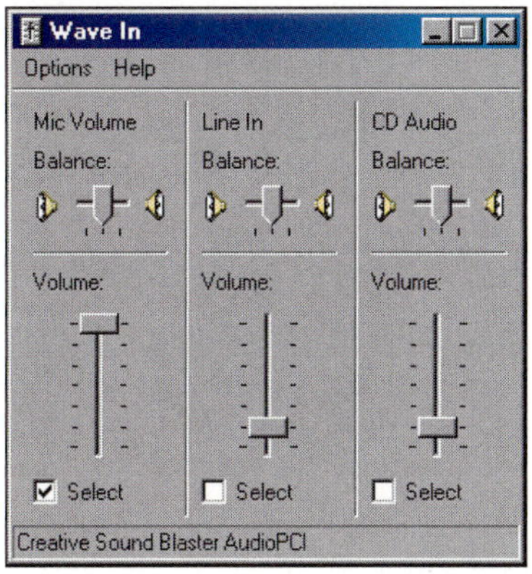

2. Start the sound-recording program. In Windows 2000, click **Start**, click **Programs** (**All Programs** in Windows XP), click **Accessories**, click **Entertainment**, and then click **Sound Recorder**.

3. Click the **Record** button (Figure 2-2) to start recording, but do not speak for a few seconds. (We'll remove your pause in the next Step-by-Step.)

FIGURE 2-2
Recording and playback controls

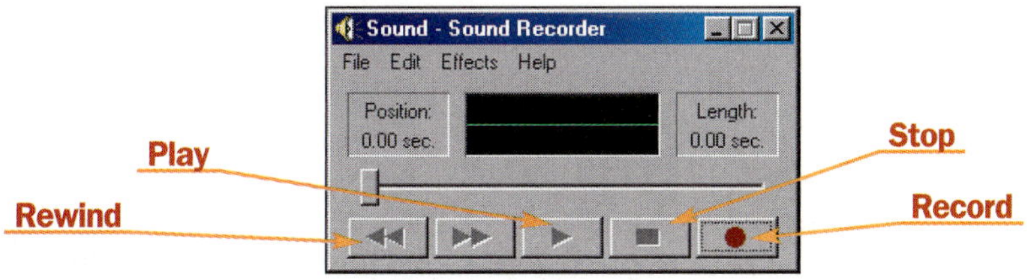

Play   Stop
Rewind   Record

4. Now read the following text into the microphone using a pleasant, yet animated, speaking voice: **Welcome to Great Outdoors Travel. Big skies. Fresh air. Fun things to do.**

5. Click the **Stop** button to stop the recording.

STEP-BY-STEP 2.1 Continued

6. Click the **Rewind** button, and then click the **Play** button to play back your recording.

7. If you're not satisfied with your recording, begin a new recording. Click **File** on the menu bar, and then click **New**. Repeat steps 3 through 6 to record again.

8. When you are satisfied with your recording, save the file as **Travel Sound**.

9. Leave the **Travel Sound** file open to use in the next exercise.

Edit a Sound File

As you recorded the sound file in the last Step-by-Step, your recording utility or application displayed a line diagram of sorts. Whenever you spoke into the microphone, the line bulged, with the magnitude of the bulge corresponding to the volume and frequency being recorded. Those bulges represent the sound's *waveform* (Figure 2-3).

> **Hot Tip**
>
> If you have selected the proper settings and you play the file but nothing has been recorded, you may need to check that your sound card is functioning properly, or you may need to turn your speakers on.

> **Note**
>
> More sophisticated programs enable you to choose a recording quality. For example, you can choose between mono (one channel) and stereo (left and right channels). You also can choose a recording quality or *sample rate*. For example, 44,100 Hz (44 kHz), 16-bit, Stereo is usually considered CD-quality sound.

FIGURE 2-3
Sound file's waveform

Sound-editing software can manipulate the waveforms to change a sound file in a variety of ways. For example, you can trim off a portion of the file or add an effect such as echo. More sophisticated editing programs enable you to edit individual channels or make corrections such as muting static in a selected section of the waveform. Sound-editing capabilities vary from program to program, but even Sound Recorder in Windows enables you to make basic changes to a wave file, such as eliminating the initial pause from the Travel Sounds file.

> **Note**
>
> Sound-editing programs typically can edit sounds only in the WAV format or another format called *RAW*. That's because compressed formats such as MP3 eliminate some of the sound data necessary for editing. So, complete all your edits to a WAV file before converting it to the MP3 format.

STEP-BY-STEP 2.2

1. With the Travel Sounds file open in Sound Recorder or your editing program, go to the position in the file just before the recorded speech begins. In Sound Recorder, you can play the file, stop it when the voice starts, and then drag the small slider above the controls to back up to a slightly earlier position (Figure 2-4). In other sound-editing programs, drag over the portion of the waveform you want to delete.

FIGURE 2-4
Editing the waveform

Position in
recording

Position slider

Make sure the line is
flat, otherwise voice
will be cropped

2. Choose the command for deleting the file information before the current position or the selected portion of the waveform. In Sound Recorder, click **Edit** on the menu bar, and then click **Delete Before Current Position**.

3. If you're prompted to confirm the deletion, click the **OK** or **Yes** button.

4. Play the file to hear the impact of the change.

5. Save your change to the file.

6. Add echo to the sound file: in Sound Recorder, click **Effects** from the menu bar, and then click **Add Echo**.

7. Play the file to hear the impact of the change.

8. Close the file without saving the echo effect change. Close your sound-editing program.

Import and Add Sound in Animations

Similar to adding graphic objects to an animation, sound objects are usually imported into the animation file. By default, you can import WAV and MP3 files into Flash MX. If you are using Flash MX on a Macintosh, you can also import AIFF files.

Most animation programs require or recommend that you insert each sound on its own layer. Insert a keyframe on the layer's Timeline where you want the sound to start playing and then import the sound or insert it from the library. After inserting the sound, you can adjust settings such as *looping* (replaying repeatedly) for the sound. You can specify streaming so a sound starts and stops with the movie, and so it loops up to 15 times.

Extra for Experts

If QuickTime 4 (or a later version) is loaded on your computer, you can import other file formats, such as AU files or sound-only QuickTime movies.

When you create or choose the sounds to include in your animation, keep the intended purpose of the animation in mind. For example, if the animation will appear on a Web site, you need to keep the overall file size small for faster downloads. Thus, you should use more compact MP3 files and loop a shorter sound segment. On the other hand, if you plan to include the animation in a presentation you'll be delivering in an auditorium equipped with a high-quality audio system, use the highest quality sound file possible.

Remember that you must use original music in professional productions such as Web animations and presentations. Otherwise, you're likely to violate copyright law. Luckily, you can use any number of inexpensive programs to combine sound loops to create original, royalty-free music for your animations and movies. Search the Web for programs that allow you to create loop-based original music.

STEP-BY-STEP 2.3

Add sounds to an animation that will form the introduction to the Web site for a company called Great Outdoors Travel.

1. Launch your animation program, if necessary.

2. Open **AV Step 2-3a** from the data files.

3. Save the file as **Great Outdoors Intro**.

4. Take a few moments to review the content of the layers in the animation. The animation includes 120 frames and multiple layers with animated objects. (You may have to use the vertical scroll bar in the Timeline to see all layers.)

5. Import the **AV Step 2-3b** MP3 file into the library. Also import the **Travel Sound** wave file you finished in the last Step-by-Step (or the **AV Step 2-3c** file if **Travel Sound** isn't available.) Rename **AV Step 2-3b** as **Music**.

> **Hot Tip**
>
> You may need to display files of all types to see the sound files in the Import dialog box.

6. Display the Library panel, if necessary. Verify that it now includes the imported sound files. If you imported **AV Step 2-3c**, rename it as **Travel Sound**.

7. Select the bottom layer, Sky, and add a new layer. Rename the new layer **Background Music** and move it to the bottom of the list of layers. (Double-click the layer name to select it and then type the new layer name. To move a layer, select it and drag it to the desired location.)

8. Add another new layer. Rename it **Voice Over**.

9. Click **frame 1** of the Background Music layer. Drag the **Music** sound file from the library (Library panel) onto the Stage.

> **Hot Tip**
>
> Add a keyframe to the layer for a sound, select that keyframe, and then add the sound to the Stage to control when a sound starts playing during an animation.

STEP-BY-STEP 2.3 Continued

10. Reselect **frame 1** of the Background Music layer. Specify the streaming and looping settings: In Flash MX, choose the **Stream** setting from the Sync drop-down list in the Property inspector and enter **5** in the Loops text box, as shown in Figure 2-5.

FIGURE 2-5
Stream the sound to sync it with movie playback

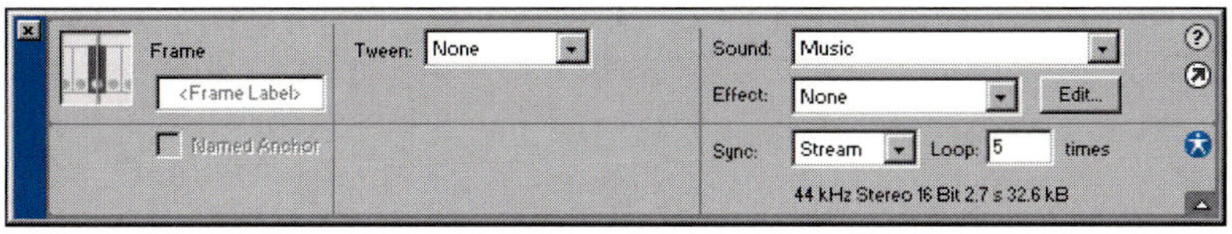

11. Click **frame 1** of the Voice Over layer. Drag the **Travel Sound** file from the library onto the Stage.

12. Save changes to the **Great Outdoors Intro** file.

13. Test the movie file in your Web browser to preview the animation with sounds added.

14. Close the Web preview. Leave the **Great Outdoors Intro** file open for the next Step-by-Step.

Extra for Experts

Sometimes when multiple sounds play simultaneously in a movie file, they may not mesh very well and may end up sounding mushy or unappealing. In this exercise, the voice may sound as if it has a lisp or an echo because of the interaction between the voice recording and the background music. Solve this problem by using the different sounds at different points in the movie, or use a full-featured sound-editing program to overlay multiple tracks in a single sound file.

Add and Animate Text

Text performs the same function in an animation as in a graphic: it gives information on the subject of the animation or directions for the viewer. In an animation program, however, you have the added option of animating the text in some way to make it even more effective.

Add a Text Object to an Animation

To add a *text object* to an animation, you use the same basic process as when adding any object. Create a layer to hold the text, choose the text tool from the toolbox, specify text settings, and then click and key the text.

Use the Property inspector or other formatting options to select a font, font size, and font style for the text object. You can also change text color and alignment. Select a text object by clicking it with an arrow or selection tool to display a blue outline. Select the text in the object using the text tool.

STEP-BY-STEP 2.4

1. In the Great Outdoors Intro file, select the top layer in the list (Campfire), and insert a new layer.

2. Rename the new layer **Fade Text**.

3. Click **frame 75** of the Fade Text layer, and insert a keyframe.

4. Zoom the Stage to approximately 50%, so most of the Stage is visible.

5. Click the tool for adding text in your animation program. In Flash MX, click the **Text** tool.

6. Adjust the text settings (in the Property inspector in Flash MX) to 36-point Arial, with a pale blue text color and center alignment.

7. Click on the Stage at a location approximately one-third of the way from the top and centered horizontally.

8. Key **Great Outdoors Travel**.

9. Click another tool such as the **Arrow** or **Selection** tool to deactivate the text tool. Your animation should now resemble Figure 2-6.

FIGURE 2-6
Position text on the Stage in the desired frame

10. Save changes and leave the **Great Outdoors Intro** file open to use in the next exercise.

Animate a Text Object

You have a number of options for animating a text object. You can have text appear and disappear in selected frames in the movie. You can create a motion animation using the same steps you used to tween the position of objects on the Stage.

In addition, you can use the Alpha color effect to make text appear to fade in or fade out. The Alpha effect adjusts opacity of an object to give the illusion of fading.

> **Note** ☑️
>
> Steps to animate text may vary quite a bit among programs, so consult your instructor if you need more specific help with a procedure in your animation program.

STEP-BY-STEP 2.5

You will modify the text object you inserted in the last exercise by using an animation effect that makes the text appear to fade into view.

1. In the Great Outdoors Intro file, click **frame 75** on the Fade Text layer.

2. Click the text object on the Stage to select it, and add a motion tween. In Flash MX, the object may now be called Tween 3 in the Property inspector.

3. To make the text object appear to fade into view, you set 0% opacity at the keyframe where the text is first inserted, then adjust opacity to 100% in a later keyframe. In Flash MX, make sure frame 75 is selected, click the **Color** drop-down list in the Property inspector, and then click **Alpha**. In the Alpha Amount box that appears beside the Color drop-down list, key **0** for 0% or use the slider to select 0. The text object disappears, because its opacity (visibility) is 0. See Figure 2-7.

FIGURE 2-7
Set Alpha amount to reduce visibility of text

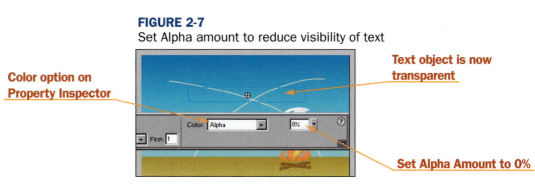

Color option on Property Inspector

Text object is now transparent

Set Alpha Amount to 0%

4. Click **frame 105** on the Fade Text layer, and insert a keyframe. The blue outline of the text object becomes visible, though the text is still invisible.

5. Click the text object on the Stage and set it to 100% opacity. In Flash MX, open the **Color** drop-down list in the Property inspector, and then click **Alpha**. In the Alpha Amount box that appears beside the Color drop-down list, key **100** for 100% or use the slider to select 100. The text object is once again completely visible.

6. If your animation program requires it, remove the tween from the Fade Text layer starting with frame 106.

7. Save your changes to the **Great Outdoors Intro** file.

8. Test the movie file in your Web browser to preview the animation with the fade text.

9. Close the Web preview. Leave the **Great Outdoors Intro** file open to use in the next exercise.

Insert Buttons in an Animation

Introducing motion into your animations makes them more attractive and interesting. But watching an animation can be a passive process for viewers. To make an animation more engaging for the viewer, you can introduce *interactive* controls such as buttons to your movie. Interactive controls allow the viewer to start a playback or exit the movie, among other functions. You can create many types of controls such as a fill-in box, a button that displays a particular Web page, a menu or a list for making selections, or a joystick that controls another object onscreen.

An interactive control requires a *script*, or program, that carries out the specific action for the control. Only the animation designer's programming abilities limit the types of controls that can be created in most animation programs. (You will learn more about scripts and how to attach them to controls in the next section.)

One of the easiest interactive controls to use in an animation is a button that performs a task when clicked. Once you have created a button symbol, you can duplicate it to ensure that all interactive buttons in your animation are similar.

Create Buttons

An interactive *button* may be as simple as a rectangle or oval formatted with an appropriate fill. To improve the visual effect, however, many designers define different button formats for the button's *rollover* states. The three common rollover states are:

- **Up:** How the button looks if the mouse pointer is not on it.
- **Over:** How the button looks if the viewer moves the mouse pointer over it.
- **Down:** How the button looks when the viewer clicks the mouse pointer on the button.

Some programs require that the designer create the button graphics for each rollover state in a separate graphics application and then import them into the animation program. In other animation programs, such as Flash MX, you can create a new *symbol* and then draw the button symbol using graphic tools. Then, you create the rollovers in Flash's symbol-editing mode.

Symbol-editing mode (Figure 2-8) provides four frames for defining rollover states, and the Stage contains a crosshair you can use to help you align symbols for each rollover. Once you have completed work on the button, you return to the main Stage to insert the buttons in the animation.

FIGURE 2-8
Symbol-editing mode

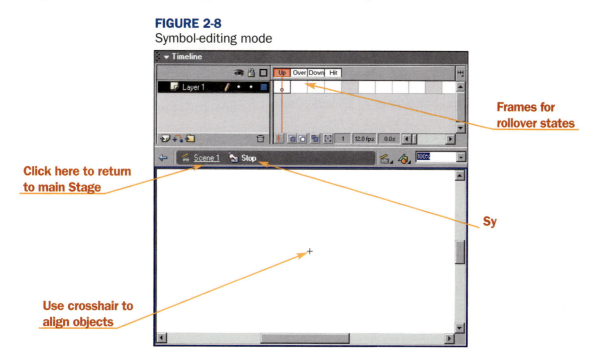

Frames for rollover states

Click here to return to main Stage

Sy

Use crosshair to align objects

S TEP-BY-STEP 2.6

You will add two buttons to the animation, one to start the animation and one to stop it. Instructions are given for Flash MX.

1. In the Great Outdoors Intro file, select the top layer in the list (Fade Text), and insert a new layer.

2. Rename the new layer **Buttons**.

3. Zoom the Stage to approximately 50%, if necessary.

4. Display the Library panel, if necessary.

5. Create a new symbol. You can click **Insert** on the menu bar, and then click **New Symbol**, or press **Ctrl+F8**.

6. In the Create New Symbol dialog box, type **Stop** in the Name text box, click the **Button** option button under Behavior, and then click the **OK** button. Symbol-editing mode opens so you can edit the symbol.

7. You will first create the button appearance for the Up rollover state (the way the button looks when the viewer first sees it in the animation). Locate the Up frame in the Timeline and notice that it already contains a keyframe.

8. Click the **Up** frame. Click the **Oval** tool, specify no stroke or outline, and apply an orange and black radial gradient fill.

STEP-BY-STEP 2.6 Continued

9. Draw a small oval button on the center of the Stage. The button should be about 55 pixels wide and 27 pixels high. (Click the oval with the Arrow tool and check its width and height in the Property inspector.)

10. Use the **Text** tool to add the word **STOP** in white, 14-point Arial bold text on the center of the button oval.

<table>
<tr><td>**Hot Tip** 🎯</td></tr>
<tr><td>You can align some part of the symbol object with the crosshair in the center of the Stage to make sure all instances of the button align with each other when inserted in the animation.</td></tr>
</table>

11. Now create the button appearance for the Over rollover state (the way the button looks when the mouse pointer is over it). In the Timeline, insert a keyframe in the Over frame.

12. Select the button oval if necessary, and lighten both of the colors in its gradient. This causes the button to appear "highlighted" when the mouse pointer is over it. See Figure 2-9. (You may need to double-click the filled area of the button to display the fill box on the Property inspector to change the gradient colors.)

FIGURE 2-9
Define Over state for button

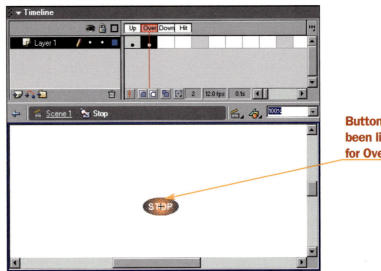

Button fill has been lightened for Over state

13. Click the **Scene 1** link in the upper-left corner of the symbol-editing stage to finish creating the button and return to the main animation Timeline.

14. Save changes and leave the **Great Outdoors Intro** file open to use in the next exercise.

<table>
<tr><td>**Note** ✅</td></tr>
<tr><td>In addition to the Up, Over, and Down rollover states, you can use the Hit state to identify the "hot" or clickable area on the button. Draw a square around the area in which viewers can click to activate the button. The square does not appear when you play the animation.</td></tr>
</table>

Duplicate Buttons

If you want to include several buttons in the animation, you can duplicate them in the library to avoid recreating the entire symbol. After duplicating, return to symbol-editing mode to make any necessary changes to the button, such as changing color or text labeling.

S TEP-BY-STEP 2.7

1. In the Great Outdoors Intro file, right-click the **Stop** symbol in the Library panel, and then click **Duplicate** on the shortcut menu.

2. Key **Start** as the symbol name in the Duplicate Symbol dialog box, and then click the **OK** button. The new symbol should open in symbol-editing mode. If it doesn't, double-click the **Start** symbol in the Library panel.

3. Click the **Up** frame, and change the text to read **START**. Edit the gradient fill to use blue and black.

4. Clear the keyframe from the Over frame. (The Start button you just created appears in the Over frame after you delete the existing keyframe.) Insert a new keyframe in the Over frame and lighten the gradient colors as you did for the Stop button.

5. Click the **Scene 1** link in the upper-left corner of the Stage to finish creating the button and return to the main animation Stage.

6. Click **frame 1** in the Buttons layer that you created earlier.

7. Add the two buttons to the lower-left corner of the Stage. In Flash MX, drag the buttons from the Library panel to the desired location. The position of your buttons should look approximately like Figure 2-10.

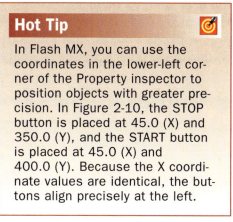

Hot Tip

In Flash MX, you can use the coordinates in the lower-left corner of the Property inspector to position objects with greater precision. In Figure 2-10, the STOP button is placed at 45.0 (X) and 350.0 (Y), and the START button is placed at 45.0 (X) and 400.0 (Y). Because the X coordinate values are identical, the buttons align precisely at the left.

FIGURE 2-10
Place the buttons on the Stage

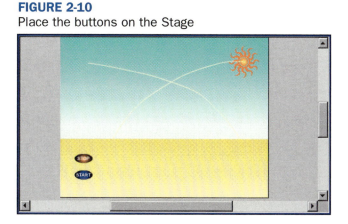

8. Save changes and leave the **Great Outdoors Intro** file open to use in the next exercise.

Use Action Scripts

After you add a button, graphic, or other item as a control in an animation, you need to give the object instructions about what it should do based on an event or user action such as a mouse click. Animation programs enable you to create scripts or *actions*—compact programming code that defines interactivity. Typically, you assign or attach a script or action to a particular object such as a button, although you can also create more general scripts that play at certain times during the animation.

JavaScript is probably the most common scripting language today, and the scripting languages used in animation programs typically resemble JavaScript. In fact, both Adobe LiveMotion and Flash MX support a similar scripting language called *ActionScript*.

In most animation applications, you select the object to which you add the script and then open a window or panel where you can insert the script code. However, applications often include tools that enable you to build scripts without your needing to memorize script commands and syntax. For example, the Flash MX Actions panel includes a number of predefined actions that you can insert into the script simply by double-clicking.

Don't be intimidated when it comes to scripting. As you gain experience building scripts, you'll be able to build increasingly complex scripts. Animation software publishers such as Macromedia include dozens of articles and example files on their Web sites to help you increase your skills. As a bonus, once you start learning the ins and outs of one scripting language, you'll be able to use other scripting languages more easily.

STEP-BY-STEP 2.8

1. In the Great Outdoors Intro file, click **frame 1** of the Buttons layer.

2. Click the **STOP** button and display the panel for attaching a script to it. In Flash MX, you can simply right-click the **STOP** button, and then click **Actions**.

STEP-BY-STEP 2.8 Continued

3. Display the category of script objects or actions for controlling the movie, and then insert the *onclick* or *on* object or action. In Flash MX, click **Actions** in the left pane of the Actions panel, click **Movie Control**, and then double-click **on**. The right side of the panel prompts you to specify a mouse event. Leave the **Release** check box checked (or check it), which specifies that the rest of the script will run after the user releases the mouse button, finishing a click on the STOP button. Figure 2-11 illustrates how the script looks so far.

FIGURE 2-11
Inserting script actions

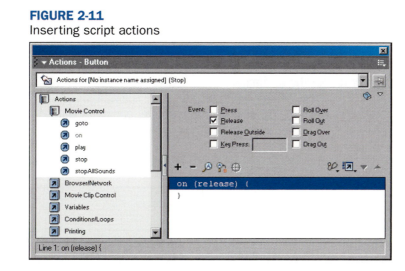

4. At the appropriate location in the script, insert the object or action for stopping the movie playback. In Flash MX, simply double-click the **stop** action in the left pane of the Actions panel. The action appears in the Actions/Movie Control folder, along with the *on* action you inserted in step 3. At this point, the finished script appears as follows:

```
on (release) {
    stop();
}
```

5. Close the scripting pane or Actions panel.

6. Click the **START** button and display the pane for attaching a script to it.

7. Repeat step 3 to insert the *on* script object or action.

> **Hot Tip**
>
> In Flash MX, use the getURL action in the Actions/Browser/Web folder in the Actions panel in a script to enable the user to jump to a Web site by clicking a button or graphic.
>
> For example, *getURL(http://www.macromedia.com)*; inserted in place of *stop();* in the script listed in step 4 to create a script that takes the user to Macromedia's home page when the user clicks the button to which the script has been attached.

STEP-BY-STEP 2.8 Continued

8. At the appropriate location in the script, insert the object or action for starting the movie playback. In Flash MX, simply double-click the **play** action in the left pane of the Actions panel. The action appears in the Actions/Movie Control folder, along with the *on* action you inserted in step 7. At this point, the finished script appears as follows:

```
on (release) {
    play();
}
```

9. Close the scripting pane or Actions panel.

10. Test the movie file in your Web browser. Click the STOP button to stop the animation, and then click the START button to restart the animation.

11. Close the Web preview, close the **Great Outdoors Intro** file, and close your animation program.

SUMMARY

In this lesson, you learned:

■ The wave format includes the original sound data but results in a large sound file. Compressed formats such as MP3, however, discard unheard sound data, resulting in a smaller, high-quality sound file.

■ Most operating system software includes a simple sound-recording utility, such as Sound Recorder in Windows. However, your system's sound card may have more sophisticated software for recording and editing sounds.

■ To record a wave file, connect the microphone or other device correctly, using the microphone (mic) in or line-in jack. Then, specify which device to record in the operating system. Finally, use the recording software to make the actual recording.

■ Sounds have waveforms that can be edited in sound-editing software. Even Sound Recorder in Windows can be used to delete part of a sound or add an echo effect.

■ Add text on its own layer in an animation project file, and then use tweening to animate the text object like any other object.

■ You can add buttons or other types of controls to enable viewers to interact with the animation.

■ When you create a button, you can define its rollover states. Duplicate a button to save time when you need more than one in an animation.

■ You build a script to define the action that should happen when an animation event occurs or the user takes an action such as clicking the mouse on the button or other control. Most animation programs include tools to make scripting easy.

VOCABULARY *Review*

Define the following terms:

Action	JavaScript	Symbol
ActionScript	Looping	Text object
Button	MP3 file	WAV (wave) file
Compression	Rollover	Waveform
Interactive	Script	

REVIEW *Questions*

TRUE / FALSE

Circle T if the statement is true or F if the statement is false.

T F   **1.** You use a microphone to record sound from a device such as an external CD player or MP3 player.

T F   **2.** Sound files can be changed once they're recorded.

T F   **3.** You can import only WAV files into Flash MX.

T F   **4.** You add each sound to a separate layer.

T F   **5.** If you intend to use an animation on a Web page, a compact format such as MP3 is best.

T F   **6.** Text in an animation can be animated like any other object.

T F   **7.** You must import text objects from a word processing program.

T F   **8.** The Alpha effect lets you control opacity of an object.

T F   **9.** You have to write all scripts from scratch.

T F **10.** The Up state shows how a button looks after it has been clicked.

WRITTEN QUESTIONS

Write a brief answer to the following questions.

1. Why are MP3 files smaller than wave files for recordings of comparable lengths?

2. What sound-recording software is on your system?

3. How do you insert a sound in an animation?

4. What is a rollover state and how do you set it up?

5. What does a script or action do?

FILL IN THE BLANK

Complete the following sentences by writing the correct word or words in the blanks provided.

1. You can use recording software to apply _____ to create a more compact audio file.

2. If you don't have special recording software, you can probably use Windows' _____ program to record sounds.

3. The _____ audio format supplies the highest quality sound.

4. Choosing the _____ setting for an inserted sound helps synchronize it with the animation.

5. _____ controls allow a viewer to perform tasks while viewing an animation.

6. The _____ state defines how a button looks when the mouse is on top of it.

7. Create a new button in a special stage area called _____.

8. A(n) _____ is compact programming code that defines interactivity.

9. The _____ panel allows you to control script for an object.

10. Flash MX and Adobe LiveMotion support the _____ scripting language.

PROJECTS

PROJECT 2-1

You are the online content developer for Trusty Insurance. You want to enhance an animation used as the Web site intro and as a presentation intro by recording and adding sound and animating text.

1. Launch your animation program, if needed.

2. Open **AV Project 2-1a** from the data files.

3. Save the file as **Trusty Intro**.

4. Hide the Second Text and Background layers.

5. On the First Text layer, add keyframes and tweening so that the text object fades in for about 15 frames and then out for about 15 frames, starting from frame 1.

6. Hide the First Text layer and redisplay the Second Text layer.

7. On the Second Text layer, add keyframes and tweening so that the text object fades in for about 15 frames and then out for about 15 frames, starting from frame 30.

8. Click **frame 1** of the Second Text layer and delete the text object there. If you correctly positioned a keyframe in frame 30, this should delete the text object from the first 29 frames.

9. Redisplay the hidden layers.

10. Insert a keyframe in frame 60 of the Background layer.

11. Save changes, and preview the animation in your animation program.

12. Use your operating system's sound-recording software to record the following brief message:

    We can help you with all your insurance needs.

13. Save the sound file as **Trusty Voice**.

14. Import the **Trusty Voice** sound file into the library of your animation program. (If you do not have access to a sound recorder, import **AV Project 2-1b** from the data files and rename it as **Trusty Voice** in the library.)

15. Add a new layer for the sound file. Rename the layer **Voice Over**.

16. Click **frame 10** in the Voice Over layer and add a keyframe.

17. Add the **Trusty Voice** sound to the Stage at keyframe 10 of the Voice Over layer.

18. Save your changes to the animation file.

19. Test the movie file in the Web browser preview.

20. Close the preview and the **Trusty Insurance** file, but leave your animation program open to use in Project 2-2.

PROJECT 2-2

You are the technology training manager for a large manufacturing company. You want to create an animation for your company intranet that users can view when they're looking for software support resources. The animation will include buttons the user can click to jump to the support pages for different software publishers.

1. Open **AV Project 2-2** from the data files.

2. Save the file as **Help Links**.

3. Add a new layer at the top of the list and rename it **Buttons**.

4. Create a button symbol using the design of your choice and at least two rollover states. Name the symbol **My Button**.

5. Return to the main Stage and add two instances of My Button, one below each program name.

6. Add a script to the first button, under *Office*, that links to http://www.microsoft.com/office/ support/default.asp. (**Hint:** Use the getURL action and key the specified Web address just as shown in this step.)

7. Add a script to the second button, under *Flash MX*, that links to http://www.macromedia.com/software/flash.

8. Save changes to the animation file.

9. Test the movie file in the Web browser preview. Test each of the link buttons to make sure they display the appropriate Web page. (You may have to connect to the Internet and switch to your Web browser window to verify that the links worked.)

10. Close the preview and the **Help Links** file, and close your animation program.

WEB PROJECT

Surf the Web until you identify at least three Web sites that have an animated introduction, tutorial, or product demonstration. Write down the URL for each site. Describe the animation for each site, including the type of content it has and any user controls that might be available. Identify what you like and dislike about each animation.

SCANS TEAMWORK PROJECT

Work in groups of five. Download the demonstration version of a sound creation program that enables you to create royalty-free music. Work together to learn how to use the program and develop some music for your animations and presentations.

CRITICAL *Thinking*

ACTIVITY 2-1

Open an animation you created in Lesson 1. Add a text object to the animation that supplies further information about the animation and animate the text object as desired. Create a new button or buttons to control the animation. Save the revised animation with a new name.

PUBLISHING AN ANIMATION

OBJECTIVES

Upon completion of this lesson, you should be able to:

- Analyze an animation movie.

- Optimize a movie.

- Publish a movie for Web delivery.

- Publish a movie to an animated or static graphic format.

- Publish a movie to an executable.

- Publish a movie to QuickTime.

Estimated Time: 1 hr.

VOCABULARY

Bandwidth

Bitmap images

Compression

Executable

GIF

JPEG

Playback rate

Plug-in

PNG

QuickTime

Standalone player

Streaming

Streaming rate

In previous lessons, you learned how to create and enhance an animation. Now you are ready to prepare your animation for delivery. In this lesson, you will learn basic concepts for preparing your animation for publication. You learn about analyzing, optimizing, and publishing a movie.

As you prepare your animation, remember the following factors that may influence your decision on how to deliver or distribute your animation:

- File size

- Content of the movie

- User's connection speed or bandwidth

- User's hardware and software (that is, RAM, processor, browser)

- Network traffic (if you work in a networked environment)

- Streaming capabilities, which involve connection speed and file size

  These factors are discussed in the next section.

Analyze a Movie File

You are already familiar with testing a movie. You have tested movies in both Lessons 1 and 2. What happens if you test your movie and it takes a long time to download or pauses during playback? How do you figure out the causes of the delays during download and playback? You do an *analysis*.

The goal of analysis is to identify potential problems while downloading and playing a movie. If you plan to download the entire movie before you play it, analysis can help you determine what parts of the movie are taking the most time to download. If you plan to deliver the movie through a *streaming* connection (playing it while downloading), your analysis should help reduce or control the pauses during downloading and playback.

Three key terms related to analyzing movie files are bandwidth or connection speed, playback rate, and streaming rate.

The *bandwidth* or *connection speed* is the speed at which a network or modem transfers data. This speed varies depending on a computer's network connection or modem, so you must try to anticipate the users who will view your animation and the network connections they may have.

The *playback rate* is how quickly the computer plays the frames of the movie. This is the *frames per second* (fps) rate that you set for an animation in Lesson 1.

The *streaming rate* is how quickly the network or modem can download frames of the movie. Streaming rate depends on two factors: the connection speed and the content of the movie. Obviously, a faster network connection can download frames of the movie faster. For a fixed connection speed, the streaming rate can still be different for different movies depending on their content: a simple movie downloads faster than a complicated one.

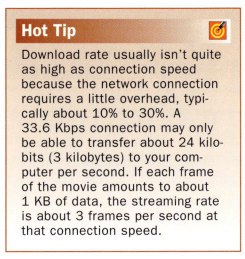

Hot Tip

Download rate usually isn't quite as high as connection speed because the network connection requires a little overhead, typically about 10% to 30%. A 33.6 Kbps connection may only be able to transfer about 24 kilobits (3 kilobytes) to your computer per second. If each frame of the movie amounts to about 1 KB of data, the streaming rate is about 3 frames per second at that connection speed.

One of the key ideas in analyzing an animation is that not only does the entire animation file have a particular size, but *each frame within the animation contains a different amount of data and has its own "size."* Each frame stores the information necessary to draw that frame, including any new images, new shapes, new text, or "tweening" information. Keyframes usually contain more data than frames that are tweened. So, the streaming rate can vary even within an animation.

Most animation programs have options to analyze your movie. For example, in Macromedia Flash MX you can use the Bandwidth Profiler and Show Streaming options. The following sections discuss these options. Of course, you can also do your own manual analysis based on what you know about the contents of your animation and the needs and resources of your users.

Generate a Size Report and Use the Bandwidth Profiler

Knowing the total file size of an animation can help you determine how quickly it will download and play. You can use a size report to prepare a printout that shows the size of each frame in an animation, as well as a running total file size for the entire animation.

To generate a size report, select an option in a dialog box that allows you to customize the export or publishing process. For example, use the Export Movie or Publish Settings command on the File menu. The size report may consist of a text file that contains the size information (see Figure 3-1). You can open this report using a simple text editor such as Windows Notepad.

FIGURE 3-1
Example of a size report

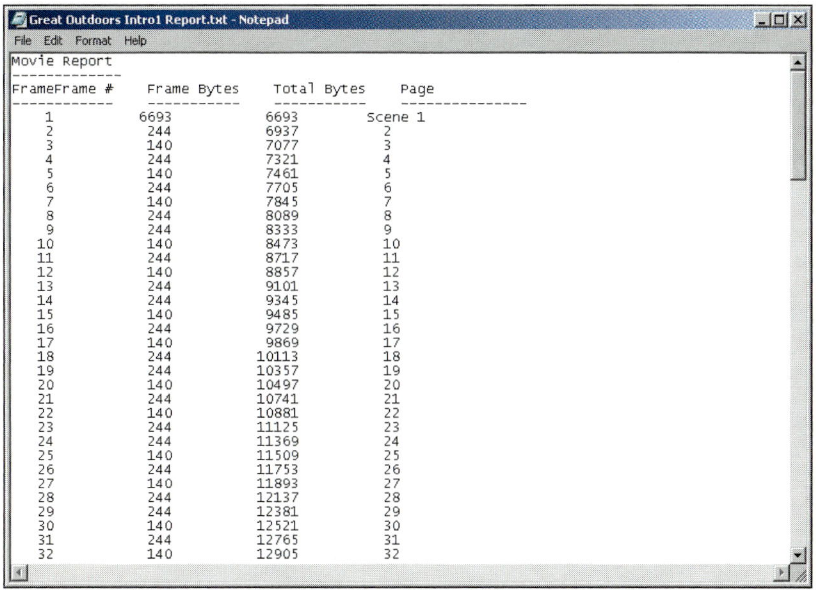
Great Outdoors Intro1 Report.txt - Notepad
File Edit Format Help
Movie Report

FrameFrame #	Frame Bytes	Total Bytes	Page
1	6693	6693	Scene 1
2	244	6937	2
3	140	7077	3
4	244	7321	4
5	140	7461	5
6	244	7705	6
7	140	7845	7
8	244	8089	8
9	244	8333	9
10	140	8473	10
11	244	8717	11
12	140	8857	12
13	244	9101	13
14	244	9345	14
15	140	9485	15
16	244	9729	16
17	140	9869	17
18	244	10113	18
19	244	10357	19
20	140	10497	20
21	244	10741	21
22	140	10881	22
23	244	11125	23
24	244	11369	24
25	140	11509	25
26	244	11753	26
27	140	11893	27
28	244	12137	28
29	244	12381	29
30	140	12521	30
31	244	12765	31
32	140	12905	32

Use a feature such as Flash's Bandwidth Profiler for a visual representation of how much data each frame of an animation contains. You can usually set a specific modem or connection speed that is represented on the graph as a horizontal red line called the *bandwidth target*. Each frame appears as a bar, similar to a bar graph.

To check the bandwidth profile of an animation, you may need to test the movie as you have done in previous lessons. In the testing window, choose the profile feature from the appropriate menu. For example, click Bandwidth Profiler on the View menu. You may also need to click a command such as Frame by Frame Graph to see information on each frame of the animation.

STEP-BY-STEP 3.1

1. Launch your animation program, and open **AV Step 3-1** from the data files.

2. Save the file as **Outdoors Analysis**.

3. Use the command for exporting the movie. In Flash MX, click **File** on the menu bar, and then click **Export Movie**.

STEP-BY-STEP 3.1 Continued

4. Key **Outdoors Analysis** in the File name box. Click the **Save** button. If asked if you want to replace the existing file with the same name, click the **Yes** button. An export dialog box opens, similar to the one shown in Figure 3-2.

FIGURE 3-2
Export Flash Player dialog box

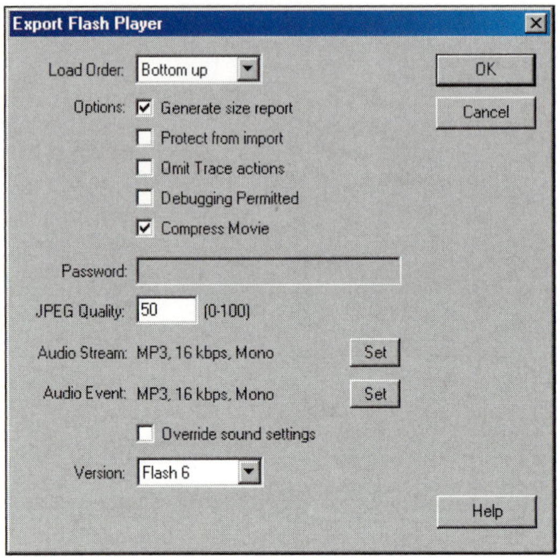

5. Click the option to generate a size report, and then click the **OK** button. The report file is saved with a .txt extension in the same folder as the Outdoors Analysis.swf file.

6. Start a simple text editor. For example, click the **Start** button on the Windows taskbar, click **Programs**, click **Accessories**, and then click **Notepad**.

7. In the Notepad window, click **File** on the menu bar, and then click **Open**. Navigate to the folder where you stored the report, click **Outdoors Analysis Report**, and click the **Open** button.

8. Scroll down the Notepad window to see all the data in the report. Then click **File** on the menu bar, and click **Print**. Click the **Print** button to print the report. Click **File** on the menu bar, and then click **Exit** to close the report and Notepad.

9. In the **Outdoors Analysis** file in your animation program, choose the command for generating a Web preview of the animation. In Flash MX, click **Control** on the menu bar, and then click **Test Movie**.

STEP-BY-STEP 3.1 Continued

10. In the testing window, issue the command that allows you to see a bandwidth profile. In Flash MX, click **View** on the menu bar, and then click **Bandwidth Profiler**. Click **Frame by Frame Graph** on the same menu if it is not already selected. Your screen should look similar to Figure 3-3.

FIGURE 3-3
Bandwidth Profiler

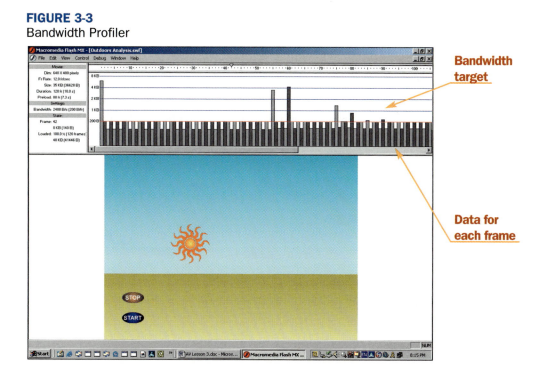

11. Locate the bandwidth target (the horizontal red line). Note the frames (gray bars) that extend higher than the bandwidth target.

12. Click the bar of the first frame to select it (it turns green when selected). Note the size of the frame, which is listed in the bottom section of the left frame of the Profiler. The file size should match that shown for Frame 1 in your report printout.

13. Close the testing window to return to the main animation program window.

14. Leave the **Outdoors Analysis** file open to use in the next exercise.

As part of your analysis, consider why frame 1 extends so far above the bandwidth target. Look at the content loaded into the first frame: all the graphics, plus two sound files. Remember, the time it takes to download a frame depends on its content.

Check Playback and Streaming Rate

At some time, you may have downloaded a movie trailer or other streaming movie from the Web. You may have noticed a bar along the bottom of the player showing the progress of the movie. On many players, you also see another progress bar showing the rate at which frames are being streamed. Figure 3-4, for example, shows both the playhead and streaming rate for a movie download.

FIGURE 3-4
Movie trailer controls showing playhead and streaming rate

Playhead  Streaming progress

In animation files, as in other movie files, you need to be aware of the bandwidth and the size of individual frames because of the way they affect playback. When you play back your file, the playback speed of the first frame cannot exceed the downloading speed of the second frame, or you experience pauses in the playing of the movie. If the playback ever catches up with the streaming (see Figure 3-5), the movie pauses. Pauses are generally not desirable.

FIGURE 3-5
Playhead exceeds the streaming rate, causing delay

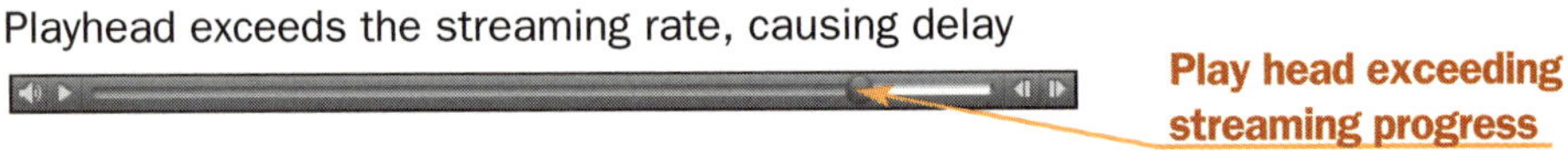

Play head exceeding streaming progress

Figure 3-6 shows how the streaming process works. Suppose that an animation plays at 5 frames per second, so each frame plays for 0.2 seconds. If the first frame takes 0.3 seconds to download, it can't start playing until after that time has elapsed. There is always an initial delay while the first frame (or, for some streaming players, the first several seconds worth of frames) is downloaded. Frame 1 starts playing while Frame 2 is downloaded. If Frame 2 is not fully downloaded before Frame 1 ends, the movie pauses until Frame 2 finishes downloading. While Frame 2 is playing, Frame 3 is downloading. By the time Frame 2 finishes playing, Frame 3 has finished downloading and Frame 4 has started downloading.

FIGURE 3-6
Illustration of data streaming

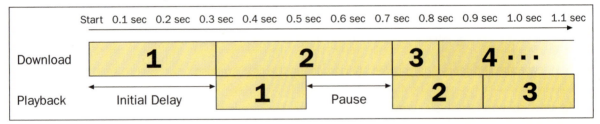

Your animation program may offer a feature that enables you to test how the animation streams and plays. In Macromedia Flash MX, for example, you use the Show Streaming command in the testing window. Click Show Streaming on the View menu to display a green bar across the top of the Bandwidth Profiler. The progress of the green bar shows the streaming rate, and a playhead indicator shows the playback rate.

Net Tip

It is a good idea to test an animation at a number of different modem speeds to make sure it can be easily viewed on a broad range of computers.

You can select a connection speed on the Debug menu to see how streaming and playback relate at faster or slower modem speeds. This helps you determine how your movie looks to viewers who are using a variety of connection speeds.

STEP-BY-STEP 3.2

1. In the **Outdoors Analysis** file, choose to test the movie to open it in the testing screen.

2. Choose the command that allows you to set the connection speed for the animation. In Flash MX, click **Debug** on the menu bar, and then click **56K** if this speed is not already selected.

3. Choose the command that shows how the animation streams and plays. In Flash MX, click **View** on the menu bar, and then click **Show Streaming**. The playhead and streaming process display, as shown in Figure 3-7. Now let's change the connection speed.

FIGURE 3-7
Playhead and streaming progress

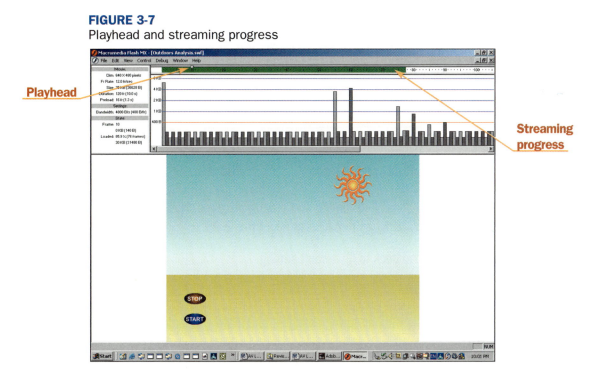

4. Change the connection speed to **28.8**. Notice that the bandwidth target drops down from its previous position.

5. Issue the command again to display streaming and playing progress. Notice that the streaming indicator now pauses at the frames that extend above the bandwidth target, such as frames 55 and 60. However, the streaming still stays ahead of the playback, so this animation plays without pauses.

STEP-BY-STEP 3.2 Continued

6. Change the connection speed to **14.4**. Notice that the bandwidth target is now slightly below a number of the frames (see Figure 3-8).

FIGURE 3-8
Bandwidth target has dropped below many frames

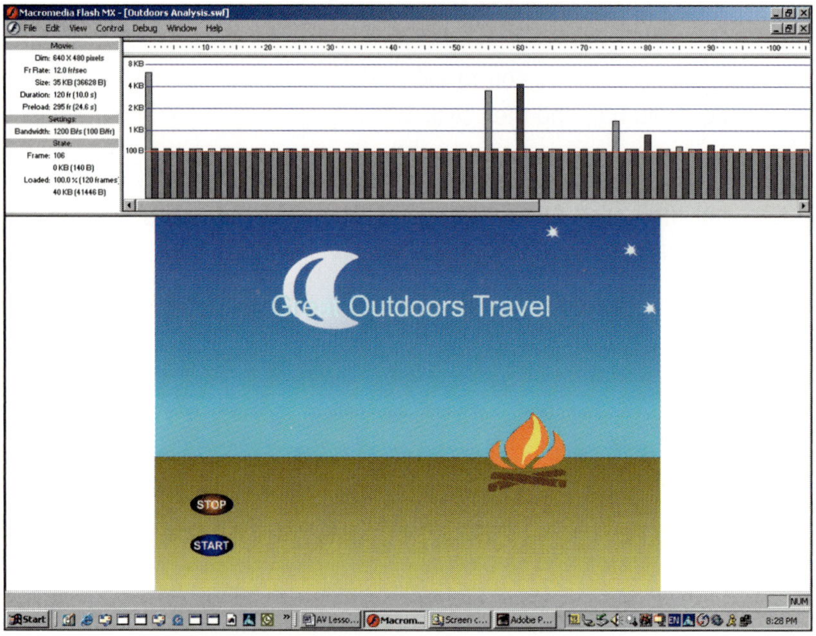

7. Issue the command to display streaming and playing progress. Notice that the streaming is much slower, and that the playback has to pause at about frame 95.

8. Set the connection speed back to its default setting.

9. Close the testing window.

10. Close **Outdoors Analysis** without saving changes, and leave your animation program open to use in the next exercise.

Optimize a Movie

You have finished your analysis of a movie and may have identified some large frames that are causing problems. What do you do now? You can optimize the file to improve the performance of your movie. The purpose is to reduce the file size of your movie and make it faster to download and smoother during playback.

The first things you should check when optimizing your file or a particular frame of the file are the kinds of data being loaded. Image files and sound files can be major problems because of their large file sizes. Ask yourself if you really need to include everything in a particular frame. Can it be simplified and still work? Can some of the content be moved to another, smaller frame?

Compression is another way to reduce file size. Text, shapes, sound, and images can all be compressed. When you compress text and shapes, no information is lost, so the quality remains the same. When compressing images and sound files, you usually have a wide range of *quality settings* you can set. A high-quality setting ensures that the image looks good or the sound plays well, but the file size remains larger than if the quality setting is lower. You can optimize a particular frame by decreasing the quality of the images and sounds in that frame, but of course, you're also giving up image or sound quality. This is the tradeoff you have to make. The more quality you are willing to give up, the smaller your files will be—and the easier and faster they will be for your users to download and play.

Optimizing your animation usually involves fine-tuning the compression settings. You can optimize at any time, or you can optimize when you publish, as discussed in the next section. For example, you can optimize the sounds in your Library by compressing to MP3 as shown in Figure 3-9.

> **Hot Tip**
>
> Flash MX has an Optimize command on the Modify menu that you can use when importing objects to remove extraneous information.

FIGURE 3-9
Optimizing a sound file

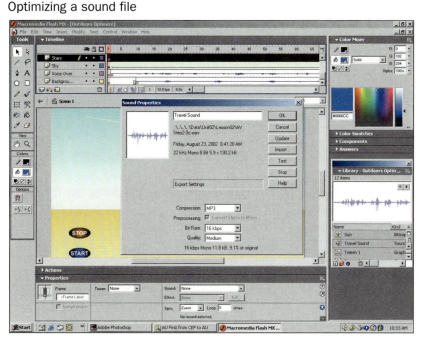

STEP-BY-STEP 3.3

1. Open **AV Step 3-3** from the data files and save the file as **Outdoors Optimize**.

2. Scroll the layer list if necessary to display the bottom two layers, Voice Over and Background Music.

3. Click **frame 1** on the Voice Over layer, then click the frame again and drag it to frame 2 to move the Travel Sound file.

STEP-BY-STEP 3.3 Continued

4. Click **frame 1** on the Background Music layer, then click the frame again and drag it to frame 10. Now the sounds do not load in frame 1 with all the other objects in the animation. Your screen should resemble Figure 3-10.

FIGURE 3-10
Sound files have been moved

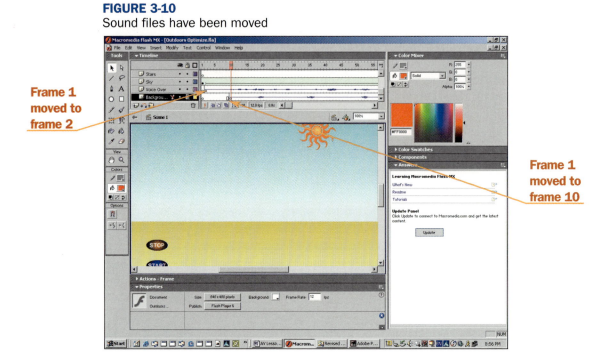

5. Open the Library panel and click the **Travel Sound**. Open the dialog box that allows you to change sound properties. In Flash MX, click the **Properties** icon at the bottom of the Library panel to open the Sound Properties dialog box.

6. Click the **Compression** drop-down arrow, and then click **MP3**.

7. Click the **Quality** drop-down arrow, and then click **Medium**. Click the **OK** button.

8. Test the movie and check the size of frames 1, 2, and 10 in the Bandwidth Profiler against the report you printed. You have managed to distribute some of the file size from frame 1 to other frames, which helps speed streaming.

9. Close the testing window. Save and close **Outdoors Optimize**, and leave your animation program open to use in the next exercise.

Publish a Movie

You've analyzed and optimized your movie so it performs better in the medium in which it will be published. Now you are ready to publish your movie.

The first step is to decide how you want to publish or distribute your animation. There are four ways of distributing your animation:

- As part of a Web page

- In a standard graphic format (such as JPG, PNG, or GIF)

- As an executable file, which bundles both the animation and the program to play it in a single file.

- As a QuickTime movie

All these formats can be delivered over the Internet or on a CD-ROM. When you distribute a graphic or an executable over the Internet, the entire file must be downloaded before you can play the animation. For animations distributed as part of a Web page or as QuickTime movies, you don't have to wait for the entire file to download before you start playing it. While you're watching what's already downloaded, your Web browser or QuickTime player can continue to download the rest of the file.

No matter which method of distribution you choose, you begin the publishing process the same way. Choose the command that opens a publishing settings dialog box. In Flash MX, for example, click Publish Settings on the File menu to open the Publish Settings dialog box (see Figure 3-11). This dialog box consists of at least one tab (Formats) that displays a list of check boxes for the different formats for publishing an animation. As you select a format, Flash MX adds a tab to the dialog box for that format. Click the tab to customize the settings for publishing to that format.

> **Note**
>
> You can select more than one format on the Formats tab. Flash MX automatically publishes in as many formats as you select.

FIGURE 3-11
Publish Settings dialog box

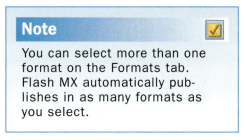

After you have selected the settings you want, click a Publish button to publish the animation and then close the dialog box. You may not see any result of this process, and your original animation remains on your screen. Your file may be published in the same folder that contains your current animation. Use a file management program such as Windows Explorer or My Computer to navigate to the published files. You can open your published files in other programs or in your Web browser.

The following sections detail how to publish to the four options listed earlier in this section using Flash MX. If you are using an animation program other than Flash MX, you should have similar tools. You may need to refer to the documentation for your animation software.

Publish a Movie for Web Delivery

One of the most common ways to distribute an animation is over the Web. Remember, file size is an issue if you are preparing an animation for the Web because you want to minimize downloading time.

Most animation programs have their own formats for their files. A user must have a player specifically for those kinds of files to play the animations. Most animation programs distribute their players free of charge over the Internet or on the CD-ROM that contains the program. These players come in two flavors: standalone programs and browser plug-ins.

A *standalone player* such as Flash Player can be installed on any computer to play animations without requiring a Web browser or access to the Internet. A browser *plug-in* is loaded into a Web browser program and takes on the job of playing an animation on a Web page when a user requests it.

When you publish an animation for Web delivery, the published animation file can be played from a Web page using the browser's plug-in or downloaded from the Web to your hard drive where you can play it by using a standalone player. You can also store the animation on a CD-ROM for distribution to another system or network.

S TEP-BY-STEP 3.4

1. Open **AV Step 3-4** from the data files, and save the file as **Outdoors Web**.

2. Click **File** on the menu bar, and then click **Publish Settings**. The Publish Settings dialog box opens.

3. Click both the **Flash** and **HTML** check boxes, if necessary.

4. Click the **Flash** tab (Figure 3-12) and review the settings available. Make sure the **Compress Movie** check box is selected. Notice the options for compress movie, JPEG quality, and Audio Stream. These options help with optimizing the animation file.

STEP-BY-STEP 3.4 Continued

FIGURE 3-12
Flash tab showing options for optimizing

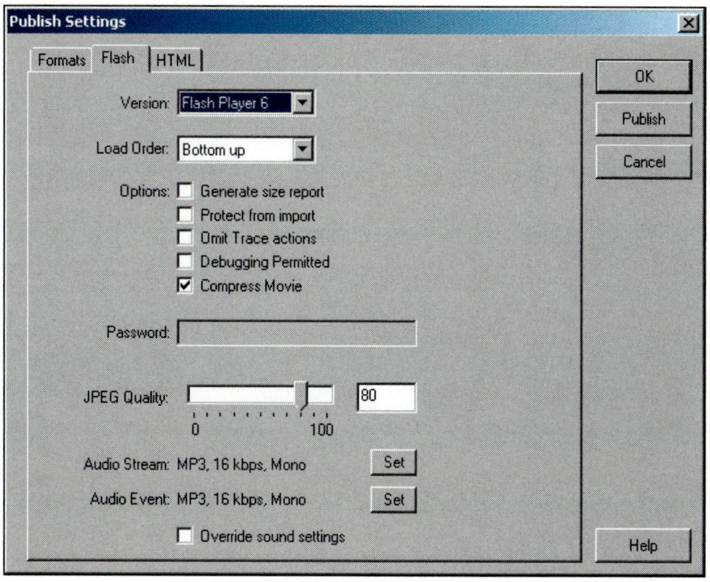

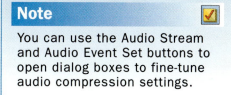

5. Click the **Publish** button. Two published files (a Flash SWF file and an HTML file) are stored in the same folder with the current animation file.

6. Click the **OK** button to close the Publish Settings dialog box.

> **Note** ☑️
>
> You can use the Audio Stream and Audio Event Set buttons to open dialog boxes to fine-tune audio compression settings.

7. Close **Outdoors Web** without saving changes and minimize the animation program. (Click the Minimize button on the program's title bar.)

8. In a file management program such as Windows Explorer or My Computer, navigate to the folder in which you stored the files for this exercise.

9. Locate the **Outdoors Web.swf** file and double-click it. If you have Flash Player on your computer, the file opens in the standalone player, as shown in Figure 3-13.

STEP-BY-STEP 3.4 Continued

FIGURE 3-13
Animation playing in standalone player

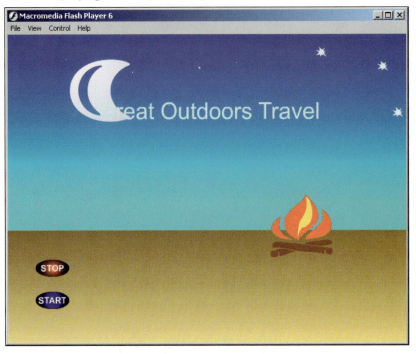

10. In the Flash Player, click **File** on the menu bar, and then click **Exit** to close the file and the player.

11. In your file management program, locate the **Outdoors Web.html** file and double-click it. The file opens in your browser, as shown in Figure 3-14.

FIGURE 3-14
Animation playing within the browser's player

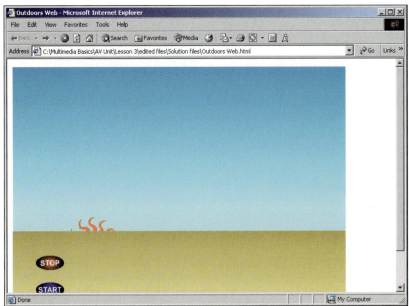

STEP-BY-STEP 3.4 Continued

12. Close the Web browser. Maximize the animation program by clicking it in the taskbar, and leave it open to use in the next exercise.

Publish a Movie to Animated or Static Graphics

You may want to publish an animation to a graphic format for a number of reasons including to create an illustration of your animation in a newsletter or brochure or to add both an animated and a static graphic file to a Web page. Besides using a published graphic on a Web page, you can store the image on a disk or CD-ROM for easy transport, or you can use the graphic in other programs such as a word processing, graphics, or presentation program. You have three file options when publishing to graphics: GIF, JPEG, and PNG.

The *GIF* graphic format is the only one that supports both animated and static images. The GIF format compresses images without losing quality, but GIF images are limited to 256 colors and are *bitmap images* that can be very large. GIFs are a good choice for simple images or animation sequences. You do not need a plug-in to play an animated GIF.

JPEG (.jpg) is a good format to use for photographs. This file type can be compressed, so you can trade off between image quality and file size. JPEG is a static graphic format.

PNG is a recently developed format intended to replace the GIF format for lossless compression (compressing an image without losing quality). Unlike GIF, it isn't limited to 256 colors. But it doesn't support animated image sequences.

When you publish to a static graphic format in some animation programs, you capture the first frame of the animation only. When you publish an animated GIF, you can choose what frames from the animation to store in the GIF, if desired, or display all of them.

Publish an Animated GIF File

The process of publishing an animated GIF file follows the basic steps of publishing any animation. Open the Publish Settings dialog box and click the GIF option on the Formats tab. On the GIF tab, make sure to select the Animated option button. You can then choose whether to loop the animation or play it a specified number of times. Use the Optimize Colors option to allow Flash MX to handle colors for best results.

STEP-BY-STEP 3.5

1. Open **AV Step 3-5** from the data files, and save the file as **Seasons GIF**.

2. Click **File** on the menu bar, and then click **Publish Settings**.

3. Deselect the **Flash** and **HTML** check boxes, if necessary. (When you deselect Flash, HTML may automatically be deselected as well.) Click the **GIF Image** check box.

STEP-BY-STEP 3.5 Continued

4. Click the **GIF** tab, and then click the **Animated** option button in the Playback section of the dialog box. Make sure the **Loop Continuously** option button is also selected (see Figure 3-15).

FIGURE 3-15
GIF tab of Publish Settings dialog box

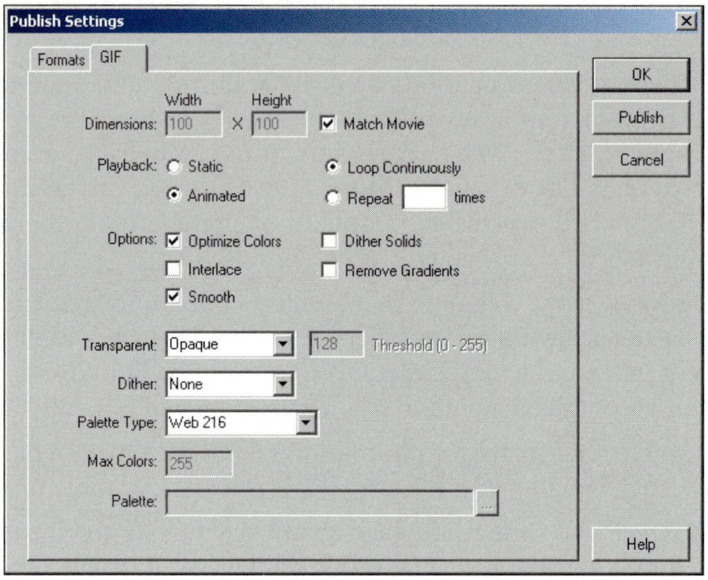

5. Click the **Publish** button, and then click the **OK** button to close the dialog box. Minimize your animation program window.

6. In a file management program such as Windows Explorer, navigate to the folder where you stored the published file and double-click **Seasons GIF.gif**. A standalone player should launch to play the animated GIF file.

7. Close the animated GIF. Close your file management program.

8. Maximize your animation program window. Close **Seasons GIF** without saving changes, and leave the animation program open for the next exercise.

Publish a Static JPG File

You may want to capture a static graphic of one of your animation files to include in the next edition of your school newspaper or a class paper. Again, this image can be inserted on a Web page, stored on a CD-ROM, or placed or imported into another program.

STEP-BY-STEP 3.6

1. Open **AV Step 3-6** from the data files, and save the file as **Brick JPG**.

2. Click **File** from the menu bar, and then click **Publish Settings**.

STEP-BY-STEP 3.6 Continued

3. Deselect the **Flash** and **HTML** check boxes, if necessary. Click the **JPEG Image** check box.

4. Click the **JPEG** tab. Notice the Quality slider. Decreasing the quality of the JPG reduces the file size, but also decreases image quality.

5. Click the **Publish** button, and then click the **OK** button to close the dialog box. The file is published in the same directory as the current animation.

6. Mimimize the animation program window.

7. Launch a graphics program such as Fireworks and open a new, blank graphic. Set the drawing area dimensions to at least 5.5 inches by 5.5 inches.

8. Click **File** on the menu bar, and then click a command such as **Import** or **Place**. Navigate to the folder where you published the JPG file.

9. Click **Brick JPG.jpg**, and then click the **Open** button. Use the pointer to drag an area about 5.5 inches square to import the picture, as shown in Figure 3-16.

FIGURE 3-16
Brick JPG in Macromedia Fireworks

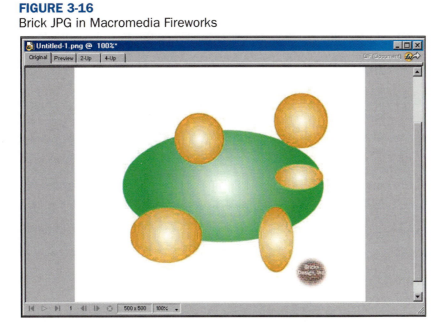

10. Save the graphic file as **Brick Graphic**. Close the **Brick Graphic** file and Fireworks.

11. Maximize your animation program. Close **Brick JPG** without saving changes, and leave the animation program open to use in the next exercise.

Publish a Movie to an Executable

Suppose you are traveling to a conference to make a presentation. You are not sure what type of software and hardware will be available at the conference. Maybe you want to share your animation with a friend who lives across town, in another state, or in another country but doesn't have animation software or a standalone player installed on his or her computer. You can create an *executable* version that can be played on a computer without a standalone player or the animation software installed. You can burn this executable version to a CD or DVD and distribute it.

The executable format is useful when you don't know whether your intended audience has a player for your animation program. The executable bundles together your data and a player so your animation can be played without using any other program. Because adding all code for the player makes the file much larger, publishing an executable also is a useful option if the size of the animation already makes it difficult for Web delivery.

Optimization is generally not as critical if you publish to an executable, but there are certain limitations. Standard audio CD-ROMs are typically 650 MB, so you are limited to that total file size if you are distributing your animation on a CD. Of course, you may also have other information on the CD, so you may have even less storage space for the animation.

S TEP-BY-STEP 3.7

1. Open **AV Step 3-7** from the data files, and save the file as **Outdoors Executable**.

2. Open the **Publish Settings** dialog box.

3. Deselect the **Flash** and **HTML** check boxes, if necessary. Click the **Windows Projector** check box.

4. Click the **Publish** button, and then click the **OK** button. Minimize the animation program window.

5. Click the **Start** button on your Windows taskbar, and then click **Run**. (See Figure 3-17.)

> **Note** ☑
>
> Windows Projector files can be played only on Windows machines. Macintosh Projector files can be played only on Apple Macintosh machines. If you want to create a hybrid CD-ROM, you need to select both versions.

FIGURE 3-17
Start menu in Windows

STEP-BY-STEP 3.7 Continued

6. Click the **Browse** button and navigate to the folder where you published the file.

7. Click **Outdoors Executable.exe**, and click the **Open** button in the Browse dialog box. Then click the **OK** button in the Run dialog box. The animation launches a standalone player if you have one and plays the animation.

8. Close the window in which the executable file is playing.

9. Maximize the animation program window. Close **Outdoors Executable** without saving changes, and leave the animation program open to use in the next exercise.

Publish a Movie to QuickTime

QuickTime is a cross-platform format that works on both Windows and Macintosh systems. It is actually a wrapper for a whole range of movie and animation technologies, even interactive ones. Publishing your animation to a QuickTime movie means it can be played on a wide range of systems without needing a player for your specific animation program. Unlike publishing to an executable, no code has to be bundled with your animation, so the file is smaller and can run on any platform supporting QuickTime.

QuickTime movies can also be imported into video-editing programs. Your users may want to add animation to their QuickTime movies, and then use the added animation in a digital video they are developing.

You can distribute your QuickTime movie via the Web, on a CD-ROM, or on videotape. QuickTime movies can be downloaded and then played, or they can be streamed.

Some versions of Flash handle QuickTime differently from others. You may need to save a Flash MX animation to a previous version of Flash to satisfactorily publish to QuickTime. You may want to check the documentation of your own animation program to see what versions of QuickTime it supports.

STEP-BY-STEP 3.8

1. Open **AV Step 3-8** from the data files. You first save this file in a different version of Flash, and then publish it.

2. Click **File** on the menu bar, and then click **Save As**. Key the filename **Outdoors QT**, click the **Save as type** drop-down arrow, and click **Flash 5 Document**.

3. Click the **Save** button.

4. Open the Publish Settings dialog box, and deselect any selected check boxes. Click the **QuickTime** check box. (If the Flash check box also becomes selected, deselect it again.)

5. Click the **QuickTime** tab (Figure 3-18), and then click the **Loop** option button in the Playback section.

FIGURE 3-18
QuickTime tab

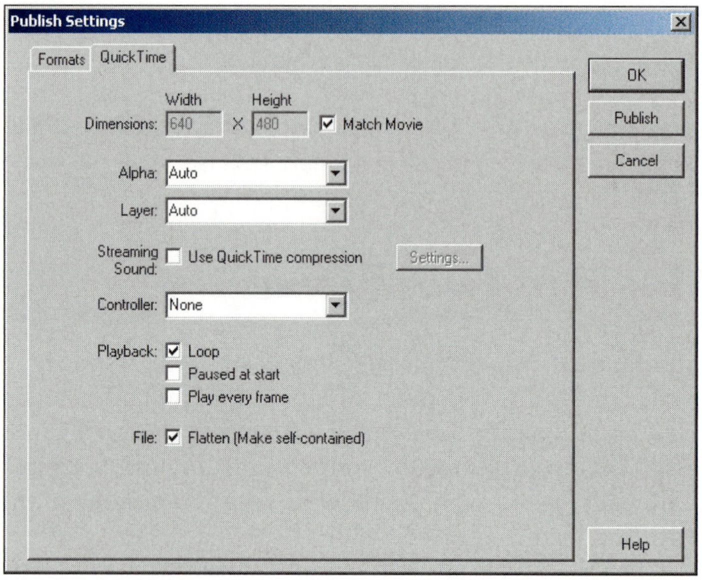

6. Click the **Publish** button, then click the **OK** button.

7. Close **Outdoors QT** without saving changes, and close your animation program.

8. Start your QuickTime player.

9. Click **File** on the menu bar, and then click **Open Movie in New Player**. Navigate to the location where you published the file.

10. Click **Outdoors QT.mov**, and then click the **Open** button.

STEP-BY-STEP 3.8 Continued

11. If the movie does not begin playing, click the **Start** button on the animation. Your screen should look similar to Figure 3-19.

FIGURE 3-19
QuickTime movie of Outdoors QT

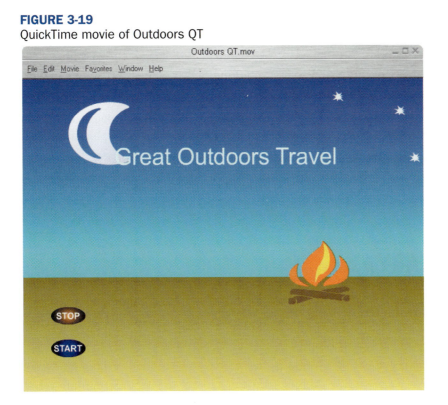

12. Close the QuickTime player.

SUMMARY

In this lesson, you learned:

■ Six factors that affect how you prepare your animation for publishing are file size, movie content, user's connection speed or bandwidth, user's hardware and software, network traffic, and streaming capabilities.

■ Data rate, playback rate, and streaming rate are concepts you use in analyzing a movie.

■ Streaming animation means that one frame of the animation can be playing while the next frame is downloading.

■ The purpose of analyzing a movie is to identify potential problems with downloading and playback.

■ The playback speed cannot get ahead of the streaming speed or a delay occurs when you play your animation.

■ Different bandwidths affect how your animation plays. The larger the animation file, the more bandwidth you need. If you have a large animation file and small bandwidth, the file requires more download time and may cause delays in playback.

■ Optimizing a movie involves reducing its file size so it downloads faster and plays more smoothly.

■ You can publish an animation to a standalone player, a Web browser's player or plug-in, an animated or static graphics format, an executable application, or a QuickTime movie.

■ GIF files are the only graphics format that supports both static images and animations. The benefit of publishing to an animated GIF is that you don't need a plug-in to play the animation.

■ Publishing to a static JPEG, PNG, or GIF captures only the first frame of the animation.

■ You can publish an animation to a QuickTime movie. QuickTime movies are cross-platform, so they can be played on both Windows and Macintosh systems.

VOCABULARY *Review*

Define the following terms:

Bandwidth	JPEG	QuickTime
Bitmap images	Playback rate	Standalone player
Compression	Plug-in	Streaming
Executable	PNG	Streaming rate
GIF		

REVIEW *Questions*

TRUE / FALSE

T F **1.** An entire animation must be downloaded to the user's computer before it starts playing.

T F **2.** Streaming data speeds up downloading a movie.

T F **3.** Every frame of an animation plays at the same speed.

T F **4.** Every frame of an animation downloads at the same speed.

T F **5.** Optimizing a movie can make playback smoother.

T F **6.** Users require special software to play an animation in a Web browser.

T F **7.** Publishing to an executable allows a user to play your animation without special software.

T F **8.** Executable animations can play on multiple platforms.

T F **9.** QuickTime movies require Flash MX.

T F **10.** Animations distributed on CD-ROM don't need to be optimized.

FILL IN THE BLANK

Complete the following sentences by writing the correct word or words in the blanks provided.

1. Watching the first part of an animation while the rest is downloading is called _____ .

2. _____ is the process of improving the download and playback of your movies.

3. _____ is a cross-platform multimedia format.

4. If you're not sure what software your user has, you might consider distributing your animation in _____ form.

5. Images and sounds can be compressed more if you're willing to give up _____ .

MULTIPLE CHOICE

Select the best response for the following statements.

1. Publishing a static graphic in Macromedia Flash MX captures
   A. The first frame of the animation.
   B. The last frame of the animation.
   C. Whatever frame of the animation you choose.
   D. All frames of the animation.

2. In order to avoid pauses, the streaming rate must be
   A. Slower than the playback rate.
   B. Faster than the playback rate.
   C. The same as the playback rate.
   D. The two are unrelated.

3. Animations can be played in a Web browser using a(n)
   A. Standalone player.
   B. Plug-in.
   C. Executable.
   D. JPEG image.

4. Which of the following image formats allow animation?
   A. GIF.
   B. JPEG.
   C. PNG.
   D. All of the above.

Research these topics and how they relate to digital animation. Put together a research plan that includes a list of what the team knows about these topics, what the team doesn't know, and what the team would like to know. Gather the answers and information, then regroup and report your findings to the team and to the class.

CRITICAL *Thinking*

ACTIVITY 3-1

Go to the Publish Settings dialog box of your animation program. Select all the possible options and review any tab menus associated with those options. Review the menus and write down questions you may have about any of the menu items. What do they mean or stand for? Use the Internet or other published resources to find the answers. Submit your answers in writing to the instructor.

ACTIVITY 3-2

Most animation programs include a tutorial to show you how to use the program. Analyze one of the native tutorial files based on a 56 Kbps modem with an actual download rate of about 4,800 bytes per second. Consider the file size, frame rate, and length of the animation as well as this data rate. Write your findings, and then compare these findings with an automated analysis using the tools in your animation program. Write a report listing the similarities and differences. **Hint:** ((playback rate × time length) / file size) / data rate = streaming rate (frames per second). Compare the streaming rate with the playback rate.

WORKING WITH VIDEO

OBJECTIVES

Upon completion of this lesson, you should be able to:

■ Set up a video project.

■ Capture video from a camera or tape.

■ Import video from other digital sources.

■ Create a video from source clips and preview a video.

■ Edit a video.

Estimated time: 2 hours

VOCABULARY

Analog

Capture

Clip

Codec

Digital

Digital video

Digital video (DV) format

IEEE 1394

In point

Insertion edit

Keyframes

Out point

Overlay edit

Rendering

Source video

Three-point editing

Timeline

Timeline marker

Lessons 4 through 6 of this unit concentrate on *digital video*. Video data has many similarities to the animations you worked with in Lessons 1 through 3, but there are many differences as well. Like an animation, video presents moving pictures. It is also organized around the idea of *frames*: distinct pictures that are played at a fixed rate. Unlike animations, frames of video data don't contain text, shapes, or images. Instead, *the entire frame is a single bitmapped image*. Figure 4-1 shows a comparison of animation frames and video frames.

FIGURE 4-1
Comparison of animation and video frames

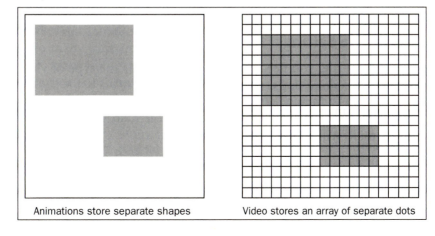

Animations store separate shapes   Video stores an array of separate dots

STEP-BY-STEP 4.1 Continued

3. Click **Window** on the menu bar, click **Workspace**, and then click **Single-Track Editing**. This loads the window configuration that we will use throughout these tutorials. As you work through the remaining tutorials, if a window configuration appears that is different from the one that is displayed after these three clicks, please repeat this step.

4. Click **Project** on the menu bar, and then click **Settings Viewer**. The Settings Viewer dialog box opens, as shown in Figure 4-5. Note the message at the bottom of the dialog box that says capture settings, project settings, and clip settings should be identical for optimal performance.

> **Hot Tip**
>
> You often see terms such as NTSC and PAL when working with video. NTSC is the format used for television broadcasts in the United States. PAL is the format used for television broadcasts in Europe.

> **Note**
>
> Premiere lays out the screen windows based on the screen size. Premiere also allows you to reconfigure the windows to best fit your working style. For these reasons, your screen may not exactly match the figures shown in this lesson.

FIGURE 4-5
Settings Viewer dialog box

Settings Viewer					
	Capture Settings	Project Settings	▾	Export Settings	OK
Video					Load...
Mode:	DV/IEEE1394 Capture	Microsoft DV AVI		Microsoft DV AVI	
Compressor:	Microsoft DV (NTSC)	Microsoft DV (NTSC)		Microsoft DV (NTSC)	
Frame Size:	720 x 480	720 x 480		720 x 480	
Frame Rate:	29.97 FPS	29.97 FPS		29.97 FPS	
Depth:	Millions	Millions		Millions	
Quality:	100 %	100 %		100 %	
Pixel Aspect Ratio:	D1/DV NTSC (0.9)	D1/DV NTSC (0.9)		D1/DV NTSC (0.9)	
Audio					
Sample Rate:	32000 Hz	32000 Hz		32000 Hz	
Format:	16 bit – Stereo	16 bit – Stereo		16 bit – Stereo	
Compressor:	Uncompressed	Uncompressed		Uncompressed	
Render					
Field Settings:	Lower Field First	Lower Field First		Lower Field First	

ⓘ For optimal performance, Capture Settings, Project Settings and Clip Settings should be identical.

5. Click the **OK** button to close the Settings Viewer dialog box. Leave Premiere open to use in the next exercise.

> **Extra for Experts**
>
> Premiere allows you to use separate settings for capturing video, working with video, and exporting video in its final form. However, if you use different settings for each of these actions, Premiere constantly converts your video from one format to another as you work on it. This may take time. To keep things as efficient as possible, use the same settings for capturing, working with, and exporting video.

Capture Video from an External Source

After you have set up your video project, the next step is to bring the video you want to work with into your program. Your video data may consist of several pieces or *clips* of *source video*. You have two options for bringing the data into your program:

- You can capture video from an external source such as a digital video camera or a tape deck.

- You can import video or still images from other files on your computer.

This section describes how to capture video from a digital camera. You learn in the next section how to import video or images already on your computer.

All data in a computer, including video, must be in *digital* form. Digital data is stored as bits or bytes like all the information stored in a computer. Today's digital video cameras record directly in digital form, most commonly the *digital video (DV) format. Analog*, or nondigital, video must be converted to digital form to be used by a computer program. Examples of analog video include television signals and VHS tapes.

The most common way of physically connecting a digital video (DV) camera to your computer is called *IEEE 1394*. This is the standard protocol for exchanging information between two digital devices. It's also sometimes called *Firewire* (Apple) or *iLink* (Sony). You need a specific type of port on your computer called an IEEE 1394 port and a specific type of card installed on your computer called an IEEE 1394 card to connect a DV camera to your computer.

Most video programs have a *capture* mode in which input from the digital camera is played in a window on the computer screen. When the part you want to record appears, you start recording, much like using a VCR. While recording, the video program captures the video and writes it to your computer's hard disk. When you stop recording, the recorded video is saved as a new source clip. You can start and stop recording as many times as you want, with each recorded segment saved as a separate source clip.

Hot Tip

If your video isn't already in digital form, you can use an *analog-to-digital converter* to convert analog video signals, such as those from television, to digital form. A converter can look like a box that sits next to your computer or a card installed in your computer (*a capture card*). If you plug the output from a VHS tape player into one of these devices and plug the device into your computer, the data looks to your computer just like digital video data.

Hot Tip

Some video-editing programs and digital video cameras allow you to control the camera from your computer. See your camera's user's manual to determine if your camera supports this.

S TEP-BY-STEP 4.2

To complete this exercise, you need a digital video camera and an IEEE 1394 card if your computer doesn't already have one built in. If you don't have the required hardware and software, you can skip this exercise and go on to the next section.

1. In Adobe Premiere, click **File** on the menu bar, click **Capture**, and then click **Movie Capture**. The Movie Capture window opens, as shown in Figure 4-6.

FIGURE 4-6
Movie Capture window

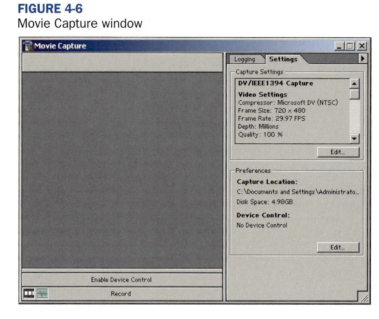

2. Connect your camera to your computer's IEEE 1394 port and turn on your camera.

3. Set the camera to Camera mode for capturing real-time video or set it to Play or VTR mode. Start your tape playing if you want to capture something you've already recorded onto your camera's tape. You should see the output from the camera displayed in the Movie Capture window. Different camera models sometimes have different controls; see your camera's user's manual for details on how to connect your camera and prepare it for transferring video to a computer.

4. Click the **Record** button at the bottom of the Movie Capture window. Premiere starts recording and displays the number of frames captured.

5. After 30 seconds, press **Esc** on your keyboard. The video should stop recording, and a Save File dialog box opens.

6. Navigate to the location where you want to store the clip. Key a filename for the clip, and then click the **Save** button.

7. A dialog box may then be displayed showing how many frames (if any) were dropped during capture. Frames may be dropped if your computer cannot keep up with the video. If this happens, click the **OK** button.

8. Close the Movie Capture window.

STEP-BY-STEP 4.2 Continued

9. Look at the Project window in Adobe Premiere. You should see a new movie clip containing the video you just captured.

10. Drag the clip to the Source (left side) view of the Monitor. It appears as shown in Figure 4-7. As you learned earlier, you work with clips in the Source view of the Monitor window, and the movie as a whole in the Program view of the Monitor.

FIGURE 4-7
Preview a clip in the Source view of the Monitor window

Source view

Playback controls

Source clip

11. Click the **Play** button in the Source view playback controls to watch the clip.

12. Click **File** on the menu bar, and then click **Close**. Leave Abode Premiere open to use in the next exercise.

Import Video Sources from Other Digital Media

Capturing video from external sources is just one way to bring source clips into your video-editing program. You can also open and import video or still image files already stored on your computer or network. These can be clips used in previous projects, video segments produced previously, animations published in video format from programs such as Macromedia Flash MX, or just about any video file already in digital form. Still images, such as those from a digital camera or produced by drawing or image-editing programs such as Adobe Photoshop, may also be imported.

You may wonder why still images would be used in a video. Once imported, still image clips can provide visual effects or be combined to create a "video collage."

Importing a source clip is different from opening a file in other programs. Your video-editing program doesn't actually edit or change the source file itself. Instead, think of your project as a series of instructions for combining source clips in the way you want. Think of how your video editor copies bits and pieces from one or more tapes to another. You can store many different video segments on different tapes, perhaps even keeping a library of source video. When you need to use this footage, you can copy all or part of each tape as needed, but never modify the original tapes. You can even put together a set of instructions for your assistant, such as "Build a video by copying tape #1 from this point to that point, then copying tape #2 from this point to that point, etc." Your video-editing program stores only these instructions, not the actual video content from the source clips.

When working with source clips, keep these things in mind:

- Your source files are not changed when you edit your video.

- You can use a single source file in many different projects.

- Your video-editing program cannot find your source clips if you rename, move, or delete them after you import them.

- If you change the content of the source clip and save it with its original filename, any existing projects using that clip as a source are affected by those changes.

The process of importing clips into your project is much like opening any other file. In many programs, you can even import entire folders of clips. Once imported, these clips are displayed using their original filenames, so some programs let you give them more descriptive aliases (nicknames).

STEP-BY-STEP 4.3

1. In Adobe Premiere, click **File** on the menu bar, and then click **New Project**. (If you did not complete the previous exercise, you may be asked to save changes to an untitled project; click the **No** button to close it without saving.) The Load Project Settings dialog box opens. In the Available Presets list, click **Multimedia QuickTime**, and then click the **OK** button.

2. Click **File** on the menu bar, and then click **Save As**. Navigate to where you want to store the project file. Key the filename **Utah**, and then click the **Save** button.

3. Click **File** on the menu bar, click **Import**, and then click **File**.

4. Locate **AV Step 4-3a.mov** in your data files, select the file, and click the **Open** button. This file should now appear in the Project window as a source clip. A movie clip icon appears to the left of its name. You can double-click on this icon to see a full-size version of the clip in a separate window. If you do, please close that window before proceeding.

5. By default, Premiere gives the clip the same name as the file you imported. We will change it to a more descriptive name. Click **AV Step 4-3a.mov** in the Name list in the Project window. Click **Clip** on the menu bar, and then click **Set Clip Name Alias**. The Set Clip Name Alias dialog box opens.

STEP-BY-STEP 4.3 Continued

6. Key **river** for the name of the clip, and then click the **OK** button. The file is renamed and still selected in the Project window, as shown in Figure 4-8.

FIGURE 4-8
Source clip in Project window

7. Click **Clip** on the menu bar, and then click **Properties**. A window opens showing the properties of that source clip. Review the properties of the clip and close the window.

8. Double-click the movie clip icon to the left of the **river** clip in the Project window. This clip should now be displayed in the Source view of the Monitor window. Click the **Play** button at the bottom of the Source view to watch it as shown in Figure 4-9.

FIGURE 4-9
Playback controls

STEP-BY-STEP 4.3 Continued

9. Repeat steps 3 through 6 to import **AV Step 4-3b.jpg** and give it the name alias **canyon**.

10. Save changes and leave the **Utah** file open to use in the next exercise.

Create and Preview a Video

Now that you have brought in source material, either by capturing it from an external source or importing it already in digital form, you are ready to create a simple video.

> **Hot Tip**
>
> You can also hold down the Alt key while you double-click the clip in the Project window to open it in a new window, but this can sometimes clutter up your workspace. This is the default setting. The effect of double-click and Alt + double-click can be reversed in Premiere's preferences. Refer to Premiere's documentation.

Central to all video-editing programs is the idea of a *timeline*. Source clips become part of the final video by being placed on the timeline. You can add as many clips or fragments of clips as you want to the timeline. When you produce the final video, these clips on the timeline are played in the order they appear in the timeline and at the time positions indicated.

The easiest way to add a clip to the timeline is to simply drag it there. If you drag the clip to an unused spot on the timeline that is too small to hold the clip, the objects already on the timeline after that point usually move ahead to make room for the new clip. If you drag the clip to a point that isn't right next to another clip on the timeline, you create a gap that becomes a blank spot in the video. In Premiere, you can drag a clip from the Source view of the Monitor window, or you can drag it from the Project window.

You can also choose to insert only part of a clip in the timeline. To do this, you specify how much of the clip you want to use. Display the clip in the Source view and use the Set Location marker beneath the clip image to mark the point where you want to start copying the clip. This is called the clip's *In point*. As you drag the Set Location marker, the movie plays in the Source view so you can judge where you want to start. You can also use the timecode readout (the green digital clock) in the Source view to start at a specific time in the clip.

Click the Mark In button on the Source view controller to mark the In point. Then move the Set Location marker to the point where you want to stop copying (the clip's *Out point*), and click the Mark Out button. When you drag the clip from the Source view to the timeline, only the part of the clip you marked is used. If you want to copy another section of the clip to the timeline, just change the In and Out points and drag the clip again to the timeline—a second occurrence of the clip appears on the timeline. This is just like using a source videotape and copying from it twice.

At any time, you can preview the video. When you preview the video, all objects on the timeline are rendered to a temporary file and played back in your Monitor window's Program view. Building a preview can take a while, but once done, you can watch it as often as you like. However, if you edit the video, parts of the preview may have to be rebuilt.

S TEP-BY-STEP 4.4

1. In the **Utah** file, drag the **river** clip to the beginning (far left) of the **Video 1** line on the Timeline as shown in Figure 4-10.

FIGURE 4-10
Timeline with a video source clip

2. Click **Timeline** on the menu bar, and then click **Preview** to see a preview of your video. After the preview is built, you should see the clip play in the Program view of the Monitor window.

3. Import the clip **AV Step 4-4.mov** from your data files and rename it with the alias **waterfall**, using the steps you learned in Step-by-Step 4.3.

4. Drag the **waterfall** clip to the Source view of the Monitor window.

5. Click the Set Location marker below the Source view and drag it to the right until you see 00:00:12:00 on the timecode readout. You can use the left or right arrow key to move the time by small increments if necessary. Click the **Mark In** button as shown in Figure 4-11. This indicates the point where Premiere will start copying the movie.

FIGURE 4-11
Set In point at 12 seconds

STEP-BY-STEP 4.4 Continued

6. Now specify the point where you want to stop copying. Drag the Set Location marker to the right until you see 00:00:17:00 on the timecode readout, and then click the **Mark Out** button as shown in Figure 4-12.

FIGURE 4-12
Set Out point at 17 seconds

7. You can now copy the portion of the video you have marked to the Timeline. Drag the **waterfall** clip from the Source view of the Monitor to the Timeline and drop it after the first clip on the Video 1 line, as shown in Figure 4-13. You may need to scroll the Timeline to see the end of the **river** clip.

FIGURE 4-13
Timeline with two video source clips

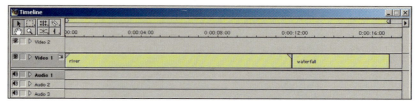

8. Press **Enter** to preview the video. You should see the first clip followed by the selected segment of the second clip play in the Program view of the Monitor window.

9. Select the **canyon** clip. This is a still image, so you need to specify how long to display it during the video. Click **Clip** on the menu bar, and then click **Duration**. The Clip Duration dialog box opens.

10. Set the duration of the clip to **00:00:07:00** seconds, and then click the **OK** button.

STEP-BY-STEP 4.4 Continued

11. Drag the **canyon** clip to the Timeline between the first and second clips already there. Notice how the **waterfall** clip moves to the right in the Timeline to make room for the new clip (Figure 4-14).

FIGURE 4-14
Timeline with a video clip, a still image clip, and a second video clip

Time ruler

Preview status
(red means it
needs to be
rendered)

12. Notice also that the Preview status for the new clip is red. This indicates that this new part needs to be rendered before it can be previewed. The **river** and **waterfall** clips don't have a Preview status indicator because they are already in the same format as the project settings.

13. Press **Enter** to preview the video. After the preview is built, notice that the **canyon** image's Preview status has turned from red to green. If you Preview the results again, this clip does not have to be rendered.

14. Save your project as **Utah1**. Leave the **Utah1** file open to use in the next exercise.

Edit Video

Once you have material on the timeline, you may need to edit the video further. You can make the following kinds of edits:

■ Rearrange or delete clips

■ Adjust a clip's In and Out points

■ Change the speed and duration of a clip

■ Cut and splice clips

■ Insert or overlay new material using three-point editing

You can also insert timeline markers that work like bookmarks to help you keep track of where certain things happen in the video.

All these edits simply alter how the source clips are used. In the next lesson, you learn more about enhancing the video with transitions, titles, and audio.

Making changes to the clips on the timeline requires you to select them. To select a clip in the timeline, click on it. A selected clip has a moving diagonal border.

As you edit your video, you may find that you have made changes you don't like, but you don't need to start over and recreate the project. Instead, you can usually use a command to throw away your recent edits and restore the file to the way it appeared when you last saved it.

Rearrange or Delete Clips

Clips can easily be rearranged on the timeline, usually by just dragging them around. Clips move as needed to make room for the clip you're moving. You can also delete clips. Be careful, though—moving or deleting clips can leave gaps in the Timeline, which cause blank segments in your video. Drag the remaining clips to close the gaps.

STEP-BY-STEP 4.5

1. In the **Utah1** file, rearrange the first two clips on the Timeline by dragging **canyon** before **river**. Drag the clip a little to the left of the beginning of the **river** clip, until the **river** clip shows a dark blue high-light with a left-pointing yellow arrow. Preview the result and notice the gap where the **canyon** clip used to be, as shown in Figure 4-15.

FIGURE 4-15
Rearranging the canyon and river clips

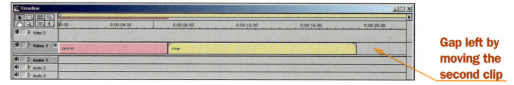

Gap left by moving the second clip

2. Remove this gap by dragging **waterfall** to the left so it appears immediately after the **river** clip. Preview the results.

3. Click **File** on the menu bar, and then click **Revert**. You are asked if you want to discard your changes. Click the **OK** button to restore the original project. (This project is reused several times throughout this lesson as you practice different editing techniques.)

4. Leave the **Utah1** file open to use in the next exercise.

Adjust In and Out Points

Some programs, including Adobe Premiere, allow you to shorten or lengthen selected clips already on the timeline by adjusting their In and Out points. Instead of recopying the clip, deleting part of it, or copying another part of it, you can simply adjust where the copying starts and stops.

STEP-BY-STEP 4.6

1. In the **Utah1** file, place the pointer near the start of the **river** clip until the pointer changes to a [shape with an arrow pointing to the right. This is the Edge Trim tool.

STEP-BY-STEP 4.6 Continued

2. Click and drag the Edge Trim tool to the right about half an inch; this shortens the segment by start-ing the copying process later in the original source clip. Notice that this also leaves a gap at the start of the Timeline, as shown in Figure 4-16.

FIGURE 4-16
Adjusting a clip's In point

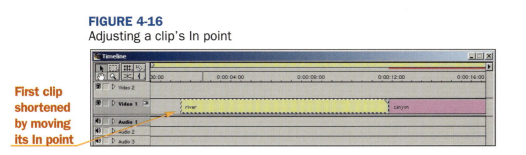

First clip shortened by moving its In point

3. Click **Edit** on the menu bar, and then click **Undo In Point** to undo step 2. Now move the pointer to the beginning of the **river** clip and press and hold down **Alt**. The Edge Trim tool looks heavier. Drag the In point as in step 2. Notice that the clip is shorter but no gap is produced.

4. Adjust the **river** clip's Out point by moving the pointer to the end of the clip until it changes to the Edge Trim tool with an arrow pointing left.

5. Press and hold down **Alt** while you drag the marker to the left half an inch. This shortens the clip by stopping earlier in the original source clip than previously. Note that you did not create a gap between the **river** clip and the **canyon** clip because you held down Alt while adjusting the Out point.

6. Adjust the In point of the **waterfall** clip by holding down **Alt** at the start of the clip and dragging its In point to the left half an inch. This *lengthens* the clip by including more at the start of the clip.

7. Preview your changes to see how the clip lengths have changed.

8. Click **File** on the menu bar, and then click **Revert**. Click the **OK** button to go back to the original project.

9. Leave the **Utah1** file open to use in the next exercise.

Adjust Speed and Duration

You can also adjust the speed at which a clip plays. You can usually specify a new speed as a percentage of the current speed. For example, to reduce the speed, key a value such as 75%. You can also specify the duration you want for the clip to play. Your program then calculates the speed that results in this duration.

STEP-BY-STEP 4.7

1. In the **Utah1** file, select the **river** clip on the Timeline.

2. Click **Clip** on the menu bar, and then click **Speed**.

3. Key **200%** in the **New Rate** box. Click the **OK** button. Notice that the first clip now takes half as much space on the Timeline.

STEP-BY-STEP 4.7 Continued

4. Adjust the positions of the **canyon** and **waterfall** clips by dragging them to the left to remove gaps in the Timeline.

5. Preview the results and see that the first clip now plays at twice (200%) its normal speed (Figure 4-17).

FIGURE 4-17
Adjusting a clip's speed

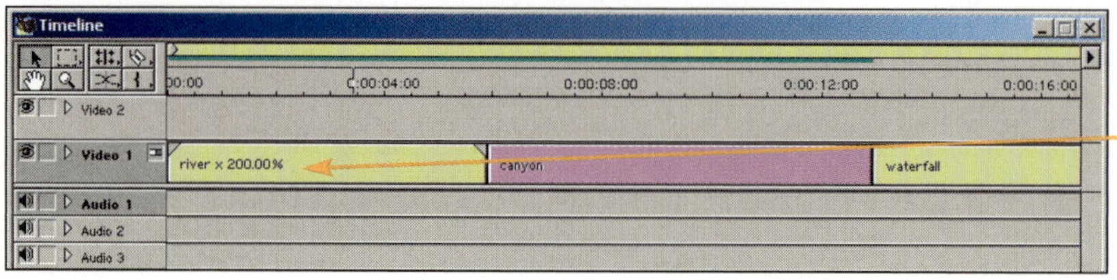

River clip now playing at 200%

6. Click **File** on the menu bar, and then click **Revert**. Click the **OK** button to go back to the original project.

7. Leave the **Utah1** file open to use in the next exercise.

Cut and Splice

As you work with most video-editing programs, you often find that there are several ways of doing the same thing. Sometimes, these methods originate from how physical videotapes or movie reels are handled. So, in addition to editing video by copying from one set of tapes to another, you can also edit tapes by "cutting" them up, rearranging or deleting parts, and then "splicing" them back together. Most video-editing programs allow you to work this way with clips on the timeline. The pieces you've cut the video into then work like separate clips copied from different segments of the same source. You can rearrange or delete them as needed.

STEP-BY-STEP 4.8

1. In the **Utah1** file, click the **Razor** tool on the Timeline's tool palette.

2. Position the pointer in the middle of the **river** clip. Notice how the pointer now looks like a razor blade once it enters a clip.

STEP-BY-STEP 4.8 Continued

3. Click the mouse to cut the clip at that point. Notice how the clip now appears as two separate pieces (Figure 4-18). Each of these pieces can be moved or deleted just like any other clip.

FIGURE 4-18
Use the Razor tool to cut a clip

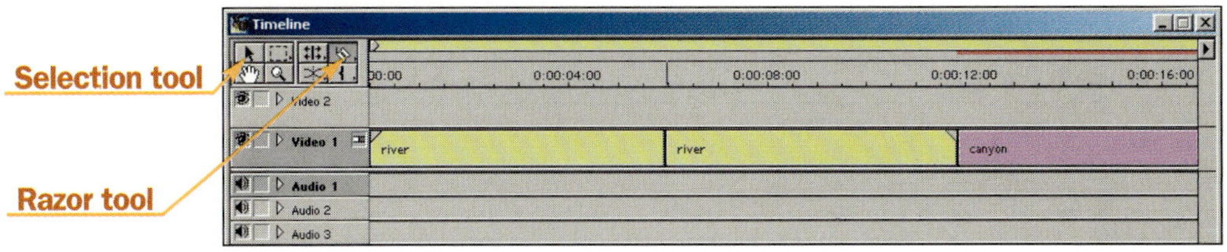

Selection tool

Razor tool

4. Click the **Selection** tool on the Timeline's tool palette. Select the second **river** clip and delete it by clicking **Edit**, then **Clear**.

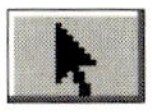

5. Adjust the positions of the **canyon** and **waterfall** clips by dragging them to the left to remove gaps in the Timeline.

6. Preview the results.

7. Click **File** on the menu bar, and then click **Revert**. Click the **OK** button to go back to the original project.

8. Leave the **Utah1** file open to use in the next exercise.

Use Three-Point Editing

The final editing technique in this section is *three-point editing*. Although this method involves adding new content to the timeline, it can also change the content on the timeline itself. This technique is reminiscent of how tape editors worked with physical tapes, plus it uses In and Out points introduced earlier.

In three-point editing, you work with a *source* and a *destination*. The source is usually a new video clip that you want to add to the current movie, which is the destination. To do a three-point edit:

1. Position the source tape to where you want to start playing (set the source's In point).

2. Specify the end of the source segment you want to copy (set the source's Out point).

3. Specify the point on the destination tape at which you want to start copying (set the destination's In point).

You don't have to specify the destination's Out point; that is determined automatically when you finish copying from the source. After you specify these three points, you can start copying from one tape to the other.

Use the Source view of the Monitor window to set the source's In and Out points, just as when specifying a portion of a movie to copy to the timeline. To set the destination's In point, you use the Set Location marker beneath the movie in the Program view of the Monitor. You can also set the destination's In point in the timeline using the *edit line* to mark where the new data starts.

You have two choices when adding data using three-point editing, as shown in Figure 4-19. If you do an *insertion edit*, the selected content of the source clip is inserted into the Timeline at the In point you set, separating the clip that's already there if necessary. This result is the same as if you cut the clip at that point into two parts and dragged the source clip in between the two parts of the old clip.) If you do an *overlay edit*, the selected content of the source clip is written to the Timeline *and overwrites whatever is there*, just as if you copied one physical tape to another. If necessary, clips already on the Timeline are split and replaced.

FIGURE 4-19
Three-point editing

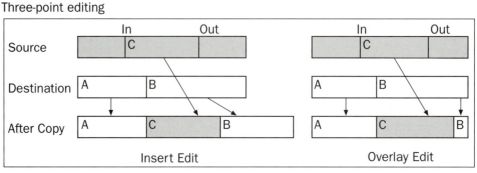

STEP-BY-STEP 4.9

1. In the **Utah1** file, select the **waterfall** clip and delete it by clicking **Edit** on the menu bar, and then **Clear**. You will put this clip back in using the three-point editing technique.

2. Select the **waterfall** clip in the Project window and drag it to the Source view of the Monitor window. Notice that the In and Out points remain at their original settings (In: 12 seconds; Out: 17 seconds).

3. To establish the destination for the three-point edit, click the Set Location marker in the Program view of the Monitor window and drag it to 8 seconds into the Program. You can see the edit line move on the Timeline as you move the marker in the Monitor, or you can watch the Program view update in the Monitor.

4. Click the Source view of the Monitor. Click **Clip** on the menu bar, and then click **Insert at Edit Line**, or click the **Insert** button below the Source view of the Monitor. Notice that this breaks the **river** clip into two parts and inserts the **waterfall** clip in between (see Figure 4-20).

FIGURE 4-20
Three-point editing using insertion editing

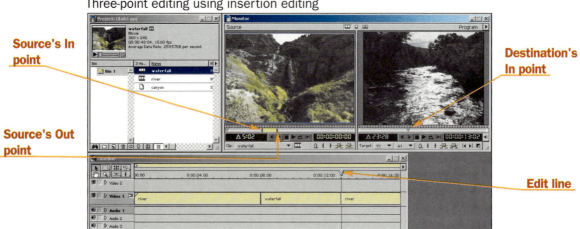

STEP-BY-STEP 4.9 Continued

5. Preview the result.

6. Click **Edit** on the menu bar, and then click **Undo Insert**.

7. Click the Source view of the Monitor. Now overlay the clip instead of inserting it by clicking **Clip** on the menu bar, and then click **Overlay at Edit Line** or the **Overlay** button in the Source view. Notice that this time, the new clip writes over the existing clips, replacing parts of both the **river** and **canyon** clips, as shown in Figure 4-21.

FIGURE 4-21
Three-point editing using overlay editing

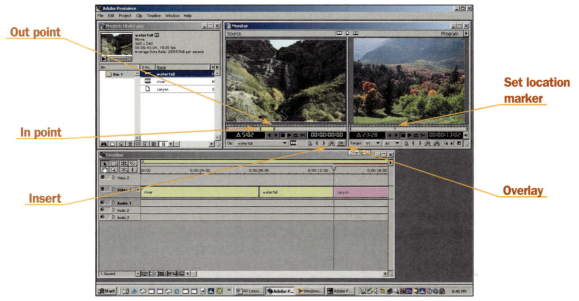

8. Preview the results.

9. Revert to the original project.

10. Leave the **Utah1** file open to use in the next exercise.

Use Timeline Markers

As you begin working with lengthier videos, it can become difficult to find a particular spot in the video—just as it can be difficult to find a specific point on a VHS tape just by fast-forwarding, stopping, and checking the tape. Most video-editing programs let you specify *timeline markers* that work like bookmarks and help you return to particular points. Using timeline markers is highly recommended for large projects.

To set a timeline marker, move the edit line in the timeline to the point where you want to add a marker. Then choose the command to set a marker. Once you have set markers, you can usually use keyboard shortcuts to jump quickly to each of them.

STEP-BY-STEP 4.10

1. In the **Utah1** file, click the **Set Location** marker in the Program view if necessary to display the edit line in the Timeline.

2. Make sure the edit line is positioned to the beginning of the Timeline. Click **Timeline** on the menu bar, click **Set Timeline Marker**, and then click **0**. You should see a portion of the 0 marker at the very beginning of the Timeline in the time ruler.

3. Move the edit line to about halfway through the **river** clip. Click **Timeline** on the menu bar, click **Set Timeline Marker**, and then click **1**. You should see the 1 marker in the time ruler. (If you can't see the **1** marker, then just move the edit line, if necessary.)

4. Move the edit line to the start of the **canyon** clip. Click **Timeline** on the menu bar, click **Set Timeline Marker**, and then click **2**. The 2 marker displays on the time ruler (see Figure 4-22).

FIGURE 4-22
Setting a timeline marker

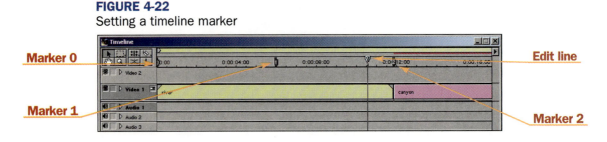

5. Press **Shift + 0** to go to marker 0 at the start of the Timeline.

6. Press **Shift + 1** to go to marker 1 in the middle of the **river** clip.

7. Press Shift + 2 to go to marker 2 at the start of the **canyon** clip.

8. Revert to the original project. Close the **Utah1** file. Close Adobe Premiere.

SUMMARY

In this lesson, you learned:

- Digital video does not store text, shapes, or other components directly. The video is stored as a sequence of frames, each of which is a separate bitmapped image.

- Because each frame is a complete image, and because there may be 10 to 30 frames appearing every second, video files are often very large and usually require compression. Video compression takes advantage of the similarity between frames by encoding each frame based on the previous one.

- Video files can also include audio tracks, which are also usually compressed.

- When the video includes text, shapes, pictures, or pieces of other video, that data must be rendered into a new sequence of frames. Rendering occurs when you preview the video or export it as a movie.

- Video-editing programs usually are based on "projects," as text programs are based on "documents." A video project contains all the pieces that go into the video, all the compression and file-handling settings, and a record of all the editing operations needed to create the video.

- A video is constructed of a number of source clips—individual video files or still images—that go into the final video production. These sources are copied, not modified, when you use them as part of a larger video project.

- Source clips can either be captured from external sources, such as a digital video camera, or imported from other data files already on your computer.

- Central to most video-editing programs is the idea of a timeline: a sequence of source clips or parts of source clips arranged in sequence.

- To see the result of the sequence of clips on the timeline, you can at any time preview the result. It may sometimes take time to build the preview if the clips must be rendered.

- You determine the part of a clip used on the timeline and in the final video by specifying In and Out points.

- After placing clips in sequence on the timeline, you can edit the result by rearranging them, adjusting their In and Out points, changing their speed and duration, cropping them, and inserting or overlaying new clips.

VOCABULARY *Review*

Define the following terms:

Analog	Digital video (DV) format	Overlay edit
Capture	IEEE 1394	Rendering
Clip	In point	Source video
Codec	Insertion edit	Three-point editing
Digital	Keyframes	Timeline
Digital video	Out point	Timeline marker

REVIEW *Questions*

TRUE / FALSE

Circle T if the statement is true and F if the statement is false.

T   F   **1.** Video-editing programs work only with digital, not analog, data.

T   F   **2.** Keyframes introduce new text or shapes that are used in later frames.

T   F   **3.** The term *codec* means "code component."

T   F   **4.** Source clips are copied, not changed, when you use them.

T   F   **5.** Previewing your video may mean waiting for your program to render the frames.

FILL IN THE BLANK

Complete the following sentences by writing the correct word or words in the blanks provided.

1. You can _____ video from external sources such as cameras or tape decks.

2. You can _____ video or still images already on your computer.

3. A video is created from a number of _____ clips.

4. The start of the segment you want to copy from a clip is called the _____.

5. The end of the segment you want to copy from a clip is called the _____.

6. The _____ stores the clips in the order you want to display them.

7. The term *codec* stands for _____ / _____.

8. _____ is the process of turning all the text, shapes, images, and pieces of video in your project into a sequence of bitmapped frames.

9. Most video frames are compressed by encoding them based on the previous frame, but _____ are encoded independently of other frames.

10. Video from VHS tapes can be captured by using a(n) _____ to _____ converter.

MULTIPLE CHOICE

Select the best response for the following statements.

1. What kinds of data can you work with in a video-editing program?
   A. Analog.
   B. Digital.
   C. Both of the above.
   D. None of the above.

2. Most video cameras connect to your computer using a connection based on which standard?
   A. NTSC.
   B. PAL.
   C. IEEE 1394.
   D. None of the above.

3. In which of these Adobe Premiere windows do you put the pieces of your video together?
   A. Project window.
   B. Monitor window.
   C. Timeline window.
   D. None of the above.

4. Which of these does *not* require your video to be rendered?
   A. Previewing your video.
   B. Exporting your video.
   C. Saving your project.
   D. All of the above require rendering.

5. Which of these points do you usually not have to specify during a three-point edit?
   A. The source's In point.
   B. The source's Out point.
   C. The destination's In point.
   D. The destination's Out point.

PROJECTS

⍦ANS PROJECT 4-1

You are a freelance video editor. You have been contracted by a client named Great Outdoors Travel to create a video to promote tourism in Utah. They have some raw video footage and still images of Utah. You will need to import the video, place video clips and still images onto the Timeline, and edit the clips and images. You will also need to add a company logo animation created in Flash to the video. The video must be no more than 40 seconds in length.

1. Launch Adobe Premiere.

2. Create a new project file and set it to Multimedia QuickTime.

3. Save the project file as **Great Outdoors Promo.**

4. Import the following data files from the Project 4-1 folder in the data files into your project file: **AV Project 4-1a.jpg** through **AV Project 4-1o.jpg, Outdoors QT.mov, AV Project 4-1p.mov,** and **AV Project 4-1q.mov. Hint:** Instead of importing each file individually as you have learned, you can import the entire folder into your project file by clicking **File** on the menu bar, clicking **Import,** and then clicking **Folder** instead of File. To expand the folder in the Premiere Project window, double-click it.

5. Key a descriptive clip name alias for each clip in your project file to make working with the clips easier. Choose clip names based on what you can see in each image. Remember, you can enlarge the images by double-clicking them in the Project window.

6. Select any seven still clips and move them to the Timeline in any order.

7. Identify a segment of either the waterfall or the river movie and move that segment to the Timeline.

8. Set up Timeline markers for each clip.

9. Rearrange the clips so they tell a story of exciting things to do in Utah. (You will be creating a written script of this video in your teamwork project.) Make sure the Great Outdoors animation is at the beginning of the Timeline. Delete any unwanted clips. Remove any gaps between clips.

10. Preview your video. **Note:** The animation **Outdoors QT.mov** was created in Macromedia Flash and exported as a QuickTime file. Premier can import the file and export it as part of your final video (more on this in Lesson 6), but because of the differences between Flash animations and bitmapped video, Premier may not be able to display this clip when you preview your video.

11. Change the speed on one clip and change the duration of another clip.

12. To shorten your movie to 40 seconds, try any of the following editing techniques:
   A. Use the Edge Trim tool to lengthen one clip and to shorten another clip. Do not adjust the length of the company logo animation.
   B. Cut one clip and delete the unwanted piece. Adjust the positions of the subsequent clips.

13. Using three-point editing, add a new movie clip to the Timeline by using either an insertion edit or an overlay edit.

14. Preview your video.

15. When you are satisfied with the movie, save changes and close the **Great Outdoors Promo** file. Close Premiere.

PROJECT 4-2

You are the owner of a video production company. Your company is small but growing. It specializes in video creation, editing, and production of weddings and special family or school events. You have been hired to videotape and photograph a school event. You will need to capture this video into a video-editing program, such as Adobe Premiere. Create a project file and import video clips and still images. Use the Timeline to rearrange the clips to tell a story. You should preview your video as you create it. The length of the video should be no more than 30 minutes, so you may need to change the speed and duration of your clips or shorten or lengthen a clip using the tools in your video-editing program. You may want to use the three-point editing method to edit clips. Save the movie under the name of your client.

SCANS WEB PROJECT

Search the Web for copyright laws and issues relating to the use of digital and video information obtained from the Internet. Possible key words to use for your search are *copyright video, royalty-free video, ethics video technology, fair use video,* and *copyright Internet video.* Write a report on your findings about the copyright laws and rules governing use of video information obtained from the Internet. Make sure you cite your sources. Submit your report to your instructor. If your school has a Web site, you may also want to post your information there.

TEAMWORK PROJECT

Working in groups of 3 or 4, write a script for the video created in Project 4-1. You will use this script in Lesson 5 to create a sound file to add to your video. Print out the script and rehearse it with the video. Adjust speed and duration of the clips as well as their order so they fit with the script. Submit your script to your instructor.

CRITICAL*Thinking*

 ## ACTIVITY 4-1

Research the impact of video technology on American society from various perspectives: economic, ethical, political, familial, and social. Use the Internet to find sources such as the technology sections of online news sites, such as CNN, MSNBC, ABC, and CBS. Make a list of questions to use for your research. Write a report of your findings.

ACTIVITY 4-2

Compare the similarities and differences between iMovie or Movie Maker and Adobe Premiere. You can investigate these programs on the Web or find information in user's guides. Identify what you like or dislike about each software program. Write a report on your findings and provide a recommendation for your instructor.

ENHANCING VIDEO

VOCABULARY

A/B roll

Audio effects

Crawling text

Cross dissolve

End title

Opening title

Rolling text

Title

Transition

Video effects

From Lesson 4, you should know how to set up a video project, capture or import source clips, put them together on the timeline, edit which parts are used, and preview your video. Now you're ready to start applying video effects, adding transitions between your clips, adding titles like those you see at the beginning and end of commercial movies, and adding your own soundtrack.

Add Effects

The first thing we'll do is add *video effects*, which change the way a particular clip is displayed. Adding effects is different from adding the special effects such as those you see in movies, which usually involves building and photographing models or using computer-generated imagery. The effects we apply don't add new content to the video, but rather change or enhance how it is rendered. These effects are like many of the filters you may find in Adobe Photoshop or other image-editing programs; the difference is that these effects are applied to each frame of the video clip instead of to a single image. These include adjusting the brightness and contrast of the video, blurring or sharpening it, distorting the spatial presentation of the video, stylizing it by enhancing edges, producing motion effects equivalent to moving the camera, and many more.

Hot Tip

Adobe Premiere has a companion product called Adobe After Effects that offers a much wider range of video effects for the serious video editor. Other companies offer plug-ins for Premiere that also add new effects.

Remember from the last lesson that your video-editing program doesn't really change the source clips. It just stores instructions for how to render and put them together into the final video. The same is true when applying effects. The source clips aren't changed. Instead, you specify that an effect is to be applied to a clip when it is rendered. You can apply more than one effect; this is similar to layering your effects on top of the original clip, as illustrated in Figure 5-1. First one effect is applied to the original clip; then a second effect is applied to the result of that one, and so on until all the effects you specify for a particular clip are applied.

FIGURE 5-1
Video effects layering

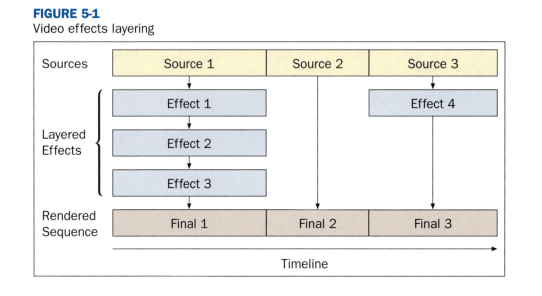

Video Effects

Adobe Premiere and similar video-editing programs usually show you in a separate window the sequence of effects applied to a particular clip. It is in this window that you usually add, reorder, or adjust the effects you want to apply. In Premiere, this is called the Effect Controls palette. As you click on different clips, the effects for that clip are displayed in the Effect Controls palette. Effects are dragged from the Transitions palette to the Effect Controls palette. As you add an effect, Premiere may ask you then to set options for the effect.

STEP-BY-STEP 5.1

1. Launch **Adobe Premiere**, and click **Cancel** to close the Load Project Settings dialog box.

2. Click **File** on the menu bar, and then click **Open**. Open **AV Step 5-1** from the data files. A Locate File dialog box may appear, asking where the source files are for this project file. Adobe searches the drive to locate these files and displays them in the list box. Select the correct filename and click the **OK** button. Repeat this for each source file.

3. Save the file as **Utah3**.

> **Note** ☑
>
> If your source files are not listed in the list box, then you need to browse to find them by clicking the down arrow located to the right of the Look in box. You may need to ask your instructor where the files are stored, especially if you are on a network. You may also have to perform this operation every time you open a project file that you have previously worked on.

STEP-BY-STEP 5.1 Continued

4. Click **Window** on the menu bar, click **Workspace**, and then click **Single-Track Editing** to make sure your windows are configured as shown in Figure 5-2. If the Effect Controls palette does not appear, click **Window** on the menu bar, and then click **Show Effect Controls**. If your Transitions palette does not appear, click Window on the menu bar, then click **Show Transitions**.

FIGURE 5-2
Single-Track Editing with Transitions palette and Effect Controls palette

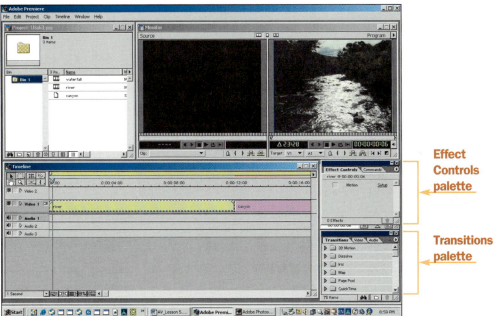

5. Position the Set Position marker to the beginning of the Timeline if it is not there already. If you do not see the marker, try scrolling around the Timeline to find it. The beginning of the **river** clip should now be displayed in the Program view of the Monitor window. Notice that the lighting is a little dark in this clip. We are going to brighten it up.

6. Click the **river** clip in the Timeline.

7. In the Transitions palette, click the **Video** tab to select video effects.

8. Click the triangle to the left of **Adjust** to expand the folder.

> **Note** ✅
>
> If your screen does not look like Figure 5-2, it may be the result of a difference in screen area between your screen and that shown in Figure 5-2. Adjust your screen area to 1024 by 768 to match Figure 5-2. To adjust your screen area in Windows 2000, select the Start menu, click Settings, and then click Control Panel. Click Display, then click the Settings tab and adjust the screen area. Or in Windows XP, click Start, then Control Panel. Click Display and find the tab where you adjust the screen area.

STEP-BY-STEP 5.1 Continued

9. Drag the **Brightness and Contrast** effect to the Effect Controls palette as shown in Figure 5-3.

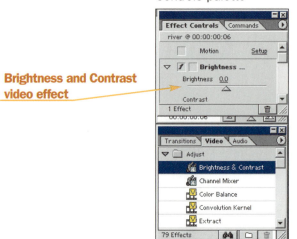

FIGURE 5-3
Brightness and Contrast effect added to the Effect
Controls palette

Brightness and Contrast
video effect

10. In the Effect Controls palette, click the triangle under Brightness and move it to the right between 45 and 50. You should see the image brighten in the Program view of the Monitor window.

11. Press **Enter** to preview the movie. This may take a little while, because the "Brightness and Contrast" effect must now be applied to every frame of the **river** clip. When the preview plays, notice that the entire **river** clip is now brighter.

Note ✅

The range of your brightness adjustment may depend on your monitor and system. You may have to set the brightness lower or higher than the amount specified here. The objective is to brighten the clip so it isn't so dark, but not to make it look washed out.

12. Save changes and leave the **Utah3** file open to use in the next exercise.

Still Image Effects

Not only can you apply visual effects to video clips, but you can apply them to still images as well. Perhaps the most common visual effect to apply to a still image is to pan through the image (move side to side) or zoom in or out of it as illustrated in Figure 5-4. The objective is to show only part of the image at any time instead of the entire image. By changing which part of the image is displayed in each frame, these effects give the image a dynamic, moving-picture quality so it has greater impact than a static picture.

FIGURE 5-4
Motion effects in a still image

Adding a motion effect is so common for still images that Adobe Premiere automatically includes a motion effect control for you in the Effect Controls palette for still images. You still have to activate the effect and edit the settings to specify how you want to move through the image.

S TEP-BY-STEP 5.2

1. The **Utah3** file should be open in Premiere. Save this file as **Utah4**. You may receive a message asking if you want to make copies of preview files. Click the **Yes** button.

2. Click the **canyon** still image clip on the Timeline. Notice the message *Edit line is outside of clip* appears along the top of the Effect Controls palette.

3. Position the Set Position marker to somewhere within the **canyon** still image clip. The canyon image should now be displayed in the Program view of the Monitor, and the message in the Effect Controls palette goes away.

STEP-BY-STEP 5.2 Continued

4. Click the check box next to the Motion effect already in the Effect Controls palette. The Motion Settings dialog box appears, as shown in Figure 5-5.

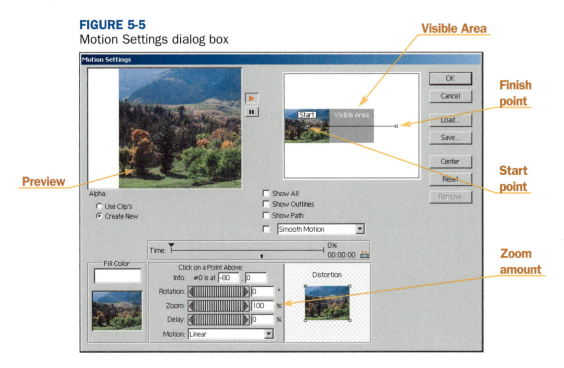

FIGURE 5-5
Motion Settings dialog box

5. Click the **Start** point, and then click the **Center** button. The image for the Start should now be centered in the Visible Area.

6. Click the **Finish** point, and then click the **Center** button. The image for the Finish should now also be centered in the Visible Area.

7. Key **200** for the zoom amount for the Finish point. The image for the Finish should now be twice its original size, and the preview for the motion effect should show a zoom from 100% to 200% magnification.

8. Click the **OK** button to close the Motion Settings dialog box.

9. Press **Enter** to preview the movie. This may again take a little while because the zoom-in effect for the canyon image must now be rendered frame-by-frame. Notice that in the preview, the canyon image clip is displayed with a zooming-in effect instead of as a single, unchanging image.

10. Save changes and leave the **Utah4** file open to use in the next exercise.

Add Transitions

Y̲ou've probably noticed when you preview your video that as soon as one clip ends and another starts, the video switches immediately from one clip to the next. This gives the video a choppy feel that may be great for an action movie, but not for animations and nature movies. Adding a *transition* helps give the video a smoother flow from one clip to the next.

Transitions involve showing the last part of one clip while at the same time beginning the next. The most common transition is a *cross dissolve* (fading out the previous clip while fading in the next one), and most video-editing programs use this as the default if you add a transition. But there are many other transitions you can apply. You may want to have one clip slide off one side of the screen while another one slides in from the other side. You may want to give the appearance of "peeling away" one video much as you'd turn the page of a book to reveal another page underneath. There are

> **Note** ✅
>
> Transitions are a great way to enhance your video and give it a more professional appearance, but be careful when adding them. It's easy to overdo it and have the effects draw too much attention to themselves and away from the video content.

many possibilities for transitions, and the best way to become familiar with your video-editing program's capabilities is to simply experiment and try them for yourself. Add different types of transitions to see how each works.

Because transitions involve overlapping clips, some video-editing programs such as Premiere allow you to view your timeline as two (or more) video tracks instead of just the single one we've been using so far. As with many digital video-editing techniques, it's useful to think about how this would work with physical tapes. If you want to do transitions, you need two tape players (call them Player A and Player B). As one clip nears completion on Player A, you start up Player B and mix the two as desired to produce the transition. Then you shut off Player A when the first clip ends and keep running Player B. While the second tape is playing on Player B, you can load another tape into Player A and have it ready to transition back. You can then go back and forth, switching between the two tapes as often as needed. Professional editors call this an *A/B roll*. Displaying this process graphically in a timeline may look like Figure 5-6.

FIGURE 5-6
A/B roll editing in Adobe Premiere

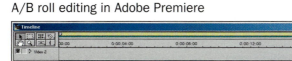

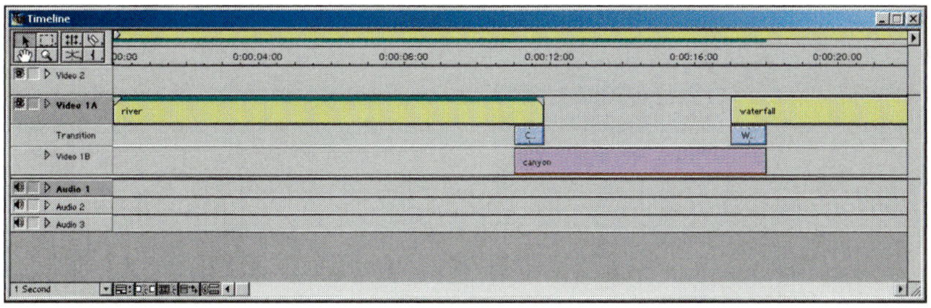

When working with A/B roll editing in a timeline, you need to make sure the clips on the A/B tracks overlap enough to produce a useful transition. The amount of overlap determines the duration of the transition. This means that when you capture, import, or select portions of clips, you should make sure to include enough material on each end for the transition.

To set up transitions in an A/B editing environment, alternate the clips between the A and B tracks. Adjust the positions of the clips on the timelines so the alternating tracks overlap in time at the ends of the clips. You then specify what kind of transition to use between the two clips.

S TEP-BY-STEP 5.3

1. The **Utah4** file should be open in Premiere. Save this file as **Utah5**. You may receive a message asking if you want to make copies of preview files. Click the **Yes** button.

2. Click **Window** on the menu bar, click **Workspace**, and then click **A/B Editing** to make sure your windows are configured as shown in Figure 5-7. Transitions can be added in either the A/B Editing or Single-Track Editing workspaces. The display in the A/B Editing workspace is a little easier to understand visually, so we use that.

FIGURE 5-7
A/B Editing configuration

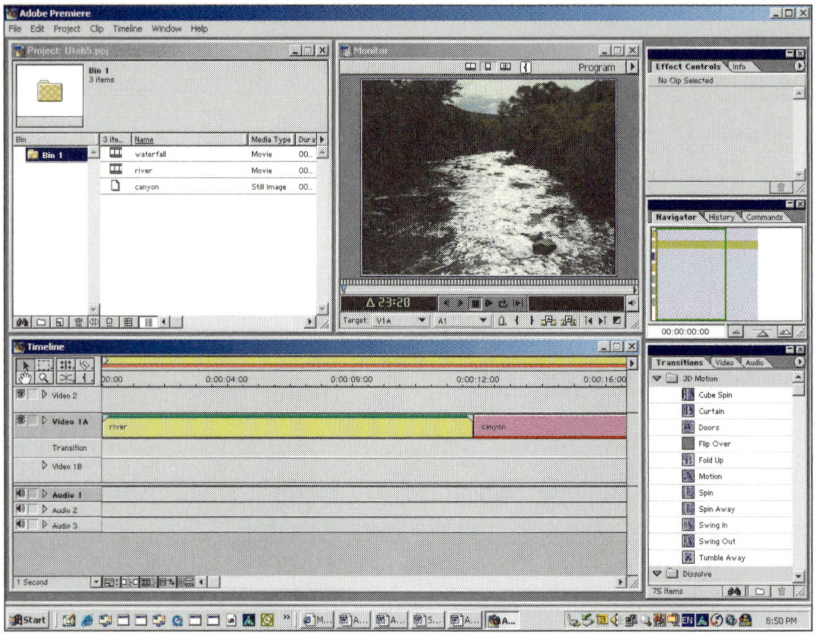

3. Click the **canyon** clip and drag it from the Video 1A track to the Video 1B track.

4. Drag the **canyon** clip on the Video 1B track so it starts at approximately 00:00:11:00 instead of 00:00:13:00.

5. Drag the **waterfall** clip on the Video 1A track so that it starts at approximately 00:00:17:00 instead of 00:00:19:00.

6. Press **Enter** to preview the movie. Notice that the clips on both tracks are played, but when there are clips on both tracks simultaneously, the clips from the Video 1A track are played instead of those on the Video 1B track, without transitions between clips.

7. Click the **Transitions** tab in the Transitions palette.

8. Click the triangle next to the Dissolve transitions.

9. Drag the **Cross Dissolve** transition to the **Transition** track of the Timeline in the space between the start of the **canyon** clip and the end of the **river** clip. Notice that the duration of the transition automatically becomes the same as the duration of the overlap between the clips.

STEP-BY-STEP 5.3 Continued

10. Press **Enter** to preview the movie.

11. Click the triangle next to the Dissolve transitions to collapse the list, and then scroll down in the Transitions palette to locate the Wipe transitions. Click the triangle next to the Wipe transitions. Scroll down the list until you see the Wipe transition.

12. Drag the **Wipe** transition to the **Transition** track of the Timeline in the space between the start of the **waterfall** clip and the end of the **canyon** clip. Your Timeline should now look like the one shown earlier in Figure 5-6.

13. Press **Enter** to preview the movie.

14. Save changes and leave the **Utah5** file open to use in the next exercise.

There are many other transitions besides the two used here. Experiment with the other transitions by dragging them from the Transitions window and dropping them onto the transitions already on the Timeline. Preview the results as usual.

Add Titles

When you go to the movies, you're probably accustomed to seeing some sort of text introducing the title of the movie and perhaps the major stars in it. At the end, you usually see a list of credits for those who worked on the movie. These are known as *titles*. The text at the beginning is known as an *opening title*, and the credits at the end are known as *end titles* or end credits. Of course, you're not limited to putting titles only at the beginning and end. You can insert them wherever you need to in your program to convey information (introducing a new sequence, subtitles, and so on).

The title-building functions in most video-editing programs are adequate but sometimes limited. If you find yourself wanting to do something more elaborate than what is offered by your program, you can use another program to build your title, and then import it into your video-editing program just as you would other clips. You could use your favorite drawing program to build a still image, or you can use one of many programs designed just for creating titles.

Create an Opening Title

The tools for creating titles usually work like those you find in simple drawing packages. You can place text, lines, shapes, logos, or other artwork in your titles. You can create colored backgrounds for your titles, or you can superimpose the title over the video content.

Once created, titles usually work just like other clips. They can be added, deleted, rearranged, and trimmed. You can apply effects or transitions between them as needed.

STEP-BY-STEP 5.4

1. The **Utah5** file should be open in Premiere. Save this file as **Utah6**. You may receive a message asking if you want to make copies of preview files. Click the **Yes** button.

2. Click **File** on the menu bar, click **New**, and then click **Title**. This opens a new window called Adobe Title Designer, as shown in Figure 5-8. The clip in the window in Figure 5-8 may not match the clip in your window, but it is not important to this exercise.

FIGURE 5-8
Adobe Title Designer window

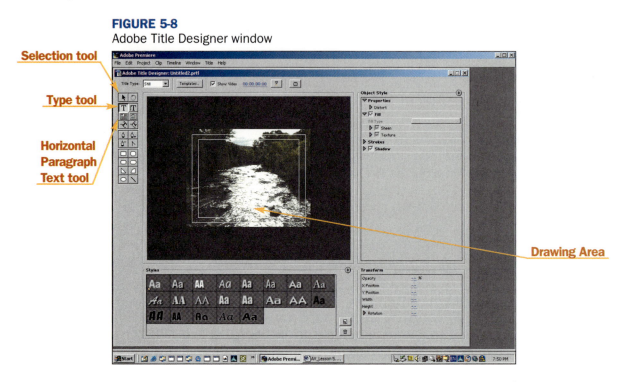

3. Click the **Type** tool to select it if necessary. Click inside the drawing area to place a text insertion point.

4. Key **Travel Utah!** to create the title for the movie.

5. Click the **Selection** tool (arrow). The title should be selected.

6. Click **Title** on the menu bar, click **Font**, click **Arial Black**, and then click **Italic**.

7. Click **Title** on the menu bar, click **Size**, and then click **Other**. Select the current size, key **36**, and then click the **OK** button.

8. Click **Title** on the menu bar, click **Position**, and then click **Vertical Center**. Click **Title** on the menu bar, click **Position**, and then click **Horizontal Center**.

9. Click **File** on the menu bar, and then click **Save As**. Navigate to the location where you saved your movie file. Key **Utah Title** as the filename, and then click the **Save** button.

10. Close the Title Designer window. Notice that the title **Utah Title** shows up as a clip in the Project window.

STEP-BY-STEP 5.4 Continued

11. Drag the **Utah Title** clip to the beginning of the Timeline on the Video 1A track. Drag it slightly to the left of the **river** clip, until the **river** clip turns blue. Everything else on the Timeline shifts to make room for the additional clip.

12. Press **Enter** to preview the movie including the new opening title.

13. Save changes and leave the **Utah6** file open to use in the next exercise.

Create End Titles

Some programs allow you to do simple animation of the text or other parts of the title. One of the most common forms of animated text is a *rolling text* similar to titles you usually see at the end of a movie. For rolling titles, you enter multiple lines of text that are smoothly scrolled through from start to finish. You can also create *crawling text*, which is a single line of text that moves from start to finish sideways across the screen.

STEP-BY-STEP 5.5

1. The **Utah6** file should be open in Premiere. Save this file as **Utah7**. You may receive a message asking if you want to make copies of preview files. Click the **Yes** button.

2. Click **File** on the menu bar, click **New**, and then click **Title**. This should again open a new window for creating titles.

3. Click the **Title Type** drop-down menu in the upper-left corner of the window, and then click **Roll**.

4. Click the **Horizontal Paragraph Text** tool in the tool palette. Click the upper-left corner inside the double-border line area and drag to the lower-right corner inside the double-border line area.

5. Click **Title** on the menu bar, click **Type Alignment**, and then click **Center** to center all the text in the rolling text area.

6. Click **Title** on the menu bar, click **Size**, and then click **Other**. Select the current size, key **24**, and then click the **OK** button.

7. Click **Title** on the menu bar, click **Font**, click **Arial Black**, and then click **Regular** to format the text.

8. Key the following text, pressing **Enter** after each word: **This movie was created by**. Press **Enter** after the last word, then key your name and press **Enter**.

STEP-BY-STEP 5.5 Continued

9. Click **Title** on the menu bar, and then click **Roll/Crawl Options**. The Roll/Crawl Options dialog box appears as shown in Figure 5-9.

FIGURE 5-9
Roll/Crawl Options dialog box

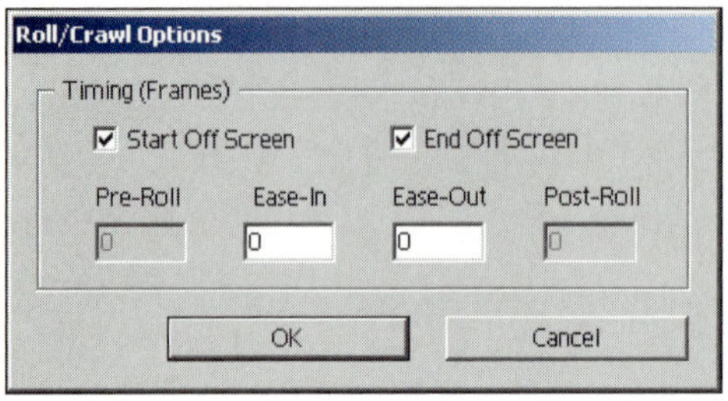

10. Click the **Start Off Screen** and **End Off Screen** check boxes. Click the **OK** button.

11. Click **File** on the menu bar, and then click **Save As**. Navigate to the location where you saved your movie file. Key **Utah end credits** as the filename, then click the **Save** button. Close the Title Designer window. The **Utah end credits** clip should now appear in the Project window.

12. Drag the **Utah end credits** clip to the Video 1A track right after the **waterfall** clip on the Timeline. Press **Enter** to preview your movie. Notice how the credits roll by at the end.

13. The default 5-second duration for the title clip is a little too fast for the rolling text. Click on the **Utah end credits** clip on the Timeline.

14. Click **Clip** on the menu bar, and then click **Duration**. Select the current duration if necessary, key **00:00:10:00** (10 seconds), and then click the **OK** button. Preview your clip and see how the text rolls by slower for the end credits.

15. Save changes and leave the **Utah7** file open to use in the next exercise.

The titles you've created here are very simple, but the drawing tools in the movie titles editing window enable you to add more text, shapes, colored backgrounds and gradient fills, and provide several other tools that you find in drawing packages. Again, if you really want to make an elaborate title, you can also use your favorite drawing program to make an image, and then import it just as you would any still image clip.

Add Audio

In addition to the video tracks, most video-editing programs can also handle audio tracks. These may include an audio track that was part of the originally captured video or sounds, music, or a voice-over that you add. When you're setting up the project, you need to specify not only the video settings but also the audio ones. These include the samples per second, the number of bits per sample, and the type of compression to use. When choosing the audio settings, think about how you plan to use audio. Speech doesn't need to have nearly the same quality as music, for example.

According to copyright law, you can use sounds from CDs or other professional sources only for personal use. If you want to publish a commercial video on your Web site or create a professional video for resale, you must use original recordings or obtain permission to use music from its creator and publisher.

Although video-editing programs have tools for capturing, importing, and editing audio, these tools usually aren't as powerful as those in programs designed specifically for sound editing. If you are serious about sound editing, you should probably look into using one of these programs.

Import an Audio Track

The process of importing an already-recorded sound file is the same as importing any other file. You import the sound file as a new source, and then you place it on the timeline with your video clips. You can add, delete, move, and trim sound file clips just like you do other clips. Just as you can apply video effects to video clips or still image clips, you can also apply *audio effects* to audio clips using the same process you learned earlier in the *Add Effects* section of this lesson.

Some video-editing programs can handle sound files only in particular formats. If you have a sound file that your video-editing program can't import, there are many third-party tools for converting sound files into different formats.

> **Extra for Experts**
>
> Audio content also takes a lot of data and requires compression. CDs use 41,000 samples per second (Hz) and 16-bit stereo (2 16-bit samples at a time). For one minute, that is $41,000 \times 16 \times 2 \times 60 = 78,720,000$ bits. That's more than 9 MB for one minute of CD-quality music. Audio CDs hold 74 minutes, or almost 800 MB. You can get a reasonable quality voice recording with just 8,000 samples per second and 8-bit mono. That's only $8,000 \times 8 \times 1 \times 60 = 3,840,000$ bits or 480,000 bytes.

S TEP-BY-STEP 5.6

In this exercise, you add music from a CD to your video. Remember that this is for personal use only. Before you can import an audio track into Premiere, you need to convert it into a file format supported by Premiere such as WAV or AIFF. To do this, you need a third-party conversion program such as WaveStudio, Sound Forge, or Audio Grabber. If you do not have one of these programs or any other way of converting CD tracks to WAV or AIFF files, you can skip this exercise.

1. Once a CD track has been converted into either a WAV or AIFF file format, click **File** on the menu bar, click **Import**, and then click **File**. Navigate to the location of the WAV or AIFF file. Select the file, and then click the **Open** button.

2. The musical track should now appear in the Project window just like your video, image, and title clips. Save the **Utah7** file as **Utah8**. You may receive a message asking if you want to make copies of preview files. Click the **Yes** button.

3. Drag the clip to the Audio 1 track of the Timeline.

4. Press **Enter** to preview your video with the accompanying audio track.

5. If your audio track is longer than the movie, you probably noticed that it continued to play after the video portion ended. Use the Razor tool to cut the audio track at the end of the end credits and delete the segment that comes after the video portion ends.

STEP-BY-STEP 5.6 Continued

6. If necessary, press **Enter** to again preview your video and accompanying audio.

7. Save changes and close the **Utah8** file, but leave the program open to use in the next exercise.

Record Your Own Audio Track

In addition to importing digital audio files, you can also capture (record) your own sound files. The process for capturing audio is described in Lesson 2 of this unit.

STEP-BY-STEP 5.7

If you are not able to convert a CD track to WAV or AIFF, you can still record a sound file. If you need to refresh your knowledge of how to make a physical connection between your computer and sound recorder and set up a microphone, please refer to Lesson 2, *Record a Sound File* section.

1. If **Utah7** is not open in Premiere, click **File** on the menu bar, click **Open Recent Project**, and then click **Utah7** to open the project. Save this file as **Utah9**. You may receive a message asking if you want to make copies of preview files. Click the **Yes** button.

2. Click **File** on the menu bar, click **Capture**, and then click **Audio Capture**.

3. You are asked to locate the audio capture program you want to use. If you don't have a third-party audio capture program, then you can use Windows Sound Recorder, as shown in Figure 5-10. (In Windows 2000, the filename is **sndrec.exe** and is probably located under **WINNT/System 32**.)

FIGURE 5-10
Windows Sound Recorder

4. If you are using Windows Sound Recorder, click the **Record** button. Quickly switch back to Premiere and start the preview. You are trying to time your reading to match what you are viewing in the preview. Read the following text into the microphone using a pleasant, animated voice.

> **Welcome to Travel Utah! Feel the beautiful flowing waters as you travel down river in a canoe. See the Fall colors as you hike the surrounding canyons and meadows. Hear the cascading waterfalls as they run down the sheer mountainsides.**

5. Click the **Stop** button to stop the recording.

6. Click the **Seek To Start** button, then click the **Play** button to play back your recording.

STEP-BY-STEP 5.7 Continued

7. If you are not satisfied with your recording, click **Seek To Start** again, and then click **Play**.

8. When you are satisfied, save the file in Sound Recorder as **Travel Utah Sound**. Close Sound Record.

9. With Premiere still open, import the **Travel Utah Sound** file to the project file.

10. Drag **Travel Utah Sound** to the Audio 1 track on the Timeline.

11. Press **Enter** to preview the file.

12. If your audio track is longer than the movie, you probably noticed that it continued to play after the video portion ended. Use the Razor tool to cut the audio track at the end of the end credits and delete the segment that comes after the video portion ends. You can also re-record and speak more quickly if the track is too long or short.

13. If necessary, press **Enter** to preview your video and accompanying audio.

14. Save changes and close the **Utah9** file. Close Premiere.

SUMMARY

In this lesson, you learned:

- You can greatly enhance the quality of your video by adding video effects, transitions, titles, and a soundtrack.

- Just like trimming and sequencing your clips on the timeline, video effects and transitions do not change the original source clips. Instead, they can be viewed as instructions for how to process the original clips to produce the final video.

- Video effects can be used to adjust the brightness or contrast of a clip, blur it, sharpen it, stylize it, or apply other enhancements to it. These effects can be layered so one effect is applied, then another, then another, and so on.

- Transitions are applied between consecutive clips on the timeline. The clips overlap slightly so part of one clip appears while the end of the preceding one disappears.

- The style of the transition controls how the old clip disappears and the new clip appears. The most common transition is a cross dissolve, but there are many other types of transitions you can use.

- Titles are text, logos, or other artwork added to a video to convey additional information. These can include *opening titles* at the beginning of the video (usually the name of the video and other information) or *end titles* at the close of the video (usually containing credits for the work). You can also use titles at various points during the video to convey additional information, such as introducing a new segment, adding subtitles, etc.

■ You can add sound to your video by importing an existing digital audio file or by recording your own sound (such as a voice-over). These audio clips are imported and added to the timeline just like other clips. You can then apply audio effects to your sound clips just as you added video effects to your video or image clips.

■ Using effects, transitions, titles, and sound to enhance your video can give your work a polished, professional look. But don't overdo it—too much can draw attention away from your video content and make the result look cluttered and busy.

VOCABULARY *Review*

Define the following terms:

A/B roll	End title	Transition
Audio effects	Opening title	Video effects
Crawling text	Rolling text	
Cross dissolve	Title	

REVIEW *Questions*

TRUE / FALSE

Circle T if the statement is true and F if the statement is false.

T   F   **1.** You can apply more than one effect to a clip.

T   F   **2.** Each effect you apply replaces your stored clip with a new one.

T   F   **3.** You have to apply a transition between each clip and the next one.

T   F   **4.** Transitions show parts of two clips simultaneously.

T   F   **5.** Motion effects show only part of the image in each frame.

FILL IN THE BLANK

Complete the following sentences by writing the correct word or words in the blanks provided.

1. Text at the beginning of your video is called a(n) _____.

2. Credits at the end of your video are also called _____.

3. The most common kind of transition is a(n) _____.

4. Using a two-tape system to produce transitions is called _____ editing.

5. Adobe Premiere can import sound files in the _____ and _____ formats.

MULTIPLE CHOICE

Select the best response for the following questions.

1. Where can titles appear in the video?
   A. At the beginning.
   B. At the end.
   C. In the middle.
   D. All of the above.

2. Rolling text moves which way?
   A. Up or down.
   B. Left or right.
   C. Either.
   D. Neither.

3. Crawling text moves which way?
   A. Up or down.
   B. Left or right.
   C. Either.
   D. Neither.

4. Effects can be applied to which of the following kinds of clips?
   A. Video clips.
   B. Image clips.
   C. Audio clips.
   D. All of the above.

5. Audio tracks from CDs use how many samples per second?
   A. 8,000.
   B. 16,000.
   C. 22,000.
   D. 41,100.

PROJECTS

PROJECT 5-1

You will continue to work with the file you created in Project 4-1. You will add transitions, effects, and an audio track (if you have the software) to your video. You will also record the script you created in the Teamwork Project in Lesson 4 as a sound file.

1. Launch Adobe Premiere, and then open **AV Project 5-1.ppj** from the data files. Save the file as **Great Outdoors Promo 2**.

2. Make sure you are in Single-Track Editing and the Effect Controls palette is displayed.

3. Experiment with video effects. Go to the online help and search for video effects. You will find a list of all the video effects. Drag three or four effects to the Effect Controls palette and experiment.

4. Choose three video effects to add to your project. Preview your video effects.

5. Add a motion effect to one of the still images. If one of the clips seems too dark, apply the Adjust video effect to one of them.

6. Change to A/B Editing to make adding transitions easier.

7. Click the following clips and move them to the Video IB track: **horse still**, **Fall landscape still**, and **hiking path 1 still**. Make sure the clips on Video 1A overlap slightly the clips on Video 1B.

> **Note** ☑️
>
> Notice that you cannot preview the opening title, **Outdoors QT.mov**, because you created this clip in Flash and published it as a QuickTime movie. You can view it in the Source view of the Monitor and when you export the file to a movie file in Lesson 6.

8. Experiment with the different transitions. If you need help, go to online help to find a description of each transition.

9. Choose six transitions and add them to the Transition track of the Timeline: one transition from the previous clip and one transition to the next clip. Preview the file. This may take a few minutes to render.

10. Add closing credits to your project. You can choose a crawling, rolling, or still title. Experiment with font, size, alignment, and color. If necessary, adjust the duration of the clip so the closing credits can be read easily. Preview the file again.

11. If you can convert a CD audio file (.cda) to either a WAV or AIFF file or if you already have a WAV or AIFF file, add this audio file to the Audio 1 track on the Timeline.

12. Create a sound file by recording the script you created in the Lesson 4 Teamwork Project. (If you did not complete the Teamwork Project, see your instructor.) Save the sound file and import it to your project file. Add the sound file to the Audio 2 track on the Timeline.

13. Preview your video and make any adjustments for the duration or length of the clips.

14. Save changes to the **Great Outdoors Promo 2** file and close the file. Close Premiere.

PROJECT 5-2

You will continue to work with the file you created in Project 4-2. Remember, you are the owner of a video production company. It specializes in video creation and editing of weddings and special family or school events. You have been hired to videotape and photograph a school event. You now need to add titles, transitions, effects, and either an audio track or sound file to the video you created in Project 4-2. Save the file under the client name.

WEB PROJECT

Search the Internet for video production companies that include examples of their videos. Write a one- to two-page paper describing what you learned about the types of titles, transitions, or effects from at least three examples.

TEAMWORK PROJECT

Work in groups of four or five. Interview two or three business owners about developing a video for their businesses. Discuss types of things to include in a video. Bring these ideas back to your class and write a video project plan, including the types of clips, titles, effects, and transitions to use or create, and the type of audio to use, either a CD track or a sound file. Include in your plan an outline of the script. You may want to create a storyboard showing each clip with the associated effect and transition as well as the script. Submit your plan to your instructor. If possible, work with your instructor and the business owner to create the video based on your plan.

CRITICAL *Thinking*

ACTIVITY 5-1

Analyze a movie trailer and break it down into the number of clips; a description of each clip; the number of titles, transitions, and effects; the types of titles, transitions, and effects; and the number of audio tracks and sound files. Keep a record of the steps you take in carrying out Activity 5-1 and write a one-page paper on your conclusion about the approach to the task. Submit the report to your instructor.

PUBLISHING VIDEO

OBJECTIVES

Upon completion of this lesson, you should be able to:

- Publish to a movie file for distribution on the Web or a CD.
- Publish to a DVD or VCD.
- Publish to a digital videotape.
- Publish to an analog videotape.
- Publish a single frame of your video as a still image.

Estimated Time: 1.5 hours

VOCABULARY

AVI

Codec

DV

DVD

Export

MPEG

QuickTime

Streaming

SVCD

VCD

The project files you've used already are great for preparing your video, but you can't use them to distribute video to friends or customers. To do this, you must first *export* the video from your video-editing program and publish the exported video as a movie file, a DVD or other videodisc, a digital videotape, an analog videotape, or still images. Publishing to some of these types of media may require additional hardware or software.

Publish to a Movie File

To publish your entire video for use on a computer, you must first export it from your video-editing program to a movie file format. There are many such formats, but the most common are *AVI* and *QuickTime*.

- AVI is the most common type of video file format used on Windows PCs. Developed by Microsoft, AVI stands for Audio Video Interleave. AVI files usually end in an .avi extension. Although most common on PCs, AVI files can be played on other computer platforms as well.

- QuickTime is a cross-platform video file format developed by Apple Computer. QuickTime movies usually end with a .mov extension. Although most commonly used on Apple Macintosh systems, QuickTime movies can also be played on other types of computers. This cross-platform compatibility makes QuickTime movies the most popular choice for CD-ROMs.

Video can also be distributed in other types of file formats, including **MPEG** (found on DVDs and other video discs), RealMedia (used for streaming video), and Windows Media Format (a multimedia file format from Microsoft).

Remember from Lesson 4, *Working with Video*, that video is usually compressed using a *codec* (compressor/decompressor). Some of the file formats listed above use just one particular compression technique, but others employ a plug-in structure and codecs to allow various kinds of compression. Different codecs are better for certain types of video and certain types of computers. For example, the Animation codec works well for 2-D animations but not for movies from video cameras. The Motion JPEG codecs work well for movies and are compatible with many systems, but they don't compress as well as a number of more recently developed codecs. The Sorenson 3 video codec produces excellent compression, but its computational requirements make it impractical for many lower-end systems. You should also be aware that not all codecs work with all file formats and computer systems.

Exporting a movie file causes the contents of the timeline to be rendered, then compressed, and then written to a file. Depending on the size of each frame, the number of frames per second, the length of the video, and the type of compression used, this may take a while—often several times the duration of the video itself.

In Lesson 3, *Publishing an Animation*, you learned how video can be transferred to a computer either by downloading the entire file before playing it or by *streaming* it (watching it while downloading). It does not matter in most video-editing programs whether you intend to download the entire file, stream it, or distribute it on a CD-ROM. The process is the same: You export the movie file from your video-editing program, and then you use other software or hardware options to distribute the file.

To distribute a file over the Web by requiring the user to download the entire file first, export the file from Premiere using one of the more common file formats such as AVI or QuickTime. Prepare a Web page that contains a description of the movie and a link to the exported movie file, and place both of these on a *Web server* (a computer on the Internet configured to distribute Web pages).

Most video-editing programs cannot directly produce streaming video. To distribute a file over the Internet using streaming,

■ Export the file in a streaming format using a special plug-in.

■ Export the entire file using one of the standard file formats, and then use a separate program to convert the video into a streaming format.

Once you have the file in a streaming format, you need to distribute it using a *streaming video server* (a computer on the Internet configured to deliver video files by streaming them to your computer instead of through normal downloading).

To distribute your file on a CD-ROM, export the file to one of the more common file formats, and then prepare and record the CD-ROM as you normally would. To your computer and the CD-ROM, your video file is just another data file. We discuss preparing your video for publication on a specialized video disc, such as a DVD or VCD, later in this lesson.

Export Your Video from Premiere

In this first exercise, you export your movie from Premiere. This produces a file that no longer requires Premiere and can be played in a video-player program such as Windows Media Player or QuickTime Player.

STEP-BY-STEP 6.1

1. Launch Premiere. Open **AV Step 6-1** from your data files. Skip previews and locate source clips as necessary to display the project in Premiere.

2. Click **File** on the menu bar, click **Export Timeline**, and then click **Movie**. The **Export Movie** dialog box opens. Notice the lower-left part of the dialog box displays the settings for the exported video file. In the future, if you want to use these settings, you can skip steps 3 to 13 and go straight to step 14.

Hot Tip

If you want to set the export settings before beginning the export processes, you can also get to the Export Movie Settings dialog box by clicking Project on the menu bar, clicking Settings Viewer, and then clicking the Export Settings tab.

3. Click the **Settings** button. The Export Movie Settings dialog box opens as shown in Figure 6-1.

FIGURE 6-1
Export Movie Settings dialog box

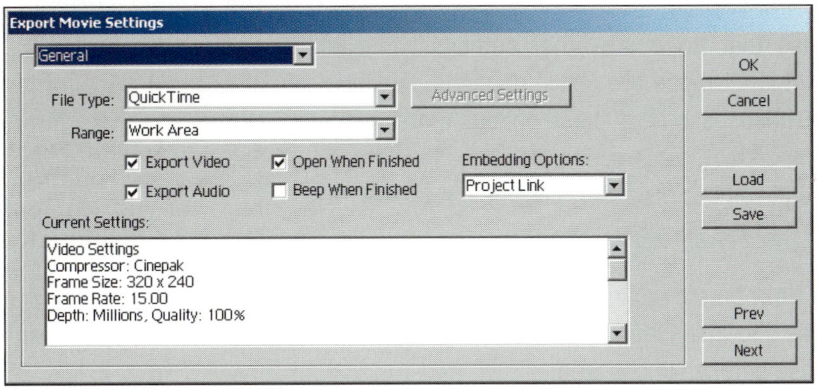

4. The Export Movie Settings dialog box displays the General settings pane. Click the **File Type** list box and then click **QuickTime** if necessary.

5. Select both the **Export Video** and **Export Audio** check boxes if necessary. Leaving one of these boxes unchecked allows you to export the movie without either audio or video. Select the **Open When Finished** check box if necessary so you can see the result of the export.

STEP-BY-STEP 6.1 Continued

6. Click the **Next** button. The Video settings pane displays as shown in Figure 6-2.

FIGURE 6-2
Video settings pane

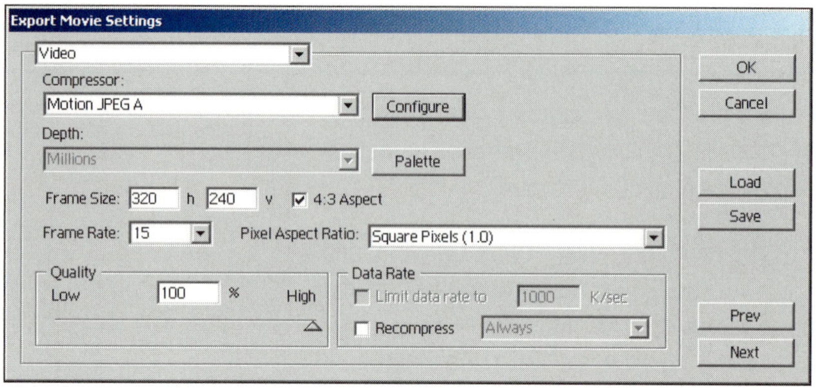

7. Click the **Compressor** list box to select which codec to be used for the exported video. For this tutorial, click **Motion JPEG A**. Notice that you can also change the frame size and frame rate for the exported video. Use the default settings shown.

8. Notice also that there are other settings you can change. Whether these are active depends on which codec you choose; some of these options aren't available for all codecs. Each codec also has specialized settings that you can access by clicking the **Configure** button next to the selected codec.

9. Click the **Next** button again. The Audio settings pane appears as shown in Figure 6-3. You can ignore the settings for video projects without audio tracks. Leave these settings unchanged.

Hot Tip

You usually want to export to a frame size and frame rate that are the same or smaller than the project settings you've used to edit the video. If you choose something larger, the rendered video often has a blocky, "pixilated" look. Remember, it's easy to reduce resolution for images and video, but it's very hard for your computer to increase resolution and make it look good.

FIGURE 6-3
Audio settings pane

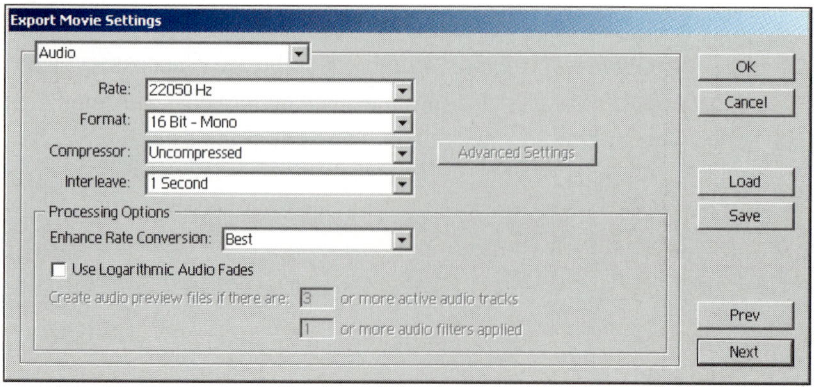

STEP-BY-STEP 6.1 Continued

10. Click the **Next** button again. The Keyframe and Rendering settings pane appears as shown in Figure 6-4. The options here allow you to control how the video is rendered, including exporting your video and audio with or without applying the effects you learned about in Lesson 5. Deselect any selected check boxes on this pane if necessary.

> **Note**
>
> For any pane in the Export Movie Settings dialog box, you can check your software program manual for an explanation of menu options. If you make changes and decide you want the default settings again, click the **Load** button.

FIGURE 6-4
Keyframe and Rendering settings pane

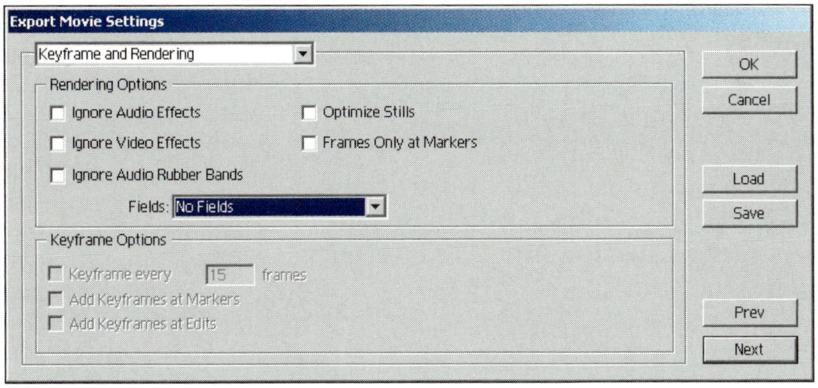

11. Click the **Next** button again. The Special Processing settings pane appears. Leave these settings unchanged.

FIGURE 6-5
Special Processing settings pane

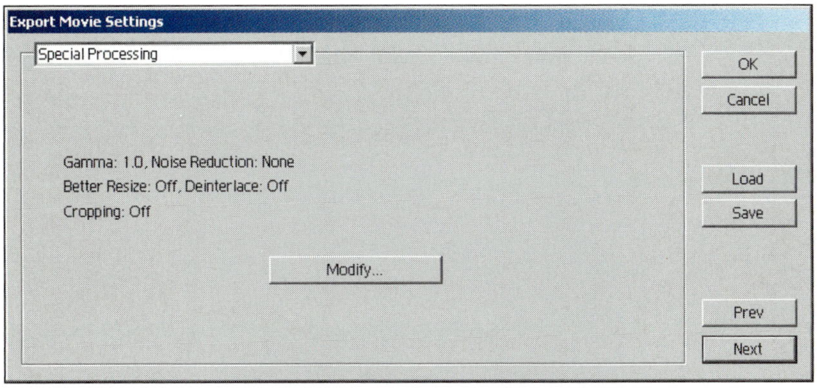

12. Click the **Next** button again. The General settings pane should appear again. You can rotate through the different settings panes using the **Next** and **Prev** buttons, or you can go right to a particular settings pane using the pane name list menu.

STEP-BY-STEP 6.1 Continued

13. Click the **OK** button. The Export Movie Settings dialog box closes and you return to the Export Movie dialog box.

14. Key the filename **Utah.mov** and navigate to the location where you want to save the file. Click the **Save** button. An Exporting dialog box appears to show you the progress of the export, and the dialog box automatically closes when the export is completed.

15. A new window opens to display the exported movie. Play the movie if you wish, and close the window when the movie is finished.

16. Leave the **AV Step 6-1** file open in Premiere to use in the next exercise.

Play Your Video in a Software Video Player

Now that you've exported your video from Premiere as a movie file, you can open it in most software video players such as Windows Media Player or the QuickTime player.

> **Hot Tip**
>
> Not all video-player programs support all file formats and codecs. If you plan to export your video for use with a specific player, you need to consider the file formats and codecs that player supports.

STEP-BY-STEP 6.2

1. Open the QuickTime player.

2. In the QuickTime player, open the file **Utah.mov** from the location where you stored it. The first frame of the movie appears as shown in Figure 6-6.

FIGURE 6-6
QuickTime player playing Utah.mov

STEP-BY-STEP 6.2 Continued

3. Click the **Play** button to view the movie.

4. Close the QuickTime player, but leave Premiere open to use in the next exercise.

Publish to a DVD or VCD

Another way to publish your video is to distribute it either on a *DVD* (Digital Video Disc, or sometimes, Digital Versatile Disc) or a *VCD* (Video CD). These discs can be played using DVD players and standard televisions.

The normal DVD disc format stores 5.2 gigabytes of data, enough for more than two hours of video. Although originally developed for distributing video (much as CDs were originally developed for audio), DVDs have commonly been used to distribute other types of data. Hence, the gradual change of terminology from Digital Video Disc to Digital *Versatile* Disc.

Frames of DVD movies are 740 × 480 pixels, and there are 29.97 frames per second. Why such a strange frame rate? DVDs are designed to work with televisions, which also display feeds at 29.97 frames per second. Each television frame takes 1/30 of a second (actually it draws all the odd lines in 1/60 of a second and all the even lines in the next 1/60 of a second), but after each half-frame, there is a very slight delay as the television's electron beam flies back from the bottom of the screen to the top. So, there are *almost*, but not quite, 30 frames per second appearing on a television screen.

VCDs are like DVDs, but the data is stored on standard CDs. Because CDs have less than one-sixth the capacity of DVDs, movies on VCDs have smaller frame sizes and lower quality than DVDs. An improved form of VCD known as *SVCD* is an attempt to improve this through better compression, but DVD quality remains significantly better. The advantage of VCDs is that they can be produced on common and less expensive CD recorders instead of on the more expensive DVD recorders. Most DVD players can also read and play VCDs.

Both DVDs and VCDs use a compression technique known as MPEG, which is one of the oldest and most popular video-compression standards. Although better techniques have been developed, MPEG continues to be widely used. VCDs use the original MPEG standard (sometimes called MPEG-1). DVDs and SVCDs use the later MPEG-2 standard.

To prepare a video for publication on a DVD or VCD, you must first export the video in MPEG format, and then use a separate program to prepare and record the DVD or VCD.

STEP-BY-STEP 6.3

1. With **AV Step 6-1** open in Premiere, click **File** on the menu bar, click **Export Timeline**, and then click **Adobe MPEG Encoder**. The Adobe MPEG Export Settings dialog box appears as shown in Figure 6-7.

FIGURE 6-7
Adobe MPEG Export Settings dialog box

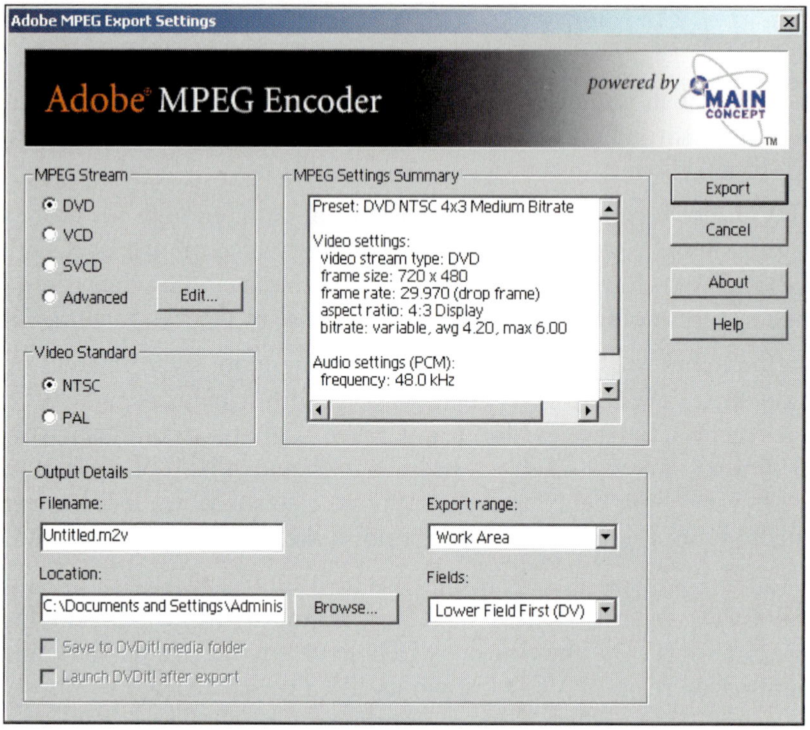

2. If necessary, click the **DVD** option for MPEG Stream and the **NTSC** option for Video Standard.

3. Key **UtahDVD** in the Filename box.

4. To the right of the Location box, click the **Browse** button to open the Output File Name dialog box. Navigate to the directory where you want to save the file. Click the **Save** button to close the Output File Name dialog box and return to the Adobe MPEG Export Settings dialog box.

5. Click the **Export** button. The Exporting dialog box appears and shows the progress of export. This process may take several minutes. When the video file is exported to MPEG, an associated WAV file called UtahDVD.wav is created.

6. Leave the **AV Step 6-1** file open to use in the next exercise.

You can now use a DVD recorder and a DVD-creation program, such as *DVDit!* (Windows) or *iDVD* (Apple), to prepare and record the DVD. Check the software manuals for these products on how to create a DVD.

Publish to a Digital Videotape

Another way to publish digital video is to write it back to a *DV* tape using a digital camcorder or a DV tape deck. In Lesson 4, you learned how to capture digital video from a digital camcorder to your computer. Now, you reverse the process. After capturing the digital video and editing it, you can write your video back to the camcorder's tape.

After recording your video to your digital camcorder, you can then connect your camcorder to a television or VCR to watch the video or copy it from digital tape (DV) to analog tape (e.g., VHS). Creating a digital videotape that contains the exported video is useful because then it can act as a master copy for making multiple analog (VHS) copies.

STEP-BY-STEP 6.4

If you do not have the necessary equipment to complete this exercise, read through these steps to understand the process.

1. To do this exercise, you need to change the project settings to work with DV. We use a copy of our current project file to do this. With **AV Step 6-1** open, click **File** on the menu bar, and then click **Save As**. Key **UtahDV** as the new project name. Navigate to the location where you are saving solution files. Then click the **Save** button.

2. Connect a digital video camera to your computer using the same process you used in Lesson 4 to capture video from the camera. This time we transfer digital video to the camera from the computer, and not the opposite. Make sure the tape in the camera is positioned to a blank part of the tape (or a part you don't mind recording over).

3. Set the digital camcorder to VTR mode (or whichever mode you use to play, rewind, and fast-forward your tapes instead of shooting new video).

4. Click **Project** on the menu bar, click **Project Settings**, and then click **General**. Click the **Playback Settings** button. The Playback Settings dialog box opens.

> **Note** ☑
>
> Playing the video on your desktop at the same time you play it (record) to an output device slows down your computer a little. If you experience pauses or delays while playing to your camera, you should deselect this option.

STEP-BY-STEP 6.4 Continued

5. Click the **Output Device** list box, and then click **Firewire**. Deselect the **Play audio on the output device only** check box, if necessary. Select the **Also play on desktop when playing to the output device** check box, if necessary.

6. Click the **OK** button to close the Playback Settings dialog box.

7. Click the **Next** button. Click the **Compressor** list box, and then click **DV/DVCPRO-NTSC** as shown in Figure 6-8. This setting tells your project to build DV data from all the clips.

FIGURE 6-8
Video settings panel in Project Settings dialog box

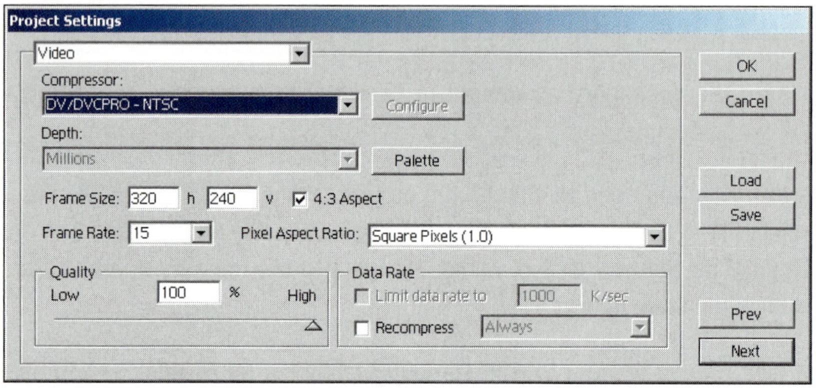

8. Click the **OK** button to close the Project Settings dialog box.

9. Press **Enter** to preview the video. This may take a few minutes, because all the previews now have to be rebuilt in the DV format. Watch your camera's viewfinder while the preview plays on your computer. The video preview should appear on both.

If your digital camcorder does not have device control, do steps 10 and 11. If your digital camcorder has device control, skip to step 12. You may have to check your camera's manual to see if it has device control, but it probably does if you have a newer model. Give it a try and see; you can always come back to this step.

10. Press **REC** on your digital camcorder to begin recording. Give it a few seconds of lead-in before you start playing the video. While the camcorder is recording, again press **Enter** to preview your video. This should again appear (and this time be recorded) on your camcorder.

STEP-BY-STEP 6.4 Continued

11. After the video finishes, again give it a few extra seconds and then press **STOP** on the camcorder to stop recording. Skip now to the end of this exercise, or try the following steps to see if your camcorder supports device control.

Steps 12 to 16 require that your camcorder have device control.

12. In Premiere, click **Edit** on the menu bar, click **Preferences**, and then click **Scratch Disks and Device Control**. The Preferences dialog box opens as shown in Figure 6-9.

FIGURE 6-9
Preferences dialog box

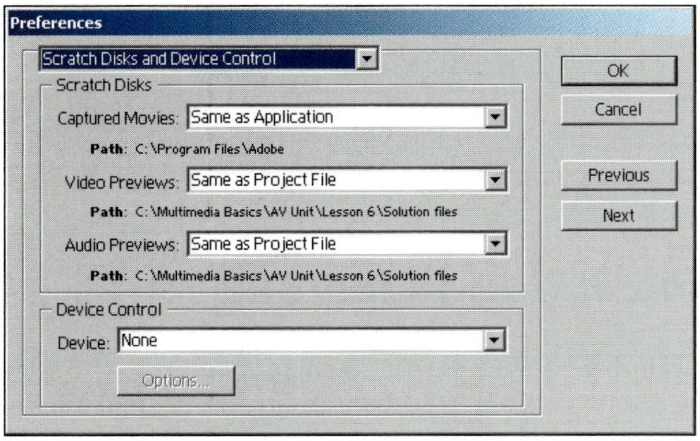

13. Under the Device Control section of the window, click the **Device** list box, and then click **DV Device Control 2.0**. The DV Device Control Options dialog box opens as shown in Figure 6-10. Click the **Device Brand** list box, and then click the brand of your camcorder. Click the **Device Type** list box, and then click the model number. If you see the word *Offline* to the right of the Check Status button, click the **Check Status** button. The computer finds the camcorder. If the displayed status does not change to Online, check your camera's connection to your computer and click **Check Status** again.

FIGURE 6-10
DV Device Control Options dialog box

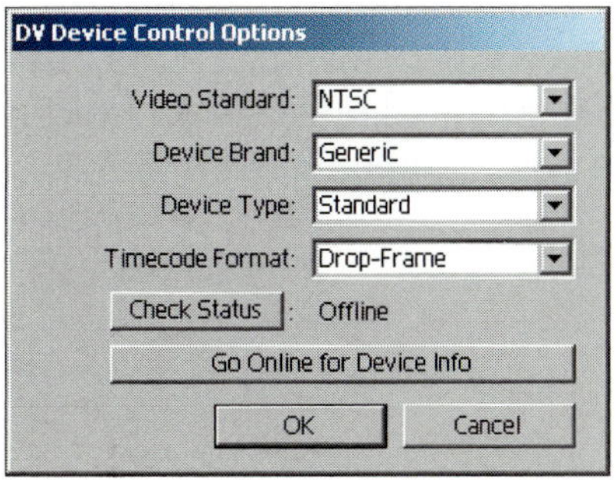

STEP-BY-STEP 6.4 Continued

14. Click the **OK** button to close the DV Device Control Options dialog box, and then click the **OK** button to close the Preferences dialog box.

15. Click **File** on the menu bar, click **Export Timeline**, and then click **Export to Tape**. The Export to Tape dialog box opens. Select the **Activate recording deck** check box if necessary. Click the **OK** button to start recording your video.

16. Premiere now uses device control to automatically start your camcorder recording. It starts playing the movie to the camcorder (and to your computer screen if you checked this option in step 5). After the video finishes, Premiere automatically stops your camcorder recording.

17. Save and close **UtahDV**, but leave Premiere open to use in the next exercise.

After you have recorded your video to your digital camcorder (either manually using steps 10 to 11 or with device control using steps 12 to 16), you can connect your camcorder to a television or VCR to watch the tape or to copy it to an analog tape format such as VHS, respectively.

Publish to an Analog Videotape

If your computer can display output to a television, you can also play your video on your computer screen and record it to a VCR. Check to see if your computer has an S-video connection, a capture card that can convert digital-to-analog as well as analog-to-digital, or some other means of connecting it to a regular television. There are also external video-conversion devices available that allow you to connect to a television through your regular monitor (VGA) port. You may have to check your computer's manual to see if there is a way to do this with your system.

If you can connect a television to your computer, you can also connect a VCR. Connect the cables so the output of the computer goes into the VCR and the output of the VCR goes into a television. Set your VCR to display and record the input from the computer. You may have to check your VCR's manual for details on how to do this.

After connecting a VCR, the process of recording your video is fairly straightforward. You start the VCR recording, start the video playing on the computer, and then stop recording when the video finishes. Many video-editing programs or software video players can display your video using the entire computer screen (perhaps blacking out the parts of the screen not used to display the video). This means that when you display and record it, you see only the video, not everything else you usually see on your computer screen.

S TEP-BY-STEP 6.5

If your computer has an analog video out port (either built-in or on a card), or you have an external device for connecting a television to your computer, use it to connect a VCR and television to your computer. The output of the computer should go to the VCR, and the output of the VCR should go to the television. You should see your computer's screen displayed on the television before proceeding.

If you do not have the necessary equipment to do this exercise, you can still read through these steps to understand the process; just ignore the instructions for starting and stopping your VCR recording.

1. In Premiere, open **AV Step 6-1** from your data files.

2. Click **File** on the menu bar, click **Export Timeline**, and then click **Print to Video**. The Print to Video dialog box opens as shown in Figure 6-11.

FIGURE 6-11
Print to Video dialog box

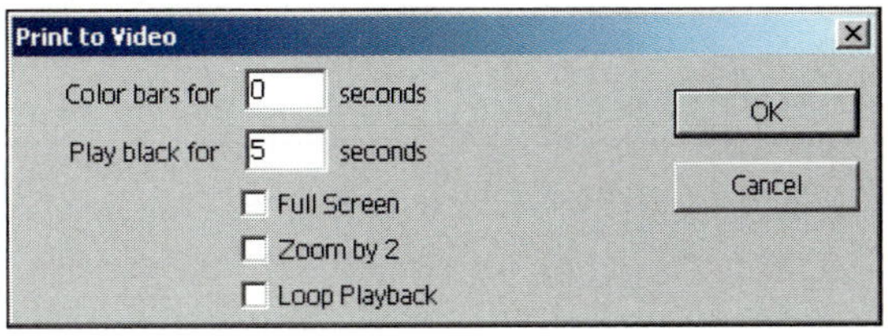

3. Key **0** in the **Color bars for ___ seconds** box, if necessary. This setting allows you to display and record color bars (like those you may sometimes see on your television) so you can later calibrate the color display on your television.

4. Key **5** in the **Play black for ___ seconds** box. This setting causes the screen to go black for a certain period of time before your video starts. This can be helpful if you want to start your video before you start the VCR.

5. Get ready to start your VCR recording. Click the **OK** button in the Print to Video dialog box. The Building Preview dialog box may appear. If so, once it completes building the preview, the video starts.

6. Both your screen and the television should go black for 5 seconds. During this time, start the VCR recording.

STEP-BY-STEP 6.5 Continued

7. After 5 seconds, your video should play on both your computer's screen and the television.

8. Once the video finishes, stop your VCR recording.

9. You can now rewind the VCR tape to the start of your video and play it on the television.

10. Leave **AV Step 6-1** open to use in the next exercise.

Publish a Single Frame of the Video as a Still Image

In Lesson 3, *Publishing an Animation*, you learned that you can publish a single frame of an animation as a still image. You can also do this with video frames, which you may want to do if you are preparing a poster, brochure, or flyer with pictures from the movie.

STEP-BY-STEP 6.6

1. In the **AV Step 6-1** file, position the edit line either in the Timeline or in the Monitor so one of the frames from the **river** clip is displayed in the Monitor.

2. Click **File** on the menu bar, click **Export Timeline**, and then click **Frame**. The Export Still Frame dialog box opens as shown in Figure 6-12. Just as in the Export Movie dialog box, the settings for the exported file should appear. In the future, if you want to use the displayed settings, you can skip steps 3 to 5.

FIGURE 6-12
Export Still Frame dialog box

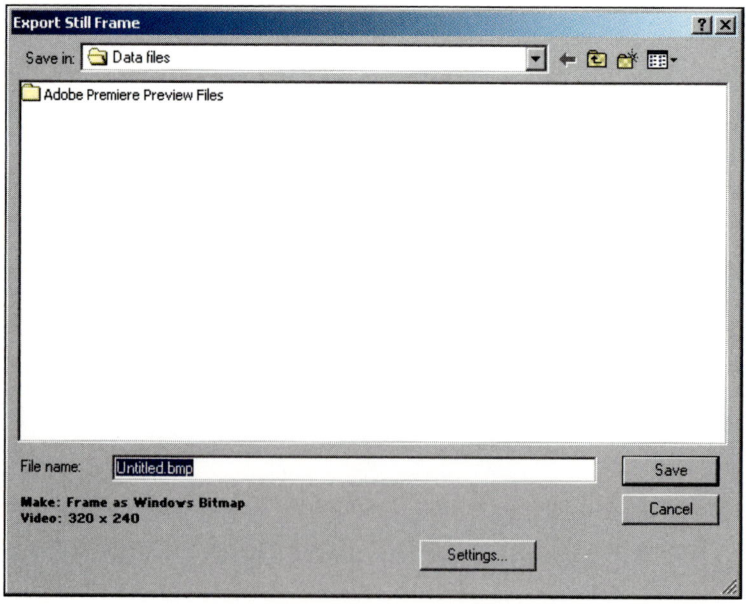

STEP-BY-STEP 6.6 Continued

3. Click the **Settings** button. The Export Still Frame Settings dialog box opens as shown in Figure 6-13.

FIGURE 6-13
Export Still Frame Settings dialog box

4. Click the **File Type** list box, and then click **TIFF**. Select the **Open When Finished** check box if necessary.

5. Click the **OK** button to close the Export Still Frame Settings dialog box.

6. Key **river** as the filename, and then navigate to the location where you are saving your solution files. Click the **Save** button.

7. A new window opens and displays the frame as a single picture. If you skipped steps 3 to 5 and the Open When Finished option was not checked, this window does not open.

8. Close the window. You should now be able to open and display this image file in any application that allows you to place TIFF files.

9. Close **AV Step 6-1** without saving changes. Close Premiere.

SUMMARY

In this lesson, you learned:

■ Projects used for video-editing programs can't be used to distribute your video to others.

■ Publishing your video requires that you export it in some fashion: as a single file (distributed by downloading, streaming, or CD-ROM), on a DVD or other type of video disc, on digital video tape (DV), on analog video tape (VHS), or as one or more still images.

■ The most common file formats for distributing video are AVI and QuickTime. These formats allow you to use one of many codecs for compression and decompression. You can use either format for distributing your file by downloading or on CD-ROM.

■ Streaming video requires a special format. Although most video-editing programs won't produce streaming video directly, you can usually use a plug-in or a separate program to convert the video file to a streaming format.

■ You can distribute your video on a disc such as a DVD, VCD, or SVCD. Video on these discs is compressed using the MPEG video standard. Not only can these discs be used on computers, but DVD players enable you to watch the video on a television set. Most DVD players can play VCDs as well.

■ You can distribute your video by writing it back out to a digital camcorder and a DV tape. You can then use the digital camcorder to play this tape on your television or to make copies of it on analog (VHS) tapes.

■ If your computer can display its screen on a television directly, you can use a VCR to record your video onto tape by playing the video on your computer screen and out to a television simultaneously.

■ You can export individual frames of your movie as still image files for use in posters, brochures, or flyers.

VOCABULARY *Review*

Define the following terms:

AVI	Export	Streaming
Codec	MPEG	SVCD
DV	QuickTime	VCD
DVD		

REVIEW *Questions*

TRUE / FALSE

Circle T if the statement is true and F if the statement is false.

T F 1. You can distribute your video by giving others your project file.

T F 2. Premiere can record DVDs.

T F 3. Most DVD players can also play VCDs.

T F 4. AVI and QuickTime files both use codecs.

T F 5. Once you export your video to digital videotape, that tape can be copied to make more tapes.

FILL IN THE BLANK

Complete the following sentences by writing the correct word or words in the blanks provided.

1. The most popular video file format for Windows computers is the _____ format.

2. The most popular video file format for distributing cross-platform CD-ROMs is the _____ format.

3. _____ use standard compact discs to record and distribute video.

4. Because DVDs are used to record other data besides video, they've increasingly become known as Digital _____ Discs.

5. Viewing a video file while downloading it is called _____.

MULTIPLE CHOICE

Select the best response for the following questions.

1. DVDs are recorded using which of the following video file formats?
   A. AVI.
   B. QuickTime.
   C. MPEG.
   D. Any of the above.

2. Which of the following video disc formats has the highest quality?
   A. DVD.
   B. VCD.
   C. SVCD.
   D. DV.

3. Digital videotapes use which of these tape formats?
   A. DVD.
   B. VCD.
   C. SVCD.
   D. DV.

4. DVDs use which of the following frame rates?
    A. 15.
    B. 20.
    C. 30.
    D. 29.97.

5. VCDs use which of the following MPEG versions?
    A. MPEG-1.
    B. MPEG-2.
    C. MPEG-3.
    D. None of the above.

PROJECTS

PROJECT 6-1

You are ready to publish the file you created in Lesson 5 for Great Outdoors Travel. The client wants to distribute this file via streaming on the company Web site.

1. Launch Premiere. Open **AV Project 6-1** from your data files and locate the source files required for the project.

2. Export the movie. Set the file type (General settings) to **Microsoft AVI** and the Compressor (Video settings) to **Cinepak Codec by Radius**.

3. Save the exported movie as **Great Outdoors Travel**.

4. Play the movie in a movie player such as the QuickTime player or Windows Media Player. Notice the Flash animation that wouldn't play in Premiere plays in the QuickTime player.

5. Close the **AV Project 6-1** file without saving changes. Close Premiere.

PROJECT 6-2

You have finished videotaping the school event from Project 5-2. You have created a video collage of the school year's events, and the school wants to export this file to a videotape so it can be sold to the graduating class. You need to deliver a master tape to the school for replication.

1. Launch Premiere.

2. Open the file you created in Project 5-2.

3. Export the file to a format that you can record to a videotape player.

4. Set the screen so it goes black for 10 seconds before your video starts playing.

5. Make sure a blank master videotape is in the VCR. Start the video playing (click **OK** in the Print to Video dialog box) and then start your VCR player recording.

6. When the video finishes, stop your VCR player from recording.

7. Rewind the master tape and play it on a television.

8. Deliver the tape to your client.

WEB PROJECT

Research on the Web the following terms: DVD, VCD, and SVCD. Before you start your research, write down what you already know about these terms and what you don't know, including this information in a report to submit to your instructor. Further, include in your report the definitions of these terms. Also explain the differences among the video formats. Cite your sources.

TEAMWORK PROJECT

Working in groups of three or four and with the permission of your instructor, contact a video-editing company in your area. Set up a visit to the company. Before you go, create a list of questions based on what you have learned from this lesson. For example, how do they publish videos? What types of software do they use? What types of hardware do they use? What types of videos do they publish? What is the cost of the software and hardware? What are some inexpensive ways to publish? How do their clients use the videos?

If you have a digital camera, you may want to take the camera on your visit to document the interview with the company. With the permission of the company, you may want to take some pictures of the facility, types of equipment and software used there, and projects worked on.

You can either prepare a written presentation to give to the class or, if you have the equipment and software, you may want to create a short video, publish it to one of the formats you have learned about in this lesson, and present it to your classmates.

CRITICAL *Thinking*

ACTIVITY 6-1

Compare and analyze the similarities and differences between animation and video. Review Lesson 1 and Lesson 4 for similarities and differences between animation and video. Review Lesson 2 and Lesson 5 for the similarities and differences between enhancing animation and enhancing video. Review Lesson 3 and Lesson 6 for the similarities and differences between publishing an animation and publishing a video. Summarize your findings in a written report to be submitted to your instructor.

ANIMATION AND VIDEO

REVIEW *Questions*

TRUE / FALSE

Circle T if the statement is true or F if the statement is false.

T F **1.** You create a motion tween for an object using blank frames.

T F **2.** You can import WAV, MP3, and AIFF files into most animation programs.

T F **3.** When you compress text and shapes, information is lost and the quality changes.

T F **4.** File size is important if you are preparing an animation for the Web.

T F **5.** Digital video stores text, shapes, and other components as one frame.

T F **6.** Rendering occurs when you preview a movie after changes have been made.

T F **7.** Video effects and transitions change the original source clips.

T F **8.** The length of the overlap determines the duration of the transition.

T F **9.** Premiere's project files are a great way to share your video with others.

T F **10.** To make DVDs, you usually need a program other than your video-editing program.

MATCHING

Match the correct term in Column 1 to its description in Column 2.

Column 1	Column 2
___ 1. Keyframe	A. Data represented by physically measurable quantities.
___ 2. Tween	B. The most popular video file format for distributing cross-platform CD-ROMs.
___ 3. WAV	C. A compression/decompression component.
___ 4. Compression	D. Editing technique where you use two video tracks.
___ 5. Bandwidth	E. The most popular video file format for Windows computers.
___ 6. Analog	F. An audio file format.

—— 7. Codec

G. Reducing the size of a data file.

—— 8. A/B roll

H. A frame that allows you to specify a change in the animation.

—— 9. AVI

I. Proper position for an object in each frame between the keyframes.

——10. QuickTime

J. Data transfer rate.

K. A type of video transition.

FILL IN THE BLANK

Complete the following sentences by writing the correct word or words in the blanks provided.

1. The ————— is the speed at which the computer plays the frames of a movie.

2. The ————— effect allows you to fade text or an object in an animation.

3. A(n) ————— consists of a blank Stage, a single frame, and a single layer.

4. The total ————— of an animation determines how fast the animation downloads and plays.

5. To identify potential problems in downloading and playing a movie, you ————— the movie.

6. Three-point editing involves a(n) ————— in point and out point and a(n) ————— in point.

7. ————— and ————— are two analog formats for television broadcasting.

8. The ————— command plays an animation in a window that simulates a Web browser.

9. DVDs are recorded using a video compression standard called —————.

10. ————— is a video disc format using standard CDs.

PROJECTS

PROJECT 1

In this project, you build an animation for the blocks logo you created in Project 2 of the Graphics Unit Review.

1. Open your animation program and create a new project file.

2. Save the file as **Toy Blocks Logo.** Set the Stage size to 550 pixels by 400 pixels if necessary.

3. Import to the library **AV Project 1a**, **AV Project 1b**, and **AV Project 1c** from the data files. If a dialog box prompts you for import settings, choose to import as a single flattened bitmap.

4. Open the Library panel if necessary.

5. Rename **AV Project 1a** to **A block**. Rename **AV Project 1b** to **B block**. Rename **AV Project 1c** to **C block**.

6. Create two new layers. Rename **Layer 1** to **C block**. Rename **Layer 2** to **B block**. Rename **Layer 3** to **A block**.

7. Drag the **C block** graphic to the Stage on the C block layer at frame 1. Zoom the stage to 75%. Resize the graphic to 160 by 160 pixels and position it at X coordinate 195 and Y coordinate 120. Insert a frame at frame 55 on the C block layer.

8. Insert a keyframe at frame 12 on the B block layer. Drag the **B block** graphic to the B block layer at frame 12 and position it in the upper-left corner of the Stage. Insert a frame at frame 55 to make sure this block stays in view as long as the C block graphic does.

9. Insert a keyframe on the B block layer at frame 24. Select frame 12 on the same layer and insert a motion tween. Select frame 24 and move the **B block** graphic to X coordinate 125 and Y coordinate 194.

10. Insert a keyframe at frame 25 on the A block layer. Drag the **A block** graphic to the A block layer at frame 25 and position it to the left of the **B block** graphic. Insert a frame at frame 55 to make sure this block stays in view with the other blocks.

11. Insert a keyframe at frame 36 on the A block layer. Select frame 25 on the same layer and insert a motion tween.

12. Insert a motion guide layer above the A block layer. Insert a keyframe at frame 25 on the motion guide layer. With this frame still selected, draw a motion path. You want to make the **A block** graphic bounce on top of the **B block**, then bounce on the top of the **C block**, curve around the right side of the **C block** graphic, and end up under the **C block** and to the right of the **B block**. To create the path, use a drawing tool to draw an arc from the center of the **A block** graphic to the top of the **B block** graphic, then to the top of the **C block** graphic, and finally around and under the **C block** graphic.

13. On the A block layer, snap the center of the **A block** graphic to the beginning of the motion path at frame 25 and to the end of the motion path at frame 36.

14. Preview the movie to test the motion. Make any adjustments necessary to improve the motion. You may, for example, want to modify the position of the block along the path to give the impression the block is tumbling.

15. Save changes and leave the **Toy Blocks Logo** file open to use in Project 2.

PROJECT 2

In this project, continue your work on the Toy Blocks Logo animation and then publish it as a QuickTime movie.

1. With the **Toy Blocks Logo** file open in your animation program, insert a new layer at the bottom of the Timeline to hold a soundtrack. Import the **AV Project 1d** file from the data files (a voice narration), and insert the file on the new layer. Or, you may import a music sound file or record and import your own voice sound file. Rename the imported file and the new layer with appropriate names.

2. Insert a new layer at the top of the layer list and rename it as **Text**. On this layer, create a text object that reads as follows: **Simple as your ABCs . . . That's ABC Toy Company**. Or, insert text that coordinates with your music or the narration you recorded. It should relate in some way to the ABC Toy Company.

3. Format the text in a 36-point serif font and change its color to blue. Center-align the text.

4. Insert a motion tween and a keyframe in frame 55 and animate the text so it fades in or out.

5. Add a button to the animation as follows:
   A. Insert a new layer above the Text layer and rename it as **Button**.
   B. Create a new button symbol named **Button**.
   C. Use a drawing tool to draw a simple button and fill it with a color or pattern of your choice. This button will be used to access a Web site, so insert the text **Web** on the button.
   D. Modify the button's Over stage so the button changes color when the mouse is over it.
   E. Insert the button on the animation near the lower-right corner of the Stage.

6. Create an action setting for the button so it opens a Web site of an online toy seller when clicked. You can use an URL such as http://www.toysrus.com or http://www.amazon.com.

7. Test your animation. Make any adjustments necessary. For example, if you created your own soundtrack, you may need to adjust the length of the animation to accommodate the sound file. Save changes when you are satisfied with the animation.

8. Publish the animation as a QuickTime movie. It may be necessary to save the movie in a different version of your animation program before publishing it to QuickTime. View your published animation in the QuickTime player. If you are logged on to the Internet, you can click your button to see if it takes you to the correct Web site.

9. Close the QuickTime player. Close the **Toy Blocks Logo** file and save changes if prompted. Close your animation program.

PROJECT 3

In this project, you create a video for ABC Toy Company promoting toy-buying during the Christmas season using the animation you published in Project 2. In your video-editing program, create a new project file and add the Toy Blocks Logo QuickTime animation to the project file.

Using a digital camera, capture five or six still images of popular toys, or locate images you can use online and save them with appropriate names (make sure you have permission to use the images for this project). Use a digital camcorder to record some video footage of a toy store near you if possible. (You may need to obtain the permission of your instructor and a toy store near you to shoot the video and still images.) Import the still images and video clips to your project file and arrange them on a timeline in the order you want. Remember to preview your results as you go. Your video should be no more than 60 seconds long, so you may need to edit it by adjusting or deleting clips, changing the duration of a clip, or cutting and splicing clips. Use three-point editing if possible for an overlay edit and an insertion edit. Remember to add timeline markers to help navigate the timeline faster.

Once you have the timeline arranged the way you want it, add at least six video effects to your still images. Add different transitions between each clip on the timeline. Add an opening title to introduce your video and closing credits. Make sure in the closing credits that you acknowledge the cooperation of the toy store.

If the toy store has a company jingle, ask if you can use it for your video. If you receive permission to use the jingle, add an audio track to your video. If not, create a script describing the toys and any discounts associated with the Christmas sale season. Record the script and add this sound file to the video.

Publish the video. You can publish it to a tape to present to your class or burn it to a CD to submit to your instructor. You may also want to share it with the toy store.

SIMULATION

JOB 1

In Job 3 of the Graphics Unit Review's Simulation, you were asked to gather a selection of pictures to market a bicycle tour in Banff National Park in Alberta, Canada. You have conducted research on the Internet and in books, magazines, and CD-ROMs. You have located eight pictures suitable for the Web and presentations. In addition to the still images, you need at least two minutes of video footage on Banff. You can obtain this footage from VHS tapes or original footage. Sources such as *National Geographic* may be useful. Remember that if you are creating a video for professional purposes, you must obtain permission to use source material. You are now going to create a 1-minute promotional video for Swift River Travel.

The first step is to animate the company logo for use as the opening frame of your video. Open **AV Job 1a** in a graphics program such as Fireworks and ungroup the graphic so the letters are separate objects. If you cannot ungroup the letters in your program, create a new graphic similar to the one in the data file. Save the letters as separate files along with the background graphic. If you want a colored background, use **AV Job1b**. Using your animation program, create a new project file. Import the graphics to the library. Using layers, set up a background and a layer for each letter. Create one motion animation and one path animation. Experiment with different effects for the animations. Make sure to preview your animation frequently. Save the animation with an appropriate name.

Add sound to the animation that forms the introduction to the video. You can use either a music sound file such as a CDA from a CD or create your own voice-over sound file, or both. Remember that if this video is for professional purposes, you must use original music for a music sound file to avoid copyright violation. Insert a layer for each sound file you create.

The company has a tag line: "Your key to adventure." Animate this tag line using tweening. Research your animation program's software manual to see what types of text animation are available and experiment.

Add three buttons to the animation: one that starts the animation, one that stops the animation, and one that launches the company's Web site. The company's Web site URL is www.swiftriver.net.

The client wants this animation to be included in the introduction of the video. It must be published to support cross-platform programs and work on both Windows and Macintosh formats. It also must be downloadable and streamable. You choose the publishing format.

Before you publish the animation, identify any potential problems that may occur while downloading and playing the movie. Use the animation program's analysis features to check the total size and streamability of the movie. For example, use a size report or the Bandwidth Profiler in Macromedia Flash MX. After you analyze the movie for problems, you may need to optimize it to reduce the file size and make it download more quickly and play back more smoothly using a feature such as the Optimize command in Flash. You may also customize your publishing settings.

JOB 2

Set up a video project file in your video-editing program and give it an appropriate name. In preparing your project, keep in mind the size of movie frames, how many frames per second, how to handle color, what compression settings to use, and how to handle sound. Capture the video you located from either a tape or a digital camera. Import the video clips as well as the still image clips and the animation file to your project file. Because the final video is only a minute in length, editing may be necessary. Rearrange clips and delete any unnecessary ones. Adjust the in and out points and the speed and duration of some clips. Cut and splice clips where needed. Use three-point editing to add some new content to the timeline. Remember that timeline markers can help you navigate the timeline more quickly as you edit.

Now enhance the video to make it more interesting and professional. Add three or four different video effects to various video and still image clips. Again, research the video-effect capabilities of your video-editing software and experiment with them. Add transitions between each clip so the video flows smoothly from one clip to the next. Add ending credits to your video using rolling text.

Add either a digital audio track and/or a voice-over track to your video. Check your video-editing program to see what types of audio file formats it supports. Apply an audio effect to your audio clip. Again, check the software program's manual for the audio effects that can be applied to audio clips.

You are now ready to export your video file. The client wants to distribute this video to both its Web site and to a VHS tape to be included with a promotional mailing piece. Determine how the video file needs to be exported so it can appear on an analog tape and Web site. Again, refer to your video-editing program's manual or to Lesson 6 in this unit.

Present the video using a media player or play it through a VCR to your client (instructor) and/or classmates for their review and approval.

PRESENTATION SYSTEMS

Unit

Estimated Time for Unit: 9 hours

WORKING WITH PRESENTATIONS

OBJECTIVES

Upon completion of this lesson, you should be able to:

- Open and save a presentation.
- Adjust the view of the presentation as you work.
- Move from slide to slide in a presentation.
- Format a presentation quickly using a preexisting design template.
- Add slides to a presentation and enter and edit slide text.
- Check for spelling errors.
- Establish transitions between slides.
- Preview a presentation.

Estimated Time: 1.5 hours

VOCABULARY

AutoCorrect

AutoRecover

Bullet

Color scheme

Content

Design template

Layout

Placeholder

Presentation program

Slide

Thumbnails

Transition

In this lesson, you will learn about *presentation programs*—programs you can use to create a professional slide presentation for a classroom, corporate training session, business seminar, or similar situation. The resulting presentation is designed to be displayed on a computer monitor or television screen connected to a computer, or projected on a screen using an overhead projector, 35mm slide projector, or multimedia projector connected to your computer.

Most presentation programs also allow you to create a slide show that runs by itself and is displayed on a computer monitor or television screen. You may create a self-running slide show if you want to present product and/or sales information at your company's booth at a trade show or convention. The slide show can be set to run continuously, or shown only when interested parties stop by your booth.

Presentation programs typically offer other presentation options as well. You may be able to use your program to deliver your presentation over the Internet or package your presentation into a self-running program that can be easily shared via e-mail, over a network, or on a CD-ROM.

Regardless of where and how you decide to use your presentation, you can print out accompanying handouts. These handouts allow your audience to follow along with your presentation and to take notes. If a computer is not available, you can use the handouts alone as your visual aides.

There are several different presentation programs available, including Corel Presentations (part of WordPerfect Office), Lotus Freelance Graphics (part of Lotus SmartSuite), and Astound Presentation. But by far the most popular presentation program is Microsoft PowerPoint, which is part of Microsoft Office. Because more than 90 percent of computer users look to Microsoft PowerPoint when creating slide presentations, this unit focuses on that program.

Explore the PowerPoint Window

Figure 1-1 shows the opening screen from Microsoft PowerPoint 2002. This is the window that opens when you launch the program. (The program window may vary depending on your version of PowerPoint.) The window contains a number of standard features such as a menu bar, the Standard and Formatting toolbars, and window control buttons (Minimize, Maximize, and Close).

FIGURE 1-1
Welcome to PowerPoint 2002

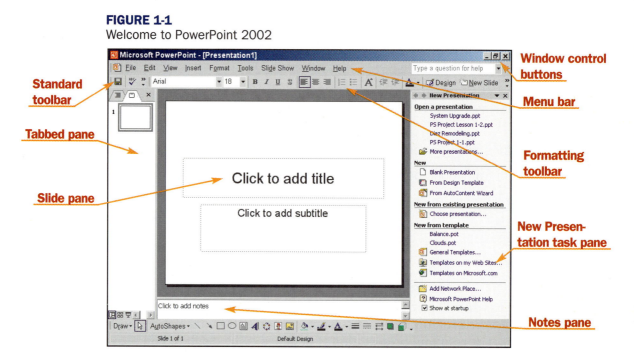

Notice that the program window has a number of different sections or panes. At the left side of the window is the *tabbed pane*, which allows you to display either an outline of the presentation or **thumbnails** of each slide in the presentation. Thumbnails are small pictures that represent the larger slides. The large area in the center is the *Slide pane*, where you view and edit slides. When you first start PowerPoint, the program displays a blank slide in the Slide pane. Below the Slide pane is the *Notes pane*, where you can enter notes you may need when presenting the slide.

At the right side of the window is the New Presentation task pane (this pane appears in PowerPoint 2002, part of the Office XP suite—not in earlier versions). This and other task panes give you quick reference to many important PowerPoint features. Use the New Presentation task pane to start a new presentation or to locate and open an existing presentation.

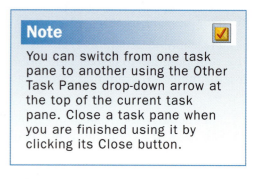

Note

You can switch from one task pane to another using the Other Task Panes drop-down arrow at the top of the current task pane. Close a task pane when you are finished using it by clicking its Close button.

STEP-BY-STEP 1.1

1. Launch PowerPoint.

2. Locate each feature of the PowerPoint window pointed out in Figure 1-1.

3. Leave the current PowerPoint file open to use in the next exercise.

Open and Save an Existing Presentation

Like most programs, presentation programs allow you to create, save, and then later reopen your presentations. When you first open PowerPoint, you can use the blank Title slide provided to start a new presentation. In the next lesson, you learn how to create your own presentations. In this lesson, you use an existing presentation to get acquainted with the program and perform routine tasks such as opening and saving a file, navigating through a presentation, making modifications, and previewing the final result.

Open a Presentation

The easiest way to open a presentation is to use the New Presentation task pane. The *Open a presentation* section of the New Presentation task pane lists the names of the presentations that have been opened recently. Open a presentation from this list by simply clicking its name.

If the presentation you want to work on is not listed, click the *More presentations* link to display the Open dialog box, shown in Figure 1-2. Then navigate to the location where the presentation file is stored, select the file, and click the Open button.

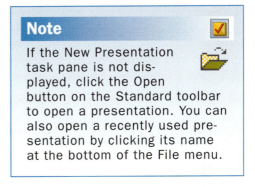

Note

If the New Presentation task pane is not displayed, click the Open button on the Standard toolbar to open a presentation. You can also open a recently used presentation by clicking its name at the bottom of the File menu.

FIGURE 1-2
Open dialog box

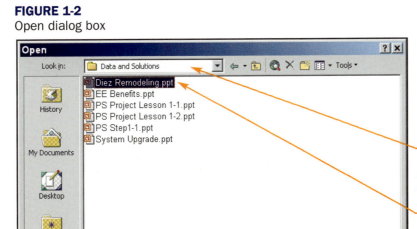

Select a folder from this list

Select the file to open from the files list

Save a Presentation

To save a new presentation that has not yet been named, use the Save As command on the File menu to open the Save As dialog box. Key the desired name for the file in the File name box and navigate to the location where you want to save it, and then click the Save button.

You can also use Save As to save an existing presentation with a new name or to a new location. You follow this procedure with the data files provided for this course. Key the new name in the Save As dialog box, or specify a new location for the file, and then click the Save button.

Once a file has been saved, simply click the Save button on the Standard toolbar or use the Save command on the File menu to save changes as you work on the presentation. PowerPoint automatically saves changes every 10 minutes. But with automatic saves, the data is not placed permanently in the original file. Instead, a list that contains just the changes is placed in an *AutoRecover* file. Should something happen before you can permanently save the file, such as a temporary power loss or a computer crash, PowerPoint 2002 (not prior versions) will attempt to reassemble your changes from this list.

This process works well, but it is not always perfect. So, your best bet to avoid the loss of any data is to manually save the file yourself using the Save button on the Standard toolbar. If the Save button is not currently displayed on the Standard toolbar, you can click the Toolbar Options button at the end of the toolbar, and click the Save button from the palette that appears. You can also click File to open the menu and click Save to save a presentation.

Extra for Experts

If you want PowerPoint to automatically save your changes more often, open the Tools menu and click Options. Click the Save tab, and key the number of minutes you want PowerPoint to wait between saves in the Save AutoRecover info every XX minutes box.

STEP-BY-STEP 1.2

1. In the current unsaved presentation file, click the **More presentations** or the **Presentations** link in the New Presentation task pane.

2. Click the down arrow on the **Look In** drop-down arrow to open the Look in list, and locate the data files folder.

STEP-BY-STEP 1.2 Continued

3. Click **PS Step 1-2** to select the file, and click the **Open** button. The presentation opens in the PowerPoint window as shown in Figure 1-3.

FIGURE 1-3
Presentation on employee benefits

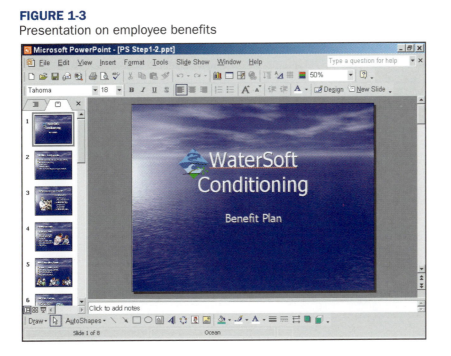

4. Click **File** on the menu bar, and then click **Save As**.

5. From the Save in list, select the location where you want to store the file.

6. In the File name box, key **EE Benefits**.

7. Click the **Save** button.

8. Leave the **EE Benefits** file open to use in the next exercise.

Change the Presentation View

Every presentation program includes several ways in which you can view your work, and PowerPoint is no exception. PowerPoint gives you a choice of three views: Normal view, Slide Sorter view, and Slide Show view. To change from one view to another, click the appropriate view button in the lower-left corner of the PowerPoint window (below the tabbed pane). You can also change views by opening the View menu and clicking Normal, Slide Sorter, or Slide Show.

Normal view, shown in Figure 1-4, is the default view in which presentations open. This is the view in which you'll do most of your work. To change to this view at any time, click the Normal View button.

FIGURE 1-4
Use Normal view for most tasks

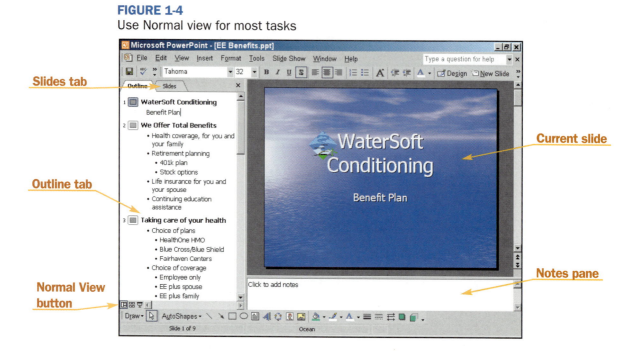

Select the Outline tab in Normal view to see the presentation in outline form—each slide and its text are displayed in order. This allows you to see the overall flow of a presentation at a glance—what came before the currently displayed slide, and what's coming after. You can also make changes to the text shown in this pane and reorder the slides—this is a quick way of structuring a new presentation or reorganizing an existing one.

Hot Tip

If the tabbed pane is taking up too much room, you can close it by clicking the X to the right of the Slides tab. Resize the pane by dragging its right side.

Click the Slides tab in Normal view to see each slide depicted as a thumbnail, so you can review the presentation's overall look and feel. You can also rearrange slides on this tab.

At the bottom of the window in Normal view is the Notes pane. You can click inside this pane and key speaker's notes that pertain to the currently displayed slide. You can print these notes to aid you when you give the presentation.

Use Slide Sorter view (shown in Figure 1-5) to rearrange the slides in your presentation. This view is most useful after most, if not all, of the presentation is complete, to reorganize the order of the slides and improve the flow of the presentation. In this view, thumbnails of the slides are presented in rows and columns so you can easily rearrange them. To change to Slide Sorter view, click the Slide Sorter View button.

FIGURE 1-5
Use Slide Sorter view to help you reorganize a presentation

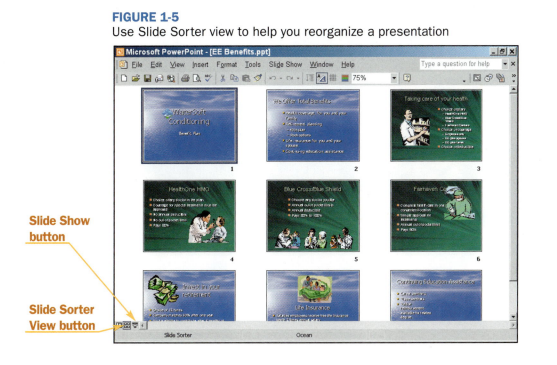

Use Slide Show view, shown in Figure 1-6, to preview how your slide show will look when presented onscreen. In Slide Show view, each slide appears at full-screen size, with no other information on the screen. This view lets you see more clearly how your slides will look during your actual presentation and is a good way to work out any kinks in the transitions and timing. To start the slide show, click the Slide Show button. You learn more about using Slide Show view later in this lesson.

Hot Tip

Zoom in on a slide by opening the Zoom list on the Standard toolbar and selecting a zoom percentage. You can also key a percentage directly in the Zoom box and press Enter to change the zoom.

FIGURE 1-6
Preview your presentation with Slide Show view

STEP-BY-STEP 1.3

1. In the **EE Benefits** file, click the **Slide Sorter View** button.

2. Click the arrow on the **Zoom** button, and then click **100%**.

3. Scroll down to fully view the last slide.

4. Click the **Normal View** button.

5. Click the **Outline** tab.

6. Leave the **EE Benefits** file open to use in the next exercise.

Navigate in a Presentation

A presentation is usually made up of a number of *slides*, so as you work on your presentation and refine its content, you will need to be able to move from slide to slide easily. In Normal view, you have several ways in which you can accomplish this task:

■ If the Outline tab is active, slides are displayed in a list format. Change from slide to slide by clicking a slide's icon in the outline (see Figure 1-7). Selecting a slide in the Outline tab displays that slide in the Slide pane. If your presentation is long, you may need to use the Outline tab's scrollbar to scroll down to a particular slide in the outline.

FIGURE 1-7
Click the icon for a slide to change to that slide

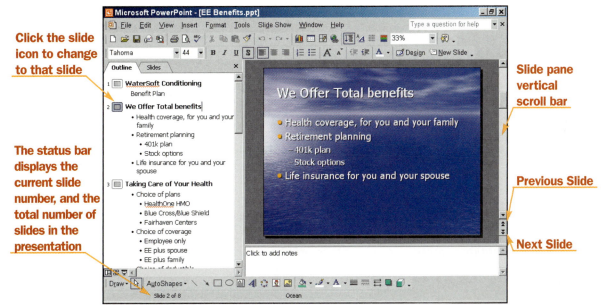

Click the slide icon to change to that slide

The status bar displays the current slide number, and the total number of slides in the presentation

Slide pane vertical scroll bar

Previous Slide

Next Slide

■ If the Slides tab is active, slides are displayed as thumbnails. To view a particular slide, click its thumbnail. Selecting a slide displays it in the Slide pane. Scroll down in the Slides tab if necessary to display the particular thumbnail for the slide you wish to view.

■ Use the vertical scroll bar in the Slide pane to quickly move to a particular slide. As you scroll, a ScreenTip appears, displaying the number of the slide you're scrolling past. When you see the number of the slide you want to view, release the mouse button to stop scrolling.

■ You can also advance from one slide to the next by clicking the Previous Slide or Next Slide buttons, located just below the vertical scrollbar in the Slide pane, or by pressing Page Up or Page Down.

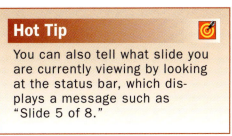

Hot Tip

You can also tell what slide you are currently viewing by looking at the status bar, which displays a message such as "Slide 5 of 8."

If you are using Slide Sorter view, the current slide is the one marked by a dark outline. To select another slide to work on, simply click it. If necessary, you can scroll down to view additional slides, and then click on the one you want to work with.

STEP-BY-STEP 1.4

1. In the **EE Benefits** file, on the Outline tab, scroll up if necessary to display the first few slides in the list.

2. Click slide 3 to view the slide in the Slide pane.

3. Click the **Slides** tab.

4. Click slide 6 to view it.

5. Click the vertical scroll box in the Slide pane and drag it up until the ScreenTip says *Slide: 1 of 8*, and then release the mouse button to stop scrolling.

6. Click the **Slide Sorter View** button.

7. Click slide 5.

8. Click the **Normal View** button. Leave the **EE Benefits** file open to use in the next exercise.

Apply a Design Template

A *design template* contains a series of formats that can be applied in a single step. Typically, the design template contains background graphics, font formatting, and bullet styles in one comprehensive package. When you apply a design template to slides within a presentation, you quickly and easily format them with a unified, professional look.

Apply a design template using the Slide Design task pane, shown in Figure 1-8. To display the Slide Design task pane, click the Slide Design button on the Formatting toolbar or click Slide Design on the Format menu. If the Slide Design task pane is already open but is not displaying design templates, click the *Design Templates* link at the top of the pane.

FIGURE 1-8
Slide Design task pane

Click this link to change the colors associated with a design template

Designs already used in the presentation appear in the *Used in This Presentation* section of the task pane. Designs used recently, either in this or some other presentation, appear in the *Recently Used* section. The *Available For Use* section lists all available design templates. Each design template has a name that relates to its appearance. Rest the mouse pointer on a design to see a ScreenTip giving the template's name.

You can apply a design template to all slides in a presentation or to selected slides. To apply a template to all the slides in a presentation, simply click the template's thumbnail in the task pane. To apply a template to selected slides, select the desired slides in the Slides tab, hold the mouse pointer over the template thumbnail, and click the arrow that appears to display the menu. Click Apply to Selected Slides.

Each design template uses a set of coordinated colors called a *color scheme*. These colors are used for the background, titles and other text, shadows, fills, bullets (and other accents), and hyperlinks. Each design template offers more than one color scheme, so you can

Note ✓

To install additional templates, scroll to the bottom of the task pane and click the Additional Design Templates thumbnail. If you do not see this thumbnail, all templates are installed.

Hot Tip ◎

To select more than one slide in the Slides tab (or in Slide Sorter view), select the first slide, hold down Ctrl, and click additional slides. Or, click the first slide of a group, hold down Shift, and click the last slide of the group to select all slides between the two slides.

swap the default color scheme for a different one, without changing the design template you have chosen. To change color schemes, display the Slide Design task pane, and then click the *Color Schemes* link. Click any color thumbnail to apply that color scheme. As with the design template, you can apply the new color scheme to all slides or only selected slides.

STEP-BY-STEP 1.5

1. In the **EE Benefits** file, click the **Design** button on the Formatting toolbar.

2. Display the Slides tab if necessary, and click slide 3.

3. Press and hold **Ctrl** as you click slides 4, 5, and 6.

4. Locate the **Beam** design template in the *Available For Use* section of the Slide Design task pane and rest the mouse pointer over it to display a drop-down arrow at the right of the thumbnail.

5. Click the drop-down arrow, and then click **Apply to Selected Slides**. The new design template is applied to the selected slides only.

6. At the top of the Slide Design task pane, click the **Color Schemes** link.

7. With slides 3 through 6 still selected, display the drop-down arrow on the teal color scheme (second row, on the right), click the arrow, and click **Apply to Selected Slides**.

8. Close the Slide Design task pane.

9. Save changes and leave the **EE Benefits** file open to use in the next exercise.

Add Slides to a Presentation

As you modify your presentation, you will very likely need to add slides to it. When you add a slide, you must select a particular slide *layout*. The layout tells PowerPoint where to place the various elements on the slide: title, bulleted text, table, chart, and so on.

A new slide is added after the current slide, so first display the slide after which you want the new slide to appear. Then click the New Slide button on the Formatting toolbar to display the Slide Layout task pane.

The Slide Layout task pane (Figure 1-9) organizes the various slide layouts by category:

■ Text layouts contain *placeholders* for different types of text, such as a title, a subtitle, or bulleted text. A placeholder is a box on the slide that indicates where text or another object will be placed on the slide.

■ Content layouts contain one or more placeholders for various types of *content*, which can include clip art, a table, an organization chart, an Excel or similar chart, or a media clip (sound or video file).

- Text and Content layouts combine bulleted text with content, such as a piece of clip art or a media clip.

- The Other Layouts category includes miscellaneous special-use layouts, such as charts of various kinds and tables.

> **Note** ☑
>
> Each slide layout has a name. Rest the mouse pointer on a layout to see its name in a ScreenTip.

FIGURE 1-9
Select layout in Slide Layout task pane

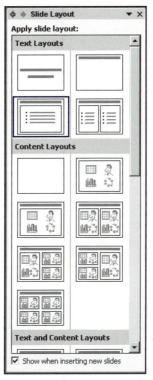

By default, a new slide displays a simple layout (usually the Title and Text layout). But you can change to any other layout. Just click the layout you want to use in the Slide Layout task pane. The new slide immediately changes to that layout.

> **Extra for Experts**
>
> You can also change the slide layout after you have added text or content to a slide. Text automatically reformats for the new layout, although you may need to adjust other content.

S TEP-BY-STEP 1.6

1. In the **EE Benefits** file, on the Slides tab, click the last slide.

2. Click the **New Slide** button on the Formatting toolbar. A new slide displays with the default Title and Text layout.

3. In the Slide Layout task pane, in the *Text and Content Layouts* section, click the **Title, Text, and Content** layout button. (First button on left in that section; rest the mouse pointer over the layout for a second or two to display a ScreenTip with its name.)

STEP-BY-STEP 1.6 Continued

4. Close the Slide Layout task pane.

5. Save changes and leave the **EE Benefits** file open to use in the next exercise.

Work with Text

A large part of creating a presentation is working with text on the slides. Text usually conveys the most important information on the slide and must be presented in a way that is easy for viewers to read and understand. Add text using the placeholders provided by the layout you've chosen for that slide. After text has been entered, you can edit it as necessary. You can also copy or move text from one location to another on a slide or from one slide to another.

Add Text to Slides

After creating a new slide and selecting a layout, it's easy to add slide text. Text placeholders contain messages such as *Click to add title*, as shown in Figure 1-10. Simply click on this message to activate the placeholder, and then begin keying. The text is automatically formatted with the font and font size specified by the current design template. In Lesson 2, you learn how to adjust these formats and others to refine the look of a slide.

FIGURE 1-10
Click the message to add slide text

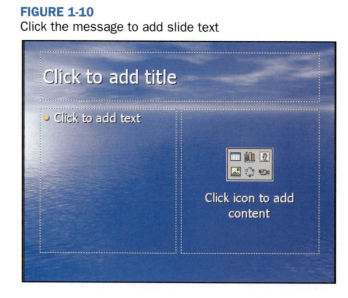

Many slides include placeholders for bulleted text—a list of items preceded by a *bullet* (such as a dot or an asterisk), which marks the start of each item. To add bulleted text to a slide, click on the *Click to add text* message to open the placeholder and begin keying the first item in the bulleted list. Press Enter to add another item to the list. When you're finished adding items, *do not press Enter*, or you'll add a lone bullet below the list.

You can create subordinate items in a bulleted list, as shown in Figure 1-11. For example, you might have the list item *Quarterly Meeting* and want to place under it these two items: *October 12th* and *Downtown Hilton, Conference Room 110*. To create a second-level bullet item, press Tab at the beginning of the bullet item. PowerPoint supplies different bullet symbols for different bullet levels. To return to the main bullet level, press Shift + Tab at the beginning of the bullet item. You should try to create at least two bullet items for any level.

FIGURE 1-11
Create subordinate bulleted items as needed

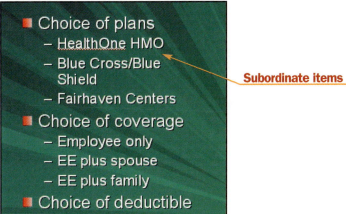

Subordinate items

Choose your words carefully when inserting slide text. In most cases, you can convey your message with a few words for each bullet item, or no more than a single sentence. The reason you want to use as few words as possible is so you can make the text large and easy to read from a distance. More text may be permissible when a presentation is most likely to be viewed by an individual (up close to a screen), rather than delivered by a speaker who can discuss each point. Also, make sure bullet items have *parallel construction*. That is, if one bullet item begins with a verb, others should as well, if possible.

Avoid crowding a slide with too many bullet items. PowerPoint tries to help you if you insert more bullet items than the placeholder is designed to hold by reducing the size of the text so it all fits, but this can make slide text look inconsistent from slide to slide—and in the worst cases, impossible to read! A better plan is to break slides with a lot of content into two or more related slides to make sure all text is easy to read.

> **Note**
>
> If a slide contains a placeholder with the message *Click icon to add content*, you must select an icon for the type of content (such as a chart or table) you want to insert. You learn how to add various kinds of content in later lessons.

Edit Text on a Slide

You can edit text either in the Outline tab or directly on a slide. Edit text using the same methods you would use in a word processing program. Insert additional text by clicking in the text to position the insertion point and then key the necessary text. Replace text by dragging the I-beam pointer to select text and then key the replacement text. Delete existing text by using the Delete or Backspace key to remove one or more characters. Or, select a block of text by dragging the I-beam mouse pointer over the text, and then press Delete to delete the entire block.

> **Hot Tip**
>
> You can select a single word by double-clicking it. To select an entire bulleted item, click its bullet.

STEP-BY-STEP 1.7

1. In the **EE Benefits** file, in the new slide you just inserted, click the **Click to add title** placeholder.

2. Key **Continuing Education**.

3. Click the **Click to add text** placeholder.

4. Key **Career seminars** and press **Enter**.

5. Key **Trade seminars** and press **Enter**.

6. Key **Tuition reimbursement available for related degrees**.

7. You've decided not to add clip art to this slide, so click **Format** on the menu bar, click **Slide Layout**, and click the **Title and Text** layout to change to that layout design. (See Figure 1-12.) Close the Slide Layout task pane.

FIGURE 1-12
Continuing Education slide

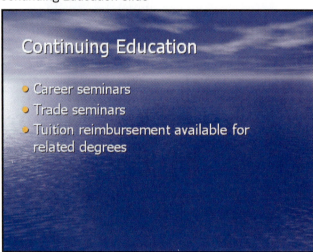

8. Click the **Outline** tab and scroll up to slide 2. Click at the end of the last bulleted item, *Life insurance for you and your spouse.*

9. Press **Enter** to add a new item to the list, and key **Continuing education assistance**.

10. Change the lowercase *b* in the slide title to an uppercase **B**. Then remove the comma in the first bulleted item.

11. Click at the end of the first item, press **Enter**, and then press **Tab** to add a subordinate item.

12. Key **Medical** and press **Enter**.

13. Key **Dental** and press **Enter**.

STEP-BY-STEP 1.7 Continued

14. Key **Eye care**. The slide looks like the one shown in Figure 1-13.

FIGURE 1-13
Additions to slide 2

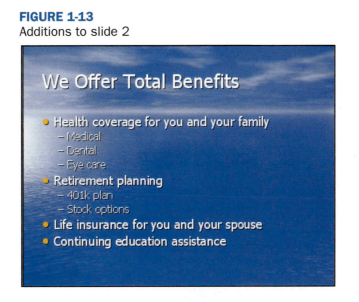

15. Save changes and leave the **EE Benefits** file open to use in the next exercise.

Copy and Move Text

After working with a presentation for a while, you will probably discover at least a few places where text is in the wrong spot and needs to be moved to another slide or another position on the same slide. You may also discover areas where you want to repeat an important message by copying text from one slide to another.

To copy or move text, select the text and then click the Copy button to copy, or the Cut button to move the text. (Or click these commands on the Edit menu.) Click on any slide (even if that slide is in another presentation) at the point where you want the text to appear, and then click the Paste button. If the Outline tab is displayed, you can also click within it at the point where you want the text to appear. These same basic steps also work when you want to copy or move text from some other document, such as a Word document, and then paste it onto a PowerPoint slide.

When copying or moving data from slide to slide, or between Office documents, the Paste Options button appears, as shown in Figure 1-14. Click it and choose the formatting option you desire: Keep Source Formatting (which retains the look of the text as it appeared in its original state) or Use Design Template Formatting (which changes the text to match the look of the text around it, based on the design template).

FIGURE 1-14
Paste Options button

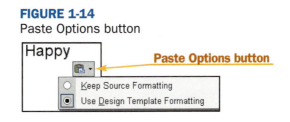

You can also use drag-and-drop editing to copy or move text from slide to slide. First, display the slide that contains the text you want to copy or move. Then click the Outline tab and scroll so you can see the destination slide. Select the text to copy or move by clicking and dragging over it. Then drag the text onto the Outline tab, and position the insertion point at the point on the destination slide where you want the text to appear. To copy the text, press and hold Ctrl while dragging, and then drop it in place by releasing the mouse button. To move the text, simply drag it and drop it.

S TEP-BY-STEP 1.8

1. In the **EE Benefits** file, change to slide 2 if necessary by clicking it in the Outline tab.

2. Select the word *assistance* by clicking and dragging over it.

3. Click the **Copy** button.

4. Scroll down to slide 9, and click at the end of the title.

5. Press **Spacebar**, and then click the **Paste** button.

6. Click the arrow on the **Paste Options** button, and click **Use Design Template Formatting**.

7. Click after the first letter *a* in *assistance* and press **Backspace**.

8. Key the letter **A**.

9. Scroll to slide 7 and select the second and third bulleted items by clicking and dragging over them. Be sure to include the space after the word *year* in the last item.

10. Drag the selection up, until the insertion point is to the left of the word *You're*. Then drop the selection by releasing the mouse button. The items are now in the order shown in Figure 1-15.

FIGURE 1-15
Your bulleted list should appear in this order

11. Save changes and leave the **EE Benefits** file open to use in the next exercise.

Check Spelling

One of the final steps in proofing any document, including a PowerPoint presentation, is to check it for spelling errors. Like Word, PowerPoint checks for errors as you enter text, and underlines any spelling errors with a red wavy line. You can correct spelling errors as they occur or wait until you have finished a presentation and use the spelling check as a final step.

To correct spelling errors as they occur, right-click any word with a red, wavy underline. A shortcut menu appears, with a list of suggested corrections, as shown in Figure 1-16. Click the correction you want to use, and the word will be changed automatically. If the word is spelled correctly, but is a word PowerPoint does not recognize, you can click Ignore All to have PowerPoint stop flagging it as an error. You can also click Spelling from this menu to start the spelling checker.

FIGURE 1-16
Select the correction you want

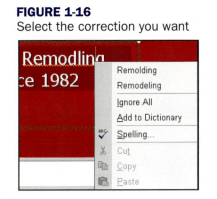

To correct the spelling in an entire presentation, press Ctrl + Home to move quickly to the top of the document—the first slide. Then click the Spelling button on the Standard toolbar, or press F7. PowerPoint checks for errors and stops when it finds one, displaying the dialog box shown in Figure 1-17.

FIGURE 1-17
Spelling dialog box

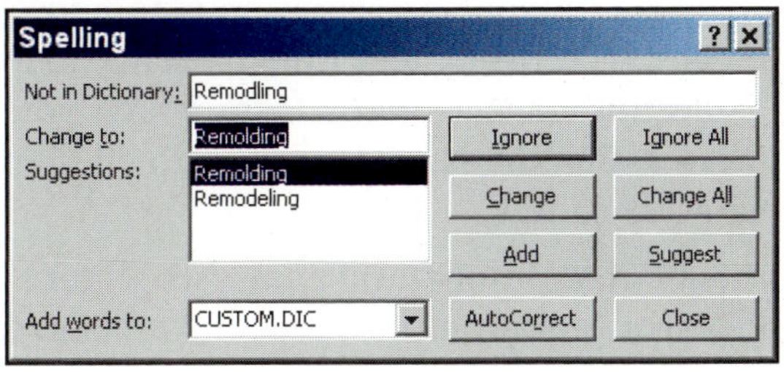

You have several options when PowerPoint displays a word it doesn't know:

■ Select a correction from the Suggestions list and click Change to change just this instance, or Change All to make the same correction throughout the presentation.

■ Key your own correction in the Change to box and click Change to change just this instance, or Change All to make the same correction throughout the presentation.

■ Click Ignore to ignore the word.

- Click Ignore All to ignore this same word throughout the presentation.

- Click Add to add the word to the spelling dictionary.

- Click AutoCorrect to add the word to the *AutoCorrect* list, which looks for common spelling errors and corrects them as you key.

- Click Close to end the spelling check before it is finished.

STEP-BY-STEP 1.9

1. In the **EE Benefits** file, press **Ctrl + Home** to move to the top of the file.

2. Click the **Spelling** button on the Standard toolbar.

3. Click **Ignore** to ignore the *WaterSoft* error.

4. Click **Ignore All** to ignore all occurrences of the spelling *HealthOne*.

5. PowerPoint suggests the correct spelling of **deductible** for the next error. Click **Change All**.

6. PowerPoint suggests the correct spelling of **limit** for the next error. Click **Change All**.

7. Click **Change All** to replace the next error with **Insurance**.

8. Click **Change All** to change the next error to **insurance**.

9. Click the **OK** button in the dialog box that lets you know the spelling check is finished.

10. Save changes and leave the **EE Benefits** file open to use in the next exercise.

Set Transitions

One of the easiest ways to jazz up your presentation is to add *transitions*. Transitions are special effects that occur when PowerPoint changes from one slide to another in Slide Show view. PowerPoint includes a vast collection of transitions from which you can select, including dissolves, wipes, and fades. You can assign the same transition to all the slides in a presentation, or select a different transition for every slide.

Set transitions using the Slide Transition task pane (see Figure 1-18). To open the Slide Transition task pane, click Slide Transition on the Slide Show menu. Display the slide you want to add a transition to, or select a group of slides that you want to have the same transition. You can use the Slides tab to select one or more slides.

FIGURE 1-18
Use the Slide Transition pane to add transitions between slides

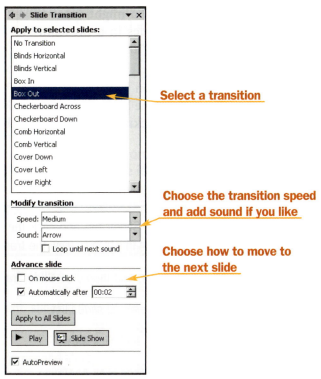

Select a transition

Choose the transition speed and add sound if you like

Choose how to move to the next slide

Click a transition in the *Apply to selected slides* list. Select the AutoPreview option in the task pane to see the transition on screen as it will appear during the presentation. If you don't like the effect, select another transition. You can choose Random Transition to apply transition effects from the list at random to the selected slide(s). You might use this option to apply a variety of transitions to a group of selected slides, without having to choose individual ones.

You can adjust the transition using settings in the *Modify transition* section of the task pane. Click the Speed drop-down arrow to change the speed at which the transition occurs from the default of Fast to Medium or Slow. Add a sound to the transition by choosing one from the Sound drop-down list. If you choose Other Sound, you can browse for a sound file on your computer and select it. Sounds play as the transition occurs, unless you choose the *Loop until next sound* option, which will cause the sound to keep playing until another sound starts.

Normally, you advance from one slide to another during a slide show by clicking the mouse. But if you want the presentation to advance to the next slide automatically without waiting for you to signal when you're ready, then click the *Automatically after* option, and select the number of seconds you want PowerPoint to wait before displaying the next slide. Notice that the *On mouse click* and *Automatically after* options are check boxes, which means that you can actually have both selected at the same time. If you select both, you can either advance the slide yourself or wait for PowerPoint to do so. Select just the *Automatically after* check box if you want PowerPoint to have complete control over advancing slides.

Extra for Experts

In Slide Sorter view and on the Slides tab, icons for each transition appear under the applicable slides or slide numbers. To preview the transition for a slide, click the transition icon. A separate notation appears only in Slide Sorter view for any time interval that might have been added.

- You can change from one presentation view to another depending on what tasks you need to accomplish.

- You can move from slide to slide using a number of options, such as the Outline tab, the Slides tab, the vertical scroll bar in the Slide pane, or the Next and Previous Slide buttons.

- Design templates let you change the font, background, colors, and bullet styles of a presentation in a single step. Apply design templates to all slides or to selected slides in a presentation. Design templates offer a number of color schemes.

- You can edit text on a slide by inserting new text, by deleting characters with the Backspace and Delete keys, or by selecting text and replacing it with new text.

- PowerPoint marks misspellings as you type and lets you correct them using a shortcut menu or the spelling checker.

- You can add transitions between slides in a presentation with the Slide Transition task bar. Apply transitions to a single slide, to selected slides, or to all slides in the presentation.

- To view your presentation as it will appear to others, use Slide Show view. You can advance slides using keys such as the Spacebar or Page Down and Page Up, or you can click the mouse.

VOCABULARY *Review*

Define the following terms:

AutoCorrect	Content	Presentation program
AutoRecover	Design template	Slide
Bullet	Layout	Thumbnails
Color scheme	Placeholder	Transition

REVIEW *Questions*

TRUE / FALSE

Circle T if the statement is true or F if the statement is false.

T   F   **1.** PowerPoint is the only presentation program in use today.

T   F   **2.** You might create a presentation to place important information on the Web.

T   F   **3.** You can create matching handouts for any presentation.

T   F   **4.** When you open a PowerPoint presentation, it's automatically saved with a new filename.

T   F   **5.** In PowerPoint, you do most of your work in Normal view.

T   F   **6.** Slide Sorter view is helpful when you want to reorganize a presentation.

T   F   **7.** You can edit the text on the Outline tab.

T   F   **8.** Press Spacebar to move from slide to slide in Normal view.

T   F   **9.** A design template contains a set of fonts, backgrounds, and colors that can be quickly applied to a slide.

T   F   **10.** A design template cannot be modified.

WRITTEN QUESTIONS

Write a brief answer to the following questions.

1. What are the various ways you can change from slide to slide in Normal view?

2. What might you use a presentation for?

3. What is an AutoRecover file, and what is it used for?

4. What two keys can you use to edit text?

5. What kinds of content can you insert on a slide that has a Content placeholder?

FILL IN THE BLANK

Complete the following sentences by writing the correct word or words in the blanks provided.

1. You can display the next slide in the presentation in Normal view by pressing the _____ key.

2. After inserting a slide, you must select the _____ you want to use.

3. A new slide is inserted _____ the current slide.

4. To enter the next item in a bulleted list, press _____.

5. To quickly select a word, _____ it.

6. To enter an item that's subordinate to the current item in a bulleted list, press _____.

7. To view the transition for the current slide, click the _____ button on the Slide Transition task pane.

8. Preserve the original formatting of copied text by clicking the Paste Options button and selecting _____.

9. If you want to copy text, drag it to its new location and press the _____ key before dropping it in place.

10. To check the spelling of a presentation, press _____.

PROJECTS

PROJECT 1-1

1. If necessary, launch PowerPoint, and then open **PS Project 1-1** from the data files.

2. Save the presentation as **Diez Remodeling**.

3. On the **Outline** tab, move to the last slide and make these changes:
   A. Add the word **New** at the beginning of the first bulleted item and change the *T* in *Tubs* to lowercase *t*.
   B. Move the item *Vinyl, tile, and hardwood flooring* up so that it is the third item in the first column.
   C. Move the items *Ceramic tile* and *Cultured marble* to the end of the list, just above the last item. (You may need to press **Enter** before the last item to move it to its own line.)

4. On the **Slides** tab, move back up to the first slide, and make these changes:
   A. Change the date to **1980**.
   B. Apply the **Clouds** design template to the first slide only.

5. Insert a slide at the end of the presentation and modify it as follows:
   A. Apply the **Title Slide** layout.
   B. Key the title **Call for an estimate today!**
   C. Key the subtitle **555-0291.**
   D. Apply the slide transition **Wheel Clockwise, 8 Spokes.** Set the speed to **Slow**, add the **Breeze** sound, and set the sound to loop. Set the advance option to advance automatically after 3 seconds, but not on a mouse click.

6. The first slide has a transition already applied. Change the transition so that the sound loops and the slide advances only on a mouse click.

7. Spell check the presentation and correct any errors.

8. Preview the presentation from the beginning. (You'll need to click to advance the first slide. The rest of the slides are set to advance automatically.)

9. Save and close the **Diez Remodeling** file, but leave PowerPoint open to use in Project 1-2.

PROJECT 1-2

1. Open the **PS Project 1-2** from the data files.

2. Save the presentation as **System Upgrade**.

3. Apply the **Balance** design template to all slides.

4. Change the color scheme to light khaki (fourth on the left).

5. Display slide 8 and copy the name of the training scheduler and her extension. Do not copy the word *Call*.

6. Paste the copied information on slide 7 after the word *contact* but before the period.

7. Add random medium-speed transitions to all the slides. Advance each slide with a mouse click. Have slides 3, 4, 5, 9, and 10 advance with a mouse click or (if the mouse click doesn't occur), advance automatically after 5 seconds.

8. Spell check the presentation and correct any errors.

9. Preview the presentation from the beginning.

10. Save and close the **System Upgrade** file. Close PowerPoint.

WEB PROJECT

Use the Office on the Web command on the Help menu to visit the Office Assistance center. In the PowerPoint center, see if you can find any help in designing professional-looking presentations.

SCANS TEAMWORK PROJECT

Discuss with your classmates the information you found about designing professional presentations. Use your discussions to design a presentation of your own to be used to inform new students about school rules. First, come up with an outline that lists the title for each slide and the order in which they should be presented. Then assign a few slides to each person, who then will write the slide text and select a layout. Remember to keep your items short and to the point. When deciding on a layout, imagine what other elements you may want on the slide to convey your message, such as clip art, a chart, or a media clip. Each person should then enter his or her own slides; don't enter any content such as clip art and tables yet. As a group, decide on the design template and color scheme to use and apply them to the presentation. Discuss whether to use transitions throughout and assign them as needed. Finally, proof the presentation for spelling errors. Present your finished product to the class and ask for comments. What improvements should you make?

CRITICAL *Thinking*

ACTIVITY 1-1

What place does color play in a presentation? What colors work well together? Use your research on the Microsoft Web site to help you learn about the color wheel, and how to select colors that contrast well so your audience can read your slide text from a distance. Put your thoughts into a 150-word report that covers the layout of a color wheel and the colors of text that are easiest to read on various colored backgrounds, such as black, light brown, red, light blue, medium blue, green, khaki, yellow, and so on. If you have access to a color printer, create samples that support your opinions.

ENHANCING A PRESENTATION

VOCABULARY

Font

Footer

Handles

Hanging indent

HSL color model

Indent

Object

Outdent

Point

RGB color wheel

Slide master

Title master

Now that you're more familiar with PowerPoint slide presentations, you're ready to create some of your own. In this lesson, you learn how to create and save a new presentation, reorganize a presentation, and apply different fonts, font sizes, alignment, line spacing, and color. You also learn how to format bulleted and numbered lists, work with slide colors and backgrounds, and make changes that affect all slides.

Create and Save a Presentation

Most presentation programs—PowerPoint included—open a new, blank, presentation for you when you start them. With PowerPoint, however, you don't have to start each presentation from scratch using that blank presentation.

Create a New Presentation

As you can see in Figure 2-1, PowerPoint allows you to create new presentations in a variety of ways. When you start the program, it creates a presentation file that contains a single slide with a plain white background. If you want to build your presentation this way and apply your own formatting and add new slides as needed, simply click the *Blank Presentation* link in the New Presentation task pane to begin work.

FIGURE 2-1
Start a new presentation from scratch if you like

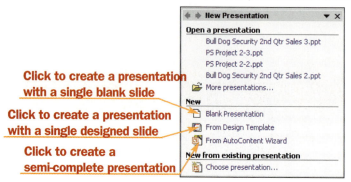

Click to create a presentation with a single blank slide

Click to create a presentation with a single designed slide

Click to create a semi-complete presentation

To create a new presentation that includes a single slide with the design template of your choice, click the *From Design Template* link in the New Presentation task pane and select a design from those shown in the Slide Design task pane that automatically opens. As you recall from Lesson 1, the design template includes a color scheme, background design, and text styles that complement each other. As you add new slides to the presentation, the design is incorporated in all the slides, giving your presentation a professional look.

To use a semi-completed presentation as the basis of your new presentation, click the *From AutoContent Wizard* link in the New Presentation taskbar. The Wizard displays a series of dialog boxes that allow you to select a presentation topic (such as a marketing plan, employee orientation, training seminar, and so on), presentation medium (screen, Web, handouts, and so on), and other options (such as displaying the date at the bottom of each slide). The Wizard will then create several slides based on a sample outline designed for the specific topic you selected. You then modify the placeholder text and graphics on each slide to personalize the presentation, add or delete slides as desired, and make other modifications to complete your presentation.

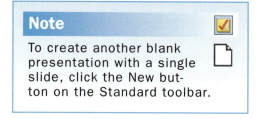

Note

To create another blank presentation with a single slide, click the New button on the Standard toolbar.

If you want to start another new presentation later on, open the File menu and click New. The New Presentation task pane reappears. Click the appropriate link to create your presentation.

STEP-BY-STEP 2.1

1. Launch PowerPoint.

2. Click the **From AutoContent Wizard** link in the New Presentation task pane, and then click **Next**.

STEP-BY-STEP 2.1 Continued

3. Click the **Sales/Marketing** button, click **Product/Services Overview**, and then click **Next**.

4. Click **On-screen presentation** if necessary, and then click **Next**.

5. Click in the **Presentation title** box and key **TapSoft Faucet Water Softener**. Leave the **Date last updated** and **Slide number** options selected. Click **Next**.

6. Click **Finish**. PowerPoint creates a slide presentation based on your selections. Close the Slide Layout task pane and leave the presentation open to use in the next exercise.

Adjust Wizard Content and Save a New Presentation

When you create a presentation using the AutoContent Wizard, the Wizard generates several slides for you, filled with suggested text that you must edit, delete, or replace with your text. In generating the slides for the presentation, the Wizard chose an appropriate layout—typically the Title and Text layout. You probably remember from Lesson 1 that the slide layout controls the placement of slide text, graphics, charts,

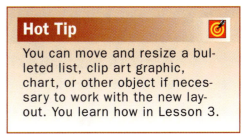

Hot Tip

You can move and resize a bulleted list, clip art graphic, chart, or other object if necessary to work with the new layout. You learn how in Lesson 3.

and other *objects*. As you make changes to the placeholder text on each slide, you may decide to add other elements as well, which means changing to a different slide layout. To change the slide layout, display the slide, open the Slide Layout task pane (by clicking Slide Layout on the Format menu), and select a new layout. If there are any objects already on the slide, such as a title and a bulleted list, they are resized and/or moved as needed, based on the slide layout you select. To apply a new layout to more than one slide, select the slides in the Slides tab and then click the desired layout.

After creating a new presentation, you should save the file to your hard disk or other storage device. Saving a presentation prevents you from accidentally losing your work should the power go out or the computer lock up. To save a presentation for the first time, click the Save button on the Standard toolbar or use the Save or Save As command on the File menu.

Hot Tip

Rather than saving all your files in the My Documents folder, create a subfolder for each project. This will make your files easier to locate. To create a new subfolder within the folder shown in the Save In box, click the Create New Folder button, key a name for the folder, and click OK.

In the Save As dialog box, navigate to the folder in which you want to save the presentation. By default, PowerPoint selects the My Documents folder to store a new presentation. To change to some other folder, open the Save In list and select the folder you want. Then key a name for the file and click the Save button.

As you work on a presentation, be sure to save often. Save your recent changes using the Save button or the Save command.

STEP-BY-STEP 2.2

1. In the new presentation file, click **File** on the menu bar, and then click **Save**.

2. Click the **Save In** list and select the location where you want to store the file.

3. Key **TapSoft Product Release** in the File name box, and then click the **Save** button.

4. Click the **Design** button on the Formatting toolbar and apply the **Eclipse** design template to all slides.

5. On slide 1, select your name and key **Product Release** to change the subtitle.

6. Display slide 2. Click **Format** on the menu bar, and then click **Slide Layout** to open the Slide Layout task pane.

7. Click the **Title, Content and Text** layout to apply it to slide 2. Close the Slide Layout task pane. The slide should look similar to Figure 2-2.

FIGURE 2-2
Slide 2 with a new design

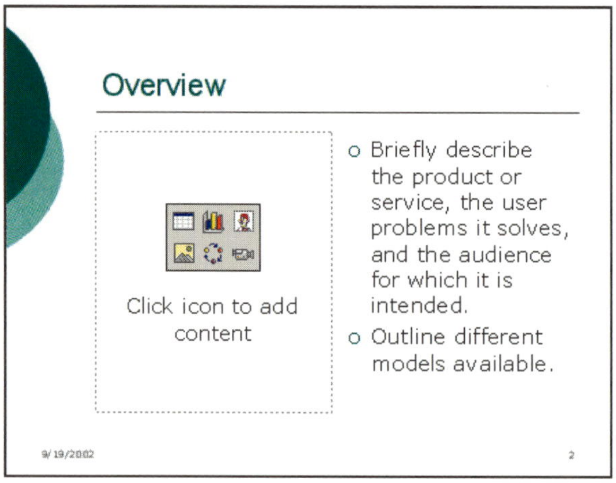

8. Save changes and close the **TapSoft Product Release** file. Leave PowerPoint open to use in the next exercise.

Delete, Duplicate, and Reorganize Slides

In the process of reviewing a presentation, you often need to copy, move, and even delete slides. You can accomplish these tasks best in Slide Sorter view, although you can also use Normal view.

Work with Slides in Slide Sorter View

To remove a slide in Slide Sorter view, click a slide to select it and then press Delete. You can remove multiple slides in a single step by selecting them and then pressing Delete. Remember that you can select multiple slides by pressing Ctrl as you click each one, or by selecting the first one in a group, pressing Shift, and clicking the last one in the group. After you delete a slide, the slides after it in the presentation are automatically moved up in the display and renumbered.

You can copy all the elements on a slide and create a new slide with them using the Duplicate command. You might do this if an existing slide is similar to one you want to create—with similar graphics, titles, layout, and so on. To duplicate a slide in Slide Sorter view, click it. Then click Duplicate on the Edit menu. The new slide appears just after the original slide. You can then make any modifications you like—replacing text, graphics, and so on.

Reorganizing slides is what Slide Sorter view was designed for. Simply click a slide and drag it to a new location. As you drag, a thin vertical bar (see Figure 2-3) marks the place where the slide will appear if you drop it. When this bar appears in the spot where you want to relocate your slide, release the mouse button to drop it in place.

> **Important**
>
> If you accidentally delete a slide you intended to keep, click the Undo button.

> **Hot Tip**
>
> You can also duplicate a slide by pressing Ctrl and dragging the copy to its new location.

> **Hot Tip**
>
> If the place where you want to move the slide is not displayed in the window, drag the slide to the top or bottom of the window, and the display scrolls to reveal the hidden slides.

FIGURE 2-3
Drag to relocate a slide

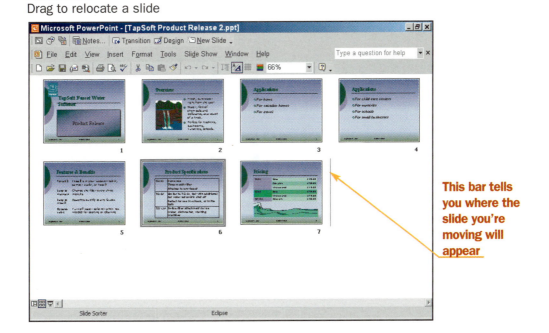

This bar tells you where the slide you're moving will appear

Work with Slides in Normal View

You can accomplish some of the same tasks in Normal view without displaying the tabbed pane, although the tasks may require more steps. For example, to delete the slide currently displayed in the Slide pane, you must click to open the Edit menu, and then click Delete Slide. Simply pressing Delete won't work, and you may end up removing the currently selected object (such as a graphic) instead.

Use the Slides tab to make it easier to delete slides: simply select a slide in the Slides tab and then press Delete, just as in Slide Sorter view. Also use the Slides tab if you want to remove multiple slides. Select the slides you want to remove, and then press Delete.

To duplicate a slide in Normal view, you do not need to display the tabbed pane. Just display the slide you want to duplicate, click Edit to open the menu, and click Duplicate. The new slide appears after the current one in the presentation. The duplicate becomes the currently displayed slide.

To reorganize slides in Normal view, use the tabbed pane. On the Slides tab, click a slide and drag it to a new location. Once again, a bar—this time a horizontal bar—marks the spot where the slide will appear when dropped (see Figure 2-4). When the bar appears in the right spot, release the mouse button to drop the slide there. To reorganize slides on the Outline tab, click the slide's icon (which appears just after its number) and drag the slide by its icon. Again, a horizontal bar guides the way. When the bar appears where you want the slide relocated, release the mouse button to drop it.

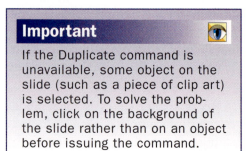

Note

If the tabbed pane is not displayed in Normal view, click View and then click Normal (Restore Panes) to open the tabbed pane.

Important

If the Duplicate command is unavailable, some object on the slide (such as a piece of clip art) is selected. To solve the problem, click on the background of the slide rather than on an object before issuing the command.

FIGURE 2-4
A bar tells you where the slide will reappear

A bar indicates the possible location of the slide you are moving

STEP-BY-STEP 2.3

1. Open **PS Step 2-3** from the data files, and save it as **TapSoft Product Release 2**.

2. On the **Slides** tab, click slide 6 to display it, and then press **Delete** to remove the slide.

3. Change to Slide Sorter view, and click slide 4 to select it.

STEP-BY-STEP 2.3 Continued

4. Click **Edit** on the menu bar, and then click **Duplicate**.

5. Click slide 3 and drag it after slide 5, in front of the *Specifications* slide.

6. Save changes and leave the **TapSoft Product Release 2** file open to use in the next exercise.

Change Font, Font Size, and Other Attributes

A *font* is a collection of characters (a typeface) that share common characteristics. Design templates (even the default blank presentation template) specify fonts as part of the design, but you may prefer another font to that used in the template. In addition to changing the font, you can change the font size; add *font styles* such as bold, italics, or underline; and change other attributes as well. In this section, you learn how to change font formatting on a slide. Later, you learn how to quickly change the font used throughout a presentation.

To change the way text looks, you should be in Normal view. You have several options for selecting text you want to change. If you want to change only a word or two, click in the text placeholder to activate the placeholder for editing, and then drag the I-beam pointer over the text you want to change. A placeholder activated for editing displays a border made up of diagonal lines, as shown in Figure 2-5. When the placeholder displays this hashed border, you must select text to format it. If you want to change all the text in a placeholder, first click in the placeholder to activate it. Then click the placeholder border to select the placeholder itself. The placeholder border changes to a border of small dots when selected. (See Figure 2-5.) For example, suppose you want to change all the text in a bulleted list. First, click anywhere in a bulleted list to activate the placeholder box. Then click the placeholder border to select the placeholder so you can change all the text inside without having to drag over the text with the pointer.

FIGURE 2-5
An active placeholder and a selected placeholder

The hashed border indicates that this active placeholder is ready for editing

The dotted border indicates that this selected placeholder is ready for formatting

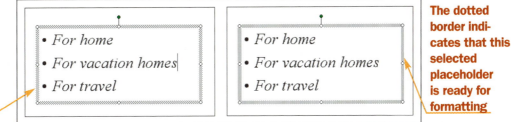

To select a new font to apply to selected text, click the drop-down arrow on the Font list on the Formatting toolbar and click the font you want from the list that appears. To add a font style such as bold, italics, underline, or shadow to the text, click the Bold, Italics, Underline, or Shadow button on the Formatting toolbar, shown in Figure 2-6.

FIGURE 2-6
Add font styles such as bold to text

Bold   Italics   Shadow   Underline

Features & Benefits

You have several options for changing the size of text. The simplest method is to click the drop-down arrow on the Font Size box and select a new size from the list. You can also key the size (in *points*) in the Font Size box and press Enter to change the font size. Another way to change font size is to click either the Increase or Decrease Font Size buttons on the Formatting toolbar. When you click the Increase Font Size button, for example, the text is increased to the next font size shown on the Font Size list. This is a convenient method when you're not sure how big you want your text to be—just that you want it to be bigger.

You can copy formats from one piece of text to another using the Format Painter button. First, click within the text that has formats you want to copy. Then click the Format Painter button. Switch slides if necessary and drag over text to copy the formats. If you double-click the Format Painter button instead of clicking, you can drag over as many different sections of text as you like, copying the same formats to all of them. When finished, click the Format Painter button to turn it off.

S TEP-BY-STEP 2.4

1. In the **TapSoft Product Release 2** file, change to Normal view and select slide 3.

2. Click within the bulleted list, and then click the placeholder border to select all its text.

3. Click the **Font** drop-down arrow on the Formatting toolbar, and then click **Times New Roman**.

4. Click the **Italics** button on the Formatting toolbar to add italics to the text.

5. Click the **Increase Font Size** button on the Formatting toolbar two times to increase the font size to 33 points.

STEP-BY-STEP 2.4 Continued

6. Click the **Format Painter** button on the Standard toolbar to copy the format of the bulleted list.

7. Display slide 4, and drag over the bulleted list to copy the formats.

8. Display slide 1, and click the border of the *Product Release* text box to select it.

9. Click the **Font** drop-down arrow on the Formatting toolbar, and then click **Times New Roman**.

10. Click the **Font Size** drop-down arrow on the Formatting toolbar, and then click **44**.

11. Save changes and leave the **TapSoft Product Release 2** file open to use in the next exercise.

Change Text Alignment

The current design template controls the way text aligns in slide placeholders. Often, for example, title text is left-aligned (placed against the left margin), but in some designs title text is centered or right-aligned. You can change the alignment of text in any placeholder using the Alignment buttons on the Formatting toolbar. You can also justify text, which causes PowerPoint to add spaces between words of each line in a paragraph to force the text to align against both the left and right margins.

To align text, change to Normal view and then click anywhere in a bulleted item, slide title, or paragraph. You can also select an entire placeholder to change all the text inside. Then click the Align Left, Center, or Align Right button, located on the Formatting toolbar. To justify text, select it and click Format, click Alignment, and click Justify.

STEP-BY-STEP 2.5

1. In the **TapSoft Product Release 2** file, change to Normal view if necessary, and select slide 6.

2. Click in front of the word *Specifications*, and key **Product**. Press the **Spacebar**.

3. Click the **Center** button on the Formatting toolbar to center the title.

4. Display slide 7.

5. Click in front of the price *$125.00*, and drag downwards to select the column of prices.

6. Click the **Align Right** button on the Formatting toolbar.

7. Save changes and leave the **TapSoft Product Release 2** file open to use in the next exercise.

Format Lists

PowerPoint allows you to create two different kinds of lists: bulleted lists (in which each item is preceded by a bullet) and numbered lists (in which each item is preceded by a number). Typically, you use bulleted lists more often in presentations, to list agenda items, important talking points, and brief descriptions, for example. A numbered list is usually reserved for listing the steps in a procedure.

Notice that none of the PowerPoint slide layouts include an option for a numbered list. If you want to change a bulleted list into a numbered list, just select its placeholder and click the Numbering button on the Formatting toolbar.

Customize a Bulleted List

When you add a bulleted list to a slide, each item is preceded by a bullet symbol specified by the current design template. You can use a different symbol or picture as your bullet, change the bullet's size, and even change its color. You can change a single bullet or all bullets in one bullet list, or you can change all bullets in an entire presentation, as you learn later in this lesson.

To change the formatting of a bulleted list, click in the bullet item (to change just that item) or select the list's placeholder. Then open the Format menu, and click Bullets and Numbering. If necessary, click the Bulleted tab, as shown in Figure 2-7. To change the bullet style, click any style shown. Adjust the size as desired—notice that the bullet size is a percentage relative to the size of the bulleted item text. If you like, click the Color list and choose a new bullet color. (You learn more about selecting colors later in this lesson.)

FIGURE 2-7
Select a new bullet style

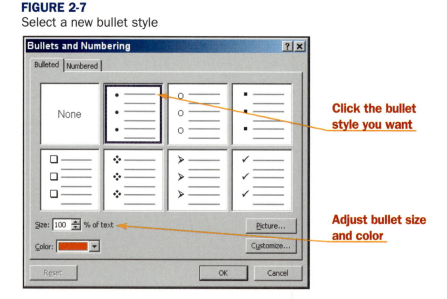

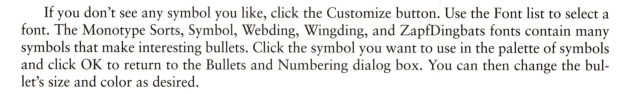

If you don't see any symbol you like, click the Customize button. Use the Font list to select a font. The Monotype Sorts, Symbol, Webding, Wingding, and ZapfDingbats fonts contain many symbols that make interesting bullets. Click the symbol you want to use in the palette of symbols and click OK to return to the Bullets and Numbering dialog box. You can then change the bullet's size and color as desired.

If you want to use a graphic as your bullet—perhaps your company's logo or a piece of clip art—click the Picture button in the Bullets and Numbering dialog box. PowerPoint opens the Picture Bullet dialog box, which is a palette of standard picture bullets included in the Clip Organizer. Click any picture and click OK to return to the Bullets and Numbering dialog box. To search for a particular piece of clip art, key a keyword such as *water* or *tree* in the Search box and press Enter. If you want to use your own graphic file, click the Import button in the Picture Bullet dialog box. Navigate to the folder containing the file, select the file, and click Add to import the file into the Clip Organizer. Click OK to apply the new bullet to the list.

Customize a Numbered List

Customizing a numbered list is similar to customizing a bulleted list. Start by selecting the list's placeholder, and then open the Bullets and Numbering dialog box. Click the Numbered tab this time, and select a numbering style from the palette of choices shown in Figure 2-8. Adjust the Size as desired—again, the size is relative to the size of the list's text. Click the Color list if you want to select a different color for the numbers. Finally, set the starting value for the list to something other than 1 by clicking the Start at spinner. Click OK to apply your selections.

FIGURE 2-8
Choose a numbering style

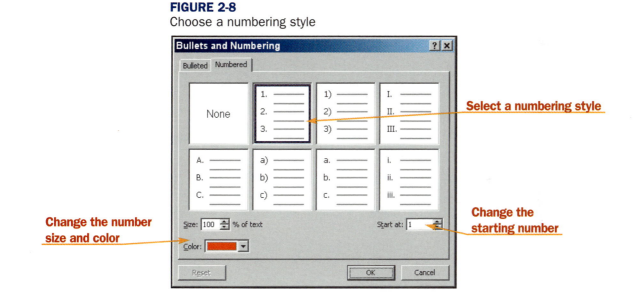

Adjust Indentation

An *indent* is an extra amount of space between the edges of a paragraph or list item and the margins. You can add an indent along the left margin for all lines or for the first line only.

In a bulleted list, the first line is *outdented*, or indented towards the left margin, in order to place the bullet away from the rest of the lines of text. You can adjust this outdent (also known as a *hanging indent*) by increasing or decreasing the amount of space between the bullet and the text.

You can adjust indents for paragraphs or lists using markers on the ruler (see Figure 2-9). Display the ruler by clicking Ruler on the View menu. Then, click within the paragraph, or drag over all the items in a bulleted list, and do one of the following:

■ To adjust the position of the bullet or to add an indent to the first line of a paragraph only, drag the first-line indent marker.

■ To adjust the distance between the bullet and the text or to adjust the distance between the lines in a paragraph and the left margin, drag the hanging indent marker (the triangle).

■ To maintain the relationship between the bullet and the text and to increase or decrease the paragraph's distance from the left margin, drag the left indent marker (the rectangle). This causes the first-line indent marker and the hanging indent marker to move together.

> **Important**
>
> If you're accustomed to Word, then adjusting indents with the ruler is not a new thing. However, unlike Word, PowerPoint does not provide an option to add a right indent.

FIGURE 2-9
Drag markers on the ruler to change indents

First-line indent marker
Hanging indent marker
Left indent marker

STEP-BY-STEP 2.6

1. In the **TapSoft Product Release 2** file, display slide 2.

2. Click the placeholder for the bulleted list.

3. Click **Format** on the menu bar, and then click **Bullets and Numbering**.

4. Click the **Customize** button in the Bullets and Numbering dialog box.

5. Click the **Font** list, and click **Webdings**.

6. Click the Earth symbol shown at right, and click the **OK** button.

7. In the Bullets and Numbering dialog box, change the Size to **80%** and click the **OK** button.

8. If necessary, click **View** on the menu bar, and then click **Ruler** to display the ruler.

9. Click at the beginning of the bulleted list and drag over all the items to select them.

10. Drag the triangle on the left indent marker to the 0.5-inch mark on the ruler to increase the distance between the bullets and the text.

11. Display slide 8, select the bulleted list items, and then click the **Numbering** button on the Formatting toolbar to change the list to a numbered list.

12. Save changes and leave the **TapSoft Product Release 2** file open to use in the next exercise.

Adjust Line Spacing

Paragraphs that don't have enough space between them are difficult to read, so PowerPoint automatically includes a little space between multiple paragraphs or bulleted items. Sometimes, however, this space may not seem great enough. You can add more space above, below, and even between the lines of a paragraph or list items.

To begin, select a bulleted list or title by clicking its placeholder. Then select the Line Spacing command on the Format menu. The Line Spacing dialog box, shown in Figure 2-10, gives you three spacing options. For each option, you can specify the spacing measurement in lines or points.

FIGURE 2-10
Line Spacing dialog box

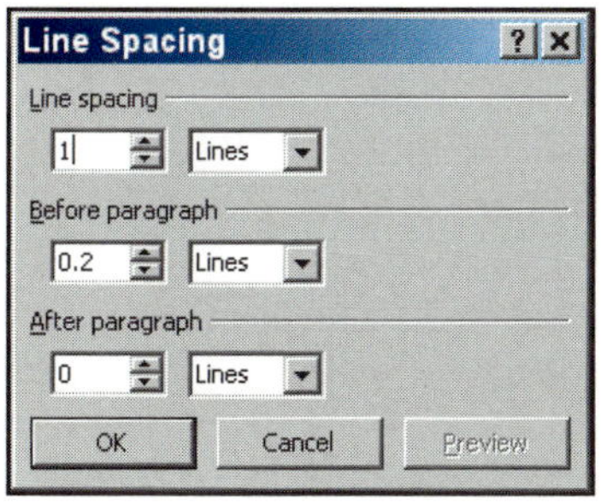

To adjust the amount of space between lines in a list or paragraph, change the Line spacing value. To add space above a paragraph or list item, adjust the Before paragraph value. To add space after a paragraph or list item, change the After paragraph value. Click the Preview button to view the changes without actually applying them. When you are satisfied with the spacing changes, click OK to apply them.

STEP-BY-STEP 2.7

1. In the **TapSoft Product Release 2** file, display slide 2.

2. Click the placeholder for the bulleted list to select it.

3. Click **Format** on the menu bar, and then click **Line Spacing**.

4. Change the **After paragraph** value to **0.15**, and click the **Preview** button to see how it looks.

5. Change the **After paragraph** value to **0.2**, and click the **Preview** button again to view the change. Click the **OK** button.

6. Save changes and leave the **TapSoft Product Release 2** file open to use in the next exercise.

Adjust Text Size with AutoFit

AutoFit is another of PowerPoint's automatic features. As you may have noticed already, when you key text into a placeholder that's not large enough for the text, AutoFit automatically decreases the size of the text so that it will fit. If you resize the placeholder to make it larger, the text size automatically increases to take advantage of the larger space.

> **Note**
>
> To resize a placeholder, click on it and then drag one of the *handles* (the small white circles on the placeholder's border) outward to make the placeholder bigger, or inward to make it smaller.

When AutoFit resizes your text, the AutoFit Options button appears, as shown in Figure 2-11. Click the drop-down arrow to reveal the menu, and click Stop Fitting Text to This Placeholder to turn the option off for just that text. If the slide uses a single-column layout, you can select from other options as well. You can split text between two slides, create a copy of the original slide so you can continue on the new slide, or change the single-column layout to a two-column layout so you can move overflow text into the second column.

FIGURE 2-11
AutoFit Options button

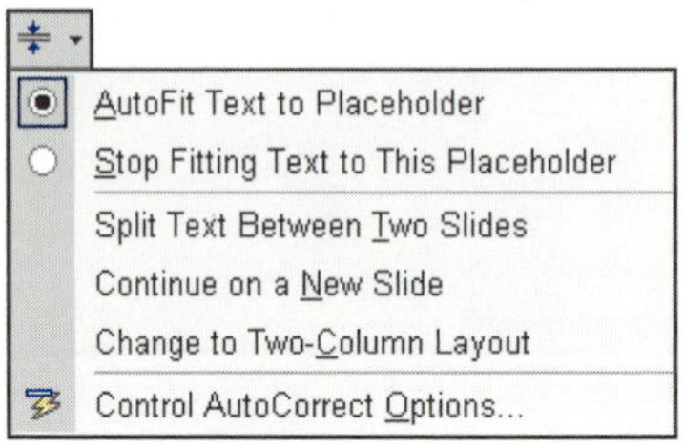

STEP-BY-STEP 2.8

1. In the **TapSoft Product Release 2** file, display slide 4.

2. Select the slide in the Slides tab if necessary, and press **Delete** to remove it.

3. Display slide 3, click **Format** on the menu bar, and then click **Slide Layout**.

4. Click the **Title and Text** layout, and then close the Slide Layout task pane.

5. In the bulleted list, click after the word *home* and press **Enter** to add a new line.

6. Key **For vacation homes** and press **Enter**.

7. Key **For travel**.

8. Click after the comma in the fourth item and press **Backspace** to remove the comma.

9. Press **Enter** and key **For** in front of the word *nurseries*.

10. Click the drop-down arrow on the AutoFit Options button, and then click **Split Text Between Two Slides**.

11. View slides 3 and 4 to see how PowerPoint split the entries.

12. Save changes and leave the **TapSoft Product Release 2** file open to use in the next exercise.

Check Styles

Creating a great presentation is difficult to do—engaging your audience and holding their attention is a critical step in getting your message across. One thing you don't want is to have little inconsistencies in your presentation draw your audience's focus away from your message and to give them the impression that your work is less than professional. To eliminate this problem, have PowerPoint spot the inconsistencies as they happen, so you can correct them on the spot.

PowerPoint can look for the following items:

- Consistent use of punctuation for slide titles and body text.

- Consistent capitalization in slide titles and body text. By default, PowerPoint assumes slide titles use Title Case, which means all words in the title are capitalized; and body text uses Sentence case, in which only the first letter of the first word of each sentence is capitalized.

- Specified number of fonts. This helps you keep fonts under control.

- Specified minimum font size. Use this style option to make sure text is large enough for your audience to read easily.

- Specified number of bullet items in a placeholder.

- Specified number of lines for a slide title or a list item.

To turn on style checking, click Options on the Tools menu. Click the Spelling and Style tab, and select the *Check style* check box. When prompted, click Enable Assistant.

You can change the types of errors the style checker looks for by clicking Style Options. The dialog box shown in Figure 2-12 appears. On the Case and End Punctuation tab, you can select the type of capitalization you want to use in slide titles and body text. You can also select the types of punctuation you want to use for slide titles and body text, so the style checker doesn't mark them as errors.

FIGURE 2-12
Adjust the case and punctuation options

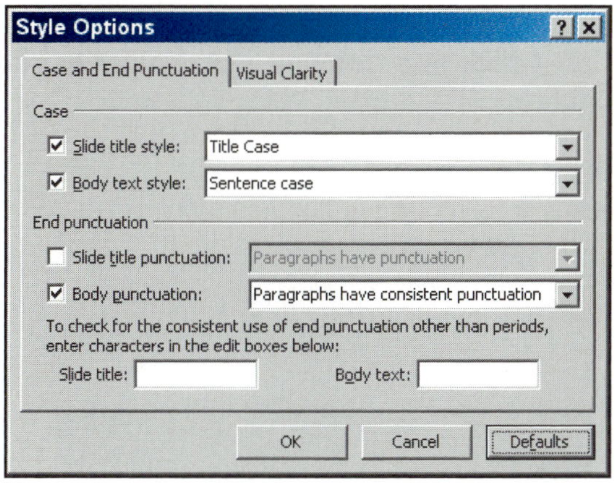

Click the Visual Clarity tab to see the options shown in Figure 2-13. Here, you can change the font limit, the minimum size for text, the maximum number of items allowed in a bulleted list, the maximum number of lines of slide text, and the maximum number of lines per bullet item. To return to the default values, click Defaults. To accept your changes, click OK.

FIGURE 2-13
Change the visual clarity options

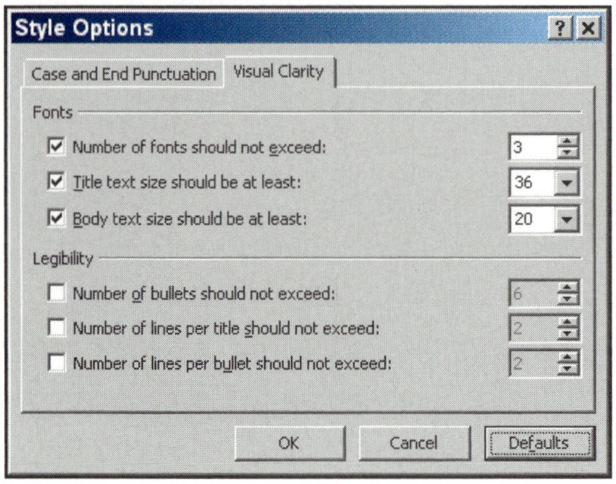

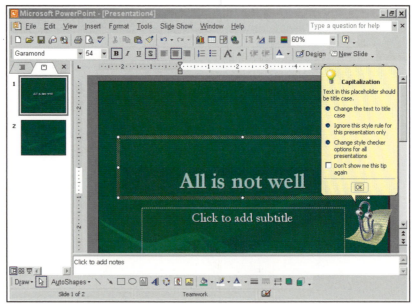

After returning to the Options dialog box, click OK to turn on style checking. Once style checking is turned on, if a style error occurs as you make changes to a slide or add new text, a light bulb icon appears. Click the icon to display the Office Assistant, which informs you of the error type and provides several options for dealing with it, as shown in Figure 2-14. Typically, you can choose to ignore the error for the entire presentation, have PowerPoint correct the error on this slide, or change the style checker options. To ignore the error for this slide only, just click OK to dismiss the message, and then click in a different placeholder or click on another slide, or the message reappears after a minute.

FIGURE 2-14
When a style error is found, the Office Assistant offers remedies

STEP-BY-STEP 2.9

1. In the **TapSoft Product Release 2** file, click **Tools** on the menu, and click **Options**.

2. Click the **Spelling and Style** tab, and click the **Check style** check box. Click the **Style Options** button.

3. On the **Case and End Punctuation** tab, click the Body punctuation drop-down arrow, and then click **Paragraphs do not have punctuation**.

4. Click the **Visual Clarity** tab, and change the **Body text size should be at least** value to **24**. Click the **OK** button twice.

5. Display slide 2 and click within the bulleted list.

6. A light bulb should appear. Click it to see what the Office Assistant suggests.

7. Click **Remove end punctuation**.

8. Click within the bulleted list on slide 8, and click the light bulb when it appears.

9. Click **Ignore this style rule for this presentation only**.

10. Save changes and leave the **TapSoft Product Release 2** file open to use in the next exercise.

Work with Design Template Colors

If your presentation uses a design template, then a set of coordinated colors (a color scheme) is automatically applied to each slide. Even if you choose not to apply a design template, you may have selected a color scheme to work with. In any case, the colors in the color scheme are used in the title and body text, slide background, bullets, object shadows and fills, and as accents. You can replace one color with another from the current color scheme, add any color to the scheme, or modify scheme colors throughout the presentation.

Replace or Add a Color

Every PowerPoint color scheme has eight colors that work well together. These colors have been applied to specific objects in the presentation. You can easily change the color of any object by selecting it and opening the dialog box or list that allows you to format the object.

For example, to change the color of text, select either the text placeholder (to change all text in the placeholder) or select a word or phrase by dragging over it. Then click the drop-down arrow on the Font Color button (located on the Formatting toolbar) to display the color palette (Figure 2-15).

FIGURE 2-15
Choose a font color

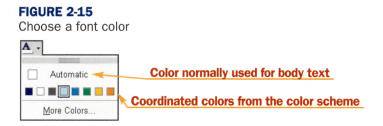

The color palette shows the eight colors of the current color scheme. The color marked as Automatic is the color assigned to body text, subtitle text, and drawn lines for the color scheme your presentation is using. To apply a different scheme color to text, select a color from the palette.

You do not need to stick to the color scheme colors, however, if you don't see one you like. You can select another color by clicking More Colors in the color palette to open the Colors dialog box, shown in Figure 2-16.

FIGURE 2-16
Colors dialog box

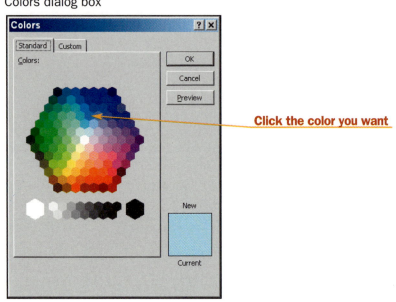

The Colors palette has two tabs: Standard and Custom. The Standard tab contains a palette of selected colors from the *RGB color wheel*. Click any color to select it. The Custom tab allows you to create your own color. Click with the crosshair pointer anywhere in the color palette (which is based on the *HSL color model*) to select a color and then adjust its value (lightness or darkness) with the slider. You can also enter the RGB values for a color in the text boxes at the bottom of the dialog box to select a color.

After choosing or creating a new color, click OK in the Colors dialog box to apply the color. This color is added to the color palette for the current presentation on a line below the default colors in the color scheme. To select that same color again, you need only click its color swatch in the palette. Follow this basic procedure to select a new color for bullets, text boxes, and other objects. For example, to change the color of bullets, open the Bullets and Numbering dialog box, click the Color drop-down arrow, and select another color from the current color scheme or click More Colors to add a new color to the scheme.

Change the Colors in a Scheme

If the colors in a particular color scheme are close but not exactly what you want, you can modify them. When you change the colors in a scheme, elements assigned to that color are automatically changed. For example, if you change the color assigned to bullets, all bullets throughout a presentation are changed to that color. This is different from changing the color of an element on a single slide, as you learned to do in the *Customize a Bulleted List* section. Keep in mind that the changes you make to the scheme are applied throughout the presentation, but only to slides using that same design template and color scheme.

To change colors in the current color scheme, display the Slide Design task pane and click the *Color Schemes* link to display the current color scheme. Then click the *Edit Color Schemes* link at the bottom of the task pane to open the Edit Color Scheme dialog box, shown in Figure 2-17. The dialog box lists the eight colors of the scheme, each labeled with the name of a specific slide element. Click the element whose color you want to change. Then click the Change Color button to open the Colors dialog box. Select or create a new color as you learned earlier and click OK to return to the Edit Color Scheme dialog box, where you can change the color of a different slide element.

> **Note** ✅
>
> Changes to a color scheme stay within the current presentation. The next time you apply that color scheme to a new presentation, the default scheme colors are applied.

FIGURE 2-17
Edit Color Scheme dialog box

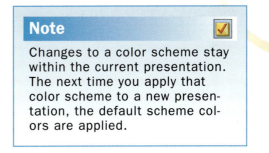

After modifying the colors in a color scheme, you can apply them throughout the presentation by clicking the Apply button. If you'd like to see how they look before committing yourself, click the Preview button instead. If you end up with a collection of colors you'd like to save permanently as a new color scheme, click Add As Standard Scheme. This adds the scheme to the collection of schemes associated with a particular template. If you apply that template to a different presentation, you can also apply the color scheme you designed and saved.

STEP-BY-STEP 2.10

1. In the **TapSoft Product Release 2** file, click the **Design** button on the Formatting toolbar.

2. Click the **Color Schemes** link, and then click the **Edit Color Schemes** link at the bottom of the task pane.

3. Click **Background**, and then click the **Change Color** button. The Colors dialog box opens.

4. Select the lightest purple on the Standard tab's color palette, and click the **OK** button.

5. Click the **Preview** button in the Edit Color Scheme dialog box to see the new background color.

6. Still in the Edit Color Scheme dialog box, click **Accent** and click the **Change Color** button. Select a color that coordinates well with the background, such as a medium purple. When you find something you like, click the **OK** button.

STEP-BY-STEP 2.10 Continued

7. Click **Title Text** and change the color of the title text for each slide to white.

8. In the Edit Color Scheme dialog box, click the **Apply** button to apply the color changes throughout the presentation. Close the Slide Design task pane.

9. Scroll through the slides to see how the color changes affect the slides. Close the Slide Design task pane.

10. Save changes and leave the **TapSoft Product Release 2** file open to use in the next exercise.

Change the Slide Background

You can change the background of a slide in a number of ways. As you just learned, one simple way is to select a new color scheme or to change the background color associated with the scheme by editing it. But PowerPoint offers you more choices than just these.

To change the slide background, click Background on the Format menu. Using the Background dialog box, shown in Figure 2-18, you can change the background of the current slide, selected slides, or all slides in the presentation. Color changes you make here affect only the background, and not any graphic that may be part of the design template background.

> **Extra for Experts**
>
> If you want to change the background of several slides but not all slides in the presentation, select the slides you want to change before issuing the Background command.

FIGURE 2-18
Background dialog box

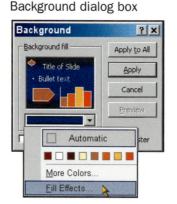

The current background color displays just below a thumbnail of the current slide. Click the drop-down arrow next to the current color to open the color palette. Choose a color in the scheme, or click More Colors to choose something different.

PowerPoint also offers four kinds of special fill effects you can apply to a slide background. Click Fill Effects on the color palette to open the Fill Effects dialog box. The Fill Effects dialog box has four tabs: Gradient, Texture, Pattern, and Picture.

On the Gradient tab, shown in Figure 2-19, you can blend two colors horizontally, vertically, diagonally, from the corners, or from the center. Start by clicking a color in the Color 1 list, and then click a different color in the Color 2 list. If you want to blend a color into black, you can save time by clicking the One color option and choosing the color to blend with black from the Color 1 list. Or you may prefer to use the preset gradient combinations PowerPoint supplies by clicking Preset and clicking one in the list.

FIGURE 2-19
Selecting a gradient

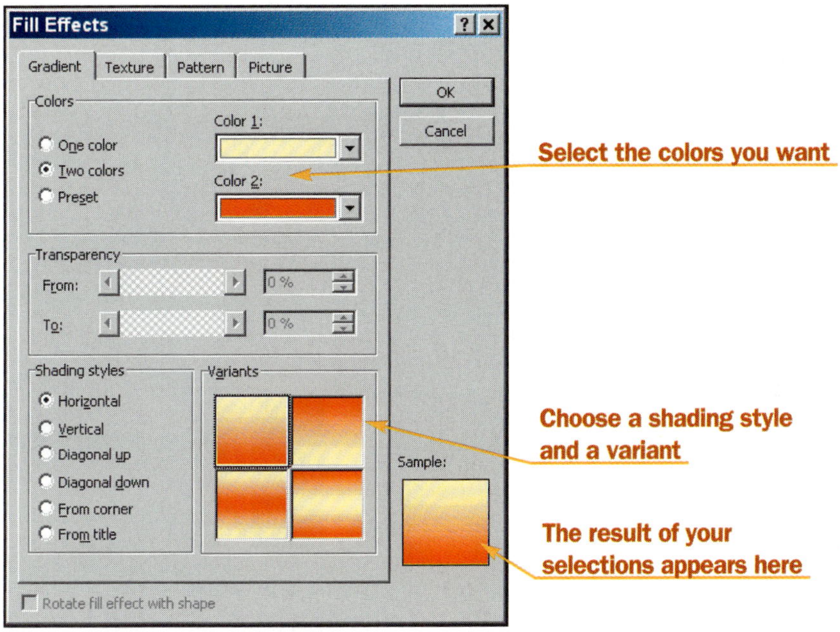

You can't adjust the Transparency of a background fill, so click a Shading style, such as Diagonal up. There are always four variants to select from within any style. A sample in the lower-right corner of the dialog box shows how the current settings look on the slide.

The Texture tab, shown in Figure 2-20, lets you apply a texture to the background instead of a flat color. Just click the thumbnail for the texture you want to use. Each texture has a name that appears below the palette of textures after you click one of the thumbnails. If you've created your own texture using a graphics editor such as PhotoShop or Paint Shop Pro, you can load it by clicking Other Texture and then navigating to your file and selecting it.

FIGURE 2-20
Apply a texture to the background

Another fill effect you might like to apply is a pattern. Click the Pattern tab to display a palette of pattern options. Select a color in the Foreground list and then a different color in the Background list, and then click the desired pattern in the palette. For best results, use two colors that are fairly light so that the pattern background does not overwhelm the slide text.

Your final choice in the Fill Effects dialog box is to use a graphic as your slide background. You may choose this option if you have a nice photograph or other graphic image that conveys the message of a particular slide or presentation or to add your company logo or other image behind the text on a slide. Click the Picture tab. Click Select Picture, click the graphics file, and click Insert to return to the Fill Effects dialog box.

After choosing a color or making a selection in the Fill Effects dialog box, you return to the Background dialog box where you have some final choices to make. To apply the new background to the currently selected slide(s) only, click Apply. To apply the new background throughout the presentation, click Apply to All. To preview the background first, click Preview. To remove a background graphic that is part of the design template you selected, click *Omit background graphics from master* before clicking Apply to All or Apply.

S TEP-BY-STEP 2.11

1. In the **TapSoft Product Release 2** file, click **Format** on the menu bar, and then click **Background**. Your current background isn't very interesting, so you want to create a more visually appealing one.

2. Click the drop-down arrow for the current background color, and click **Fill Effects**.

3. Click the **Texture** tab, and click the **Blue tissue paper** texture (the first thumbnail in the third row).

4. Click the **OK** button, and then click the **Preview** button to see the new background on the current slide.

5. This isn't quite what you want, so display the Fill Effects dialog box again.

6. Click the **Gradient** tab, click **Preset**, and then click **Fog** in the Preset colors list.

7. Click the **Horizontal** option for Shading, if necessary, and click the first of the **Variants**. Then click the **OK** button.

8. Click the **Preview** button to see the new background. That's more like it!

9. In the Background dialog box, click the **Apply to All** button.

10. Scroll through the slides to see the new background in place.

11. Save changes and leave the **TapSoft Product Release 2** file open to use in the next exercise.

Change Formatting on Slide Masters

Up to now, the formatting changes you've learned have affected only the current slide (or selected slides). To change the font, font size, alignment, spacing, or bullet style for all the slides in a presentation, you must make your changes to the *slide master*. You can also add a graphic to the slide master to have it appear on all slides. The slide master is the part of a design template that contains all its global formatting information such as font and font size, bullet styles, alignment options, and so on. If you have applied a design template to your presentation, you have a slide master you can change. If you have applied multiple design templates, then your presentation has multiple slide masters.

Slide masters come in sets of two—a slide master that controls the format and styles used in most of the slides in a presentation, and a *title master*, which controls any slide using the Title layout. You typically have only one title slide—the first slide—although you may want to break up a long presentation into smaller sections with a title slide for each section.

Make Changes to a Master

To display the slide master, click the View menu, click Master, and click Slide Master. The master for the current slide is displayed on the screen. If you are viewing a title slide when you issue this command, the title master displays. If you are viewing a slide other than the title slide, the slide master appears, as shown in Figure 2-21.

FIGURE 2-21
Make changes to the slide master

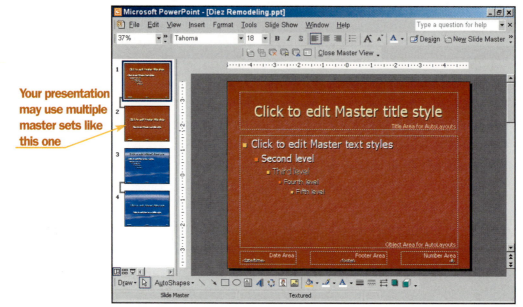

The slide master contains two major placeholders—one for the slide title and one for body text. Each placeholder contains text that tells you how to change it. For example, the top placeholder on the slide master says, *Click to edit Master title style.* You don't need to edit or delete this text. Instead, concentrate on changing its format to the text style you want to use for the title of a slide. Change the title's font, font style, alignment, color, or position on the slide.

The larger placeholder on the slide master controls body text. It displays a sample of each bullet level. You can change individual bullet styles (for example, change the bullet symbol for a specific bullet level), or you can select the entire placeholder to make changes to all levels at once. You can change font, font size, font color, alignment, and so on.

Changes you make to the title style on the slide master also affect the title style on the title master automatically. For example, if you change the title style on the slide master from 44 to 46 point, the title style on the title master changes proportionately, from 51 to 53 point. Likewise, if you change the font, font size, or style of the top bullet level text, a similar change is automatically made to the subtitle style on the title master because the two are designed to coordinate with each other. For these reasons, you should make changes to the slide master first, and then make any final adjustments to the title master's title and subtitle styles.

You can resize any placeholder by dragging one of its handles (small white circles that appear around its perimeter when the placeholder is clicked). You may do this if you want to change the default size of a body text placeholder throughout a presentation. To move a placeholder, click between the handles on the perimeter and drag.

Change to the title master, shown in Figure 2-22, by clicking it in the Slides pane. Click in the placeholders as directed to make any changes to font, font size, alignment, line spacing, or other attribute. Changes made on the title master affect only the slide text—they do not automatically change the slide master styles. So, for example, if you change the font size of the title style on the title master from 51 to 53 point, the title style on the slide master *is not affected at all.*

Note

Figures 2-21 and 2-22 shows two sets of masters, because in this presentation, two design templates are used. Each pair of masters is associated with a different design template.

FIGURE 2-22
Make changes to the title master

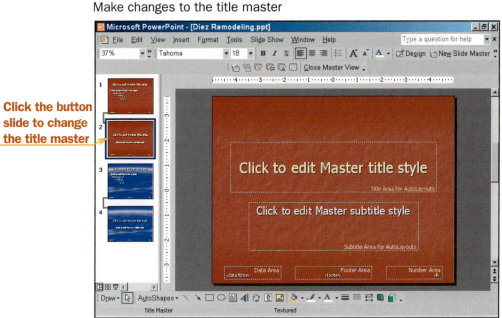

When you're finished making changes to the slide master and title master, click Close Master View on the Slide Master View toolbar. Before you do, however, you may want to add a footer to your slides.

Add Footer Information

You may have noticed on both the title and slide masters that there are placeholders for *footer* information—text or graphics that appear at the bottom of every slide. You need to provide the content for those placeholders if you want items such as a date, a slide number, or a footer to appear on the slides. To do that, while in Slide Master view, click Header and Footer on the View menu to open the Header and Footer dialog box, shown in Figure 2-23.

FIGURE 2-23
Header and Footer dialog box

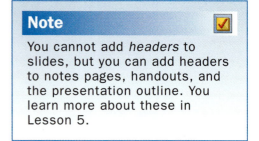

You have two options for including a date and time on slides. Make sure the Date and time box is selected, and then choose either *Update automatically* or *Fixed*. The automatic update option updates the date and time each time you open or print the presentation. You can select from a number of date and time formats. Choose the fixed option to display a date that stays the same. You must then key the date and time in the box as you want them to be shown.

> **Note**
>
> You cannot add *headers* to slides, but you can add headers to notes pages, handouts, and the presentation outline. You learn more about these in Lesson 5.

To have the slide numbers appear on each slide, click Slide number. To add additional information, click Footer and key what you want in the box. You might add your name, the company's name, the name of the presentation, and so on. If you don't want this data to appear on the title slide, click *Don't show on title slide*. Then click Apply to All.

On the slide master or title master, you can click any of the footer placeholders to format the text. You can drag the placeholders to change their location on the slides. To change what appears in the footer, you should open the Header and Footer dialog box again.

> **Hot Tip**
>
> If you want to change the footer for selected slides, change to Normal view and display the Header and Footer dialog box again. Make your changes and click Apply.

STEP-BY-STEP 2.12

1. In the **TapSoft Product Release 2** file, click **View** on the menu bar, click **Master**, and then click **Slide Master**.

2. Select the slide master if necessary (first in the Slides tab list), and click the **Click to edit Master title style** placeholder in the slide pane.

STEP-BY-STEP 2.12 Continued

3. Click the **Font** drop-down arrow on the Formatting toolbar, and click **Times New Roman**.

4. Click the **Font Size** drop-down arrow on the Formatting toolbar, and click **40**.

5. Click the **Bold** button on the Formatting toolbar.

6. Click the **Click to edit Master text styles** placeholder. Display the Bullets and Numbering dialog box and change the bullet color to a dark gray (third from left on the list of current scheme colors).

7. Select the title master in the Slides tab, and click the **Click to edit Master title style** placeholder. Click the **Font Size** drop-down arrow on the Formatting toolbar, and click **40**.

8. Click **View** on the menu bar, and then click **Header and Footer**.

9. Click the **Update automatically** option, and click a format similar to **August 30, 2005**.

10. Click the **Footer** check box and key your name in the text box.

11. Click the **Apply to All** button.

12. Click the **Close Master View** button.

13. Scroll through the slides in the presentation to see your changes.

14. Save changes and close the **TapSoft Product Release 2** file. Close PowerPoint.

SUMMARY

In this lesson, you learned:

- You can create a new presentation using a blank presentation, a design template, or the AutoContent Wizard.

- You must save your presentations often to avoid data loss.

- You can copy, move, or delete slides as desired to improve the flow of your presentation.

- Buttons on the Formatting toolbar allow you to change the font and font size of text, to add bold or italics, to change the color of text, and to adjust text alignment.

- There are several ways to change the size of text—with the Font Size list, or with the Increase/Decrease Font Size buttons.

- You can change the bullets used in bulleted lists by adjusting their size, their shape, and their color. Use symbols from other fonts or picture bullets to add special interest to bulleted lists.

- PowerPoint helps you fit text in a placeholder using the AutoFit Text feature.

- You can check styles in a presentation to prevent inconsistencies in punctuation, capitalization, and font size. You can also establish limits on the number of fonts used, the number of items in a list, and the number of lines in a title.

- You can change the color of any object on a slide to another color in the color scheme, or you can add a color to the scheme or create your own colors. You can edit color scheme colors to change colors throughout a presentation.

- When changing the background of a slide, you can apply a flat color, gradient, pattern, texture, or picture. You can also remove the background graphic from the design template if you like.

- The slide master and title master control the styles used throughout a presentation, although you can change individual slides as desired. Use Slide Master view to insert footer data that appears on every slide.

VOCABULARY *Review*

Define the following terms:

Font	HSL color model	Point
Footer	Indent	RGB color wheel
Handles	Object	Slide master
Hanging indent	Outdent	Title master

REVIEW *Questions*

MULTIPLE CHOICE

Select the best response for the following statements.

1. You can create a new presentation that incorporates a design template by
   A. Clicking the New button.
   B. Clicking the Design button.
   C. Clicking the AutoContent Wizard button.
   D. Clicking the From Design Template link.

2. After creating a new presentation, save it by
   A. Clicking the Save File button.
   B. Clicking the Print and Save button.
   C. Clicking the Save button.
   D. Turning on AutoSave.

3. If you add an automatic date to the footer in a presentation, it will be updated whenever you
   A. Print.
   B. Save.
   C. Run the slide show.
   D. Spell check.

4. The best way to remove a slide from a presentation while in Slide Sorter view is to
   A. Press Delete.
   B. Click Remove.
   C. Press Esc.
   D. Click Edit, Delete Slide.

5. The best way to remove a slide from a presentation while in Normal view is to
   A. Press Delete.
   B. Click Remove.
   C. Press Esc.
   D. Click Edit, Delete Slide.

6. Use the Duplicate command to
   A. Copy a presentation.
   B. Copy a slide.
   C. Copy a graphic from one slide to another.
   D. Repeat a word.

7. If the Duplicate command is currently unavailable, it's because
   A. You're in Slide Sorter view.
   B. You've selected an element on a slide.
   C. You're in Normal view.
   D. You've selected multiple slides.

8. You can change the font
   A. In a slide title and subtitle.
   B. Throughout a presentation.
   C. In all the elements of a slide.
   D. All of the above.

9. Fonts that use serifs are
   A. More popular on the Web.
   B. Compatible on all computer systems.
   C. Easier to read at a distance.
   D. No longer made.

10. You can change a bullet's
    A. Number and position.
    B. Color and size.
    C. Size and number.
    D. Number and shape.

FILL IN THE BLANK

Complete the following sentences by writing the correct word or words in the blanks provided.

1. A(n) _____ is created by gradually blending one color into another.

2. It's easiest to reorganize slides in a presentation while in _____ view.

3. A(n) _____ is a collection of characters that form a typeface.

4. The height of a font is measured in _____.

5. If text is centered, that means its edges are equally distant from the left and right _____.

6. It's easier if you work in _____ view when applying formatting to text.

7. PowerPoint lets you create bulleted lists and _____ lists.

8. A(n) _____ is the amount of space between the left edge of a paragraph and the margin.

9. The _____ feature automatically changes the size of text to fit the size of its placeholder.

10. To make global changes throughout a presentation, make them to the _____.

PROJECTS

PROJECT 2-1

1. Launch PowerPoint and start a new presentation with the **Glass Layers** template.

2. Save the presentation as **Bull Dog Security 2nd Qtr Sales**.

3. On the title slide:
   A. Key the title **Bull Dog Security**.
   B. Key the subtitle **Second Quarter Sales Report**.

4. Change the subtitle text to 28-point Verdana.

5. Add a second slide with the **Title, Text, and Content** layout:
   A. Key the title **Predictions for Second Quarter**.
   B. Add the following bulleted list:

   New wireless system would increase sales by 25%

   Installation time would increase by 2 hours on average

   Net Income would rise by only 10% due to increased labor costs

6. Click the title placeholder and click the **Decrease Font Size** button two times, to 36 points.

7. Add a third slide:
   A. Use the **Title Only** layout.
   B. Key the title **So what were the results?**

8. Display slide 2 and click the bulleted list placeholder. Open the Bullets and Numbering dialog box.

9. Click the **Picture** button. In the Picture Bullet dialog box, click **Import**, change to the data files folder, click the file **PS Project 2-1**, and click **Add**.

10. In the Picture Bullet dialog box, click the bull dog bullet, and click the **OK** button.

11. With the bulleted list placeholder still selected, change the line spacing after each paragraph to **0.1 Lines**.

12. Save changes and close the **Bull Dog Security 2nd Qtr Sales** file, but leave PowerPoint open to use in Project 2-2.

PROJECT 2-2

1. Open **PS Project 2-2** from the data files.

2. Save the file as **Bull Dog Security 2nd Qtr Sales 2**.

3. In Normal view, display slide 9. Duplicate this slide.

4. Display slide 9 again, and edit the subtitle to read **Sales are up**. Change the percentage to **28%**.

5. Right-align the subtitle.

6. Display slide 10, and edit the title to read, **And…**

7. Change to Slide Sorter view. Click the *Summary* slide (slide 8) and drag it to the end of the presentation to move it.

8. Click the *Training Costs* slide (slide 5) and delete it.

9. Turn on style checking, set body text punctuation to none, and increase the minimum body text size to 28 point.

10. Click the title on slide 3 and fix the title case error. Reduce the font size to 40 so the edited title fits on one line.

11. Click the bulleted list on slide 4 and fix the problems with sentence case and font size.

12. Click the bulleted list on slide 5 and ignore the suggestion to fix the punctuation (for this slide only), and fix the problem with font size.

13. Save changes and leave the **Bull Dog Security 2nd Qtr Sales 2** file open to use in Project 2-3.

PROJECT 2-3

1. In the **Bull Dog Security 2nd Qtr Sales 2** file, display the slide masters for the presentation.

2. Select the slide master if necessary (the first slide in the Slides tab), and click the title style placeholder.

3. Change the color of the title text to a light blue.

4. While still in slide master view, open the Header and Footer dialog box.

5. Turn off the date and time display.

6. Turn on slide numbering. Then click in the **Footer** box and key **Confidential - Office Use Only**. Apply the footer information to all slides, and then close the slide master view.

7. Display the Design Template task pane and choose to edit the current color scheme.

8. Change the Accent color to a medium turquoise blue and apply the change.

9. Save changes and close the **Bull Dog Security 2nd Qtr Sales 2** file. Close PowerPoint.

SCANS 🌐 **WEB PROJECT**

Display the New Presentation task pane, click the *Templates on Microsoft.com* link, and explore the many templates available on Microsoft's Web site. You'll need to dig through the categories listed there—each category contains a mix of templates for programs such as Word, Excel, and Access.

Locate the "Selling Your Ideas" template, download it, and create a presentation with at least five slides using the template. Assume you are a mid-level manager at a big company, and this is your chance to impress your boss with a new proposal and move up to a better position in the company. Your idea is to fix the problem of low client retention (not many clients staying with the company after one year of service) by issuing laptop computers to the installation team so they can download client data on site, make requested changes, and upload and test them before they leave the client. This process will ensure that changes are made in a timely fashion and that the client is happy when the installer leaves—but it also means spending a lot of money buying computers, training personnel, and increasing the size of the MIS department so the installers have technical support for the new laptops. Research the cost of new laptops for a team of 10 installers and the cost of training them in using Windows, Word, and Excel. Include those costs in your presentation. Research the average starting salary for technical support personnel, and include that cost as well. Use the template to focus your ideas and present them in a convincing manner.

Once you've entered the text, apply a different design template and/or color scheme—or replace the background completely with one you've created and choose a color scheme to work with. Adjust the colors in the scheme to suit your taste. Turn on the style checker so you can make sure your presentation uses consistent formatting, punctuation, and capitalization. You'll be presenting this program in a conference room to a group of five upper-level executives. Spell check and proofread your presentation as well.

SCANS 🤝 **TEAMWORK PROJECT**

With your classmates, create a new presentation. Assume you are a dental hygienist in a pediatric dentist's office, and that you are creating a presentation to play on TV monitors installed in each exam room that kids can watch while getting their teeth cleaned. The presentation is a demonstration of proper teeth brushing/flossing procedure. But you need to make it fun and light-hearted as well, because the intended audience is children.

Create an outline that breaks the procedure down into easy-to-remember steps. Include suggestions in the outline for graphics that you'll add later in this unit. Choose a background and colors that appeal to your audience, and enter the text for the presentation. Make sure the text is large because the TVs are mounted high on the wall. Keep the text simple and easy to read. Apply interesting transitions and sounds that hold your young audience's attention, and adjust the timing so slow readers can read each slide before the next one is presented.

CRITICAL *Thinking*

ACTIVITY 2-1

Create a new presentation on swimming safety using the design template of your choice. First, do some research online or at the library. What are the most important things a swimmer must remember in order to have fun and yet stay safe while swimming? Create a title slide for a presentation that demonstrates the Dos and Don'ts in swimming and at least three other slides. You can select layouts with spaces for clip art, charts, and so on, but do not add those elements just yet. Instead, work on the order of the information in your presentation. What data do you want to share with your audience of swimmers (all ages)? In what order should that data be presented? What elements do you want on each slide other than text? Save the presentation with the name Swimming Safety.

ACTIVITY 2-2

Open the Swimming Safety presentation, and concentrate now on refining the look of the presentation. Change the fonts used for the titles. Play around with the colors in the color scheme, changing those you don't like. Select or create a background for your slides, and choose a coordinating color scheme. You can modify some of the colors in the scheme to suit your taste. See if you can find swimming-related bullets for your bulleted lists. Adjust line spacing and alignment if necessary to fit text attractively. Add a footer to your presentation that gives your name.

ACTIVITY 2-3

Examine the options for the style checker again. Why do you think a presentation should follow these rules? If a presentation didn't follow the style rules, what might go wrong? When might it be a good idea to bend these rules? What other rules do you think good presentations should follow? Write your thoughts in a 200-word report. Then open a presentation you've created and examine it for errors. Correct the errors you find.

WORKING WITH GRAPHIC OBJECTS

OBJECTIVES

Upon completion of this lesson, you should be able to:

- Add clip art to a slide.
- Insert graphic images from files on a slide.
- Import images directly from a digital camera or scanner.
- Locate and download graphics on the Internet.
- Draw text boxes, rectangles, circles, and other objects.
- Format and manipulate graphics and objects.
- Organize slide data in a table.
- Create charts to illustrate data.
- Add a diagram to a slide.

Estimated Time: 2 hours

VOCABULARY

Adjustment handle

Aspect ratio

AutoShape

Cell

Chart

Clip art

Datasheet

Diagram

Legend

Rotation handle

Table

Graphic images are often critical in underscoring your intended message, keeping your audience's interest, and even adding much-needed humor to a presentation. In this lesson, you learn everything you ever wanted to know about using graphics in PowerPoint—including clip art; graphic images stored on your computer or network; and images imported from a digital camera, scanned with your scanner, or downloaded from the Internet. You learn how to manipulate graphics by resizing, moving, rotating, flipping, and even adjusting the color, brightness, and contrast of a graphic as needed. If pre-made graphics do not provide you with the illustration you're looking for, you can create your own objects using PowerPoint's drawing tools, and format and manipulate them as well.

Graphic pictures and drawn objects are not the only illustrations you can add to a slide, however. In this lesson, you learn how to organize and present data in a table format, create charts to display data visually, and insert diagrams such as organization charts. You also learn how to format tables, charts, and diagrams to make them more presentable.

PowerPoint's content placeholders include a palette of icons for objects such as clip art, stored images, tables, charts, and diagrams. Click the appropriate icon to insert the graphic object on your slide. However, you can always add one of these content items even if there isn't a placeholder for it. In such a case, PowerPoint typically creates a placeholder for the content by changing to an appropriate layout. PowerPoint also offers many layouts designed specifically for graphic objects, such as the Title and Table layout or the Title and Chart layout. In some cases, you may decide to use these layouts to maximize the space on the slide for your content.

Insert Clip Art

PowerPoint gives you access to Microsoft Office's large collection of *clip art*, photos, and even sounds and movie clips. You can insert clip art to emphasize the message of a particular slide, to provide visual interest in a slide, or to add some comic relief to a long presentation.

You have several options for inserting clip art images. In a content slide layout, click the Insert Clip Art icon to open the Select Picture dialog box, which displays pictures stored on your system in a small, easy-to-use dialog box. You can also click Picture on the Insert menu and then click Clip Art, or click the Insert Clip Art button on the Drawing toolbar to display the Insert Clip Art task pane, shown in Figure 3-1. This task pane provides you with a rich set of tools for locating exactly the image you want and previewing it in a larger format prior to inserting it on a slide.

FIGURE 3-1
Use Insert Clip Art task pane to add a clip art image

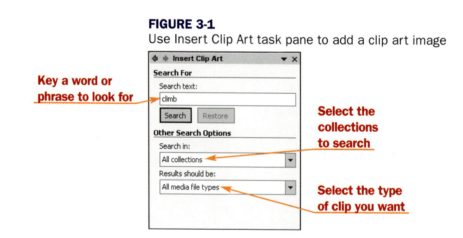

Although PowerPoint provides many slide layouts that contain placeholders for graphic content, you do not have to use a specific slide layout to insert a clip art picture. Select the placeholder you want to hold the clip art picture, or don't select any placeholder if you want PowerPoint to insert the picture as a movable object on the slide. Actually, you're free to move the picture anywhere on the slide, even if you have inserted it in a placeholder.

You can easily search for the clip art picture you want in the Insert Clip Art task pane, making it a simple job to illustrate any slide. Key a word or phrase in the Search text box. This might be a key word from your slide or a phrase related to the slide's meaning, such as *challenge, money, finish, strong*, and so on. You can limit the search to a particular clip art collection by clicking the Search in arrow and clicking the collection(s) to search.

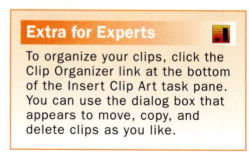

Extra for Experts

To organize your clips, click the Clip Organizer link at the bottom of the Insert Clip Art task pane. You can use the dialog box that appears to move, copy, and delete clips as you like.

In the *Results should be* drop-down list, you can choose the kind of image you need. Select either Clip Art or Photographs, or click both check boxes to find clip art graphics as well as photographs. Notice that you can also search for movies and sound files. You learn about these types of files in the next lesson.

Click the Search button in the task pane to begin the search based on your criteria. PowerPoint displays a panel of thumbnails of images matching your description. If you don't see anything you want to use, click the Modify button and change your criteria. Click an image to add it to the slide. If you click the drop-down arrow on the thumbnail, you can select any of the options shown in Figure 3-2 rather than insert the picture.

FIGURE 3-2
Other actions you can take with a clip art image

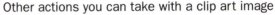

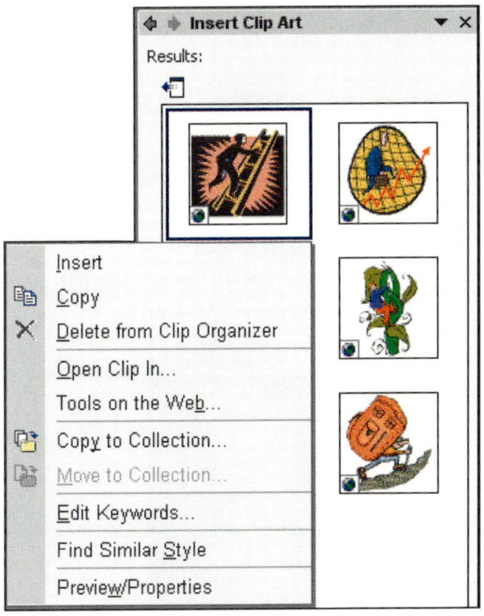

S TEP-BY-STEP 3.1

1. Launch PowerPoint, and open **PS Step 3-1** from the data files. Save the file as **Senior Security**.

2. On slide 1, click **Insert** on the menu bar, click **Picture**, and then click **Clip Art**. The Insert Clip Art task pane opens. (If the Add Clips to Organizer dialog box appears, click **Don't show this message again** and click **Later** to continue.)

3. In the Insert Clip Art task pane, key **senior** in the **Search text** text box.

4. If necessary, click **Everywhere** in the Search in list.

5. Click the **Results should be** drop-down arrow and click only **Photographs**. (If Clip Art, Movies, or Sounds are selected, deselect them by clicking each option to turn it off.) Click the **Search** button.

> **Note** ☑
>
> Depending on your system setup, you may have only a limited number of clip art files on your computer. You may need to use the Microsoft Office Media Content CD-ROM to access a wider selection of pictures.

STEP-BY-STEP 3.1 Continued

6. Locate an image similar to the one shown in Figure 3-3 and click it to insert it into the center of slide 1. (You may be prompted to insert a CD-ROM to insert the picture.)

FIGURE 3-3
Insert this or a similar photograph

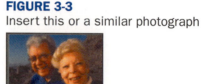

7. Display slide 2. In the Insert Clip Art task pane, click the **Modify** button.

8. Key **receptionist** in the Search text box, and then click the **Search** button.

9. Click the image shown in Figure 3-4 or a similar one to insert it. Close the Insert Clip Art task pane.

FIGURE 3-4
Insert this or a similar photograph

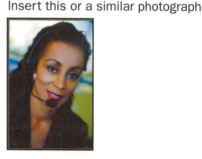

10. Save and close **Senior Security**. Leave PowerPoint open to use in the next exercise.

Insert Pictures from Other Sources

You are not limited to clip art images that come with PowerPoint. You can also insert other graphic images stored on a hard disk, CD-ROM, or similar device. You can import images from your digital camera or scanner directly into a presentation. The Internet is another major source of images.

Insert Picture from Files

If the graphic you want to use on a slide is already stored on a hard disk or similar device, you can insert it easily by clicking the Insert Picture icon in a content placeholder or on the Drawing toolbar. You can also click Picture on the Insert menu, and then click From

File. Any of these actions opens the Insert Picture dialog box, shown in Figure 3-5. Navigate to the folder that contains the file, click the file to select it, and click Insert to add it to a slide.

FIGURE 3-5
Insert Picture dialog box

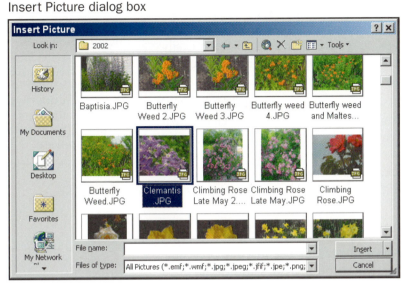

Import Images from a Scanner or Digital Camera

You can import images directly from your digital camera or scanner into a PowerPoint presentation. After you have properly connected your computer to a scanner or digital camera, click the placeholder on the slide in which you want the image to appear. Click Picture on the Insert menu, and then click From Scanner or Camera to open the Insert Picture from Scanner or Camera dialog box, shown in Figure 3-6.

Extra for Experts

Click Picture on the Insert menu and then click New Photo Album to create a presentation based on a series of graphic files. Select the graphic files you want to use, pick a layout, add text boxes where needed, and PowerPoint creates a new presentation with the selected images.

FIGURE 3-6
Import an image from your camera or scanner

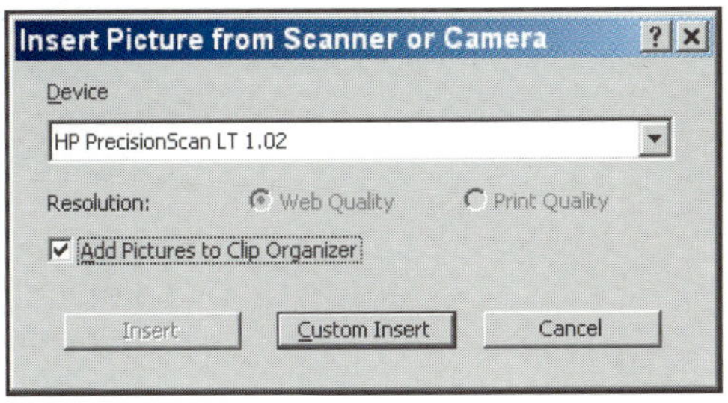

Click the Device drop-down arrow and select the device you want to import from (scanner or camera). With most scanners, you can probably initiate the scan directly from this dialog box. Simply click the resolution you want (Web Quality or Print Quality) and click Insert to begin the scan procedure. To add the image to the Clip Organizer so you can access it more easily later, click the Add Pictures to Clip Organizer check box before clicking Insert.

With a digital camera or non-compatible scanner, click Custom Insert. This launches the device's own program so you can use it to initiate a scan, sort and select images on a camera, adjust resolution, and so on. Again, before clicking Custom Insert, you can indicate whether you want the selected image added to your clip art collection.

Download Images from the Internet

Another source of images for use in your presentations is the Internet. Microsoft provides additional clips in the Design Gallery Live portion of its Web site. There are also many sites on the Internet that provide clip art and photos copyright free; in other words, you can use them for your own purposes without paying a fee.

To import images from Microsoft's Web site, click the *Clips Online* link at the bottom of the Insert Clip Art task pane. Your Web browser displays the Design Gallery Live on Microsoft's Web site. To search the site for clips, type a key word in the Search for box. As on the Insert Clip Art task pane, you can limit the search to specific types of clip art collections and files. You can also choose the order in which the results will appear by clicking the Order by arrow and making a selection. Click Go or press Enter to begin the search.

> **Important**
>
> Importing directly from a camera or scanner may produce mixed results, depending on the exact model you're using. The device must support TWAIN or WIA protocols for this procedure to work. Before attempting to import an image, make sure the device is properly connected to your computer and you've installed the software that came with the device.

> **Important**
>
> Just because you find an attractive graphic, photo, video, or sound file on a Web site doesn't mean you can download it to your system and use it however you like. Even if a Web site does not tell you so specifically, images, videos, and sounds created by others are their property, *not yours*. Download and use files only if you've been given specific permission to do so. Ignoring a copyright is not only unethical, it is illegal.

> **Note**
>
> If you click an icon on the Design Gallery Live home page to display a collection of featured clips, you cannot select individual clips in that group. Instead, click the Download Collection link to download the collection.

Figure 3-7 shows a search results page. Click a thumbnail to preview the clip in a larger size. To select a clip to download, click its check box. To select all the clips, click the *Select All* link. If you select a single clip, you can continue selecting as many clips as you want. A running total appears at the top of the window. In most cases, you'll have several pages of clips to browse through. To display the next page, click the Click for More Clips icon. To return to a previous page, click the Click for Previous Clips icon. You can also click a specific page to view from the drop-down list.

FIGURE 3-7
Click the clips you want to download

When you're ready to download your clips, click the *Download X* clips link. You'll see a summary page listing the number of clips selected for download and their total size. Click Download Now! and the files are copied to your computer's hard disk. The Clip Organizer opens, and the clips are automatically placed in its My Collections\Downloaded Clips collection. Use the dialog box to reorganize your clips as desired, and then close it.

There are many other sources of clip art and photos on the Internet, some offering free access and others requiring a fee for use. In some cases, the fee gives you the right to use the image however you want—in print, on the Web, or within an onscreen presentation (but not saved to CD, DVD, or published in any form). Other images come with more limited usage rights, so be sure to read carefully any legal notices you may find on the sites you visit. Still other clip art Web sites simply claim not to know for sure whether the images are copyright protected, and that the illegal use of any image on the site is your problem. It's typically best to avoid using clips found on such sites because you can't verify your right to use them.

STEP-BY-STEP 3.2

1. Open **PS Step 3-2a** from the data files. Save the file as **Senior Security 2**.

2. Display slide 4, and click the **Insert Picture** button in the content placeholder on the left. The Insert Picture dialog box opens.

STEP-BY-STEP 3.2 Continued

3. Navigate to the data files folder, and click the file **PS Step 3-2b**. Click the **Insert** button.

4. Change to slide 5. Search the Internet for a copyright-free photo you can use to illustrate the slide. Study the other images already in use and the text on this slide, before deciding which image you want to use.

5. Download and insert the image on slide 5 in the content placeholder provided.

6. Save changes and leave the **Senior Security 2** file open to use in the next exercise.

> **Note** ☑
>
> Don't worry if your image is not the right size, or if it covers up some text. You learn how to adjust object and placeholder size and how to create a text box to add a photo credit later in the lesson.

Format Images

Sometimes, after inserting a graphic image or piece of clip art, you may decide that the image is a bit too dark or that portions of it are unnecessary. Although you can make these kinds of modifications and a whole lot more in a graphics editor such as Photoshop, PowerPoint's tools on the Picture toolbar can help you make certain minor adjustments without leaving your presentation.

> **Note** ☑
>
> The buttons on the Picture toolbar affect only the copy of the image stored in the presentation—not the actual image file stored in the Clip Organizer or on your computer's hard disk.

When you click a picture—either a graphic image or clip art—it's surrounded by handles. In addition, the Picture toolbar is usually automatically displayed on your screen. If it doesn't appear, select the View menu, click Toolbars, and choose Picture Toolbar. Table 3-1 contains a brief description of each button in the Picture toolbar and its purpose.

TABLE 3-1
Picture toolbar buttons

BUTTON	NAME	DESCRIPTION
	Insert Picture	Inserts a graphic file.
	Color	Changes an image from full color to grayscale (gray, black, and white), black and white, or washout.
	More Contrast	Increases the contrast in an image by making the light areas lighter and the dark areas darker.
	Less Contrast	Decreases the contrast in an image by making the light areas more dark and the dark areas more light.
	More Brightness	Lightens the image without affecting the contrast.
	Less Brightness	Darkens the image without affecting the contrast.

TABLE 3-1 Continued
Picture toolbar buttons

BUTTON	NAME	DESCRIPTION
	Crop	Hides part of an image from view. Click the Crop button and drag a handle inward to hide (crop) that part of the image. After cropping, click the Crop button again.
	Rotate Left	Rotates the image 90 degrees.
	Line Style	Adds a border around a graphic.
	Compress Pictures	Reduces the size of presentation file by compressing all or selected images, and/or reducing their resolution.
	Recolor Picture	Lets you change the colors in clip art stored in WMF (Windows metafile) format to the colors in your color scheme, or to any colors you choose.
	Format Picture	Opens a dialog box where you can adjust various image properties in one step.
	Set Transparent Color	Makes a selected color clear (transparent) so objects underneath that area of the image can be seen. Does not work on clips stored in animated GIF format, and some clip art.
	Reset Picture	Reverses changes to an image to restore original appearance.

STEP-BY-STEP 3.3

1. In the **Senior Security 2** file, display slide 3.

2. Click the photo in the upper-left corner to select it. If the Picture toolbar does not automatically appear when you select the picture, click **View** on the menu bar, click **Toolbars**, and click **Picture**.

3. Click the **Crop** button on the **Picture** toolbar.

4. Drag the middle handle on the right side of the photo towards the left, cropping the right side of the photo as shown in Figure 3-8.

FIGURE 3-8
Crop the right side of the photo

STEP-BY-STEP 3.3 Continued

5. Click the **Crop** button again to turn it off.

6. Display slide 4 and click the photo on the left to select it.

7. Click the **More Brightness** button on the **Picture** toolbar two times.

8. Save and close the **Senior Security 2** file. Leave PowerPoint open to use in the next exercise.

Draw Your Own Objects

Like most Microsoft Office programs, PowerPoint has a Drawing toolbar that contains simple drawing and formatting tools. Although you probably do not want to try to create complex illustrations with these tools, they can be very useful for adding shapes and lines to your slides. For example, you can draw a graphic arrow to point out a specific bullet item, design a simple and yet effective slide background, or create shapes to illustrate slide content. You can also add text boxes, which enables you to place text wherever you want it on a slide.

Draw a Simple Shape

To draw an object such as a rectangle, click on the appropriate tool on the Drawing toolbar, as shown in Figure 3-9. For example, click the Rectangle tool. Then click anywhere on the slide and drag the crosshair until the object is the desired size. Press Shift while you drag to make the height and width of the object equal. Press Ctrl while you drag to draw the object outward from its center, rather than from a corner. New objects use a default line style and color and the fill color specified by the design template's color scheme. You can easily change these and other formats, as you learn later in this section.

FIGURE 3-9
Drawing tools

If you draw a text box, the insertion point automatically appears within it. To add your text, select the font, font size, and other attributes you want from the Formatting toolbar. To create a bulleted or numbered list, be sure to click the Bullets or Numbering button. To create regular text, simply key it.

Create an AutoShape

Luckily, with PowerPoint's AutoShape feature, you don't need to create every shape from scratch. An *AutoShape* is a complex, pre-drawn object, such as a hexagon, star, callout bubble, or block arrow. To create an AutoShape, click the AutoShapes button on the Drawing toolbar, click a category such as Block Arrows, and then click the object you want to draw from the palette of objects that appears. Click on the slide and drag the crosshair to create the shape.

The Lines category of AutoShapes contains some tools that require a bit more explanation. To use the Curve tool, click to start and then click where you want the line to curve. Double-click to end the line. To use the Freeform tool, click to start, and then drag the pencil pointer just as if you were drawing with a pencil. Double-click to end the line.

Format Objects

After creating any shape, you can change any of the format settings you like. Use the tools at the right end of the Drawing toolbar, shown in Figure 3-10, to change object formats.

FIGURE 3-10
Use these tools to format an object

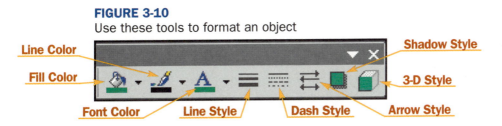

To start formatting, click the object to select it. If you like, you can press Ctrl and click several objects to format them all in a similar manner. Then click the drop-down arrow on the Fill Color, Line Color, or Font Color button to choose a new color. If you simply click one of these buttons, you apply the color shown on the button. The fill color controls the color inside an object's borders, the line color controls the color of the object's outline, and the font color controls the color of any text. Notice that you can also apply patterns, such as those you used for slide backgrounds, to an object's fill. You can also apply a pattern to an object's outline or a drawn line using the Patterned Lines option on the Line Color palette.

Click the Line Style, Dash Style, Arrow Style, Shadow Style, or 3-D Style button to display a palette of styles, and then click the style you want. Line Style changes the thickness of the outline around an object, or the style of a drawn line. Dash Style changes the solid outline of an object to a dashed style. It also changes a solid drawn line to a dashed one. Arrow Style adds an arrowhead to either or both ends of a drawn line. Shadow Style adds a shadow to an object or line; 3-D Style makes that object or line appear to have three dimensions. Most of the palettes contain a command such as More Lines or More Colors, which causes a dialog box with additional style or color options to appear. The Shadow Style and 3-D Style palettes contain a command that causes a special toolbar for modifying the shadow or 3-D effect to appear.

STEP-BY-STEP 3.4

1. Open **PS Step 3-4** from the data files, and save the file as **Senior Security 3**.

2. Display slide 6. Note the gray and tan square at the bottom right of the slide. You will modify this object in the next several steps.

3. Click the **Rectangle** tool on the Drawing toolbar. If the Drawing toolbar is not displayed, click **View**, click **Toolbars**, and click **Drawing**. Start on the diagonal line between colors about ⅛ inch from the top of the object. Draw a rectangle as shown at the left in Figure 3-11. The lower-right corner of the rectangle should be on the diagonal line between colors at the lower-right side of the object.

4. Click the **Fill Color** drop-down arrow on the **Drawing** toolbar, and click the **Follow Fills Scheme Color** swatch (the fifth color from the left). PowerPoint may select this color automatically.

5. Click the **Text Box** tool on the Drawing toolbar, and draw a box across the width of the rectangle you just added.

6. Change the font to **Times New Roman**, **66** point size, **Center** alignment, and select the **Follow Accent and Hyperlink Scheme Color** font color (second color from right). Key **help**. The object now looks like the one shown on the right in Figure 3-11.

FIGURE 3-11
Completed help button

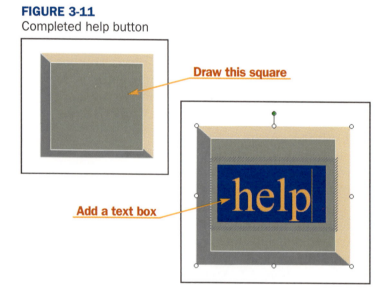

Draw this square

Add a text box

7. Display slide 4. Click the **Text Box** tool and drag across the width of the white area on the right.

8. Select **Times New Roman**, **60** point, and the font color **Follow Background Scheme Color**. Key **Never feel alone again**.

9. Display slide 5. Insert a text box on the slide to provide permission information about the photograph used on the slide. Key **Permission granted for use in this presentation only.** Change the font size to **12** point and adjust the font color if desired to contrast well against the photograph.

10. Save changes and leave the **Senior Security 3** file open to use in the next exercise.

Manipulate Objects and Graphics

When PowerPoint adds clip art, photos, or other graphic images to a slide, their sizes are automatically adjusted to fit the placeholder in which they are inserted. If you don't insert a graphic into a placeholder, it is inserted at its original size. In any case, you can resize a graphic as desired, move it, and even remove it when needed. You can modify drawn objects such as text boxes, rectangles, and ellipses in the same way. For special effects, you can rotate objects or adjust their shapes. Use the Draw menu on the Drawing toolbar to further manipulate objects.

Resize, Move, Copy, or Delete Objects

First, select the object (graphic image or drawn object) you want to resize, move, or delete by clicking it. The handles that appear around the selected object's perimeter (or on the placeholder perimeter) let you know that PowerPoint is ready for you to work with that object. To resize an object, drag any handle outward to make the object bigger, or inward to make it smaller. If you drag by a corner handle, you can maintain the object's *aspect ratio*, or the relationship of height to width. Maintain the aspect ratio to prevent distortion of the image.

To move an object, click it first to select it. Move the mouse pointer over the object until it changes to a four-headed arrow. Click and drag the object wherever you want on the slide. To move the object onto a different slide or into a different presentation, click it and then click the Cut button on the Standard toolbar. The object temporarily disappears. Click on the slide where you want to move the object, and click the Paste button. To copy an object, select it, click the Copy button on the Standard toolbar, and then click the Paste button. If the original slide is still displayed, the copy will appear on top of the original object. If you change to a different slide, the copy will appear in the same relative position on the slide.

To delete an object, click it and press Delete. If the object is in a placeholder, the placeholder remains on the slide. You can use the placeholder to add content in the object's place, such as a table, or you can remove the placeholder by clicking it and pressing Delete again, or by changing to a different layout.

Rotate and Adjust Objects

In addition to the white selection handles, selected drawn objects and images have a green *rotation handle*, like the one shown in Figure 3-12. Click and drag the handle to rotate the drawn object, clip art, or graphic image.

FIGURE 3-12
Rotate an object with its rotation handle

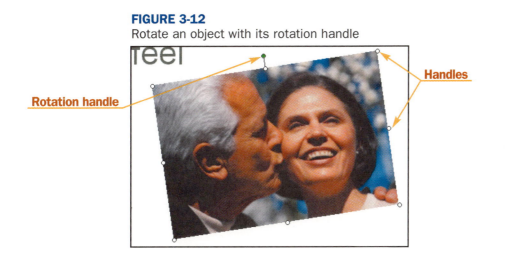

Handles

Rotation handle

Most AutoShapes also include a yellow *adjustment handle*, shown in Figure 3-13, which you can use to adjust the shape. For example, use the adjustment handle to change the size of the arrowhead on a block arrow, adjust the pointer on a callout balloon, change the depth of a star's points, and so on. To make the adjustment, click the handle and drag inward or outward.

> **Hot Tip** 🎯
>
> Placeholders do not have a rotation handle, but text boxes do, which means that you can rotate text if you place it in a text box rather than use a placeholder provided by a slide layout.

FIGURE 3-13
Click the adjustment handle to change the size and width of the arrowhead

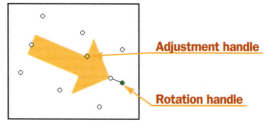

Manipulate Objects with the Draw Menu

The Draw menu allows you to manipulate objects in a number of ways. To display the Draw menu, click the Draw button on the Drawing toolbar. Here are some useful commands you'll find on the Draw menu:

- **Group, Ungroup, Regroup**—Group selected objects so they can be resized, moved, deleted, copied, and formatted as one unit. You can later ungroup objects to apply separate formatting, and then regroup the same objects again.

- **Order**—Use this command to change the order of an object in a stack of objects. You can bring an object to the front or bring it forward one layer, or send an object to the back or send it backward one layer.

- **Nudge**—Move object(s) by a very small amount in the direction you select.

- **Align or Distribute**—Align object(s) along the selected edge or position, such as their top edge, or their centers, or distribute (space) them evenly, either vertically or horizontally. If you turn on the Relative to Slide option, these commands change the positions of object(s) relative to the slide instead of each other.

- **Rotate or Flip**—Rotate an object around its center, or flip an object over its horizontal or vertical axis.

S TEP-BY-STEP 3.5

1. In the **Senior Security 3** file, display slide 6, and click the *help* text box you added to the button. When clicking the text box, be sure to click its border so that you select the box itself and not the text inside.

2. Press and hold **Shift** as you click the square you drew and the gray and tan square beneath it.

STEP-BY-STEP 3.5 Continued

3. Click **Draw** on the Drawing toolbar, and then click **Group**.

4. Drag the rotation handle on the help button object and rotate it as shown in Figure 3-14.

FIGURE 3-14
Move the button into position

5. Click the edge of the help button object and drag to move it into the position shown in Figure 3-14.

6. Display slide 5. Click the permission text box. Use the rotate handle to rotate the text box 90 degrees to the left so it is vertical, and position the text box at the right side of the slide so the text begins in the lower-right corner.

7. Display slide 3, and click the photo on the right. Drag it to position it in the upper-left corner of the accent color area.

8. Resize the photo by dragging its lower-right handle until the right edge of the photo touches the edge of the slide. Part of the photo hangs over the lower edge of the slide.

9. Click the **Crop** button on the **Picture** toolbar, and drag the bottom middle handle of the photo up, cropping the area that hangs over the lower edge of the slide, as shown in Figure 3-15. Click the **Crop** button again to turn it off.

FIGURE 3-15
Crop the photo to fit

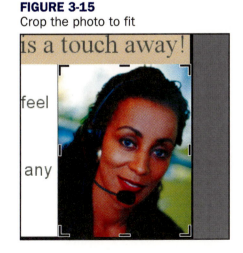

STEP-BY-STEP 3.5 Continued

10. Display slide 4, and adjust the text box width if needed to display two lines of text, with two words on each line. Drag the rotation handle on the text box to the left so the text box fits diagonally between the picture and the right edge of the slide.

11. Display slide 5, and resize your photo if needed so it fills the content area, leaving a small strip of background color on the left, like other slides. Use the **Crop** tool on the Drawing toolbar if needed to make the photo fit the content area.

12. Click the **Draw** button, click **Order**, and click **Send to Back** to place the photo behind the text box. Change the text color if needed so the text in the text box shows up clearly.

13. Save changes and close the **Senior Security 3** file. Leave PowerPoint open to use in the next exercise.

Add a Table

One type of content you can add to a slide is a *table*—a collection of data organized in columns and rows. Data is entered into the individual *cells* of the table. For example, in a presentation detailing the sales revenue from the last quarter, you might include a table such as the one shown in Figure 3-16, comparing that revenue with the previous quarter's revenue.

FIGURE 3-16
A table presents data in an organized fashion

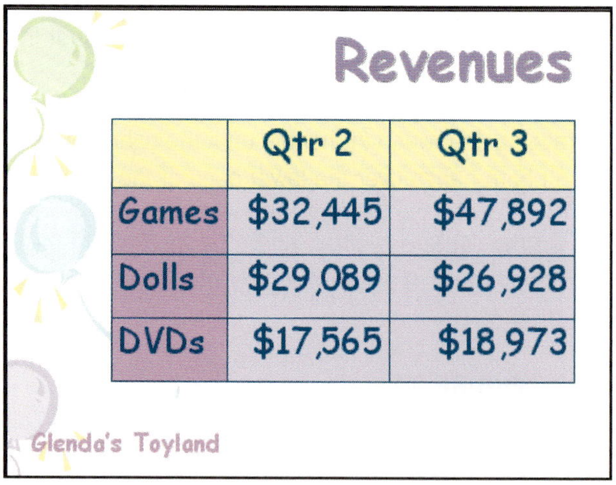

Revenues

	Qtr 2	Qtr 3
Games	$32,445	$47,892
Dolls	$29,089	$26,928
DVDs	$17,565	$18,973

Glenda's Toyland

Insert a Table

To add a table to a slide, apply the Title and Table layout or some other content layout. After applying the layout, click or double-click the table icon to display the Insert Table dialog box. Select the number of columns and rows you need and click OK. Be sure to include an extra row for headings at the top of each column, and an extra column on the left for row headings.

The insertion point appears in the first cell. Key the data for that cell and press Tab to move to the next cell, or click in any cell and key data. If you press Tab in the last cell of the table, you automatically create another row. When you key numerical data, be sure to key dollar signs, commas, and periods if you want to display them, because they cannot be added with formatting. Also, you must key any totals yourself. Unlike Word tables and Excel worksheets, PowerPoint tables do not have a function to calculate totals for you.

> **Important**
>
> Keep in mind that if your table contains a lot of data, the type will be small and hard to see. So limit the number of columns and rows to as few as possible. In some cases, you should consider using a chart instead, to show the data in a graphical manner.

Modify a Table

After entering data into a table, you may find it necessary to add or delete rows or columns. Click a cell next to where you want to add a new column or row. Then click the Table button on the Tables and Borders toolbar, and click Insert Columns to the Left, Insert Columns to the Right, Insert Rows Above, or Insert Rows Below. To remove columns or rows (and the data they contain), select the columns or rows, click the Table button, and click Delete Columns or Delete Rows.

Another way to modify a table is to draw the cells you want to add and erase the cells you want to remove. You can also merge two cells together (forming a single cell) or divide a cell into multiple cells, as shown in Figure 3-17. To draw a border, click the Draw Table button. You can then choose border formats from the Tables and Borders toolbar. Select the border style you want from the Border Style list. Select a border thickness from the Border Width list. Click the Border Color drop-down arrow and select a color for the border—remember that the colors in your color scheme appear in a row just under the Automatic color. Once your selections are made, drag with the pencil pointer to draw a new border. For example, click in the middle of a cell and drag downwards to split the cell into two cells. Add as many borders as you like. When you're done, click the Draw Table button again to display the normal mouse pointer.

> **Hot Tip**
>
> To insert more than one column or row, select the number of columns or rows you want to insert, and then use the appropriate Insert Columns or Insert Rows command to add that number of columns or rows to the table.

> **Hot Tip**
>
> You can draw a border diagonally across a cell if you want.

FIGURE 3-17
Draw the table you want

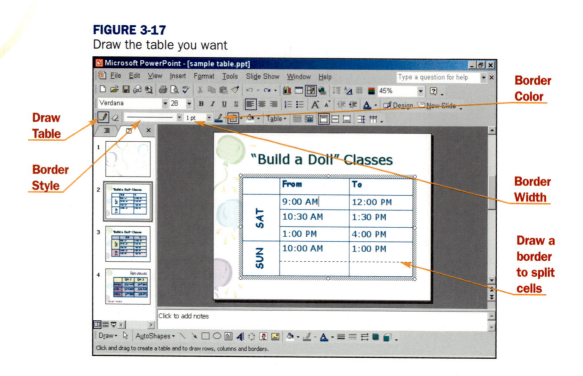

To erase a border and merge two cells together, click the Eraser button on the Tables and Borders toolbar, and click on any border to remove it. Click the Eraser again to turn it off.

At some point, you may need to adjust the width of the columns and the height of the rows to fit the data more precisely. Simply drag a column's border left or right, or a row's border up or down to adjust width or height.

Format a Table

Formatting a table is as easy as selecting the rows, columns, or cells you want, and then applying the formatting you desire. Select a row or column by dragging over its cells, and select a cell by clicking in it. Apply text formatting using the tools on the Formatting toolbar, such as the Font, Font Size, Font Color, and alignment buttons. You can also format a table with tools on the Tables and Borders toolbar, such as Fill Color, Border Style, and the vertical alignment buttons.

Hot Tip

One quick way to resize the rows or columns in a table is to resize the table itself, and then distribute the space evenly by clicking either the Distribute Rows Evenly or Distribute Columns Evenly button, located on the Tables and Borders toolbar.

STEP-BY-STEP 3.6

1. Open **PS Step 3-6** from the data files, and save the file as **Senior Security 4**.

2. Display slide 7, and click the **Insert Table** icon in the placeholder. The Insert Table dialog box opens.

3. Key **3** for **Number of columns**, and key **5** for **Number of rows**. Click the **OK** button.

STEP-BY-STEP 3.6 Continued

4. Key the data shown below. Remember to press **Tab** to move from cell to cell.

	Senior Security	911
	Senior Security	911
Answer call	Instantly	1 min.
Get information	On file	6 min.
Help arrives	6 min.	7 min.
Total wait time	6 min.	14 min.

5. Click the table placeholder, and click **32** in the Font Size list. Click the **Bold** button.

6. Drag over the three cells in the top row, click the **Table** button on the Tables and Borders toolbar, and click **Borders and Fill**. The Format Table dialog box opens.

7. Click the **Fill** tab. Click the **Fill color** check box, click the arrow on the **Fill Color** list, and click the last color on the right (tan), in the row of color scheme colors just under the Automatic color. Click the **Semitransparent** check box, and then click the **OK** button.

8. Drag over the first cells on the left, in rows 2, 3, and 4. Repeat steps 6 and 7 to add a semitransparent, light tan fill to these cells.

9. Drag over the three cells in the bottom row. Repeat steps 6 and 7, this time applying a semitransparent gold fill by clicking the second to the last color on the right in the row of color scheme colors.

10. Drag the right border of column 1 to the right, until the row heading *Get information* displays on one line.

11. Drag the right border of column 2 to the right, until the column heading *Senior Security* also displays on one line.

12. Drag over the two column heading cells to select them, and then click the **Center Vertically** button on the Tables and Borders toolbar. The table should look like the one shown in Figure 3-18.

FIGURE 3-18
Completed table

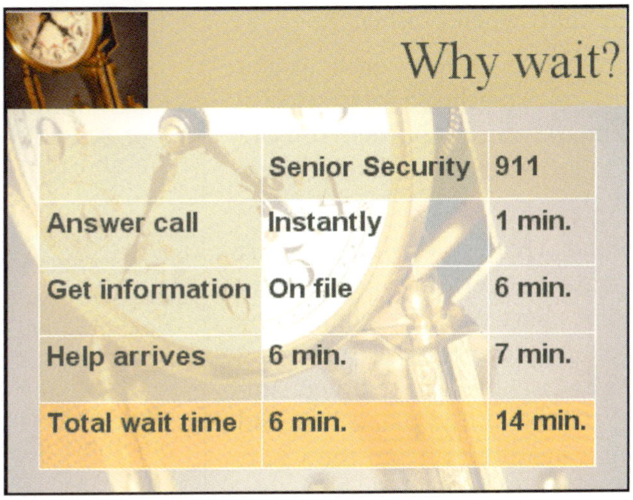

13. Save changes and leave the **Senior Security 4** file open to use in the next exercise.

Create a Chart

Another way to share numerical data with your audience is to create a *chart*—a graphical representation of table data. You can create a chart on any slide that includes a content placeholder. Depending on the amount of data you want to chart, you may prefer to use the Title and Chart layout.

Insert a Chart

To create a chart, click the Insert Chart button within a content placeholder, or double-click the chart icon on a Title and Chart layout. A sample *datasheet* appears, as shown in Figure 3-19. Click in any cell and key new data to replace the sample data. Unlike in a table, you do not have to type dollar signs, commas, or insignificant zeroes. You can add this formatting using toolbar buttons. As you key new data, the default chart displayed behind the datasheet changes automatically. When finished, click on the chart to make changes and close the datasheet if you want. Click on the slide to deselect the chart and see how it looks on the slide.

FIGURE 3-19
Enter data into the datasheet

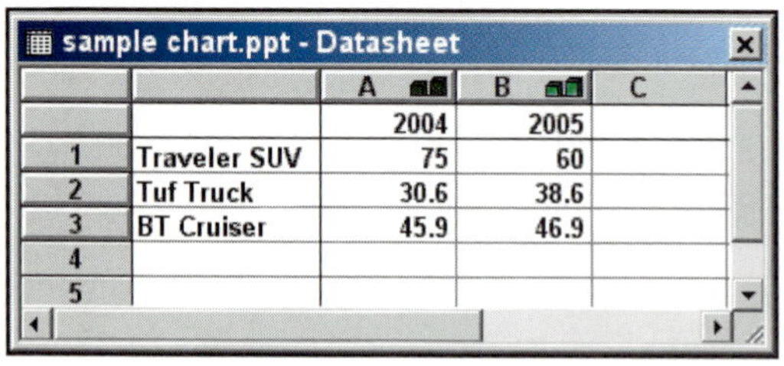

		A	B	C	
		2004	2005		
1	Traveler SUV	75	60		
2	Tuf Truck	30.6	38.6		
3	BT Cruiser	45.9	46.9		
4					
5					

sample chart.ppt - Datasheet

Modify and Format a Chart

After creating a chart, if you notice an error in the data, you can change it easily. Simply double-click the chart to open it for editing, and then make the needed changes to the datasheet. (If the datasheet does not appear, click the View Datasheet button on the Standard toolbar.) Click outside the chart when finished.

You can copy, move, resize, or delete a chart as you can any other object. Click once on the chart to select it and display handles around the object's border. You can then manipulate its size or location as you like or press Delete to remove it altogether.

By default, PowerPoint creates a column chart when you insert a new chart. For certain types of data, you may prefer a different chart type. To change the chart type, double-click the chart to open it for editing (if needed). If the chart is already open for editing, simply click the chart. Click Chart on the menu bar, and click Chart Type. Click a general type from the Chart type list, and click a specific type from the Chart subtype palette. Then click OK to apply the new chart type to your existing data. Click outside the chart when done.

> **Important**
>
> The datasheet contains three rows and four columns of sample data. If you don't need to use a particular column or row, you should remove it (rather than just deleting the data in the cells). To remove an unwanted row or column, right-click its heading (such as 1, 2, 3 or A, B, C) and click Delete on the shortcut menu.

> **Important**
>
> Not all charts are interchangeable. You cannot, for example, successfully change a column chart to a pie chart, because a pie chart uses only one column or one row of data.

You can add formatting to the data in the datasheet, such as dollar signs or extra decimal points. Drag over the cells in the datasheet that you want to format. Click the Currency Style, Percent Style, or Comma Style button on the Formatting toolbar to apply that style format. (See Figure 3-20.) You can also click the Increase Decimal or Decrease Decimal buttons as many times as needed to add or remove decimal places.

FIGURE 3-20
Use Formatting toolbar buttons to change value formats

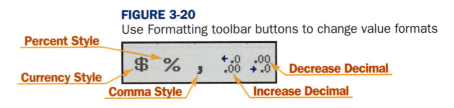

You can remove any unwanted element of a chart, such as its *legend*, by simply clicking the element and pressing Delete. You can also format any element you like, such as the value axis, plot area, chart area, gridlines, and so on. Various chart elements are identified on Figure 3-21. Either double-click the element you want to format, or click it in the Chart Objects list on the Standard toolbar. Then click the Format *Object* button, located next to the Chart Objects list. The name of this button changes with the object selected from the Chart Objects list. Clicking this button displays a dialog box with options for formatting that specific element. Click the options you want and click OK to apply the formatting. For example, you might select Chart Area from the Chart Objects list, click the Format Chart Area button, and change the font used throughout a chart.

FIGURE 3-21
Chart elements

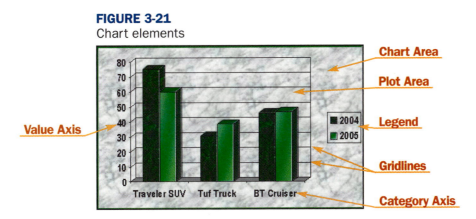

After making modifications and applying formatting to a chart, click outside the chart to deactivate it and return to normal slide editing.

STEP-BY-STEP 3.7

1. In the **Senior Security 4** file, display slide 10 and click the **Insert Chart** button in the content placeholder.

2. Key the following data into the datasheet, replacing the existing data.

	Audio unit	Installation	Monthly fee
Senior Security	15	10	25
Always Alert	25	25	30

STEP-BY-STEP 3.7 Continued

3. Right-click the **3** row heading and click **Delete** to remove that row.

4. Right-click the **D** column heading and click **Delete** to remove that column.

5. In the datasheet, drag over the data cells and click the **Currency Style** button on the Formatting toolbar. Click the **Decrease Decimals** button two times.

6. Close the datasheet. Click the **Chart Objects** drop-down arrow, and then click **Chart Area**. Click the **Format Chart Area** button on the Standard toolbar, just to the right of the Chart Objects list. The Format Chart Area dialog box opens.

7. Click the **Font** tab. Click the **Color** drop-down arrow, and click **Dark Green**. (Move the mouse pointer over a color, and a ScreenTip appears with the name of that color.) Change the font size to **22**. Click the **OK** button to apply these formats.

8. Click the **Chart Objects** drop-down arrow, and then click **Value Axis Major Gridlines**. Click the **Format Gridlines** button. The Format Gridlines dialog box opens.

9. On the **Patterns** tab, click the **Color** drop-down arrow, and click **Dark Green**. Click the **OK** button.

10. Repeat steps 8 and 9 to apply dark green to the **Walls border**, **Value Axis lines**, **Legend border**, and **Legend font**. Click outside the chart. The chart should look like the one shown in Figure 3-22.

FIGURE 3-22
Completed chart

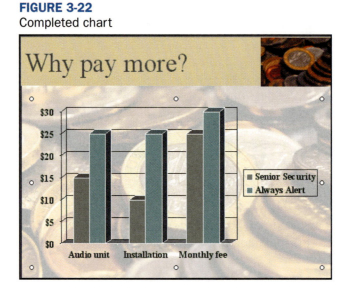

11. Save changes and leave the **Senior Security 4** file open to use in the next exercise.

Create a Diagram

In addition to graphical charts that compare values, PowerPoint allows you to add conceptual charts, or *diagrams*, to your slides. An organization chart, a common type of diagram, is shown in Figure 3-23. You can create several different types of diagrams in PowerPoint:

FIGURE 3-23
Organization chart

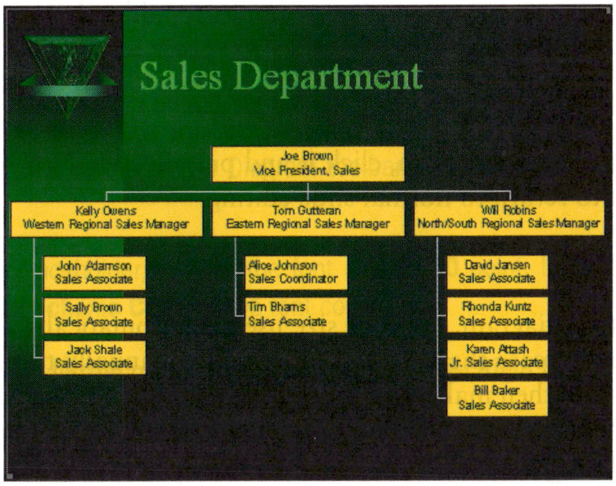

- **Organization**—This type of diagram depicts the relationships between people within a group such as a company or volunteer organization. An organization chart includes these basic relationships: superior, assistant, subordinate, and coworker. A *superior* is a person within an organization whose powers and responsibilities are above those of another group of people. A manager is one type of *superior*. An *assistant* is a person who assists a superior in his or her work. A *subordinate* is a person who reports to a superior. A *coworker* is a person who reports to the same superior as someone else.

- **Cycle**—This type of diagram is used to chart some kind of cyclical process, such as the life cycle of a tree or the design and production of a computer chip.

- **Radial**—This type of diagram illustrates the relationship of several items to a single item. For example, use a Radial diagram to show how the phones in a particular department are connected to a single incoming phone line.

- **Pyramid**—This type of diagram shows the proportions of individual elements in a whole. A good example is the Food Pyramid, which shows the proportionate amounts of each food group you should consume in a single day.

- **Venn**—This type of diagram depicts items with overlapping characteristics, such as the secondary and tertiary colors in a color wheel that are comprised of two primary/secondary colors.

- **Target**—This type of diagram illustrates items that build on each other, such as the steps toward a specific goal. For example, you might use a target diagram to list the steps for mixing a cake or building a house.

SUMMARY

In this lesson, you learned:

- PowerPoint provides a vast collection of clip art and photos you can use to enhance a slide. To open the Insert Clip Art task pane, use the Clip Art button on the Drawing toolbar or click Picture on the Insert menu and then click Clip Art.

- You can use key words to search for the exact clip or photo you want. Modify the search if you don't find a clip you like.

- Photos or other images can be imported directly from a scanner or digital camera by clicking Picture on the Insert menu and then clicking From Scanner or Camera.

- The Insert Picture icon in a content placeholder is for adding graphics stored on a hard disk, network, or similar device.

- Click the Clips Online link at the bottom of the Insert Clip Art task pane whenever you want to add to your clip art collection with new clips stored on Microsoft's Design Gallery Live Web site.

- You can adjust the contrast and brightness of images using the Picture toolbar. You can also crop, recolor, rotate, compress, and add a border with the tools on the Picture toolbar.

- All graphics can be moved, resized, copied, or deleted.

- You can create your own shapes for slides using the tools on the Drawing toolbar. You can also format those shapes with the Fill Color, Line Style, Line Color, Shadow Style, and 3-D Style buttons on the Drawing toolbar.

- Add a block of text anywhere on a slide using the Text Box tool. That text can be rotated and flipped just like any other object.

- The Draw button on the Drawing toolbar contains commands for grouping, flipping, rotating, aligning, and precisely arranging selected objects.

- A table is a series of cells created by the intersection of rows and columns.

- A chart can be used to graphically depict table data.

- A diagram is a conceptual chart, typically showing the relationship between items such as people in a group.

- Tables, charts, and diagrams can all be formatted using special toolbars that appear when they are opened for editing.

VOCABULARY *Review*

Define the following terms:

Adjustment handle	Chart	Legend
Aspect ratio	Clip art	Rotation handle
AutoShape	Datasheet	Table
Cell	Diagram	

REVIEW *Questions*

TRUE / FALSE

Circle T if the statement is true or F if the statement is false.

T   F   **1.** To adjust the size of an object, use its adjustment handle.

T   F   **2.** An object can be manipulated separately from other slide elements.

T   F   **3.** All the clip art you will ever need is stored on your computer.

T   F   **4.** You can add both a 3-D effect and a shadow to a drawn object.

T   F   **5.** The color inside an object can be changed using the Fill Color button.

T   F   **6.** The border surrounding an object cannot be changed or removed.

T   F   **7.** To add a drawn object to a slide, change to a slide layout that uses a content placeholder.

T   F   **8.** Parts of some images can be made transparent so that the background shows through.

T   F   **9.** The Format Picture dialog box is used to recolor parts of an image.

T   F **10.** Any image you find on the Web can be downloaded and used in a presentation.

FILL IN THE BLANK

Complete the following sentences by writing the correct word or words in the blanks provided.

1. A(n) _____ is a device that uses a process similar to a copier to convert a paper image into a digital one.

2. The relationship between an object's height and width is called its _____.

3. Use the _____ handle to change the shape of an AutoShape object.

4. To place one object behind another object, use the _____ commands on the Draw menu.

5. Images, sounds, and videos that are not in the public domain may be protected by _____.

MATCHING

Match the correct term in Column 2 to its description in Column 1.

Column 1

_____ 1. Datasheet

_____ 2. Chart

_____ 3. Legend

_____ 4. Group

_____ 5. Target diagram

_____ 6. AutoShape

_____ 7. Table

_____ 8. Organization chart

_____ 9. Rotate

_____ 10. Cycle diagram

Column 2

A. Objects that can be manipulated and formatted as a unit.

B. A pre-designed object you can draw in one step.

C. Shows the steps in a process.

D. Shows the relationship between values.

E. Shows the relationship between people in a group.

F. Move an object around its center.

G. A special window into which you enter chart data.

H. Charts how items in a group build on each other.

I. Displays the name and color assigned to each data series in a chart.

J. Data organized in columns and rows.

K. An object that's automatically formatted for you.

PROJECTS

PROJECT 3-1

1. Launch PowerPoint. Open **PS Project 3-1** from the data files, and save the file as **Fiesta Mexicana**.

2. Display slide 4 and insert a photo background:
   A. Open the Insert Clip Art task pane, and search for photos matching the key word *chiles*.
   B. Insert an appropriate photo from the search results.
   C. Resize the photo so it takes up the entire slide area. Crop the photo as necessary to fit neatly on the slide.

3. Use the **Freeform** AutoShape tool (in the Lines palette) to create a freeform object flowing across the right corner of the slide, as shown in Figure 3-25. Apply the **Follow Accent and Followed Hyperlink Scheme Color** (blue) fill color to the object.

4. Add a text box to the slide, and insert text as follows:
   A. Key **Tortilla-making classes** and press **Enter**.
   B. Key **Jalapeno-eating contest** and press **Enter**.
   C. Key **Miss Fiesta pageant**.
   D. Right-align the text and change the font to 36-point Arial Narrow.
   E. Position the text as shown in Figure 3-25.

FIGURE 3-25
Completed slide

5. Display slide 5 and add a table with 3 columns and 4 rows.
   A. Key the following data:

	Start	End
Fri	11 AM	12 PM
Sat	12 PM	1 AM
Sun	12 PM	6 PM

   B. Change the font for the entire table to 32-point Arial Narrow.
   C. Center the row headings in the first column.
   D. Add a white transparent fill to all cells in the table.

6. Save and close the **Fiesta Mexicana** presentation, but leave PowerPoint open to use in Project 3-2.

PROJECT 3-2

1. Open **PS Project 3-2** from the data files, and save the file as **Fiesta Summary**.

2. Display slide 2, and click the **Insert Chart** icon in the content placeholder.

3. Key the following data into the datasheet, and remove the unused columns:

	Adults	Children
Fri	15665	3874
Sat	18502	7898
Sun	16458	6322

4. Apply the **Comma Style** to all data cells, and do not display any decimal places.

5. Apply **Arial, 24 pt, bold** font to the entire chart area.

6. Change the chart on slide 4 to a **3-D Pie Chart**. Display the legend. (Click the **Legend** button on the Standard toolbar.)

7. Drag the legend below and to the right of the pie chart, and remove the legend fill. (Set the Fill for Area on the Patterns tab to None.)

8. Resize the plot area to maximize the size of the chart. Remove the border from around the plot area. Reposition the chart as necessary to center it on the slide. Click outside the chart.

9. Modify the table on slide 3 as follows:
   A. Resize each column so that the data just fits.
   B. Apply a semitransparent fill color using the Follow Fills Scheme Color (yellow, fifth from left) to the cells in the top row.
   C. To the lower three cells in the first column, add a semitransparent fill color using Follow Shadows Scheme Color (orange, third from left).
   D. Center the table on the slide if needed.

10. Save and close the **Fiesta Summary** presentation. Close your PowerPoint.

SCANS WEB PROJECT

Tourism is down in New York City, and it's your job to pump it up with an exciting presentation to be played on a large monitor at an important conference for travel agents next month. You need to provide the agents with data that will excite their customers into booking vacations in your fair city. Address the issues of crime and terrorism, which are major concerns for visitors. Research statistics and create charts and tables for your presentation that show how safe the city is becoming. Search the Web for sites that offer copyright-free graphics, and browse for clip art and photos you can use.

SCANS TEAMWORK PROJECT

Add graphic elements to the presentation you created in Lesson 1 on school rules. First, as a team, decide which slides need illustration, and decide the types of graphic elements to use—clip art, photos, drawn objects, tables, charts, or diagrams. Be sure to include at least one table, chart, and diagram in the presentation. Decide if the layout should be changed on each slide to accommodate the graphic element—will the graphic be used as a background, on half the slide, on a slide by itself? Assign a person the task of locating or creating the graphic element(s) for each slide. Preview the results and write down your thoughts: Did the illustrations improve the presentation or detract from it too much? Did they add humor at just the right moment? Did they fit the topic of that slide well enough, or should you look further? Were the charts, tables, and diagrams easily understandable? Did they quickly convey the message you wanted to send?

CRITICAL *Thinking*

ACTIVITY 3-1

You are the head of one of the design teams at a large telecommunications firm, and it's your job to convince upper management to use your design proposal. You're convinced that your team has come up with a new way to communicate and send data via a portable device similar to a cellular phone or PDA. This presentation must wow your bosses and convince them to finance the device's development. Create an outline for your presentation. Decide what you need to say about the new device, and how best to say it. Include development costs and target dates in the presentation. With your outline, create a five-slide presentation using a variety of content.

ACTIVITY 3-2

Add graphic elements (clip art, photos, tables, charts, and diagrams) to the swimming safety presentation you created in Lesson 2. Present the completed project to your classmates. Design a survey they can use to critique your work. How could you have communicated the need for safety more clearly? Did they understand the tables, charts, and diagrams you included? What did they think of the clip art and photos you chose? Gather the comments and prepare a 150-word report that summarizes the effectiveness of your presentation.

WORKING WITH SOUND AND ANIMATIONS

<table>
<tr><td>

OBJECTIVES

Upon completion of this lesson, you should be able to:

- Insert sound objects such as clips, files, CD tracks, or recorded sounds.
- Record narration for an entire presentation.
- Add an animated GIF file to a slide.
- Insert video clips.
- Apply an animation scheme to a slide.
- Create custom animations in a presentation.

Estimated Time: 1 hour

</td><td>

VOCABULARY

Animation scheme

Codec

Embed

Link

Loop

MIDI

Motion path

Movie

MP3

Music loop

Trigger

WAV

</td></tr>
</table>

Although graphics play a critical role in a great presentation, they tell only part of the story. A picture may be worth a thousand words, but a movie clip can be worth a whole lot more. And if you plan to play your presentation automatically (in self-running mode) or publish it on the Web, sound not only reinforces the text on the slides, but can also make the presentation more authoritative and convincing. In this lesson, you learn how to add both movie and sound objects to a slide.

You also learn how to animate objects on a slide in this lesson. Just as slide transitions control how each slide is displayed, object animation controls how objects on a slide appear, disappear, become temporarily more noticeable, and/or move across a slide.

Insert a Sound Object

PowerPoint supports many sources for sound within a presentation. You can easily add a sound clip from the Clip Organizer, your hard disk, or a network. You can search for a sound file on the Web. You can also set up a slide to play one or more tracks from a CD during a presentation. Another way to add sound to slides is to record a sound or record narration for an entire presentation, as you learn to do in the next section.

The sound file format you choose to insert depends on the nature of the sound you want your presentation to play. If you're looking for a beep, a whirr, or a click—for instance, during a transition between slides or highlighting a bullet point—the sound effect you need is probably a *WAV* file. Such a file carries the .wav extension. Virtually all WAV files can be played in Windows and PowerPoint. The contents of a WAV file are digital waveforms—digits that represent segments of sound waves.

If you need full musical background, consider a *MIDI* (Musical Instrument Digital Interface) file. Instead of digital waveforms, a MIDI file (with a .mid or .midi extension) contains digits that represent notes on a musical scale and designate the musical instruments that play those notes. Most Windows computers include software that performs the job of a synthesizer, simulating the sound of these instruments. However, some networked systems (especially Windows NT and 2000) are set up with MIDI synthesis turned *off*, so the background score you choose for a presentation may be silent on some systems.

As an alternative, you can choose an *MP3* file (.mp3) as your background score. Like WAV files, MP3 files contain digital waveforms that reproduce recorded sound or musical tracks. Unlike a WAV file, an MP3 file is mathematically compressed to consume less storage space. So, while a WAV file containing a track from a musical CD may consume 50 to 100 MB of storage, an MP3 file containing exactly the same track may consume a mere 3 MB.

To add a sound object to a slide, you use the Movies and Sounds command on the Insert menu, and then select an option from the pop-out menu to locate the sound object. After you locate and select the sound object, PowerPoint opens a dialog box asking if you want the sound to play automatically when the slide appears. Click Yes to have the sound play automatically as soon as the slide appears in Slide Show view. Click No if you want to control the sound yourself. After you make this choice, PowerPoint displays an icon for the sound on the slide. If you have chosen to control the sound manually, you click this icon to play the sound whenever you want during the presentation.

The sound icon is like any other object on a slide. You can move it by dragging it or change its size using a selection handle. To remove the sound icon, select it and press Delete. You can drag the icon off the slide if you don't want the icon to appear on the slide in Slide Show view. However, drag the icon off a slide only if you have set the sound to play automatically, because you will not see the icon or be able to click it during the presentation.

To play a sound while viewing a slide in Normal mode, double-click the sound icon. To stop the sound, click anywhere in the Slide pane or change to a different slide. To have the sound play continuously until you advance to the next slide, you must change the sound's settings so it *loops*, or repeats. To do that, right-click the sound icon and click Edit Sound Object on the shortcut menu. Click Loop until stopped and then click OK.

Add Sound from Clip Organizer

To add a sound from the Clip Organizer, click Movies and Sounds on the Insert menu, and then click Sound from Clip Organizer. The Insert Clip Art task pane appears, displaying thumbnails for the Clip Organizer's sound collection. Scroll through the list and click a thumbnail to insert that sound. To display a selected list of sounds, click the Modify button, key a word or phrase in the Search text box, select Sounds in the *Results should be* list box, and click the Search button. To hear the sound before you insert it, move the mouse pointer over the thumbnail, click the arrow, and click Preview/Properties. The sound automatically plays. Use the controls to replay the sound as shown in Figure 4-1.

FIGURE 4-1
Preview a sound before adding it to a slide

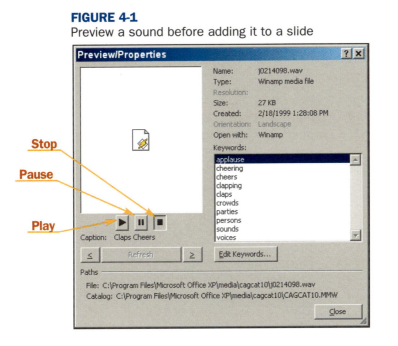

Add Sound File

Adding a sound file from your hard disk or network is similar to adding a sound from the Clip Organizer. Start by clicking Movies and Sounds on the Insert menu, and then click Sound from File. Navigate to the folder that contains the sound file, click it, and click OK to add it to the slide. Once again, you'll be asked if you want the sound to play automatically when the slide is viewed.

If the sound file is larger than 100 KB, it will be *linked* to the presentation file, rather than *embedded* in it. Linking means that PowerPoint stores only a shortcut to the file in the presentation itself, rather than storing the entire sound. This helps keep your presentation file to a manageable size. However, you may need to relink (reinsert) the file to the presentation if you move the presentation to a new location. To make it easy to relink, you can store sound files in the same folder with the presentation.

Add Sound from the Web

Just as the World Wide Web is an excellent source of clip art and other images, it is an abundant source of sound files. Most search engines allow you to search for

> **Note** ☑
>
> You can also insert a sound from the Clip Organizer by clicking the Insert Media Clip icon in any content placeholder. All media clips (sounds and movies) stored in the Clip Organizer appear. Key a word or phrase in the Search text box and click Search to narrow the listing.

> **Hot Tip** ◎
>
> To change the file size value PowerPoint uses to decide whether to link, click Tools on the menu bar, click Options, and click the General tab. Change the value in the *Link sounds with file size greater than* box, and click OK. Also, to avoid having to relink, use Pack and Go to move the presentation.

specific multimedia files such as sounds or movies. A number of Web sites allow you to create your own *music loops* for downloading without dealing with copyrights or permissions.

Microsoft's Design Gallery Online is as good a source for sounds as it is for images. Click the Clips Online link in the Insert Clip Art task pane to jump to this online site. Use the search features on the site to locate sounds that match your key words.

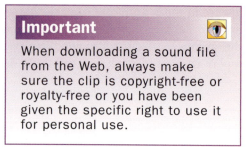

Important

When downloading a sound file from the Web, always make sure the clip is copyright-free or royalty-free or you have been given the specific right to use it for personal use.

Download a sound from the Web the same general way you download an image file. You can store the sound in the Clip Organizer or save it in a specific folder. Use the Sound from Clip Organizer or Sound from File command to locate and insert the sound.

Add Sound from CD-ROM

You can link to sound track(s) on a CD-ROM and play music with one or more slides. Insert the CD you want to use into its drive, and then click Movies and Sounds on the Insert menu. Click Play CD Audio Track. The dialog box shown in Figure 4-2 opens.

FIGURE 4-2
Select the CD track you want to play

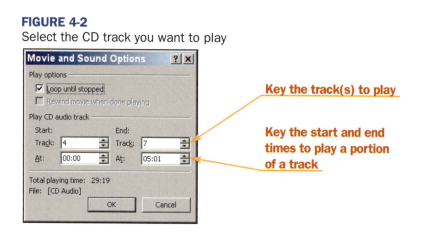

To play the track continuously until you advance to the next slide, click the Loop until stopped check box. Key the starting and ending track numbers in the Track boxes. To play only one track, key the same number in both boxes. If you want to play a portion of a track, key the starting and ending time in the At boxes. When you click OK, you'll be asked if you want the sound to begin playing when the slide is viewed. Click Yes or No, and a CD-ROM icon appears on the slide. To play the track manually at any time, double-click the CD-ROM icon.

Hot Tip

You can customize how and when music plays during a presentation by applying a custom animation. For example, you can play the CD track during the presentation of several slides, instead of just one. To do that, display the Custom Animation task pane, select the CD-ROM icon, and on the Effect tab of the Effect Options dialog box, key the number of slides with which you want the music to play. You learn more about custom animation later in this lesson.

S TEP-BY-STEP 4.1

1. Launch PowerPoint. Open **PS Step 4-1a** from the data files, and save the file as **Senior Security SV** (SV stands for sounds and video).

2. Display slide 6. Click **Insert** on the menu bar, click **Movies and Sounds**, and then click **Sound from Clip Organizer**. The Insert Clip Art task pane opens.

3. Click the **Modify** button. Key **clock** in the Search text box. If necessary, click only the **Sounds** option and then turn off the options in the Results should be list, and then click the **Search** button.

4. Click the **Metal Clock Tick** clip to insert it. (You may be prompted to insert the Media Content CD-ROM.) Click **Yes** when asked if you want the sound to play automatically. The sound icon appears in the middle of the slide. Drag the icon off the slide.

5. Click the **Modify** button in the Insert Clip Art task pane. Key **alarm** in the Search text box, and then click the **Search** button.

6. Click the **Short Bell Alarm** clip to insert it. (If you do not see this file after your search, ask your instructor for help.) Click **Yes** to play the sound automatically, and drag the icon off the slide next to the previous clip. Close the Insert Clip Art task pane.

7. Display slide 3. Click **Insert** on the menu bar, click **Movies and Sounds**, and then click **Sound from File**. Navigate to the data files folder, select **PS Step 4-1b**, and click **OK**. Click **Yes** to play the file automatically, and then drag the icon off the slide.

8. Display slide 1. Search the Web for an upbeat music loop and download it to your system. Store the music clip in the solution files for this lesson.

9. Click **Insert** on the menu bar, click **Movies and Sounds**, and then click **Sound from File**.

10. Navigate to the folder where you stored the downloaded sound file, click the file to select it, and click the **OK** button. Click **Yes** to play the file automatically, and then drag the icon off the slide.

11. Test the sound file on slide 1 by double-clicking it. Click anywhere on the slide to stop the music.

12. With slide 1 still displayed, click the **Slide Show** view button to start the slide show. Listen to your music loop on slide 1, and then advance through the slides by clicking the mouse button. You should hear the sound you inserted on slide 3, and both sounds you inserted on slide 6.

13. Save changes and leave the **Senior Security SV** file open to use in the next exercise.

Record a Sound on a Slide

The Record Sound command on the Movies and Sounds submenu also allows you to add sound to a slide by recording sound effects, vocals, or narration. You need a good microphone, sound card, and speakers on your computer to record the sound.

Start by clicking Movies and Sounds on the Insert menu, and then click Record Sound. The Record Sound dialog box, shown in Figure 4-3, opens. Key a name for the sound file in the Name box. This name enables PowerPoint to identify the object. Click the Record button to begin recording. When you're through, click the Stop button. To replay the recording to check it, click the Play button. When you're satisfied, click OK to save the file and create a sound icon on the slide.

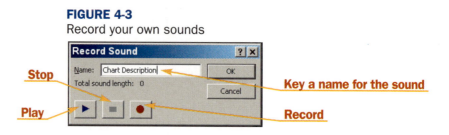

FIGURE 4-3
Record your own sounds

STEP-BY-STEP 4.2

1. In the **Senior Security SV** file, display slide 3.

2. Click **Insert** on the menu bar, click **Movies and Sounds**, and then click **Record Sound**.

3. In the Name box, key **Hello** as the title of the sound clip you will record.

4. Click the **Record** button.

5. In a normal tone, read the following text into the microphone:
   Senior Security. How may I help you?

6. Click the **Stop** button. Then click the **Play** button to check the recording.

7. Click the **OK** button. Position the sound icon in the lower-right corner of the slide.

8. Play the slide show. On slide 3, after the phone pickup sound file plays, click the sound icon to hear your recorded sound.

9. Save changes and close the **Senior Security SV** file. Leave PowerPoint open to use in the next exercise.

Record Narration

If your presentation will be played as a self-running slide show at a kiosk, conference center, or other venue, you may want to accompany it with some narration. Narration reinforces the message of the slide text, and allows you to add further comments or expand on the text. To record a narration, your computer must be set up with a microphone, sound card, and speakers.

PowerPoint's Record Narration feature streamlines the process of adding narration to slides. Click Record Narration on the Slide Show menu to open the Record Narration dialog box, as shown in Figure 4-4.

FIGURE 4-4
Record Narration dialog box

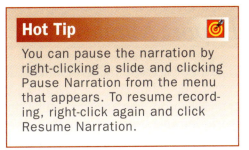

Adjust the recording level

Adjust the quality of the recording

Link rather than embed the sound

Establish the proper recording level by clicking Set Microphone Level, speaking some test phrases, dragging the slider right or left as needed to keep the recording in the green level, and then clicking OK. You may notice that the slider adjusts by itself as you speak, but you can still make your own adjustments to keep the level in the green band. You can click Change Quality to select the sound quality you want. Higher quality sound increases the presentation's file size, so keep that in mind. You can choose to save the narration in a separate file and link it to the presentation, rather than embedding the data in the presentation file, by clicking *Link narrations in*, clicking Browse, selecting a folder in which to save the file, and clicking Select. Click OK when you are ready to begin recording.

You don't have to begin recording narration with the first slide. To begin on a different slide, display that slide before you issue the Record Narration command. If you select a slide other than the first slide to begin your narration, PowerPoint displays a dialog box after you click OK in the Record Narration dialog box, asking if you want to begin the narration with the current slide or the first slide.

PowerPoint displays slides in Slide Show view, beginning with the slide you selected. As you record your narration, PowerPoint displays each slide in turn, so you can recall what you want to say about it. Speak into the microphone to record your narration for the displayed slide. If you want to view your speaker's notes while you're recording, right-click the slide and click Speaker Notes. Click Close to remove the notes window so you can display the next slide. To move to the next slide, click on the slide or press Page Down.

Important

You can play only one sound at a time on a slide, so if you've added an automatic sound to a slide, the narration overrides it. The solution is to have the sound play on your click, instead of automatically. That way, you can play the sound after the narration. If you want to play a sound automatically along with a narration, record the two together by playing the sound on a stereo system as you record your narration.

Hot Tip

You can pause the narration by right-clicking a slide and clicking Pause Narration from the menu that appears. To resume recording, right-click again and click Resume Narration.

When you reach the end of the presentation, click to return to regular editing mode. PowerPoint displays a message asking if you'd like to also save your timings—the time you took to present each slide. Timings are used to automatically advance from one slide to another. To save them, click Save; otherwise, click Don't Save. You can always record timings separately if you like, as you learn to do in Lesson 6.

In the next exercise, you record narrations for an entire presentation. If you do not have a microphone, go through the steps anyway to become familiar with this process.

S TEP-BY-STEP 4.3

1. Open **PS Step 4-3** from the data files, and save the file as **Katie's Cafe**.

2. Display slide 1, if necessary. Click **Slide Show** on the menu bar, and then click **Record Narration**. The Record Narration dialog box opens.

3. Click **Set Microphone Level**, adjust the microphone level for a normal speaking voice, and then click the **OK** button to return to the Record Narration dialog box.

4. Click the **OK** button to begin recording. PowerPoint displays the first slide in Slide Show view.

5. Right-click the slide and click **Speaker Notes**. Read the note into your microphone. When you have finished, click the **Close** button, and then click to move to slide 2.

6. Right-click the slide and click **Speaker Notes**. Scroll to the top, read the note, click the **Close** button, and then click to move to slide 3.

7. Right-click the slide and click **Speaker Notes**. Read the note, click the **Close** button, and then click twice to end the presentation.

8. Click the **Save** button to save your slide timings. PowerPoint displays the timings below each slide in Slide Sorter view.

9. Click slide 1, if it is not already selected, and then click the **Slide Show** view button to play the slide show and listen to your narration.

10. Save changes and close **Katie's Cafe**. Leave PowerPoint open to use in the next exercise.

Import Movies

In PowerPoint, the term *movies* means one of two objects: a simple animated GIF file, or an actual video clip. The Clip Organizer contains a collection of animated GIFs you can use, or you can easily add your own to a slide. In addition, you can add video clips from a hard disk, network, intranet, or the World Wide Web.

PowerPoint borrows the services of Windows Media Player to play video files along with a presentation. There are several versions of Windows Media Player, and each version can be customized with different *codecs* (video encoding formats). So, the types of video files PowerPoint can display on any Windows computer is always limited to the types of video files that Media Player can display on that same computer.

To sidestep a very confusing topic, we can boil down video formats to two types: those expressly designed for use with Media Player, and those not designed for Media Player. There are literally hundreds of formats belonging to both categories, but you don't need to know them all to import a movie into PowerPoint.

The original set of formats designed for Media Player is stored using the .avi extension. Most installations of Windows enable PowerPoint to play AVI files. A second set of formats for Media Player is stored using the .wmv extension. Only Windows computers containing Media Player version 6 or later will enable PowerPoint to play WMV files. A third set of formats for Media Player is stored using the .asf extension. Some versions of Media Player version 6 may have been retrofitted and can play ASF files, although some may not. The only way you can see if your version 6-equipped computer can play ASF files is if you try it. Media Player version 7, and all versions since, play ASF files.

The majority of video files not intentionally designed for Media Player are stored under the .mpg or .mpeg extension. Whether your Windows computer enables PowerPoint to play an MPEG file depends on whether Media Player has been set up with the proper software to decode the audio and video channels encoded in that file. There are hundreds of different codecs under the MPEG umbrella. As a result, you may encounter the occasional MPEG video file that does not play through PowerPoint on one computer, but plays through PowerPoint on another. The only reliable way to determine whether an MPEG plays well on a specific computer is to test it.

The two most important types of video files that probably do not play through PowerPoint are QuickTime (.qt extension, designed by Apple and popular on the Macintosh platform) and Real Media (.rm and .ram extension; these are streaming files designed for Windows and other computers, but they are not supported by Media Player). Software has been designed to enable both types of files to play in Media Player, and therefore in PowerPoint. However, QuickTime and Real Media files do not play in recent versions of Media Player and on earlier versions that have been "patched" or upgraded. As a result, a QuickTime or Real Media file may play well through PowerPoint on one day, and following an administrator upgrade to the network, fail to play anymore. As a result, unfortunately, you should avoid using these two formats for PowerPoint presentations.

Add Movies from Clip Organizer

Unless you've added your own video clips to the Clip Organizer, the only movie files it contains are animated GIF files. An animated GIF is a clip art drawing that has some element of animation in it.

To add an animated GIF, click Movies and Sounds on the Insert menu, and then click Movie from Clip Organizer. The Insert Clip Art task pane displays thumbnails for its entire movie collection. Click a thumbnail to insert the clip. Search for a particular clip by clicking the Modify button, keying a word or phrase in the Search text box, and clicking the Search button. If the clip you inserted is a video clip, you'll be asked when you want it to play. Click Yes to play the video automatically when the slide is displayed during a presentation or click No if you want to click to start it manually.

Animated GIFs and videos from the Clip Organizer are inserted in a rather small size, regardless of the placeholder you may have chosen for them. Because the clips are essentially objects, you can resize them as you like. If you enlarge a video considerably, it may appear grainy when viewed unless the resolution was quite high when it was recorded. Be sure to drag by a corner handle when resizing so you don't change the aspect ratio of the video window and distort its image. To view the animated GIF in motion, click the Slide Show view button. To view a video clip, double-click it.

Add a Video File

Adding a video file from your hard disk is easy: Click Movies and Sounds on the Insert menu, and then click Movie from File. Navigate to the folder that contains the video, click it, and click OK. You'll be asked if you want the video to play automatically when the slide is viewed. Click Yes or No, and the first frame of the movie appears on the slide.

Video files can be quite large, so they may be linked to the presentation rather than embedded in it. It is a good idea to store video clip files in the same folder that holds your presentation, and then insert it from that location so the files remain properly linked.

Video files offer a few more options. Right-click the video and click Edit Movie Object. In the dialog box that appears, shown in Figure 4-5, click *Loop until stopped* to keep replaying the movie during the presentation until you move to the next slide. Click *Rewind movie when done playing* to have the first frame of the video appear after the video is finished playing during the presentation. Click OK after selecting the options you want.

Important

To resize the video so it appears as clearly as possible without skipping, click the video, click Format to open the menu, click Picture, and click the Size tab. Click *Best scale for slide show* and click OK.

Hot Tip

It is not necessary to include a title on a slide. If you want to remove a slide's title to make more room for a video, click the title placeholder and press Delete.

FIGURE 4-5
Choose options for your video

Net Ethics

There are many places on the Internet where you may find a video clip for use in a presentation. You often find sound clips on the same Web sites. But before you download and use these clips, make sure you obtain the proper permission. And, if you plan on publishing your work to the Web or in any other format, be sure you have permission to do that, as well. Many sites allow you to download clips for personal use, but not if they are to be published elsewhere. Some other sites require only that you link your Web site to the original source or provide some type of credit line.

STEP-BY-STEP 4.4

1. Open **Senior Security SV**, the file you worked on earlier in this lesson. Save the file as **Senior Security SV 2**.

2. Display slide 7. Click **Insert** on the menu bar, click **Movies and Sounds**, and then click **Movie from Clip Organizer**.

3. Click the **Modify** button, key **healthcare**, and if needed, click **Movies** from the Results should be list and deselect any non-Movie options. Then click the **Search** button.

4. Click the clip shown in Figure 4-6 to insert it. If you do not see this clip after your search, ask your instructor for help. The inserted clip automatically changes the slide layout.

5. Click **Undo** to undo the automatic layout change. Drag the clip into position as shown in Figure 4-6.

FIGURE 4-6
Drag the clip into position

Help arrives in minutes

Drag the movie clip and position it just under the heading

6. Click the **Modify** button, key **pager**, and click the **Search** button. Insert the clip you find on the slide, Undo the layout change, and move the GIF below the text *Press alarm button*. Close the Insert Clip Art task pane.

7. You need to place your video files in the same folder where you save this presentation. Use a file management program such as Windows Explorer or My Computer to copy **PS Step 4-4a** and **PS Step 4-4b** to your solution folder.

8. Display slide 10. Click **Insert** on the menu bar, click **Movies and Sounds**, and then click **Movie from File**.

9. Navigate to the solution folder, if necessary, click **PS Step4-4a**, and click the **OK** button. Click **Yes** when asked if you want the movie to play automatically. Resize the video object to make it as large as possible without losing its aspect ratio. Center the video in the white area of the slide.

10. Display slide 11. Click **Insert** on the menu bar, click **Movies and Sounds**, and then click **Movie from File**.

11. Click **PS Step 4-4b** and click the **OK** button. Click **Yes** when asked if you want the movie to play automatically. Resize the video object and center it as you did in step 9.

12. Display slide 7, and click the **Slide Show** view button to see your animated GIFs. Advance through the slides to slide 10 and watch the video. Advance to slide 11 by clicking outside the video on slide 10, and view the video on the slide.

13. Save changes and close the **Senior Security 2** file. Leave PowerPoint open to use in the next exercise.

> **Important**
>
> If you click on a video while it's playing, the video will stop. If you click on a video after it has played, it will play again. So always click outside the video to advance to the next slide during a slide show.

Use an Animation Scheme

In Lesson 1, you learned how to add transitions between slides to a presentation. A slide transition controls how each slide is displayed—a slide might fade into view, or zoom in from the side, for example. These transitions add movement and excitement to a presentation and help you to keep your audience's attention.

In this section, you learn how to add *animation schemes*—animations that control how text is displayed on a slide. You can combine slide transitions with animation schemes if you like and have a blank slide appear in an interesting way, followed by the appearance of the slide title and each item in the bulleted list.

Animation schemes are packages applied to the entire slide. For example, the Wipe scheme fades in the slide title and wipes on each bulleted item. You can't break up the package and have the wipe apply to the title as well, for instance. But you can customize an animation scheme after you apply it. The next section of this lesson covers custom animation effects.

To apply an animation scheme, first select the slide or slides you want the scheme to affect. Then click Animation Schemes on the Slide Show menu. The Slide Design task pane opens with the Animation Schemes information active, as shown in Figure 4-7. The *Apply to selected slides* list contains several sections of animation schemes including Recently Used schemes (schemes

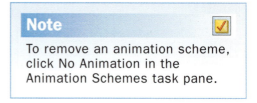

> **Note**   ☑️
>
> To remove an animation scheme, click No Animation in the Animation Schemes task pane.

that have been applied to recent presentations; if you have never used schemes before, this list will be empty) and three categories of schemes labeled Subtle, Moderate, and Exciting. Click an animation scheme from the list, and it is applied to the selected slide(s). You can also apply the same scheme to all slides by clicking the Apply to All Slides button.

FIGURE 4-7
Apply an animation scheme

After you select the animation scheme, it previews on the slide in Normal view so you can see how the scheme controls objects on the slide. You can click the Play button to see the preview again. Note that although bulleted items display automatically in the preview in Normal view, you have to click the mouse button to display them when you view the presentation in Slide Show view.

<table>
<tr><td>**Extra for Experts**

You can apply animations to the slide master to have the animation scheme affect all slides, even slides you may add later on.</td></tr>
</table>

S TEP-BY-STEP 4.5

1. Open **Katie's Cafe**, a presentation you worked on earlier in this lesson. Save the file as **Katie's Cafe 2**.

2. Switch to Normal view if necessary. Display slide 1 if necessary. Click **Slide Show** from the menu bar, and then click **Animation Schemes**. The Slide Design task pane opens with the Animation Schemes options active. If the narration begins to play while you are applying the scheme, click anywhere in the Slide pane to stop the narration.

3. Click the **Float** scheme in the Exciting section of the Apply to selected slides list. You may also find this scheme in the Recently Used section of the list.

4. Display slide 2. Click the **Descend** scheme in the Moderate section of the Apply to selected slides list.

5. Display slide 3. Click the **Pinwheel** scheme in the Exciting section of the Apply to selected slides list.

6. Change back to slide 1. Play the presentation in Slide Show view.

7. Save changes and close the **Katie's Cafe 2** file. Leave PowerPoint open to use in the next exercise.

Customize Animations

An animation scheme is a quick way to apply animation effects to the text on a slide. If you want more control over the animations, you can apply custom animations. When you use custom animations, you can animate any of the objects on a slide, such as graphics, charts, diagrams, and tables, as well as text objects such as titles and bullet lists. Use custom animation to modify an animation scheme or to start animating from scratch.

To apply custom animations, click Custom Animation on the Slide Show menu to display the Custom Animation task pane, as shown in Figure 4-8. To apply animation to an object, select it and then click the Add Effect button in the Custom Animation task pane. A drop-down list appears, with the following choices of events to animate:

- *Entrance* controls how the element comes into view on the slide.

- *Emphasis* adds an animation to the element after the object is displayed.

- *Exit* controls how the element is removed from the slide.

- *Motion Paths* allows you to specify a path along which an object will travel.

- *Sound Actions* allows you to control when a sound is played, paused, or stopped.

FIGURE 4-8
Custom Animation task pane

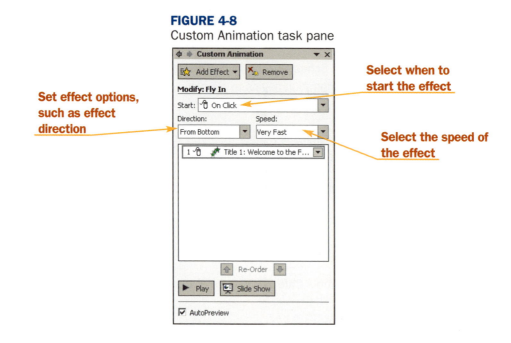

Set effect options, such as effect direction

Select when to start the effect

Select the speed of the effect

Each event has a submenu that displays a list of effects you can apply. For example, to have a title fade into view when the slide appears, click Entrance and then click the Fade effect. You can click More Effects at the bottom of the menu to display a complete list of effects for that category.

You can select more than one effect for a single object. As you select effects for the objects on a slide, they appear in the Custom Animation list in the order you chose them. Figure 4-8 shows one effect in the Custom Animation list, the animation for a slide title.

You have a number of options for controlling the animation. Open the Start list and click when you want the effect to occur: *On Click* holds the effect until you click during the slide show. *With Previous* starts the effect when the effect listed above it in the Custom Animation list begins (or immediately after the slide appears, for a title effect). *After Previous* starts the effect after the effect above it. Next, change any properties associated with the effect. For example, for the Fly In effect shown in Figure 4-8, you can select the direction from which the text flies in. Finally, open the Speed list and click the speed at which you want the effect to occur.

To view the animation sequence for the current slide, click the Play button in the Custom Animation task pane. Animations are displayed one after another, in the order in which they appear in the list. If you want to see the animations using any Start delays you may have set up, click the Slide Show button.

Note

To remove an animation effect, click it in the list and click Remove.

Change the Order of Effects

You can change the order in which the effects play by moving effects in the Custom Animation list. Click an effect to select it (it is surrounded by a dark outline when selected) and drag the effect. A dark horizontal bar shows the progress of the move. Drop the effect when the dark bar is where you want the effect to appear. You can also use the Re-Order button to move selected effects up or down the list.

S TEP-BY-STEP 4.6

1. Open the **Senior Security SV 2** file you worked on earlier in this lesson, and save it as **Senior Security SV 3**.

2. Select slides 2 through 11. Click **Slide Show** on the menu bar, and then click **Animation Schemes**. In the Apply to selected slides list, click **Elegant**. It is in the Moderate section.

3. On slide 1, click **Slide Show** on the menu bar, and then click **Custom Animation** to display the Custom Animation task pane. You should see three objects in the Custom Animation list. Drag the last item, the sound file, to the top of the list.

4. Click the **Start** drop-down arrow, and click **On Click**. This command allows you to start the music when the presentation begins.

5. Still on slide 1, click the picture to select it. Click the **Add Effect** button in the task pane, click **Entrance**, click **More Effects** at the bottom of the submenu, and scroll to find the **Grow & Turn** effect in the Moderate section. Click the **OK** button to apply the effect.

6. Drag the picture effect up the list and drop it just below the music effect. Click the **Start** drop-down arrow and click **With Previous**. This starts the picture effect when the music begins. Click the **Speed** drop-down arrow and click **Very Slow**. Click **Play** to preview the animation.

7. On slide 3, in the Custom Animation task pane, drag the first effect (*Help is a touch away!*) to just above the PS Step 4-1b sound item. Click the **Start** list and click **On Click**.

8. Click the Media 6 item. Click the **Start** list and click **After Previous**.

9. Click the PS Step 4-1b item. Click the **Start** list and click **With Previous**. Click **Play** to preview the animation sequence. You may notice that the Media 6 sound file does not play automatically; we will fix this in the next exercise.

10. Save changes and leave **Senior Security SV 3** open to use in the next exercise.

You have further options for customizing each effect in the animations list. To see the effect options, select the effect in the Custom Animations list to display a list arrow at the right. Click the drop-down arrow and select Effect Options to open a dialog box with options for the effect. These options, shown on the Effect tab, are specific to the type of object selected (text, chart, sound file) and the effect you applied. (See Figure 4-9.) The Effect Options dialog box changes its title depending on the effect chosen, as shown in Figure 4-9, which depicts the available options for the Fly In effect applied to a text object. The following sections discuss some of the more common effect options for various objects. In addition, the dialog box always contains a Timing tab. Use the settings on this tab to change the timing of the effect. For example, you can delay the start of an effect by a few seconds, repeat the effect (loop it), and make other timing changes.

FIGURE 4-9
Adjust the effect to suit your taste

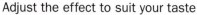

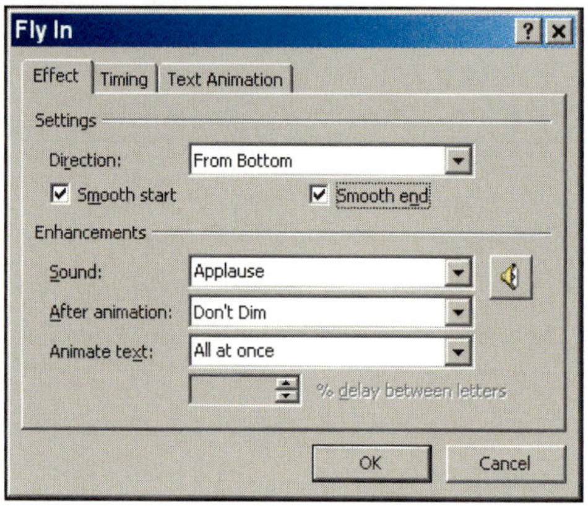

Text Effect Options

For text objects, the dialog box that appears when you select Effect Options has three tabs that allow you to fine-tune the effect settings, set timing options, and control how the text is animated. On the Effects tab, you can select a sound to play with the effect, choose to dim text after the effect, and specify whether the text appears all at once, word by word, or letter by letter. On the Timing tab, change the Start and Speed options, set a start delay, choose to repeat the animation, and set *triggers* that allow you to coordinate the start of one effect with the start of another one on the same slide. By the way, you can also display the Timing tab in by clicking an item in the animation list, clicking the drop-down arrow, and clicking Timing.

On the Text Animation tab, shown in Figure 4-10, you can control how bullet items appear. *As one object* displays all items at once. *By 1st level paragraphs* displays the main bullet items one at a time. If any bullet items have subordinate bullet items, the subordinate bullet items appear with their main bullet item. *By 2nd level paragraphs* displays main bullet items one at a time and subordinate bullet items one at a time also. You can also add a time delay between the appearance of items, animate the text box with the text, and reverse the order of the appearance of the items in the list.

> **Note** ☑️
>
> Small number tags appear next to each object on a slide to which an animation effect has been applied. To select the effect so you can customize it, simply click this numbered tag. Then click the arrow in the listing and click Effect Options.

FIGURE 4-10
Adjust the effect of text animations

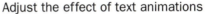

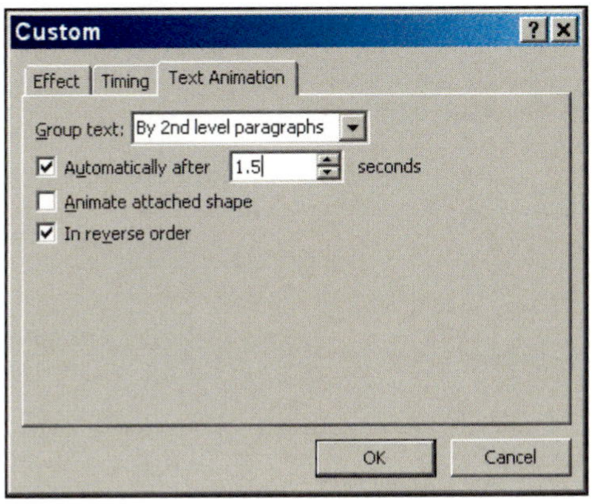

Chart and Other Object Effects

If you choose to animate a chart, the Effect Options dialog box includes the usual Effect and Timing tabs and the Chart Animation tab. Here, you can opt to have various elements of the chart appear separately and to animate the gridlines and legend (or to have the chart area, gridlines, and legend simply appear before the animation of the chart elements begins). If the object is an organization chart or diagram, the dialog box includes the Diagram Animations tab instead of the Chart Animations tab. Here, you can choose to animate the entire diagram as a unit; as separate elements, but at the same time; or as separate elements in a clockwise fashion around the diagram.

When you choose to animate an object by its separate parts, such as the levels in a bulleted list or parts of a chart, the Custom Animation list collapses the animation for each subordinate item under the main effect. You can see all the animation effects associated with an object (such as a bulleted list) by clicking the gray bar to expand the display. (See Figure 4-11.) Click it again to collapse the display. With the list expanded, you can select individual parts of the animation sequence (such as a single bulleted item) and modify its animation effects separately from the others.

FIGURE 4-11
You can animate the individual elements of a chart, diagram, or bulleted list

Click to expand or collapse effects

You can animate other objects, such as pictures, videos, and animated GIFs, in the same way you animate text and chart objects. Pictures, videos, and animated GIFs have only two tabs in the Effect Options dialog box, one to fine-tune the effect itself, and one to set up timings.

STEP-BY-STEP 4.7

1. In the **Senior Security SV 3** file, display slide 2. If needed, click the gray bar to collapse the animation listing for the bulleted list. By collapsing the listing to a single item, you can make a global change to the animation of the list.

2. Click the effect's drop-down arrow, and click **Effect Options**. On the Text Animation tab, click the Group text list, and then click **By 2nd level paragraphs**. Click the **OK** button.

3. On slide 3, click the **Media 6** item in the animation list. Click the drop-down arrow and click **Timing**.

4. Click **Animate as part of click sequence**. Click the **OK** button.

5. Display slide 7. Click the diagram, click **Add Effect**, click **Entrance**, and click **Fade**. You may need to click **More Effects** to locate this effect in the Subtle section and then click the **OK** button.

6. With the diagram item still selected in the animation list, click the effect's drop-down arrow and click **Effect Options**. On the Diagram Animation tab, click the **Group diagram** list, and then click **Clockwise**. Click the **OK** button. Click the gray bar to expand the listing of effects for the diagram.

STEP-BY-STEP 4.7 Continued

7. Click the animated GIF under *Press alarm button*. Click **Add Effect**, click **Entrance**, and click **Ease In**. You may need to click **More Effects** to locate the effect in the Moderate section and then click the **OK** button. Click the **Start** list, and then click **With previous**. Drag the effect up the list, and drop it just under the *Press alarm button* item (1).

8. Repeat step 7 to animate each GIF, and then place each animated GIF in the animation sequence under its associated diagram text.

9. Display slide 9. Click the chart to select it, and then apply an entrance effect of **Fade**. Click the effect's drop-down arrow, and then click **Effect Options**. Click the **Chart Animation** tab. Group the chart **By series**, deselect the **Animate grid and legend** check box, and then click the **OK** button.

10. Display slide 1. Select the **Title 1** effect. Click the **Start** list, and then click **With Previous**. Click the effect's drop-down arrow, and then click **Timing**. Set the Delay to **7** seconds, and then click the **OK** button. Click the effect for the bulldog graphic (the last effect in the list), click the **Start** list, and then click **With Previous**. Click the effect's drop-down arrow, click **Timing**, and set the delay to **9** seconds. Click the **OK** button.

11. Click the **Slide Show** button in the task pane to test your animations in Slide Show view. Click to advance each slide and see the animations. On slide 7, click to display each diagram item. On slide 9, click to display the chart and each series.

12. After the presentation ends, save changes and leave the **Senior Security SV 3** file open to use in the next exercise.

Create a Motion Path Animation

One of the most interesting ways to animate objects on a slide is to create a *motion path*. A motion path animation causes an object to move on the slide from one location to another.

To create a motion path animation, select the object to animate, and then click Motion Paths on the Add Effect list. Select a direction for the object to travel from the submenu. The default directions are straight lines, but you can choose Draw Custom Path to draw your own path using standard Drawing tools, or More Motion Paths to choose from a wide range of basic shapes, special shapes, and lines and curves.

After you select a direction, the object follows the path you choose. After the preview stops, the motion path appears with a green and red arrowhead marking its beginning and end. (See Figure 4-12.) Drag these arrowheads to adjust the length of the path or its starting and ending positions.

FIGURE 4-12
Use Motion Path to move an object across a slide

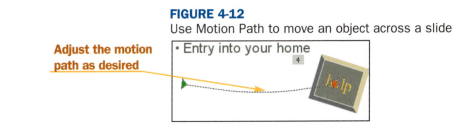

Adjust the motion path as desired

Fine-Tune Timing

Earlier, you learned you could make adjustments to the timing of an effect using the options on the Timing tab of the Effect Options dialog box. Sometimes, to get the timing just right, you need to watch the animation play several times. That's hard to do if you have to make a change in the dialog box, exit, play the animation, and then repeat the process a number of times. Instead of playing the slide show again and again, you can adjust the timing of an animation effect using the Advanced Timeline. Click the arrow on any item in the list and click Show Advanced Timeline. The timeline appears at the bottom of the Custom Animation task pane, as shown in Figure 4-13.

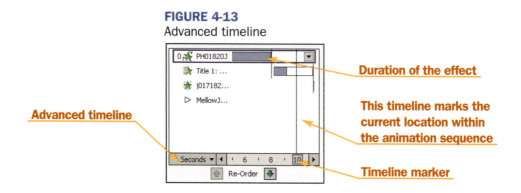

FIGURE 4-13
Advanced timeline

Duration of the effect

This timeline marks the current location within the animation sequence

Advanced timeline

Timeline marker

After displaying the timeline, click the Play button to play the animations on a slide. A vertical line crosses the task pane as each animation is played. In addition, a time block representing the timing for each effect appears as the associated object is animated. To use the timeline to change the timing of an effect, click the effect you want to change, and then drag either end of the time block to adjust the start or ending times and the length of the effect. You can also adjust the time delay on an effect by dragging the time block left or right. The timeline marker on the Advanced Timeline lets you know where you are within the animation sequence.

Extra for Experts

Change the scale of the timeline by clicking the Seconds button and choosing Zoom In to make the scale larger and allow fine-tuning of microseconds, or Zoom Out to make the scale smaller and allow you to see longer expanses of time on the timeline.

STEP-BY-STEP 4.8

1. In the **Senior Security SV 3** file, display slide 6.

2. Click the clock graphic to select it. Click the **Add Effect** button, click **Motion Paths**, and then click **Down**. The clock drops down the side of the table.

STEP-BY-STEP 4.8 Continued

3. When the motion stops, click the red arrowhead at the bottom of the path and drag it downward to lengthen the path, as shown in Figure 4-14. You can click and drag when the pointer is a double-headed arrow. You may need to move the green triangle back up to the center of the clock after you make this adjustment.

FIGURE 4-14
Extend the path of the clock

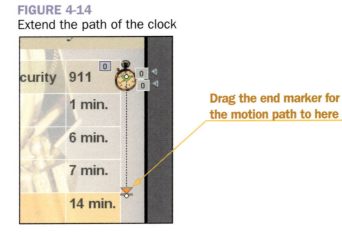

Drag the end marker for
the motion path to here

4. With the clock effect still selected, click the upward-pointing Re-Order arrow twice to move the effect just below the Title effect, so it's now the second item in the list.

5. Click **After Previous** in the Start list. Click **Very Slow** from the Speed list.

6. Click the clock graphic again to select it, click **Add Effect**, click **Emphasis**, and click **Blink**. You may need to click **More Effects** to locate the effect in the Exciting section and then click **OK**. If the Add Effect button says Change, you have not selected the clock graphic; you have selected the current effect. Click directly on the clock graphic to select it.

7. Display the Effect Options dialog box for the Blink effect. On the Timing tab, click **5** in the Repeat list and click the **OK** button.

8. Drag this Blink animation up one position in the list, so it's now the second from the last item in the list. You can click and drag when the pointer is a double-headed arrow. Click **After Previous** in the Start list.

STEP-BY-STEP 4.8 Continued

9. Click the **Media 31** item in the list, and click **With Previous** in the Start list. Click the **Media 32** item in the list, and click **With Previous** in the Start list. The Custom Animation task pane now looks like the one shown in Figure 4-15.

FIGURE 4-15
Your list should look similar to this one

10. Click the Title effect to display the drop-down arrow, and then click **Show Advanced Timeline**. Click **Play** to view the entire animation sequence.

11. Display slide 1 and play the entire presentation in Slide Show view.

12. Save and close the **Senior Security SV 3** file. Close PowerPoint.

SUMMARY

In this lesson, you learned:

■ Commands on the Insert menu's Movies and Sounds submenu are used to insert sounds from the Clip Organizer, from a file, or from a CD, or to record your own sound. You can also locate sound files by searching the World Wide Web.

■ Sounds can be made to play automatically when the slide appears during a presentation, or played only when you click the sound icon.

■ With the Record Narration command, you can run through a presentation and record a narration to accompany it.

■ The Clip Organizer contains animated GIF files you can add to a slide instead of static clip art.

■ A presentation can be energized with a video you add to a slide, using the Movie from File command.

■ Animation schemes combine a set of entrance animations for the slide title and body text into a neat, easy-to-apply package. Apply an animation scheme using the Animation Schemes command.

■ The Custom Animation command provides the tools to animate other objects on a slide, such as clip art, text objects, videos, and sound files.

VOCABULARY *Review*

Define the following terms:

Animation scheme	Loop	MP3
Codec	MIDI	Music loop
Embed	Motion path	Trigger
Link	Movie	WAV

REVIEW *Questions*

TRUE/FALSE

Circle T if the statement is true or F if the statement is false.

T F **1.** A MIDI file is the appropriate format choice if you want to create a short sound effect.

T F **2.** An MP3 file is smaller in size than the same recording saved as a WAV file.

T F **3.** You can play sound from a CD-ROM as long as you insert a custom animation.

T F **4.** PowerPoint can play any movie file that's supported by Windows Media Player.

T F **5.** With an animation scheme, you can animate the individual parts of a chart, diagram, or bulleted list.

FILL IN THE BLANK

Complete the following sentences by writing the correct word or words in the blanks provided.

1. _____ is often added to a presentation designed to be run automatically.

2. If you want to initiate a sound manually during a presentation, the _____ must appear somewhere on the slide.

3. Large sound files are _____ to a file, and not embedded in it.

4. To automatically play a sound file multiple times until you advance to the next slide, set it up so that it _____.

5. To record a narration, your computer must have a(n) _____, sound card, and speakers.

6. During a presentation, you can play _____ sound(s) at one time.

7. In PowerPoint, animated GIF files and videos are called _____.

8. You can combine slide transitions and _____ on the same slide.

9. A custom animation allows you to change the _____, emphasis, and exit of various objects, such as a chart, diagram, title, and text on a slide.

10. To start an animation so it coincides with the animation above it in the Custom Animation list, set the Start value to _____.

MATCHING

Match the correct term in Column 2 to its description in Column 1.

Column 1	Column 2
___ 1. Loop	A. Clip art that moves.
___ 2. Track	B. A recorded message that accompanies a presentation.
___ 3. Kiosk	C. Controls the appearance, emphasis, and exit of objects on a slide.
___ 4. Motion path	D. Replays a sound multiple times.
___ 5. Narration	E. Controls the appearance of text onto a slide during a presentation.
___ 6. Timings	F. Location of an interactive presentation.
___ 7. Animated GIF	G. One song on a CD-ROM.
___ 8. Animation scheme	H. Used to advance to the next slide automatically during a presentation.
___ 9. Custom animation	I. Starts the animation of one object when you click another object on the slide.
___ 10. Trigger	J. An animation effect.
	K. The sequence of animation effects on a slide.

PROJECTS

PROJECT 4-1

1. Open **PS Project 4-1a** from the data files.

2. Save the presentation as **KDDC Advertising**.

3. Display slide 4. Search the Clip Organizer for animated GIFs using the key word **earth**.

4. Insert a graphic of your choice and undo the layout change. Position the graphic to the left of the bulleted list and enlarge it if necessary.

5. Display slide 5. Search the Clip Organizer for animated GIFs using the key word **award**.

6. Insert a graphic of a plain gold cup with no background. Resize and position the graphic in the lower-right corner of the slide. Close the Insert Clip Art task pane.

7. Display slide 1. Insert the sound file **PS Project 4-1b.** You may first want to save the sound file in the same folder with your solution and give it a new name such as **newstheme.wav.**

8. Set the sound to play automatically when the slide is displayed. Loop the sound as well. Drag the sound icon off the slide so it is not visible.

9. Display slide 3 and record the narration below to explain the chart. Use the name **Ad Rates** for the sound. Leave the sound icon on the slide.
KDDC-TV 51 offers both broader distribution and sharper focus throughout the day to better target your message to your customer. In the morning, [pause for the count of 2] noon, [pause again for the count of 2] and prime-time bands, KDDC-TV's advertising rates meet or beat our competitors'. Let the Heart of Kansas City produce, adapt, and target your message for any customer, any time of day, and to meet any budget.

10. Drag the sound icon off the slide.

11. Display slide 2. (Don't worry that the text on the slide appears to overlap; it's all part of the animation sequence you are building.) Insert the movie file **PS Project 4-1c.** You may first want to save the video clip in your solution folder, with a new name such as **Ad Sales.mpg.** Do not allow the video to play automatically.

12. Size and position the video so it exactly covers the gold rectangle object on the slide. (**Hint:** If you have trouble positioning the video exactly, click **Draw** on the Drawing menu, click **Grid and Guides,** and deselect **Snap objects to grid.**) Display the Custom Animation task pane and position the video effect at the top of the list.

13. Display slide 1 and play the presentation in Slide Show view to see your animations and hear the sound files. You will need to click on slide 2 to start the video. Click the sound icon on Slide 3 to hear your recorded narration.

> **Important**
>
> If the animation on slide 2 does not play with the video, then open the Custom Animation task pane, click the first object under the video in the listing, display the Timing tab in the Effect Options dialog box, select With Previous from the Start list again, set the Delay to 8.5 seconds and click OK. This should reset the effect and the effects after it in the list.

14. Save changes and leave the **KDDC Advertising** open to use in Project 4-2.

PROJECT 4-2

1. Save the **KDDC Advertising** file as **KDDC Advertising 2.** (If you were unable to record the narration for the presentation in Project 4-1, see your instructor for help.)

2. Display the slide master. Select the graphic in the upper-left corner and apply the **Thread** entrance effect, starting **With Previous.** Apply the same effect to the graphic on the title master. Applying these effects in master view will animate the graphic on all slides in the presentation.

3. Apply the **Unfold** entrance effect for the titles on all slides in the presentation except the title slide, starting **With Previous.** Use the **Fast** speed. Close slide master view.

4. Display slide 1. Apply the **Color Wave** emphasis effect to the title. Change the Color to a medium gold, and set the Speed to **Very Fast**. Apply the **Thread** entrance effect to the subtitle. Set the Speed to **Very Fast**. Start the effect after the slide title effect.

5. Display slide 3. Drag the sound icon off the slide. Start the sound file With Previous. Remove the trigger by changing the animation effect timing so that the sound effect is animated as part of the click sequence.

6. Add the **Wipe** entrance animation effect to the chart, and choose the direction to wipe. Animate the chart by category. Do not animate the grid and legend. Set the Speed to **Fast**.

7. Start the chart effect with the sound file, but delay the start of the category 1 effect by **11 seconds**.

8. Start the category 2 effect with the sound file as well, but delay it by **12 seconds**. To see the category 2 effects, expand the chart effect by clicking the gray bar.

9. Start the category 3 effect with the sound file and delay it by **13.5 seconds**.

10. Preview the slide animation, and adjust the timing of the chart categories if necessary so the chart columns appear at the proper time in the narration.

11. Apply the **Rise Up** animation scheme to slides 4, 5, and 6. Modify the bullet list effect on at least one of these slides to add some variety. You might apply a different effect to the list, add a sound effect, display text by 2nd level paragraphs, create time delays, and so on. You may also animate the graphics on slides 4, 5, and 6 if you like.

12. Play the slide show from the beginning, and then adjust any animations that need more work.

13. Save and close **KDDC Advertising 2**. Close PowerPoint.

SCANS WEB PROJECT

The governor is hosting a conference on pollution, and it's your job to create a presentation on greenhouse gases. Mayors and other city officials from throughout the state will attend. Attendees will be given a copy of the presentation so they can modify it for use in a city-wide conference, planning meeting, town meeting with ordinary citizens, and so on. The presentation needs to explain the causes of greenhouse gases and the damage they cause in simple terms. You've been instructed to include information on what various nations are doing to reduce greenhouse gases—especially in the United States, Mexico, and Europe. Provide an analysis that compares your state's greenhouse emissions with those of other states, using charts and tables. Include information on recent changes in the law or in policy, and prepare a forecast of future trends. Add appropriate clip art, photos, animated GIFs, and videos that support your presentation text. For example, you might include a short video featuring the "governor" (played by a classmate or friend) that details the simple things families, businesses, and schools can do to reduce greenhouse gases in their city.

SCANS TEAMWORK PROJECT

Create a presentation for the school board that describes how the school meets the Title IX funding requirement for girls' sports programs. Break into pairs, and assign research duties to each pair: What conditions must the school meet in order to prove Title IX compliance? How many females/males attend your school? How many females/males participate in sports? How much money is spent per female/male athlete? Compare this information using appropriate charts and tables. Conduct interviews on video of athletes who tell how sports have affected their lives in a positive way. In areas where the school may be lacking, come up with a plan that helps the school meet the guidelines and present your ideas. For example, what might be done to increase a girl's interest in sports? If a girl chooses not to participate, what reasons does she give? Survey a sampling of girls of various ages, ethnicity, and economic backgrounds, and prepare a statistical analysis of their reasons for not participating. Do any patterns emerge? How can the more frequent reasons for not participating be overcome? As a team, prepare an outline for the presentation, and key in text and chart/table data. Add video, sound, and animations to enliven the presentation.

CRITICAL *Thinking*

ACTIVITY 4-1

The mayor wants a presentation to support her urban renewal program, so she's asked everyone on her staff to create one. The presentation will be used to encourage young families to purchase homes in the old Trevor Hills neighborhood and, using low-interest financing, fix them up. Include video, sound clips, and graphics that illustrate the benefits of living downtown in an old neighborhood that's undergoing renewal. Add video testimonials and other endorsements. Create a rubric (a chart with criteria for judging the quality of some work) to be used by the mayor in judging which presentation does the best job. Then, use this rubric to compare your presentation to others produced by your class.

ACTIVITY 4-2

Research the appropriate use of sound, movies, and animation effects in a presentation and prepare a 200-word report. Is there such a thing as too much? How do sound, movies, and animation enhance a presentation? What tips did you find on creating quality sound/video clips? Are there any quality standards you should abide by? Are there any standards on the use of animations? Do the standards change if you plan to use the presentation in front of a large group, in a trade booth, at a kiosk, or on the Web? Does any particular color background help enhance video and/or animated GIFs? What equipment produces the best results, but still is affordable?

ACTIVITY 4-3

Complete the teeth brushing demonstration you created in Lesson 2. First, remember that the presentation is to be self-running, so make the appropriate changes to the presentation setup. Add graphics, video, and narration to help the text explain proper brushing technique. Keep the presentation lively and fun, since it will be viewed by children as they are having their teeth cleaned.

CREATING SUPPORT MATERIALS

OBJECTIVES

Upon completion of this lesson, you should be able to:

- Enter notes about your presentation.
- Print notes pages for your use or for your audience.
- Design handouts with illustrations of each slide.
- Print handouts in a variety of formats.
- Print a presentation outline.
- Create overheads and 35mm slides.
- Export notes, handouts, or outline data to Word for further processing.

Estimated Time: 1 hour

VOCABULARY

Embed

ftp

Header

Landscape

Portrait

Service bureau

The purpose of a presentation is to impart information. That information, of course, can take many forms: you may be informing customers about the advantages of a product; proposing a change in policy; reporting on past sales and predicting future trends; or teaching new skills. Obviously, you've already chosen to pass on this important information using a PowerPoint presentation. But to help your audience remember what you present, you need to reinforce your message with support materials.

You have several options. You can print a copy of each slide and pass them out to the participants. Or, you can create handouts, which include a small thumbnail of each slide and usually some room for taking notes. You can create your own notes, too, and use them when giving a presentation.

An even more fundamental question you should have asked yourself by now is, "How am I going to share this presentation?" If you have a large video screen or monitor that can be connected to a desktop or laptop computer, then you can display your presentation on it. If a video screen/monitor is not available, then perhaps you can project your presentation onto a screen using a multimedia projector connected directly to your computer/laptop, an overhead projector and overhead transparencies of your slides, or a slide projector and 35mm slides of your presentation. If flexibility is what you desire, then you may want to come prepared for any situation by creating handouts, notes, slides, and overheads of your presentation. You learn how to create all of these materials in this lesson.

Use Notes Pages

The main reason for creating notes is to help you remember what to say when you give the presentation. In your notes, you may include several short sentences or entire paragraphs of text, a numbered or bulleted list, supporting charts and tables, or even a photo or a map. There are limits, however: You can create only one notes page for each slide.

Even if your presentation is destined for the Web and not meant to be displayed in front of an audience, you still may want to create notes. When you publish your presentation to the Web, you can decide whether to include the notes. These notes can help a viewer better understand the data presented on each slide.

You may have already noticed the Notes pane that appears beneath the Slide pane in Normal view (see Figure 5-1). You type your notes and add objects (charts, tables, graphics, and so on) directly into this pane. Simply click anywhere inside the pane and key the note text or use the Insert menu to add graphics. You can resize the Notes pane if you like by dragging the border that separates it from the Slide pane. The size of the slide displayed in the Slide pane automatically adjusts.

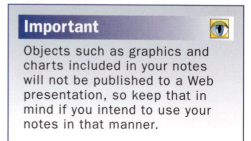

Extra for Experts

When desired, you can export your notes to Word and create more than a single page of notes for a slide. You learn how later in this lesson.

Important

Objects such as graphics and charts included in your notes will not be published to a Web presentation, so keep that in mind if you intend to use your notes in that manner.

FIGURE 5-1
Key quick notes directly into the Notes pane

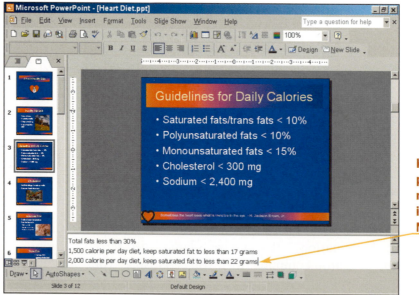

Key your presentation notes directly into the Notes pane

The Notes pane is convenient when you're creating a presentation and think of a few things you want to remember. However, to enter large amounts of text, long lists, graphics, and other objects, you may find it more convenient to switch to Notes Page view (Figure 5-2) by clicking Notes Page on the View menu. Click beneath the picture of the slide, and key the note text.

FIGURE 5-2
When adding lots of notes, use Notes Page view instead

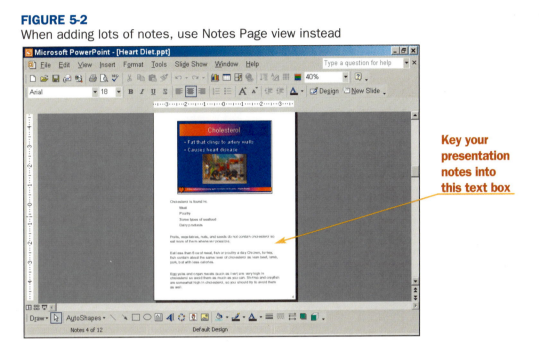

Key your
presentation
notes into
this text box

Format Notes Pages

As you key the note text, use the buttons on the Formatting toolbar to change the font, font size, font style, alignment, font color, and so on. You won't see some formatting or inserted objects in Normal view (at least, not typically—see the Extra for Experts), but you do see them when you change to Notes Page view.

To make room for more notes, you can reduce the size of the slide while in Notes Page view by dragging a corner handle. You can also reposition the slide place-holder by dragging it. To apply a design template, color scheme, or background to the notes pages, use the commands on the Format menu. Your selections do not affect the slides themselves.

Extra for Experts

To display formatting, such as a different font, in the Notes pane while in Normal view, click the Show Formatting button on the Standard toolbar.

To make global changes to your notes pages, use the notes master. Click Master on the View menu, and then click Notes Master. The notes master, shown in Figure 5-3, is similar to the slide and title masters you learned about in Lesson 2. Like the slide and title masters, the notes master displays standard placeholders for text and objects that appear on each page, such as the body text placeholder; the slide placeholder; and the header, date, footer, and number placeholders.

FIGURE 5-3
Notes master

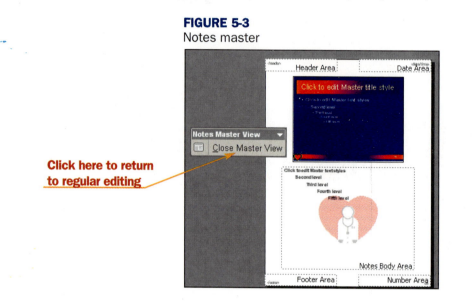

Click here to return to regular editing

Changes you make here affect all notes pages. For example, if you click the body text place-holder and change the font, that font appears on all notes pages. If you resize the slide, you set that size for all pages. You can insert a graphic, such as a company logo or an image from your slide background, to have it appear on all pages, as well.

To remove a placeholder, click it and press Delete. For example, you may remove the footer placeholder so you can enlarge the body text placeholder. If you remove a placeholder that you later decide you need, click the Notes Master Layout button on the Notes Master View toolbar to display a dialog box that allows you to redisplay it. When you are finished making changes, click Close Master View.

While in notes master view, you can add a *header* or footer to print on your notes pages by clicking Header and Footer on the View menu to open the Header and Footer dialog box you worked with in Lesson 2. Click the *Date and time* option if desired, and choose an automatic or fixed date. Click in the Header box and key text that you want to appear at the top of each notes page. Click in the Footer box and key text to appear at the bottom of every notes page. To display page numbers, click the *Page number* option. The pages start with page 1, unless you change the starting page number in the Page Setup dialog box. You learn more about the Page Setup dialog box later in this lesson. Finally, click Apply to All to apply the header and footer information to all notes pages.

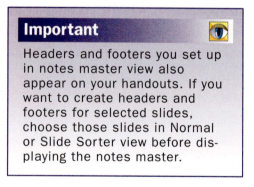

> **Important**
>
> Headers and footers you set up in notes master view also appear on your handouts. If you want to create headers and footers for selected slides, choose those slides in Normal or Slide Sorter view before displaying the notes master.

Preview and Print Notes Pages

It's best to preview your notes pages prior to printing them to make sure they look
exactly the way you want them to. Click the Print Preview button on the Standard toolbar to
display the Print Preview window, shown in Figure 5-4. If needed, click the Print What list
and click Notes Pages to display your notes pages. Switch between *portrait* and *landscape* orientation by clicking the appropriate buttons on the toolbar. Click the Options button to reveal a menu
with commands that let you create headers and footers; adjust the size of the data to fit the size of
the paper you've selected in the Page Setup dialog box; and add a frame around the slide on each
page. The Color/Grayscale command allows you to print your notes pages in full color, grayscale,
or black and white. Although printing in color is perhaps more eye-catching, this uses a lot of
expensive color inks; may take more time than grayscale or black and white printing; and, if large
areas are printed in the same color, may even result in some smearing and smudging.

FIGURE 5-4
Print Preview window

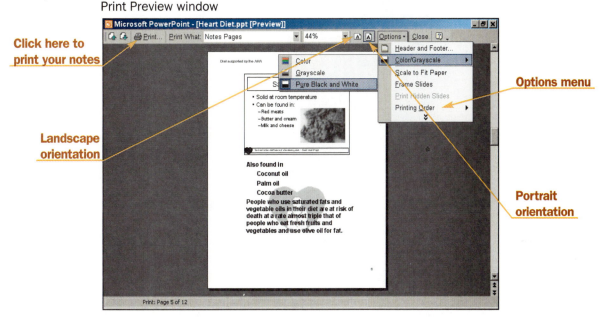

After making your selections and previewing the results, click the Print button on the toolbar to display the Print dialog box, shown in Figure 5-5. You have some additional choices here: In the Print range area, you can choose to print all notes pages, or just the ones that correspond to the current slide, selected slides, or the slides whose numbers you enter in the Slides box.

Note

To insert a comment on a slide, click Insert on the menu bar, and click Comment.

The Copies area allows you to print multiple copies at one time and collate the copies into sets. Click the *Include comment pages* option to print any comments you may have added to the slides. These comments print on a separate page or pages, after the handouts. Click OK to print your notes pages.

FIGURE 5-5
Print dialog box

Select which slides or pages to print

Print multiple copies if you want

Print your comments as well

STEP-BY-STEP 5.1

1. Launch PowerPoint, and open **PS Step 5-1** from the data files.

2. Save the file as **Heart Diet**.

3. On slide 2, click in the Notes pane and key: **Diet plans approved by the American Heart Association will be available at the back of the lecture hall after the presentation.** If necessary, enlarge the Notes pane by dragging the top border upward to provide more room to key the text.

4. Click **View** on the menu bar, and then click **Notes Page**.

5. Select the note text, and click **18** on the Font Size list.

6. Click **View** on the menu bar, click **Master**, and then click **Notes Master**.

STEP-BY-STEP 5.1 Continued

7. Click the **Line** button on the Drawing toolbar, and draw a line the width of the text box, beneath the slide and above the text box.

8. Click the **Line Style** button, and click **2¼ pt**. Click the arrow on the **Line Color** button, and click the **Follow Accent Scheme Color** (third from right). Click the **Close Master View** button.

9. Click the **Print Preview** button on the Standard toolbar. Click the **Print What** list and click **Notes Pages**.

10. Click the **Options** button on the Print Preview toolbar, click **Color/Grayscale**, and then click **Pure Black and White**.

11. Click the **Print** button on the Print Preview toolbar. The Print dialog box opens. Click the **OK** button to print the notes. Click the **Close** button on the Print Preview toolbar to return to Notes Page view.

12. Save changes and leave the **Heart Diet** file open to use in the next exercise.

Prepare Audience Handouts

While notes pages are designed for speaker use, handouts are designed to be used by your audience. Like notes pages, handouts include a picture of each slide in the presentation. You can choose how many slide thumbnails appear on each handout: 1, 2, 3, 4, 6, or 9 thumbnails per page. On the three-slide layout, a lined area is automatically included alongside each slide for your audience to use when taking their own notes.

Extra for Experts

Even though the other handout layouts do not include a lined area for notes, you can add your own lines to any of the other layouts by resizing the slide images and adding lines with the Line tool. You can also export handout data to Word and create your own custom layouts using its tools if you prefer.

Format Handouts

To format handouts, use the handout master: Click Master on the View menu, and then click Handout Master. Shown in Figure 5-6, the handout master is similar to other masters. With the buttons on the Handout Master View toolbar, you can quickly display various handout layouts. As with other masters, you can add graphics, apply a design layout or color scheme, and format the background. In addition, you can add text with a text box, draw lines for taking notes, and add other objects. The changes you make in the master affect every handout page you print in the current presentation. Remember that headers or footers you create or change while in handout master view affect the headers/footers on your notes pages because these masters share header/footer information. When you are through making changes, click Close Master View.

FIGURE 5-6
Handout master

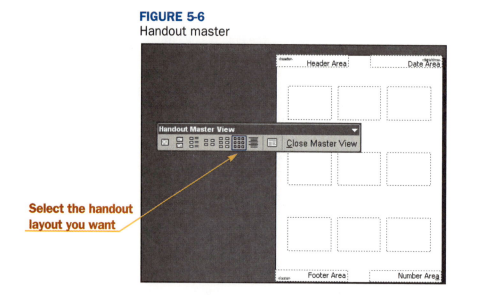

Select the handout layout you want

Preview and Print Handouts

To check your handouts, change to Print Preview by clicking the Print Preview button on the Standard toolbar. Click the Print What list and click the handout layout you are using, such as Handouts (2 slides per page). Switch between portrait and landscape orientation by clicking the buttons on the toolbar. Click the Options button to change the headers and footers, change to grayscale or black and white printing, adjust the size of the data to fit the size of the current paper selection, or add a frame around the slide on each page.

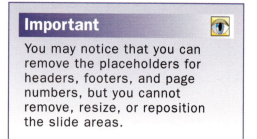

Important

You may notice that you can remove the placeholders for headers, footers, and page numbers, but you cannot remove, resize, or reposition the slide areas.

In addition, particular layouts allow you to change the order in which the slides appear on the page. By default, the printing order is horizontal. For example, in a four-slide layout, slide 1 appears in the upper-left corner, slide 2 appears next to it horizontally, slide 3 appears in the lower left corner, and slide 4 appears in the lower-right corner. You can change the print order by clicking Printing Order on the Options menu. If you change to a vertical print layout, slide 2 appears below slide one (moving vertically), slide 3 appears in the upper-right corner, and slide 4 appears below it in the lower-right corner.

When you're ready to print, click the Print button on the toolbar. Select options as described in the *Preview and Print Notes Pages* section, and click OK.

S TEP-BY-STEP 5.2

1. In the **Heart Diet** file, click **View** on the menu bar, click **Master**, and then click **Handout Master**.

2. Click the **Show positioning of 3-per-page handouts** button.

3. Click **View** on the menu bar, and then click **Header and Footer**.

4. Click in the **Footer** box, and key **Presentation by Heart Happy Diets, Inc.** Click the **Apply to All** button.

5. Click the **Close Master View** button.

6. Click the **Print Preview** button on the Standard toolbar.

7. Click the **Print What** list and click **Handouts (3 slides per page)**.

8. Click the **Options** button, click **Color/Grayscale,** and then click **Color**.

9. Click the **Print** button, and then click the **OK** button in the Print dialog box to print the handouts. Click the **Close** button on the Print Preview toolbar.

10. Save changes and leave the **Heart Diet** file open to use in the next exercise.

Print an Outline

The outline of the text in a presentation appears on the Outline tab in Normal view. You can print this outline for your own review or as an additional handout for your audience. In Normal view, display the Outline tab. Click the Expand All button on the Standard toolbar, if needed, to display all levels of text. To hide the text on a particular slide, double-click its slide icon, as shown in Figure 5-7. To hide all slide text and display only the slide titles in the outline, deselect the Expand All button.

FIGURE 5-7
Display the outline text you want to print

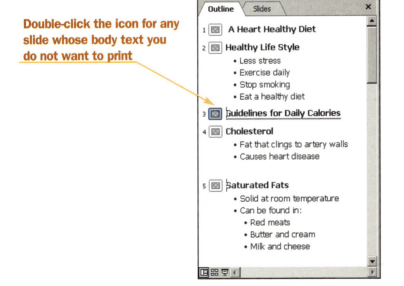

Double-click the icon for any slide whose body text you do not want to print

After displaying the text in the outline that you wish to print, you can preview the outline view the same way you preview notes pages and handouts. Click Outline View on the Print What list. Click the Options button and change options as desired. The design template, color scheme, background, headers, and footers shown in Outline View are those you selected for handouts. When you're ready to print the outline, click the Print button on the toolbar, and then click OK.

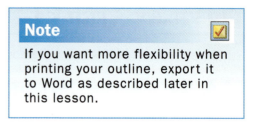

Note ☑

If you want more flexibility when printing your outline, export it to Word as described later in this lesson.

STEP-BY-STEP 5.3

1. In the **Heart Diet** file, click the **Normal View** button, and then click the **Outline** tab if necessary to display the outline.

2. Double-click the slide icons for slides 9 and 10 to hide the body text on both slides.

3. Click the **Print Preview** button on the Standard toolbar.

4. Click the **Print What** list, and click **Outline View**.

5. Click the **Print** button, and then click the **OK** button to print the presentation outline. Close Print Preview.

6. Save changes and leave the **Heart Diet** file open to use in the next exercise.

Create Overheads and 35mm Slides

If you plan to give your presentation before a live audience, you're not limited to displaying the slides on a television monitor or large digital screen/wall display. When needed, you can display your presentation on a regular portable AV screen using a simple overhead projector. Or, you can have your presentation processed into slides and use a slide projector. In this section, you will learn how to produce both types of materials. Before you create overheads or 35mm slides, however, you may need to make some changes in the design and layout of your presentation.

Design Considerations for Overheads and 35mm Slides

Unlike a presentation viewed on a computer monitor or similar device, presentations that use overheads or 35mm slides are projected onto a screen using a light, so there are illumination issues to consider. For example, does the same color show up as well when using a slide projector as it does with an overhead projector? There are also some rules for color choices, as discussed below.

The first thing you must think about is the slide background. When creating overheads, it's typically recommended that you use a light background such as white, with dark text such as black or dark blue. This combination seems to work best with the kind of light source in most overhead projectors. When creating 35mm slides, the exact opposite is often true—the recommendation here is to use a dark background with light text. Dark blue with light yellow or white text works especially well for projected slides. Again, the medium of projection is different, so your color choices change.

Clear, sans serif fonts such as Arial and Tahoma, in a minimum 24-point size, work best when projected, so consider using them when creating overheads or slides. To quickly change the font throughout a presentation, display the slide master and apply sans serif fonts to the text placeholders as described in Lesson 2.

Consider adding slide numbers to your presentation. They are invaluable should you ever accidentally drop your overheads or 35mm slides. Add slide numbers using the Header and Footer command on the View menu.

For 35mm slide presentations, it's usually best to avoid templates with patterns because they don't always render well to a slide. Because overheads are usually produced by running transparency sheets through a printer, patterns should be avoided with this medium as well, because there is a good chance the patterns will look splotchy and grainy.

With 35mm slides, you may encounter problems if the slide background contains a semi-transparent graphic, such as the graphic backgrounds of the Stream and Competition design templates. Most slide printers render graphics to PostScript format first, and PostScript does not deal with transparency correctly.

After looking over your presentation and making changes in its design and layout to accommodate the medium you intend to use, you are ready to create your overheads or slides.

Create Overheads

The process of creating overheads from a PowerPoint presentation is simple. You print your slides on special transparency film, readily available at most office supply stores, computer stores, or on the Internet.

Before printing the overheads, make any changes to the design template or color scheme necessary to display your slide content clearly on the transparencies. If you're not sure how your design and colors will appear, you can always print one slide onto transparency film, and then test it by standing at the back of the room you intend to use and judging how clear the text is. You

Hot Tip

Make sure you select the correct transparency film for your printer. Film for a laser printer is different from film for an inkjet printer. You may also want to purchase transparency frames or protectors to protect your transparencies from scratches, dust, and so on.

may also want to modify your slide layout. If you intend to use frame protectors on your transparencies, for example, you may need to adjust the position of the text placeholders on the slide master to ensure at least a half-inch margin all around.

When you're ready to print your slides, click Page Setup on the File menu to display the Page Setup dialog box (see Figure 5-8). Click the Slides sized for list, and click Overhead. Click OK to close the dialog box.

FIGURE 5-8
Page Setup dialog box

Select the type of media associated with the presentation

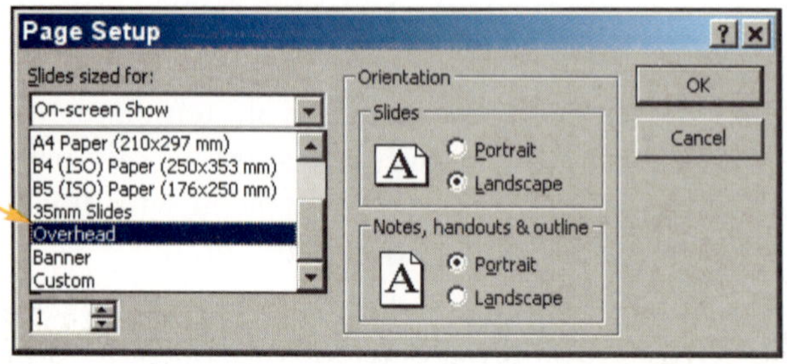

Next, you can preview your slides before you print them. Click the Print Preview button on the Standard toolbar and change any options as desired. To maximize the slide on the transparency, click the Options button and click Scale to Fit Paper. Adding a frame around the slide with the Frame Slides command is especially useful for defining the edges of the slide if you change from color to black and white or grayscale with the Color/Grayscale command on the Options menu. To print, load the transparency film in the printer and click the Print button on the toolbar. Click OK to begin printing.

Extra for Experts

Because transparency film tends to have a lot of static, you may find it helpful to load only one transparency into the printer's feed bed at a time, and print only the current slide by clicking the Current slide option in the Print range area of the Print dialog box.

STEP-BY-STEP 5.4

1. In the **Heart Diet** file, click the **Design** button on the Formatting toolbar and click **Color Schemes**. Click the first scheme on the right (you may need to scroll up). Close the Slide Design task pane.

2. Click **View** on the menu bar, click **Master**, and then click **Slide Master**.

3. Change to the slide master if needed, and click the **Master title style** placeholder. Click the arrow on **Fill Color** button on the Drawing toolbar and select a medium red. Click the arrow on the **Font Color** button and click white.

4. Click the gradient-filled rectangle at the bottom of the slide. Click the **Fill Color** button again to apply the same red color.

5. Change to the title master, click the **Master title style** placeholder, and click the **Fill Color** button to apply the same red color. Click the **Font Color** button and click white. Click the gradient-filled rectangle at the bottom of the slide. Click the **Fill Color** button and choose the same fill as the rectangle on the slide master. Click the **Close Master View** button.

6. On slide 1, click the text box for the quote, which is located at the bottom of the slide. Click the **Font Color** button and click white. Change the quotation text on all the slides to white.

STEP-BY-STEP 5.4 Continued

7. Click **File** on the menu bar, and then click **Page Setup**. The Page Setup dialog box opens.

8. Click the **Slides used for** list, and click **Overhead**. Click the **OK** button.

9. Click the **Print Preview** button. Click **Options** on the toolbar, and then click **Scale to Fit Paper**. Scroll through the slides to see how they will look as overheads. Close Print Preview.

10. Save and close the **Heart Diet** file, and leave PowerPoint open to use in the next exercise.

Create 35mm Slides

Unlike the other support materials you have learned about in this lesson, 35mm slides cannot be created using your desktop printer. To create 35mm slides from your PowerPoint presentation, you need to prepare the PowerPoint file and take it or send it to a *service bureau* for processing. If you can't find a service bureau locally, you can search for one on the Internet. Many online service bureaus can create slides for you—simply transfer the PowerPoint file to them via *ftp*, and they ship the slides back to you after processing. FTP is a file transfer utility that allows for quick transfer of files across the Internet.

Because you provide a copy of the PowerPoint file to the service bureau and expect 35mm slides in return, all the information the service bureau needs to properly create those slides must be contained in the file. Therefore, you must take several steps to prepare the file properly:

■ First, change the page setup so PowerPoint knows you want to output to 35mm slides. To do that, open the Page Setup dialog box, click the Slides sized for list, and click 35mm Slides.

■ Once PowerPoint understands that the output is intended to be on 35mm slides, it adjusts the size of the slides accordingly. The default placement of the text placeholders should ensure that none of your information is covered by the slide mount, but you may want to adjust the position of the text placeholders on the slide master to increase the margins slightly to avoid any possible problems. A minimum half-inch margin all around is typically recommended.

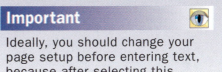

Important

Ideally, you should change your page setup before entering text, because after selecting this option, the size of your on-screen slides changes. You need to recheck your text on each slide to make sure it is still placed where you want it.

■ For best results, use only standard Windows TrueType fonts to avoid any problems caused by the service bureau substituting your fonts for whatever they happen to have that's close in style.

■ Some bureaus may be able to accept other font files on disk so you can use specialty fonts when needed. You can also *embed* TrueType fonts in the file and avoid font problems that way. Embedding fonts makes the file larger, which may cause some slide output machines to run out of memory and not print the slides. As long as you don't embed too many fonts, however, you should be fine. To embed fonts when saving a presentation, click the Tools button in the Save As dialog box, and then click Save Options. Click Embed TrueType Fonts and click OK. Then click Save to save the file.

■ Keep in mind that bullet symbols typically come from a font (unless you use a graphic image for the bullet), and that the font you use must be either a Windows standard font, a font embedded in the file, or a font you supply in a separate file to the service bureau.

■ The slides in your presentation file are oriented in landscape. If you need some slides in portrait orientation, you need to move them to a different file because PowerPoint can handle only one orientation per presentation for slides. To change the orientation of your slides, click the appropriate button in the Print Preview window, or select the option you want from the Page Setup dialog box.

■ Graphics used on your slides can raise a number of issues. First, don't use so many that the presentation file becomes too large for the service bureau's equipment to handle. Ask if they have any guidelines on file size. If your presentation is too large, consider removing unneeded graphics, compressing them, or creating multiple PowerPoint files for processing.

■ Every service bureau has its own recommendations for graphics file types, but most recommend using TIFF, JPG, and PICT for imported graphics, and CGM, WMF, and PCX for clip art, whenever possible.

■ Rotated text may not reproduce in the color you see onscreen. Sometimes, on a slide it appears as black text in a red text box. Ask your service bureau if this is true on their equipment.

■ Grouped images (including charts and tables imported from Word) may not be rendered properly unless they are ungrouped first. You won't be able to change data linked to a chart after ungrouping, so don't ungroup objects until you're ready to send your file to the service bureau. To ungroup a grouped object, right-click it, click Grouping, and click Ungroup.

S TEP-BY-STEP 5.5

1. Open **PS Step 5-5** from the data files, and save it as **Heart Diet 2**. This is another version of the presentation you worked with earlier in this lesson.

2. Click **File** on the menu bar, and then click **Page Setup**.

3. Click the **Slides sized for** list, and click **35mm Slides**. Click the **OK** button. You should notice immediately that the slide currently displayed changes dimensions.

4. Click the **Slide Sorter View** button.

5. After checking that the layout of each slide fits the new dimensions, return to Normal view.

6. Click **View** on the menu bar, and then click **Header and Footer**.

7. Click **Slide number** and then click the **Apply to All** button.

8. Save changes and leave the **Heart Diet 2** file open to use in the next exercise.

Export Notes, Handouts, or an Outline to Word

Everyone likes having choices, and although PowerPoint provides some flexibility when it comes to printing your notes, handouts, and presentation outline, it may not be enough for you. That's why PowerPoint makes it easy to export your data to Word so you can use Word's tools to manipulate the presentation data. Simply click Send To on the File menu, and then click Microsoft Word. The Send To Microsoft Word dialog box opens, as shown in Figure 5-9.

FIGURE 5-9
Send To Microsoft Word dialog box

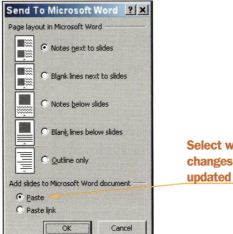

Select whether you want changes to be automatically updated in Word

As you can see, the dialog box provides many options. You can send thumbnails of your slides along with your notes to Word, with notes positioned to the right or below the slide thumbnails. If handouts are your goal, click either *Blank lines next to slides* or *Blank lines below slides*. To print the presentation outline, click *Outline only*. Click *Paste* to simply copy the data to a Word document. Click *Paste link* to link the data so that it's updated automatically if changes are made to the presentation at a later time. After making your selections, click OK. Microsoft Word starts automatically and creates the document that corresponds to your choice.

If you choose either of the "next to" options, Word creates a three-column table. Slide captions (Slide 1, Slide 2, and so on) appear in the first column, the slides are displayed in the second column, and the notes or blank lines appear in the third column. The slides are resized so that three fit on a page. If your notes take up more room in the table row than the slide, fewer slides may fit on a page.

If you choose one of the "below" options, a single slide and its corresponding notes or blank lines display on each page of the Word document. If you select *Outline only*, each slide title becomes a level 1 heading. Subtitles and body text are assigned lower levels.

After the data appears in Word, you can change it however you like, rearranging the number of slides per page, adding a background, inserting a graphic, formatting text, and so on. If you know how to work with Word tables, you can adjust column width and row height to display notes and slides more compactly, or even delete columns or rows you don't need.

Extra for Experts

You can also import an outline into a presentation. Use this method to create a presentation or add to it with data already stored in another form. In PowerPoint, click Slides from Outline on the Insert menu. Select the file containing the outline, and click OK. The outline can be in a variety of formats including HTML, text, Word, Lotus, or Excel format. For best results when importing a Word outline, the text you want to appear as slide titles should be formatted in the Heading 1 style.

STEP-BY-STEP 5.6

1. In the **Heart Diet 2** file, click **File** on the menu bar, click **Send To**, and then click **Microsoft Word**.

2. Click the **Notes next to slides** option, click the **Paste** option if necessary, and click the **OK** button. Microsoft Word starts and takes a few moments to create a three-column table.

3. In Word, move the I-beam pointer over the column border to the right of the *Slide 1* caption until it changes to a double-pointed arrow. Drag the column border to the left to reduce the width of the first column. You may find this easier to do if you turn the ruler on with the Ruler command on the View menu.

4. Move the I-beam pointer to the top of the third column until it changes to a dark downward-pointing arrow. Click to select the entire third column. From the Font list on Word's Formatting toolbar, select a serif font such as Times New Roman. Change the font size to 10 point.

5. If desired, drag row borders up to reduce row height and make the document more compact. Dragging the row markers on the vertical ruler may be easier than trying to position the I-beam pointer just so. When you are satisfied with the look of your document, click the **Print** button on the Standard toolbar to print the document.

6. Save the Word document as **Slide Notes**.

7. Close the document and exit Word.

8. Save and close the **Heart Diet 2** file and close PowerPoint.

SUMMARY

In this lesson, you learned:

■ Notes about the presentation that you want to remember can be entered in the Notes pane in Normal view or in Notes Page view, which displays each slide on its own page with its corresponding note.

■ Notes can include text, graphics, charts, tables, or any object. Apply formatting to note text using the buttons on the Formatting toolbar.

■ To make global changes to notes pages, use the notes master.

■ You can print handouts that include an image of each slide in a variety of layouts. Make global changes to handout pages using the handout master.

■ You can add a design template, color scheme, or background to notes, handouts, and outline pages.

■ Print notes, handouts, or a presentation outline from the Print Preview window.

■ Clicking the Options button in the Print Preview window displays commands you can use to change from color to grayscale or black and white printing, add a frame around the printout, and change the order of slides on handout pages.

- You can also change the page orientation of notes, handouts, and the outline in the Print Preview window.

- Printouts sized for overhead transparency film can be created by selecting the Overhead option in the Page Setup dialog box. Overheads typically require a light background and dark text for best readability.

- To create 35mm slides, take or send a PowerPoint presentation file to a service bureau. To set up a presentation file for 35mm slide development, select 35mm Slides in the Page Setup dialog box.

- For best visual appearance, 35mm slides typically require a dark background and light text.

- For more choices in creating and formatting handouts and outlines, send a presentation to Microsoft Word.

VOCABULARY *Review*

Define the following terms:

Embed	Header	Portrait
ftp	Landscape	Service bureau

REVIEW *Questions*

FILL IN THE BLANK

Complete the following sentences by writing the correct word or words in the blanks provided.

1. When preparing a presentation to be printed on 35mm slides by a service bureau, it's best to use _____ fonts.

2. You can create _____ notes page(s) per slide in PowerPoint.

3. Notes can also be included when you save your presentation to the _____.

4. Large amounts of note text are easier to enter in _____

5. In the Notes pane, you don't normally see _____ and objects you may have inserted in a note.

6. To add text that appears at the top of each notes page, add a(n) _____.

7. To print multiple copies of your notes or handouts in sets beginning with page 1, select the _____ option in the Page Setup dialog box.

8. To print lines for taking notes alongside the slides printed in your handouts, choose the _____ handout layout option.

9. In the Print Preview window, select the item you want to print from the _____ list.

10. To print slide text in an outline, click the Outline tab and then the _____ button.

MATCHING

Match the correct term in Column 2 to its description in Column 1.

Column 1	Column 2
___ 1. Notes master	A. Prints using black, white, and gray tones.
___ 2. Portrait	B. Typically uses a dark background and light text.
___ 3. Overhead	C. Allows you to make global changes to outline pages.
___ 4. Grayscale	D. Places text so it reads across the narrowest dimension of a page.
___ 5. Transparency	E. Used for transferring files over the Internet.
___ 6. Landscape	F. Allows you to make global changes to notes pages.
___ 7. 35mm slides	G. Flourishes that appear at the ends of basic letter shapes in particular fonts.
___ 8. Handout master	
___ 9. ftp	H. Typically uses a light background and dark text.
___ 10. Serif	I. Prints notes, handouts, or an outline in black and white.
	J. Clear film onto which you can print your presentation.
	K. Places text so it reads across the largest dimension of a page.

WRITTEN QUESTIONS

Write a brief answer to the following questions.

1. What changes might you make to a presentation to prepare it for printing as 35mm slides?

2. What changes might you make to a presentation to prepare it for printing overheads?

3. When might you want to send notes, handouts, or outline data to Word?

4. What is the difference between notes and handouts?

5. What kinds of global changes could you make to notes using the notes master?

PROJECTS

PROJECT 5-1

1. Launch PowerPoint, and open **PS Project 5-1** from the data files.

2. Save the presentation as **System Upgrade 2**.

3. Add the following headers/footers to the notes and handout pages:
    A. Add a fixed date: **9/22/04**.
    B. Add a header: **Computer Systems Upgrade**.
    C. Add a footer: **Lindh, Lopez, and Williams**.

4. Prepare notes pages as follows:
    A. Change the font size to 14 point.
    B. Change the font size back to 12 point on page 7 only.
    C. Add a frame around all the notes pages.
    D. Print the notes pages.

5. Prepare handouts as follows:
    A. Change to the 4 slides per page layout.
    B. Draw four lines for taking notes under each slide.
    C. Print the handouts.

6. Prepare an outline of the presentation as follows:
    A. Send the data to Word as Outline only and save it as **System Upgrade Outline**.
    B. Add 12 points of space before each slide title. (**Hint:** Click **Format** on the menu bar, click **Paragraph**, and key **12** in the Before box.)
    C. Add page breaks where needed to make sure that the text for each slide appears on the same page. (**Hint:** To insert a page break, click at the beginning of the line you want to move to the next page, and then press **Ctrl + Enter**.)
    D. Print the outline.

7. Save and close the **System Upgrade Outline** document. Close Word.

8. Save and close the **System Upgrade2** presentation, but leave PowerPoint open to use in Project 5-2.

PROJECT 5-2

1. Open **PS Project 5-2** from the data files and save the file as **KDDC Advertising Slides**.

2. Change the page setup to 35mm Slides.

3. Move the footer on the slide master so that it is located at least 0.5 inches from the edge. Repeat for the title master.

4. Make the trophy graphic on slide 5 slightly smaller so it does not crowd the text so much.

5. Save changes to the file.

6. Resave the file with the filename **KDDC Advertising Overheads**.

7. Change the page setup on this new file to Overhead.

8. Change the color scheme colors so they are more suitable for overheads:
   A. Change the background to white.
   B. Change the text and lines color to black.
   C. Change the shadow color to light yellow.

9. Change colors on the slide and title masters as well:
   A. Change the slide titles to dark red.
   B. Change the bullets to medium red.

10. To make the dark text clearer on this light background, remove the **Shadow** style from the slide titles, body text, and footers.

11. Save and close the **KDDC Advertising Overheads** file. Close PowerPoint.

WEB PROJECT

Create a 35mm slide presentation to help parents and students at your school prepare for the costs of college. Use the Web to accumulate information on the costs of attending at least two different states' universities for one year. You may include information for other universities as you like. Include charts or tables that list this year's fees and next year's, if available. From that information, create a prediction of the cost of these same colleges when you'll be old enough to attend. Arrange the charts/tables so parents and students can easily make comparisons. Include admission information, forms, and phone numbers to contact. Gather details about financial aid and scholarships. What aid packages and scholarships are available? How does someone qualify? What are the deadlines for applying? If a state university has extension(s) located near or in your city, include information about them as well. What can you do now to prepare for college and its costs? After entering text, graphics, and proofing the presentation, locate a service bureau on the Web that can print 35mm slides of your presentation in two days. Make changes to your presentation as needed, following any requirements provided by the service bureau.

TEAMWORK PROJECT

Prepare a presentation to be printed on overhead transparency film that informs parents about teen drug use. Design a survey for collecting data; then divide into teams. Interview students in at least three separate age groups about their knowledge of addictive substances and substance abuse. Do not collect names, but rather *opinions*: What do you consider a drug? What drugs do you consider dangerous? What would you do if your best friend started using something you thought was dangerous? Would you ask for help, and if so, from whom? What causes someone to abuse dangerous substances? What compels someone to avoid these dangers? What can parents do to help their children avoid drugs? Prepare a table or chart with your interview findings. Gather statistics on the Web about drug abuse today. Prepare charts and tables that report on past and current trends, and with the help of your teammates, speculate on how changes in both public policy and personal attitudes could affect these trends in the future.

CRITICAL *Thinking*

ACTIVITY 5-1

Add graphics (clip art, photos, charts, diagrams, and tables) to the client retention presentation you created in Lesson 2. For example, you may want to create a diagram that shows how the data from the installers' laptops will be processed by the main computer to update the client's permanent file and then retransmitted back to the laptops for testing. Enter and print your notes for the presentation. Print an outline as well. You'll be using your notes as handouts, so proof them for spelling errors and add appropriate formatting, graphics, and support materials such as charts and tables. Because you may be giving your presentation before a larger audience than expected and in a room equipped with only an overhead projector and screen, make the appropriate changes to the presentation to prepare it for overhead transparencies.

ACTIVITY 5-2

Search the Web for information on effective layout and design in a PowerPoint presentation. What constitutes good design? What constitutes poor design? Write a 200-word report on your findings. Include as many examples of good and poor design as you can, and explain what makes them so.

Insert Hyperlinks

A hyperlink is a word or phrase, a graphic, or other object that when clicked causes PowerPoint to display a particular slide, file, Web page, or e-mail message. You might include hyperlinks in a presentation to enable you to jump to a specific slide whenever a particular issue or question comes up or to launch a program and display supporting data. If you click a text hyperlink and later return to the same slide, you'll notice that the text has changed color. This is to let you know you've already visited that particular hyperlink. The color of text hyperlinks (visited and unvisited) is controlled by the color scheme, so you can make adjustments as desired.

Create a Hyperlink to a Slide in the Current Presentation or a Custom Show

To create a hyperlink to a slide in the current presentation or to a slide in a custom show you've set up, select the text, graphic, or other object you want to use as the hyperlink. Click the Insert Hyperlink button on the Standard toolbar to open the Insert Hyperlink dialog box. In the Link to bar, click Place in This Document to display a list of the current presentation's slide titles and custom shows, as shown in Figure 6-3.

FIGURE 6-3
Link to a slide in the current presentation

Click the slide or the custom show you want to link to. If linking to a custom show, be sure to click the *Show and return* check box if you want PowerPoint to return to the slide containing the hyperlink after displaying the slides in the custom show. Click OK when finished.

Create a Hyperlink to a Slide in Another Presentation

To create a hyperlink to a slide in a different presentation, select the text, graphic, or other object you want to use as the hyperlink and then click the Insert Hyperlink button. In the Link to bar, click Existing File or Web Page. Use the Look in list to change to the folder that contains the presentation you want to link to, and click the presentation file to select it. Click Bookmark to open the Select Place in Document dialog box, which lists the slides in the selected presentation

(Figure 6-4). Click the slide you want to link to in this list, and then click OK twice to close all dialog boxes.

FIGURE 6-4
Link to a slide in another presentation

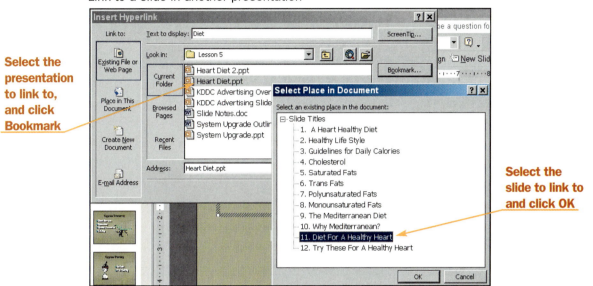

Select the presentation to link to, and click **Bookmark**

Select the slide to link to and click OK

Create a Hyperlink to an E-Mail Address

To create a hyperlink that displays an e-mail message window pre-addressed to a particular e-mail address, simply key that address on a slide, and PowerPoint automatically creates a hyperlink that opens the default e-mail program when clicked. If you want to use some other text, graphic, or object as the hyperlink, then select it and click the Insert Hyperlink button. In the Link to bar, click E-mail Address. The Insert Hyperlink dialog box changes its appearance, as shown in Figure 6-5. Key the address to link to in the E-mail address box, or click an address in the Recently used e-mail addresses list. Key a description for the message in the Subject box and click OK.

FIGURE 6-5
Link to an e-mail address

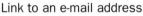

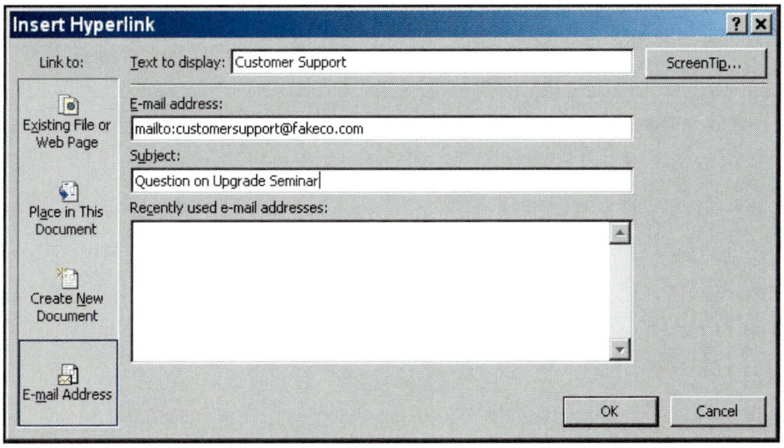

Create a Hyperlink to a Data File or Web Page

To create a hyperlink to a data file (such as a Word document or an Excel workbook) or to a Web page, select the text, graphic, or other object you want to use as the hyperlink. Click the Insert Hyperlink button. In the Link to bar, click Existing File or Web Page. The Insert Hyperlink dialog box is displayed as shown in Figure 6-6.

FIGURE 6-6
Link to a data file or Web page

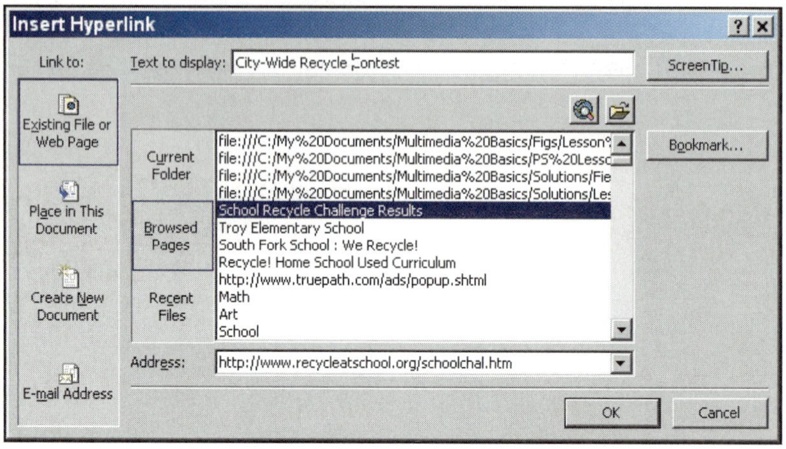

Change to the folder containing the data file and then click it in the list, or key the path to the Web page you want to link to in the Address box. To display the files in any folder, click the Current Folder button and select the folder from the Look in list. To display a list of files *and* Web pages you've viewed lately, click the Browsed Pages button. To view recently used files only (and not Web pages), click the Recent Files button. You can click the Browse the Web button to launch your Web browser and navigate to the Web page that way if you prefer. Click OK when finished.

Hot Tip

You can create a hyperlink to a Web page instantly by simply typing the Web address on a slide.

Create a Hyperlink to a New Document

To create a hyperlink to a file and create the file at the same time, select the hyperlink text, graphic, or other object. Click the Insert Hyperlink button. In the Link to bar, click Create New Document. The Insert Hyperlink dialog box shown in Figure 6-7 opens.

FIGURE 6-7
Link to a new document

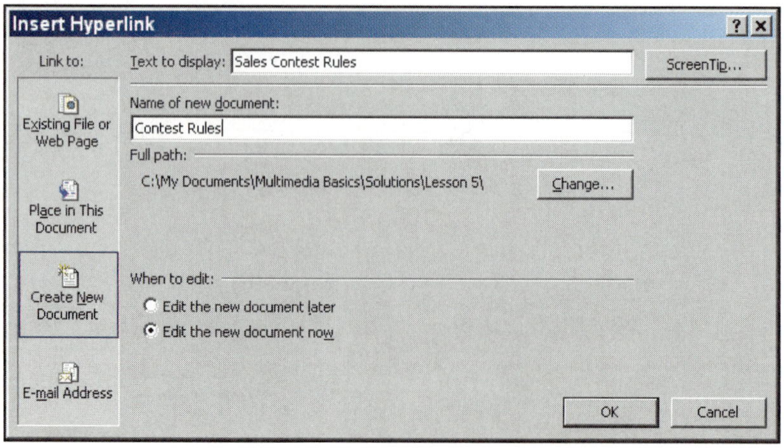

Key the name of the new file in the Name of new document box. Click Change and change to the folder in which you want the new file saved, and then click OK. Click either the *Edit the new document later* option button or the *Edit the new document now* option button, and then click OK to close the dialog box. If you elected to edit the new document now, the file is created and the associated program is launched so you can begin to enter data.

Create a Hyperlink Base

When you link to another file, that file must of course remain in exactly the same folder as it was when you created the hyperlink, or PowerPoint cannot locate it when you give your presentation. If you plan to move your presentation file to another computer when you give the presentation, you may want to establish a *hyperlink base*—a folder in which all linked files are stored. You can easily change this hyperlink base later on, without needing to edit each hyperlink so it points to the new folder location. To create a hyperlink base, click File on the menu bar and click Properties. Click the Summary tab. In the Hyperlink base box, key the path to the folder that contains the files you want to hyperlink to, and then click OK.

Add Action Buttons

Action buttons are typically added to a self-running presentation to help the viewer move through it. After adding the action button you want, you can specify an action setting that displays the appropriate slide (in the current presentation, in a custom show, or even in a different presentation), starts a video, plays a sound, opens a Web page, launches a program, and so on.

To insert an action button, select the slide(s) on which you want it to appear and click Slide Show on the menu bar. Click Action Buttons and then click the type of button you want to add. Although you can assign any action setting regardless of the button style you choose, try to select a button whose purpose will be obvious to your audience from its appearance. Click and drag on the slide to draw the button in the size and position you want it to appear. Because the button is an object, you can always adjust its size and position later. The Action Settings dialog box, shown in Figure 6-8, opens when you finish drawing the button.

FIGURE 6-8
Action Settings dialog box

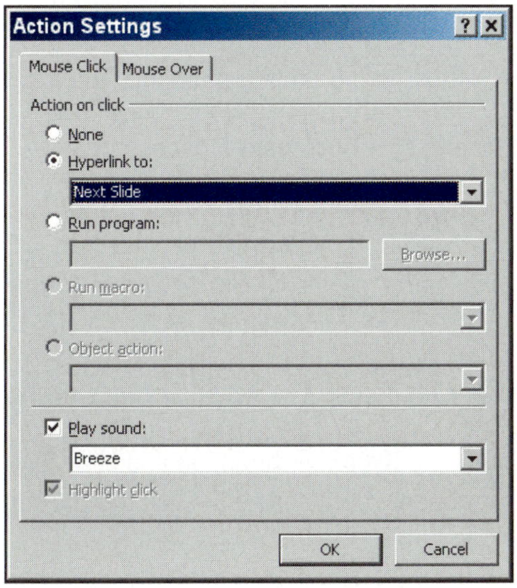

Note that the Action Settings dialog box has two tabs, Mouse Click and Mouse Over, that offer the same action settings. Mouse Click settings take effect when you click the mouse on the action button. Mouse Over settings take effect when you move the mouse pointer over the action button. These two tabs allow you to specify two different action settings for the same button, if you like.

On either tab, you have three main action options. You can make the action button a hyperlink and use the drop-down list to select the slide, custom show, Web page, or other target you want to link to. You can choose to run a program and then select the program you want to start. To have the action button play a sound, choose the Play Sound option and then select the sound from the drop-down list or navigate to the location of a sound file. Some action buttons display default selections in the Action Settings dialog box. For example, if you choose the Next Slide action button, Hyperlink to Next Slide automatically is displayed in the Action Settings dialog box when it opens. However, you can change to a different action setting if you like—although doing so may confuse your users.

> **Extra for Experts**
>
> If you place an action button on the slide master, it appears on every slide. If you place it on the title master, it appears on every slide that uses the Title layout.

STEP-BY-STEP 6.2

1. Open **PS Step 6-2** from the data files, and save the file as **Fiesta Guide**.

2. On slide 1, click the **Espanol** text box.

3. Click the **Insert Hyperlink** button on the Standard toolbar. The Insert Hyperlink dialog box opens.

4. In the Link to bar, click **Place in This Document**.

5. Click the **Espanol** custom show. Click the **Show and return** check box. This will cause PowerPoint to redisplay slide 1 after a person presses Esc to end the show. Click the **OK** button.

6. Display slide 8 and select the text *Comidas y bebidas*.

7. Click the **Insert Hyperlink** button on the Standard toolbar. The Insert Hyperlink dialog box opens.

8. In the Link to bar, click **Place in This Document** if necessary.

9. Click slide 12 in the list of slides, and then click the **OK** button.

10. Display slide 12. Click **Slide Show** on the menu bar, click **Action Buttons**, and then click **Action Button: Information**.

11. Draw the button in the lower-right corner. The Action Settings dialog box opens.

12. On the Mouse Click tab, click the **Hyperlink to** option and click **Slide** in the drop-down list. When the Hyperlink to Slide dialog box opens, click slide 13. Click the **OK** button twice.

STEP-BY-STEP 6.2 Continued

13. Run the slide show from slide 1. Test the **Espanol** hyperlink on slide 1 to see the Espanol custom show. On the first slide of the custom show, try the hyperlink you added. Try the action button you added to the *Comidas y bebidas* slide. Use the other action buttons to navigate in the custom show. Press **Esc** to return to slide 1, and then press **Esc** again to end the show.

14. Save and close the **Fiesta Guide** file. Leave PowerPoint open to use in the next exercise.

Set Up Slide Timings

In Lesson 1, you learned how to add slide transitions to a presentation and to tell PowerPoint when you want it to advance to the next slide. As you may recall, the Slide Transition task pane gives you two choices for advancing a slide—on a mouse click or automatically after a set amount of time. If you choose both the *On mouse click* and the *Automatically after* options, PowerPoint waits until you click or the allotted time has passed (whichever happens first) and then advances the slide.

There is another way you can add automatic timings to a presentation, and that involves rehearsing your presentation and advancing the slides as you would during the show. PowerPoint makes a note of how much time you spend displaying each slide and uses those timings to set up your show.

To use the rehearsal method to enter slide timings, click Rehearse Timings on the Slide Show menu. PowerPoint displays the first slide in Slide Show view, along with the Rehearsal toolbar shown in Figure 6-9. To move to the next slide, click the Next button on the Rehearsal toolbar or just click on the slide. Pause the timing if you like by clicking the Pause button. Click the Pause button again to resume your rehearsal. If you need to repeat the timing of a slide, click the Repeat button.

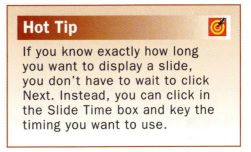

> **Hot Tip**
>
> If you know exactly how long you want to display a slide, you don't have to wait to click Next. Instead, you can click in the Slide Time box and key the timing you want to use.

Continue advancing slides as you rehearse what you are going to say. You'll notice that the total presentation timing is displayed at the right end of the Rehearsal toolbar. When you reach the end of the show, PowerPoint asks if you want to save your timings. Click Yes to save the timings or click No if you want to throw them away.

FIGURE 6-9
Rehearsal toolbar

Display the next slide

Repeat

Pause

Set Up the Show

Prior to presenting your program, you should establish the settings you want to use. For example, you must tell PowerPoint whether you plan to display the presentation in front of an audience or have it run by itself at a kiosk. To set up a show for presentation, click Set Up Show on the Slide Show menu. The Set Up Show dialog box opens, as shown in Figure 6-10.

FIGURE 6-10
Set Up Show dialog box

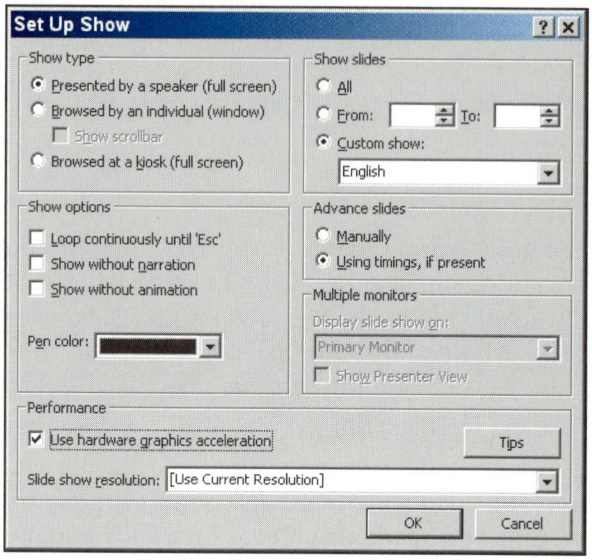

First, select the type of show you want to run from the Show type options. Next, select the slides you want to include in this presentation—all of them, a range of slides, or just the slides in a custom show. From the Show options area, select the options you want for this show. For example, you may prefer to turn off any narration you may have recorded for a previous show. You can change the pen color you use to draw on the slides during a presentation by clicking the arrow on the Pen color list and then clicking a color. In the Advance slides area, select how you plan to advance from slide to slide—manually or with the timings you may have recorded. To improve the performance of your presentation, you may want to select the *Use hardware graphics acceleration* check box, if you know that the computer you are using has it. Finally, click the arrow on the Slide show resolution box and select the resolution you want to use during the presentation. This should match the resolution of the monitor/projector you plan on displaying the presentation on. Click OK to close the dialog box.

S TEP-BY-STEP 6.3

1. Open **PS Step 6-3** from the data files, and save the file as **Heart Diet Show**.

2. Print notes pages so you can use them when rehearsing slide timings: Click **File** on the menu bar, and then click **Print**. In the Print dialog box, click the drop-down arrow on the **Print what** list, and click **Notes Pages**. Click the **OK** button.

3. Click **Slide Show** on the menu bar, and then click **Rehearse Timings**.

4. Read the text on the title slide. Click the **Next** button to advance to the next slide.

5. Continue reading the text on each slide, clicking to display each bullet item. After reading the text on each slide, read the notes for that slide as well, and then click to advance to the next slide.

STEP-BY-STEP 6.3 Continued

6. When you reach the end of the show, click **Yes** to save the timings.

7. Click **Slide Show** on the menu bar, and then click **Set Up Show**.

8. In the Show type area, click **Presented by a speaker (full screen)** if necessary.

9. In the Show options area, make sure no check boxes are selected. In the Show slides area, click the **All** option if necessary.

10. In the Advance slides area, click **Using timings, if present** if necessary.

11. In the Performance area, click **Use hardware graphics acceleration**. Click the **OK** button.

12. Save changes and leave the **Heart Diet Show** file open to use in the next exercise.

Package a Presentation for Use on Another Computer

If you plan to display a PowerPoint presentation on a computer other than the one used to create it, you can use the Pack and Go Wizard to package all the applicable files together so they are available wherever you take the presentation. Included in this package are any files linked to the presentation, such as graphics, sounds, and videos. You can embed any TrueType fonts you may have used in the package file. You can also include the PowerPoint viewer, a sort of miniature version of PowerPoint specifically designed for displaying presentations. You will need the viewer if the computer on which you intend to show your presentation does not have PowerPoint installed.

> **Important**
>
> If a presentation has been password protected, you cannot display it using the viewer. You must use the full PowerPoint program instead.

> **Important**
>
> Some features are not supported by the viewer, which means that you must have the full version of PowerPoint 2002 installed to include those features in your presentation. Those features include graphic bullets, animated gifs, automatic numbering of numbered lists, Visual Basic for Applications, and ActiveX controls.

When you're ready to package your presentation, click Pack and Go on the File menu. The Pack and Go Wizard opens. Click Next to start the Wizard. Select the presentation to pack (usually the active presentation). Choose the location where you want to pack the files, such as a floppy drive, Zip drive, or a file location on your system. Select whether to include linked files and/or to embed TrueType fonts. Select whether to include the viewer. If the viewer is not installed on your system, you need to click Download the viewer to install it. Click Finish to pack the files.

After you copy the package file to the computer on which you plan to run your presentation, you must un-package it to make its file(s) ready to use. Start Explorer and change to the folder in which you copied the package file. Double-click the Pngsetup.exe file. After the package file is unpacked, a message appears asking if you want to run the presentation now. Click Yes or No as desired.

STEP-BY-STEP 6.4

1. In the **Heart Diet Show** file, click **File** on the menu bar, and then click **Pack and Go**. The Pack and Go Wizard dialog box opens.

2. Click the **Next** button to start the Wizard. Make sure **Active presentation** is checked, and then click the **Next** button.

3. Click the **Choose destination** option and click the **Browse** button. Navigate to the location of your solution files, and then click the **New Folder** button in the Choose Directory dialog box. Key **Heart Diet** as the name of the folder to hold your packed files. Click the **OK** button. Click the **Select** button to return to the Wizard.

4. Click the **Next** button. Click the **Embed TrueType fonts** check box to select it, if necessary, and then click the **Next** button.

5. Make sure the **Don't include the Viewer** option is selected, click the **Next** button, and then click the **Finish** button. PowerPoint packs the presentation files and stores them in the folder you created.

6. Save changes and close the **Heart Diet Show** file. Leave PowerPoint open to use in the next exercise.

> **Hot Tip**
>
> You can store only one packed presentation in a directory. If you pack another presentation to the same directory, PowerPoint overwrites the previous packed file. To prevent this from happening, store your packed presentations in separate folders.

Deliver On-Screen Presentations

If you want to display your presentation on a monitor or large screen, you have two basic options—present the show in front of a live audience or set it up to run by itself. Each method has its particular requirements, as you will soon see.

Live Presentations

When presenting a show in front of a live audience, you must first connect a large monitor or projector to your computer or laptop. Follow the manufacturer's instructions to install and test the device. You are then ready to begin the show. However, you may want to consider installing and using a secondary monitor.

Use a Secondary Monitor

Whenever possible, you may want to connect a second monitor to your computer so you can display your notes, open ancillary programs and files, and perform other tasks without your audience's knowledge. To use two monitors on a single computer, that computer must use Windows 98, Windows Me, Windows 2000, or Windows XP. After connecting the second monitor, open the Control Panel, double-click the Display icon, click the Settings tab, select a monitor, and designate it as the main monitor (the one you wish to use for viewing) by clicking Use this device as the primary monitor (if needed). Click the icon for the secondary monitor (the one the audience will see) and click *Extend my Windows desktop onto this computer*. Click OK. Then, in PowerPoint, rerun the setup for the presentation by clicking Slide Show on the menu bar and clicking Set Up Show. Click the arrow on the Display slide show list, and select the monitor you want the presentation displayed on. Click the *Show Presenter View* option and click OK.

Presenter view, which is displayed on your private monitor during a presentation, provides controls you can use to quickly navigate through the presentation, view your notes, and perform other tasks, as shown in Figure 6-11. Click the Start Show button to start the show. Click the left or right arrow buttons to move to the next or previous slide. Click a slide thumbnail to jump directly to that slide. You can also press Spacebar to display the next slide, and press Backspace to display a previous slide. Press Page Up or Page Down to scroll the speaker's notes. If you want to darken the screen temporarily so your audience is not distracted by its text or graphics, click the Black Screen button.

FIGURE 6-11
Presenter view

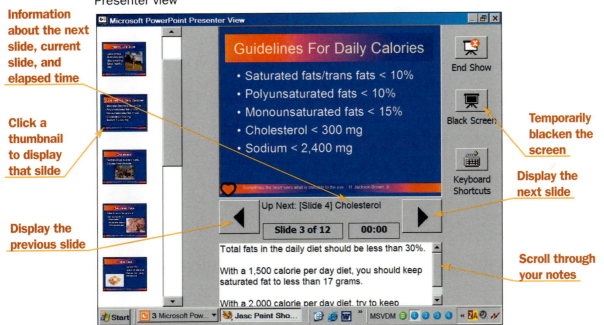

Run the Show

After setting up the show and installing a secondary monitor (if desired), you are ready to start the presentation. Click the Slide Show button or press F5 to start a show from within PowerPoint. You can also start a presentation from within Windows Explorer by right-clicking the file and clicking Show from the shortcut menu. If you installed the PowerPoint viewer on your system after unpacking presentation files, click Start, click Programs, and click PowerPoint 97 Viewer. Then select the presentation you want to display, and click Show.

Important

If you want to use any of the commands described in Table 6-1 while in Presenter view, you need to move your mouse pointer onto the secondary screen by dragging it to the right until it appears on the audience screen. Right-click, and the command menu appears; click the command you want to use as described in the table.

Control the Show

After starting a presentation, you have many options for controlling the show and performing tasks during the show. Table 6-1 summarizes the actions you can take. Note that there may be more than one way to perform some of these tasks. For example, you can right-click to display a shortcut menu with many useful commands and features. You can also display this shortcut menu by clicking the button in the lower-left corner of the slide. Choose the method that is most comfortable for you to display this menu.

TABLE 6-1
Slide show navigation and actions

TO	DO THIS
Display the next slide	Press Spacebar, Page Down , down arrow, Enter, or click the mouse.
Display the previous slide	Press Backspace, up arrow, or Page Up.
Jump to specific slide	Key the slide number and press Enter.Or right-click on the slide/click the button in the lower-left corner of the screen, click Go, click By Title, and click the slide you want to display. Or right-click, click Go, click Slide Navigator, and select a slide title.
Display a hidden slide	Right-click, click Go, and click Slide Navigator. Hidden slides are listed with their slide numbers in parentheses. Click the hidden slide you want to display, and click Go To.
Blank the screen	Right-click, click Screen, and click Black Screen. To return to the show, click the screen.
Hide/display the mouse pointer	By default, the mouse pointer appears during a slide show but disappears after 15 seconds of inactivity. To hide the mouse pointer, right-click, click Pointer Options, and click Hidden. To display the pointer regardless of inactivity, right-click, click Pointer Options, and click Arrow.
Mark on a slide	Right-click, click Pointer Options, and click Pen to turn the pen on. To use the pen, drag with the mouse. To change pen color, right-click, click Pointer Options, click Pen Color, and then click a color. Annotations automatically disappear from a slide when you move to the next slide, but to erase them while still viewing the slide, press E. When the pen is turned on, you cannot move to the next slide by clicking, so use an alternate method to advance the slide.
View speaker's notes	Right-click and click Speaker Notes. Add to the notes by keying right into the large text box. Click Close when finished.

TABLE 6-1 Continued
Slide show navigation and actions

TO	DO THIS
Record action items	*Action items* are reminders to do something. Right-click and click Meeting Minder. Click the Action Items tab, key a title for the item in the Description box, key the description in the large text box, and then click OK. Action items are added to an extra slide placed at the end of the show. You can also export them to Outlook or to Word. To display the Meeting Minder after a show is over, click Tools on the menu bar and click Meeting Minder.
Record meeting minutes	Right-click, click Meeting Minder, click the Meeting Minutes tab, and key your notes into the large text box.
End the show	Press Esc or right-click and click End Show.

STEP-BY-STEP 6.5

1. Open **PS Step 6-5** from the data files, and save the file as **KDDC Advertising Show**.

2. Click the **Slide Show** button to start the show.

3. Click to display the graphic, then click to begin the music. After the music and animation stop on slide 1, click the mouse to continue to slide 2.

4. Wait for the graphic and title to automatically appear. After reminding the audience that KDDC offers the best value for your advertising dollar, click the chart to begin the recording.

5. After the recording stops, take a moment to answer a question from the audience. Because the question does not pertain to the chart and you want to prevent your audience from being too distracted, right-click, click **Screen**, and then click **Black Screen**. After answering the question, click the slide to redisplay it.

6. The audience seems to be very interested in primetime advertising, so key **5** and press **Enter** to jump to slide 5. Wait for the graphic to automatically appear. Click to display each of the three bullets as you explain each one. Then click three more times as you introduce each of your lead anchors and their names appear on-screen.

7. Key **2** and press **Enter** to jump back to slide 2, which contains the chart.

8. Right-click, click **Pointer Options**, and then click **Pen**. Right-click, click **Pointer Options**, click **Pen Color**, and click **Red**. Explain the chart again, circling each group of columns as you point out that KDDC's advertising rates are at or only slightly higher than their competitors', even though the station's ratings are much higher.

9. Right-click, click **Pointer Options**, and click **Automatic** to redisplay the mouse pointer. Press **down arrow** to move to slide 3, which discusses morning advertising. Wait as the graphic automatically appears. Click to display each of the three bullets as you explain each one. Take a moment to answer another question.

STEP-BY-STEP 6.5 Continued

10. Press **Page Down** to move to slide 4, which discusses noon advertising. Wait for the graphic to appear. Click to display each of the four bullets as you explain each one.

11. In response to a request for more details, tell the audience that you will have copies made of the most recent Mandatron ratings. Then tell them you want to make a note of that right now so you'll be sure to follow up. Right-click the slide and click **Meeting Minder**. Click the **Action Items** tab. In the **Description** box, key **Print copies of Mandatron**. In the **Assigned To** box, key your name. Change the **Due Date** to tomorrow. Click the **Add** button. Click the **OK** button.

12. Because the audience has already seen the next slide and discussed it in depth, press **Esc** to end the show. Print a copy of the action item, which is located on the last slide. Display the last slide in Normal view, then click **File** on the menu bar, click **Print,** click **Current slide**, and click the **OK** button.

13. Save and close the **KDDC Advertising Show** file. Leave PowerPoint open to use in the next exercise.

Self-Running Presentations

When designing a presentation that's going to run by itself, several items need to be considered:

- Should you include information normally communicated by a presenter? If so, create a narration—either for one slide or for the entire presentation. See Lesson 4 for help.

- How will the slides advance during the presentation? You can set up automatic timings, or allow the user to advance by clicking the slide. See Lesson 1 and this lesson for help. To give the user the most control, add action buttons and/or hyperlinks as explained in this lesson.

With a self-running presentation, most likely you want the show to automatically restart after the last slide appears. You probably want the show to be displayed in full screen view so your text and graphics are as easy to see as possible.

Use the Set Up Show dialog box, which you learned about earlier in this lesson, to choose settings that allow you to control a self-running presentation. In the Show type area, click Browsed at a kiosk (full screen). When you select this option, the Loop continuously until "Esc" option is automatically selected because it is understood that at a kiosk, you want your presentation to automatically loop. You can of course choose which slides to display or to present a custom show.

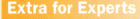

Extra for Experts

If you want to gather information from the viewer, such as name, gender, preferences, and so on, then add ActiveX controls to a slide and program them to collect the data in a file. See Microsoft Visual Basic Help for more information.

STEP-BY-STEP 6.6

1. Open **PS Step 6-6** from the data files, and save the file as **Katie's Cafe Kiosk**.

2. Click **Slide Show** on the menu bar, and then click **Set Up Show**.

3. In the Show type area, click the **Browsed at a kiosk (full screen)** option, and then click the **OK** button.

STEP-BY-STEP 6.6 Continued

4. Click the **Slide Show** button to test the presentation. After the presentation loops two times, press **Esc** to stop it.

5. Save and close the **Katie's Cafe Kiosk** file. Leave PowerPoint open to use in the next exercise.

Deliver Online Presentations

When giving a presentation in front of a live audience is inconvenient (it's too difficult to get everyone together at the same time, or too costly), you can present your show another way—through the Internet or a private intranet. As you learn in this section, there are a number of ways to utilize the power of the Internet to get your message out.

Publish a Presentation

The easiest way to share your presentation with a large group of people is to *publish* it to the Internet/intranet. The process of publishing involves saving the presentation in *HTML* format so it can be interpreted and displayed correctly in a Web browser. The publishing process also allows you to make some decisions as to what data you want to include (such as notes, animations, and so on) and how you want the data packaged—in a series of related files or in a single *Web archive*.

Preview a Presentation

Prior to publishing a presentation, you may want to preview how it looks first, and make any minor adjustments. To preview your presentation, click Web Page Preview on the File menu. The presentation appears in your Web browser, as shown in Figure 6-12.

FIGURE 6-12
Preview a presentation before publishing it

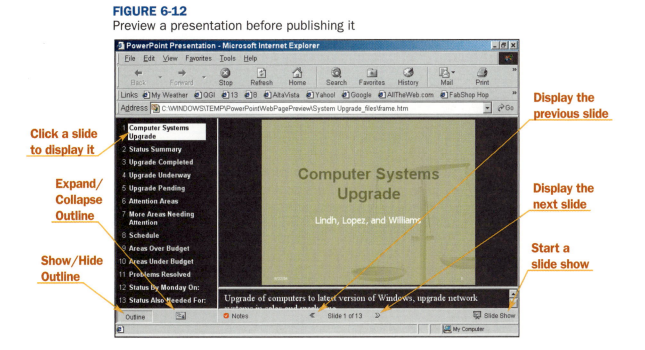

The preview is not exactly the same as what your user will see, but it's a reasonable facsimile. On the left is the presentation outline. To move to any slide, click its title in the outline. You can also click the arrow buttons at the bottom of the window to move to the next or previous slide. Click the Show/Hide Outline button to display or hide the outline pane. Click the Expand/Collapse Outline button to display/hide body text in the outline. Click the Slide Show button to display the slides full screen. This hides the controls too, and simulates what a user might see in a full-screen version. Press Esc to return to the normal view. When you're done previewing the presentation, close the browser window.

Publish after Previewing

After previewing a presentation and fixing any problems you may have noticed, it's time to publish the presentation. Click File on the menu bar and click Save as Web Page to open the Save As dialog box shown in Figure 6-13. Change to the folder in which you want to save the Web file(s). The folder should be located in a place that your users can access—a local intranet or a folder on a Web server. Key a name for the Web file in the File name box. Click the arrow on the Save as type list, and click the type of file you want to create—Web page or Web archive. The title from the first slide is used as the title of the Web page (it appears in the title bar of the user's Web browser when the page is viewed). To change this title to something else, click Change Title, key a new title, and click OK.

FIGURE 6-13
Save a presentation as a Web page or Web archive

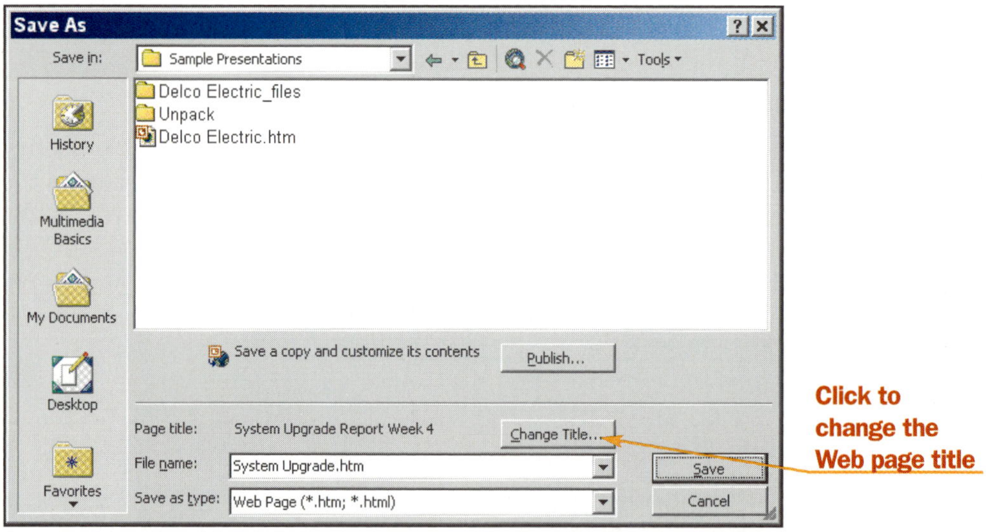

Click to change the Web page title

If you choose to save the presentation as a Web page, PowerPoint saves the presentation in HTML format and creates a folder to hold the files required to create the pages. For example, the folder contains clip art graphics used on the pages, buttons, and design elements applied by the current design template. If you choose to save as a Web archive, PowerPoint stores all this information in one file. This makes it easier for you to manage all the files required for the presentation.

You can simply click Save in the Save As dialog box to save your presentation as either a Web page or a Web archive. If you want more control over the Web presentation, however, click the Publish button to open the Publish as Web Page dialog box, shown in Figure 6-14. Select the slides you want to publish—all of them, a range of slides, or just those in a custom show. Click the *Display speaker notes* option if you want to make your notes visible to the user. Even if you've recorded a narration to accompany the presentation, including the text of the narration in your notes helps users who are deaf or hard of hearing. These notes also serve as a backup should the sound on your system malfunction.

FIGURE 6-14
Publish as Web Page dialog box

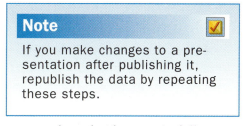

Use the Browser support area to select the type of browsers you want to support. Your selection here affects the overall quality of the presentation and the size of the resulting file(s). You may want to prevent users with very old browsers from viewing the presentation, for example, because some features do not work in browser versions prior to Internet Explorer 4.0. Older browsers cannot display animations, slide transitions, sounds and videos, or in full-screen mode, for instance.

> **Note** ☑
>
> If you make changes to a presentation after publishing it, republish the data by repeating these steps.

Click the Web Options button to open the Web Options dialog box, shown in Figure 6-15, where you have more options for displaying the presentation. On the General tab, you can decide whether to include navigation controls (these are separate from any controls you might have already placed on the slides), animations, and resizable graphics. On the Browsers tab, you can fine-tune the type of browser support you wish to give. On the Files tab, you can choose how files are organized and named. On the Pictures tab, you can set the resolution you want to use; on the Encoding tab, you can select which language you want to use; and on the Fonts tab, you can select the default font sets. After making selections, click OK to return to the Publish as Web Page dialog box. Click the *Open published Web page in browser* check box to display the completed file(s) in your browser for previewing. Then click Publish.

FIGURE 6-15
Web Options dialog box

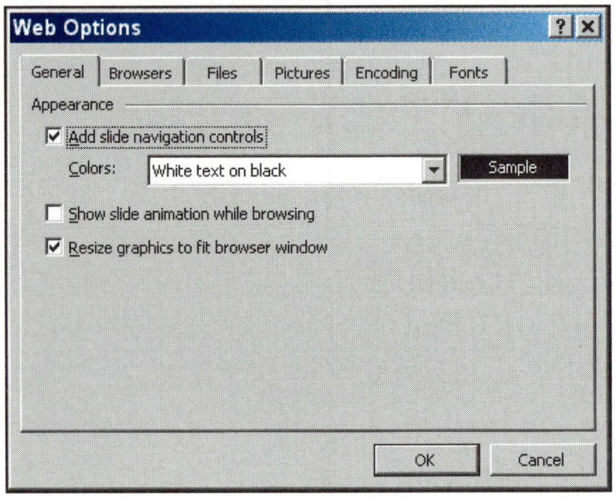

Broadcast a Presentation

Another way to deliver your presentation using the Internet is to **broadcast** it. A broadcast is normally done live, and it can contain live video and sound from you, the presenter. The broadcast is also recorded in a file that can be manually replayed on a Web browser by anyone who wasn't able to attend. First, if you want to include live video or sound, connect a video camera and/or microphone to your computer and test them. Then, to start an online broadcast, click Slide Show on the menu bar, click Online Broadcast, and then click Start Live Broadcast Now. After PowerPoint prepares the presentation, you'll see a message telling you that it is ready to begin. Click Broadcast. The Live Presentation Broadcast dialog box appears, as shown in Figure 6-16.

FIGURE 6-16
Live Presentation Broadcast dialog box

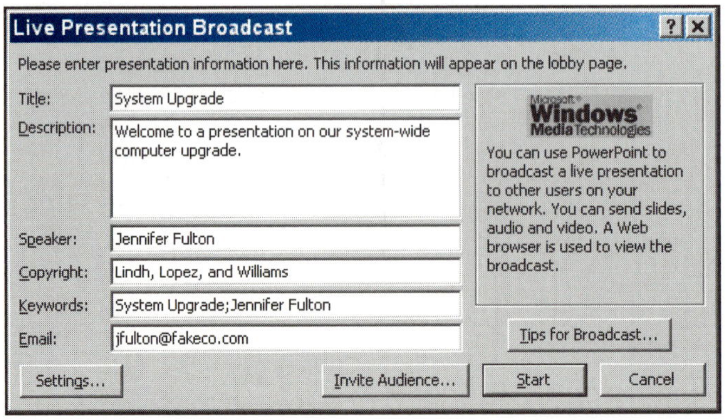

In the Description box, key any message you want to appear on the *lobby page*—a Web page that appears in the user's browser window as he or she is waiting for the broadcast to begin. Click Settings to open the Broadcast Settings dialog box, shown in Figure 6-17.

FIGURE 6-17
Broadcast Settings dialog box

In the File location area, click Browse and change to the folder in which you want to save the recording of the broadcast. Click Select to return to the Broadcast Settings dialog box. In the Audio/Video area, select whether you want to transmit live audio and video, live audio only, or none. Click OK to return to the Live Presentation Broadcast dialog box.

Click the Invite Audience button to create e-mail messages with the URL address of the broadcast. Key any message and click Send.

> **Important**
>
> To broadcast your presentation to 10 people or fewer, all you need (besides PowerPoint) is Internet Explorer 5.1 or later. To broadcast to a bigger audience, you need to use a Windows Media Server. If you don't have access to one, there are many Windows Media service providers to assist you.

When you are ready to begin the broadcast, click Start. The Broadcast Presentation dialog box opens. If you are transmitting live video and audio, the connections are tested. You can click Recheck Microphone to recheck the microphone before you begin transmitting; click Audience Message to recheck the message to the audience on the lobby page; or click Preview Lobby Page to display a preview of what the audience is currently seeing. When you are ready, click Start to begin the broadcast. After you end the broadcast (by ending the slide show), you can opt to replay the recording of the broadcast or to continue working in PowerPoint.

You may prefer to schedule your live broadcast prior to actually giving it, by sending out e-mails ahead of time. To do that, click Slide Show on the menu bar, click Online Broadcast, and click Schedule a Live Broadcast. Click Settings and follow the steps given here to select the settings for the broadcast, the location of the files, and so on. Click Schedule, and Outlook displays a meeting request. Enter the e-mail addresses of your invitees into the To box. Type a description in the large text box. Adjust the Start and End time for the broadcast and click Send. When you're ready to give your broadcast, click Slide Show on the menu bar, click Online Broadcast, and click Start Live Broadcast Now. Select the presentation you wish to broadcast and click Broadcast.

■ Prepare a presentation for use on another computer with Pack and Go Wizard. Choose where to store the packed presentation, decide whether to include linked files and fonts, and whether you need the Viewer. Unpack the presentation at its final destination by double-clicking the Pngsetup.exe file created by the Pack and Go Wizard.

■ Presentations can be delivered on-screen or over the Internet/intranet. When presenting on-screen, you can display the presentation live in front of an audience or as a self-running presentation in a kiosk.

■ When giving a presentation in front of a live audience, you may prefer to set up a second monitor so you can view your notes and other programs off-line.

■ To control the presentation while it is running, right-click on any slide to display a shortcut menu that displays useful commands and options. You can also display this menu by clicking the button at the lower-left of the slide.

■ To set up a presentation for use at a kiosk, choose the Browsed at a kiosk (full screen) option and consider adding narration, slide timings, and action buttons.

■ Preview how a presentation will look on the Web using Web Page Preview on the File menu. A presentation can be saved as a Web page or a Web archive. Publish the presentation for more control over the final Web presentation.

■ If you have access to the Internet or an intranet, you can broadcast a presentation live using the Online Broadcast feature. After you set up your presentation for broadcasting and invite your audience, start the presentation. The presentation is stored for future use as a Web presentation.

VOCABULARY *Review*

Define the following terms:

Action item	HTML	Lobby page
Broadcast	Hyperlink base	Publish
Custom show	Kiosk	Web archive

REVIEW *Questions*

TRUE/FALSE

Circle T if the statement is true or F if the statement is false.

T F **1.** A custom show cannot include hidden slides.

T F **2.** In most presentations, the colors used for text hyperlinks are controlled by the user's Web browser.

T   F   **3.** Using a hyperlink base saves you time and trouble if you ever move a presentation that contains hyperlinks.

T   F   **4.** You can program an action button to perform some task when the mouse moves over it.

T   F   **5.** Slide timings allow you to keep track of how much time you have left in a presentation so you don't run over the allotted time.

T   F   **6.** You can draw on slides during a presentation.

T   F   **7.** To use a secondary monitor when giving a presentation, you must have a laptop computer.

T   F   **8.** To view a presentation on someone else's computer, that computer must have PowerPoint 97 (or above) installed.

T   F   **9.** When the pen is active during a presentation, you can advance to the next slide by pressing the down arrow key.

T   F   **10.** You can invite attendees to an online broadcast of a presentation several days before the event.

WRITTEN QUESTIONS

Write a brief answer to the following questions.

1.   What special .features might you utilize when designing a presentation to be displayed in a kiosk at a trade show?

2.   What kinds of things can you create a hyperlink to? When might you include hyperlinks in a presentation?

3.   What features might you utilize when preparing to give a presentation in front of a live audience?

4. What special design issues must be considered if you plan on publishing your presentation to the Internet?

5. What should you do to prepare for an online broadcast of a presentation?

FILL IN THE BLANK

Complete the following sentences by writing the correct word or words in the blanks provided.

1. To present selected slides to a particular group of people, create and use a(n) _____.

2. Controls that allow a user to navigate a presentation are called _____.

3. To prepare a presentation for use on another computer, use the _____.

4. Using _____ view, you can view notes, display data in other programs, and perform other tasks without the audience seeing what you are doing.

5. Self-running presentations are typically displayed at a(n) _____.

6. If you want to remember to follow up on some concern or question that comes up during a presentation, create a(n) _____.

7. To redisplay the first slide after the last slide has been viewed, set the presentation to _____ until the Esc key is pressed.

8. Web pages use _____ format.

9. Before you publish a presentation, you should _____ it first.

10. If you want all the data and supporting files for a presentation stored in a single file, then save it as a(n) _____.

PROJECTS

PROJECT 6-1

1. Launch PowerPoint, and open **PS Project 6-1** from the data files.

2. Save the presentation as **Diez 2Q Sales Report**.

3. Create a custom show:
   A. Name the show **Management**.
   B. Include slides **1, 3, 4, 5, 6, 7, and 9**.

4. Display slide 9. Select the text *Home-a-rama* and use it to create a hyperlink to the Web site **www.homearama.com**.

5. Set up the show for a live audience:
   A. You're going to present the Sales custom show.
   B. Use the timings you will create in step 6.
   C. Match the presentation to your monitor resolution, and utilize graphics acceleration if your computer has it.

6. Establish timings for each slide:
   A. Rehearse timings, reading the text on each slide, slowly. (Only the slides associated with the Sales custom show appear.)
   B. Pause for at least 10 seconds before changing to the next slide.
   C. When you come to a chart or a table, pause long enough to fully absorb its meaning.
   D. Save the timings.

7. Run the presentation, pretending to explain each slide to your "live audience."
   A. Use the pen on at least one chart.
   B. Create at least two action items.
   C. At some point, jump back to a previous slide.
   D. After the presentation, send your reminders to Word: Click **Tools** on the menu bar, and then click **Meeting Minder**. Click the **Action Items** tab. Click the **Export** button to export all items. Deselect the **Post action items to Microsoft Outlook** check box, and then click the **Export Now** button. Save the Word file as **Action Items**.

8. Publish the presentation as a Web page for the sales people who could not attend:
   A. Preview the presentation as a Web page first.
   B. Use the filename **Diez 2Q Sales**.
   C. Change the page title to **Diez 2nd Qtr Sales Report**.
   D. Create a Web file, not an archive.
   E. Save only the slides in the Sales custom show.
   F. There aren't any speaker notes.
   G. Use Microsoft Internet Explorer 4.0 support.
   H. Display the result in your Web browser.

9. Close the Web browser. Save and close the **Diez 2Q Sales Report** presentation, but leave PowerPoint open to use in Project 6-2.

PROJECT 6-2

1. Open **PS Project 6-2** from the data files, and save the file as **Open House**.

2. Add action buttons to the slide master as follows:
   A. Insert previous and next buttons.
   B. Place the buttons in the lower-left corner, just to the right of the crayons. Eliminate the Date/Time footer area to make room.
   C. Do not place the buttons on the title master.

3. Set up the presentation for use at a kiosk:
   A. Include all the slides.
   B. Use the timings.
   C. There is no animation or narration.
   D. Use graphics acceleration if your computer has it.

4. Package the presentation so you can copy it to another computer:
   A. Create a folder to store the packed presentation in named **Open House**.
   B. Include TrueType fonts.
   C. Do not include the viewer.

5. Use the packaged file to display the presentation as a slide show to make sure that it looks all right.
   A. Create a new folder in which to unpack the file, named **Unpack**, so it does not override your current presentation.
   B. Unpack the presentation into the Unpack folder, and then open it and view it.

6. Save and close the **Open House** file. Close PowerPoint.

WEB PROJECT

Use the Web to research smoking so you can create a "How to Stop Smoking" demonstration. The presentation will be placed on a local hospital's Web site, so people who are trying to quit can get some help. Your focus should be on successful techniques a person can use to quit smoking. Provide a step-by-step plan or other details so the techniques are clear and easily understood. Include the names of any resources available for people trying to quit—such as clinics, seminars, support groups, and so on. Include hyperlinks to these resources (Web sites or e-mail addresses), if possible. Include appropriate graphics, tables, charts, videos, and sound files. Add action buttons to aid in navigation, and then save the presentation for use on the Web.

TEAMWORK PROJECT

You and your teammates work in the marketing department of a large pharmaceutical company. It's the job of your team to develop a presentation for an upcoming stockholder's meeting. The presentation needs to impress them so they continue to invest. Include a report on current earnings and a prediction of future earnings as well. Your company's latest "promising cancer cure" was turned down recently by the FDA, so you need to address this disappointment, too. The company has several new drugs in the channels, so you present them at the meeting, but none of them will be ready for FDA approval for at least a year or more.

Break the team into smaller groups to create a viable outline, supporting charts and tables, and a video message from your CEO. As a team, write a script for the designated "presenter," and type this script into the Notes area of the appropriate slides. Set up the presentation for a live audience. Have the presenter rehearse the presentation and add timings. Then, if possible, create a live broadcast of the presentation, with live video and audio.

CRITICAL*Thinking*

ACTIVITY 6-1

You're concerned about the environment, and you want to do your part to help encourage the kids at your school to recycle. Use the Web to come up with as many ideas as you can, and create a presentation that you can customize for the school board (with changes they might institute at the school), and for the students (with things they can do at school and at home). For example, you might propose that the school use recycled shredded tires under the playground equipment instead of mulch, that recycle bins be placed throughout the school so the kids can recycle paper cups and aluminum cans, and that both the kids and the school start recycling used ink jet cartridges from their computer printers. Include hyperlinks to Web sites that explain the importance of recycling and identify recycling drop-off sites, successful campaigns at other schools, and so on. Create two Web presentations to be placed on the school Web site—one for students and one for the school board.

ACTIVITY 6-2

You work at a large automobile insurance company, and it's your job to come up with a presentation that schools can use in their driver's education courses to help improve teen driving safety. Present tips that teens can follow to improve their chances of either avoiding an accident or at least surviving one. Include statistics on traffic accidents and fatalities, broken down by age groups. Make the presentation lively and teen-oriented, with music, videos, and animations—but remember that your purpose is a serious one: to encourage teens to drive more safely. Include hyperlinks to your insurance company's Web site and your e-mail address, in case the teachers want to access them. Package the presentation so it's ready to be used by any teacher—and be sure to include the PowerPoint viewer because you don't know for sure that each school has access to PowerPoint.

ACTIVITY 6-3

Use the Web to do research on how to give an effective presentation. What techniques do the professionals use? Have you tried any of these when giving your own presentations? What techniques have worked for you? What hasn't worked well? Create a 200-word report on your findings.

PRESENTATION SYSTEMS

REVIEW *Questions*

TRUE / FALSE

Circle T if the statement is true or F if the statement is false.

T   F   1.   PowerPoint's spelling checker also checks for obvious grammar errors.

T   F   2.   An automatic date that appears in a header or footer is updated each time you open the presentation.

T   F   3.   Typically, you must request specific permission to use any graphic, sound, or video file that is copyrighted.

T   F   4.   Use Outline view to display a listing of slide titles.

T   F   5.   AutoFit automatically adjusts the size of text when you change the size of the placeholder.

T   F   6.   To quickly format a presentation, apply a design template.

T   F   7.   Action buttons help you navigate through a presentation.

T   F   8.   Changes to the slide master affect every slide.

T   F   9.   If a sound icon is placed off a slide, the associated sound file does not play during a presentation unless it is part of an animation sequence.

T   F   10.   You can create multiple notes pages for a slide when needed.

MATCHING

Match the correct term in Column 1 to its description in Column 2.

Column 1	Column 2

____ 1. Indent

____ 2. Color scheme

____ 3. Embed

____ 4. MIDI

____ 5. Transition

____ 6. Animation effects

____ 7. Layout

____ 8. MP3

____ 9. Link

____ 10. Aspect ratio

A. Arrangement of data on a slide.

B. A sound file format in which sound is recorded as a compressed digitized waveform.

C. Relationship between the height and width of an object.

D. One part of a design template.

E. To copy a Web presentation and its supporting files in a single file.

F. Pointer to a file associated with a presentation.

G. Allows you to delay the appearance of objects on a slide during a presentation.

H. Controls how PowerPoint displays the next slide during a presentation.

I. Place a copy of fonts or sounds in a presentation within the file, so they are available on whatever computer the presentation is displayed on.

J. A file format in which sound is recorded as individual musical notes.

K. Extra space between the margin and the left edge of a paragraph or bulleted list item.

FILL IN THE BLANK

Complete the following sentences by writing the correct word or words in the blanks provided.

1. You can display another slide, a data file created in another program, or an e-mail message by clicking a(n) _____.

2. To add your own comments or descriptions to a presentation, record a(n) _____.

3. You enter the data for a chart on its _____.

4. After rehearsing a presentation, you can tell PowerPoint to save the _____ so that it can automatically advance each slide during the real show.

5. To make an object stand out during an animation sequence, add a(n) _____ effect.

6. To share a presentation with coworkers located in another city, _____ it over the Internet.

7. To drag an object around its center, use its _____ handle.

8. To change the shape of an AutoShape object, drag its _____ handle.

9. To use animation to make an object move across a slide, add a(n) _____ effect.

10. To start the animation of one object at the same time you click a different object, set a(n) _____ .

PROJECTS

PROJECT 1

1. Launch PowerPoint. Open **PS Project 1** from the data files. Save the presentation as **Ozone**. In this project, you add text, notes, and slides to a presentation on the ozone layer.

2. Insert a slide at the end of the presentation, accepting the default **Title and Text** layout. Key the title **Effects**. Key the following bullet items:

   Lung damage

   Nausea

   Throat irritation

   Chest pains

   Difficulty breathing

3. Click in the Notes pane and key **Particularly damaging in hot dry weather, when ozone levels are higher. Elderly and children more susceptible.**

4. Insert a slide after slide 6. Apply the **Title and Chart** layout. Key the title **Changing Size of Ozone Hole**. Add the note **Chart depicts minimum size of ozone hole over Antarctica for that year.**

5. Insert another slide after the slide you just created, accepting the default **Title and Text** layout. Key the title **Ground Level Ozone**. Key the following bullet items:

   Burning fossil fuels such as gasoline

   Industrial emissions

   Chemical solvents

   Burning forests

6. Change to Notes Page view and key the following notes:

Ground level ozone created by burning fossil fuels (cars and trucks, 37%) gets trapped in the troposphere, along with chemical solvents (5%) and industrial emissions (58%). These are sources of VOC (volatile organic hydrocarbons).

Nitrogen oxides (NOx) sources include cars and trucks (49%), fuel combustion from industrial, commercial, and residential use (13%), utilities (28%), and other sources (10%).

Hot, sunny weather with low winds increases concentrations of ground ozone.

7. Insert a slide at the end of the presentation. Apply the **Title and Table** layout. Key the title **Air Quality Index**. Key the following notes:

Air Quality

Good: Little risk.

Moderate: Acceptable risk.

Unhealthy for sensitive people: Bad for children, seniors, and people with respiratory problems.

Unhealthy: Affects everyone; sensitive people may be affected seriously.

Very unhealthy: Everyone experiences more risk, more serious effects.

Hazardous: Emergency conditions.

8. Change to Slide Sorter view. Drag slide 3, *What Is The Ozone Layer?*, in front of slide 2, *UV Radiation*.

9. Check the spelling and make corrections as needed. Turn on Style Check and check each slide for errors in style, using the default style settings. In most cases, you should correct errors as suggested, but feel free to use your own judgment.

10. Save changes and leave the **Ozone** presentation open to use in Project 2.

PROJECT 2

1. Save the **Ozone** file as **Ozone 2**. Now that you have the text entered, you'll turn your attention to graphics, videos, and sound files.

2. Insert the graphic **PS Project 2a.gif** from the data files into the placeholder on slide 2. Resize the graphic to make it fit the slide.

3. On slide 4, insert the graphic **PS Project 2b.jpg**. Undo the layout change so the text placeholder is full size. Reposition the graphic in the lower-right corner of the slide. Resize the graphic so it is as large as possible without crowding the text.

4. On slide 5, insert the graphic **PS Project 2c.gif**.

5. On slide 6, insert the movie file **PS Project 2d.mpeg**. Set the movie to play automatically when the slide is displayed. Resize the movie to make it as wide as the slide title. As a test, double-click the movie to play it.

6. Change to slide 8. Search the Clip Organizer for a piece of clip art using the keyword **exhaust**. Select an image and insert it. Undo the layout change. Resize and position the graphic in the lower-right corner.

7. Change to slide 10. Search the Clip Organizer for a piece of clip art using the keyword **cough**. Select an image and insert it. Change to the **Title, Clip Art, and Text** slide layout. Increase the text size to 32 point. Move the graphic up and resize it if necessary. Then drag the top of the bulleted list placeholder down so the graphic and text appear as shown in Figure UR-1.

FIGURE UR-1
Reposition the graphic and the text

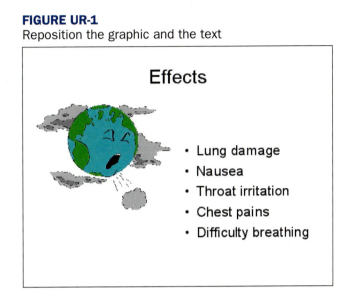

8. Locate a suitable music file on the Internet for the presentation, and insert it on slide 1. Set it to play automatically, and drag the icon off the slide. Use the Text Box tool if needed to create a credit line for the sound file and place it on the slide.

9. Locate a suitable photo on the Internet for slide 1 and insert it behind the title. Enlarge the photo to fit the slide, crop as needed, and send the photo behind the text on the slide. Again, use the Text Box tool to create a credit line for the photo if needed.

10. Increase the font size of the title text on slide 1 to 60. Change the font color if needed, so the title text contrasts well with the photo and is easy to read.

11. On slide 9, click on the slide with the Text Box tool and key a capital letter **X**. Set the font to **Arial**, the size to **250** points, and the color to red. Center the text box over the three graphics on the right-hand side of the slide. Group the objects together so they can be resized or moved as a unit.

12. Save changes and leave the **Ozone 2** presentation open to use in Project 3.

PROJECT 3

1. Save the **Ozone 2** file as **Ozone 3**. In this project, you polish your presentation with color and animation and add a chart and a table.

2. Apply the **Beam** design template to all slides but slide 1.

3. On the slide master, change the bullet color on the first-level bullet style from the red and white picture currently used to the standard, square, color-filled bullet style in the Bullets and Numbering dialog box, adjusted to 150% of text size, and changed to golden yellow.

4. Change the font size for the Master text style to **34**. Change the Master title style to **48** point. View each slide and adjust the size of the graphics if needed so they do not crowd the bullet text. Change the slide title on slide 7 to **46** pt.

5. On slide 7, add a chart using the following data:

    Min. Size

1980	209
1982	205
1984	189
1986	146
1988	110
1990	124
1992	117
1994	94
1996	111
1998	90
2000	94

6. Display chart data by columns by clicking the **By Columns** button on the Standard toolbar. Change the chart type to Line with markers displayed at each data value. Remove the legend. Change the value axis scale **minimum** to **85** and the **maximum** to **225**. Format the data series called "Min. Size," changing the line color to yellow and the foreground and background color on the marker to yellow as well.

7. On slide 11, add the following table:

Air Quality	Condition
0 - 50	Good
51 - 100	Moderate
101 - 150	Unhealthy for sensitive people
151 - 200	Unhealthy
201 - 300	Very unhealthy
301 - 500	Hazardous

8. Apply the following color fills to the rows of the table: row 2: green; row 3: yellow; row 4: orange; row 5: red; row 6: purple; row 7: magenta.

9. Apply the **Title arc** animation scheme to all slides but slide 1. Apply the **Faded wipe** animation scheme to slide 1.

10. Adjust the animation on slide 1 so the sound file loops until you click the slide.

11. On slide 7, add the **Fade** entrance effect to the chart. Start the effect automatically after the title effect. Set the Speed to **Medium**. Have the line appear by category. Animate the grid and legend as well.

12. On slide 11, apply the **Rise Up** entrance effect to the table. Start the effect automatically after the title effect. Set the speed to **Slow**.

13. Display slide 1, and click the **Slide Show** button to play the slide show and view the animations.

14. Save changes and leave the **Ozone 3** presentation open to use in Project 4.

PROJECT 4

1. Save the **Ozone 3** file as **Ozone 4**. In this project, you prepare the presentation for your lecture and print supporting materials.

2. Set up the presentation for printing on slides. After changing the page size, review each slide and make any necessary adjustments, leaving an approximately half inch margin on all sides.

3. Preview the notes pages. Apply grayscale to the color graphics. Add a header that includes the title of the presentation, **Our Disappearing Ozone**. Add a footer that includes your name and the page number. Do not include the date.

4. Print your notes.

5. Preview the handouts in 6 slides per page format. Change to landscape orientation. Restore the color to the graphics.

6. On the handout master, draw three lines under each graphic for notes.

7. Copy the graphic on slide 1 to the handout master. Resize the graphic and place it in the upper-left corner. Move the header box to the right to make room for the graphic. Remove the date/time box.

8. Print the handouts.

9. Save changes to the **Ozone 4** presentation, and close your presentation program.

SIMULATION

You are a marketing assistant for Swift River Travel, a travel agency. The owner has been aware for some time that the travel industry is changing because the Internet makes it so easy for customers to book their own vacations. So she has asked you to create a presentation about the impact of technology (specifically, the Internet) on the travel industry. You also need to include suggestions on how to overcome this problem and a plan to implement those suggestions at the agency.

JOB 1

To create your presentation, first do some research on the Internet. Visit travel agency–related Web sites and search for reports that deal with the problem of an Internet-savvy customer. Note any statistics you find, such as how much the industry has been affected (for example, perhaps local business has gone down 10%, even though 45% of people report they make online travel purchases). Note any other problems you encounter during your research, such as airline-based Internet Web sites, low commissions, depressed travel market following September 11, 2001, and so on.

What benefits can a local travel agency offer that the Internet does not? What steps have other agencies taken to build a loyal customer base? Do incentives and other loyalty programs work? What local agencies have a Web site, and what do their Web sites offer? Do they offer information only, or is there an online ticketing system? Do they offer information or booking for related services such as hotel rooms and car rental?

What are the most popular travel Web sites? What conveniences do they offer? What can your agency offer a customer that online sites cannot?

Key your findings into a word processing document, such as a Word document. Save the document as **Internet Travel**. If you like, use your word processor's outline feature to organize your thoughts and prepare the outline for the presentation.

JOB 2

Launch PowerPoint and start a new presentation. Save the presentation as **Internet Impact**. Using the outline contained in the **Internet Travel** document, key the titles for the slides you want in your presentation. You can also use PowerPoint's Slides from Outline command on the Insert menu to import an outline directly into PowerPoint. Reword the text on each slide as necessary so it is short, to the point, and easily read. Key supporting information into the notes area of each slide.

After keying titles and text for your slides, add at least one chart, table, or diagram. For example, if you gathered statistics on Internet travel usage, organize that data in a table or chart. Add graphics such as photos or clip art to your slides.

Add sound and movie files to the presentation to liven it up. For example, you can add music or narration for the sound. For movie files, consider creating a short travelogue of popular vacation spots. Or perhaps you could record an interview with a company travel coordinator, or a neighbor or relative who uses the Internet regularly to book vacations or business travel.

Add polish to your presentation by applying a design template and modifying it to suit your preferences, or by creating a custom slide master with your own graphics, colors, and fonts. Make sure your design enhances the presentation's message of travel and the Internet. Add animation schemes, slide transitions, and custom animations to hold the interest of your audience. Preview your presentation and make adjustments to the animations as needed.

Prepare the presentation for a live audience. Create handouts and print your notes, then give your presentation to a small group of classmates. Gather feedback from your audience on your performance and the presentation itself. What worked and what didn't? What changes might you make for future talks? Prepare a 150-word report with your conclusions, and save it as **Internet Presentation Review**.

DESKTOP PUBLISHING

Unit

Estimated Time for Unit: 10.5 hours

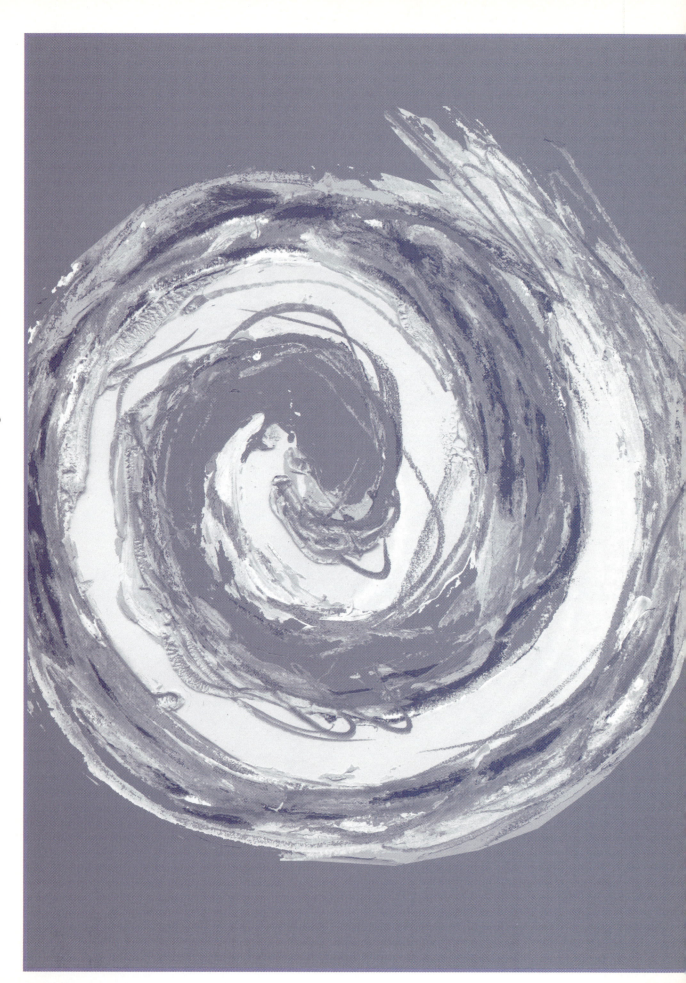

WORKING WITH DOCUMENTS

Desktop publishing is used to design and produce printed documents such as business cards, brochures, booklets, nametags, product packaging, posters, banners, calendars, invitations, and newsletters. Although all desktop publishing programs have features you can use to arrange and format text and graphics, the programs differ in their level of sophistication. For example, programs designed for professional use, such as Microsoft Publisher or Adobe PageMaker, include features used to prepare a document for commercial printing, while home-use programs, such as Microsoft Greetings or Microsoft Works, assume you will print your documents on a desktop printer. Some word processing programs also offer low-level desktop publishing features for simple documents such as letters, memos, and reports. In this book, you will learn how to use a full-featured desktop publishing program to design, create, and publish professional-level documents.

No matter which program you use, there are six basic steps to producing a desktop publishing document:

1. Plan the document.
2. Select a design.

3. Insert text.

4. Insert graphics.

5. Prepare the document for publication.

6. Print the document.

In this lesson, you will learn to use these steps to create a document quickly and easily. Later lessons cover these steps in greater detail.

Plan a Publication

The first phase of desktop publishing is to plan the basic format for your document. You must make decisions about the physical aspects of the document, such as the page size, the paper stock, color scheme, single-sided or double-sided printing, *binding* options, and the number of copies.

As you think about these issues, you should keep your budget in mind. The amount of money you have available significantly affects the type of document you can produce. For example, color printing costs more than black and white, and paper stocks range widely in price.

You should also consider the program you are using. Make sure it supports all the features you want to include, and that it is *compatible* with other programs and *hardware devices* you may need to use. A compatible program can exchange data easily with another program or device. A device is a piece of equipment attached to your computer, such as a scanner. For example, can you use your desktop publishing program to create graphics, or will you need to import graphics from another source, such as a graphics program, a scanner, or a digital camera? Can you easily enter as much text as you need, or will you need to copy the text from a word processing program?

You also need to make decisions about the content of the document: Who will be reading it? What is its goal? There are many different reasons for creating a publication. Marketing publications, such as direct mail postcards, are designed to sell a product, while informational publications, such as corporate newsletters, are designed to educate and inform. Invitations, playbills, and product packaging have very different purposes, and therefore require different approaches. The content of a brochure to be distributed at a conference for neurosurgeons will certainly differ from the content of a flyer that is part of a mass mailing to the customers of a retail store.

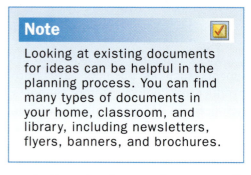

Note

Looking at existing documents for ideas can be helpful in the planning process. You can find many types of documents in your home, classroom, and library, including newsletters, flyers, banners, and brochures.

To ensure the success of your publication, you should create a *mock-up* or prototype. A mock-up is a rough draft or sample of the publication that represents the finished product, without including fine details. Creating a mock-up lets you experiment with *page size, sheet size*, and *orientation* as well as positioning text and graphics. It is important to note that in desktop publishing, page size and sheet size are not the same thing. Page size is the dimensions of the finished document page, while sheet size—which is sometimes called *paper size*—is the size of the paper on which the document is printed. Orientation is the position of the paper in relation to the printed content. *Portrait orientation*—sometimes called *tall*—prints the content across the short side of the page, while *landscape orientation*—sometimes called *wide*—prints the content along the long side of the page.

Although you may be able to use your desktop publishing program to preview sample documents, the most effective method for creating a mock-up is to actually take a piece of paper the same size and shape that you envision for the finished product, and then mark it with the location of text and graphics. For example, you can create a mock-up of a tri-fold brochure by folding a standard 8.5-inch by 11-inch sheet of paper into thirds. Or you can create a mock-up of a postcard mailer by using a ruler to draw a rectangle the size of the postcard on a sheet of paper, and then using a pencil to indicate the placement of an address label, text, and graphics.

STEP-BY-STEP 1.1

1. Hold a blank sheet of 8.5-inch by 11-inch paper with the 8.5-inch sides at the top and bottom. This is portrait orientation. You are going to make a mock-up of a postcard mailer. The page size of the mailer is approximately 8.5 inches wide by 5.5 inches high, which is about half the sheet size. The postcard has two pages—the front and the back.

2. Fold the top edge of the sheet down to meet the bottom edge, and then unfold the page. If you plan to print on 8.5-inch by 11-inch paper, you can fit two postcards on a page. However, you need to create a mock-up of only one. In this case, use the top half of the sheet.

3. Using a ruler, draw 0.5-inch margins on all sides of the rectangle, and then mark the locations where you would position a headline, informational text, and a picture. Refer to Figure 1-1.

FIGURE 1-1
Mock-up of a postcard mailer

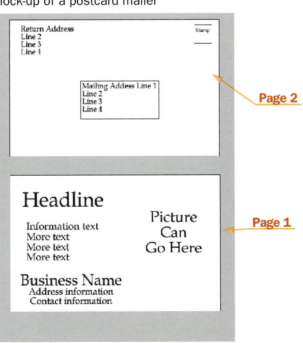

4. Draw the same margins on the back, and then mark the locations of the mailing address, return address, and stamp.

5. Keep this sheet of paper as a reference for creating a postcard mailer in the rest of this lesson.

Create a New File

To create a new desktop publishing file, use the New command on the File menu, or click the New button on the main or standard toolbar. There are many variations or options for creating a new publication, depending on the program you are using. Some programs automatically create a blank file using the *default* settings for options, such as page size and orientation, but most programs display a dialog box where you can select the *publication type*—such as a newsletter or a calendar—and then select the publication design, or *template,* or where you can customize the settings. The default settings are the standard options already selected in the program. A template is a file used as a model for creating other files. It usually contains page layout and text formatting settings as well as objects such as sample text and graphics.

Using a template is the fastest and easiest way to create a professional-looking document, because it already has a coordinated font scheme, color scheme, and layout. All you have to do is replace the sample text and graphics. You can select options to customize the individual settings at any time.

An alternative to creating a publication from a template is to create a blank document and build it from scratch. You will learn how to create a publication this way in a later lesson.

Depending on your program, the available publications are listed in a New dialog box, a Templates dialog box, or New Publication task pane, similar to the one in Figure 1-2. When you select a publication type, most programs list the designs or templates available for that type. In some programs, actual thumbnail-sized previews appear in the dialog box or in a window called a Design Gallery. Click the design or template you want to use to create the new document, and then, if necessary, click a button such as Open or Create Publication.

FIGURE 1-2
Publication types listed in a task pane

New files usually have a generic name such as Publication or Untitled and are numbered consecutively. So, the first file you create is Publication1; the second is Publication2; and so on. You customize the name when you save the file. Most programs let you have more than one file open at a time, although only one can be *active*. The active file is the one in which you are currently working.

Some desktop publishing programs use contact information such as names and phone numbers to automatically enter data in a new publication. You may have supplied some of this information when you installed the program. If the contact information has not already been filled in, the program prompts you to enter it when you create a new document. Simply select a category for the information set, such as home or business, and key the desired information. This contact information will be used in most future publications created with a template or design.

S TEP-BY-STEP 1.2

1. Launch your desktop publishing program. The New dialog box, Templates dialog box, or New Publication task pane displays. If the program is already open, or the dialog box is not open, click **File** on the menu bar, and then click **New**. If you are using Adobe PageMaker 7and the Templates dialog box is not open, click **Window**, click **Plug-in Palettes**, and then click **Show Template Palette**.

Note ✅

In some programs, publication types are sorted into categories to help you quickly locate an appropriate design. Click the publication type to expand the list to display categories, and then click a category to scroll quickly to the designs for that category.

Did You Know? 🗽

You can edit the contact information at any time. Click Edit on the menu bar and then click the command to open the information set. Select the set you want to use, make the changes, and then click the Update button.

STEP-BY-STEP 1.2 Continued

2. Select a postcard mailer publication type. A postcard mailer is usually a simple, two-page document similar to the mock-up you created in the previous exercise. One page is set up for entering text and graphics and the other page is set up for entering address information and postage. Once you select a publication type, the available designs are displayed on the screen, as shown in Figure 1-3.

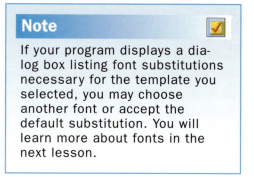

> **Note** ☑️
>
> If you cannot find postcards in the list of publications, your program probably uses a different name, such as mailers, or lists them as a category under cards. Also, don't worry if your screen looks different from the one in the illustration. You may be using a program that lists the publications and designs in a different format, such as in a dialog box or without previews.

FIGURE 1-3
Sample designs for postcard mailers

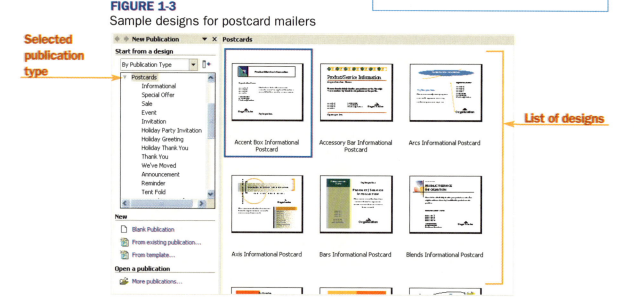

Selected publication type

List of designs

3. Scroll through the list of designs to see what is available, and then click a simple design such as the Level Informational design in Microsoft Publisher or the 2000640.pmt template in Adobe PageMaker 7. If necessary, click the **Open** or **Create Publication** button to create the document.

4. If prompted, cancel the dialog box that asks you to enter contact information. Your program creates and displays the publication on screen with default sample information. Depending on your program and the publication type, options for changing the layout and content may be displayed as well.

> **Note** ☑️
>
> If your program displays a dialog box listing font substitutions necessary for the template you selected, you may choose another font or accept the default substitution. You will learn more about fonts in the next lesson.

STEP-BY-STEP 1.2 Continued

5. If available, select the option to change the size of the document from quarter page (4.25 inches × 5.5 inches) to half page (5.5 inches × 8.5 inches). The document should look similar to Figure 1-4.

FIGURE 1-4
Sample page of postcard mailer document

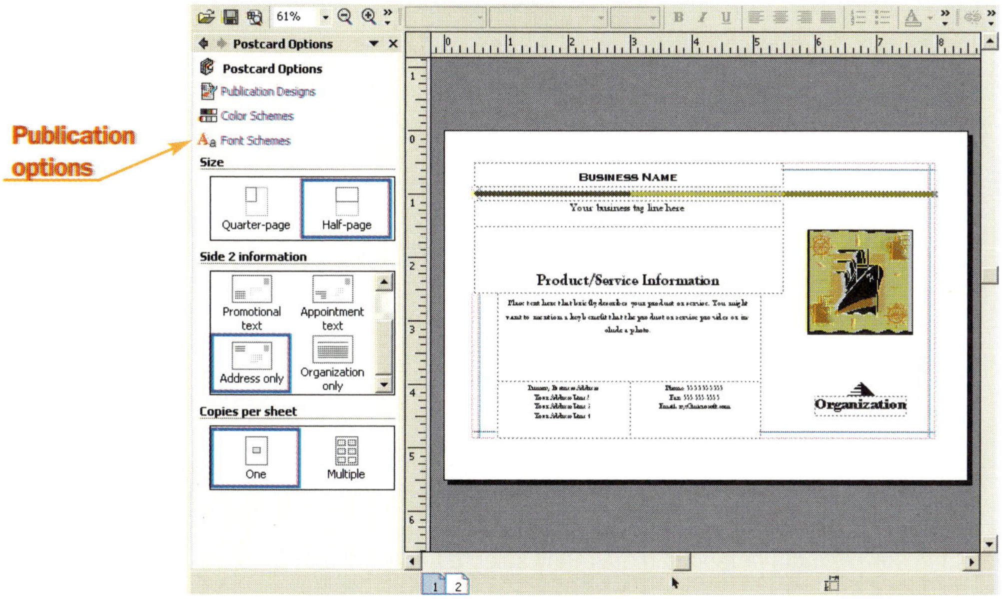

6. Leave the publication open to use in the next exercise.

Save, Close, and Reopen a Document

The first time you save a publication, use the Save As command on the File menu to give it a name and select a storage location. As with all new files, you should use filenames that help to identify the file contents, and, of course, you must follow standard filename rules. That means you cannot use the following characters: /, \, >, <, *, ?, ", !, :, ;, .

By default, most programs save a new publication file in the My Documents folder on your local hard disk, or in the same folder where you most recently saved a file. However, you can select a different location. You can save a file on a local hard disk, on a network drive, or on removable media, such as a 3½-inch disk or a CD-R.

STEP-BY-STEP 1.3

1. Click **File** on the menu bar, and then click **Save As**. The Save As dialog box opens, as shown in Figure 1-5.

FIGURE 1-5
Save As dialog box

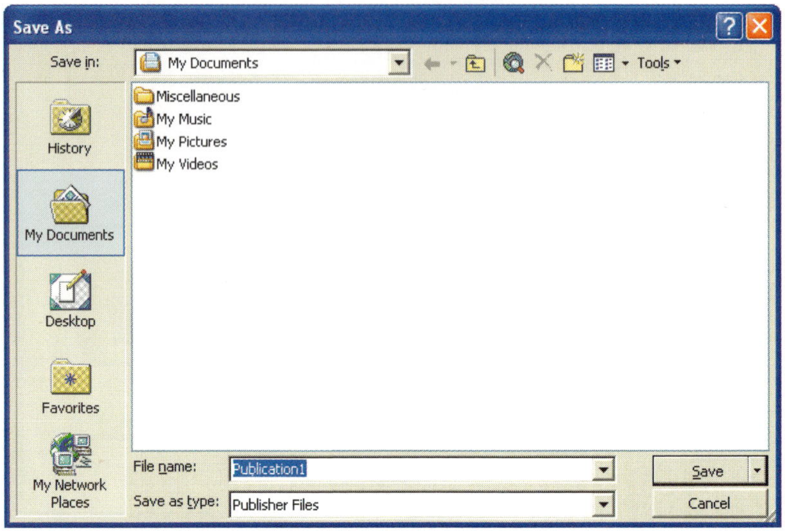

2. In the **File name** box, with the default name already selected, key **Postcard**. This will be the name of the new file.

3. From the **Save in** list, select the location where you want to store the file.

4. Click the **Save** button in the dialog box. The file is saved with the new name in the selected storage location.

5. Leave the **Postcard** file open to use in the next exercise.

Once you have saved a file for the first time, you can use the Save As command to save the file with a new name or in a new location. The original file will remain unchanged.

Close a File

When you have finished using a publication file, you should close it. You can close a file by using the Close command on the File menu. Some programs remain open after you close a file so you can continue using it, while others close unless there are other publication files still open.

If you have not saved the file before selecting the close command, the program displays a dialog box asking if you want to save. Click the Yes button to save the changes and close the file. Click the No button to close the file without saving the changes. Click the Cancel button to close the dialog box and continue working in the file. If you close the file without saving, all changes that you made since the last time you saved will be lost.

STEP-BY-STEP 1.4

1. Click **File** on the menu bar, and then click **Close**. The **Postcard** file closes.

2. Leave your desktop publishing program open to use in the next exercise.

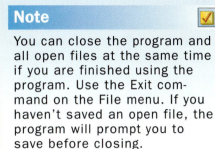

> **Note** ☑
>
> You can close the program and all open files at the same time if you are finished using the program. Use the Exit command on the File menu. If you haven't saved an open file, the program will prompt you to save before closing.

Open an Existing File

To work again with a file you have already closed, you must open it in your desktop publishing program. You can use the Open button on the main or standard toolbar or the Open command from the File menu to display the Open dialog box. By default, the Open dialog box displays the files in the My Documents folder. Or the dialog box may display the location from which you last opened a file. You can use the Open dialog box to locate and select the file you want to open.

STEP-BY-STEP 1.5

1. Click **File** on the menu bar, and then click **Open**. The Open or Open Publication dialog box appears, as shown in Figure 1-6. Don't worry if your Open dialog box does not look exactly the same as the one in the figure.

FIGURE 1-6
Open Publication dialog box

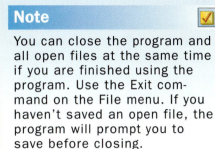

2. If the Postcard file is not listed in the dialog box, click the **Look in** list drop-down arrow and then select the location where the file is stored.

3. In the list of files, click **Postcard**.

4. Click the **Open** button in the dialog box. The file opens in the program window.

5. Leave the **Postcard** file open to use in the next exercise.

Change the Document View

When a publication file is open, it may appear in a program window similar to Figure 1-7. The appearance of the screen depends on the program you are using as well as on default options set for your computer, so don't worry if your screen doesn't look exactly the same as the one in the illustration. However, most desktop publishing programs have a number of standard screen elements in common, such as a document window, menu bar, toolbars, scroll bars, rulers, and panels or task panes where you can select options.

FIGURE 1-7
Typical desktop publishing window

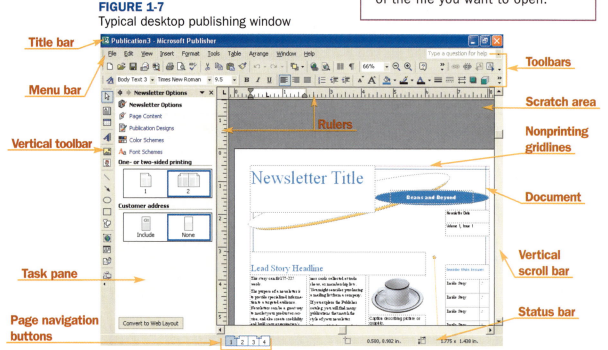

In addition, your program probably has nonprinting gridlines that help you align objects on a page; page navigation buttons, which are icons you can click to shift the display to show a different page; and a *scratch area*, which is a portion of the screen where you can temporarily store text and graphics. Even if the element names are not the same in all programs, the functions are similar.

View Options

While you are working in your desktop publishing program, you may want to change the *view* to get a different look at your publication. The view is the way your file is displayed onscreen. Most programs let you display your file in different view modes such as normal or standard, whole page or two-page spread, or preview. You can also choose to show or hide specific elements such as the rulers, the task pane, the guides, and the toolbars.

Most of the commands you use to change the view are located on the View menu. Other commands may be on a different menu, such as the Arrange menu or the Window menu, or available as buttons on a toolbar. Notice that many commands controlling the way a program is displayed are *toggles*, which means they are either on or off. Each time you select the command, it switches from on to off, or off to on. When a command is on, it usually has a check mark beside it on the menu.

S TEP-BY-STEP 1.6

1. In the **Postcard** file, click **View** on the menu bar, and then click a command such as **Rulers**. If the rulers were not displayed before, this command toggles them on. If they were displayed, the command toggles them off.

2. Choose the command that shows or hides the toolbars. For example, in Microsoft Publisher click **View** on the menu bar, click **Toolbars**, and then click **Formatting** on the submenu. This toggles the Formatting toolbar on or off. Or, in Adobe PageMaker click **Window** on the menu bar, and then click **Hide Tools**.

3. Repeat steps 1 and 2 until the rulers and the Formatting toolbar are displayed. In other words, toggle the rulers and toolbar on.

4. Use the page navigation feature in your program to display page 2 of the postcard. For example, click the page 2 icon on the Status bar. Page 2 in the Postcard document is the reverse side of the mailer, as shown in Figure 1-8. Use the same feature to display page 1 again. In some programs, you can press the Page Up or Page Down key to change pages.

FIGURE 1-8
Page 2 of the postcard mailer

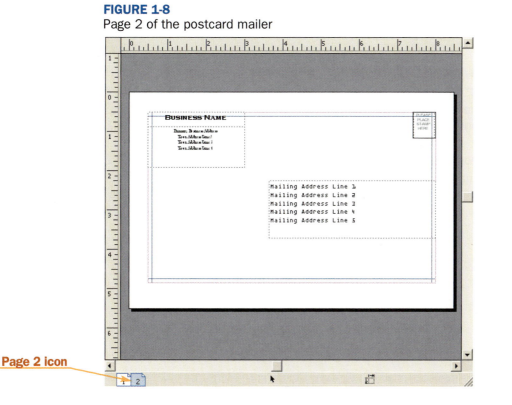

Page 2 icon

5. If your program has a task pane or panel displayed, select the command to close it. For example, click **View** on the menu bar, and then click **Task Pane**.

STEP-BY-STEP 1.6 Continued

6. Practice toggling other elements on and off to change the view, including options that may be on different menus. For example, show and hide special characters or boundaries and guides.

7. Leave the **Postcard** file open to use in the next exercise.

> **Did You Know?**
>
> Most panels and task panes have close buttons in the upper-right corner. Click the button to close the task pane. They may also have drop-down arrows you can click to display option menus.

Change the Zoom

When you need to get a closer look at a publication, *zoom* in. Zooming increases or decreases the magnification of the file on your screen by a percentage of its original size. For example, zoom in to 200% to display the file at twice its actual size, or zoom out to 50% to display it at half its actual size. Zooming in gives you a closer look and makes it easier to see and work with a particular area, while zooming out makes the publication look smaller and lets you get an overall look at the composition.

You can use the Zoom or Zoom To command on the View menu to select a magnification percentage from a list. You may be able to use a Zoom box on a standard toolbar to key a specific percentage. You can also simply click the Zoom In tool to zoom in or the Zoom Out tool to zoom out.

> **Did You Know?**
>
> In some programs, you can click the drop-down arrow next to the Zoom box on the toolbar to display a list of magnifications like the one available on the Zoom submenu.

STEP-BY-STEP 1.7

1. In the **Postcard** file, use the **Zoom** or **Zoom To** command on the **View** menu to change the magnification to **200%**. The magnification increases so you get a closer look at the publication.

2. Click the **Zoom Out** tool on the toolbar, or click **View** on the menu bar, click **Zoom**, and then click **150%**. The magnification decreases.

STEP-BY-STEP **1.7** Continued

3. Adjust the zoom to 75%. For example, click the **Zoom Out** button repeatedly until the magnification is 75%, or click the **Zoom** box on the Standard toolbar, key **75**, and press **Enter**. The magnification is adjusted to 75% of the document's actual size. It should look similar to Figure 1-9.

FIGURE 1-9
File displayed at 75% of its actual size

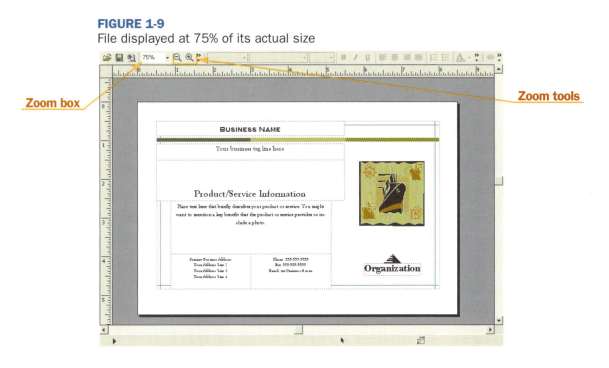

Zoom box

Zoom tools

4. Leave the **Postcard** file open to use in the next exercise.

Add and Edit Text

Text in a desktop publishing file is inserted in a ***text box*** or *frame*. A text box or frame is an object you can easily move and resize, which makes it easy to position and format the text in the publication. (Some programs have an additional feature called a text block, which is also used for holding text.) When you create a publication file based on a design or template, your program automatically inserts text boxes to hold the contact information and sample text. You replace the sample text to customize the publication. You can also enter new text and edit existing text at any time, as well as insert new text boxes. You learn more about working with text in Lesson 2.

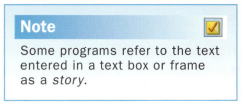

Note

Some programs refer to the text entered in a text box or frame as a *story*.

Enter Text

In some programs, such as Microsoft Publisher, you simply click the mouse pointer in the text box to position the insertion point so you can enter and edit text. In other programs, such as Adobe PageMaker, you first select the Text tool in the toolbox, and then click in the text box. When the insertion point is inside the text box, a border and sizing handles may appear, as shown in Figure 1-10. In some programs, a rotation handle displays as well. To select the text box, click its border with the mouse pointer, or click the selection tool in the toolbox and then click the border.

FIGURE 1-10
Select text box

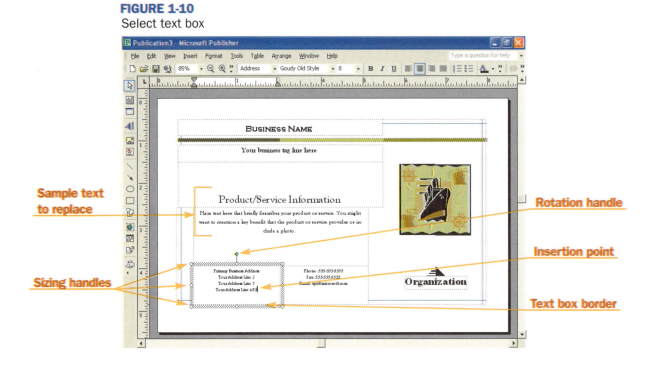

Sample text to replace

Rotation handle

Insertion point

Sizing handles

Text box border

In most desktop publishing programs, you use the same standard text entry, editing, and selection commands that you use in other programs to move the insertion point within a text box or frame and to make changes to the text. For example, to select text, simply drag the mouse across it, or, with the keyboard, position the insertion point at the beginning of the selected text; press and hold Shift; and then press arrow keys to define the selection. To insert new text, simply position the insertion point and begin keying. Table 1-1 describes some of the common keystrokes used to work with text.

TABLE 1-1
Common text-editing keystrokes

PRESS THIS KEY	TO DO THIS
↑	To move insertion point up one line.
↓	To move insertion point down one line.
←	To move insertion point one character to the left.
→	To move insertion point one character to the right.
← BACKSPACE	To delete the character to the left of the insertion point.
DELETE	To delete the character to the right of the insertion point.
↵ ENTER	To start a new paragraph.

As you type in a text box, the text is automatically formatted according to the settings determined by the publication type and design. For example, the text may automatically be centered within the text box, or aligned to the right or left. Usually, the text is automatically sized to fit within the text box. Also, you do not have to press Enter to start a new line, because the text *wraps* within the text box. When text wraps, it automatically starts a new line when the current line is full. If automatic hyphenation is on, words that are split from one line to the next are automatically hyphenated. Although you can change the formatting, in most cases, the default design formatting is appropriate for the publication type and design you have selected.

STEP-BY-STEP 1.8

1. In the **Postcard** file, replace sample information with specific company information as follows. (You may have to switch pages to enter all the information, and some information may be entered more than once.)

> **Note** ☑️
>
> Some programs use sample text designed to help you decide where to enter replacement text, while other programs may use gibberish or foreign language text as placeholders.

   a. Locate sample text for the company name (such as *Business Name* or *Organization*) and zoom in, if necessary, to get a better view. Then, key **Beans and Beyond**.

   b. Locate sample text for the company address and key the following street address:
   622 Elm Street
   Sudbury, MA 01776

   c. Locate sample text for other contact information and key the following replacement text:
   Phone: 555-555-5555
   Fax: 555-555-5555
   Email: vmcgill@mail.com

   d. If you see sample text for a company tag line or slogan, key **Fine Coffee and Tasty Treats from Around the World**.

STEP-BY-STEP 1.8 Continued

2. Locate the sample headline (such as *Product/Service Information*) in the publication and select the sample text. (If necessary, switch to page 2.)

3. Key **Jazz in the Mornings**. The new text replaces the selected text.

4. Click the sample text in the text box below the headline, or wherever there is a text box for entering information, and key the following text. Remember, you do not have to press Enter to begin a new line.

Beans and Beyond is pleased to announce a series of Sunday morning jazz concerts beginning the first Sunday in September and continuing through the end of the year. Each week will feature a different ensemble or solo artist, specially selected to complement your weekend. Join us for a relaxing blend of music, beverages, and pastry delights. 9:30 a.m. until 2:00 p.m.

5. Locate the sample mailing address for the postcard and replace it with your name and address.

6. Replace any other sample text in the document. For example, click the sample text *Organization* and replace it with the text **Beans and Beyond**. Notice that the text is automatically resized to fit within the text box. Delete any text boxes you do not need, such as a text box giving information about the template used to create the publication. Now, go back and edit some existing text.

Note

To delete a text box, click the text box border, and then press Delete.

7. Click the text *Jazz in the Mornings* with the pointer or text tool. The insertion point appears where you clicked.

STEP-BY-STEP 1.8 Continued

8. Select the text *in the* and replace it with the text **on Sunday**. The document should look similar to the one in Figure 1-11.

FIGURE 1-11
Postcard with replacement text

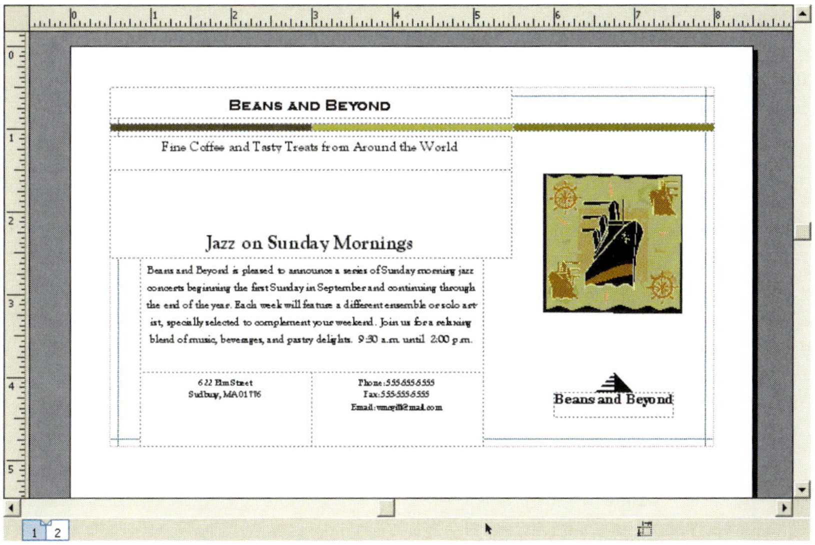

9. Leave the **Postcard** file open to use in the next exercise.

Use Undo and Redo

If you are unhappy with the results of a command or selection in your desktop publishing program, you can use the Undo command to reverse it. Undo lets you reverse the most recent action, or, in some programs, a series of actions. You can use the Redo command to reverse the results of an Undo action. Undo and Redo are available as commands on the Edit menu and may also be available as buttons on a toolbar. The first time you use the command, the most recent action is reversed. Repeat the command to reverse the action prior to that, and so on.

> **Note**
>
> Some programs let you automatically undo or redo a series of commands. Click the drop-down arrow on the Undo toolbar button to display a list of commands that can be reversed. When you click an item in the list, it and all items above it are undone. You can use the same steps on the Redo button to redo a series of actions.

STEP-BY-STEP 1.9

1. In the **Postcard** file, select the **Undo** command from the **Edit** menu, or click the **Undo** button on the toolbar. Your program undoes the most recent action, which is the replacement of the text *in the* with the text *on Sunday*.

2. Select the **Redo** command from the **Edit** menu, or click the **Redo** button on the toolbar. The previous action is reversed.

3. Leave the **Postcard** file open to use in the next exercise.

Save Changes to a File

You can quickly save changes to a file by clicking the Save button on the toolbar, or by using the Save command on the File menu. Saving changes ensures that you don't lose your work if there's a problem with your computer or the software. In some programs, depending on the edits you have made, a dialog box may ask if you want to save changes to your contact information. Click Yes to save the changes to the contact information, or click No to save the file, but leave the contact information unchanged.

> **Important**
>
> Save your files frequently! In the event of a mechanical problem or a power failure, all data you have entered or edited since the last time you saved will be lost. Saving is the only way to ensure that your work is safe.

STEP-BY-STEP 1.10

1. Click **File** on the menu bar, and then click **Save**. If a dialog box asks if you want to save the changes to your contact information, click **No**. The changes are saved.

2. Leave the **Postcard** file open to use in the next exercise.

Insert a Picture

When you create a publication file based on a design or template, your program may automatically insert sample *graphics*, sized and positioned to enhance the document. Graphics are picture files that are generally inserted as objects directly in your desktop publishing files, although in some programs you must insert them into frames. Depending on the publication type and design, the sample graphics may be *shapes* or *clip art* pictures. Shapes are exactly that—lines, ovals, rectangles, and polygons inserted and formatted to enhance the appearance of the document. Clip art pictures are images already saved in a graphics file format. (You learn more about working with graphics and other objects in Lesson 4.)

While you probably want to keep the shapes that are part of the publication design, you may just as likely want to replace the sample clip art in your document with something that represents the content of the publication. To replace the clip art, you open a dialog box in which you locate and select the graphics file you want to insert instead.

In some programs, you first select the object you want to replace, then click Insert on the menu bar, click Picture, and then click From File to open the Insert Picture dialog box. Once you locate and select the file you want, click the Insert button to insert it in the publication. In other programs, you must first delete the sample graphic, then use the Place command on the File menu to open the Place dialog box. Once you locate and select the file, click the Open button, then drag the insertion pointer to define the size and location where you want the picture placed in the publication. For example, drag where the previous clip art image was positioned.

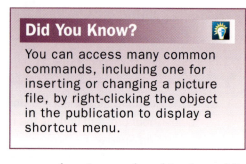

> **Did You Know?**
>
> You can access many common commands, including one for inserting or changing a picture file, by right-clicking the object in the publication to display a shortcut menu.

STEP-BY-STEP 1.11

1. In the **Postcard** file, select the picture you want to replace. (If you are using Adobe PageMaker, you should delete the sample LOGO graphics objects first.)

2. Select the command to open the dialog box where you can locate and select the picture file you want to insert.

3. Locate and select **DP Step 1-11** from the data files.

4. Click the **Insert** or **Open** button in the dialog box. If necessary, click **Yes** to accept information about the picture file size and then click and drag the insertion pointer to insert the picture where the original object(s) had been and size it at about 1.25 inches square. The replacement graphic should look similar to Figure 1-12.

FIGURE 1-12
Replacement picture in the Postcard file

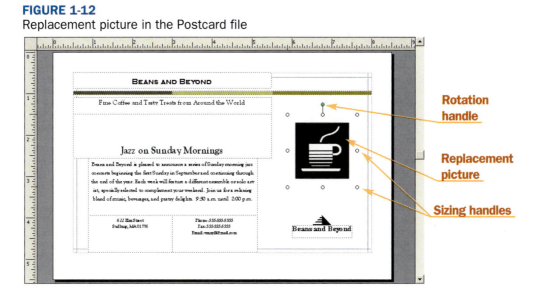

5. Save changes and leave the **Postcard** file open to use in the next exercise.

Check Spelling

At a minimum, most desktop publishing documents include some text, such as a caption on a poster, and often they include a lot of text, such as an eight-page newsletter. Spelling errors can take all the credibility out of a publication, so it is very important to check the spelling in a publication before you print it or send it to be published.

All desktop publishing programs include a spelling checker feature that you can use to locate and correct spelling errors. The spelling checker compares the words in the document to a built-in dictionary. If the spelling checker cannot find the word, it highlights the word. You can correct the spelling, ignore the word, or add the word to the dictionary so that it will not be marked as incorrect in the future.

Some programs also offer a feature that checks spelling as you type and automatically flags words that may be incorrect with a visual mark on the screen, such as a wavy colored underline. You can ignore the flag and continue typing, correct the spelling, or add the word to the dictionary.

Of course, even the best spelling checker won't catch all spelling errors. For example, if you key the word *threw* when you mean to key *through*, the spelling checker does not identify the mistake. The only way to be certain your text is correct is to proofread it carefully.

Extra for Experts

If your program automatically inserts text stored in your contact information into a publication file, it will not mark the text as misspelled, even if it includes a proper name or an unusually spelled word. The program recognizes that these words may not be in its dictionary.

To start a spelling checker in your desktop publishing program, click in the text box you want to check, then click the Spelling button on the toolbar, or select the check spelling command. Your program may open the text box's text in a *story editor* window, which is a separate window used for editing text. When the spelling checker identifies a word that is not in the dictionary, it displays a dialog box similar to the one in Figure 1-13. Select the correct spelling in the list and then click the Change or Replace button, or click one of the other command buttons, such as Ignore or Add to Dictionary. There may also be an option to extend the spell check to all text boxes (or stories) in the document.

FIGURE 1-13
Check Spelling dialog box

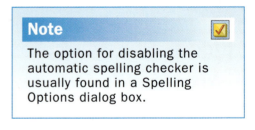

If your program has an automatic spelling checker, you may already have noticed flagged words. The program checks the spelling as you key new text and marks words that are not in the dictionary. To correct the spelling, you can delete the error and rekey the text, or you can right-click the word and select an option from the shortcut menu that displays. Usually, you can choose the same options that are available in the

Note

The option for disabling the automatic spelling checker is usually found in a Spelling Options dialog box.

spelling dialog box, including selecting the correct spelling, ignoring the error, or adding the word to the dictionary.

STEP-BY-STEP 1.12

1. In the **Postcard** file, click in the headline text *Jazz on Sunday Mornings* and change the *a* in *Jazz* to an **e**, then change the *d* in *Sunday* to a **b**. Click the text box border to select the text box. If your program has an automatic spelling checker, it probably flagged the incorrectly spelled words *Jezz* and *Sunbay*.

2. If your program displays a wavy underline beneath the word *Jezz*, right-click on the word. A shortcut menu displays, similar to the one in Figure 1-14.

FIGURE 1-14
Spelling shortcut menu

3. Click the correctly spelled word *Jazz* on the shortcut menu. Your program corrects the spelling. Now use the spelling checker to locate other errors in the publication.

4. Click the **Spelling** button on the toolbar, or select the command to start the spelling checker. You may need to click the **Start** button in the spelling dialog box if the text opens in a story editor window.

5. If you have not already corrected the word *Jezz*, your program will highlight it. Click the **Change** or **Replace** button to replace the incorrect word.

6. The spelling checker highlights the word *Sunbay*. Click the **Change** or **Replace** button, or key the correct spelling.

7. Select the option to check all text boxes or stories in the publication. You may need to ignore the proper names used in the address. When the check is complete, close all open dialog boxes and/or the story editor window(s).

8. Save changes to the **Postcard** file and leave it open to use in the next exercise.

Historically Speaking

Before computers took over so many publishing tasks, authors and editors checked text on long sheets of proofs called *galleys*. They marked the text using standard *proofreaders' marks* that printers and typesetters understood to specify changes in the text. Although computers have automated a good part of document production, some jobs are still best done the old-fashioned way, and that includes proofreading. For best-quality results, final proofs should still be printed, read, and marked by hand. Reading a document for errors is a vital part of creating a first-class publication.

Figure 1-15 illustrates just a few of the standard proofreaders' marks used to indicate errors and changes. One mark is made in the margin beside the text, and one mark is made in the text itself. An editor or production specialist reading the marked copy knows immediately how to correct the document. You can find a complete list of proofreaders' marks in most standard dictionaries or on the Internet.

FIGURE 1-15
Common proofreaders' marks

INSTRUCTION	MARK IN MARGIN	MARK IN TEXT
Delete		the happy dog
Insert	happy	the dog
Let it stand	stet	the happy dog
Make capital	cap	the dog
Make lowercase	lc	the Dog
Set in italics	ital	the dog
Set in boldface	bf	the dog
Transpose	tr	dog the
Close up space		d og
Insert a space	#	thedog
Start a paragraph	¶	"where is the dog?" "Over there."
Move left	[	[the dog
Move right	]	the dog
Align	‖	the dog / the dog / the dog

Preview and Print a Document

The goal of creating a desktop publishing document is to see it in print. Even if you intend to have the actual publication prepared by a commercial printer, you can use your program to preview the publication onscreen the way it will look when it is printed and to quickly print a sample copy.

To preview a document before printing, you can simply change the zoom setting or use a Print Preview button or menu command if available. Programs with Print Preview usually display the entire first page, as shown in Figure 1-16. The Print Preview may also have a toolbar with buttons you can use to change pages, display multiple pages at the same time, change the zoom, change some printer settings, and print the document.

> **Note** ☑
>
> Not all desktop publishing programs have a Print Preview feature. This may be because in regular view, the publication is displayed the way it will print.

FIGURE 1-16
Postcard in Print Preview

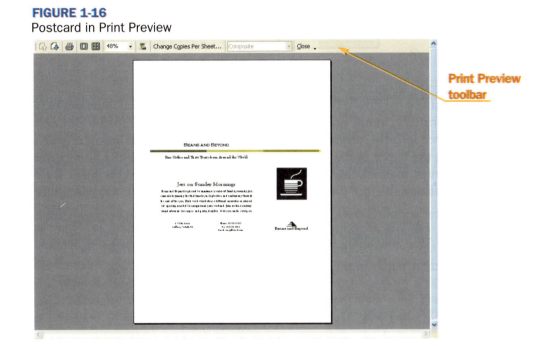

Print Preview toolbar

To quickly print a single copy using the default print settings, you can usually simply click the Print button on the toolbar. If you want to change any print settings, you must select the Print command from the File menu to open the Print dialog box. The Print dialog

REVIEW *Questions*

TRUE / FALSE

Circle T if the statement is true or F if the statement is false.

T   F   **1.** Zooming in increases the size of the publication displayed on your screen.

T   F   **2.** A template is another word for newsletter.

T   F   **3.** Some word processing programs offer desktop publishing features that can be used to create simple publications.

T   F   **4.** To include text in a desktop publishing document, you must import it from a word processing file.

T   F   **5.** Most desktop printers can print on two sides of a sheet of paper at the same time.

T   F   **6.** Automatic spelling checkers flag misspelled words as soon as you type them.

T   F   **7.** Once you insert a picture in a publication, you cannot replace it.

T   F   **8.** When you create a publication using a template or design, your program may automatically insert graphics and sample text in the document.

T   F   **9.** When you type in a text box, the text is automatically formatted according to the current settings.

T   F   **10.** Many programs display nonprinting gridlines onscreen in a publication to help you align objects on a page.

WRITTEN QUESTIONS

Write a brief answer to the following questions.

1. What are some things to consider when you plan a publication?

2. What are some reasons for using a publication design or template instead of creating a blank publication?

3. List at least five types of publications you can create with a desktop publishing program.

4. Why would you want to change the zoom while working with a publication?

5. Why should you check the spelling in a publication?

FILL IN THE BLANK

Complete the following sentences by writing the correct word or words in the blanks provided.

1. To quickly print a single copy of a publication using the default print settings, click the _____ button on the toolbar.

2. Graphics are _____ files that are usually inserted as objects directly into a desktop publishing file.

3. Use the _____ command to reverse the results of the Undo command.

4. You do not have to press Enter to start a new line if the text is set to _____ in the text box.

5. Another term for text box is _____.

6. When a command is _____ on, it usually has a check mark beside it on the menu.

7. Some programs automatically customize publications by inserting contact _____.

8. While planning a publication, you can create a(n) _____ to represent what the finished product will look like.

9. The first time you save a publication, you use the _____ dialog box to enter a filename and select a storage location.

10. Some programs have a(n) _____, which is a portion of the screen where you can temporarily store text and graphics.

PROJECTS

PROJECT 1-1

1. Launch your desktop publishing program and choose to create a flyer.

2. Select a simple design or template appropriate for advertising an event.

3. Save the file as **Speaker**.

4. Close the task pane if there is one, and then zoom in to 75%.

5. Replace the sample text with the following information:

Event title: Guest Speaker

Date: Date: April 22

Time: Time: 12:00 p.m.

Location: Location: Building 8, Cafeteria B

Contact: Contact person: 555-7777, ext. 3456

Description: Dr. Keith Lancaster, a specialist in retirement planning, will be giving a lecture about investing for the future, targeted toward those nearing retirement age. At the end of the talk, Dr. Lancaster will answer questions from the audience.

> **Note**
>
> If you are using a template from a program such as Adobe PageMaker, you may need to adjust fonts, font sizes, and text boxes to fit information, and you may also have to decide how to arrange the information given above. Ask your instructor for help if necessary.

6. Replace the sample picture with **DP Project 1-1** from the data files. Adjust the size of the graphic frame if necessary.

7. Check the spelling in the file. Remove any unnecessary text boxes, frames, or graphics.

8. Preview the file, and then print a single copy.

9. Save changes and close the **Speaker** file, but leave your desktop publishing program open to use in Project 1-2.

PROJECT 1-2

1. In your desktop publishing program, choose to create a business card.

2. Select a design or template, such as the Punctuation template in Microsoft Publisher or the 1000768.pmt template in Adobe PageMaker 7.

3. Save the file as **KeithL**.

4. Close the task pane if there is one, and then zoom in to 150%.

5. Replace the sample text with the following information. (You may need to adjust fonts, font sizes, and text box sizes in some programs.)

Company name: Lancaster and Associates

Name: Keith Lancaster

Title: Retirement Specialist

Address: 5454 Main Street
Suite 7B
San Jose, CA 95110

Phone: 408-555-5555

Fax: 408-555-5666

Email: klanc@mail.com

Logo, organization, or other text: Retirement Planning

6. Check the spelling in the publication. If your template includes more than one business card on the page, you need modify only the first sample. Delete any text boxes or graphics you don't need.

7. Preview the publication, and then print one copy.

8. Save changes, close the **KeithL** file, and close your desktop publishing program.

WEB PROJECT

Use the Internet to look up and compare the features of at least two desktop publishing programs. You might try searching for desktop publishing, or looking up the Web sites of software companies you know sell desktop publishing programs, such as Microsoft and Adobe. Try to find a program designed for professional use and one designed for home use. Look for information that you can use to decide whether to buy the program. For example, most sites have feature lists that you can save or print, as well as pricing information. Compare the information you find and see if you can pick a program you would like to own.

TEAMWORK PROJECT

As a group, plan the development and production of a publication. Start by deciding the type of publication you want to produce as well as the target audience and the message you want the publication to convey. Agree on how you want the finished product to look, how it will be printed, and how it will be distributed. If possible, research the costs of producing the publication, including paper costs, printing costs, and delivery costs. You can call or write to a commercial printer to ask for a price list. Your school may even have a resource you can ask about paper and copying costs. Enter the pricing information into a spreadsheet, or write it on paper. See if you can save money by changing some of the project specifications. For example, could you print fewer copies, use fewer pages, or distribute the publication by hand instead of mail? Once you have settled on a budget and a publication plan, try making a mock-up that you can share with the class.

CRITICAL *Thinking*

ACTIVITY 1-1

Use your desktop publishing program to create an invitation to a party at your school or home. Start by planning how you want the invitation to look. For example, do you want it to be a single, unfolded sheet of paper, or do you want it to be folded card? Look at the designs or templates available in your program for ideas; then, create a mock-up. Create the document by selecting the publication type and design. Replace the sample text and graphics with customized text and graphics. Before you print the invitation, be sure to check the spelling.

WORKING WITH TEXT

VOCABULARY

Clipboard
Color scheme
Font
Font effects
Font size
Font style
Horizontal alignment
Indents
Insertion point
Kerning
Leading
Margins
Points
Sans serif font
Serif font
Tabs
Tracking
Vertical alignment
White space

Text is an important component of most desktop publishing documents. Sometimes, the text makes up the bulk of the publication, such as in a newsletter that includes lengthy articles. Other times, the text is used to highlight or complement other content, for example, in a sales flyer that may use short bullet lists or a travel brochure that may have photo captions. All desktop publishing programs include tools that help you enhance the appearance of your publications and ensure that the text is easy to read. Most of the tools are similar to those found in word processing programs that allow you to apply boldface or indent a paragraph. Other tools are designed specifically for fine-tuning documents for publication, such as adjusting spacing between lines, characters, and paragraphs. In this lesson, you learn how to create a blank document, insert and delete text boxes, format text, and control text flow.

Create a Blank Document

In Lesson 1, you learned to create a publication using your program's built-in designs or templates. If none of the templates or designs is suitable for your publication, you can create a new blank document and start from scratch. Once you create a blank document, you insert text and graphics and apply formatting to design your publication.

Although some desktop publishing programs start with a new blank document open on the screen, most start displaying a dialog box or task pane listing designs or templates. Click the option for creating a blank document or publication to display a default blank document. Alternatively, click the New button on the toolbar. Some programs first display a Document Setup dialog box in which you can select settings to control the appearance of the new document or just click OK to create a document with the default settings. In most programs, the default blank document is a full 8.5-inch by 11-inch page with 1-inch *margins* marked by margin guides on all sides. Margins are the area between the edge of the page and the objects in the publication. Some programs may have different default margins.

S TEP-BY-STEP 2.1

1. Launch your desktop publishing program. If necessary, close the template dialog box or window.

2. If necessary, click the option to create a blank full-page document, or click the **New** button on the toolbar. If your program displays a Document Setup dialog box, key **1** in each of the margin boxes and then click the **OK** button. Your program creates and displays a document similar to the one shown in Figure 2-1.

FIGURE 2-1
Blank full-page document

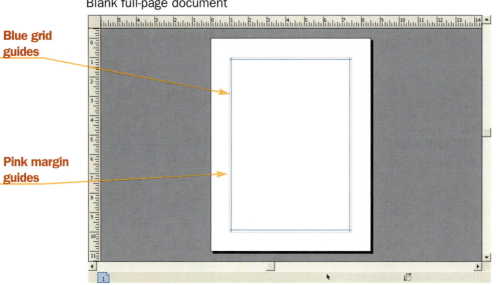

Blue grid guides

Pink margin guides

3. Save the file as **Meeting** and leave it open to use in the next exercise.

Work with Text Boxes

As you have already learned, text in a desktop publishing document is inserted in a text box, which is sometimes called a *frame* or *text frame*. When you create a document based on a template or design, your program automatically inserts and formats text boxes. You can manually insert text boxes at any time, and you can delete text boxes you no longer need. Once a text box is inserted in a document, you can easily change its size and/or position on the page.

> **Note** ✓
>
> Some programs let you create two types of text boxes—text blocks and text frames. For the exercises in this lesson, you should use text frames.

Insert and Delete Text Boxes

To insert a text box, use a tool or command such as Text Box, or use a frame tool. Click the appropriate tool and then click and drag the mouse pointer to define the size and position of the object on the page. As you drag, guidelines appear on both the horizontal and vertical ruler. Use these lines to help you gauge the text box dimensions. When you release the mouse button, the new text box is inserted in the document, and it is selected. The appearance of a selected text box varies depending on the program you are using. Most display sizing handles and a nonprinting border, like other selected objects. Some display a thin black printing border called a *stroke* and *windowshade handles* on the top and bottom. You learn how to add, modify, and remove strokes in Lesson 4.

Usually, the new text box has an ***insertion point*** flashing in it, but in some programs, you have to click a text tool and then click in the new frame to place the insertion point. The insertion point is a flashing vertical bar that indicates where keyed text will be inserted. New text is generally inserted to the left of the insertion point. You use standard text entry

> **Note** ✓
>
> You should always use proper typography and keyboarding when keying text in a publication.

and editing techniques to key text in a desktop publishing program. To delete a text box, click its border to select it, and then press Delete, or choose Delete or Clear from the Edit menu.

STEP-BY-STEP 2.2

1. In the **Meeting** file, adjust the zoom to at least 75% so you have a good look at the top part of the document.

2. Click the tool that allows you to insert a text box or rectangular frame, and then position the mouse pointer at the top margin halfway across the page, at about 4.25 inches on the horizontal ruler.

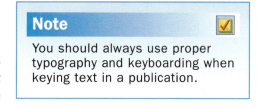

> **Extra for Experts**
>
> In some programs, you can drag the rulers closer to the work area so you can measure the objects in your publication.

STEP-BY-STEP 2.2 Continued

3. Press and hold the mouse button and drag diagonally down and to the right to draw a box about 1 inch high and 3 inches wide. Use the rulers for help sizing the object. Release the mouse button to insert the object in the file. It should look similar to Figure 2-2. Don't worry if your text box or frame has a stroke, or line, around it.

> **Note** ☑
>
> If you want to remove the stroke, select None from the Stroke list in the Fill and Stroke dialog box.

FIGURE 2-2
Blank text box

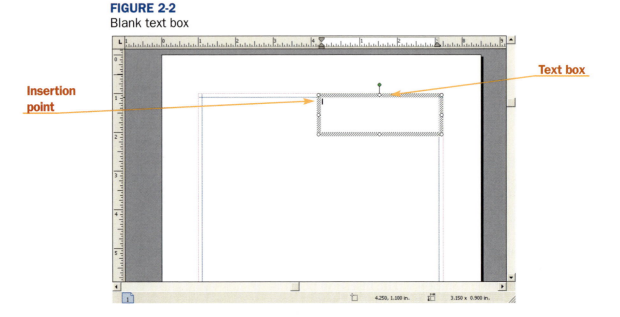

4. If necessary, click in the text box with the text tool to position the insertion point, and then key the text **Leadership Association Meeting**. The text displays in the default formatting. You learn how to change the formatting later in this lesson.

5. Click the text box or frame tool again, and then position the mouse pointer in the lower left corner of the document.

6. Press and hold the mouse button and drag diagonally up and to the right to draw a box about 2 inches high and 6 inches wide. Again, use the rulers to help size the object. Release the mouse button to insert the object in the file.

7. Key the text **Join us on Friday**. Now, try deleting a text box.

8. Use the pointer or selection tool to click the border of the text box you drew in step 6 to select it, and then press **Delete**. The text box is removed from the file.

9. Save changes and leave the **Meeting** file open to use in the next exercise.

Resize, Position Text Boxes

When you select a text box, sizing handles display around its border. Drag a sizing handle to quickly resize the text box. When the mouse pointer is positioned over a sizing handle, it may change to a double-headed arrow and include the word *Resize*. Drag a top or bottom handle to change the text box height. Drag a side handle to change the width, or drag a corner handle to change both the height and width at the same time.

To position a text box, simply place the mouse pointer over the object's border and then drag the object to a new location. When the mouse pointer is over the border, it may change to a four-headed arrow and include the word *Move*.

> **Note** ✅
>
> Most programs display the *X* and *Y coordinates* of a text box or frame, as well as the width and height of the object, in the status bar or in a control palette. You can use these coordinates and measurements to position or size a text box precisely.

STEP-BY-STEP 2.3

1. In the **Meeting** file, select the text box.

2. Position the mouse pointer over the object's border (the Move pointer may appear), and then press and hold the mouse button and drag the object to the upper-left corner of the document, where the top and left margins meet. Release the mouse button to move the object.

3. Position the mouse pointer over the sizing handle in the lower-right corner of the text box.

4. Press and hold the mouse button and drag across to the right margin and down to the 3-inch mark on the ruler, as shown in Figure 2-3. As you drag, the mouse pointer may change to a cross-hair, and a dashed line may define the text box size. Release the mouse button to resize the object.

FIGURE 2-3
Resize a text box

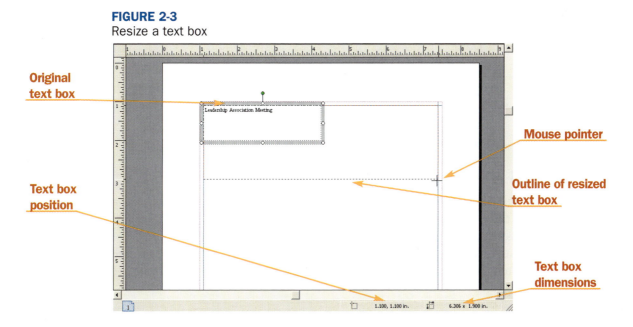

Original text box

Mouse pointer

Outline of resized text box

Text box position

Text box dimensions

Leadership Association Meeting

1.100, 1.100 in.   6.306 x 1.900 in.

5. Save changes and leave the **Meeting** file open to use in the next exercise.

Work with Fonts

Change the look of text in a publication using font formatting. A *font* is the typeface or design of a set of characters, including letters, numbers, and symbols. Although the main goal in selecting a font is to make text easy to read, appropriate use of fonts can also make an impact in your publications and help define the tone and message you want to convey. Fonts can be elaborate or simple, decorative or plain. It is worth spending some time to select just the right font or combination of fonts to complement your publication.

In addition to selecting a font, you can set font size, font style, font effects, and font color. You can apply font formatting to selected text, or you can select the options before you key new text. Many font formatting options can be set using toolbar buttons, palette options, or menus. In addition, most programs have a Font or Character Specifications dialog box similar to the one shown in Figure 2-4, in which you can select any of the font formatting options. To open the Font dialog box in most programs, click Format on the menu bar and then click Font. To open the Character Specifications dialog box in PageMaker, click Type on the menu bar and then click Character.

FIGURE 2-4
Font dialog box

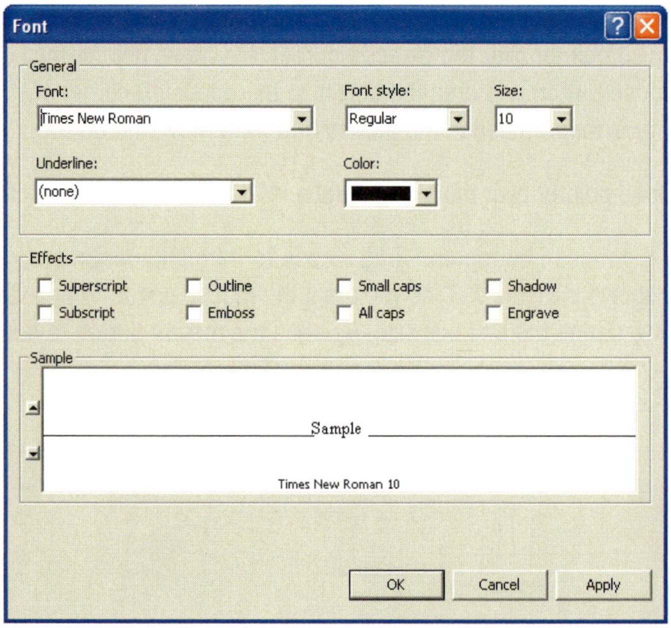

Select a Font and Font Size

There are two basic types of fonts: serif fonts and sans serif fonts. *Serif fonts* have short lines and curlicues at the ends of the lines that make up each character. Serif fonts are generally easy to read and so are often used for lengthy paragraphs, reports, or letters. Some common serif fonts include Times New Roman, Garamond, and Century. *Sans serif fonts* have straight lines without serifs and are often used for headlines and titles. Some common sans serif fonts are Arial, Impact, and Tahoma. Other types of fonts include script fonts, which imitate handwriting decorative, or fantasy fonts, and symbol fonts, which include sets of symbols you can insert as characters into text. Figure 2-5 shows examples of different fonts.

FIGURE 2-5
Sample fonts

Serif Fonts	Script Fonts
Times New Roman	Brush Script MT
Sylfaen	Edwardian Script ITC
Georgia	Freestyle Script

Sans Serif Fonts	Decorative or Fantasy Fonts
Arial	Chiller
Comic Sans MS	CASTELLAR
Gill Sans MT	Curlz MT
	Jokerman
	Ravie

Your program probably has a default font and font size for text inserted in a blank document. For example, in Microsoft Publisher, the default font is 10-point Times New Roman. To choose a font, locate your program's font list on a menu, toolbar, or in a dialog or task pane. In most cases, the fonts are listed in alphabetical order, and you can sometimes see a preview of a font when you select it in the list. Most desktop publishing programs come with a long list of built-in fonts, and you may have other fonts available on your computer as well. You can buy and install font sets you need, or locate free fonts on the Internet.

Extra for Experts

Some programs let you scale the width of selected text by a percentage of its original size. For example, scale text to 200% to stretch it to twice its original width. Scale text to 50% to shrink it to half its original width.

Too many fonts can make a publication difficult to read. In general, you should try to use no more than three fonts on a page, and you should avoid mixing similar fonts on the same page. For example, use a serif font for body text and a sans serif font for headlines. You can add a third font for captions or subheadings, or better yet, change the size and/or style of one of the other fonts you are already using.

Font size is the height of an uppercase letter in the font set, measured in ***points***. There are 72 points in an inch. Select a new font size by locating your program's font size list on a toolbar, menu, or palette, or in the Font dialog box. You can choose one of the sizes on the list or key a size in the font size box. Many programs have Increase Font Size and Decrease Font Size toolbar buttons that you can use to quickly change the font in 1-point increments.

STEP-BY-STEP 2.7 Continued

3. Click the **OK** button in the dialog box. The text should look similar to Figure 2-9.

FIGURE 2-9
Text is centered vertically and horizontally

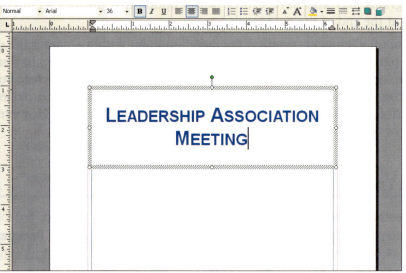

4. Print one copy of the **Meeting** file.

5. Save changes and close the **Meeting** file. Leave your desktop publishing program open to use in the next exercise.

Set Indents and Tabs and Create Lists

You can set indents and tabs within a text box in much the same way you do in a standard word processing document. *Indents* are used to set temporary margins for a paragraph or series of paragraphs. *Tabs* are used to adjust the horizontal position of text across a single line. To set indents and tabs for a single paragraph, simply position the insertion point in the paragraph and then select the options you want to apply. To format multiple paragraphs, select the paragraphs before selecting the options. You can also select the options before you key new text. Indents and tabs are carried forward to new paragraphs when you press Enter.

Lists are an effective way to present information so that readers can quickly identify and digest the important points you are trying to make. In addition, lists are useful for breaking up the layout of a page to make it more interesting and appealing. Use numbered lists when the order of items matters and use bulleted lists when the order does not matter. For example, number directions to a building and bullet facts about a product or service.

Most programs offer many different methods to apply indents, tabs, and lists. Usually, you can set precise values or select options in a dialog box or control palette, but it is often faster and easier to simply drag the indent or tab markers on the horizontal ruler or on the Indents/Tabs ruler.

Set Indents

Most programs offer five types of indents, as shown in Figure 2-10. A first-line indent indents the first line of a paragraph from the left margin. A left indent indents all lines in a paragraph from the left margin. A right indent indents all lines from the right margin. A double or quotation indent indents all lines from both the left and right margins. A hanging indent indents all lines except the first line from the left margin.

FIGURE 2-10
Sample indent styles

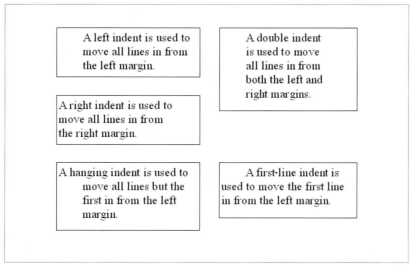

Indents may be set by dragging indent markers on a ruler, by specifying values in a Control palette, or by using a dialog box. Some programs have Increase Indent and Decrease Indent toolbar buttons that you can use to quickly adjust a left indent in 0.5-inch increments. To open the Indents and Lists dialog box, click Format on the menu bar and then click Indents and Lists. To open the control palette, click Window, Show Control Palette. (You may have to click the Paragraph formatting button to make the indents options available.) To display the Indents/Tabs ruler, click Type on the menu bar and then click Indents/Tabs. Your instructor may want you to use a particular method to complete the following exercise. If not, select the method you want to use.

STEP-BY-STEP 2.8

1. In your desktop publishing program, open **DP Step 2-8** from the data files. This publication is similar to the Meeting file you worked with earlier in this lesson, but it includes additional text.

2. Save the file as **Meeting2**.

3. Increase the zoom to at least 75%, and then select the text of the quotation, including the quotation marks, but not the speaker's name or title.

4. Apply a double or quotation indent by indenting the text 0.5 inches from both the left and right margins. You can do this by dragging the indent markers on the horizontal or Indents/Tabs ruler, or by setting values in the Indents and Lists dialog box or Control palette.

STEP-BY-STEP 2.8 Continued

5. Select the speaker's name and title and indent the lines 3 inches from the left margin. When you deselect the text, the text box should look similar to the one in Figure 2-11.

FIGURE 2-11
Indents applied to text

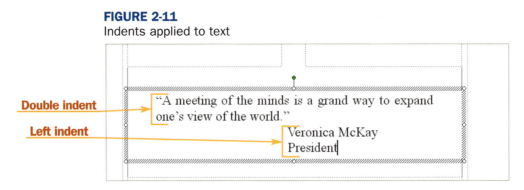

6. Save changes and leave the **Meeting2** file open to use in the next exercise.

Set Tabs

A tab is a stopping point at a specific point along the horizontal ruler. Each time you press the Tab key, the insertion point advances to the next tab stop. There are four types of tab stops in most programs. Left sets text to start flush with the tab stop. Right sets text to end flush with the tab stop. Center centers text on either side of the tab stop. Decimal aligns decimal points or periods flush with the tab stop. Most programs have default left tab stops set every 0.5 inch. In most programs, you can also set *tab leaders*, which are characters repeated on the line preceding the tab stop. Common tab leader characters include dots, lines, dashes, and bullets.

Set tabs by selecting the type of tab stop in the tab stop box near the ruler and then clicking on the horizontal ruler or the Indents/Tabs ruler to position the tab, or by using the Tabs dialog box.

You can usually change one type of tab to another by double-clicking the tab to display a dialog box where you can select the new tab type. Move a tab if necessary by simply dragging it on the ruler. To delete a tab, drag it off the ruler or use a dialog box to delete it.

STEP-BY-STEP 2.9

1. In the **Meeting2** file, position the insertion point to the right of the colon after the word *Date:* in the last text box on the page.

2. Set a left tab stop at 1.25 inches on the horizontal ruler or on your program's Indents/Tabs ruler. You can set the tab stop by clicking on the ruler or, in some programs, by using the Tabs dialog box.

3. Press **Tab**, key **Saturday, March 22**, and then press **Enter**. (You may need to close the Indents/Tabs ruler before you can begin working with the text.)

4. Key **Time:**, press **Tab**, and key **10:00 a.m.**

tracking
the line
specify t
top, bott
the text

Set Ch

The
You can
ing. Ker
word. Un
kerning

Track
box, or y
on a co
Format
Spacing.
the menu
may hav
ter form
as a perc
program
which d
spacing.
acters by
spacing
automati
ters whe

S **T**

1.

2.

3.

4.

5.

5. Press **Enter**, key **Location:**, press **Tab**, and key **Midtown Hotel**. The text box should look similar to the one in Figure 2-12.

FIGURE 2-12
Align text using tabs

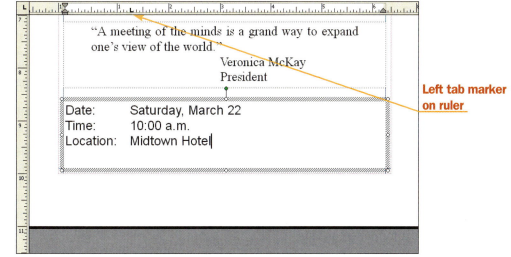

Left tab marker on ruler

6. Save changes and leave the **Meeting2** file open to use in the next exercise.

Create Lists

To create a list, you simply apply a list format or style to the current paragraph or to selected paragraphs. Most lists are formatted automatically using a hanging indent, but in some programs, such as Adobe PageMaker, you must adjust the indents manually on the Indents/Tabs ruler. Usually, the formatting is carried forward when you press Enter. You can also select the list format before you key new text.

Most programs include a set of built-in bullet styles that you can quickly apply to lists. Click the Bullets button on the toolbar to apply the default bullet style or the most recently used bullet style to the current paragraph, or select the bullet size and other options in a dialog box. In some programs, you must specify how many paragraphs you want formatted as part of the list.

Likewise, most programs include built-in number formats. Click the Numbering button on the toolbar to quickly apply the default number style or the most recently used number style to the current paragraph. Options for customizing the *separator character* and indent are usually found in a dialog box.

Set Line and Paragraph Spacing

Line spacing, or leading (pronounced to rhyme with *wedding*), is important because if there is too much or too little space between lines, the reader's eye has trouble following from one line to the next. In general, you want the space between lines to be greater than the space between words, but some situations, such as short lines of text, call for tighter leading.

In most programs, you can set the leading in a Line Spacing dialog box or using the Leading menu accessed from the Type menu. To open the Line Spacing dialog box, click Format on the menu bar and then click Line Spacing. You can usually use either lines or points as the unit of measure. If you use lines and then change the font size, the line spacing adjusts automatically. If you use points, the line spacing remains constant, no matter what font size you apply.

Paragraph spacing helps break content into chunks that are easier to locate and read than one long continuous stream of text. You usually set the amount of space to leave before and after the current paragraph in points.

You should set paragraph and line spacing instead of pressing Enter to insert extra lines. Setting spacing options gives you greater control over the appearance of your publication and makes editing and rearranging text much easier. Both paragraph spacing and line spacing can be applied to the current paragraph, to selected paragraphs, or to new paragraphs before you key the text. The formatting is carried forward to the next paragraph when you press Enter. Line and paragraph spacing options are usually available in a dialog box or in a control palette.

> **Note**
>
> If you set space lines too close together, *ascenders*, which are the parts of characters that extend above the rest of the text, may run into the text in the line above, and *descenders*, which are the parts of characters that extend below the baseline, may run into the text in the line below.

> **Note**
>
> Display special characters to show nonprinting paragraph marks at the end of each paragraph in your document. To display special characters, click the Special Characters button on the toolbar, or select the appropriate command from the View menu.

> **Note**
>
> Instead of trying to fit many paragraphs into one text box, you can break the text up into multiple text boxes. Using multiple text boxes gives you more flexibility in terms of position, size, alignment, and other options.

S TEP-BY-STEP 2.12

1. In the **Meeting2** file, select all of the text in the text box containing the quotation.

2. Using the appropriate dialog box or menu, set the leading or line spacing to 18 points. You may have to type the unit of measure (such as *pt*, which is the abbreviation for point) in order to switch from lines to points. Setting the spacing to 18 points decreases the amount of space between lines.

3. Deselect the text and then position the insertion point anywhere within the quotation.

STEP-BY-STEP 2.12 Continued

4. Set the spacing before the paragraph to 3 points and the spacing after the paragraph to 6 points. You may have to type a unit of measure in a Control palette box such as p3 or p6 to set the spacing in points. When you are finished, the text box should look similar to the one in Figure 2-14.

FIGURE 2-14
Adjusted line and paragraph spacing

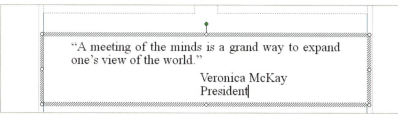

5. Save changes and leave the **Meeting2** file open to use in the next exercise.

Set Margins in a Text Box

To control the amount of space between text and the text box border, set the text box margins, which are sometimes called the *frame inset*. Your program probably has a narrow default text box margin size, such as 0.04 inch. You can increase a margin by increasing the width, or decrease a margin by decreasing the width. Each margin can be set independently of the other margins. In most programs, the text box margins are set in a dialog box. You can set the margins for one text box or for selected text boxes at the same time.

STEP-BY-STEP 2.13

1. In the **Meeting2** file, select the two text boxes containing the lists. To select both boxes at the same time, select one, press and hold Shift, and then select the other.

2. Open the dialog box in which you can set text box margins. For example, click **Format** on the menu bar, click **Text Box**, and then click the **Text Box** tab.

3. Set the left, right, top, and bottom margins to 0.1 inch, and then click the **OK** button in the dialog box. The margins in the text boxes increase, as shown in Figure 2-15.

FIGURE 2-15
Increase text box margins

4. Save changes and leave the **Meeting2** file open to use in the next exercise.

Copy, Move, and Import Text

To save yourself the trouble of rekeying, you can easily copy, move, or import text into a desktop publishing document. The Copy, Cut, and Paste commands are used in all Windows programs to copy and move text as well as objects from one location to another. The copied or cut items are stored temporarily on the *Clipboard*, which is a temporary storage area in your computer's memory. When you select the Paste command, the item is inserted at the current location. A cut item is removed from the original location, while a copied item remains in both the original and new locations. Cut, Copy, and Paste commands are available as toolbar buttons or on the Edit menu.

> **Note** ☑
>
> In some programs, if you include the paragraph mark at the end of a paragraph when you copy or move text, you include the paragraph formatting, too.

Using the Clipboard, you can copy or move selected text within a text box or from one text box to another. You can also copy or move an entire text box and its contents. You can even copy and move text from one document to another, even if the documents are different types. For example, you can copy a chart from a spreadsheet into a publication document, or a paragraph from a word processing document into a text box in a publication.

When you want to import an entire text file into your desktop publishing document, you use the Insert Text File command or the File Place command. Locate and select the file you want to insert, and then click OK. Depending on your program, you may be able to insert text-only files, or you may be able to import and preserve text that has been formatted in a word processing document. When you insert a file, all of the file is inserted into a text box.

> **Extra for Experts** 📊
>
> Some programs let you use the Import command to import a word processing or other type of file. When you use the Import command, the file is converted to a new desktop publishing document.

When copying or importing text, you may find that the text box or frame is not large enough to hold all text. If a text box cannot show all text, it usually displays a symbol near the bottom, such as A… or a red triangle in the bottom handle of the frame. If you see such a symbol, adjust the size of the text box or frame until it disappears to make sure you have all text showing.

STEP-BY-STEP 2.14

1. In the **Meeting2** file, select the text *Guest speaker: Ms. Catherine Huang* in the bullet list. Try not to include the paragraph mark at the end of the line. You want to copy this text into the headline text box at the top of the page.

2. Use the **Copy** button or command to copy the text to the Clipboard. Position the insertion point at the end of the headline text in the text box at the top of the page, and press **Enter** to start a new paragraph.

3. Use the **Paste** button or command to paste the text at the insertion point location. If you copied the paragraph mark, too, the line will retain its bullet list formatting. Simply click the **Bullets** button on the toolbar to remove the bullet. You may also need to center the text horizontally.

STEP-BY-STEP 2.14 Continued

4. Click the **Text Box** or rectangular frame tool on the toolbar and insert a new text box between the headline text box and the text boxes containing the lists. Size the box to fill the open area—about 6.3 inches by 1.2 inches.

5. Select all the text in the quotation text box, including the speaker's name and title. Use the **Cut** button or command to cut the selection to the Clipboard. Then click in the new text box and use the **Paste** button or command. The text moves to the new text box. If a dialog box is displayed asking if you want to use AutoFlow, click No to continue. Don't worry if some of the text is hidden. You can adjust the size of the box later. The top part of your document should look similar to Figure 2-16.

FIGURE 2-16
Copy and move text in a document

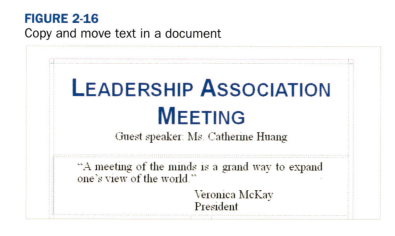

6. Position the insertion point in the text box where the quotation originally appeared. This box should be empty now.

7. Select the command to insert a text file. For example, click **Insert** on the menu bar, and then click **Text File**. Locate and select **DP Step 2-14** from the data files, and then click **OK**. The text is inserted into the empty text box. If you are using Adobe PageMaker, first select the empty frame, then click **File**, click **Place**, and locate and open the data file.

8. Select the inserted text and change the font to **Arial**.

9. If your program has a copy fitting option, select the command to automatically size the text to fit in the text box. If not, set the font size to **14** points.

10. Set the left and right indents to **0.25** inches.

11. Justify the horizontal alignment.

STEP-BY-STEP 2.14 Continued

12. Display the document in Print Preview, if that option is available, or change the zoom to display the entire page. It should look similar to Figure 2-17. If some of the text is hidden, adjust the size and position of the text boxes until all text is displayed.

FIGURE 2-17
Completed publication

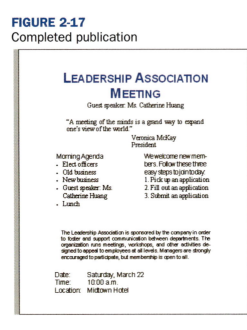

13. Print one copy of the file. Close the Print Preview window if necessary.

14. Save changes and close the **Meeting2** file. Leave your desktop publishing program open to use in the next exercise.

> **Note**
>
> In some programs, such as PageMaker, you cannot insert columns in a text box. Instead, use text blocks to constrain text to the width of a column on the page.

Control Text Flow

In some desktop publishing programs, you can control the way text flows within a text box by dividing the text box into newsletter-style columns. In newsletter-style columns, text flows from the bottom of a column to the top of the next column to the right. With newsletter-style columns, the columns are fixed within the size and position of the text box, so you do not have a great deal of flexibility when it comes to arranging the text in the publication.

To provide more flexibility, some programs let you connect text boxes so text that does not fit in the first text box automatically flows into the next connected text box. When you use connected text boxes, you can size and position each text box independently. You can even connect text boxes on different pages.

> **Extra for Experts**
>
> Most desktop publishing programs have features for controlling hyphenation and the way words break from one line to the next. You can usually use options in the Hyphenation or Type dialog box to insert *discretionary* and *manual hyphens*, change the width of the *hyphenation zone*, and turn automatic hyphenation off or on. You can also insert *em dashes* rather than double hyphens for punctuation, and *en dashes* in place of the words to or through.

Divide a Text Box into Columns

If your program offers a feature for dividing a text box into columns, you use a columns dialog box usually accessed by clicking a button in the Format Text Box dialog box. Key the number of columns you want to apply, and then specify the amount of space to leave between columns. When you type in the text box, text is entered in the left-most column. When you reach the bottom of the left-most column, the text automatically wraps to the top of the next column to the right.

If your program does not have a feature for dividing text boxes into columns, save the data file as instructed in the exercise below and then go on to the next section.

S TEP-BY-STEP 2.15

1. In your desktop publishing program, open **DP Step 2-15** from the data files.

2. Save the file as **Reminder**.

3. Increase the zoom to at least 75%, and then select the second text box from the top.

4. Open the Columns dialog box. For example, click **Format** on the menu bar, click **Text Box**, click the **Text Box** tab, and then click the **Columns** button.

5. Key **2** in the Columns box and key **0.25** in the Spacing box. Click the **OK** button in the Columns dialog box, and then click the **OK** button in the Format Text Box dialog box. The text box is formatted into two newsletter-style columns, with 0.25 inches of space between the columns.

> ### Extra for Experts
>
> Some desktop publishing programs have Paragraph Specifications commands for keeping paragraphs and lines together on a page or in a column. Options include keeping lines together, keeping a paragraph with the next paragraph, and controlling widows and orphans—words or short lines of text displayed at the top or bottom of a column or page.

6. Save changes and leave the **Reminder** file open to use in the next exercise.

Connect Text Boxes

In most programs, you connect text boxes by selecting the first text box, clicking a linking tool such as Create Text Box Link, and then clicking the next text box to connect. Or you may be able to simply click the bottom *windowshade* handle of one frame and then click in the next frame with the link pointer. The box to connect must be blank, but the first box may contain text. Repeat the procedure to connect additional boxes. The text will flow from one box to the next in the order in which you connect the boxes. To break the link connecting boxes, click in the box and then use a tool such as Break Forward Link.

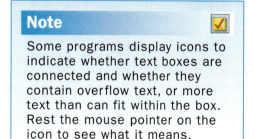

> ### Note
>
> Some programs display icons to indicate whether text boxes are connected and whether they contain overflow text, or more text than can fit within the box. Rest the mouse pointer on the icon to see what it means.

If your program does not offer support for connected text boxes, skip the following exercise, close your program, and continue with the Lesson Review.

STEP-BY-STEP 2.16

1. In the **Reminder** file, click in the text box containing the text *Register now or you'll miss the following.*

2. Display the Connect Frames toolbar or the toolbar in your program that has the buttons for connecting text boxes, and then click the **Create Text Box Link** button. If you are using Adobe PageMaker, click in the bottom windowshade handle.

3. Click the next blank text box. The two boxes are now connected.

4. Click back in the previous text box and position the insertion point at the end of the text *Register now or you'll miss the following:*, and press **Enter** to start a new line. Notice that the insertion point jumps to the connected text box.

5. Key the following lines:

   Guest speaker Catherine Huang

   Election of officers

   Lunch

6. Press **Enter**, and key **Call 555-5555 to register now!** Notice that the last line does not fit in the text box.

7. Link the current text box to the next blank text box. The overflow text displays in the newly connected box.

8. Select the text box that contains the text entered in step 5, and increase the width slightly so that the name Catherine is not hyphenated.

9. Display the document in Print Preview. It should look similar to Figure 2-18.

FIGURE 2-18
Completed document

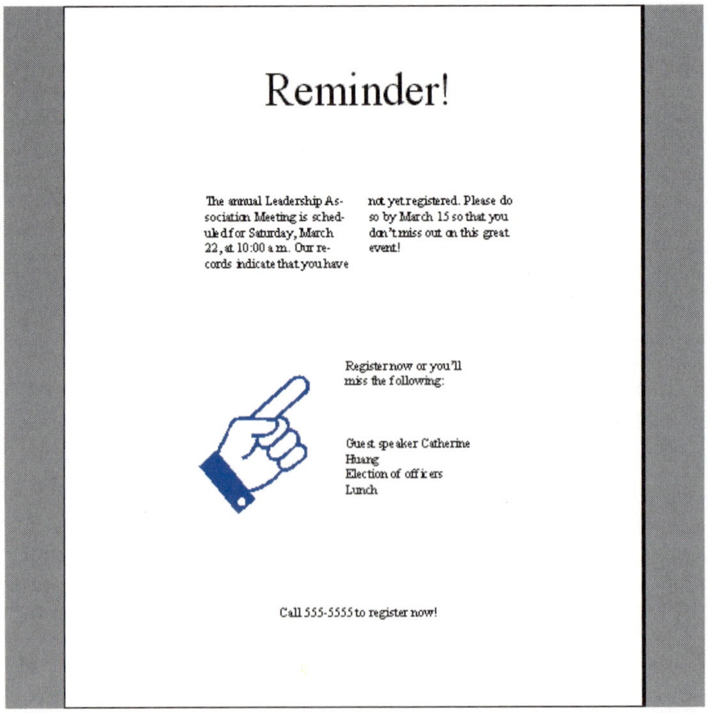

STEP-BY-STEP 2.16 Continued

10. Print one copy of the document.

11. Save changes and close the **Reminder** file. Close your desktop publishing program. You have completed the exercises in this lesson.

SUMMARY

In this lesson, you learned:

- When you want to create a publication from scratch, create a blank publication.
- You can create new text boxes at any time, and delete text boxes you no longer need.
- Apply font formatting to enhance the appearance of a publication and make the text easier to read.
- Horizontal alignment controls the position of text relative to the left and right text box margins, and vertical alignment controls the position of text relative to the top and bottom text box margins.
- Set indents to create temporary margins for a paragraph in a text box.
- Set tabs to position text along a single line.
- Lists are an effective way to communicate important points of information. Use bullet lists when order doesn't matter, and use numbered lists when order matters.
- You can change the spacing between characters, lines, and paragraphs to make your text easier to read and to control the amount of white space in a document.
- The Clipboard is the easiest way to copy and move text and objects, but you can also insert an entire text file into a text box.
- You can control text flow by creating columns within a text box or, in some programs, connecting text boxes.

VOCABULARY *Review*

Define the following terms:

Clipboard	Indents	Sans serif font
Color scheme	Insertion Point	Serif font
Font	Kerning	Tabs
Font effects	Leading	Tracking
Font size	Margins	Vertical alignment
Font style	Points	White space
Horizontal alignment		

REVIEW *Questions*

TRUE / FALSE

Circle T if the statement is true or F if the statement is false.

T   F   **1.** Set a left tab when you want to align all of the text in a text box with the left margin.

T   F   **2.** The default font is always 12-point Arial.

T   F   **3.** Use tracking to control the spacing between all characters in a selection.

T   F   **4.** Use kerning to control the spacing between pairs of characters.

T   F   **5.** Use a quotation or double indent to indent a paragraph from both the left and right margins.

T   F   **6.** Font size is usually measured in inches.

T   F   **7.** Keyed text is inserted to the right of the insertion point

T   F   **8.** Drag a corner handle to resize the height and width of a text box at the same time.

T   F   **9.** Use a numbered list when the order of items in the list doesn't matter.

T   F   **10.** Connect text boxes to place the overflow from one text box into the next text box.

WRITTEN QUESTIONS

Write a brief answer to the following questions.

1. How many fonts should you use in a publication?

2. What are some reasons for creating a blank publication instead of using a publication design or template?

3. What is the difference between kerning and leading?

4. What are the four types of horizontal alignment?

5. List at least three instances when you could use lists in a publication.

FILL IN THE BLANK

Complete the following sentences by writing the correct word or words in the blanks provided.

1. In some desktop publishing programs, you can control the way text flows within a text box by dividing the text box into _____ .

2. Items that are cut or copied are stored in the _____ until you paste them in a new location.

3. You can control the amount of white space between text and the text box border by changing the text box _____ .

4. The amount of space allotted for the width of each character is determined by the _____ set.

5. Font size is measured in _____ .

6. Lists are usually formatted using a(n) _____ indent.

7. Tab _____ are characters such as dots that are repeated on the line preceding the tab stop.

8. Font _____ are attributes applied to characters.

9. When you connect text boxes, the first box may contain text, but the box to connect must be _____ .

10. _____ fonts have short lines and curlicues at the ends of the lines that make up each character.

PROJECTS

PROJECT 2-1

1. Launch your desktop publishing program and create a new blank document with 1-inch margins.

2. Save the file as **Sale**.

3. Insert four text boxes or frames as follows:
   A. Draw one text box starting in the upper-left corner of the document, where the left and top margins meet. Size the box approximately 2 inches high and 6.5 inches wide (the width of the page from margin to margin).
   B. Start the second text box immediately below the first (with no space between the boxes), and size it to approximately 2.5 inches high and 6.5 inches wide.
   C. Repeat step B above to draw a third text box immediately below the second.
   D. Draw the fourth text box immediately below the third, sizing it to fill the remaining area at the bottom of the document—approximately 2 inches high by 6.5 inches wide.
   E. If you are using Adobe PageMaker, change the margins of each frame to 0.05 on all sides and set the stroke for each frame to None.

4. Click in the first text box at the top of the page, and key and format text as follows:
   A. Select a sans serif font such as Gill Sans MT in 48 points and key **Hip Hop Music**.
   B. Press **Enter**, change the font size to **36**, and key **Grand Opening Sale**.
   C. Center the text horizontally and vertically in the text box.
   D. Select the text in the text box and apply the Small caps font effect.

5. Click in the next text box down, and key and format text as follows:
   A. Using the same sans serif font you used in step 4, in 26-point font size, key the text **Join in the Excitement**, and then press **Enter** to start a new line.
   B. Change to a serif font such as Georgia in 18 points and set a left indent of 2 inches.
   C. Key the following five lines of text, pressing **Enter** after each line:
      Contests
      Food
      Live music
      Giveaways
      Special guests
   D. Select all five lines and apply bullet list formatting. (In some programs you may want to adjust the space between the bullet and the text.).
   E. Center the first line of text in the text box, then select it and apply bold, italics, and an underline.
   F. Set the paragraph spacing to leave 12 points of space after the selected paragraph.
   G. Select the *E* and the *x* in the word *Excitement* and expand the kerning to add space, then select the *x* and the *c* and collapse the kerning to remove space.

6. Click in the third text box, and key and format text as follows:
   A. Using the same sans serif font you used in step 4, in 26-point font size, key the text **Enter to Win**, and then press **Enter** to start a new line.
   B. Change to a serif font such as Georgia in 18 points. Set a left indent of 1.25 inches and a right indent of 1 inch.
   C. Key the following three lines of text, pressing **Enter** after each line:
      Fill out an entry form
      Drop it off at any Hip Hop Music store
      Wait for the call announcing you're the winner!
   D. Select all lines but the first and apply number list formatting. You may need to adjust the hanging indent in PageMaker.
   E. Center the first line of text in the text box, then select it and apply bold, italics, and an underline.
   F. Set the paragraph spacing to leave 12 points of space after the selected paragraph.

7. Click in the last text box, and key and format text as follows:
   A. Set a left indent at 1.5 inches.
   B. Using the same serif font you used earlier, in 18-point font size, key the text **Hip Hop Music** and then press **Enter**.
   C. Change the font size to **16** points, and then key **5151 South City Turnpike**. Press **Enter**, key **West Hill, NH 03300**, and then press **Enter** to start a new line.
   D. Remove the left indent (set the indent to 0), and then set a left tab stop at 2.5 inches on the horizontal ruler.
   E. Change the font size to **14** points and key the text **Monday – Saturday**. Press **Tab** and key the text **10:00 a.m. until 9:00 p.m.** Press **Enter** to start a new line.
   F. Key the text **Sundays,** press **Tab**, and key the text **12:00 p.m. until 9:00 p.m.** Press **Enter** to start a new line.
   G. Delete the left tab stop and set a right tab stop at 5.7 inches on the horizontal ruler. Key the text **For information contact**, press **Tab**, and key **Jay Hewitt, Store Manager**. Press **Enter** to start a new line.
   H. Press **Tab** and key **555-555-5433**.
   I. Click anywhere on the line with the city, state, and ZIP code, and set spacing to leave 6 points of space after the current paragraph.
   J. Set the vertical alignment in the text box to bottom.

8. Check the spelling in the document and make corrections as necessary. If necessary, adjust text box size and position to display all text.

9. Print one copy of the document.

10. Save changes and close the **Sale** file, but leave your desktop publishing program open to use in Project 2-2.

PROJECT 2-2

1. In your desktop publishing program, create a new blank full-page document with 1-inch margins.

2. Save the file as **Invite**.

3. Insert a text box the full size of page 1.

4. Select a decorative font, such as Comic Sans MS in 36 points, change the font color to blue, set the horizontal alignment to center, and key the text **Hip Hop Music is having a Grand Opening Sale!**

5. Press **Enter** to start a new line, change the font color to black, the font size to 26 points, and key the following lines of text. (Press **Enter** at the end of each line.)

   You're Invited!
   Friday April 10
   4:30 p.m.

6. On a new line, change the font size to 20 points and key the following lines:

   5151 South City Turnpike
   West Hill, NH 03300

7. Select all text in the document and, if necessary, set the horizontal alignment to center, and set the line spacing to leave 6 points of space before and after each paragraph.

8. Start a new line, and then insert **DP Project 2-2** from the data files into the text box.

9. Select the newly inserted text and change the font to a casual script, such as Freestyle Script in 24 points, and justify the alignment.

10. Set line spacing to leave 36 points of space before the paragraph.

11. Check the spelling in the document and then print it. Fold the printed page into an invitation.

12. Save changes and close the **Invite** file. Close your desktop publishing program.

WEB PROJECT

For a project on China, use the Internet to research the Chinese alphabet. See if you can find information about different characters and what they mean, and which are considered lucky or unlucky. Then see if you can find a Chinese character font that you can download for free to use in a publication. For example, you may design a poster or banner using the Chinese characters. If you have trouble locating a Chinese character font, see if you can find an English-language font that is designed to simulate Chinese characters.

TEAMWORK PROJECT

As a group, plan and design a publication announcing an upcoming event at your school or in your community. For example, you may want to create a flyer, banner, or poster to announce a concert or play, a sporting event, a parade, or a meeting. You can work together on each stage of creating the flyer, or you can assign tasks.

Write the text you want on the flyer, and then create a mock-up of the flyer so you can determine the page size and how you want the text positioned on the page. For example, determine whether all the text should be in one text box, or if you should split it into multiple text boxes, and then indicate spacing and alignment on the mock-up as well. Decide which text should be large and which should be smaller, and discuss the types of fonts you want to use. You can use your desktop publishing program to test different fonts, font sizes, and font effects. Try to find a combination of two or three fonts that you think work well together, and print sample text to see how they look when printed. Finally, create the flyer document.

You can start with a blank document, or use a template or design that matches your mock-up. Apply font formatting, spacing, and alignment to make the flyer look appealing and be easy to read. When you are finished, check the spelling and then print the flyer.

CRITICAL *Thinking*

ACTIVITY 2-1

Use your desktop publishing program to create a business card for yourself. Create a mock-up so you can size and position all the information you want to include. You can use your actual information, or make up a job you would like to have. Include at least your name, address, phone number, and e-mail address. When you are ready, start with a blank document, or use one of your program's templates or designs. Use text boxes to position the text the way you planned on the mock-up. Use two fonts, and any colors, styles, and effects that you think enhance the card. Try different alignments and spacing. When you are finished, check the spelling and print one copy. If you are happy with the result, you can purchase blank cards and print additional copies.

FORMATTING PAGES

VOCABULARY

Binding

Color scheme

Facing pages

Field

Font scheme

Footer

Gutter

Header

Layout guides

Master page

Mirrored pages

Page layout

Paper size

Style

Two-page spread

Good page formatting uses the basic principles of design, including *contrast*, *balance*, and *consistency*, to capture a reader's attention. Your desktop publishing program has many tools to help you use these principles when you format your publication. When you create a document using a template or design, your desktop publishing program automatically applies page formatting options suitable for the publication type. The formatting includes a *page layout* that controls settings such as page size, margin width, the number of pages in the publication, and the page orientation. You can also format pages on your own by selecting options manually. For example, you may set a custom page size for a brochure, change the orientation for a booklet, or add pages to a catalog. That way, you can customize built-in designs, and you can create your own designs from scratch. You can even save your own designs as a template for creating future documents. In this lesson, you learn how to format pages by applying layouts and other options.

Set up Pages

Page setup options usually include the *page size*, *margins*, and *page orientation*. As you learned in earlier lessons, the page size is the height and width of the printed page, the margins are the space between the edges of the page and the content, and the page orientation is the position of the paper in relation to the content. You may also be able to set other options, such as the *paper size*, which is the size of the actual sheet of paper on which the publication is printed. Paper size is sometimes called the sheet size.

Margins are usually set for the top, bottom, left, and right of a page. If you are going to bind or fold a publication, you need to leave extra space along the inside page edges, or *gutter*—usually, the left edge of right-hand or odd-numbered pages, and the right edge of left-hand, or even-numbered pages. *Binding* is the way pages or sections of a book or booklet are secured together using stitching, staples, or glue. Sometimes, depending on the program and publication type, the left and right margin settings are actually called inside and outside margins. "Inside" refers to the edge that may be bound or folded, and "outside" refers to the edge opposite the binding or fold.

In all desktop publishing programs, you can change these settings manually. In some programs, you can select built-in options in a task pane or dialog box to automatically apply the changes.

Change Page Setup Options Manually

Often, page setup options depend on the publication type and are set automatically when you select a template or design, or when you select the publication type in a Document Setup or Page Setup dialog box similar to the one in Figure 3-1. The Document Setup dialog box in your program may also have options for setting the number of pages in the publication, specifying *double-sided printing*, and creating a *two-page spread*. A two-page spread consists of two *facing pages* that are sometimes called *mirrored pages* because their layout and margins are not identical, but reversed.

> **Note** ☑️
>
> If the margin settings are not in the Page Setup dialog box, you set them by adjusting the margin guides. Working with guides is covered in the next exercise.

FIGURE 3-1
Page Setup dialog box

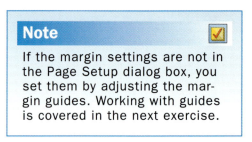

S TEP-BY-STEP 3.1

1. Launch your desktop publishing program, and if necessary click the **New** button on the toolbar to create a new document. If the Document Setup dialog box opens, skip step 2. (If the Template dialog box opens, close it.)

2. Click **File** on the menu bar, and then click **Page Setup** or a similar option, such as or **Document Setup** to open the appropriate dialog box.

3. Set the orientation to Landscape, or Wide.

4. Click **Custom** in the publication type or page size list and then set the page size dimensions to 7 inches wide by 5 inches high.

5. If the margin settings are in the dialog box, set them to 1 inch on all sides, and clear all other options. Don't worry if there are no margin setting options in the dialog box. You learn how to set margins using guides later in this lesson.

6. Click the **OK** button in the dialog box. The publication should look similar to the one in Figure 3-2.

FIGURE 3-2
Custom page size

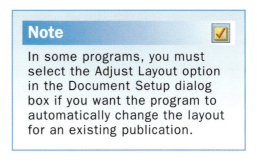

7. Save the file as **Notice**.

8. Open the Page Setup or Document Setup dialog box again.

9. Click **Postcard** in the Publication type list, and then click ¼ **page Letter** in the Page size list. Alternatively, set the custom page size to 5.5 inches wide by 4.25 inches high.

10. Click the **OK** button. The changes are applied to the document layout.

11. Save changes and leave the **Notice** file open to use in the next exercise.

> **Note** ✅
>
> In some programs, you must select the Adjust Layout option in the Document Setup dialog box if you want the program to automatically change the layout for an existing publication.

Apply Built-In Options

In some programs, you can apply built-in options to change the appearance of pages. The options are usually displayed in the task pane. They change depending on the current publication type, and sometimes even depending on the current page. To apply a built-in option, open the task pane and select the type of option you want to change, or select the type of option directly from the Format menu. Then, click the option to apply it. Again, the available options depend on the type of publication you are working on and possibly, even the current publication page.

For example, if you want to include a customer address on the back of a catalog publication, click Catalog Options in the task pane or on the Format menu. Then, click Include in the customer address section. Your program automatically changes the layout and design of the back page of the catalog to include the address. To remove the address, click None. To change a catalog page from two columns of all text to one column with graphics, click Page Content in the task pane or on the Format menu, make the page you're planning to modify active, and then click the option to apply it.

Not all programs offer built-in options. For example, Adobe PageMaker does not. If your program does not, skip this exercise, close the Notice file, but leave your desktop publishing program open to use in the following exercise.

STEP-BY-STEP 3.2

1. In the **Notice** file, click **Format** on the menu bar, and then click **Quick Publication Options**.

2. In the task pane, click the **No picture** layout. It may be the second choice from the bottom in the middle row. Rest your mouse pointer on each layout option to display a description of it.

3. Click the **No heading** layout in the task pane. The publication changes to reflect the selection.

4. Close the task pane. The file should look similar to the one in Figure 3-3.

FIGURE 3-3
Apply a built-in layout option

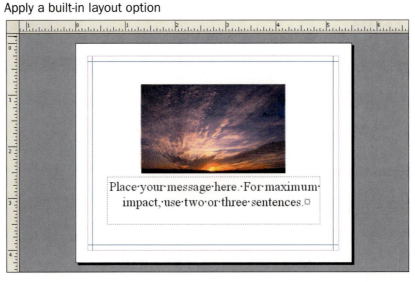

Place·your·message·here.·For·maximum·
impact,·use·two·or·three·sentences.

5. Save changes and close the **Notice** file. Leave your desktop publishing program open to use in the next exercise.

Set Guides

Page layout, or the way you organize and arrange objects and white space on a page, significantly affects the overall impact of a publication. Page layout involves the use of alignment, size, and position to lead the reader's eye across the page and makes it easy for the reader to locate and absorb information. All desktop publishing programs have *layout guides* or non-printing gridlines that can be displayed on the screen while you work to help you position and align objects.

Different programs use different terms to identify guides. Your program may use column guides or grid guides to define columns and rows; margin guides to define the top, bottom, left, and right margins; and ruler guides to define any point along the vertical or horizontal ruler. Usually, each type of guide is displayed in a different color so you know differentiate them. In most programs, you set column, grid, and margin guides for the entire publication, but you can set ruler guides on any page. In the next section, you learn about creating guides on master pages to make sure they are consistent on every page. Figure 3-4 shows different guides in a desktop publishing document.

> **Note** ☑
>
> If you select a layout option that has more or fewer pages than the current publication, your program displays a dialog box asking you to confirm the insertion or deletion of additional pages. Click Yes to apply the option and continue.

> **Note** ☑
>
> In programs that have text blocks as well as text frames, you must use text frames if you want to overlap defined columns. Text blocks are constrained within the column borders.

FIGURE 3-4
Color-coded guides in a blank publication

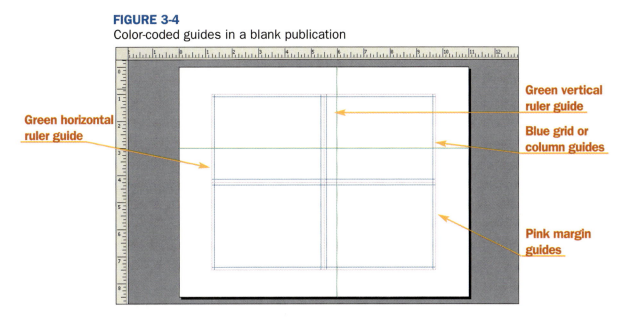

Green horizontal ruler guide

Green vertical ruler guide

Blue grid or column guides

Pink margin guides

To set guides, you usually use a dialog box such as Column Guides or Layout Guides, shown in Figure 3-5. In some programs, you set margins in the Document Setup dialog box, as you learned earlier. Some guides you toggle on or off using a menu, and then move them into the desired position by pressing Shift and dragging the line with the mouse. To remove a guide, change the settings or select a menu command to clear the guides.

> **Hot Tip**
>
> In some programs, you insert ruler guides simply by clicking or Shift-clicking on the ruler and then dragging the guide into to the document window.

FIGURE 3-5
Layout Guides dialog box

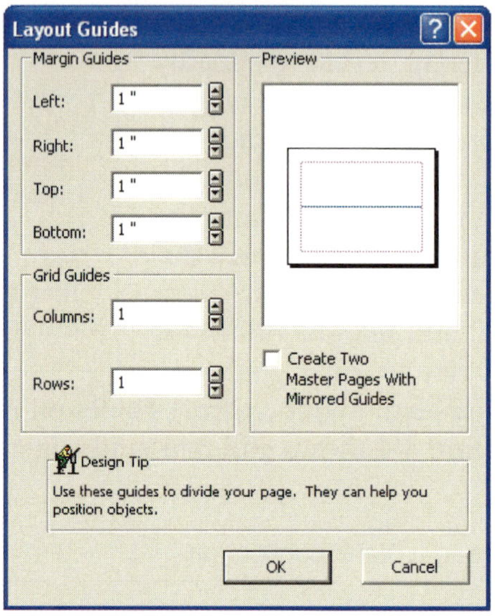

STEP-BY-STEP 3.3

1. In your desktop publishing program, click the **New** button and create a new blank 8.5-inch by 11-inch single-page document. If you are using a program that prompts you for document setup options, clear the **Facing pages** and **Double-sided** options.

2. Save the file as **Safety**.

3. Select the command to open the dialog box for setting margin guides. For example, click **Arrange** on the menu bar, and then click **Layout Guides**.

4. In the margins section, key **1.25** in the Left (Inside), Right (Outside), Top, and Bottom boxes and then click the **OK** button. This sets the margin guides to 1.25 inches from the edge of the page on all sides.

5. Select the command to open the dialog box for setting grid or column guides. This may be the same dialog box that you used in step 3, or you may have to click **Layout** on the menu bar and then click **Column Guides**. Key **2** in the Columns box, and then click the **OK** button.

> **Note**
>
> If guides are not displayed on your screen, you may have selected the command to toggle them off. Click View on the menu bar, and then click the command to show guides.

STEP-BY-STEP 3.3 Continued

6. Select the command to display a horizontal ruler guide, or press and hold **Shift** and then click and drag a guide off the horizontal ruler. If necessary, zoom in to at least 66% to get a closer look at the page.

7. Move the horizontal ruler guide so it is 3 inches below the top of the page. Depending on your program, either drag or Shift-drag the guide to move it. The pointer might change to a double-headed arrow and include the word *Adjust*.

8. Insert a text box or text frame between the top margin and the horizontal ruler guide, sized to the width of the page. If you are using Adobe PageMaker, set the stroke for the frame to None and change the frame margins to 0.05 inches on all sides. Select a sans serif font such as Arial; set the font size to 48; apply boldface; and set the horizontal alignment to center.

9. Key the text **New Security Rules**. The file should look similar to the one in Figure 3-6.

FIGURE 3-6
Text added to Safety file

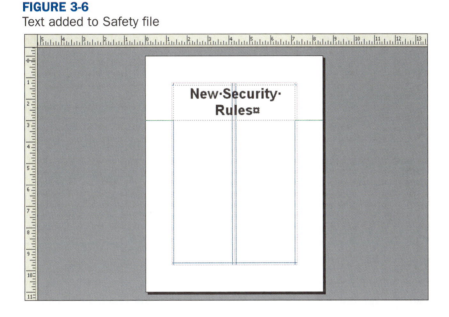

10. Save changes and leave the **Safety** file open to use in the next exercise.

> **Did You Know?**
>
> You can change the unit of measure in most desktop publishing programs to inches, centimeters, *picas*, or points.

Use Master Pages

Most desktop publishing programs include some form of *master page* to help you maintain consistency through a multipage publication, but these features may be used differently depending on your program. For example, in Microsoft Publisher, a master page is used to store objects that are repeated on every page of a publication, such as page numbers, a *watermark*, or a logo that you want in the corner of every page. In Adobe PageMaker, master pages are used like layout templates to help you maintain consistent formatting throughout a publication. They store basic page setup options as well as objects.

To understand master pages, imagine a background that displays standard and consistent elements on every page in a publication. On each page of the publication, you overlay a sheet of tracing paper. You can see through the tracing paper to the background elements, but you can insert different content on the tracing paper to customize the foreground of each page.

No matter which program you use, changes that you make to a master page affect every page formatted with that master, while changes that you make to the foreground page affect only that page. To modify a master page, you must switch to that page. Otherwise, the changes are applied to the foreground page only.

In programs that use simple master pages to store objects to be displayed on every page, you can have a single master page for an entire document. You can also have a master page spread, which creates a left page master page and a right page master page suitable for publications that have facing pages or two-page spreads, such as booklets. You create a master page spread by selecting the option in the Layout Guides dialog box. To work on master pages in these programs, simply switch to Master Page view by choosing Master Page on the View menu, and then apply the settings and objects you want on the page.

In programs that use master pages to control layout, you can have one master page (called a *document master*) for an entire publication, or you can have different master pages for different pages. In these programs, a document master is created automatically using the default document setup options when you create a new document. If you change the page setup, the changes are automatically applied to the master. You can also create additional master pages using the options in the Master Page palette. To work on a master page in these programs, select the specific master page by selecting it from a list on a shortcut menu, on the Layout menu, or in the Master Page palette. Some programs always display a Master Page icon on the horizontal scroll bar. Click the icon to switch to the master page. Other programs display the Master Page icon only when you are in Master Page view. The Master Page icons are usually in a different color from the regular page icons, and probably display an L for left or an R for right.

S TEP-BY-STEP 3.4

1. In the **Safety** file, switch to Master Page view. For example, click **View** on the menu bar and then click **Master Page,** or click the Master Page icon if it is available. Elements that you entered on the foreground page are no longer displayed, while elements on the master document, such as margin guides and, in some programs, column guides, are.

STEP-BY-STEP 3.4 Continued

2. Insert a text box or frame along the bottom margin. (Don't forget to remove the stroke, if necessary.) Select a sans serif font such as Arial, set the font size to **18**, and the horizontal alignment to **Center**. Key the text **These rules will be strictly enforced at all times.** If necessary, set the vertical alignment to bottom so the text runs across the bottom margin. The page should look similar to Figure 3-7.

FIGURE 3-7
A master page

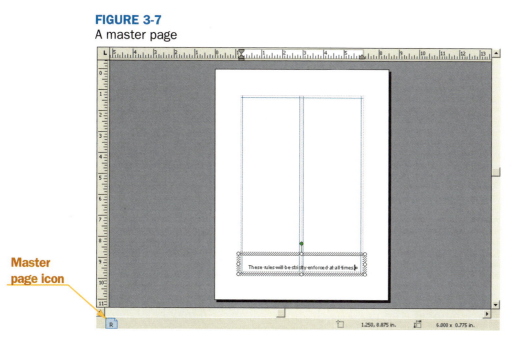

Master page icon

3. Change back to regular page view. The content on the master page and the foreground page appears.

4. Save changes and leave the **Safety** file open to use in the next exercise.

Insert Page Numbers

Page numbers are an important feature of multi-page documents. For example, page numbers in a catalog help readers locate specific items and may also be used for ordering. In most desktop publishing programs, page numbers are inserted on a master page as a *field* or marker. A field is a code instead of an actual number so the page number updates if you add, delete, or move pages within the publication. Usually, page numbers are inserted in either the page *header* or *footer*. A header displays information repeated at the top of every page in the area between the top margin and the top edge of the page, and a footer repeats information at the bottom of every page in the area between the bottom margin and the bottom edge of the page.

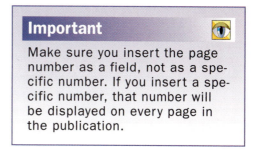

Important

Make sure you insert the page number as a field, not as a specific number. If you insert a specific number, that number will be displayed on every page in the publication.

To insert page numbers, switch to the master page and then select the Page Numbers command on the Insert menu. Most programs display a page numbers dialog box similar to the one in Figure 3-8 in which you can select options such as the location of the number on the page, the number format, and whether a number should appear on the first page.

Extra for Experts

In some programs, you change the page numbering or the page number format in the middle of a publication by creating a new master page. In other programs, you can do it by creating a *section*. Click Section on the Insert menu, then select to start a new section on the current page and set numbering options.

FIGURE 3-8
Page Numbers dialog box

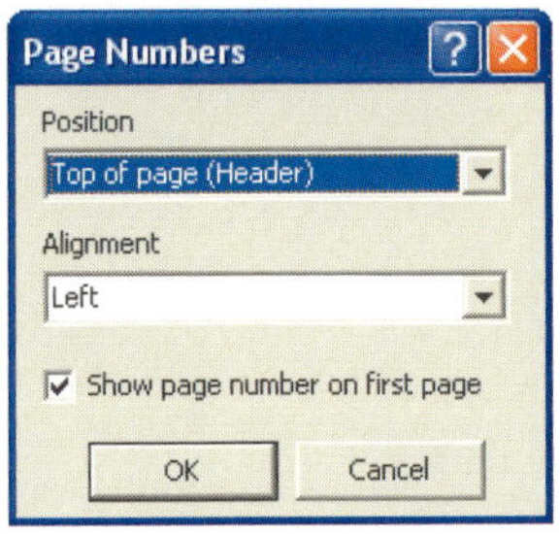

If there is no page number command on the Insert menu, you may be able to key the code for inserting page numbers directly on the page by clicking the text tool in the toolbox, clicking on the page where you want the numbers displayed, and then keying the code for your program or pressing a shortcut key combination such as Ctrl + Alt + P or Ctrl + Shift + N. Use the Document Setup dialog box to set numbering options.

You can insert any information that you want on every page into a header or footer. You can always create headers and footers manually by inserting the data in that part of the document, but some programs have commands you can use to quickly create headers and footers. To use a command to create a header or footer, select the Header and Footer command on the View menu. Key data into the text boxes, or use the toolbar buttons described in Table 3-1.

TABLE 3-1
Header/footer toolbar buttons

ICON	BUTTON NAME	CLICK TO
[#]	Insert Page Number	Insert automatically updating page numbers.
[📅]	Insert Date	Insert current date.
[🕐]	Insert Time	Insert current time.
[⊞]	Show Header/Footer	Switch between the header and footer areas.
Close	Close	Click to close the toolbar and return to the previous document view.

STEP-BY-STEP 3.5

1. In the **Safety** file, change to Master Page view.

2. Insert page numbers in the center of the footer. For example, click **Insert** on the menu bar, and then click **Page Numbers**. In the Page Numbers dialog box, select **Bottom of page (Footer)** from the Position list, and select **Center** from the Alignment list. Make sure the option to display numbers on the first page is selected, and then click the **OK** button. If you are using PageMaker, click the text tool in the toolbox, select a 10 point font size, click at the horizontal center of the page in the footer area, and then press **Ctrl + Alt + P**.

3. Zoom in on the bottom of the page to at least 100% magnification. It should look similar to Figure 3-9. Because you are in Master Page view, the code is displayed instead of the actual page number.

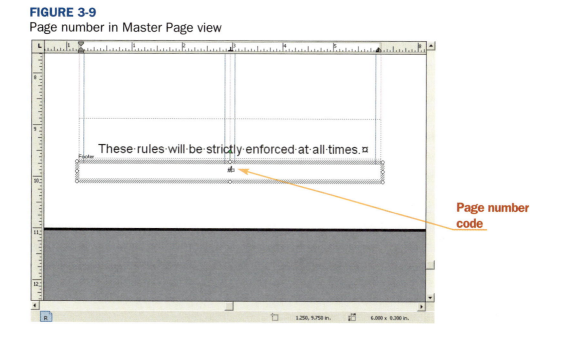

FIGURE 3-9
Page number in Master Page view

Page number code

STEP-BY-STEP 3.5 Continued

4. Change to regular page view. The footer area should look similar to Figure 3-10.

FIGURE 3-10
Page number in regular page view

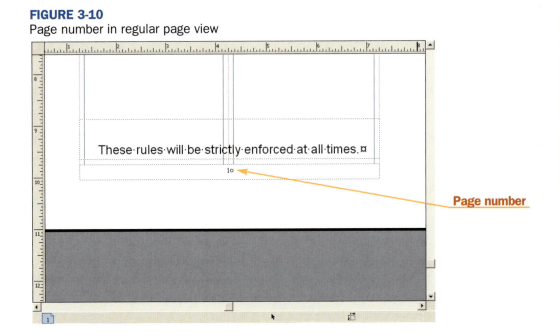

5. Change back to Master Page view.

6. Create a header with the current date left aligned. For example, click **View** on the menu bar, and then click **Header and Footer**. Click the **Date** button on the Header and Footer toolbar, and then click the **Close** button on the **Header and Footer** toolbar. If your program does not have a Header and Footer feature, simply use the text tool to key the date in the header area.

7. Change to regular page view.

8. Save changes and leave the **Safety** file open to use in the next exercise.

Insert and Delete Pages

A fundamental way to change the layout of a publication is to change the number of total pages. In most programs, you can easily insert new pages or delete pages you don't need. To insert a new page, use the Page command on the menu bar or the Insert Pages command on the Layout menu. Usually, a dialog box

> **Note** ✓
>
> Keep in mind that if you change the number of pages in a book-style publication by an odd number, it affects the layout of the entire document. For example, left-hand pages, which are usually even-numbered, may become right-hand pages, which are usually odd-numbered.

similar to the one in Figure 3-11 displays, in which you select options such as how many pages to insert, where to insert them, and whether to create content on the new page(s). In some programs, you also select the master page to apply to the new pages. To delete a page, make it active and use a command such as Delete Page on the Edit menu or Remove Pages on the Layout menu. Usually, but not always, a dialog box appears that asks you to select options or to confirm the deletion. Be careful deleting pages, because all the content on the page is deleted at the same time.

FIGURE 3-11
Insert Page dialog box

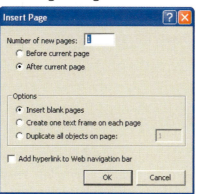

STEP-BY-STEP 3.6

1. In the **Safety** file, make sure you are in regular page view, and then select the command to insert one blank page after the current page. The new page is displayed on the screen. It should look similar to Figure 3-12. Notice that all the content you inserted on the master page is on the new page, but the content you inserted on the foreground page is not.

FIGURE 3-12
New page 2

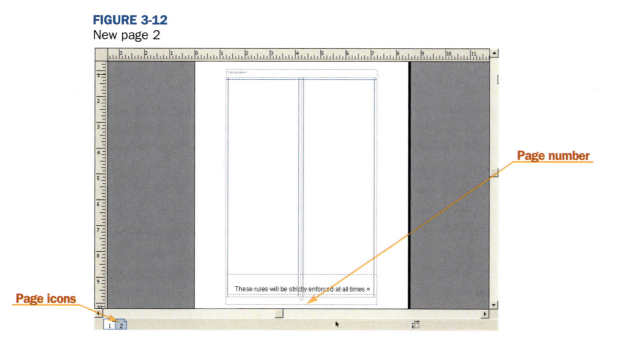

STEP-BY-STEP 3.6 Continued

2. Insert another new blank page. Now, the publication has three pages. Try deleting a page.

3. Switch to page 2, and then select the command to delete it. For example, click **Edit** on the menu bar, and then click **Delete Page**. If necessary, click the **OK** button in any confirm dialog boxes to complete the deletions.

4. Save changes and leave the **Safety** file open to use in the next exercise.

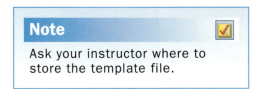

Extra for Experts

In some programs, you can reposition pages within a document by dragging the page icons. However, in many programs, the only way to move a page is to insert a new blank page, then copy and paste the content from the original page to the new blank page.

Create a Template

Once you have a publication set up just right, you can save it as a template so you can base future documents on it. Saving a publication as a template ensures that new documents are created with uniform page setup and formatting characteristics. In addition, your template can include elements that you want to be the same in every new document, such as page numbers, disclaimer text, and even a corporate logo.

Save a Publication as a Template

Save a publication as a template using the familiar Save As command. In the Save As dialog box, key a template name and select the template file type from the Save as type drop-down list. In some programs, the template file is automatically stored in the Templates folder with other publication templates. In other programs, you can store the template file in any folder.

STEP-BY-STEP 3.7

1. In the **Safety** file, click **File** on the menu bar, and then click **Save As**. The Save As dialog box opens.

2. Key **2 Page Rules** in the File name box. It is a good idea to use a name that describes the template.

3. Click **Template** or a similar option, such as **Program Name template**, from the Save as type list.

4. If necessary, select the location where you want to store the template. For example, select the location where you have been saving all your files.

Note

Ask your instructor where to store the template file.

STEP-BY-STEP 3.7 Continued

5. Click the **Save** button in the Save As dialog box. The file is saved as a template.

6. Close the **2 Page Rules** file, and leave your desktop publication program open to use in the next lesson.

Create a Publication Based on a Custom Template

There are two basic ways to create a new document based on a custom template, depending on your program. In some programs, you open the New Publication task pane or dialog box and then click *From template* to open the Open Template dialog box, which should look similar to the one in Figure 3-13. Click the template you want to use, then click the Create New button. In other programs, you click Open on the File menu to display the Open dialog box. You locate and select the template file; make sure the Copy option button is selected; and then click the Open button in the dialog box. Your program opens a copy of the template that you can save as a new file with a new name. If you click the Original option button instead of the Copy button, your program opens the original template file, which you can edit.

FIGURE 3-13
Open Template dialog box

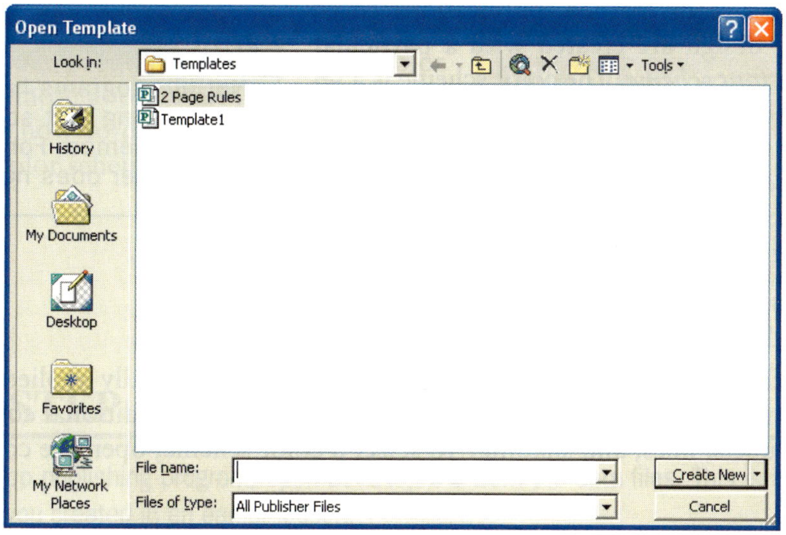

Use Styles

A *style* is a collection of formatting settings that you can apply to text and, in some programs, to objects all at once. For example, a style might include the font, the font size, the alignment, and the font effect. Most programs include a list of styles for formatting text, headings, lists, and other parts of a publication. Styles can be very useful in helping you maintain consistent formatting throughout a document, and they can save you time. To apply a style, click in the paragraph to format, or select the text to format, and then open the Styles task pane or palette. For example, click Format on the menu bar and click Styles and Formatting, or click Window on the menu bar, click Show Styles, and then click the style to apply. You can also select a style and then key new text.

> **Note** ☑️
>
> Some programs have a Style box on the Formatting toolbar. Click the drop-down arrow to display the style list, or key the style name directly in the Style box, and then press **Enter**.

STEP-BY-STEP 3.11

1. In the **Postcard2** file, open the task pane or palette that lists styles. For example, in Publisher, click **Format** on the menu bar, and then click **Styles and Formatting**. In PageMaker, click **Window** on the menu bar, and then click **Show Styles**.

2. Click anywhere in the company name text *Beans and Beyond* in the lower-right corner of the document, and then scroll through the list of styles. In some programs, such as PageMaker, you must click the text tool before you click the text. Click the first body text style in the list. It may be called Body Text or simply Body. The style is applied to the text.

3. Scroll through the list of styles and click the second organization or company name style or the Subhead 2 style. (In some programs, such as PageMaker, you may also want to apply the Subhead 2 style to the *Beans and Beyond* text at the top of the card.)

STEP-BY-STEP 3.11 Continued

4. Click in the headline *Jazz on Sunday Mornings*, and then click the second organization or company name style again, or the Headline style. The document should look similar to the one in Figure 3-18.

Note ☑

You may notice that even though the same style is used to format different text, the font sizes vary. This is because the AutoFit option is set to automatically size the text to fit in the text boxes.

FIGURE 3-18
Text formatted with styles

5. Save changes without modifying the personal information, and then print the publication.

6. Close the **Postcard2** file and your desktop publication program.

SUMMARY

In this lesson, you learned:

■ Page formatting controls the layout and organization of objects on a page.

■ The basic page setup options include page size, margins, and page orientation.

■ There are three types of guides in most desktop publishing programs: column or grid guides, margin guides, and ruler guides.

■ Guides help you arrange and position objects on a page.

- Master pages help you maintain consistency in multipage documents.

- In some programs, master pages store objects that are the same on every page, and in other programs they store page layout and formatting settings for the publication.

- You should insert page numbers on a master page.

- You can insert and delete pages at any time.

- You can save a document as a template so that you can create new documents based on it.

- Some programs have color schemes and font schemes you can quickly apply to any publication.

- Use a style to quickly apply a set of formatting characteristics to text in a publication.

VOCABULARY *Review*

Define the following terms:

Binding	Footer	Mirrored pages
Color scheme	Gutter	Page layout
Facing pages	Header	Paper size
Field	Layout guides	Style
Font scheme	Master page	Two-page spread

REVIEW *Questions*

TRUE / FALSE

Circle T if the statement is true or F if the statement is false.

T   F   **1.** Changes you make to a master page affect all pages that use that master page.

T   F   **2.** A header is the area between the top margin and the top edge of the page.

T   F   **3.** Page numbers inserted as a field are updated when pages are added or deleted.

T   F   **4.** A font scheme is a collection of formatting settings you can apply to text all at once.

T   F   **5.** Page size is the term used for the height and width of the printed page.

T   F   **6.** If you plan to bind or fold a publication, be sure to leave extra space along the outside edges of the pages.

T   F   **7.** If you don't want guides to print, you must delete them from your publication.

T   F   **8.** To save a file as a template, use the Save As command.

T   F   **9.** Use ruler guides to set up columns on a page.

T   F   **10.** To modify a master page, you must switch to Master Page view.

WRITTEN QUESTIONS

Write a brief answer to the following questions.

1. What is the primary benefit of using master pages?

2. Name one principle of design that can be applied to page layout, and then list some of the desktop publishing features that help you use that principle.

3. Why are left and right margins sometimes called inside and outside margins?

4. How many fonts are included in a typical font scheme?

5. What are some of the formatting settings frequently included in a style?

FILL IN THE BLANK

Complete the following sentences by writing the correct word or words in the blanks provided.

1. Some programs have one master page called a(n) _____ master that is used for the entire publication.

2. The _____ is the space along the inside page edges.

3. Create a two-page _____ when you want to set up facing pages.

4. Another term for sheet size is _____ size.

5. Page numbers are usually inserted as a(n) _____ or marker so they are updated if you add, delete, or move pages.

6. The area between the bottom margin and the bottom edge of the page is called the _____.

7. Save a file as a(n) _____ so you can base future documents on it.

8. A(n) font _____ is a set of coordinated fonts.

9. A(n) _____ is a collection of formatting settings that you can apply to text.

10. You can set _____ guides to define any horizontal or vertical point in a publication.

PROJECTS

PROJECT 3-1

Before beginning this project, create a mock-up of a two-sided 8.5-inch × 11-inch newsletter with two columns on both pages and a *banner headline* that extends across the top of the first page. You need space for four articles on each page, but the articles may not be of equal length.

A. Use a ruler and a pencil to draw columns on both sides of a letter-sized sheet of paper.

B. Use a ruler and a pencil to draw horizontal rules indicating the location of the banner headline on page 1 and possible divisions for positioning the four articles on each page.

1. Launch your desktop publishing program and open **DP Project 3-1** from the data files. This file contains all the content you need to create a two-sided newsletter, already formatted and divided into text boxes. However, you must size and position the text boxes to create a layout that is appealing and easy to read.

2. Save the file as **CNONews**.

3. Increase the zoom to at least 75% and take some time to examine the content. Look at both pages. Notice that some of the text boxes are overflowing with text. At least one is overlapping the margins.

4. Zoom out to show the whole page and divide both pages into two columns of equal width.

5. Make page 1 active and move all text boxes except the one at the top of the page out into the scratch area (the gray area around the outside of the page).

6. Format the page as follows:
   A. Set horizontal ruler guides at 2.25, 2.5, and 6.75 inches on the vertical ruler. You can check the position of your ruler guides using the coordinates in the status bar or Control palette.

   B. Size and position the remaining text box to fit vertically between the top margin and the first ruler guide, and horizontally across the width of the page.
   C. Size and position the text box containing the date and volume number vertically between the first and second ruler guides, and horizontally across the width of the page.
   D. Now move the second ruler guide down 0.25 inch, to the 2.75 inch mark on the vertical ruler.
   E. Size and position the text box with the headline *Annual Fundraiser* vertically between the second and third ruler guides and horizontally within the left column.
   F. Move the third ruler guide down 0.25 inch to the 7 inch mark on the vertical ruler. Size and position the text box with the headline *Volunteer News* vertically between the third ruler guide and the bottom margin, and horizontally within the left column. Notice that there is still overflow text.
   G. Insert a new blank text box or frame sized and positioned vertically between the second and third ruler guides and horizontally within the right column. If you are using Adobe PageMaker, remove the stroke from the text frame and change the frame's margins to 0.05 inches on all sides. Connect the text box at the bottom of the left column with the blank text box at the top of the right column. The overflow text should flow into the new text box. If necessary, improve the appearance of the publication by increasing the tracking in the last paragraph in the left column to force additional lines to the top of the right column.
   H. Size and position the remaining text box vertically between the third ruler guide and the bottom margin, and horizontally within the right column. Page 1 is now complete.

7. Make page 2 active and drag all of the text boxes into the scratch area.

8. Format the page as follows:
   A. Insert a horizontal ruler guide at 5 inches on the vertical ruler.
   B. Size and position the text box with the headline *Officer Nominations* to fit vertically between the top margin and the horizontal ruler guide, and horizontally within the left column.
   C. Size and position the text box with the *masthead* list of editors and officers to fit vertically between the ruler guide and the bottom margin, and horizontally within the left column.
   D. Move the ruler guide up to 2.5 inches on the vertical ruler, and then size and position the text box containing the text *Don't Forget!* to fit vertically between the top margin and the ruler guide and horizontally within the right column.
   E. Move the ruler guide down to the 2.75 inch mark on the vertical ruler, and then size and position the remaining text box within the remaining space.

9. Print both pages, either on separate sheets of paper or on a double-sided sheet.

10. Save changes and close the **CNONews** file, but leave your desktop publishing program open to use in Project 3-2.

PROJECT 3-2

Before beginning this project, create a mock-up of a side-fold card using a blank letter-sized sheet of paper:
A. Fold the sheet in half top to bottom, then in half again left to right.
B. Mark the front, back, and two inside pages, and then unfold the sheet. Note that the sheet is divided into four pages and that only one side of the sheet of paper will display content.

1. Create a new blank document in your desktop publishing program. In the Page Setup dialog box, set options to create a Side-fold card with pages sized 4.25 inches wide by 5.5 inches high in Portrait orientation. If necessary in your program, set margins to 0.25 inches on all sides; make sure the Facing pages option is selected; and set the number of pages in the document to 4.

2. If your program asks permission to add pages, click the **OK** button.

3. Save the file as **CNOInvite**.

4. Increase the inside margin to 0.75 inches.

5. Change to Master Page view and set up the pages as follows:
   A. Insert two horizontal ruler guides. Position one across the top of the sheet at the 0.5 inch mark on the vertical ruler, and position the other across the bottom of the sheet at the 5 inch mark on the vertical ruler.
   B. Draw four text boxes—one at the top of each page between the ruler guide and the top margin and one at the bottom of each page, between the ruler guide and the bottom margin. (If you are using Adobe PageMaker, you may want to use text blocks instead of text frames. In that case, skip this step and proceed with the next step.).
   C. Using the default font in 8 points in both top text boxes, key **Community Network Organization**. Left-align the text on the left page and right-align the text on the right page. Drag the text block if necessary so the bottom border of the box aligns with the ruler guide.
   D. Using the same font and font size in both bottom text boxes, key **Page**, leave a space, and then insert the page number field. Again, left-align the text on the left page and right-align the text on the right page.

6. Change to regular page view and make page 1 active if necessary. Set up the page as follows:
   A. Insert three horizontal ruler guides positioned at 1.5, 2.5, and 3.5 inches on the vertical ruler.
   B. Draw two text boxes sized to fit between the inside and outside margins—one between the first and second ruler guides you just added and one between the second and third ruler guides. If necessary, remove the stroke and set frame margins to 0.05 on all sides.

7. Enter and format text in the text boxes as follows:
   A. Display the Font Schemes list and select a decorative but sophisticated font scheme such as **Etched**, which uses Copperplate Gothic and Garamond. If your program does not offer font schemes, use Copperplate Gothic for all headings and Garamond for lists and other text in the rest of this exercise.

B. In the top text box that you just created, key **CNO**. Display the Styles list and apply the **Title** style to the text. If the title style is not available, apply a style such as **Headline** style. If necessary, set the font size to **48**, and adjust the frame size to accommodate the text.

C. In the bottom text box that you just created, key **Needs Your Help**. Apply the **Title 5** style to the text. If the Title 5 style is not available, apply a style such as **Subhead 1**. Change the font size to **22**.

D. Center the text in both text boxes horizontally and vertically.

8. Display pages 2 and 3 and insert two vertical ruler guides. Position one 1 inch from the left edge of page 2 and the other 1 inch in from the right edge of page 3. (In some programs, that is at 1 inch and 7.5 inches on the horizontal ruler. In other programs, it is 3.25 inches on each page.)

9. On page 2, insert a text box sized to fit between the text boxes on the top and bottom and the vertical ruler guide on the left and the margin on the right (inside). If necessary, remove the stroke and change frame margins to 0.05 on all sides. Enter and format text as follows:
   A. Apply the **Heading 7** style (or use a 12-point font) and key **Entertainment provided by:** and then press **Enter** to start a new line.
   B. Apply the first **List Bullet** style, or if that style is not available, use a **Hanging indent** and then apply bullets to each line, but change the font size to 14 points and key the following list:

   The Davis Brothers
   Lisa Dianne
   The Shindig Dancers
   Comedy by George

   C. Center the text vertically in the text box.

10. On page 3, insert a text box sized to fit between the text boxes on the top and bottom, the margin on the left (inside), and the vertical ruler guide on the right. If necessary, remove the stroke and set the frame margins to 0.05. Enter and format the text as follows:
    A. Apply the **Title 5** style (or use a 14-point font) and key **Please join us at our annual fundraising drive on October 11.**
    B. Press **Enter** to start a new line and change to the **Normal** or **Hanging indent** style, but increase the font size to 16 points.
    C. Key **Tickets in advance**, press **Tab**, and key **$25**. Press **Enter**, key **Tickets at the door**, press **Tab**, and key **$35**.
    D. Click in the first paragraph on the page and set the spacing after the paragraph to 24 points.
    E. Center the text vertically in the text box.

11. Make page 4 active and draw a text box sized to fit between the top and bottom and left and right margins. If necessary, modify the stroke and margin settings as usual. Enter and format text as follows:
    A. Apply the **Heading 1** style (or use a 16-point font), key **Special Thanks To**, and then press **Enter** to start a new line.

B. Apply the **List Bullet** style, or if that style is not available, apply a **Hanging indent.** Then, add a bullet to the list items, but increase the font size to 12 points; set the line spacing to leave 12 points of space before and no space after; and key the following list:

> **Note** ✓
>
> Your program may automatically apply an accent mark to the word Cafe.

Main Street Cleaners
Bumpy's Breakfast Cafe
Center Karate Studios
The Mayor
Auto Mile Gas and Service Station
Electrical Supply
Midtown Hotel

C. Center the text vertically in the text box.

12. Check the spelling of the document and then print it. Fold the printed page into an invitation.

13. Save changes and close the **CNOInvite** file and your desktop publishing program.

SCANS WEB PROJECT

Use the Internet to research desktop printers. Look up types of printers, such as ink jet, bubble jet, and laser, and the features they offer. Are some designed for a specific purpose? Do some offer features that make them more suitable for desktop publishing than others? Take note of specifications such as resolution and speed. Pick three to five printers and make a comparison chart. You can use a spreadsheet program if you have one, or write the chart by hand. When you have compiled all of the information you need, decide which printer you think is the best value.

SCANS TEAMWORK PROJECT

As a group, plan and design a newsletter for your class or for a school or community organization. You should decide the page setup, including the number of pages, and whether you will print the newsletter double-sided or single-sided. Make a mock-up so you have a general idea of the size, layout, and appearance, and any objects you want displayed on all pages. If so, plan to use master pages. Assign articles to each member of the team, then research the topics, and write enough text to fill the publication.

When you are ready, use your desktop publishing program to create the publication. Use the page setup tools to organize it, including layout and ruler guides. Take turns entering and positioning the text on the page. Select a font scheme, and use styles to format the headings and the body text. You can modify the formatting if you want to change the alignment, indents, or font formatting. When you are finished, check the spelling and then print the newsletter. With your instructor's permission, print enough copies to distribute to the class.

CRITICAL*Thinking*

ACTIVITY 3-1

Use your desktop publishing program to create a side-fold card as an invitation, greeting card, or thank you card. Create a mock-up so you can size and position all of the information you want to include. Remember that page 1 is the front cover, pages 2 and 3 are facing pages in a two-page spread, and page 4 is the back cover, and design the publication accordingly. Look at cards you have received for ideas. When you are ready, start with a blank document, or use one of your program's templates or designs. Use layout guides and ruler guides to set up the pages, and then insert text boxes to enter the content. Use a font scheme, or select any fonts you want to use. Don't forget to use text formatting such as alignment, lists, and color to enhance the publication. When you are finished, check the spelling and print one copy.

WORKING WITH OBJECTS

OBJECTIVES

Upon completion of this lesson, you should be able to:

- Identify types of objects.
- Draw shapes.
- Modify fills and strokes.
- Acquire objects.
- Size and crop objects.
- Position and arrange objects.
- Set text wrap.

Estimated Time: 2 hours

VOCABULARY

Bitmap

Crop

Distribute

Download

Embed

Fill

Flip

Floating object

Group

Link

Object

Picture frame

Pixels

Rotate

Scale

Scanner

Stack

Stroke

Vector

*O*bjects are the text boxes, charts, shapes, pictures, and other elements you insert in a publication to provide information, organize a page, and improve visual appeal. You can draw objects such as shapes and text boxes directly in a publication file, or you can import objects from a variety of sources, including digital cameras, graphics programs, and scanners. Once an object is placed in a publication, you use your desktop publishing program to size, position, and enhance it on the page. For example, you can crop a photograph to eliminate unnecessary content, or you can increase the size of a shape to make it a focal point. Most desktop publishing programs provide many tools for working with objects. In this lesson, you learn how to insert objects in a publication, how to acquire objects from different sources, and how to size and position the objects on a page.

Identify Types of Objects

You have already learned how to create text box objects in a publication, how to insert a picture file, and how to insert a text file. Depending on your program, you may have worked with picture or text frame objects as well. These are only a few of the types of objects you can include in a desktop publishing document. For example, you can create *drawing objects*,

Microsoft Excel worksheet objects, or Adobe Table objects. You can also insert graphics files and possibly, other types of files as objects. In general, you can create new or import existing objects in any format that is *compatible* with your program.

When you work with graphics files, keep a few basic concepts in mind. The two types of graphics used in computer applications are **bitmap** and **vector**. Vector graphics consist of lines and curves—called *vector paths*—that are defined by mathematical objects called vectors. Shapes you draw with the drawing tools are usually vectors. Bitmaps, which are sometimes called *raster images*, use colored dots—called **pixels**—arranged in a grid to define an image. Digital photographs are usually bitmaps.

In addition, there are different types of graphics file formats. Three of the most common are:

■ Tagged Image File Format (.tif or .tiff). *TIFF* files are used for storing bitmap images and are frequently used in desktop publishing because they support transparency and reproduce well when printed.

■ Joint Photographic Experts Group (.jpg or .jpeg). *JPEG* files are used for photographs and other images that incorporate a great many colors. JPEG files can be compressed to save disk space, but they do not support transparency.

■ Graphics Interchange Format (.gif). *GIF* files can contain up to 256 colors and support transparency. They are frequently used for cartoons, logos, and animations on the World Wide Web.

Draw Shapes

You can use your program's drawing tools to draw basic shapes such as rectangles, ovals, lines, and arrows. To use a drawing tool, click on it to select it. The mouse pointer changes to a crosshair. Hold down the mouse button and drag in the publication window to create the shape. The shape is inserted with a thin black **stroke** and no **fill**. The stroke is the line used to draw a shape, and the fill is the area inside a shape. You learn about changing the stroke and fill later in this lesson. New shapes are selected by default and have sizing handles around their edges. In some programs, a rotation handle may be displayed as well.

In some programs, you use a polygon tool to draw a multisided shape, but other programs offer a special tool for quickly inserting complex shapes that are sometimes called AutoShapes. Use AutoShapes to easily insert whimsical shapes such as lightning bolts and smiley faces and to quickly draw outlines for banners, stars, and *callouts*.

To draw an AutoShape, click the AutoShape tool on the toolbar, click the category of shape, and then click the shape you want to insert. Drag in the document to draw the shape. To draw a polygon, first set options such as the number of sides and star angle insets in a dialog box. For example, click Element on the menu bar, and then click Polygon Settings. Key the settings, then click OK. Click the Polygon tool in the toolbox and drag to draw the shape.

> ### Hot Tip
>
> Hold down the Shift key while dragging to constrain the shape. For example, use the Shift key with the Ellipse or Oval tool to draw a perfect circle. Use it with the Rectangle tool to draw a perfect square. Use it with the Line tool to draw lines at 45-degree angles.

STEP-BY-STEP 4.1

1. Launch your desktop publishing program, and open **DP Step 4-1** from the data files.

2. Save the file as **Eyes**. This publication is a reminder postcard that already contains two text box objects. You are going to draw basic shapes to create a picture of eyeglasses.

3. Click the **Oval** tool and then click and drag in the white space in the upper-left corner of the page to draw an oval shape approximately 0.5 inches high and 1 inch wide. When you release the mouse button, the shape is inserted. It should look similar to Figure 4-1. (Not all programs display a rotation handle.)

FIGURE 4-1
Oval shape in the publication

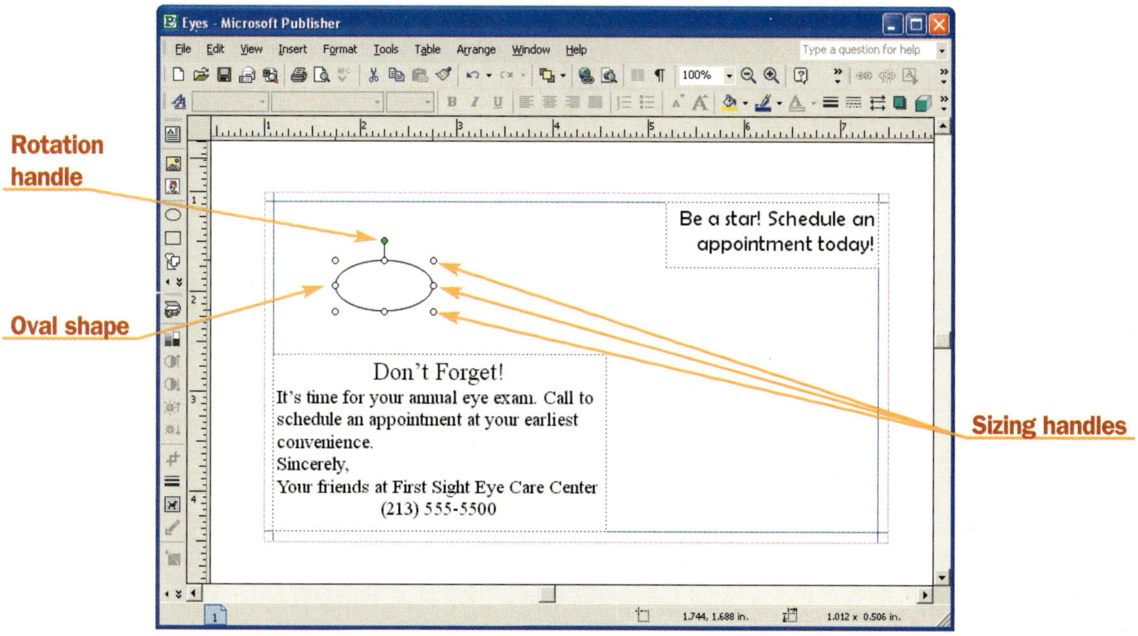

4. If necessary, click the **Oval** tool again, click about 0.25 inches to the right of the first shape, and draw another oval shape of approximately the same size.

5. Click the **Line** tool and draw a line between the ovals.

6. Click the **Line** tool again and draw a diagonal line about 0.5 inches long starting from the left end of the oval on the left side of the page and heading toward the upper-left corner of the page.

STEP-BY-STEP 4.1 Continued

7. Click the **Line** tool again and draw another diagonal line about the same angle and length as the first, starting from the right end of the oval on the right side of the page. The file should look similar to Figure 4-2. Now insert a star shape.

FIGURE 4-2
Basic shapes combine to make a picture

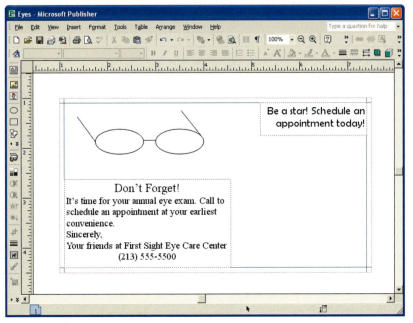

8. Select the tool for drawing a 5-pointed star with 50-degree angles or star insets. For example, click the **AutoShapes** tool, click **Stars and Banners**, and then click the **5-Point Star**. In a program such as Adobe PageMaker, you may need to click **Element**, then click **Polygon Settings** to specify a 5-sided shape with 50-degree star insets, and then click the **Polygon** tool.

FIGURE 4-3
Star shape added to the postcard

ST **STEP-BY-STEP 4.1 Continued**

9. Click and drag to draw the shape approximately 2 inches high and 2 inches wide in the white space in the lower-right corner of the page. The file should look similar to Figure 4-3.

10. Save changes and leave the **Eyes** file open to use in the next exercise.

Modify Fills and Strokes

B y default, when you draw a shape, it is displayed with no fill and a thin black stroke. Some objects, such as text boxes, have no fill and no stroke. In most programs, you can modify the fill and stroke by changing the color or style using the options in a dialog box, such as Format AutoShape, which is shown in Figure 4-4, or Fill and Stroke. You may also be able to select the options from a menu or palette. For example, click the Line/Border Style tool or click Element and then click Stroke to display a palette of stroke options.

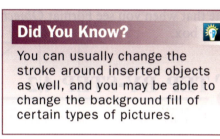

Did You Know?

You can usually change the stroke around inserted objects as well, and you may be able to change the background fill of certain types of pictures.

FIGURE 4-4
Stroke and fill options in a dialog box

A

top
an
for
cli
fro
ate
sho

de
Th
so
de
co
en
Cl
ter
su

Usually, you can apply a solid or pattern fill color and set the transparency or tint. For strokes, you can usually select a color and a weight—or width—and sometimes you can select a style, such as a double line or a dotted line.

To make changes to an object, you must first select it. To select a shape, click the selection pointer on the

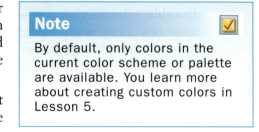

Note

By default, only colors in the current color scheme or palette are available. You learn more about creating custom colors in Lesson 5.

4. Click the **OK** button in the Insert Object dialog box. The chart object is inserted into the publication file. It should look similar to Figure 4-17. If necessary, drag the object into position as shown.

FIGURE 4-17
Chart object in the publication

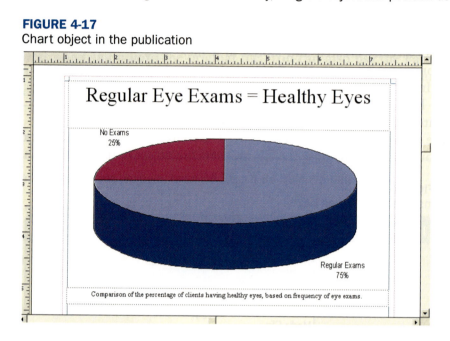

5. Save changes and leave the **Eyead** file open to use in the next exercise.

Size and Crop Objects

Once an object is inserted in a publication file, you can easily change its size to integrate it on the page. There are basically three ways to change an object's size. You can simply resize the object to change its height and/or width. You can *scale* the object, which means to change its size by a percentage of its original size. Or, you can *crop* the object, which means to remove one or more of its outer edges.

Resize or Scale an Object

To resize an object quickly, simply drag a sizing handle in or out. Drag a top or bottom handle to change the height, drag a side handle to change the width, or drag a corner handle to change the height and width at the same time.

To set a precise size or scale for an object, use the options in a dialog box such as the Format *Object* dialog box or a palette such as the Control palette. Key the dimensions or scale percentage in the appropriate boxes, and then click the OK or Apply button.

S TEP-BY-STEP 4.10

1. In the **Eyead** file, select the picture of the glasses near the bottom of the page.

2. Drag the sizing handle at the lower-left corner of the object to the corner where the left and bottom margins meet, and then drag the sizing handle at the upper-right corner of the object to the corner where the right margin and the lower text box meet. This increases the size of the object significantly. Try scaling the object.

3. Click the object to select it, and then choose the command to open the dialog box or palette where you set precise dimensions. For example, click **Format** on the menu bar and then click **Object**. If necessary, click the **Size** tab.

4. In the Size section, click in the **Height** box and key **2.5**, and then click in the **Width** box and key **4.75**. Click the **OK** or **Apply** button to apply the change. The bottom half of the page should look similar to Figure 4-18. If necessary, drag the object into position as shown.

FIGURE 4-18
Resize the object precisely

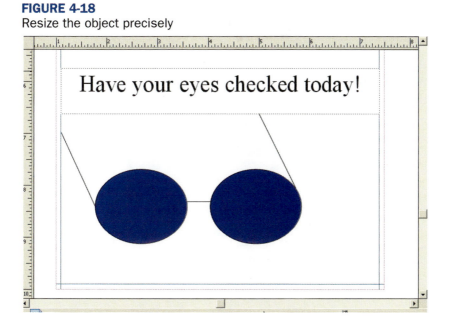

Have your eyes checked today!

5. Save changes and leave the **Eyead** file open to use in the next exercise.

Crop an Object

When you want to remove the outer portions of an object, you crop it. To crop an image in most programs, click the Crop tool on the Picture toolbar or in the toolbox to display cropping handles around the object. Drag the handles to define the area you want to remove. For example, drag a top handle down to remove the upper edge of the object. To crop by a precise amount, use the options in the Format *Object* dialog box or the Control palette.

S TEP-BY-STEP 4.11

1. In the **Eyead** file, click the chart object to select it. From the location of the sizing handles, you can see that the object has a lot of extra space around it. Try cropping the object to remove the extra space.

2. Click the **Crop** tool on the toolbar or in the toolbox. You may need to display the Picture toolbar to locate the Crop tool.

3. Drag the upper-middle crop handle down about 2.25 inches, or until the top edge of the object is located just above the text *No Exams*. When you release the mouse button, the object is cropped.

4. Drag the left crop handle to the right until the left edge of the object is just to the left of the edge of the chart, then drag the right crop handle to the left until the right edge of the object is just to the right of the text *Regular Exams*. Finally, drag the lower crop handle up about 2 inches so the bottom edge of the object is just under the text *75%*. The top half of the page should look similar to Figure 4-19. If necessary, resize the object and drag it into position as shown.

FIGURE 4-19
Cropped object

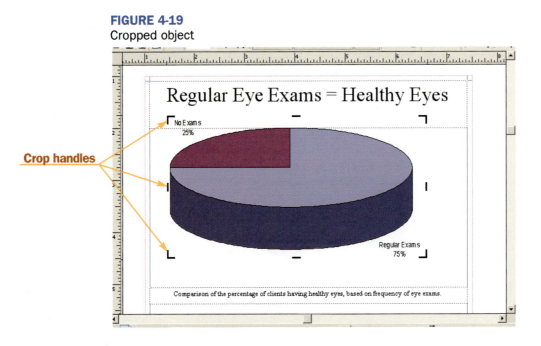

Crop handles

5. Deselect the object, save changes, and leave the **Eyead** file open to use in the next exercise.

Position and Arrange Objects

As you have already learned, the way you position and arrange objects on the page is one of the most important factors in creating a successful publication. The easiest way to position an object is to select it and then drag it to a new location, but most programs include tools for fine-tuning position, including alignment options, precise positioning, and layering, or stacking.

In most programs, objects are modified based on a *reference point*, which is a fixed spot used as a control for moving and modifying objects. The default reference point depends on the program you are using, but it is often the center of the object or the upper-left corner. While many programs do not let you move the reference point, some programs do, and it can greatly affect modifications made to the object. For example, if you set the precise position of two identical objects to 2 inches horizontal and 2 inches vertical, and then set one reference point at the center of an object and the other in the upper-left corner of the object, the objects will be positioned in different places on the page. The following exercises assume that the default reference points have not been moved.

Position an Object Precisely

To position an object precisely in some programs, you use the Format *Object* dialog box to specify the horizontal and vertical location relative to either the upper-right corner, the upper-left corner, or the center of the page. In other programs, you set the horizontal (X) and vertical (Y) *coordinates* in a palette such as Control. The coordinates are specific points laid out in an invisible grid that starts in the upper-left corner of the page, with the coordinates of 0, 0. As you move an object to the right, the X coordinate increases. As you move down, the Y coordinate increases.

STEP-BY-STEP 4.12

1. In the **Eyead** file, select the chart object if it is not already selected.

2. Choose the command to open the dialog box or palette where you enter values to position an object. For example, click **Format** on the menu bar, and then click **Object**. Click the **Layout** tab if necessary.

3. Click in the **Horizontal** or **X** box and key **1.75**. If necessary, click the **From** box and select **Top Left Corner**.

4. Click in the **Vertical** or **Y** box and key **2.24**. Again, if necessary click the **From** box and select **Top Left Corner**.

5. Click the **OK** button or the **Apply** button. The object moves to the specified position. If the object does not appear to be centered in the space, you may have to drag it into position.

6. Save changes and leave the **Eyead** file open to use in the next exercise.

Align Objects

You have already learned how to use guidelines to visually align objects on a page. Most desktop publishing programs also have tools for making sure objects are precisely aligned. You can toggle on the Snap to feature if you want objects to automatically align to the guides. You can use the Nudge command or the arrow keys to move an object up, down, left, or right in small increments. In some programs, you can align an object to adjust its position horizontally relative to the left and right margins, and vertically relative to the top and bottom margins.

If you are using a program such as Adobe Page-Maker that does not have options for aligning or distributing individual objects, you can complete the following exercise by dragging the objects or setting the X and Y coordinates.

> **Extra for Experts**
>
> Many programs also have a **distribute** command you can use to space multiple objects evenly between either the top and bottom margins or the left and right margins.

S TEP-BY-STEP 4.13

1. In the **Eyead** file, click the picture of the glasses on the bottom half of the page.

2. Select the command to center align the object between the left and right margins. For example, click **Arrange** on the menu bar, click **Align or Distribute**, and then click **Align Center**. The object is centered horizontally between the margins. If necessary, drag the object into position, or set the X and Y coordinates.

3. Select the command to align the object with the bottom margin. For example, click **Arrange** on the menu bar, click **Align or Distribute**, and then click **Align Bottom**.

4. Use the Nudge command to nudge the object up so it is even with the bottom layout guide. For example, click **Arrange** on the menu bar, click **Nudge**, and then click **Up**. Repeat the command nine more times, or press the Up arrow key on the keyboard nine times. The publication should look similar to the one in Figure 4-20.

FIGURE 4-20
Objects aligned in publication

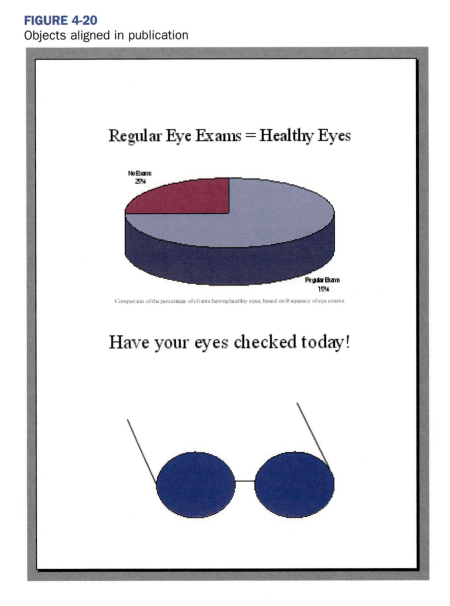

STEP-BY-STEP 4.13 Continued

5. Print one copy of the **Eyead** file.

6. Save changes and close the **Eyead** file. Leave your desktop publishing program open to use in the next exercise.

> **Note** ✅
>
> If the commands on the Align or Distribute menu are dimmed, click the Relative to Margin Guides command to activate them.

Group and Reorder Stacked Items

When you want to apply the same changes to more than one object at once, you can select all of the objects and then apply the changes. Alternatively, you can *group* multiple objects. Grouped objects can be selected and modified as one unit. That way, you don't have to worry about selecting all items each time you want to make changes.

To create a group, simply select the objects you want to include and then click the Group button, or click the Group command on a menu such as Arrange or Element. Selection handles surround the entire group, rather than the individual objects in the group. Use the Ungroup button or command to turn off grouping so you can work with the individual objects again.

As you insert objects, they *stack* in the document, even if they do not actually overlap each other. The first object is at the bottom or back of the stack, and the most recent object is at the top or front of the stack. You sometimes need to rearrange the stacking order of objects to make sure that an object is displayed properly or to create overlapping effects.

The command to rearrange the stacking order varies depending on the program you are using. It may be the Arrange command on the Element menu, or the Order command on the Arrange menu. There may even be an Order button on the toolbar. Once you locate the command and select it, a menu of stacking options is displayed. Most programs give you four options for adjusting stacking order: Send to Back, Send Backward, Bring Forward, and Bring to Front. Send to Back moves an object behind all other objects, while Bring to Front positions an object in front of all other objects. Send Backward and Bring Forward move objects forward or backward one position at a time. To change the stacking order, select the object you need to change and then select a command.

> **Extra for Experts** 📊
>
> Do not confuse the stacking order with layers. Some programs have a Layers feature you can use to separate a document into individual transparent planes. Layers are used for creating complex publications and certain special effects.

STEP-BY-STEP 4.14

1. In your desktop-publishing program, open **DP Step 4-14** from the data files. This is another version of the original reminder postcard.

2. Save the file as **Eyes4**.

STEP-BY-STEP 4.14 Continued

3. Select all of the shapes that comprise the picture of the glasses. Sizing handles are displayed around each shape, and in some programs the Group button is displayed.

4. Click the **Group** button, or select the command to group the objects. For example, click **Arrange** on the menu bar, and then click **Group**. The objects are grouped into a single unit. Notice that sizing handles are displayed around the entire group. In some programs, the Group button changes to the Ungroup button.

5. Resize the entire group to about 1 inch high by 3 inches wide, if necessary.

6. Select the large blue star and position it horizontally 5 inches and vertically 2 inches from the upper-left corner of the page.

7. Set the stacking order for the large blue star to send it to the back. For example, select the star, click **Arrange** on the menu bar, click **Order**, and then click **Send to Back**.

8. Position the four smaller stars relative to the top left corner as follows:

   Black star: horizontally 6 inches and vertically 1.75 inches

   Yellow star: horizontally 4.5 inches and vertically 1.75 inches

   Orange star: horizontally 6 inches and vertically 2.75 inches

   Purple star: horizontally 4.5 inches and vertically 2.75 inches

9. Select the black star and change its stacking order to send it to the back.

10. Select the purple star and change its stacking order to send it to the back. The publication should look similar to the one in Figure 4-21.

FIGURE 4-21
Grouped and stacked objects

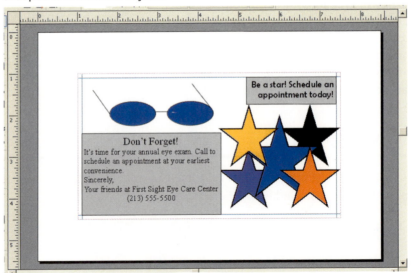

STEP-BY-STEP 4.14 Continued

11. Print one copy of the **Eyes4** file.

12. Save changes and close the **Eyes4** file. Leave your desktop publishing program open to use in the next exercise.

Rotate and Flip

Two other methods of changing the way an object is positioned on the page are rotating and flipping, which is sometimes called *reflecting*. When you **rotate** an object, it pivots around its reference point. When you **flip** an object, you reverse the image either horizontally (left to right) or vertically (top to bottom).

In some programs, such as Microsoft Publisher, a rotation handle is displayed with certain shapes when an object is selected. Simply drag the rotation handle to rotate the object around a center reference point. In other programs, such as Adobe PageMaker, you must first click the Rotate or Free Rotate tool in the toolbox or select the Free Rotate command from a menu to display rotation handles. Drag any handle to rotate the object. In some programs, the handle you drag becomes the reference point. Some programs also have a menu command for rotating an object in 90-degree increments left or right, and most programs also let you rotate an object by a precise amount by entering a specific value for the rotation in a dialog box such as Format *Object* or a palette such as Control.

To flip an object, choose either the Flip Horizontal or Flip Vertical command on a menu such as Arrange, or click the Reflect button on a toolbar or in a palette such as Control.

STEP-BY-STEP 4.15

1. In your desktop publishing program, open **DP Step 4-15** from the data files.

2. Save the file as **Eyes5**.

3. Select the purple star and rotate it to the right until the top point is pointing to the upper-right corner of the page (approximately 35 degrees).

4. Select the black star and drag the rotation handle about 0.25 inches to the left (approximately −25 degrees).

5. Select the orange star and drag the rotation handle about 0.25 inches to the right (approximately 25 degrees).

6. Select the lightning bolt and flip it horizontally.

STEP-BY-STEP 4.15 Continued

7. Flip the lightning bolt vertically. The publication should look similar to Figure 4-22. If necessary, adjust the position of the objects.

FIGURE 4-22
Objects rotated and flipped

8. Save changes and leave the **Eyes5** file open to use in the next exercise.

Set Text Wrap

Y ou can set text wrap to adjust the width, shape, and position of white space between text and objects on a page. You have already learned that text automatically wraps within a text box from the end of one line to the beginning of the next line. Most desktop publishing programs also have a selection of text wrap styles and options you use to control the way text wraps to make room for objects. Most programs offer five wrapping styles, as described in Table 4-1.

TABLE 4-1
Text wrap styles and options

BUTTON	STYLE NAME	DESCRIPTION
	Square	Wraps text evenly around four sides of an object.
	Tight	Wraps text along the contours of an object.
	Through	Continues lines of text through transparent backgrounds of objects.
	Top and Bottom	Wraps text evenly on the top and bottom of an object.
	None	Does not wrap text. Instead, text is stacked behind or in front of the object.

In most programs, the text wrapping options are listed in a dialog box, such as Format *Object* or Text Wrap. Simply select the object, and then open the dialog box and select the style you want to apply. Alternatively, click the Text Wrap button on a toolbar such as Picture, and then click the style on the pop-up palette that is displayed. Depending on the style you select and your program, you may also be able to set text flow options to control the way text flows around the object. For example, if you select Square, Tight, or Through, you can select whether to wrap the text on both sides of the object, only the left side, only the right side, or just on the largest side of the object. If you select the Square wrapping style, you can enter the specific distance you want to maintain between the object and any of its four sides, sometimes called the *standoff*.

STEP-BY-STEP 4.16

1. In the **Eyes5** file, select the lightning bolt shape and set the wrapping style to **Tight**. For example, click the shape, click the **Text Wrap** button on the toolbar, and then click **Tight**. You may need to display the Picture toolbar to locate the Text Wrap button.

2. Select the orange star and set the wrapping style to **Square**.

3. Select the black star and set the wrapping style to **Square**.

STEP-BY-STEP 4.16 Continued

4. Select the purple star and set the wrapping style to **Tight**. The publication should look similar to Figure 4-23. If necessary, adjust the size and position of objects. If your program has Standoff settings, you may have to adjust the measurements to a value such as 0.01 all around.

FIGURE 4-23
Text wrapped around objects

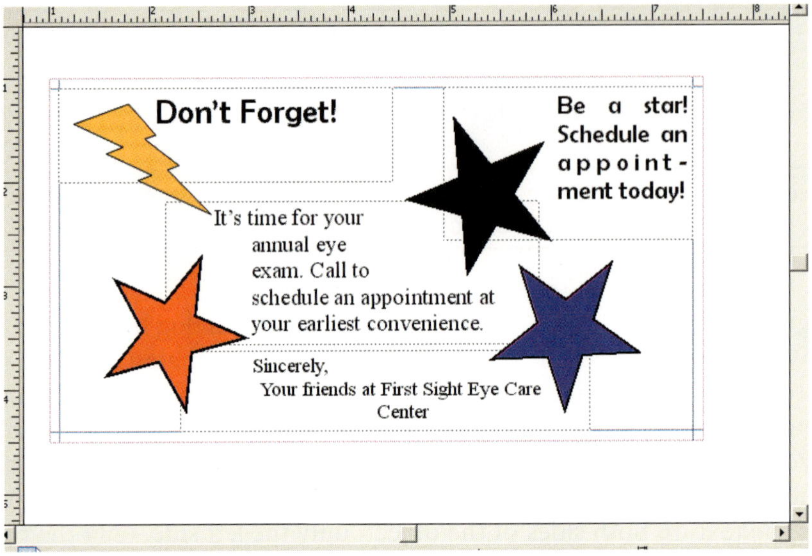

5. Print one copy of the **Eyes5** file.

6. Save changes and close the **Eyes5** file and your desktop publishing program.

SUMMARY

In this lesson, you learned:

■ There are many types of objects you can insert in desktop publishing documents.

■ Most desktop publishing programs have drawing tools you can use to draw basic shapes.

■ You can insert many types of graphics files in a desktop publishing program.

■ Use a scanner to convert printed material into an object or graphics file.

■ You can transfer files from a digital camera to a computer, and then insert them into a publication.

■ Most desktop publishing programs come with clip art, or you can download clip art from the Internet.

■ It is important to obey copyright laws and to cite sources of material you acquire from other sources.

- One of the easiest ways to insert an object in a publication is to use the Copy and Paste commands.

- You can modify objects by changing the color and style of fills and strokes.

- You can resize, crop, and position objects using precise values or by dragging handles with the mouse.

- To integrate objects with text, you can select from several text wrapping styles.

VOCABULARY *Review*

Define the following terms:

Bitmap	Floating object	Rotate
Crop	Group	Scale
Distribute	Link	Scanner
Download	Object	Stack
Embed	Picture frame	Stroke
Fill	Pixels	Vector
Flip		

REVIEW *Questions*

TRUE / FALSE

Circle T if the statement is true or F if the statement is false.

T F   **1.** By default, when you draw a shape, it is displayed with no fill.

T F   **2.** An ISP is a Web site that helps you locate a Web page even if you don't know the page's address.

T F   **3.** Use a scanner to convert a graphics file into a printed document.

T F   **4.** By default, pasted objects are linked to a publication.

T F   **5.** When you want to move an object up, down, left, or right by a very small amount, use the Nudge command.

T F   **6.** Scale an object to remove one or more of its outer edges.

T F   **7.** Bitmap graphics use colored dots arranged in a grid to define an image.

T F   **8.** To select more than one object at a time, press and hold Shift and then click each object.

T F   **9.** When you rotate an object, you reverse the image.

T F **10.** Select a text wrap style to control the way text makes room for objects on the page.

WRITTEN QUESTIONS

Write a brief answer to the following questions.

1. Name at least two hardware devices you can use to acquire graphics objects.

2. What are some of the modifications you can make to a shape's stroke or fill?

3. What is the benefit to using a frame when you insert a picture?

4. Name at least two graphics file formats and list some characteristics of each.

5. What is the difference between linking an object and embedding an object?

FILL IN THE BLANK

Complete the following sentences by writing the correct word or words in the blanks provided.

1. Select the _____ text wrapping style to wrap text along the contours of an object.

2. _____ graphics consist of lines and curves that are defined by mathematical objects.

3. The _____ is the area inside a shape.

4. The _____ is the line used to draw a shape.

5. You can align _____ relative to the left and right margins.

6. To position an object so it _____ other objects, change its stacking order to Bring to Front.

7. _____ an object to change its size by a percentage of its original size.

8. Use a(n) _____ to convert printed material into a graphics file.

9. _____ are colored dots arranged in a grid to define an image.

10. Some programs have a(n) _____ feature you can use to quickly draw whimsical objects such as lightning bolts and smiley faces.

PROJECTS

PROJECT 4-1

1. Launch your desktop publishing program and open **DP Project 4-1a** from the data files. This file is a version of the CNO newsletter you worked with in Lesson 3. You are going to enhance it by inserting pictures and shapes.

2. Save the file as **CNONews2**.

3. Insert the graphics file **DP Project 4-1b** from the data files into a frame in the upper-left corner of page 1 to complement the newsletter title.
   A. Size the frame to about 1.25 inches high by 1.5 inches wide, if necessary. You can do this before inserting the picture, or you can resize the picture after you insert it in the publication.
   B. Position it along the left margin (about 1.1 inches from the top left corner horizontally and vertically).
   C. If the text and the picture overlap, set the text wrap for the picture to Square.

4. Locate a clip art picture of wrapped presents. You may look in the clip art collection that came with your program or in other clip art you have on a CD or installed on your system, or you may want to download a picture from the Internet.

5. Insert the clip art to illustrate the story with the headline *Holiday Helpers Needed* in the lower-right corner of page 1. Format the picture as follows:
   A. Size the picture to about 0.75 inches high by 0.75 inches wide.
   B. Set the text wrap for the clip art to **Tight** or adjust the standoff as necessary to allow for tight wrapping.
   C. Position the clip art to the left of the headline, overlapping the column guides. Fine-tune the position as necessary so that all of the text fits in the text box.

6. Change to page 2 and draw a smiley face on the page near the letter to the editor. You may draw the face using an AutoShape, or by using basic shapes.
   A. Size the smiley face to 0.5 inches by 0.5 inches.
   B. Fill the shape with the color yellow.
   C. Set the text wrap to **Square**.
   D. Position the shape to the left of the text *Dear Editor*, then fine-tune the position so all of the text fits in the text box.

7. Print both pages, either on separate sheets of paper or on a double-sided sheet.

8. Save changes and close the **CNONews2** file. Leave your desktop publishing program open to use in Project 4-2.

PROJECT 4-2

1. In your desktop publishing program, open **DP Project 4-2a** from the data files. This is a version of the invitation you worked with in Lesson 3.

2. Save the file as **CNOInvite2**.

3. On page 1, insert the graphics file **DP Project 4-2b** from the data files and format the object as follows:
   A. Resize the object to about 3 inches wide by 2.75 inches high.
   B. Position it in the white space on the bottom half of the page.
   C. Center it horizontally between the margins.

4. On page 2, insert a picture of entertainment. You may acquire the picture from any source you want. For example, insert clip art, a scanned picture, a picture acquired from a digital camera, or a picture you draw on a graphics tablet. Format the object as follows:
   A. Size and position the object to fit in the white space at the top of page 2.
   B. Try flipping or rotating the object to create an interesting effect.

5. On page 3, insert a different picture of entertainment. You may want to use a different source from the one you used in step 4 to acquire the image. Format the object as follows:
   A. Size and position the object to fit in the white space at the bottom of page 3. This balances the object on page 2.
   B. Apply a similar effect to the object that you used for the object on page 2. This provides consistency.

6. On page 4, insert objects to decorate the white space along the outside margin and the bottom of the page. For example, insert shapes, such as stars or hearts, or clip art, or a drawing that you scan or create with a graphics tablet. Use color to highlight the objects, and rotate and position them to create interesting angles and juxtapositions. Create a pattern by repeating the shapes, or by grouping shapes and repeating the group. Try overlapping the objects and changing the stacking order to make the page exciting and festive.

7. When you are satisfied with page 4, print the publication and fold it into an invitation.

8. Save changes and close the **CNOInvite2** file and your desktop publishing program.

SCANS ## WEB PROJECT

The copyright laws that govern the use of material found on the Internet may be complex, but you can find Web sites that list the dos and don'ts in simple, straightforward language. Use the Internet to find some basic rules to keep in mind when you download information such as a picture from a Web site. See if you can find information about the proper way to request permission for using a picture, and then use a word processing program to write such a letter. Finally, look up different ways to cite sources for Internet data. Ask your instructor which method he or she prefers, and then use that method to cite sources.

ANS **TEAMWORK PROJECT**

As a group, plan and design a flyer or brochure about a historic or famous site in your community. You need to agree on the site and then research it so you have the correct information to include in the publication. If possible, use a digital camera to take pictures of the site to include in the document. Alternatively, find pictures that have already been printed that you can use. As with other publications, you should decide the page setup, including how many pages to include, and whether you will use double-sided or single-sided printing. Then, mock up the publication so you have a general idea of its size, layout, and appearance.

When you are ready, use your desktop publishing program to create the publication document. Insert all text and objects, and position them on the pages so the document is appealing and easy to read. When you are finished, check the spelling and then print the publication.

CRITICAL*Thinking*

ACTIVITY 4-1

Enhance one of the publications you created in a previous lesson by inserting objects. For example, add clip art pictures or digital photos to the side fold card, and/or draw basic shapes. Open the file and save it with a new name so you can make the changes without affecting the original publication. Insert graphics files, or create the objects directly in the publication. Once you insert the objects, use the tools in your desktop publishing program to adjust the size and position for the best impact. For example, scale the objects to make them larger or smaller, or crop out parts you don't need. You can rotate or flip the images and change the stroke and fill if you want. Adjust the text wrap to control the white space around the pictures. When you are finished, check the spelling and print one copy.

ENHANCING PUBLICATIONS

OBJECTIVES

Upon completion of this lesson, you should be able to:

- Work with color.
- Enhance objects.
- Enhance text.
- Insert horizontal rules.
- Apply border art.
- Create a watermark.
- Use design objects.

Estimated Time: 1.5 hours

VOCABULARY

CMYK

Color system

Dot leader

Dropped capital

Gradient

Horizontal rule

Hue

Letterhead

Logo

Masthead

Pattern

Process color

RGB

Shadow

Spot color

Table of contents

Texture

Tint

Transparency

Watermark

Maybe you can't judge a book by its cover, but an exciting, attractive book jacket can certainly capture a potential reader's attention. When you add visual details and enhancements to a document, you make the publication more appealing. You can also use enhancements to create *brand recognition*. For example, if you repeat a color or shape in print—think of the blue and yellow of a Blockbuster Video sign or the black and white cow print of the boxes Gateway computers come in—people associate certain colors or shapes with specific organizations. In this lesson, you learn how to use desktop publishing tools to enhance publications with special effects and color. You can add shadows and 3-D effects to objects to make them stand out on a page. You can apply borders and rules to visually separate elements on a page, and you can add borders and watermarks to pages as decoration or part of an overall publication design. You can even use text as a decoration by turning it into a graphics object or starting a paragraph with a dropped capital letter.

Work with Color

Color, also called *hue*, is frequently the first thing a reader sees and responds to. While some publications, such as some newspapers, use only two colors—black and white—many incorporate at least one additional color for emphasis and effect, and some use a wide spectrum of colors for reproducing photographs and other full-color images.

You have already learned how to select a color scheme and apply standard colors to text, fills, and strokes. You can also define custom colors. The options available for working with color vary depending on your desktop publishing program, but in general you select the element you want to color, and then open a dialog box where you can select or define a custom color. The custom color is then added to the palette so you can apply it to other elements in the publication.

Understand Color Systems

When you work with color in a desktop publishing program, the most important thing to keep in mind is that the way colors are displayed on your computer screen is not necessarily the way they will look when printed. Many factors affect the way colors appear on your screen and in print, including the specific printer model, the specific monitor model, and your software program. But the most important factor is that printers and monitors use different *color systems*. A color system is a method for defining standard colors. It may also be called a *color model*.

The color system used for displaying colors on a monitor is called **RGB**. The RGB system creates colors by combining different values of red, green, and blue. The main color system used for defining colors in print is called **CMYK** (or CMY). The CMYK system creates colors by combining percentages of cyan (blue), magenta (red), yellow, and black. These colors—often called *process color*—are the colors of the ink used in four-color printing. Process color is usually used for publications that contain many colors, such as brochures that include photographs or high-definition graphics.

When a publication designer wants to use a specific color of ink instead of mixing the color during printing, he or she can select a *spot color* from a color system or library such as the *Pantone Matching System*. A spot color is ink that is premixed before the printing process. You use spot colors when it is necessary to have an exact color such as matching a client's logo color, or when printing with only one or two colors, or when using special inks for emphasis. You can use both spot

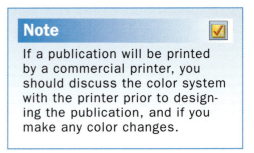

Note ☑

If a publication will be printed by a commercial printer, you should discuss the color system with the printer prior to designing the publication, and if you make any color changes.

colors and process colors in the same publication. Spot color printing on its own is usually less expensive than process color printing.

Create Custom Colors

There are two basic methods for defining a custom color, both of which use a color dialog box similar to the one in Figure 5-1.

FIGURE 5-1
Create custom colors

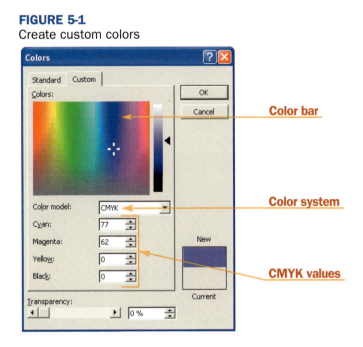

The first method, which may not be available in all programs, is to simply select a color from a *color bar*. A color bar displays a spectrum of colors across a rectangle from left to right. To apply a custom color using a color bar, start by selecting the element to color and opening the standard color scheme palette. Select the option to open the colors or custom colors dialog box, click the color you want to apply, and then click OK.

The other method for defining a custom color is to key the color system values for a particular color in the dialog box. To apply a custom color by keying a color system value, select the element to color and open the standard color scheme palette. Select the option to open the custom colors dialog box, select the color system from a drop-down list, and key values for each color. Units used for values differ by system. For example, RGB values usually range from 0 to 255, but CMYK values use percentages.

In some programs, you simply click OK to apply the color to the element, while in other programs you must key a name for the custom color, save it, and then apply it from the standard color scheme palette. In either case, the custom color is added to the color palette for that publication.

Net Tip

Look on the Web to find color system tables listing values for the entire range of colors. Such a table can save you time in experimenting with color values to find the one you want.

Some programs come with color charts for particular color systems that you can use to select a specific color. When you select the color system from the drop-down list in the custom color dialog box, a color chart dialog box similar to the Pantone Colors dialog box shown in Figure 5-2 opens. Click the color you want to use, and then click OK.

Did You Know?

RGB, CMYK, and the Pantone Matching System are not the only color systems. Other common process color systems include HSL (Hue, Saturation, Lightness) and Grayscale, which uses percentages of black to create shades of gray. Other spot color systems include Toyo Color Finder and DIC Color Guide.

FIGURE 5-2
Pantone color chips

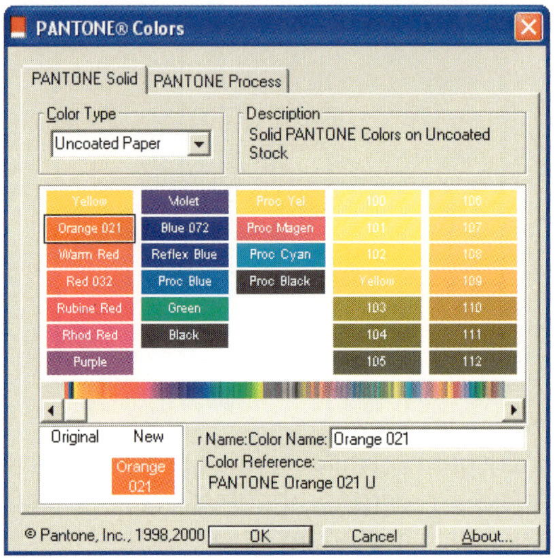

You can also usually modify a color by changing its ***tint*** and/or ***transparency***. Tint, which is sometimes called *brightness*, is the range of a color from black to white. When you add white to a color, you increase its brightness. Add black to shade or decrease the brightness. Transparency, which is sometimes, called opacity, measures the degree to which you can see through a color. To make a color completely opaque, set the transparency to 0%. To see through a color, increase the transparency. The options for changing tint and/or transparency may be found in the Colors dialog box or palette.

Extra for Experts

You can make colors in some bitmap graphics and clip art files transparent so they do not show when printed. Select the Set Transparent Color tool or command in your desktop publishing program, and then click the color in the image.

STEP-BY-STEP 5.1

1. Launch your desktop publishing program, and open **DP Step 5-1** from the data files.

2. Save the file as **Coffee**. This publication is a flyer announcing coffee tasting at the Beans & Beyond coffee shop.

STEP-BY-STEP 5.1 Continued

3. Insert an 8-point star shape in the upper left of the publication. (Set the star inset to 17% if necessary.) Size the shape to 3 inches high by 3 inches wide, and position it horizontally 1.25 inches from the upper-left corner and vertically 1 inch from the upper-left corner. If necessary, rotate the shape so one point of the star is vertical.

4. With the star shape selected, open the Fill color custom colors dialog box. For example, click the **Fill Color** tool on the toolbar, click **More Fill Colors**, and then click the **Custom** tab.

5. Select the CMYK color system and key the following values: Cyan: **70**; Magenta: **30**; Yellow: **5**; Black: **0**. If necessary, name the color Star Blue.

6. Click the **OK** button as many times as necessary to close all dialog boxes and apply the color to the shape. If necessary, click the new color in the color palette to apply it. The shape should look similar to Figure 5-3.

FIGURE 5-3
Custom color fill

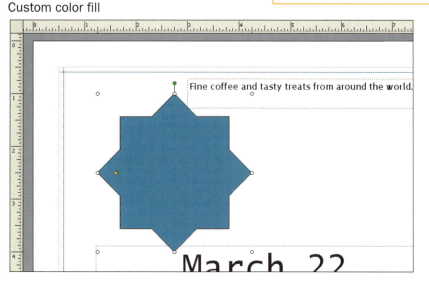

7. Save changes and leave the **Coffee** file open to use in the next exercise.

Enhance Objects

Many programs provide options for formatting objects with special effects such as shadows, 3-D, textures, gradients, and patterns. Patterns, textures, and gradients are applied as fill or stroke effects, while shadows and 3-D effects are used to format entire objects. The methods for applying special effects to objects vary depending on your program, and not all programs offer all types of effects. In programs that offer only basic effects such as patterns, you select a fill or stroke effect from a menu or in the Stroke and Fill dialog box as you learned in Lesson 4. In programs that offer many special effects, you use the appropriate dialog box or toolbar button.

To apply fill effects such as gradients, textures, or patterns, you usually select the object to format, open the basic fill color palette, then click Fill Effects to open the Fill Effects dialog box. There may be multiple tabs in the dialog box, each one offering options for applying specific fill effects. Locate the effect you want to use, click it, and then click OK. To apply a stroke pattern, you usually select the object to format, open the basic stroke color palette, and then click Patterned Lines to open the Patterned Lines dialog box. Locate the pattern you want to use, click it, and then click OK.

Apply Patterns, Textures, and Gradients

Patterns are simply repetitive designs such as grids or hatchmarks. By default, they are black on white, but you can usually select a foreground color and a background color. Patterns may be applied to both fills and strokes. *Textures* are bitmap graphics files used as fills. You can select from a list of built-in textures, or select a picture file to use as a texture.

Gradients are a blend of colors that gradually change in brightness or tint. You usually select one or more colors to include in the gradient, and then select a pattern or style. For example, a *radial gradient* blends colors out from a central point, while a *linear gradient* blends the colors horizontally. There may be other gradient options available in your program as well, such as variations of the selected style or a list of preset colors and styles. Shadows and 3-D effects are applied to an entire object.

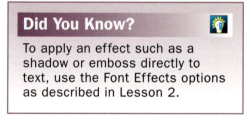

Did You Know?

To apply an effect such as a shadow or emboss directly to text, use the Font Effects options as described in Lesson 2.

STEP-BY-STEP 5.2

1. In the **Coffee** file, select the star shape if it is not already selected.

2. Open the dialog box that contains options for applying texture fill effects. For example, click the **Fill Color** tool on the toolbar, click **Fill Effects**, and then click the **Texture** tab. If you are using a program such as PageMaker that does not offer texture effects, open the dialog box or menu for applying fill patterns.

3. Click a blue, heavy texture, such as Denim. Click the **OK** button as many times as necessary to apply the effect to the shape. It should look similar to Figure 5-4. If your program does not offer texture effects, select a large grid pattern.

STEP-BY-STEP 5.2 Continued

FIGURE 5-4
Texture fill effect

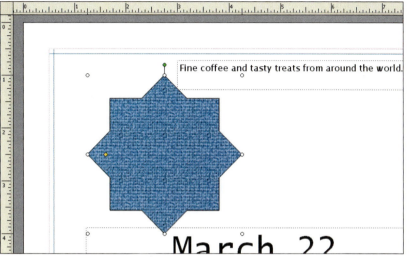

4. Open the dialog box that contains options for applying gradient fill effects. For example, click the **Fill Color** tool on the toolbar, click **Fill Effects**, and then click the **Gradient** tab. If your program does not offer gradient effects, open the dialog box or menu for applying fill patterns.

5. Click a radial gradient style that shades one color from the center out. Click the **OK** button as many times as necessary to apply the effect to the shape. If your program does not offer gradient effects, select a small grid pattern.

6. Open the dialog box or menu for applying stroke pattern effects. For example, click the **Line Color** button on the toolbar, click **Patterned Lines**, and then click the **Pattern** tab.

7. Click a dark horizontal line pattern, and then click the **OK** button as many times as necessary to apply the effect to the shape. The shape should look similar to Figure 5-5. If your program does not support patterned lines, select a 3-point dashed line as the stroke.

STEP-BY-STEP 5.2 Continued

FIGURE 5-5
Gradient fill and patterned line effects

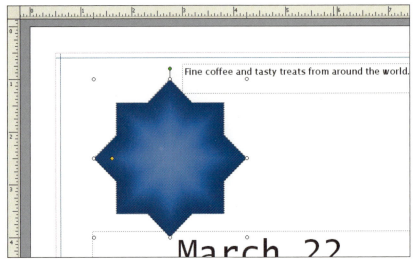

8. Save changes and leave the **Coffee** file open to use in the next exercise.

Apply Shadows and 3-D Effects

A *shadow* adds shading on one side of the outer edge of an object to create the illusion of depth and highlights. A 3-D effect also creates the illusion of depth by adding or extending shapes along one or two sides of an object. To apply a shadow, select the object to format, and then select the command to open a palette of available styles. For example, click the Shadow Style button on the toolbar. Click the style you want to apply. You may also be able to use toolbar buttons to adjust options such as the position, color, and size of shadows.

The procedure for applying 3-D effects is basically the same. Select the object to format, then click the button to open a palette of 3-D styles. For example, click the 3-D Styles button on the toolbar. Click the style you want to apply. You also may be able to use toolbar buttons to adjust options such as the depth, direction, tilt, and lighting of the 3-D effect.

Usually, you cannot combine shadows and 3-D effects on the same object. Not all desktop publishing programs have features for applying shadows and 3-D Effects. If you are using a program such as PageMaker that does not, skip the following exercise.

STEP-BY-STEP 5.3

1. In the **Coffee** file, select the star shape and then open the dialog box or menu for applying a shadow. For example, click the **Shadow Style** button on the toolbar.

STEP-BY-STEP 5.3 Continued

2. Click the style that applies a long shadow extending from the bottom of the shape up and to the right. For example, select shadow style 12. It should look similar to Figure 5-6.

FIGURE 5-6
Shadow effect

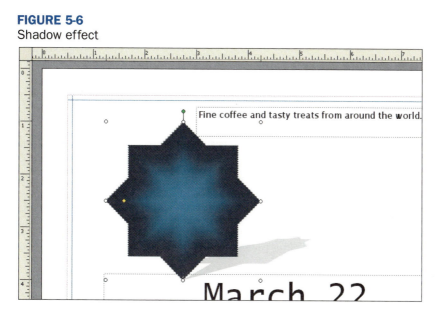

3. Open the dialog box or menu for applying 3-D effects. For example, click the **3-D Style** button on the toolbar.

4. Click the style that tilts the face of the object down and to the right, and extends the top and left sides of the object up and to the left. For example, select 3-D style 18. It should look similar to Figure 5-7.

FIGURE 5-7
3-D effect

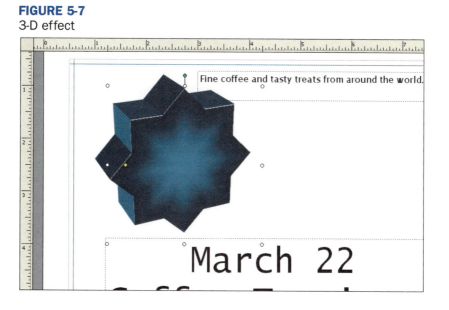

5. Save changes and leave the **Coffee** file open to use in the next exercise.

Enhance Text

In addition to formatting text with fonts and font formatting, many desktop publishing programs provide tools for creating sophisticated effects using text. Most programs have a feature for creating a *dropped capital*—sometimes called a *drop cap*—a decorative effect in which the first character in a paragraph is larger than the other characters. The drop cap may be offset to the left of the lines of text in the paragraph or inset to the right. Some programs offer a utility that lets you create text objects that include special effects formatting such as shadows and 3-D, and some programs let you simply add text to shapes.

Create Dropped Capitals

Dropped capital letters are often used to dress up the first paragraph of a chapter in a book or for emphasizing the first paragraph in a newsletter or magazine article. When you apply a dropped capital, the first letter in the paragraph is scaled to the specified size, which is usually measured in lines. In some programs, you can select additional options for formatting the dropped capital, including whether you want the character to drop down into the paragraph or extend up above the paragraph. You may also be able to select more than one character to drop and to change the font formatting. Some programs come with a selection of built-in dropped capital styles.

To apply a dropped capital, position the insertion point in the paragraph to format, and then open the Drop Cap dialog box. For example, click Format on the menu bar, and then click Drop Cap, or click Utilities on the menu bar, click Plug-ins, and then click Drop cap. Some Drop Cap dialog boxes have a tab displaying a list of built-in styles as well as a Custom Drop Cap tab

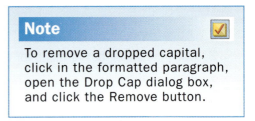

Note

To remove a dropped capital, click in the formatted paragraph, open the Drop Cap dialog box, and click the Remove button.

that displays formatting options. Key the number of lines you want the character to drop, or select alternative formatting options, and then close the dialog box to apply the formats.

STEP-BY-STEP 5.4

1. In the **Coffee** file, position the insertion point in the paragraph of text beginning with *The baristas*.

2. Open the Drop Cap dialog box. For example, click **Format** on the menu bar, and then click **Drop Cap**. Click the **Custom Drop Cap** tab, if necessary.

STEP-BY-STEP 5.4 Continued

3. Key **2** for the number of lines to drop the capital. Click the **OK** or **Apply** button to apply the dropped capital to the paragraph. It should look similar to Figure 5-8.

FIGURE 5-8
Dropped capital

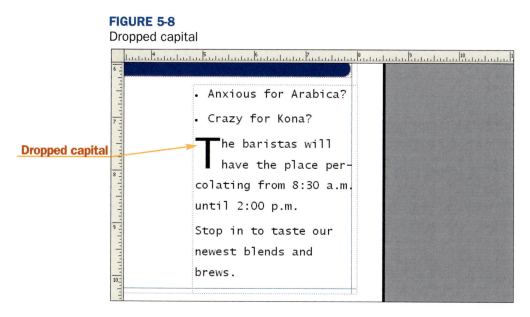

Dropped capital

• Anxious for Arabica?

• Crazy for Kona?

The baristas will have the place percolating from 8:30 a.m. until 2:00 p.m.

Stop in to taste our newest blends and brews.

4. Save changes and leave the **Coffee** file open to use in the next exercise.

Create Text Art

Some desktop-publishing programs, such as Publisher, have a feature that lets you turn your text into graphics objects. Creating an object from text characters lets you remove the constraints of the text box and adds flexibility in terms of formatting, sizing, and positioning the text. For example, you can format the object with special effects such as fills and shadows, scale it, and position it anywhere on the page. However, not all desktop publishing programs include a feature for creating text art. If you are using a program such as PageMaker that does not, you may be able to create a text art object in a different program and insert it into your publication.

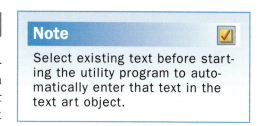

To create a text art object, start the utility provided with your program. For example, click Insert on the menu bar, click Picture, and then click WordArt. Alternatively, click the appropriate toolbar button to start the utility. In most cases, you then select a style and click OK. Key the text you want included in the object and select font formatting. Click OK to create the object.

Note ☑

Select existing text before starting the utility program to automatically enter that text in the text art object.

You can use standard techniques to format the entire object, such as scaling, moving, and rotating. In addition, buttons on a toolbar enable you to modify the text art itself. For example, you may be able to change the shape, edit the text, or select a different style for the text. Other options may include changing to vertical text, adjusting character height and spacing, and selecting an alignment.

STEP-BY-STEP 5.5

1. In the **Coffee** file, delete the text box that contains the text *March 22 Coffee Tasting*.

2. Start the utility for creating text art. For example, click the **Insert WordArt** button on the toolbar. If your program does not support text art, locate and insert **DP Step 5-5** from the data files into the **Coffee** file and then continue with step 5 below.

3. Click a style that displays simple black text in a shape that arcs up in the middle, and then click the **OK** button.

4. Key the text **Coffee Tasting** to replace the sample text, and then click the **OK** button. Your program creates the text object and inserts it in the publication.

5. Resize the object to 1.25 inches high by 6.5 inches wide.

6. Position the object vertically 4.25 inches from the upper-left corner and horizontally 1 inch from the upper-left corner (centered between the left and right margins). It should look similar to Figure 5-9.

FIGURE 5-9
Text as a graphics object

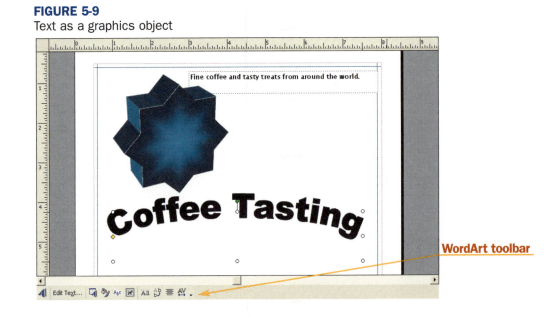

WordArt toolbar

7. Save changes and leave the **Coffee** file open to use in the next exercise.

Add Text to Shapes

In some programs, such as Publisher, you can add text to shapes inserted in a publication. Simply select the shape and key the text. The program automatically inserts a text box that is sized and positioned to constrain the text within the shape. You can key and format the text as you would in any text box. Not all programs—including PageMaker—have a feature for adding text to shapes, but you may be able to create the same effect by layering a text box on top of the shape.

S TEP-BY-STEP 5.6

1. In the **Coffee** file, select the star shape.

2. Key the text **March 22**. If your program does not support adding text to shapes, insert a text box or frame sized to fit within the star. Format the text box with no fill and no stroke, and then key the text in the text box.

3. Select the text and format it as follows: Use a serif font such as Times New Roman. Set the font size to 36 points and set the font color to white. (If the text does not show up well in white, use black.) Center-align the text vertically and horizontally in the text box. It should look similar to Figure 5-10.

FIGURE 5-10
Text added to a shape

4. Save changes and leave the **Coffee** file open to use in the next exercise.

Insert Horizontal Rules

Horizontal rules are printing lines that can be inserted before or after a paragraph of text. In most programs, you apply a rule using a dialog box such as Horizontal Rules or Paragraph Rules. First, position the insertion point in the paragraph to be formatted. Next, open the dialog box for applying rules and select the option to apply a rule before the paragraph and/or after the paragraph. For example, click Format on the menu bar, and then click Horizontal Rules. Or, click Type on the menu bar, click Paragraph, and then click the Rules button. Select formatting options for each rule. For example, select the line weight, the line style, and the line color. You can also specify to indent the rule from the left and/or right text box margin, and you may be able to specify how much space to leave between the text and the rule. Click OK to apply the rule. To remove a rule, open the dialog box and deselect the option for applying the rule before and/or after the paragraph.

STEP-BY-STEP 5.7

1. In the **Coffee** file, click in the first bullet item, and then open the dialog box for applying horizontal rules.

2. Select options to apply a 2-point, single-line rule before the paragraph. Change the line color to the custom blue you created earlier in this lesson, then click the **OK** button as many times as necessary to close all dialog boxes and apply the rule.

3. Position the insertion point in the last paragraph of text in the same text box and open the dialog box for applying horizontal rules.

4. Select options to apply a 2-point, single-line rule after the paragraph. Change the line color to the custom blue you created earlier in this lesson, and then click the **OK** button as many times as necessary to close all dialog boxes and apply the rule. When deselected, the text box should look similar to Figure 5-11.

FIGURE 5-11
Horizontal rules applied before and after paragraphs

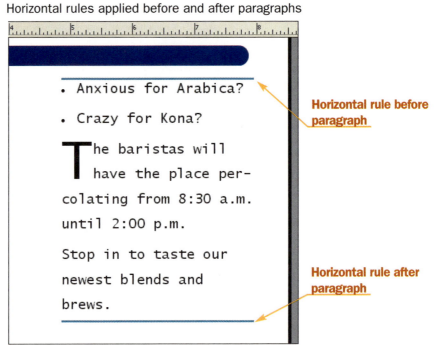

Horizontal rule before paragraph

Horizontal rule after paragraph

5. Save changes and leave the **Coffee** file open to use in the next exercise.

Apply Border Art

Some desktop-publishing programs, such as Publisher, come with a collection of built-in border art pictures you can apply around rectangular objects such as text boxes and squares. To apply border art, select the object, and then open the Format *Object* dialog box. Click the Border Art button to open the Border Art dialog box. Click the border you want to apply, and then click OK. Click OK again to close the Format *Object* dialog box and apply the border.

In some programs, you can create a custom picture border. Simply click the Create Custom button in the Border Art dialog box and then click the Select Picture button. Locate and select the picture file you want to use, and then click OK. Key a name for the new border and then click OK again. The new border is added to the list of available borders.

> **Note** ☑️
>
> To create a page border, draw a text box the size of the margins on the master page, and then apply a border to it. The border then appears in the background on all pages in the publication.

STEP-BY-STEP 5.8

1. In the **Coffee** file, select the text box containing the slogan at the top of the page.

2. Open the Border Art dialog box. For example, click **Format** on the menu bar, click **Text Box**, click the **Colors and Lines** tab, and then click the **Border Art** button. If you are using a program such as PageMaker that does not have a feature for applying border art, apply a blue 6-point triple line stroke on all sides of the object, and then skip to step 4.

3. Select the **Classical Wave** border, and then click the **OK** button as many times as necessary to close all dialog boxes and apply the border. If the Classical Wave border is not available, select any border.

4. Center-align the text horizontally in the text box. If the text appears too close to the border, align it vertically in the text box as well, or resize the text box if necessary.

5. Select the star shape and align it on the left, relative to the left and right margins. The page should look similar to Figure 5-12.

FIGURE 5-12
Border art around a text box

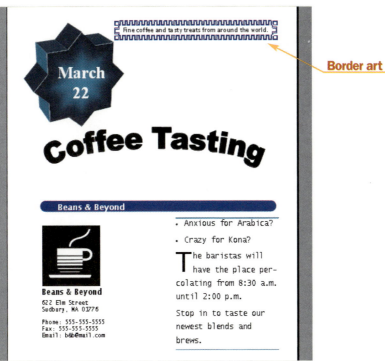

6. Save changes and leave the **Coffee** file open to use in the next exercise.

Create a Watermark

A *watermark* is a semitransparent image usually inserted in the background of printed publications. Watermarks can be found on many types of publications but are often used on stationery, business cards, and even currency and checks, as they are difficult to forge and can be proof of authenticity. In most programs, watermarks must be created from a picture file. You insert the picture file on the page and adjust its size and position. Then, adjust the image control settings to make the picture semitransparent. The image control settings may be in a dialog box or on a toolbar, such as the Picture toolbar. Send the image to the back of the stacking order so it is layered behind all other objects on the page.

> **Extra for Experts**
>
> If you want to use an object that is not a picture file, you can save it as a picture. Right-click the object and click Save as Picture on the shortcut menu to open the Save As dialog box. Key a name, select a storage location, and then click the Save button.

Some programs have options that automatically adjust the color and transparency to settings appropriate for a watermark. For example, in some programs you click the Color button on the Picture toolbar and then click Washout. In other programs, you must manually adjust the settings to at least 70%. For example, click Element on the menu bar, click Image, and then click Image Control. Increase the lightness and contrast settings as necessary (click Apply to see the change without closing the dialog box), and then click OK.

Most programs let you control the transparency of any image, but some programs, such as Adobe PageMaker, provide image control only for black and white or grayscale bitmaps. In that case, you may need to convert an image to grayscale in a different program and then insert it into your publication.

> **Note**
>
> If you want a watermark to appear on every page of a publication, insert it on a master page.

STEP-BY-STEP 5.9

1. In the **Coffee** file, delete the picture of the cup of coffee near the lower-left corner of the page.

2. Change to Master Page view.

3. Insert the picture file **DP Step 5-9** from the data files on the master page.

4. Resize the picture to approximately 7.5 inches high by 7.5 inches wide, and center it horizontally and vertically relative to the page margins.

STEP-BY-STEP 5.9 Continued

5. Set the image control to washout, or set the lightness to 85% and the contrast to somewhere between 20% and 50%, then click the **OK** button.

6. Switch back to regular page view. The page should look similar to the one in Figure 5-13.

FIGURE 5-13
Watermark in the background

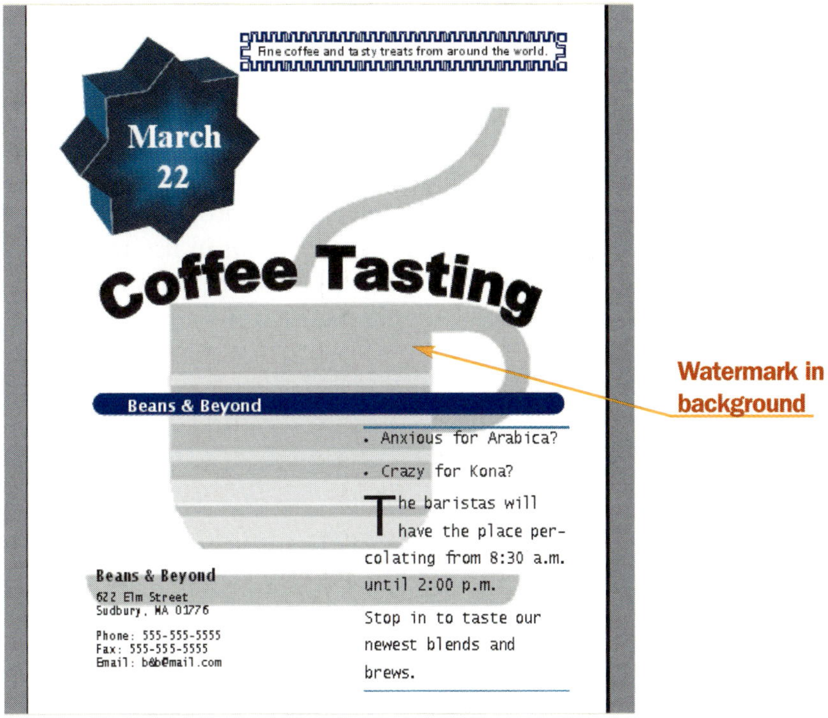

Watermark in background

7. Print one copy of the **Coffee** file.

8. Save changes and close the **Coffee** file. Leave your desktop publishing program open to use in the next exercise.

Use Design Objects

Many desktop-publishing programs, including Publisher, come with tools for automatically setting up and formatting elements of a publication that otherwise have to be created manually. For example, you may be able to quickly insert such features as tables of contents, logos, forms, pull-quotes, and mastheads. Unfortunately, not all desktop publishing programs include tools for automating the creation of these features. If you are using a program such as PageMaker that does not, you can manually insert and format text and graphics and design these features on the page.

If your program includes pre-designed publication elements, they are probably listed in a design gallery or dialog box. To open the gallery, click the Design Gallery Object button on the toolbar, or click Insert on the menu bar, and then click a command such as Design Gallery Object. In the gallery, click the category of the element you want to create, click the design you want to use, and then click Insert. The element is inserted as an object, or a group of objects, in the publication. You can customize the object by replacing sample text and graphics, by sizing it and positioning it on the page, and even by changing formatting. For example, you can change the font or color scheme or apply special effects.

Mastheads

A *masthead* is simply the information displayed across the top of a newsletter or newspaper, including, but not limited to, the title, the date, and the volume number. A masthead usually includes graphics elements such as borders or rules. Some include quotes, slogans, color, and pictures. You can set up a masthead manually by positioning text boxes and graphics across the top of the page and applying formatting. However, if your program can automatically set up a masthead, you can easily select one from the program's built-in list and insert it in your publication. To customize the masthead, replace the sample text with the correct information and make any formatting changes you want, such as modifying the color or font scheme.

STEP-BY-STEP 5.10

1. In your desktop publishing program, open **DP Step 5-10** from the data files.

2. Save the file as **Brew**. This is the front page of a newsletter.

3. Open the gallery or dialog box that lists available design objects. For example, click **Insert** on the menu bar and then click **Design Gallery Object**.

> **Note**
>
> If your program does not offer design objects, you can set up the masthead yourself using text boxes and formatting. Ask your instructor for more information.

4. Select the **Masthead** category, and then click the **Accessory Bar** masthead design. Click the **Insert Object** button to insert the object into the publication.

5. Align the object vertically with the top of the page, relative to the page margins.

6. Replace the sample text *Newsletter Title* with the text **What's Brewing?**

STEP-BY-STEP 5.10 Continued

7. Replace the sample text *Business Name* (or *Your organization*) with the text **Beans & Beyond**.

8. Replace the sample text *Newsletter Date* with the text **Spring/Summer**.

9. Change the color scheme to Sienna. The top portion of the newsletter should look similar to Figure 5-14.

FIGURE 5-14
Masthead object in publication

10. Save changes and leave the **Brew** file open to use in the next exercise.

Tables of Contents

Use a *table of contents* to direct the reader to specific articles, stories, or chapters in a publication. Although traditionally associated with long publications, a table of contents can be useful in short publications such as newsletters, as well. A table of contents usually includes a list of the headlines or titles on the left and the page numbers where the items begin on the right. It may or may not have *dot leaders* along the line between the two columns.

Extra for Experts

A few programs, including Page-Maker, have features for generating a table of contents that automatically updates the page numbers if you add, delete, or rearrange content. First, you apply styles to mark the paragraphs you want to include in the table, and then you select the command to generate the table and insert it in a text box.

If your program can automatically set up a table of contents, you simply select the design you want to use, replace the sample text with the correct headlines, titles, and page numbers, and then size and position the object in the publication. If you are using a program such as PageMaker that does not include design objects, either manually create a table of contents as shown in Figure 5-15, or skip the following exercise.

STEP-BY-STEP 5.11

1. In the **Brew** file, open the gallery or dialog box that lists available design objects.

2. Select the **Tables of Contents** category, and then select the **Accessory Bar** design. Click the **Insert Object** button to insert the object into the publication.

3. Size and position the object to fit in the left column between the masthead and the existing article.

4. Replace the list of titles (*Inside Story*) with the following list so it looks similar to Figure 5-15:

   Perc or Drip? Which Brewing Method's Right for You

   Costa Rica: A Central American Paradise

   Meet the Owner: An Interview with Vera McGill

   Letters to the Editor

   Just for Laughs

   Check This Out! Links to Interesting Web Sites

   Taste Test

FIGURE 5-15
Table of contents in publication

5. Save changes and leave the **Brew** file open to use in the next exercise.

Logos

A *logo* is a symbol representing a company or organization, which may include graphics, or both. Usually, logos are designed using a different program, such as a graphics program, or by hand, but they are often printed in publications as part of stationery *letterheads*, in the masthead of a newsletter, or even as a watermark. A letterhead is the area on a sheet of stationery where the name, address, and other information about a company or individual are printed. If a logo has been saved as a graphics file, you can simply insert it in a publication as you would any graphics file. If it has been drawn or printed, you can scan it in. If you don't have an existing logo, you may be able to use your desktop publishing program to create one by inserting, sizing, and positioning text and graphics.

If you are using a program such a Publisher that can automatically create a logo, you simply select the logo design you want to use, replace the sample text with the name of your organization, and then replace the sample picture with the picture of your choice. You can size and position the logo anywhere in the publication. The result is a professional-looking logo in minutes.

S TEP-BY-STEP 5.12

1. In the **Brew** file, open the dialog box or gallery that lists available design objects. Alternatively, insert the graphics file **DP Step 5-12a** into the white space in the lower-right corner of the page, and then skip to step 6.

2. Select the **Logos** category, and then select the **Open Oval Logo** design. Click the **Insert Object** button to insert the object into the publication.

3. Drag the object over into the white space in the lower-right corner of the page.

4. Replace the picture (the pyramid shape above the text) with the picture file **DP Step 5-12b** from the data files.

5. Replace the sample text with the text **Beans & Beyond**.

STEP-BY-STEP 5.12 Continued

6. Resize the object to fill the white space—about 3 inches wide by 1.5 inches high. When you are finished, the whole page should look similar to Figure 5-16.

FIGURE 5-16
Completed page

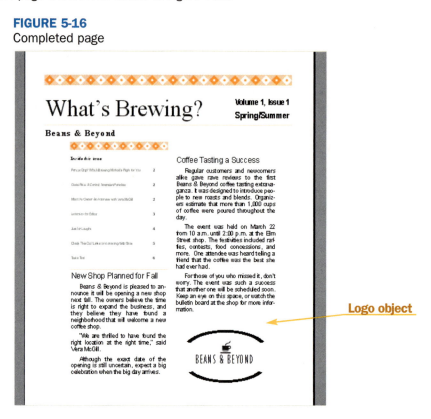

7. Print one copy of the **Brew** file.

8. Save changes and close the file. Close your desktop-publishing program.

SUMMARY

In this lesson, you learned:

- The RGB color system is used to define color on monitors, and the CMYK color system is used to define color in print.

- You can define custom colors by using a color bar or by keying a color system value.

- You can add a gradient, pattern, or texture to a fill, and a pattern to a stroke.

- Shadows and 3-D effects create the illusion of depth on the page.

- A dropped capital is a decorative effect that makes the first letter in a paragraph stand out from the rest of the text.

- Some programs have utilities that let you turn text into graphics objects, and some programs let you add text to shapes.

- You can insert horizontal rules before and/or after a paragraph.

- Some programs let you apply pictures as borders around rectangular objects.

- You can insert a watermark in the background of any page in a publication.

- Some programs come with objects already designed for use as logos, mastheads, and tables of contents.

VOCABULARY *Review*

Define the following terms:

CMYK	Letterhead	Spot color
Color system	Logo	Table of contents
Dot leader	Masthead	Texture
Dropped capital	Pattern	Tint
Gradient	Process color	Transparency
Horizontal rule	RGB	Watermark
Hue	Shadow	

REVIEW *Questions*

TRUE / FALSE

Circle T if the statement is true or F if the statement is false.

T   F   **1.** The color system used for displaying colors on a monitor is called CMYK.

T   F   **2.** CMYK values are usually entered as percentages.

T   F   **3.** Transparency measures the amount of white added to a color.

T   F   **4.** Patterns may be applied to both fills and strokes.

T   F   **5.** A radial gradient blends colors out from a central point.

T   F   **6.** All desktop publishing programs have features for transforming text into graphics objects.

T F 7. You can place rules only on the left and right of a paragraph of text.

T F 8. Watermarks are sometimes used as proof of authenticity.

T F 9. Logos may be included as part of a letterhead.

T F 10. A shadow is the only special effect that creates the illusion of depth.

WRITTEN QUESTIONS

Write a brief answer to the following questions.

1. Name at least two reasons for using spot color when printing a publication.

2. What is the difference between a texture fill and a pattern fill?

3. What is a common use for a dropped capital?

4. List at least two benefits of converting text to a graphics object.

5. Name at least two ways to apply borderlines to text boxes.

FILL IN THE BLANK

Complete the following sentences by writing the correct word or words in the blanks provided.

1. A(n) _____ is a symbol representing a company or organization.

2. Use a(n) _____ to direct a reader to specific articles, stories, or chapters in a publication.

3. A(n) _____ is a semitransparent image usually inserted in the background of printed publications.

4. A(n) _____ is a decorative effect in which the first character in a paragraph is larger than the other characters.

5. Use a(n) _____ gradient to blend colors horizontally across a shape.

6. _____ is the range of a color from black to white.

7. To make a color completely see-through, set the _____ to 100%.

8. The colors of ink used in four-color printing are often called _____ color.

9. The Pantone Matching System is an example of a(n) _____ color system.

10. The *K* in CMYK stands for _____.

PROJECTS

PROJECT 5-1

1. Launch your desktop publishing program and create a new blank full-page document with 1-inch margins.

2. Save the file as **GHA**. You are going to design letterhead stationery for a medical office.

3. Change to Master Page view. Because you want the letterhead information displayed on all pages, you will insert the data on the master page.

4. Insert a horizontal ruler guide at 2 inches on the vertical ruler, and another one at 9 inches on the vertical ruler.

5. Insert a text box 7 inches wide by 1.5 inches high. Align the bottom of the text box on the top ruler guide, and center it horizontally between the margins.

6. Insert and format text as follows:
   A. On the first line in the text box, use a 36-point serif font such as Sylfaen and key **Good Health Associates, Inc.**
   B. Center the text horizontally and vertically in the text box.
   C. Insert a 1-point horizontal rule below the paragraph, sized to extend from the left margin to the right margin.

7. Insert another text box 7 inches wide by 1.5 inches high. Align the top of the text box on the bottom ruler guide, and center it horizontally between the margins.

8. Insert and format text as follows:
   A. On the first line in the text box, use the same serif font you used in step 6 in 14 points to key **320 Matheson Street ~ Healdsburg, California ~ 95448**, and then press **Enter**.
   B. Key **Telephone (707) 555-5555 ~ Fax (707) 555-6666 ~ Email mail@gha.com**.
   C. If the tilde characters (~) appear too high in relation to the other text on the line, format them using the Subscript font effect.
   D. Center all lines horizontally, and align them vertically with the bottom of the text box.
   E. Position the insertion point in the first line of text, and insert a 1-point horizontal rule above the paragraph, sized to extend from the left margin to the right margin.

9. Insert a heart shape near the top of the page, sized at 0.5 inches by 0.5 inches. (If you cannot draw a heart using your program's drawing tools, draw a different shape such as a star.) Format the shape as follows:
   A. Position the shape horizontally 1 inch from the upper-left corner and vertically 0.5 inches from the upper-left corner. Set the text wrap to None.
   B. Open the custom color dialog box and select the CMYK system.
   C. Enter the following values: Cyan: 0; Magenta: 55; Yellow: 15; Black: 0. Name the color if necessary.
   D. Click the **OK** button until all dialog boxes are closed and the color is applied.
   E. If possible, apply a 3-D effect to the shape, such as style 10, which tilts the face down and to the right and extends the top and left sides.

10. Use the **Copy** and **Paste** commands to duplicate the shape. Flip or reflect the shape horizontally, and then position the duplicate horizontally 1 inch from the upper-right corner and vertically 0.5 inches from the upper-right corner.

11. Create a watermark as follows:
    A. Insert a clip art picture of a medical staff. If you cannot locate a suitable picture, use **DP Project 5-1** from the data files.
    B. Set the image control color to washout, or adjust the lightness and contrast as necessary. (Try 85% lightness and somewhere between 15% and 55% contrast.)
    C. Size the picture to about 5.5 inches square, and center it horizontally and vertically relative to the margins.

12. Change back to regular view.

13. Print one copy of the publication.

14. Save changes and close the **GHA** file. Leave your desktop publishing program open to use in Project 5-2.

PROJECT 5-2

1. In your desktop publishing program, open **DP Project 5-2** from the data files. This is a version of the CNO Newsletter you worked on previously. You are going to enhance the document with borders, lines, dropped capitals, and other effects.

2. Save the file as **CNONews3**.

3. On page 1, insert a masthead design object in a simple style, such as Checkers. Format the object as follows. (If your program does not have masthead design objects, use text boxes to insert the masthead information.)
   A. Center the object horizontally between the left and right margins, and position it 0.5 inches from the upper-left corner of the page.
   B. Replace the sample text *Newsletter Title* with the text **CNO News**.
   C. Replace the sample text *Business Name* (or *Your organization*) with the text **Community Network Organization**.
   D. Replace the sample text *Newsletter Date* with the text **Fall/Winter**.
   E. Change the color scheme to Harbor, or any scheme that uses dark green. If no color schemes are available, create a custom dark green. (For example, CMYK: C: **67**; M: **31**; Y: **37**; K: **36**.) If the green appears too dark, select or create a brighter green.

4. On page 1, insert a table of contents design object in the same style you used for the masthead. Format the object as follows. (If your program does not have table of contents design objects, use text boxes to insert the information.)
   A. Replace the first three story names (*Inside Story*) with the following: **Officer Nominations, Holiday Helpers Needed, Letters to the Editor**. Each story is on page 2.
   B. Delete the remaining items in the table. (Select all of the information, click **Table** on the menu bar, click **Delete**, and then click **Rows**.)
   C. Size and position the object to fit in the white space in the lower-right corner of the page.

5. Position the insertion point in the first paragraph under the headline *Annual Fundraiser*, and apply a dropped capital letter sized to drop 3 lines. Adjust the text box depth, if necessary, to display all text again.

6. Position the insertion point in the headline text *Volunteer News*, and apply a 2-point dark green horizontal rule before the paragraph.

7. Switch to page 2 and select the text box containing the headline *Letters to the Editor*. Apply a simple art border, such as solid block checks, around the object. If your program does not have art borders, apply a heavy, dashed line border. If necessary, adjust the line spacing in the text box to 1 line, and the paragraph spacing to 6 points after each paragraph to fit all text in the text box.

8. Insert dark green 2-point horizontal rules before the first paragraph in each text box in the left column.

9. Position the insertion point in the first paragraph under the headline *Holiday Helpers Needed* and create a dropped capital letter that drops 2 lines. Adjust text boxes as necessary to show all text.

10. Print one copy of each page—either using double-sided printing or on two sheets.

11. Save changes and close the **CNONews3** file. Close your desktop publishing program.

SCANS WEB PROJECT

For a history or social studies project, use the Internet to research a major holiday celebrated in a country other than the United States. For example, you might research the Indian holiday of Diwali, Chinese New Year, or Cinco de Mayo. Look for information about the history of the holiday and ways in which the holiday is observed or celebrated. When you have finished the research, use your desktop publishing program to create a greeting card for the holiday, including pictures and text.

SCANS TEAMWORK PROJECT

As a group, plan and design an advertisement for a travel destination you would like to visit. Think of four or five possible spots, and then vote to select one. Look up information about the location, either in books and magazines or on the Web. If you have time, you might contact a travel agent for information. Make a list of the highlights appealing to visitors, and try to think up a slogan or catch phrase that would catch a reader's attention. Locate pictures to illustrate the ad. Consider using a watermark, logo, or other design element.

When you have the information you need, plan the advertisement publication. Decide on the page setup, including the page size, sheet size, and orientation. For example, you may want to make a poster, a postcard mailer, or a banner. Mock-up the ad so you can see where to place text and graphics. When you are ready, use your desktop publishing program to create the publication document. Insert all text and objects, and position them on the pages so the document is appealing and easy to read. When you are finished, check the spelling and then print the publication.

CRITICAL*Thinking*

ACTIVITY 5-1

Use your desktop publishing program to design and create a book jacket for a book you have read, or for a report you are preparing. Plan the publication carefully, considering the page size and sheet size and all the components that must be included. For example, the document will be printed only on one side, but it will probably have five pages: a back page, a front page, and a spine (the strip along the binding between the back and front), as well as folds for the front and back covers. Use a ruler to measure the actual book so you know how large a sheet to use and how large the pages must be. Write the text and either create or locate the graphics, and then insert the data into the publication. Adjust the size and position of all objects, and enhance the publication using color, horizontal rules, and other effects. When you are satisfied with the publication, check the spelling, print it, and share it with your class.

PUBLISHING A DOCUMENT

OBJECTIVES

Upon completion of this lesson, you should be able to:

- Plan for publication.
- Perform prepress checks.
- Set properties for desktop printing.
- Enable trapping.
- Print a composite and color separations.
- Save a file for commercial printing.
- Deliver files to a commercial printer.

Estimated Time: 1.5 hours

VOCABULARY

Bleed

Camera-ready

Composite

Compress

Crop

Crop marks

PostScript

PostScript Printer Description file

Print properties

Printer's spreads

Proof

Publish

Reader's spreads

Separations

Trapping

A document created with a desktop publishing program is not really complete until it is *published*. Publishing is the method you use to output the document so you can distribute it to readers. The two main methods of publishing are printing the document on your desktop printer or having it printed by a commercial printer. A third option is to print a copy on your desktop printer, and then have it reproduced at a copy shop. In this lesson, you learn how to decide the type of publication best suited for a particular project and how to prepare a document for publishing.

Plan for Publication

You make some decisions regarding publication before you even start a project. As you learned in Lesson 1, you should always start by determining the physical aspects of the publication, such as page size, paper stock, method of binding, number of colors, and the number of copies you will need. And, of course, you must consider your budget. All these factors affect the decision of how to publish the completed document. For example, if your desktop printer cannot

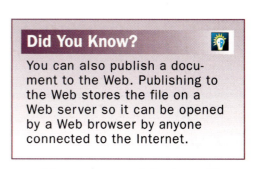

Did You Know?

You can also publish a document to the Web. Publishing to the Web stores the file on a Web server so it can be opened by a Web browser by anyone connected to the Internet.

accommodate the paper size you want to use, you must consider a commercial printer. If you plan to fold a booklet or staple a newsletter in the upper-left corner, you might not need a commercial printer. But if you want a more sophisticated binding you may have no other choice. Other things to consider include how fast you need the document published; the quality you expect in the finished product; and extra options, such as embossing or foil stamping.

Select a Publication Method

As mentioned, the basic choices for publishing a document are to use your desktop printer, a commercial printer, or a copy shop. Use the following guidelines for deciding which method is best for a particular job.

■ In general, if you need only a few copies of a publication and are working within a tight budget, your desktop printer may be the best choice. Keep in mind, however, that the quality of the publication depends a great deal on the specific printer you are using. A laser printer provides the best quality output, followed by an inkjet printer. Other considerations include the time you must spend manning the printer, the cost of ink or toner, the necessity of folding or binding by hand, and whether your printer can handle the project specifications such as page size, color, or double-sided printing.

■ Use a copy shop if you need to produce many copies, if you have a tight budget, or if you need the publication in a hurry. A copy shop may also be able to handle folding or basic binding techniques such as stapling. When you use a copy shop, the quality of the finished product depends on the quality of the original being reproduced, as well as on the available equipment. Before you commit to a copy shop, consider generating a test copy so you can determine if it meets your standards.

■ Finally, you should use a commercial printer if you want the highest quality product and if you can afford it. Other benefits of using a commercial printer include access to more binding options, the ability to handle special orders, and the knowledge and advice an experienced printer can provide.

Select a Commercial Printer

If you decide to use a commercial printer, then the next step is choosing one. The cost of the job should not be the only factor to influence your decision. You will have to work closely with the printer from the very outset of the project, so you should find someone you are comfortable with and who you trust. Following are some of the questions you should ask a commercial printer before you even begin designing the publication:

■ What type of color will be used—spot, process, or a combination—and must you use a specific color matching system?

■ Does the commercial printer want the document file in a particular format, such as PostScript, or is your program's file format suitable?

■ How does the commercial printer want the file delivered? Can it be on a disk or CD or sent electronically on the Internet?

■ Does the printer have in stock the type and quantity of paper you've selected?

■ Does the printer have the necessary facilities for folding or binding the publication as required?

■ What type of proof do you need to submit? Can you print a composite and color separations on your desktop printer, or does the printer require *camera-ready* film? Camera-ready film is film made of the finished pages that can be used to publish the document.

■ For bound or folded publications, should you submit pages formatted as *printer's spreads* or *reader's spreads*? Reader's spreads are basically facing pages—such as page 2 on the left and page 3 on the right. In printer's spreads, the pages are arranged in the order that they must be printed for the page order to be correct when the publication is bound. For example, in a 4-page folded booklet, page 4 is on the left of the sheet and page 1 is on the right of the sheet.

Perform Prepress Checks

No matter which method of publication you select, before you publish the document, you should be sure to use a spelling checker and to proofread the file for errors. (Checking spelling is covered in Lesson 1.) You should also look over the design and layout to determine if there are any improvements to make. For example, you may need to nudge the location of a headline in a newsletter, or expand the size of a text box so all the text is displayed.

Check Page Design

Some desktop-publishing programs, such as Publisher, include tools for checking the design of a publication. A design checker works similar to a spelling checker. It locates and highlights design problems, such as too much text to fit in a text box, and may find grammar and punctuation problems as well. To start the checker, click Tools on the menu bar, and then click Design Checker. The design checker may display a dialog box asking which pages to check. Click OK to check them all, or key the specific page numbers. Click OK to start the check. When the checker finds a problem, it displays a dialog box similar to the one in Figure 6-1. You can choose to ignore the problem, ignore all occurrences of the problem, or close the dialog box. You cannot continue the check until you select an option or fix the problem. You do not have to close the dialog box to fix the problem. Simply drag the box out of the way and work in the publication. Click the Explain button to start the Help program and display information about how to fix the problem. When the problem is corrected, click the Continue button to restart the check.

FIGURE 6-1
Design Checker dialog box

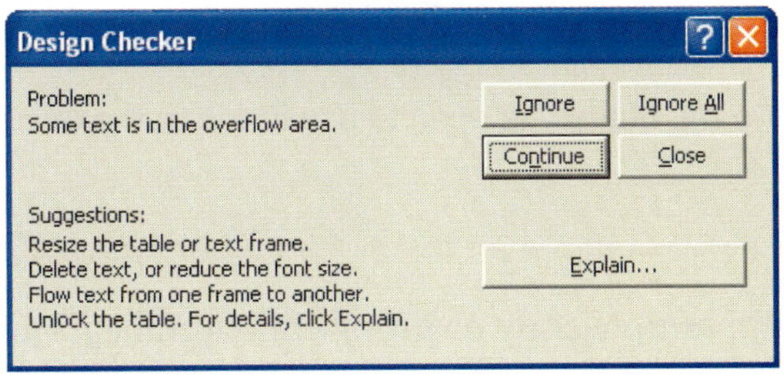

If your program has a design checker, use it to complete the following exercise. If you are using a program such as PageMaker that does not have a design checker, you can complete the exercise simply by examining the publication on your computer screen to find problems and correct them.

STEP-BY-STEP 6.1

1. Launch your desktop publishing program, and open **DP Step 6-1** from the data files.

2. Save the file as **Mailer**. This publication is a version of the postcard mailer you used in previous lessons.

3. Run a spelling checker to identify spelling errors. If the checker finds any errors, correct them.

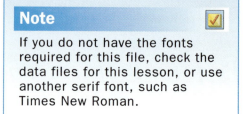

Note

If you do not have the fonts required for this file, check the data files for this lesson, or use another serif font, such as Times New Roman.

4. Start the design checker if one is available in your program. For example, click **Tools** on the menu bar, and then click **Design Checker**. Click the **OK** button to check the publication with the default settings. The program stops when it comes to the first problem—a text box that is too small to display all of the text it contains. If your program does not have a design checker feature, try to locate the text box on page 1 that is too small to display all text.

5. Select the problem text box, and resize it so it is about 1.3 inches high. You can do this by dragging the top sizing handle up or by keying the value in the appropriate dialog box. Once the box has been resized, all of the text appears. If necessary, move the text box up so it doesn't overlap other content on the page.

6. Click the **Continue** button to resume the check. A text box on page 2 is also too small to display all the text it contains. This time, correct the problem by changing the font size.

7. If your program has an AutoFit or Copy fitting feature, select it to automatically resize all the text in the text box to fit. If not, resize the text to 12 or 13 points.

8. Click the **Continue** button to resume the check. The checker should locate two spaces following a period in a text box on page 1. Typing two spaces after a punctuation mark is an incorrect keyboarding technique.

9. Delete one of the spaces. (If necessary, display nonprinting characters so you can see the spaces.)

10. Click the **Continue** button to resume the check. Correct or ignore any other problems that the Design Checker identifies, and then click the **OK** button to complete the check.

11. Save changes and leave the **Mailer** file open to use in the next exercise.

Print Page Proofs

You should always print a sample copy or *proof* of the publication to review before you print all copies or send the publication to a commercial printer. You should proofread the printout for spelling errors that your spelling checker does not catch, and for design problems such as inconsistent line weight, misaligned objects, or mismatched colors that show up more clearly in print. Also, you can see the entire publication at once, and even give it to someone else to check as well. For desktop printing, you can also use a proof to determine if the colors you have selected reproduce the way you expect.

Some desktop publishing programs and some desktop printers have options to control the quality of the output when you print proofs. For example, you may be able to set your desktop printer for a lower quality printing in order to use less ink, or, if you want to check the text but are not concerned with the graphics, you may be able to set your program so it does not print graphics objects. Likewise, if you want to simply scan the proof to see if objects are aligned, you may be able to print thumbnails of each page, which saves paper. These options are usually selected in the Print dialog box, or in one of the print or printer properties dialog boxes. You learn more about print properties in the next exercise.

Before printing, make sure the desktop printer is correctly set up for use with your computer. This means it is physically attached to your computer or network and the printer driver software has been correctly installed. You should also make sure that the proper size paper is correctly loaded in the printer and the printer is turned on. You may want to install fresh ink cartridges or toner to ensure the best color quality.

As you have already learned, to print a copy of a publication on your desktop or network printer, click File on the menu bar and then click Print. A Print dialog box similar to the one in Figure 6-2 opens. Set properties as necessary, and then click the OK or Print button in the Print dialog box to generate the file. Alternatively, to print a single copy of the document using the default settings, click the Print button on the toolbar.

FIGURE 6-2
Print dialog box

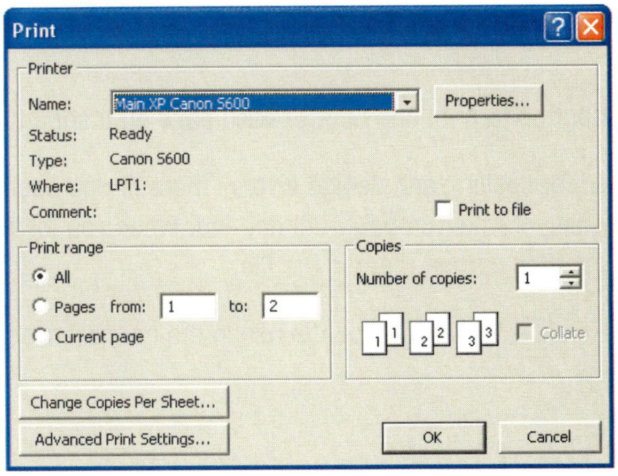

S TEP-BY-STEP 6.2

1. With the **Mailer** file open in your desktop publishing program, click **File** on the menu bar and then click **Print**.

STEP-BY-STEP 6.2 Continued

2. If your printer is capable of different quality output, select the option for draft printing. This option is probably available in your printer's Properties dialog box, which should look similar to Figure 6-3. To open the dialog box, click a button such as **Properties** or **Setup** in the Print dialog box. Select an option such as Draft or Fast, and then click the **OK** button.

FIGURE 6-3
Properties dialog box for a Canon inkjet printer

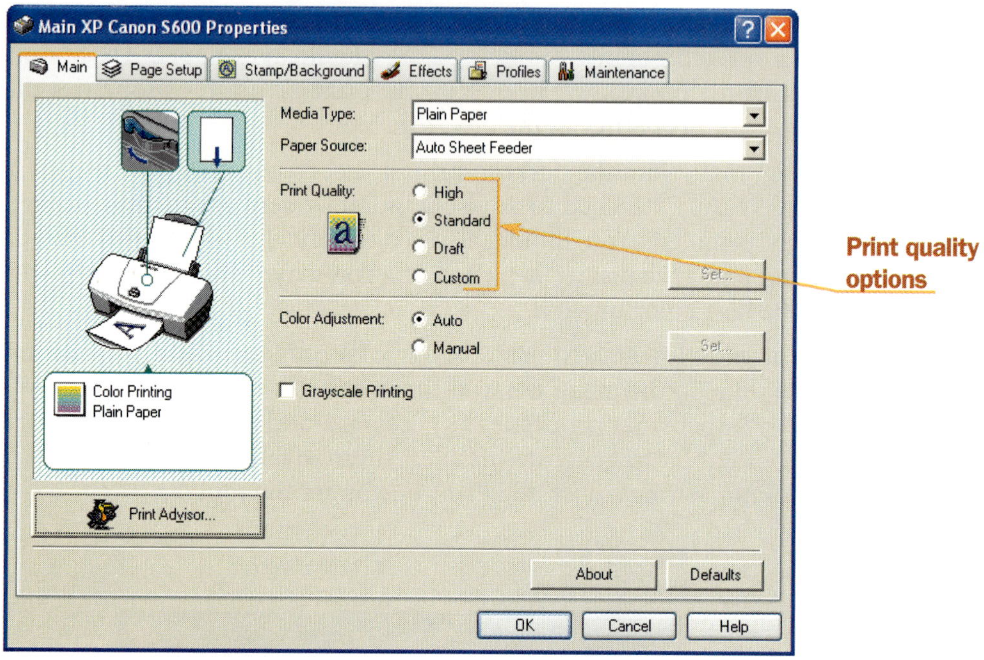

3. Click the **OK** or **Print** button to print one copy of each page on a separate sheet of paper.

4. Proofread the printout for spelling and design errors. There is one spelling error and one grammatical error that the spelling checker probably did not find. When you locate the errors, circle them on the printout in red, and then correct them in the file.

5. Save changes and leave the **Mailer** file open to use in the next exercise.

Set Properties for Desktop Printing

*P*rint properties are the settings that control the way a publication prints on your desktop printer. They fall into two basic categories: *printer options*, which are specific to the printer model you are using; and *print options*, which are specific to the program and the publication document. For example, printer options may include the draft quality, while print options might include whether to print graphics or how many copies of a page to print on one sheet of paper.

You access the print properties through your program's Print dialog box. The available options and the way they are organized depend on your desktop publishing program, your printer, and the publication you are working with. Usually, however, you click a button such as

Properties or Setup to open your printer's Properties dialog box. You click a different button such as Advanced Print Settings or Options to open a Print Settings or Print Options dialog box, similar to the one in Figure 6-4. There may be other buttons for accessing other dialog boxes as well. In each dialog box, select the appropriate options, and then click OK to return to the Print dialog box. When you have set all the necessary properties, click the OK or Print button in the Print dialog box to print the publication.

FIGURE 6-4
Print Settings dialog box

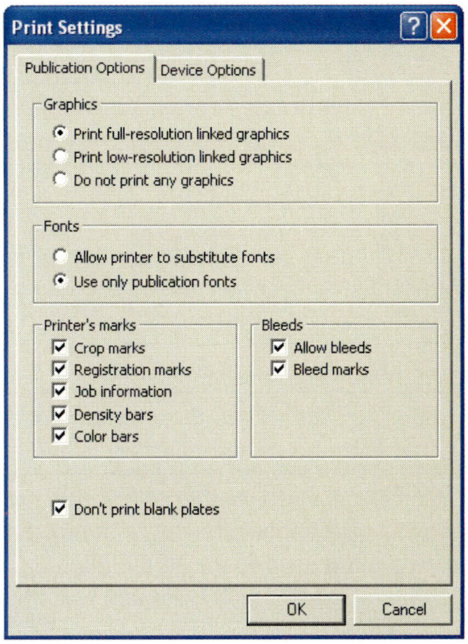

In addition to properties, keep in mind that certain types of publications require special setup or handling to print correctly. For example, duplex (double-sided) printing may require you to print one page, then reinsert the paper correctly in the printer to print the next page. Banners and posters may print on multiple sheets of paper, which must then be arranged to create the complete publication. Conversely, you may be able to print more than one postcard on the same sheet, and then trim them to size.

Some effects also require special handling. For instance, you print a *bleed*, which is an effect created by an object running off the edge of the page, by using options in the Page Setup dialog box to set the publication to print on a sheet size larger than the page size. Position the object in the document so it extends beyond the edge of the page. After printing, you *crop*, or trim, the paper to the appropriate page size.

Table 6-1 lists some common print properties. Keep in mind, however, that because the specific properties available on your computer depend on the printer and the program you are using, you may not have all the properties listed, or you may have more.

TABLE 6-1
Common print properties

PROPERTY	DESCRIPTION
Printer	Select the printer to print the document. Other options may change depending on the printer selected.
Number of copies	Key the number of copies of each page that you want to print.
Collate	Select this option to print pages consecutively. Deselect this option to print all copies of each page before proceeding to the next page.
Print range	Use these options to specify the exact pages to print. Select All to print all pages, key a range separated by a hyphen to print all pages within the range, and/or key specific page numbers separated by commas to print only those pages. Other options may be available, such as printing the current page only, printing only odd- or even-numbered pages, or printing blank pages.
Orientation	Select either landscape or portrait orientation.
Reverse	Select this option to print pages from the end of the document to the beginning, rather than from the beginning to the end.
Printer's marks	Use these options to specify whether to print elements such as **crop marks,** which indicate where the paper should be cut or trimmed down to the correct page size, or color bars, which are used to gauge the printed colors. Marks are displayed only if the paper size is at least 1 inch taller and wider than the page size.
Fonts	Use these options to specify whether to allow font substitution.
Page setup	Depending on your printer, you may be able to scale the output by a percentage of the original size or select an option to control the way the document fits on the printed page. For example, you may be able to select Poster printing or Banner printing, to print thumbnails of each page, and to choose how many copies of each page to print per sheet. Other options may include printing reader's spreads or printer's spreads and tiling the pages.
Graphics or Proof	Use these options to specify whether to include graphics in the printout.
Print quality	Select the quality level you want to use. The higher the quality, the better the output. This option usually determines the resolution, the amount of ink, or number of colors used to print a document.
Color	Use these options to specify grayscale, black and white, or four-color printing. In some programs, or for some publications, you may be able to set options for printing color separations, screens, and/or bleeds.

STEP-BY-STEP 6.3

1. With the **Mailer** file open in your desktop publishing program, click **File** on the menu bar and then click **Print**.

2. If available, select the option for double-sided printing. You may find this option in your printer's properties dialog box. If the option is not available, select to print only page 1. This option is in the Print dialog box.

3. Select the option to print crop marks. You may find this option in the Print Settings or the Print Options dialog box.

4. Click in the Copies or Number of copies box and key **2**.

> ### Did You Know?
> Some desktop printers have a nonprintable region, which is the area on the top, bottom, left, and right of a page on which data cannot be printed. If your printer has a nonprintable region, it is listed in the printer-specific Properties dialog box. You should take your printer's nonprintable region into consideration when designing a document.

5. Click the **OK** or **Print** button to print two copies. If you have duplex printing, both sides of the postcard should print. If not, only page 1 should print. If both pages printed, skip to step 9. Otherwise, continue with the following steps to complete the publication.

6. Reinsert the printed sheets into your printer, positioned correctly to print page 2 on the reverse side.

7. In the **Mailer** file, make page 2 active, click **File** on the menu bar, and then click **Print**.

8. Select to print only page 2, and then repeat steps 3 through 5. You should now have two copies of the **Mailer** publication.

9. Using the crop marks as guides, trim the paper to the publication page size. You can use scissors, but to get a straighter edge, use a paper cutter.

10. Save changes and leave the **Mailer** file open to use in the next exercise.

Enable Trapping

Sometimes adjoining colors are printed slightly out of register, which means they are not aligned properly. When that happens, there may be gaps or overlaps between the colors. *Trapping* is a technique used to adjust the position of adjoining colors to avoid such gaps or overlaps. Most desktop publishing programs have automatic trapping that you can turn off or on. By default, your program uses typical trapping settings appropriate for most publications. You can adjust the trapping settings in most desktop publishing programs to fine-tune the way trapping is applied. For example, you may be able to specify the trap width or set custom trapping for objects.

To enable trapping for a publication, open the trapping preferences dialog box, which should look similar to Figure 6-5. For example, click Tools on the menu bar, click Commercial Printing Tools, click Trapping, and then click Preferences. In some programs, you simply click File on the menu bar, click Preferences, and then click Trapping. Select the option to enable trapping, and then click OK.

FIGURE 6-5
Trapping Preferences dialog box

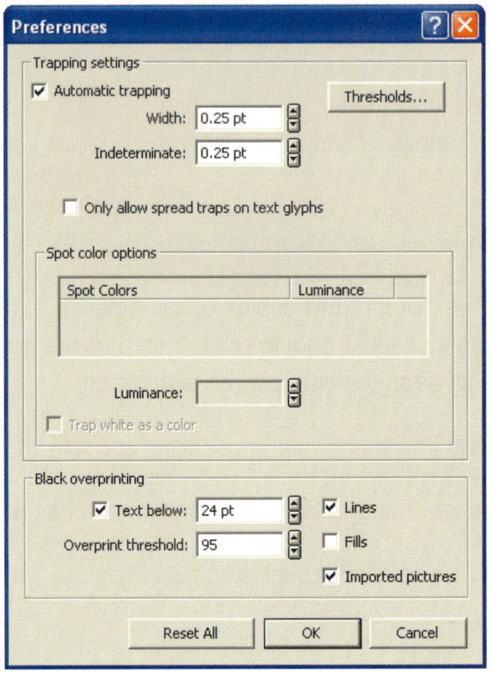

S TEP-BY-STEP 6.4

1. In the **Mailer** file, open the trapping preferences dialog box.

2. Select the option to enable trapping, and then click the **OK** button.

3. Save changes and leave the **Mailer** file open to use in the next exercise.

Prepare a Composite and Color Separations

A commercial printer will probably want you to submit a final *composite* proof, which is an accurate copy of the publication, as well as *separations*, which are printouts showing the layout of each color—black, cyan, magenta, and yellow for process color printing, and each spot for spot color printing—on separate sheets of paper. A composite is the default method of printing. All components and all colors are printed on each page. You printed a composite of the Mailer file earlier in this lesson. If you want to print separations, you must select that option in the Print dialog box. You may also select whether to print a separation page for each color in the publication, or for only a selected color. Note that separations generally print in black and white because they are used to note the position of each color, not to match colors.

In some programs, such as PageMaker, the options for printing separations are always available in one of the print properties dialog boxes. In other programs, however, the color printing options are not available until you set up the file for commercial color printing.

Set Up a File for Commercial Color Printing

If you are using a program such as Publisher that requires you to set up the file for commercial color printing, click Tools on the menu bar, click Commercial Printing Tools, and then click Color Printing. A Color Printing dialog box similar to the one in Figure 6-6 is displayed. Select the type of printing process you want to use, and then click OK. You can select spot color, process color, or a combination of the two. Your program may also offer RGB or single-color options.

FIGURE 6-6
Color Printing dialog box

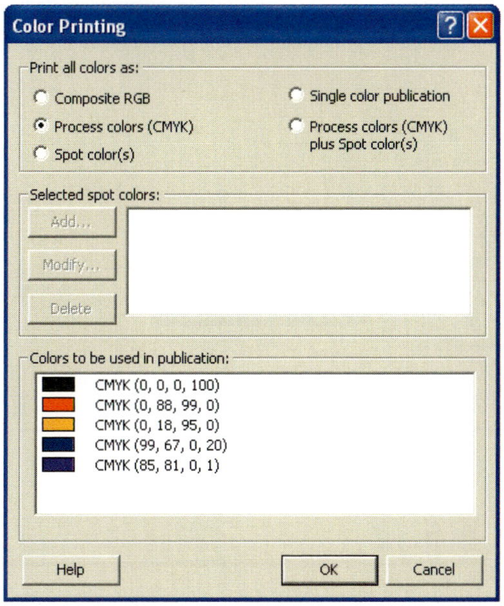

If you are using a program that requires you to set up the publication for commercial printing, complete the following exercise. If not, you can skip to the next exercise.

S TEP-BY-STEP 6.5

1. In the **Mailer** file, click **Tools** on the menu bar, click **Commercial Printing Tools**, and then click **Color Printing**.

2. Click the **Process colors (CMYK)** option button, and then click the **OK** button.

3. Save changes and leave the **Mailer** file open to use in the next exercise.

Print Separations

If your publication is set up for commercial printing, or if your program lets you print separations for all publications, the option for printing separations is found in a print properties dialog box. For example, click File and then click Print. If the Composite and Separations options are not listed, click the Color button. When you select the option to print separations, the list of available colors becomes active, as shown in Figure 6-7. Select All to print all colors, or select the specific color you want to print.

FIGURE 6-7
Options for printing separations

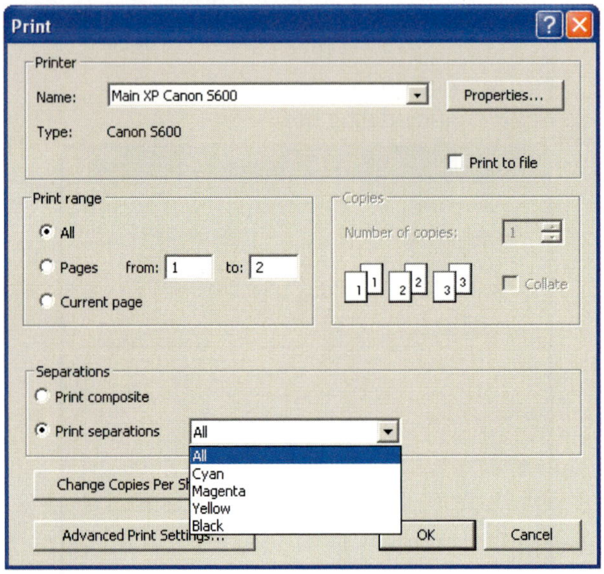

STEP-BY-STEP 6.6

1. In the **Mailer** file, click **File** on the menu bar, and then click **Print**. The Print dialog box opens. Select the option to print all separations. If the option is not listed in the Print dialog box, click the **Color** button and then select the option.

2. Click the **OK** or **Print** button to print the separations. One page prints for each color.

3. Save changes and leave the **Mailer** file open to use in the next exercise.

Save a File for Commercial Printing

Before you deliver a publication to a commercial printer, you must correctly prepare your publication files. Usually, that means saving the file in a format that the commercial printer can use and making sure that all graphics and fonts used in the publication are available. If your commercial printer uses the same program you use, or has the capability to convert your file, you may be able to submit the file in its native, or default, file format. You must, however, be sure that all graphics and fonts are embedded in the file, or you must submit the graphics and font files as well.

Luckily, most desktop publishing programs have a tool for preparing a file for commercial printing. This utility, which is usually called something like Pack and Go or Save For Service Provider, automatically sets up all the files needed to generate the publication, including the publication file, fonts, and graphics. In some cases, it actually packs all the files together in one new file. In other cases, it simply copies and organizes the necessary files.

If the commercial printer cannot use your file in its default file format, you may have to convert to a different format. Many commercial printers request files in *PostScript* format. PostScript is a page description language used to define page layout and design for printing specifically on PostScript printers, which are printers that use the PostScript language.

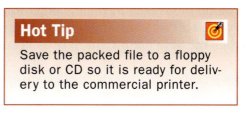

Hot Tip

Always consult your commercial printer before submitting files and proofs. Most printers have a list of requirements detailing exactly what you need to provide.

Pack the Publication Files

To reproduce the document correctly, the commercial printer must be able to open and use all components of the publication file including the fonts and graphics. If fonts and graphics are embedded in the publication, your commercial printer should be able to use them. You can manually make sure all the files are available, but it is easier to use a file preparation utility that comes with your desktop publishing program. In addition to compiling the necessary files and packing them into a single file, most programs also generate a list of the packed files, including information such as whether a font is embedded and a graphics file is linked. Usually, the utility also creates a Readme or Report file that contains information about the packed publication and possibly, how to extract the data.

The steps for using an automatic file preparation utility vary depending on the program you are using. Usually, you start the utility and then select options to control where the packed file is saved and exactly what is included in it. In any case, you start the utility by clicking File on the menu bar, clicking Pack and Go, and then clicking Take to a Commercial Printing Service. Select options, if necessary, and click the Next button to proceed through the steps necessary to complete the process. Alternatively, you may have to click Utilities on the menu bar, click Plug-ins, and then click Save For Service Provider. Select options and then click Package. Set options as desired, and then click Save.

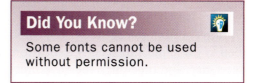

Hot Tip

Save the packed file to a floppy disk or CD so it is ready for delivery to the commercial printer.

The file preparation utility usually automatically names the files that it generates. It may use the name of the original publication file, or it may use a name such as packed01.

If your program does not have an automatic file preparation feature, you must make sure to deliver all font and graphics files to the commercial printer along with the publication file. Most printers will request a file list as well.

Did You Know?

Some fonts cannot be used without permission.

S TEP-BY-STEP 6.7

1. Create a new folder named **DP Step 6-7** that you can use to store the packed files. Ask your instructor where to place the folder.

STEP-BY-STEP 6.7 Continued

2. In the **Mailer** file, start the file preparation utility that comes with your program. For example, click **File** on the menu bar, click **Pack and Go**, and then click **Take to a Commercial Printing Service**.

3. Click the appropriate button to continue. For example, click **Next**, or click **Package**.

4. Select or key the location where you want to store the packed file—the DP Step 6-7 folder you created in step 1—and then select the options you want to use for the packed file. You may have to click **Next** to select the options.

5. Click the **Save** or **Finish** button to complete the procedure. If a dialog box prompts you to print separations or composites, clear the selections, then click the **OK** or **Close** button to close the utility. The packed file is stored in the specified location.

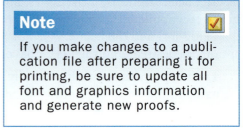

Extra for Experts

Even if you do not use an automatic file preparation utility, your program may have tools for managing graphics and fonts. Consult your program's Help files for more information.

6. Leave the **Mailer** file open to use in the next exercise.

Save a PostScript File

Most desktop publishing programs have tools for converting a file to PostScript format. In some programs, you start off using the Save As command just as you do to save the file in any other format. However, if you select PostScript from the Save as type list and then click the Save button, the Save as PostScript File dialog box opens. You *must select a PostScript printer from the Printer list*, as well as other print properties for printing the PostScript file. Click the Save button to save the file. If you do not have a PostScript printer available, you will not be able to save the file in PostScript format.

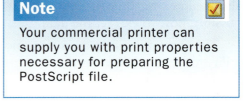

Note

Your commercial printer can supply you with print properties necessary for preparing the PostScript file.

In other programs, you create the PostScript file using the Print Options dialog box. Click File on the menu bar, and then click Print. From the Printer list, select a PostScript printer, and then select the appropriate *PostScript Printer Description file* (PPD), which is a file that provides information about the printing device, from the PPD list. (You should ask your commercial printer which printer and PPD to use.) Click the

Note

If you make changes to a publication file after preparing it for printing, be sure to update all font and graphics information and generate new proofs.

Options button, select the Write PostScript to File check box in the Print Options dialog box, and then key a name and specify a location for the PostScript file. Select additional printer options as necessary, and then click the Save button to save the file.

STEP-BY-STEP 6.8

1. In the **Mailer** file, select the command for saving the file in PostScript format. In some programs, this is the **Save As** command on the **File** menu, and in other programs it is the **Print** command on the **File** menu.

STEP-BY-STEP 6.8 Continued

2. Select **PostScript** as the file type, or select a PostScript printer and PPD, and the option to write to a file.

3. If necessary, select the location where you want to store the file.

4. Click the **File name** box, and then key the filename **PSMailer**.

5. Select properties, or click the **Save** button to open the Save As PostScript File dialog box so you can select properties, including a PostScript printer if it is not already selected. You must select a PostScript printer in order to save the file in PostScript format.

6. Click the **Save** button to save the file. (If a message box appears, click **OK** to continue.)

7. Save and close the **Mailer** file and your desktop publishing program.

> ### Extra for Experts
>
> To save a copy of a publication file in a format other than PostScript, click File on the menu bar, click Save As, select the file format from the Save as type list, and then click the Save button. The formats in the Save as type list vary depending on the program you are using.

Deliver Files to a Commercial Printer

When the files are 100% ready to go, you must deliver them to the commercial printer. You usually have two choices for delivery: on removable media, such as a CD-R or CD-RW, or electronically via the Internet. Ask your printer which method you should use.

Remember, you may have to deliver the font and graphics files in addition to the publication file. Font files are stored in the Fonts folder, which is in the Windows folder on your hard drive (or network). A Fonts folder window is shown in Figure 6-8. Be sure to deliver font files for all styles of the font used in the publication. For example, include the bold and italic versions of the font.

FIGURE 6-8
Fonts folder window

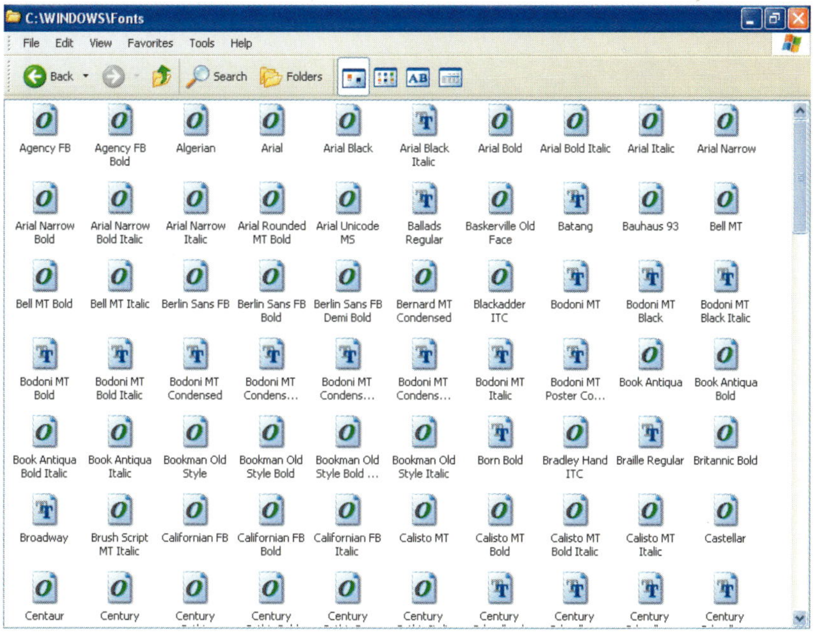

If you are submitting more than one file, your commercial printer may want you to *compress* or zip them into one file. A compressed file is smaller than a lot of individual files and is usually easier to manage. The printer can unzip or extract the files as necessary.

Compress Files

Although you do not have to compress the files before delivery, it is easier to send one compressed file over the Internet instead of many other files. Also, the printer may request a compressed file. Some versions of Windows come with a compression utility you can use to zip or compress the files, or you can use any compression utility. Select all the files you want to compress, then right-click the selection and click the appropriate command for zipping or compressing the files. For example, with the Windows compression tool, click Send to. On the submenu, click Compressed (zipped) Folder. Windows compresses the files into one folder. You can identify the zipped folder because its icon has a zipper on it, as shown in Figure 6-9. By default, the zipped folder has the same name as the first compressed file. To rename the folder, right-click it and click Rename. Key the new name and then press Enter. To extract the files, right-click the zipped file or folder and click Extract All.

FIGURE 6-9
Compressed folder icon

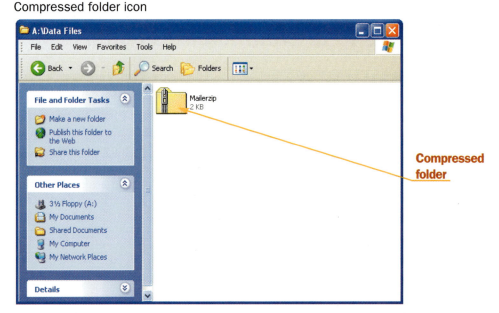

In the following exercise, you use data files and font files supplied with this book. Your instructor may want you to use the actual PostScript file or the packed files you created in previous exercises, as well as the font files stored in the Fonts folder in the Windows folder on your computer.

Note

If you are using a different file compression utility, you may have to specify a storage location and name for the zipped folder or file.

STEP-BY-STEP 6.9

1. From the Windows desktop, use My Computer or Windows Explorer to navigate to the folder where the data files are stored.

2. Press and hold **Ctrl** and click the following files to select them: **DP Step 6-9a** (the PostScript file), **DP Step 6-9b** (a TIFF graphics file), **GOUDOS** (Goudy Old Style font), **GOUDOSI** (Goudy Old Style Italic font), **GOUDOSB** (Goudy Old Style Bold font), **COPRGTB** (Copperplate Gothic Bold font), and **TCCM____** (Tw Cen MT Condensed font).

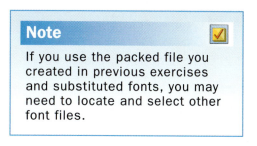

> **Note** ☑
>
> If you use the packed file you created in previous exercises and substituted fonts, you may need to locate and select other font files.

3. Use your compression utility to compress the files. For example, if you are using the Windows compression utility, right-click the selection and click **Send to** on the submenu, then click **Compressed (zipped) Folder**. (You may have to supply a name and click the Add button before your program compresses the files. See the next step to supply the filename.)

4. Right-click the compressed folder and click **Rename**. Key the filename **Mailerzip**, and then press **Enter**.

5. If you did not store the **Mailerzip** folder in the folder where you have stored others files for this lesson, right-click the **Mailerzip** folder, click **Cut**, navigate to the folder where you have stored other files for this lesson, right-click a blank area in the folder window, and click **Paste**.

Deliver Files on Removable Media

If your commercial printer requests the file(s) on a disk or CD, simply copy the necessary files to the disk. If you are copying a lot of files, you may want to compress or zip them first. You copy files to a disk using your operating system. First, insert the destination disk in the appropriate storage device. For example, insert the CD-R in the CD-R drive. Then, navigate to the window where your publication files are stored. Select the file or files to copy, click Edit on the menu bar, and then click Copy. Navigate to the My Computer window and select the storage device that contains the destination disk. Click Edit on the menu bar, and then click Paste. You should attach a label to the disk and write the filename, your name, and the date on it, as well as any other information to help the commercial printer identify the contents. You can then hand deliver or ship the disk along with the composite and separations and a file list.

> **Hot Tip** 🎯
>
> You can also use shortcut keystrokes, the Copy and Paste buttons on the toolbar, the Copy this file command in the Explorer Bar, or the Copy and Paste shortcut menu commands.

STEP-BY-STEP 6.10

1. Insert the destination disk into the appropriate storage device. For example, insert a CD-R or CD-RW into a CD-R drive, or insert a floppy disk into a floppy disk drive.

2. From the Windows desktop, navigate to the folder where the data files are stored.

STEP-BY-STEP 6.10 Continued

3. Click the **DP Step 6-10** compressed folder to select it. Click **Edit** on the menu bar, and then click **Copy**.

4. Navigate to the My Computer window and select the device that contains the destination disk.

5. Click **Edit** on the menu bar, and then click **Paste**. Windows copies the folder to the disk.

6. Remove the disk and label it with the filename, your name, and the date. It is now ready to deliver to the commercial printer.

7. Use a word processing program, a text editor, a database program, a spreadsheet program, or a piece of paper and a pen to create a list of all the files you have copied to the disk.

Deliver Files Electronically

If your commercial printer requests the file(s) electronically, send them via e-mail using your e-mail account. Log on to the Internet using your ISP account, and then start your e-mail program. Create a new message and key the recipient's e-mail address in the Send to box. Key descriptive information in the Subject box, such as the job number or the publication name. Attach the file or compressed file to the message, and then send the message. Ask the printer to confirm receipt. You may need to ship the file on a disk as well, along with all proofs and file lists.

> ### Extra for Experts
> Your printer may have an FTP site to which you can upload files. To use an FTP site, you need FTP client software, an account number, and a password.

STEP-BY-STEP 6.11

1. Log on to your Internet Service Provider, and start your e-mail program.

2. In the To box, key the address of the commercial printer.

3. In the Subject box, key **Files for postcard mailer**.

4. In the message text area, key **Please reply to confirm receipt**, and then key your name and e-mail address.

5. Click the button for attaching a file, then locate and select the **DP Step 6-11** compressed folder.

6. Click the **Send** button in your e-mail program to send the message and its attachment.

7. Close your e-mail program and log off. If necessary, disconnect from the Internet.

SUMMARY

In this lesson, you learned:

- You can use a desktop printer to publish a document if you need only a few copies or are concerned about the cost.

- You can have a copy shop reproduce a publication if you need many copies, are in a hurry, and are concerned about the cost.

- You should have a commercial printer publish a document if you want the best quality, need many copies, have special printing requests, and have enough money in the budget.

- Before printing, you should check the spelling and design in a publication.

- Some programs have a design checker utility that can locate problems such as too much text in a text box, or double spaces after punctuation.

- You set print properties to control the way a document prints, but the properties vary depending on your printer, your desktop publishing program, and the publication.

- Commercial printers usually require a composite proof and separations.

- Trapping helps eliminate gaps and overlaps between adjoining colors.

- Many programs have a utility that automatically prepares a file for commercial printing.

- You may have to save a file in PostScript format for your commercial printer.

- You can deliver a publication file to a commercial printer on disk or electronically.

- In some cases, you must deliver font and graphics files as well.

VOCABULARY *Review*

Define the following terms:

Bleed	PostScript	Proof
Camera-ready	PostScript Printer	Publish
Composite	Description file	Reader's spreads
Compress	Print properties	Separations
Crop	Printer's spreads	Trapping
Crop marks		

REVIEW *Questions*

TRUE / FALSE

Circle T if the statement is true or F if the statement is false.

T   F   **1.** You can print a PostScript file only on a PostScript printer.

T   F   **2.** All printers have the same printer properties.

T   F   **3.** Once you run a spelling checker, you don't have to worry about spelling errors in your publication.

T   F   **4.** Use a copy shop to reproduce a publication if you need it in a hurry.

T   F   **5.** To avoid overlapping between adjoining colors, you should adjust the separation.

T   F   **6.** Commercial printers always have all the font files needed for printing a publication.

T   F   **7.** One way to deliver files is to copy them onto a CD-R and then ship the CD-R to the printer.

T   F   **8.** Compressed files usually take up less disk space than files that have not been compressed.

T   F   **9.** Font files are usually stored in the Type folder.

T   F **10.** Use the collate print option to print pages consecutively.

WRITTEN QUESTIONS

Write a brief answer to the following questions.

1. List at least two pros and two cons of publishing a document on your desktop printer.

2. List at least three questions you should ask a commercial printer.

3. What is the difference between a printer's spread and a reader's spread?

4. List at least two situations in which you need a special setup or handling to print a publication on a desktop printer.

5. Why do color separations print in black and white?

FILL IN THE BLANK

Complete the following sentences by writing the correct word or words in the blanks provided.

1. A(n) _____ is a file that provides information about a PostScript printing device.

2. If a font is not _____ in the publication file, you must send the font file to the commercial printer.

3. Print _____ to show the layout of colors in a publication.

4. _____ is a technique used to adjust the position of adjoining colors during printing.

5. Printed _____ indicate where paper should be trimmed or cut to the correct page size.

6. A(n) _____ is an effect created by an object running off the edge of the page.

7. You should always review a(n) _____ of the publication before you have it published.

8. Use a(n) _____ to publish your document if you want the highest quality.

9. Print _____ are the settings you use to control the way a publication prints on your desktop printer.

10. A(n) _____ is an accurate copy of your publication, including all graphics and colors.

PROJECTS

PROJECT 6-1

1. Launch your desktop-publishing program, and open **DP Project 6-1** from the data files. This is a version of the CNO Newsletter you have worked with in previous lessons.

2. Save the file as **CNONews4**.

3. Run the spelling checker. Ignore all proper names, and correct any other spelling errors as necessary.

4. Run the design checker to locate and fix the following problems, and any other problems you or the checker find. If your program does not have a design checker, manually look for and fix design problems.
   A. The text box containing the headline *Annual Fundraiser* is not large enough to fit all the text. Fix the problem by decreasing the spacing after paragraphs to 8 points.
   B. The text box containing the headline *Officer Nominations* is also not large enough to fit all the text. This time, increase the height of the text box as necessary.
   C. There is a double space following a period in the text box in the right column on page 1. Delete the extra space.

5. Set printer properties to print one draft-quality proof of each page on separate sheets of paper.

6. Print the proofs.

7. Proofread the proofs for spelling and grammatical errors that the spelling checker did not catch, and for design problems that the design checker did not catch. Mark the problems on the printed proofs, and fix them in the publication file.
   A. There are two spelling/grammatical errors in the story headlined *Volunteer News*.
   B. There are two spelling/grammatical errors in the story headlined *Officer Nominations*.
   C. There are design problems with two horizontal rules on page 2. One rule is thicker than the other rules on the page and is not aligned with the left margin. Another rule is not aligned with the right column margin.
   D. There is a design problem with the alignment of the text box at the top of the right column on page 1. It would look better if the text were aligned vertically with the text in the left column.

8. Set printer properties to print two high-quality, double-sided color copies of the **CNONews4** file. If necessary, print page 1, then reinsert the sheet in the printer and print page 2 on the reverse side.

9. Save changes and close the **CNONews4** file. Leave your desktop-publishing program open to use in Project 6-2.

PROJECT 6-2

1. In your desktop-publishing program, open the file **DP Project 6-2a**. This is a version of the invitation you worked with previously.

2. Save the file as **CNOInvite3**.

3. Run the spelling checker and design checker to identify and correct errors.

4. Set print properties to print a draft-quality proof of the document.

5. Print the draft, and then proofread for spelling, grammatical, and design problems. Correct any problems that you find.

6. Enable trapping.

7. If necessary, set up the publication for commercial color printing using both spot and process colors.

8. Print a composite of the publication.

9. Print separations of the publication.

10. If your program has an automatic file preparation utility, use it to prepare the publication files for the commercial printer. Save the files on a floppy disk, a CD-R, or a new folder set up for this purpose, named **DP Project 6-2**. (If your program asks you to locate the clip art files inserted on pages 2 and 3, you will need access to the CD from which they were inserted, or you can navigate to the data files for this lesson and select and open DP Project 6-2c and DP Project 6-2d.)

11. Save a copy of the publication in PostScript format, with the name **PSCNOInvite3**. You must have a PostScript printer available in order to save the file in PostScript format.

12. Compress the PostScript file and all necessary graphics and font files together and rename the compressed folder **CNOzip**. Locate the files on your computer, or use the data files provided. (If you use an automatic file packing utility, don't worry if there are fewer graphics files than are listed below. Some programs may have fewer graphics files in the publication. Also, if your program substituted fonts, you may need different font files.)
    Graphics files: DP Project 6-2b, DP Project 6-2c, DP Project 6-2d, DP Project 6-2e, DP Project 6-2f, DP Project 6-2g.
    Font files: GARA, GARDBD, GARAIT, COPRGTB, COPRGTL

13. Copy the **CNOzip** folder to a floppy disk or CD.

14. Save changes and close the **CNOInvite3** file. Close your desktop-publishing program.

WEB PROJECT

In addition to the options of printing a publication on the desktop, using a copy shop, or using a commercial printer, a fourth option is to publish to the Web. Use the Internet to research some of the differences between designing a page for printing and designing a page for publishing on the World Wide Web. Start by looking for information about the basic principles of design as used for printed documents and for Web pages. Look for the different ways to use color; for example, most printed documents use dark text on a light background, while many Web pages use light text on a dark background. Are there different concepts concerning alignment or white space? See if you can find information about fonts that look better onscreen than in print, or why you should select certain types of graphics for use on the Web and others for use in print. Use the information you find to write a report using a word processing program or create a chart using a spreadsheet program comparing print publishing design with Web publishing design.

TEAMWORK PROJECT

As a group, use a telephone book or other business directory to compile a list of commercial printers and copy shops in your community. If you have a database program or a spreadsheet program, use it to enter information about each business, including the name, address, telephone number, fax number, and e-mail address. You may want to include additional information such as specialties, a contact's name, or even the hours of operation. If you do not have a database or spreadsheet program, you can record the information in a notebook.

Think of a publication you would like to create for your class, school, or community. You can pick any type of publication, such as a newsletter, a poster, a banner, a flyer, a brochure, an advertisement, or a booklet. If you like, you can even use one of the publications you planned and created in an earlier lesson. Plan the publication from scratch, including paper stock, sheet size, color, page setup, and number of copies. Contact at least two commercial printers on your list and ask them for assistance planning the publication. Tell them up front that this is a class project, and that it is unlikely you will actually be contracting with them to print the publication. If they are uncooperative, thank them and then try a different business in your list. For example, ask them the type of color process they use, what type of files they prefer working with, and how they like the files delivered. Ask them if they have any advice about paper stock, what the time frame for completing the job would be, and, of course, how much it would cost. Record the answers along with the other information about the printer.

Contact at least two copy shops and ask them for information about reproducing copies of the publication. Ask them if they have color copying, if they have self-service options, and if they have any advice based on the type of publication and the number of copies you need. Also, remember to ask them the cost, and how long it would take.

Based on the information you have gathered, decide whether you would want to use a commercial printer, a copy shop, or simply print the publication yourselves on your desktop printer. Use a word processing program to write a proposal for producing the publication. Include specifications about the publication and a recommendation for how and where to publish the document. Include the reasons for your recommendation. If you do not have a word processing program, handwrite the proposal. Present the proposal to your class.

CRITICAL *Thinking*

ACTIVITY 6-1

Design and create a booklet providing tips and hints about desktop publishing that could be used as a handout in a desktop publishing class. Start by planning the booklet from scratch. Think about the audience and how you want to present the information. Consider how the booklet will be published, its size and its length, and whether you will use color in it or just black and white text and graphics. Also consider how long it will take to create the booklet and develop a realistic schedule to guide you through the process. Build in time to have your classmates review your work at each stage so you can improve it as you go along. Record specifications in a word processing or spreadsheet document so you can refer to them as you create the booklet.

Next, organize the information to include in the booklet. Do you want to include technical information about printers and software programs, or just information about design and organization? If necessary, research the information to include using books or the Internet, or by talking to an instructor or commercial printer. Use a word processing program or text editor to store the information electronically.

Plan how to format the text in the booklet. Will you simply key paragraphs of information, or do you want to use different elements to break up the text and make the booklet more appealing visually? Look at other publications to see how they do it. (Look at this book for ideas, such as the list of objectives at the beginning of each lesson, the way the headings are formatted, and how tips and notes are presented in boxes.) Select or create a font scheme, and select the appropriate font sizes to use for each element. Record the specifications in a word processing or spreadsheet document so you can refer to them when you create the booklet. Having specifications ensures consistency throughout the booklet.

Decide what type of graphics to include. Do you want to use lines or borders? Are there pictures to include? If so, are they already in a graphic file format, or do you need to convert them or create them? Do you have permission to use them? Prepare the graphics files so you have them ready to insert. Think of a title for the booklet and how you want the cover page to look.

Use your desktop publishing program to create the booklet. Set up the pages to match the specifications that you planned. Copy and paste the text from the word processing or text editor document, or key the text directly into the publication. Apply the text formatting specifications you selected. Insert, size, and position graphics objects to complement the text. Print a draft copy of the booklet and ask your classmates to review it and make comments. If necessary, make changes or adjustments to improve the booklet.

Prepare the booklet for publication. Check the spelling and the design. Print another proof and review it carefully for errors. Make improvements, if necessary, and then review it again. When you are satisfied that the booklet is complete, print it and share it with your class.

DESKTOP PUBLISHING

REVIEW *Questions*

TRUE / FALSE

Circle T if the statement is true or F if the statement is false.

T F **1.** Using a commercial printer is usually the fastest way to publish a document.

T F **2.** Prepare separations for a publication to avoid gaps or overlaps between adjoining colors during printing.

T F **3.** Horizontal alignment adjusts the position of paragraphs in relation to the left and right margins of a text box.

T F **4.** Tabs are used to adjust the horizontal position of text across a single line.

T F **5.** Layout guides do not print.

T F **6.** A headline is repeated at the top of every page in a publication.

T F **7.** Some clip art Web sites require you to register and pay for downloading pictures.

T F **8.** A spot color is ink that is mixed during printing.

T F **9.** Horizontal rules do not print.

T F **10.** By default, text wraps from the end of one line in a text box or frame to the beginning of the next line.

MATCHING

Match the correct term in Column 1 to its description in Column 2.

Column 1   **Column 2**

___ 1. Reader's spread   **A.** A prototype or sample of a publication

___ 2. Gutter   **B.** Pages that must be printed on the same sheet of paper so the page order is correct when the publication is bound

___ 3. Footer

   C. Pages that are printed in consecutive order

___ 4. Printer's spread

   D. The file format used for digital photographs

___ 5. Color scheme

   E. A decorative text effect used to highlight the first character in a paragraph

___ 6. GIF

   F. The area between the bottom margin and the bottom of the page

___ 7. Mock-up

   G. The inside page edges

___ 8. JPEG

   H. The area on a page that has no text or graphics

___ 9. Dropped capital

   I. The file format used most often for cartoons and logos

___ 10. White space

   J. A set of coordinated colors

   K. The area between the top margin and the top of the page

FILL IN THE BLANK

Complete the following sentences by writing the correct word or words in the blanks provided.

1. Set the _____ to adjust the space between two specific characters.

2. The method used to attach the pages of a publication to one another is called the _____.

3. _____ formatted files are often used for graphics in desktop publishing documents because they reproduce well when printed and support transparency.

4. Use a(n) _____ to quickly apply a set of formatting settings to text in a publication.

5. In many programs, you insert graphic objects into a(n) _____ frame.

6. When you _____ an object in a publication, the object is not connected to the source file in any way.

7. A(n) _____ is a hardware device that uses light to capture a digital version of printed or handwritten data.

8. When you _____ an object, it pivots around its reference point.

9. To print across the wide side of a page, select _____ orientation.

10. Use the _____ around the edges of a page displayed on screen to temporarily store objects.

PROJECTS

PROJECT 1

1. Launch your desktop publishing program and create a new blank document using the default settings.

2. Save the document as **Poster**.

3. Set up the page layout for the **Poster** publication as follows:
   A. Publication type: Poster
   B. Page size: 18 inches wide by 24 inches high
   C. Paper size: Letter
   D. Orientation: Portrait
   E. Page overlap: 0.5 inches. (In some programs you specify overlap—or tiling—when you print, not when you set up the page layout.)
   F. Margins: 1.5 inches on all sides
   G. No double-sided printing

4. Insert a horizontal ruler guide at 13 inches on the vertical ruler.

5. Search your program's clip art collection to locate pictures of a band or orchestra, and then insert the picture into the **Poster** publication. Resize and position the picture to fill the space above the horizontal ruler guide—approximately 14.5 inches wide by 11 inches high.

6. Insert another horizontal ruler guide at 16.75 inches on the vertical ruler, and then insert a text box or text frame sized to fit in the space between the two horizontal ruler guides—approximately 14.75 inches wide by 3.5 inches high.

7. In a 42-point sans serif font, such as Arial Rounded MT Bold, key the following five lines of text.

   Calling All Musicians!

   Perfect Pitch Community Band

   Needs You!

   All Band Instruments

   All Levels of Ability

8. Format the text as follows:
   A. Apply the Small Cap text effect to the second line of text.
   B. Adjust the paragraph spacing before and after the second line of text to 12 points.
   C. Change the leading or line spacing between the last three lines of text to 0.9 lines. All the text should fit within the text box, but if not, increase the text box height slightly.
   D. Center all text horizontally.

3. Save the document as **Brochure**.

4. Change the page layout for the **Brochure** publication as follows:
   A. Publication type: Custom
   B. Orientation: Landscape
   C. Page size: 11 inches wide by 8.5 inches high
   D. Paper size: Letter
   E. Margins: 0 inches on all sides
   F. No double-sided printing

5. Switch to Master Page view and divide the page into 3 columns, leaving no space between columns, then switch back to regular page view. Remember, on page 1 is the content for the inside panels of the brochure, and on page 2 is the content for the outside panels of the brochure. The middle panel on page 2 is the back panel, and the right panel on page 2 is the front panel.

6. If available, select the Binary font scheme. On both pages 1 and 2, insert two horizontal ruler guides—one at 2 inches on the vertical ruler and one at 6 inches on the vertical ruler.

7. Position the text boxes as follows:
   A. On page 1:
   Place the Bretton Woods text box in the left column between the top margin and the first horizontal ruler.
   Place the Sunday River text box in the middle column between the top margin and the first horizontal ruler.
   Place the Mont Tremblant text box in the right column between the top margin and the first horizontal ruler.
   B. On page 2:
   Place the Okemo Mountain text box in the left column between the top margin and the first horizontal ruler guide.
   Place the two-line Swift River Travel text box in the right column between the top margin and the first horizontal ruler guide.
   Position the seven-line Swift River Travel text box centered horizontally and vertically in the middle column.

8. Format all except the text box in the middle column of page 2 as follows:
   A. Change the text box margins (or inset) to 0.5 inches on the top, left, and right and 0.04 inches on the bottom. (**Hint:** Select and modify all text boxes on page 1 at the same time, and then all text boxes on page 2 at the same time.)
   B. Apply the **Heading 2** style to all resort names (16-point Verdana, bold, with a 0.14-inch space after each resort name) and the **Body Text 2** style to the locations (12-point Georgia).
   C. In the third column on page 2, apply the **Title 3** style to the text *Swift River Travel* (28-point Verdana, bold, with a 0.14-inch space after the paragraph) and the **Tagline** style to the text *"Your Key to Adventure"* (9-point Georgia, bold, italic).
   D. Center all text horizontally.
   E. Apply a blue, 2-point horizontal ruler after the second paragraph in each text box, except for the middle box on page 2, which is formatted in the next step.

9. Format the text in the text box in the middle column of page 2 as follows:
    A. Apply the **Heading 2** style to the first line (16-point Verdana, bold).
    B. Apply the **Tagline** style to the second line (9-point Georgia, bold, italic).
    C. Apply the **Address** style to the remaining lines (8-point Georgia).
    D. Center all text.
    E. Apply a 2-point blue line before the first line and after the last line. If necessary, increase the spacing between the rule and the baseline of the text.

10. In all three columns on page 1, and in the left and right panels on page 2, insert a text box between the two horizontal guides. Size it to fill the space (approximately 3.5 inches wide by 4 inches high). Set the text box margins (or inset) to 0.5 inches on the left and right and 0.04 inches on the top and bottom. Using the information you gathered in Part 1, key or copy information into the text boxes in the panels under a resort name. Alternatively, use the information in **DP Job 1b**, a data file in Microsoft Word format.
    A. Enter one or two sentences describing the resort, or something unique about the resort. Press **Enter** and key **Fast Facts:** and then press **Enter** again. Key a list of five or six facts about the resort.
    B. Apply the **Body Text 2** style (12-point Georgia, with 9 points of space after each paragraph) to the list items and the description sentence(s), and apply the **Heading 5** style (12-point Georgia, bold, with 9 points of space after each paragraph) to the text *Fast Facts*.
    C. Apply a basic small round bullet to the list items.
    D. Justify the description sentence(s).
    E. If necessary, improve the design by adjusting the line or paragraph spacing. For example, change the line spacing in the middle panel of page 1 to leave 36 points of space before the text *Fast Facts*.

11. In the right column on page 2, key the following

    Check It Out!

    Super Winter Escapes

    Packaged tours to four thrilling resorts:

    Bretton Woods, New Hampshire

    Sunday River, Maine

    Mont Tremblant, Quebec, Canada

    Okemo Mountain, Vermont

12. Format the text as follows:
    A. Line 1: **Title 4** style (18-point Verdana, bold), centered horizontally. If you did not apply a style, increase the leading to add some space between lines.
    B. Line 2: **Heading 6** style (12-point Verdana, bold), centered horizontally. If you did not apply a style, increase the leading slightly to improve appearance.
    C. Line 3: **Body Text 5** style (10-point Verdana, bold, italic, with 9 points of space after the paragraph), aligned left.
    D. Lines 4, 5, 6, and 7: **Body Text 2** style (12-point Georgia, with 9 points of space after each line), aligned left.
    E. Center the text vertically in the text box.

13. In all three columns on page 1, and in the left column on page 2, insert pictures of each resort into the space between the lower horizontal ruler guide and the bottom margin. Size each picture to approximately 3 inches wide by 2 inches high and align the tops of the pictures with the horizontal ruler guide. If you do not have picture files, insert **DP Job 1c** for Bretton Woods; **DP Job 1d** for Sunday River; **DP Job 1e** for Mont Tremblant; and **DP Job 1f** for Okemo.

14. Create a text box along the bottom edge of each picture and key the source information for the text and graphics in 8-point Georgia, centered. For example, for Bretton Woods, key **Source for data and picture: www.brettonwoods.com**. Include other source data as necessary, such as the date.

15. In the right column on page 2, insert a clip art picture of a skier into the space between the bottom margin and the lower horizontal ruler guide.

16. Prepare the document for publication on your desktop printer.
    A. Check the spelling and design.
    B. Print a draft-quality proof.

17. Print the **Brochure** file, using double-sided or duplex printing. Save it and close the file, but leave your desktop publishing program open to use in Job 2.

SCANS JOB 2

Your supervisor has asked you to initiate a monthly internal newsletter to help keep the staff up to date on company news. First, you need to design a template for the newsletter that you can save and use as a starting point each month. Then, you insert graphics and text to complete the publication.

Part 1

1. In your desktop publishing program, create a new blank publication using the default settings.

2. Save the file as **SRTNews**.

3. Adjust the page setup as follows:
    A. Publication type: Full page
    B. Orientation: Portrait
    C. Page size: 8.5 inches wide by 11 inches high
    D. Paper size: Letter
    E. Margins: 1 inch on all sides
    F. No double-sided printing
    G. No facing pages

4. Insert a new page so there are a total of two pages in the publication, and then create two columns on each page.

5. If available, insert the Crossed Lines Masthead design object, and align it with the top of the page vertically, centered horizontally. Replace the sample text *Organization Name* (or *Your Organization*) with the text **Swift River Travel**. Replace the sample text

Newsletter Name with the text **SRT Update**. Replace the sample text *Newsletter Date* with the text **Winter**. If the design object is not available, create the masthead as follows:

A. Insert a text box sized about 0.5 inches high and 5 inches wide, aligned with the top and left of the page. In the text box, key the text **Swift River Travel**, using a 13-point serif font (such as Times New Roman) in bold all-capital letters. Fill the text box with a bright blue color, and change the font color to white. Apply a 1-point white (or paper) horizontal rule after the paragraph.

B. Insert another text box sized about 1.25 inches high and 5 inches wide. Position it vertically so its top is aligned with the bottom of the other text box, and horizontally with the left of the page. Using the same serif font in about 56 points, key the text **SRT Update**. Fill the box with the same bright blue, and change the font color to white.

C. Insert two more text boxes, each sized about 0.5 inches high by 1.5 inches wide. Position them to the right of the other text boxes, one above the other, so the top of one is aligned with the bottom of the other. The top box should be aligned with the top margin of the page. Using a sans serif font, such as Arial Narrow, key **Volume 1, Issue 1** in the top text box, and **Winter** in the bottom text box. Adjust font size and style as desired.

D. If necessary, adjust the size and position of the text boxes to improve the appearance of the masthead. Select all four text boxes and group them.

6. Change to Master Page view and insert page numbers in the lower-right corner of the page. Precede the number with the word **Page**. You can do this by creating a footer or by inserting a text box or text block.

7. Change back to regular page view.

8. On page 1, insert a horizontal ruler guide at 3 inches on the vertical ruler on page 1.

9. On page 2, insert a text box sized to approximately 3 inches wide by 4.75 inches high.

10. Key the following lines of text
SRT Update is published by employees of Swift River Travel for internal use only. Information contained in this newsletter is not meant as any type of advertising or promotion. It is not meant for distribution to outside clients or other agencies.
For more information, call (941) 555-5555.

11. Format the text with an 18-point serif font, such as Times New Roman. Justify the text. Apply a light gray fill or shade to the text box and a 4-point bright blue border line on all sides. Set paragraph spacing to leave 6 points before and after each paragraph. Align the text box in the lower-left corner of the page.

12. Save the changes, and then save the **SRTNews** file as a template file named **Newstemp**.

13. Close all open files.

Part 2

1. In your desktop publishing program, create a new document based on the **Newstemp** template.

2. Save the file as **SRTNews2**.

3. Insert two text boxes on page 1, each one sized to 3 inches wide by 6.5 inches high. Position one in the left column, with its top aligned with the horizontal ruler guide; and position the other in the right column, also with its top aligned with the horizontal ruler guide.

4. Switch to page 2, and insert three text boxes as follows
   A. Size one text box to approximately 3 inches wide by 3.25 inches high and position it in the upper-left part of the page.
   B. Size one text box to approximately 3 inches wide by 1.5 inches high, and position it in the upper-right part of the page.
   C. Size the third text box to approximately 3 inches wide by 4.75 inches high and position it in the lower-right part of the page.

5. Open the file **DP Job 2** from the data files. You may open this text file in your desktop publishing program, or in a text editor such as Notepad. Copy and paste the text from the text file into the text boxes in the **SRTNews2** publication as follows. (Note that if you open the text document in Notepad, each paragraph may appear as a single line.)
   A. Copy and paste the first four paragraphs of text into the text box in the left column of page 1.
   B. Copy and paste the next four paragraphs of text into the text box in the right column of page 1.
   C. Copy and paste the next eight paragraphs of text into the text box in the upper-left part of page 2.
   D. Copy and paste the next two paragraphs of text into the text box in the upper-right part of page 2.
   E. Copy and paste the last three paragraphs of text into the text box in the lower-right part of page 2.

6. Close the **DP Job 2** text file without saving any changes.

7. Format the text as follows:
   A. Format all headlines (the first line in each text box) with a sans serif font, such as Arial, in 16 points.
   B. Format the remaining text with a serif font, such as Times New Roman, in 12 points.
   C. Set the line spacing of all text to 1 space between lines and 6 points before and after each paragraph.
   D. Apply a 4-point blue horizontal rule before the first paragraph (the headline) in the three text boxes you inserted on page 2. (You may need to adjust the spacing options for the rules if they crowd the text.)

8. Insert clip art pictures as follows:
   A. Insert a picture of a snowboarder or skier on page 1. Size the picture to about 2 inches wide by 1.5 inches high. Position it about 2.5 inches from the left edge of the page and about 7.25 inches from the top of the page. Set the text wrap to square.
   B. Insert a picture of a beach on page 1. Size the picture to about 2 inches wide by about 1.8 inches high. Position it to align with the right margin horizontally, and about 4 inches from the top of the page. Set the text wrap to square.
   C. Insert a picture of a computer class on page 2. Size it to about 3.25 inches wide by about 2 inches high. Position it about 4 inches from the left edge of the page and about 2.75 inches from the top of the page. Set the text wrap to square. Apply a 0.75-point border line around all sides of the picture.
   D. Insert a picture of a family on page 2. Size it to about 2 inches wide by about 1.5 inches high, and then center it horizontally in the text box at the bottom right of the page. Set the text wrap to Top and Bottom.

9. Adjust the size and position of text boxes as necessary to make sure they are neatly aligned and large enough to display all text. For example, try to align the horizontal rule at the top of the text box in the lower-right part of page 2 with the top border of the text box in the lower-left part of the page. You may also try nudging the pictures to adjust the way text wraps around them.

10. Prepare the document for publishing by a commercial printer.
    A. Check the spelling and the design.
    B. If necessary, enable color printing for commercial printers, using the CMYK process color system.
    C. Enable trapping.

11. Print a composite proof and separations for all colors.

12. Use your program's automatic file preparation utility to pack all necessary files onto a removable disk, such as a floppy disk or a CD.

13. Save the **SRTNews2** file and close it. Close your desktop-publishing program.

WEB SITE DEVELOPMENT

Unit

Estimated Time for Unit: 10 hours

CREATING A WEB PAGE

OBJECTIVES

Upon completion of this lesson, you should be able to:

- Describe how the Web is organized.
- Find Web sites and Web pages.
- Create folders to contain Web page material.
- Enter HTML structural tags.
- Save an HTML text file.
- View a Web page.
- Add and modify Web page text.
- Format text using HTML tags.

Estimated Time: 2 hours

VOCABULARY

ANSI (American National Standards Institute)

ASCII (American Standard Code for Information Interchange)

Attribute

Domain name

HTML (Hypertext Markup Language)

Hypertext Transfer Protocol

Tags

Text editor

Truncate

URL (Uniform Resource Locator)

Web browser

Web clients

Web pages

Web servers

Web sites

Welcome page

You are probably familiar with the Internet (also called the Net) and the World Wide Web. This fascinating system links people and places together in ways that could only be dreamed about as recently as 1990. People who "surf the Net" are actually jumping from one Web page to another in search of information that interests them. In this unit, you learn how to create Web pages using a variety of programs, features, and tools.

In this lesson, you begin your study of Web site development by using a text editor such as Windows Notepad to create a simple Web page. You learn how to enter the HTML tags that provide page content, modify tags and text, and use tags to format text on the Web page. In later lessons, you use a high-end Web design program, such as Macromedia Dreamweaver or Microsoft FrontPage, to create and format Web pages. You also learn how to use other applications, such as a word-processing program, presentation program, or spreadsheet program, to create Web pages and add information to a Web site.

How the Web Is Organized

The World Wide Web is a collection of Web servers, Web clients, Web sites, and Web pages. The basic unit of this structure is the Web page.

Web pages are text documents that contain content such as text, graphics, multimedia effects, or some combination of all three (see Figure 1-1). A Web page can be of any length. However, individual Web pages are generally short. If more information is available on a given topic, links are created to other Web pages that provide more detail.

FIGURE 1-1
A Web page contains text, graphics, and multimedia effects

Web sites are collections of Web pages. Once two Web pages on a similar topic are linked, a Web site is born! Generally, Web pages on a Web site deal with different aspects of the same topic. For example, the Microsoft Web site at www.microsoft.com concerns itself with Microsoft products, service, and support. The Library of Congress Web site at www.loc.gov considers aspects of American history and government.

Web servers can host any number of Web sites and Web pages. Servers communicate with other computers when Web pages are requested by the users of those computers.

Web clients are software programs that talk to the Web and display Web pages. When you use your Web browser to visit a Web site, you are using a client to request pages from a server (see Figure 1-2). A *Web browser* interprets the coding on a Web page to display it on your screen. There are a number of Web browsers on the market, including Internet Explorer, Netscape, Mozilla, and Opera.

FIGURE 1-2
Web servers communicate with Web clients

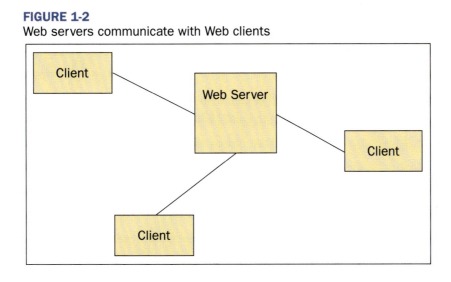

These important elements can best be understood by viewing examples. In Step-by-Steps 1.1 and 1.2, you visit the World Wide Web and learn about Web servers, clients, sites, and pages firsthand.

STEP-BY-STEP 1.1

1. Launch your Web browser.

2. What is the name of your Web browser or client software? Enter its name here.

_____

3. When you start your Web browser, the first page you see is your personal default Web page. Briefly describe this page.

_____

_____

_____

4. Is your personal default Web page part of a larger collection of pages, i.e., a Web site?

_____

STEP-BY-STEP 1.1 Continued

5. What is the name of the organization or business that maintains your personal default Web page? Briefly explain if the Web site sponsor is a school, business, government agency, or other organization.

_____

_____

_____

6. Briefly describe the organization listed in step 5 above that hosts your default Web page. What is the organization's purpose in maintaining the site? What does the organization gain from making a site available to you?

_____

_____

_____

7. Leave your Web browser open to use in the next exercise.

Find Web Sites and Web Pages

People find specific Web pages by using *Uniform Resource Locators*, or *URLs*. Contained in every URL on the Web is a path statement that describes how to get to the page, just as a home address written on an envelope enables letters to be delivered to the correct individual's house. Understanding the path is the key to finding Web pages.

Understand an URL

To understand the parts of an URL, let's dissect this example:

http://www.course.com/folder/subfolder/webpage.html

All Web addresses properly begin with the characters *http://*, as shown in Figure 1-3. *Http* stands for ***Hypertext Transfer Protocol***, a communications system used to transfer data over the World Wide Web between servers and clients.

URL in
Address bar

The *www* in the URL stands for *World Wide Web*. These letters designate a Web server. A Web server stores Web pages to be shared with Web-browsing clients. A server is a fast computer with the ability to send millions of pages to clients all over the world.

Net Tip

You usually don't have to enter either http:// or www when entering a Web address in a browser's Address bar.

The letters *course.com* describe a ***domain name***. A domain name is owned by a business, organization, or institution. In this case, the course.com domain name is owned by Course Technology, the publishers of this textbook.

The *.com* portion of the domain name course.com is called the *top-level domain name*. Top-level names describe the type of site being visited. The top-level domains .com and .biz are used for commercial and business sites. Other top-level names are used for education (.edu), for public service and nonprofit organizations (.org), or government-controlled Web sites (.gov). Network service providers often use the .net designation. There are many other top-level domain names, including country designations such as .us for the United States or .mx for Mexico.

Any letters, numbers, or names surrounded by two slashes represent a folder. For example, in the URL *www.course.com/folder/subfolder/webpage.html*, the section */folder/subfolder/* represents two folders, one inside the other. You have probably seen or created this type of organization on your own personal computer. For example, on a Windows computer, folders are often organized by primary folders and subfolders as shown in Figure 1-4. Web sites use folders to organize multiple Web pages into topics and subtopics.

FIGURE 1-4
Folders are organized on computers

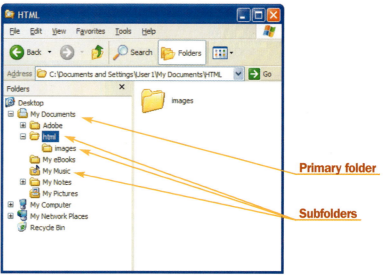

The last part of the domain name, *webpage.html*, is the actual name of the Web file you are looking for. This Web file is found inside the folder and subfolder on the Web server known as www.course.com. Does it all make sense now?

All Web sites contain a ***welcome page*** or home page that opens first when you access the site. This page welcomes new visitors and directs them to other informative Web pages found on the site. In the next exercise, you visit the welcome page of a widely respected government-sponsored Web site, the Library of Congress, famous for its catalogs of historical and government-related information.

STEP-BY-STEP 1.2

1. If necessary, log on to your ISP. In the browser's Address bar, enter **www.loc.gov** and press **Enter**. The Library of Congress's welcome page opens (see Figure 1-5). Because this Web site is updated frequently, your page will differ from the one shown in the figure.

STEP-BY-STEP 1.2 Continued

FIGURE 1-5
Library of Congress Web site

2. To visit another Web page on the same Web site, click any of the hypertext links, hyperlinked graphics, or any underlined words that interest you.

3. Notice how the URL or path in the address bar changes after you click a link (Figure 1-6). Write the full path of this new Web page here, including the domain name, top-level domain name, any folders or subfolders, and the name of the actual page itself, if possible.

_____

STEP-BY-STEP 1.2 Continued

FIGURE 1-6
View another page on the same site

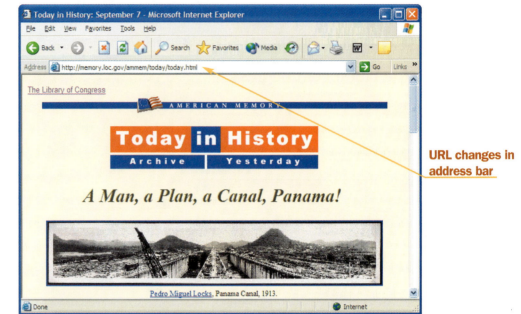

URL changes in
address bar

4. Try another hypertext link to visit another Web page on the same Web site. Write the full path to this Web page here.

_____

5. Leave your browser open to use in the next exercise.

Display HTML Source Code

In this lesson, you will create a Web page using *HTML*. HTML is an acronym, short for *Hypertext Markup Language*. HTML is a document-description language. HTML tags define and describe text, graphics, hypertext links, and other multimedia elements found on World Wide Web pages. HTML uses *tags* to mark up documents. The mark-up tags describe how multimedia Web documents should be displayed.

> **Did You Know?**
>
> You can usually tell you are visiting a page in the same Web site if pages look similar, or if a group of pages on a related topic has the same domain name.

HTML tags allow an interpreter, such as a Web browser client, to display a Web page document according to the instructions provided by the tags. Figure 1-7 shows a typical Web page as well as the tags that actually describe the page.

FIGURE 1-7
HTML tags create Web page content

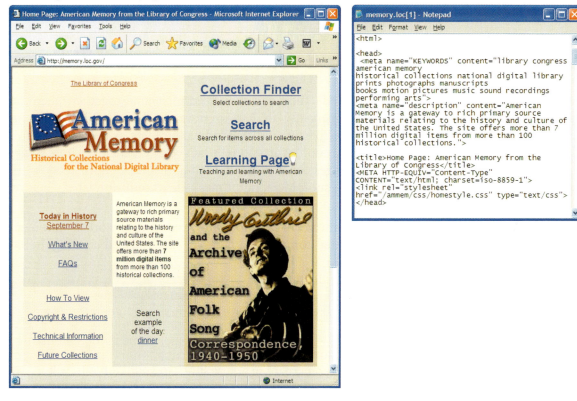

You can use your Web browser to view the HTML code of any page on the World Wide Web. Use a command such as Source or Page Source on the View menu to display the current page's HTML code in a window.

Note

The HTML code usually appears in your default text editor. You learn more about text editors later in this lesson.

S TEP-BY-STEP 1.3

1. In your Web browser, enter **www.loc.gov** in the Address bar to open a page on the Library of Congress Web site.

2. Click **View** on the menu bar, and then click **Source** (in Internet Explorer) or **Page Source** or **Document Source** (in Netscape) to open a window containing the page's HTML code. If you are using another browser, search for a similar command on a menu such as View.

3. Scroll down in the HTML code to see the kinds of tags used to create the page.

STEP-BY-STEP 1.3 Continued

4. When you have finished examining the code, click **File** on the code window's menu bar, and then click **Exit** to close both the document and the text editor.

5. Log off from your ISP and close your Web browser.

Create HTML Web Site Folders

A Web site can consist of many HTML files, and they need to remain together when they are placed on a Web server. Web designers use folders to store the HTML files for a site. Generally, you create one main folder for the site and then add subfolders as necessary to hold related files. For example, it is considered good professional practice to create a separate *images* or *graphics* subfolder to save all the images for a Web site. It takes a little more work in the beginning to organize your Web site using subfolders, but it means less confusion later when you can neatly store your related files in the proper subfolders.

You can create all your Web pages, organize all your graphics, and store any other multimedia files in your Web site folder on your personal computer. When you have finished creating the site, you upload the contents of this folder to a Web server. Once placed on a Web server with a URL identified for the site, the contents of your Web site become available to anyone in the world who has a browser.

For this lesson, you create a folder for your Web site called *html* and then create a subfolder named *images* within the html folder. You store the files you create in this lesson in the html folder. You can create the folders using your computer's file management feature, such as Windows Explorer or My Computer.

> **Did You Know?**
>
> It is considered good form to use lowercase letters for all file and folder names. You can use uppercase letters, but if you do, visitors to your Web site will need to capitalize words the same way you do to find your pages, which could be confusing.

STEP-BY-STEP 1.4

1. Launch a file management program such as My Computer or Windows Explorer.

2. Navigate to the folder where you want to store the Web site folders.

3. Click **File** on the menu bar, click **New**, and then click **Folder**.

4. Enter **html** as the folder name.

STEP-BY-STEP 1.4 Continued

5. Double-click the new html folder to open it. Repeat step 3 to create a subfolder within the html folder. Enter **images** as the subfolder name. The subfolder should resemble Figure 1-8.

FIGURE 1-8
New html folder with the images subfolder

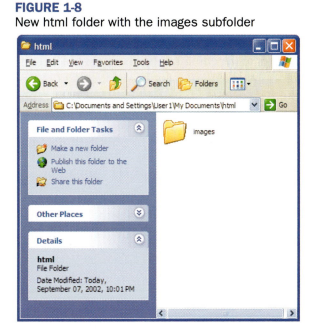

6. Close the file management program.

Use a Text Editor to Enter HTML Structural Tags

Now that you have seen a variety of Web pages and even looked at a few HTML tags, it's time to create a simple Web page of your own. Every HTML document is a simple text document. Text documents are created with *text editors*. There are many kinds of text editors—simple ones, word processors, and specialized HTML editors—that all do the trick.

When you are just starting out, it's helpful to use a simple text editor without a lot of extra features so you can concentrate on entering the HTML tags. A text editor such as Windows Notepad is a good choice for a beginner, although you can also use any word processor, as long as you save the files properly. (See the next section for more information on saving.)

Text editors such as Notepad contain a number of familiar features if you have used a word processor. You can save and print documents. You can use commands such as Cut, Copy, and Paste, for example, to move or copy text. You can select text and use Backspace and Delete to remove text. But your options for formatting

> **Did You Know?**
>
> Text files created in a text editor use *ASCII* or *ANSI* characters. ASCII is short for *American Standard Code for Information Interchange*. ANSI is short for *American National Standards Institute*. ASCII and ANSI consist of a set of standard text-based characters that all computers can read and understand, including the letters, numbers, and symbols found on a typical keyboard, along with some other special characters. This limited set of characters is what must be used in HTML text documents.

text are very limited. Because you will be applying HTML codes to format your Web page text, you don't have to worry about the text editor's formatting capabilities.

In the next Step-by-Step exercise, you use a text editor to enter some simple HTML structural tags. These tags form the basic backbone and structure for Web pages. You should be aware of some HTML basics as you begin your Web page:

■ An HTML tag begins with a < character and ends with a > character. Between these characters is the actual tag name, such as BODY or FONT. A correct tag thus looks like this: <BODY>.

■ Most tags appear in pairs of an opening tag (such as <HTML>) and a closing tag (such as </HTML>). The difference between an opening and closing tag is simply the slash (/) in front of the tag name in the closing tag. Not all HTML codes require both an opening and closing tag.

■ Text that you enter between HTML tags is formatted with the code specified by those tags. For example, if you enter <H1>Graphics</H1>, a browser will turn on H1 formatting and apply it to the word *Graphics*, and then turn off H1 formatting at the end of the word.

■ You can use either uppercase or lowercase letters when entering HTML tags. For example, a Web browser will interpret <HTML> and <html> the same way. In this text, we use all uppercase letters to denote tags so you can spot them easily in your text pages.

S TEP-BY-STEP 1.5

1. Launch your text editor. For example, to start Notepad, click the **Start** button on the Windows taskbar, click **Programs**, click **Accessories**, and then click **Notepad**. A new, untitled document opens, as shown in Figure 1-9.

FIGURE 1-9
New Notepad window

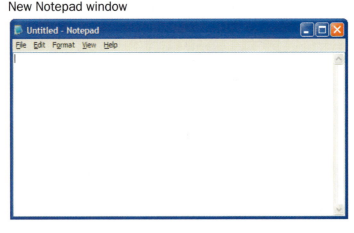

STEP-BY-STEP 1.5 Continued

2. Start your Web page by entering the following structural tags exactly as shown here. Your text editor window should resemble Figure 1-10 when you finish.

```
<HTML>
<HEAD> <TITLE> </TITLE> </HEAD>
<BODY> Hello, World Wide Web!</BODY>
</HTML>
```

FIGURE 1-10
HTML structural tags

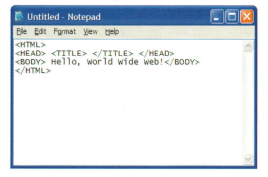

3. Leave the document open to use in the next exercise.

Save HTML Text Documents

You save an HTML text document the same way you save files in other programs. Use Save or Save As on the File menu to open a Save As dialog box, navigate to the location where you want to store the file (such as in your html folder), and then enter a name for the file. After you make changes to a previously saved file, use the Save command to save new changes.

When saving an HTML document, you must be careful to save it using the correct *file extension*. You may not have noticed, but every file you save on a computer has a file extension. These file extensions are often hidden from view so as not to confuse novice computer users. Nevertheless, these file extensions are important because they tell your computer, and your Web browser, the types of files that have been saved.

You may have already learned about file extensions for graphics and other file formats. For example, Microsoft Word documents are saved with a .doc extension, while Web graphics are often saved with .gif or .jpg file extensions.

HTML documents must be saved with an .htm or an .html file extension. Both of these file extensions tell Web browsers that the files being opened are text documents designed to be interpreted by Web browsers. The traditional naming convention for HTML files was .html as the extension. However, in 1995, Microsoft began to change some tried and true Web-based standards. For example, they truncated .html file extensions to .htm, which better matched the way Microsoft saved its files. To *truncate* means to shorten. Now, Web browsers recognize both file extensions, .html and .htm.

Traditionally, the first page a Web browser looks for when it finds a new Web site is the index.html file. Increasingly, browsers use other file names to find the main or welcome page of a Web site, such as default.html or default.asp. However, save your file as index.html.

S TEP-BY-STEP 1.6

1. Click **File** on the menu bar, and then click **Save As**. The Save As dialog box opens.

2. Navigate to the html folder you created in Step-by-Step 1.4, and open the folder.

3. In the **File name** box, with the default name already selected, enter **index.html** as shown in Figure 1-11.

FIGURE 1-11
Save the text file

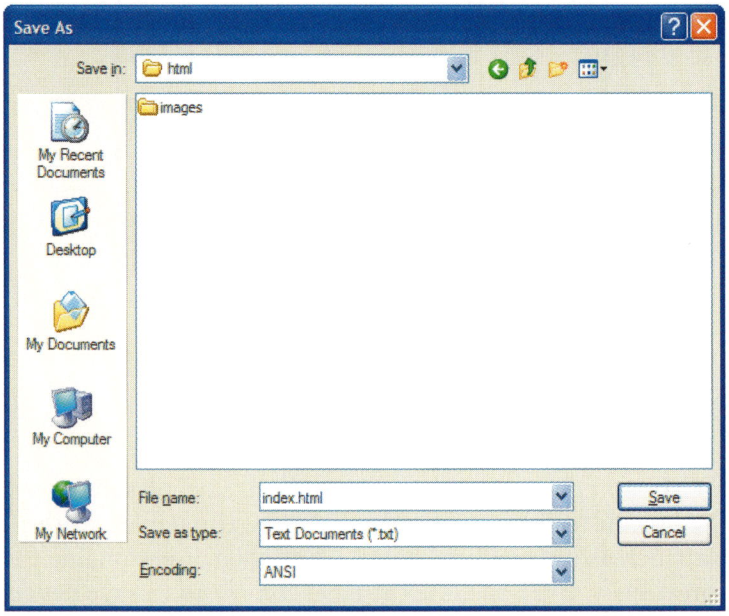

4. Click the **Save** button.

5. Leave the **index.html** file open in your text editor to use in the next exercise.

After you save a file in your text editor, you may want to close the file. In most text editors, closing the file also means exiting the program. To do so, use the Exit command on the File menu, or click the Close button on the program's title bar.

Extra for Experts

If you use Word or WordPerfect as a text editor, save your Web page as an ASCII text file. Enter a file-name that includes an .htm or .html extension and select the plain text file type in the Save As dialog box. Do not try to save HTML tags using the Save As Web Page or HTML command found in these powerful word processors.

View a Web Page

Now that you have created a Web page, it's time to look it over. It won't look like much to start with, but you'll make improvements in the next few sections.

View a Web page using a Web browser such as Internet Explorer. Because the page you want to look at is stored on your computer (or local network), you do not need to connect to your ISP and search for the page. Instead, use the browser's Open command to locate the page. Click File on the menu bar, and then click Open to display a dialog box you can use to enter the path to the page. You can also click the Browse button to navigate to the page location, select the file, and then open it.

Chances are, you will want to view your pages frequently as you create them to check layout and format. You do not need to reopen a page each time you want to view it. Leave the page open in your browser and simply click the browser's Refresh button to see your latest changes.

The exercise below gives instructions for viewing a page using Internet Explorer on a Windows computer. The instructions for your browser may vary slightly from these steps.

> **Note** ☑
>
> Refreshing the browser shows the latest changes you have saved. Be sure to save any new changes in your text editor before you refresh the browser, or you will not see the latest version.

STEP-BY-STEP 1.7

1. Launch your Web browser. You do not have to connect to your ISP.

2. Click **File** on the menu bar, and then click **Open** to display the Open dialog box.

3. Click the **Browse** button and navigate to your html folder.

4. Click the **index.html** file, as shown in Figure 1-12.

FIGURE 1-12
Locate and select the index.html file

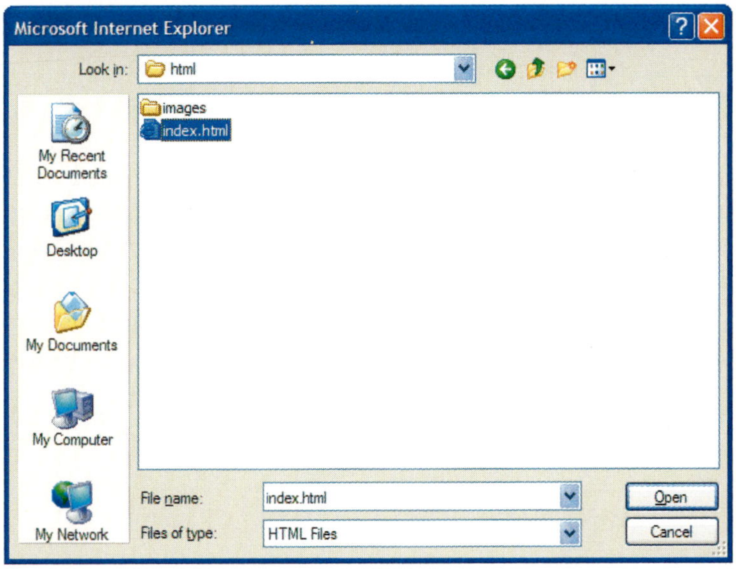

STEP-BY-STEP 1.7 Continued

5. Click the **Open** button, and then click the **OK** button in the Open dialog box. Your page displays in the browser and should look similar to Figure 1-13.

FIGURE 1-13
View your Web page

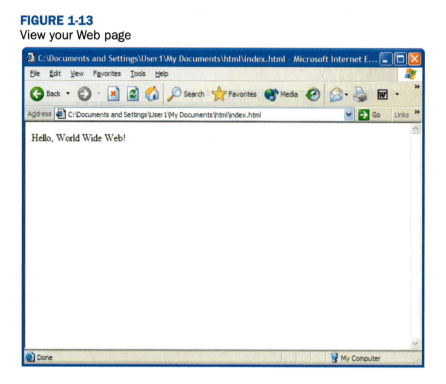

6. Close or minimize your browser.

7. Click **File** on the text editor menu bar, and then click **Exit**. The document and the program both close.

Modify a Web Page

Truthfully, your Web page looks a little thin right now. You need to create some content fast! Content can include any information to be shared with others. Because graphics are such an important part of any professional Web site, we're going to use *Graphics* as the primary topic of this practice Web site.

The main content of a Web site is enclosed by the <BODY> </BODY> tags. Anything that is placed within the body tags displays in the main viewing area in a Web browser.

If you need to open the HTML document to modify its content, you may not see it at first in the folder where you stored it. If the HTML file does not appear, select All Files from the Files of type list, as shown in Figure 1-14.

Choose All Files from the Files of type box

STEP-BY-STEP 1.8

1. Launch your text editor. For example, click **Start**, click **Programs**, click **Accessories**, and then click **Notepad**.

2. Click **File** on the menu bar, and then click **Open**. In the Open dialog box, navigate to your html folder and open it. If you do not see the index.html file, click the **Files of type** drop-down list and click **All Files**.

3. Click **index.html**, and then click the **Open** button.

4. Select the words *Hello, World Wide Web!* between the <BODY> </BODY> tags and press **Delete** to remove the text.

STEP-BY-STEP 1.8 Continued

5. Press **Enter** after the <BODY> tag and then enter the list shown in bold below.

```
<HTML>
<HEAD> <TITLE> </TITLE> </HEAD>
<BODY>
Graphic and Multimedia Formats
Portable Network Graphic
Joint Photographic Experts Group
Graphics Interchange Format
Bitmap
Wireless Bitmap
Tagged Image File Format
Apple Macintosh PICT Format
</BODY>
</HTML>
```

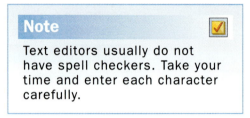

Note

Text editors usually do not have spell checkers. Take your time and enter each character carefully.

6. Click **File** on the menu bar, and then click **Save** to save your changes.

7. Launch your browser if necessary. Open the **index.html** page and view your changes. Note that the content does not appear quite as you would like it. In fact, it's a bit of a mess, as seen in Figure 1-15.

FIGURE 1-15
View your changed content

D:\Multimedia book\Final lesson 1\index1-15.html - Microsoft Internet E...

File   Edit   View   Favorites   Tools   Help

Back   Search   Favorites   Media

Address   C:\Documents and Settings\User 1\My Documents\html\index.html   Go   Links

Graphic and Multimedia Formats Portable Network Graphic Joint Photographic Experts Group Graphics Interchange Format Bitmap Wireless Bitmap Tagged Image File Format Apple Macintosh PICT Format

Done   My Computer

8. Close or minimize your browser. Leave the **index.html** file open in your text editor to use in the next exercise.

Add Paragraph and Line Breaks

The list of file formats you created in Step-by-Step 1.8 looks absolutely horrible! Even though you entered the items in a list in your text editor, they run together in one long, unbroken string. A Web browser does not move an item to a new line unless you insert the correct tag to start a new paragraph or line.

You need to add paragraph and line break tags to make the list look more presentable. The paragraph tag, <P> </P>, starts a new paragraph with space automatically added after it. The line break tag, <BR>, starts a new line but not a new paragraph, so text coded with this tag does not have extra space after it.

The break tag does not need a closing tag. You simply insert the tag at the end of one line to move the next item to a new line. Most Web developers use both opening and closing paragraph tags.

STEP-BY-STEP 1.9

1. In the **index.html** file, add the tags shown in bold below to your Web page.

```
<HTML>
<HEAD> <TITLE> </TITLE> </HEAD>
<BODY>
<P> Graphic and Multimedia Formats </P>
Portable Network Graphic <BR>
Joint Photographic Experts Group <BR>
Graphics Interchange Format <BR>
Bitmap <BR>
Wireless Bitmap <BR>
Tagged Image File Format <BR>
Apple Macintosh PICT Format <BR>
</BODY>
</HTML>
```

2. Save changes in your text editor.

3. Open or maximize your browser, and use the Open command or click the **Refresh** button to display the latest version of your page. It should resemble Figure 1-16.

4. Close or minimize your browser. Leave the **index.html** file open in your text editor to use in the next exercise.

FIGURE 1-16
Paragraph and line breaks on a Web page

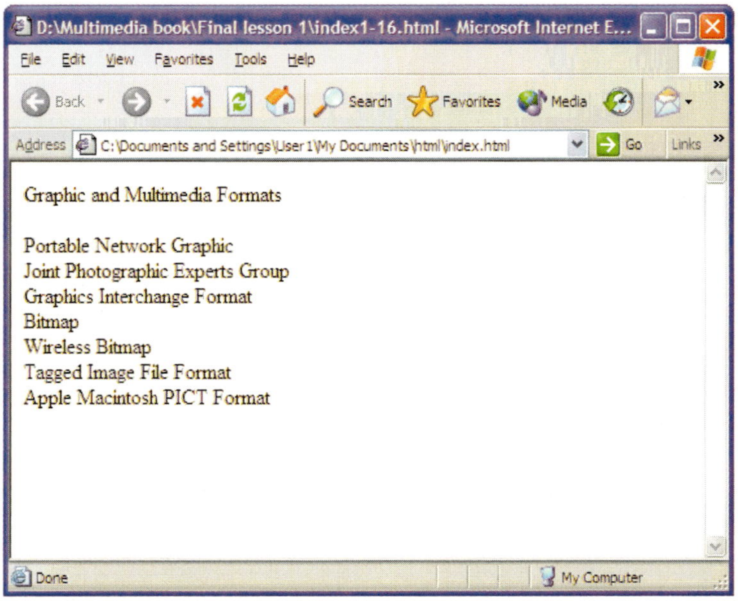

Add a Title

You've probably been wondering what some of the tags above the body tag are used for and why they are important, such as:

```
<HEAD> <TITLE> </TITLE> </HEAD>
```

Information stored within the head tags does not show in the main display area of the browser, but it is still important. For instance, any information placed within the title tags, <TITLE> </TITLE>, displays in the title bar region of the Web browser, as seen in Figure 1-17. This information helps Web page visitors orient themselves so they know exactly what Web site they are visiting and its theme or topic.

Extra for Experts

In a later lesson, you learn that other information can be placed between the <HEAD> </HEAD> tags as well, including programming information used when developing interactive Web pages.

FIGURE 1-17
Information between the title tags appears in the title bar

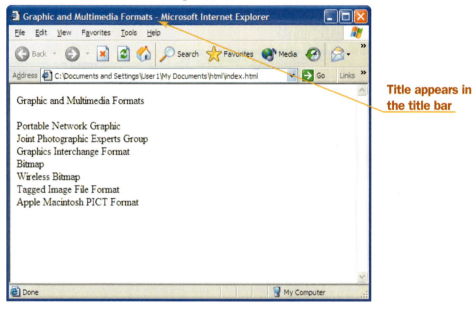

Title appears in the title bar

STEP-BY-STEP 1.10

1. In the **index.html** file, add the text shown in bold below between the <TITLE> </TITLE> tags on your Web page.

```
<HTML>
<HEAD> <TITLE> Graphic and Multimedia Formats </TITLE> </HEAD>
<BODY>
<P> Graphic and Multimedia Formats </P>
Portable Network Graphic <BR>
Joint Photographic Experts Group <BR>
Graphics Interchange Format <BR>
Bitmap <BR>
Wireless Bitmap <BR>
Tagged Image File Format <BR>
Apple Macintosh PICT Format <BR>
</BODY>
</HTML>
```

2. Save changes in your text editor.

3. Open or maximize your browser, and use the Open command or click the **Refresh** button to display the latest version of your page. Locate the new title in the title bar of the browser.

4. Close or minimize your browser. Leave the **index.html** file open in the text editor to use in the next exercise.

> **Hot Tip**
>
> If you don't see the change in the title bar, you did not save your file first in the text editor. Display the text editor, click the Save command, and then refresh your browser to see the latest version of the file.

Format Text with HTML Tags

Your page is starting to look a little better. But currently, all the text is the same size and thus appears to be of the same importance. However, you can use HTML tags to apply heading tags and font size tags to emphasize portions of your Web page text.

Use Heading Tags

Some parts of your Web page need to stand out from surrounding text. Most pages, for example, have a main heading at the top of the page that indicates what the page is about. Many pages also use subheadings to identify different sections of content. You can use heading tags to format headings on a page.

HTML provides six heading levels, identified by heading tags from 1 to 6:

```
<H1> Very Large Heading </H1>
<H2> Large Heading </H2>
<H3> Medium Size Heading </H3>
<H4> Slightly Smaller Heading </H4>
<H5> Small Heading </H5>
<H6> Very Small Heading </H6>
```

These simple tags can change the look of your text quickly, as is shown in the next exercise. Don't forget that these are paired tags, so you should always key a closing tag for every opening tag.

S TEP-BY-STEP 1.11

1. In the **index.html** file, insert the heading tags shown in bold below into your file.

```
<HTML>
<HEAD> <TITLE> Graphic and Multimedia Formats </TITLE> </HEAD>
<BODY>
<H1> <P> Graphic and Multimedia Formats </P> </H1>
<H6> Portable Network Graphic </H6> <BR>
<H5> Joint Photographic Experts Group </H5> <BR>
<H2> Graphics Interchange Format </H2> <BR>
<H3> Bitmap </H3> <BR>
<H4> Wireless Bitmap <H4> <BR>
<H2> Tagged Image File Format </H2> <BR>
<H6> Apple Macintosh PICT Format </H6> <BR>
</BODY>
</HTML>
```

2. Save changes in the text editor.

3. Open or maximize your browser, and use the Open command or click the **Refresh** button to display the latest version of your page. It should resemble Figure 1-18.

FIGURE 1-18
Heading tags change the size of text

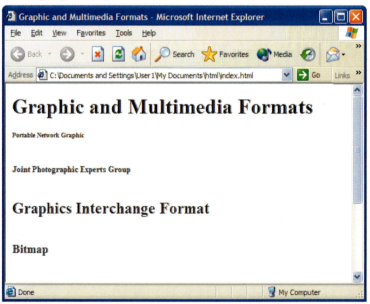

4. Close or minimize your browser. Leave the **index.html** file open in the text editor to use in the next exercise.

Format Text Expertly with the Font Tag

Using heading tags is considered a crude way to change the size of text. Another tag, called the <FONT> </FONT> tag, can change the size of text much more precisely. The font tag is very powerful and can accomplish a number of changes.

To tell the browser exactly how to display text, font tags use *attributes*. Attributes define more exactly what a tag is asked to do than the H1, H2, etc., of heading tags. Attributes appear immediately after the tag they modify and are followed by an = and often, by quotation marks (" "), as in this example:

```
<FONT SIZE="number"> </FONT>
```

In this case, the SIZE attribute tells the browser to change the size of the text to the number that is enclosed in quotation marks. With the SIZE attribute, you can use a range of numbers from 1 (smallest) to 7 (largest). In reality, however, using the smaller numbers results in text that is simply too small to read in certain fonts.

STEP-BY-STEP 1.12

1. In the **index.html** file, delete the heading tags from your file as shown below.

```
<HTML>
<HEAD> <TITLE> Graphic and Multimedia Formats </TITLE> </HEAD>
<BODY>
<P>Graphic and Multimedia Formats </P>
Portable Network Graphic <BR>
Joint Photographic Experts Group <BR>
Graphics Interchange Format <BR>
Bitmap <BR>
Wireless Bitmap <BR>
Tagged Image File Format <BR>
Apple Macintosh PICT Format <BR>
</BODY>
```

2. Add the font tags shown in bold below to your file. To save time, you can use your text editor's Copy and Paste commands to insert the font tags and then change the size numbers as necessary.

```
<HTML>
<HEAD> <TITLE> Graphic and Multimedia Formats </TITLE> </HEAD>
<BODY>
<P>Graphic and Multimedia Formats </P>
<FONT SIZE="7"> Portable Network Graphic </FONT> <BR>
<FONT SIZE="6"> Joint Photographic Experts Group </FONT> <BR>
<FONT SIZE="5"> Graphics Interchange Format </FONT> <BR>
<FONT SIZE="4"> Bitmap </FONT> <BR>
<FONT SIZE="3"> Wireless Bitmap </FONT> <BR>
<FONT SIZE="3"> Tagged Image File Format </FONT> <BR>
<FONT SIZE="3"> Apple Macintosh PICT Format </FONT> <BR>
</BODY>
</HTML>
```

STEP-BY-STEP 1.12 Continued

3. Save changes in your text editor.

4. Open or maximize your browser, and use the Open command or click the **Refresh** button to display the latest version of your page. It should resemble Figure 1-19.

FIGURE 1-19
Font tags can also change the size of text

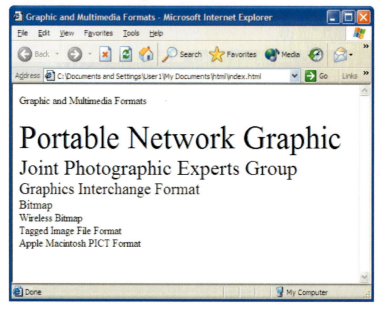

5. Close or minimize your browser. Leave the **index.html** file open in the text editor to use in the next exercise.

Use Heading and Font Tags Together

In the previous section, you experimented with font tags. However, this is not exactly how they would be used in the real world. You can achieve more professional results with less effort by combining heading and font tags. Rather than format every line of text with a different font tag, you can enclose a number of lines within one pair of font tags to apply that font formatting to all lines at once.

S TEP-BY-STEP 1.13

1. In the **index.html** file, delete the font tags from your file as shown below.

```
<HTML>
<HEAD> <TITLE> Graphic and Multimedia Formats </TITLE> </HEAD>
<BODY>
<P>Graphic and Multimedia Formats </P>
Portable Network Graphic <BR>
Joint Photographic Experts Group <BR>
Graphics Interchange Format <BR>
Bitmap <BR>
Wireless Bitmap <BR>
Tagged Image File Format <BR>
Apple Macintosh PICT Format <BR>
</BODY>
</HTML>
```

2. Add the font and heading tags shown in bold below to your file.

```
<HTML>
<HEAD> <TITLE> Graphic and Multimedia Formats </TITLE> </HEAD>
<BODY>
<H2> <P>Graphic and Multimedia Formats</P> </H2>
<FONT SIZE="4"> Portable Network Graphic<BR>
Joint Photographic Experts Group <BR>
Graphics Interchange Format<BR>
Bitmap<BR>
Wireless Bitmap <BR>
Tagged Image File Format<BR>
Apple Macintosh PICT Format <BR> </FONT>
</BODY>
</HTML>
```

3. Save changes in your text editor.

STEP-BY-STEP 1.13 Continued

4. Open or maximize your browser, and use the Open command or click the **Refresh** button to display the latest version of your page. It should resemble Figure 1-20.

FIGURE 1-20
Font and heading tags working together

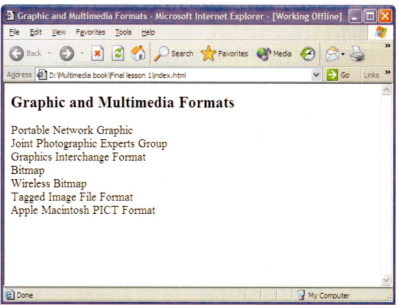

5. Close your browser. Close the **index.html** file and exit your text editor.

SUMMARY

In this lesson, you learned:

- The World Wide Web is a collection of Web pages, Web sites, Web servers, and Web clients.

- The component parts of a URL allow a Web browser to find a specific page in a Web site.

- Use a Web browser to locate pages on the World Wide Web and interpret their HTML tags to display content.

- You should create folders and subfolders before beginning a Web site to hold the files you will create for the site.

- You can use a simple text editor such as Notepad to enter HTML tags. Tags allow you to properly display a title on the Web page, headings, and other text content. Save an HTML file in a text editor so you can reopen it to modify text.

- You can use your browser to view your page without logging on to the Internet.

- Use paragraph and break tags to display paragraphs and list items in a Web page.

- Use FONT SIZE to modify the size of text on a page.

VOCABULARY *Review*

Define the following terms:

ANSI (American National Standards Institute)

ASCII (American Standard Code for Information Interchange)

Attribute

Domain name

HTML (Hypertext Markup Language)

Hypertext Transfer Protocol

Tags

Text editor

Truncate

URL (Uniform Resource Locator)

Web browser

Web clients

Web pages

Web servers

Web sites

Welcome page

REVIEW *Questions*

TRUE / FALSE

Circle T if the statement is true or F if the statement is false.

T   F   1. Clients share Web pages with servers.

T   F   2. A Web site usually includes different aspects of related topics.

T   F   3. HTTP is used to mark up Web pages.

T   F   4. The *www* in a URL domain name is the top-level portion of the domain name.

T   F   5. The *net* designation is often used by educational and governmental organizations.

T   F   6. HTML is an acronym for *Hypertext Markup Language.*

T   F   7. It is considered good professional practice to create separate folders for graphics and images.

T   F   8. Macromedia's Dreamweaver is the simplest and most basic of text editors.

T   F   9. Unfortunately, word processors and presentation programs cannot create Web pages.

T   F   10. Web pages are saved as text files with an .html or an .htm extension.

WRITTEN QUESTIONS

Write a brief answer to the following questions.

1. What are Web pages?

2. What are Web sites?

3. What is a Web server?

4. What is a Web client?

5. What is HTML?

FILL IN THE BLANK

Complete the following sentences by writing the correct word or words in the blanks provided

1. You should begin an HTML page with a(n) <_____> tag.

2. Place information for the title bar between the <_____> </_____> tags.

3. Automatically add space after a line of text by using the <_____> </_____> tags.

4. Start a new line without extra space below it by using the <_____> tag.

5. The information that is displayed in the main viewing area of a browser is placed between the <_____> </_____> tags.

6. The heading tags that create the largest font size or text are the <_____> </_____> tags.

7. The heading tags that create the smallest font size or text are the <_____> </_____> tags.

8. The attribute used with the font tag to determine the size of words is <FONT _____ ="7"> </FONT>.

9. The _____ top-level domain name is often used for public service or nonprofit organizations.

10. The filename extension .html can be _____ to .htm.

PROJECTS

ANS PROJECT 1-1

Now it's your turn to create a Web site on a topic of your choice. In the next three projects, you'll have a chance to decide on a topic and create a page for it.

First, brainstorm five possible topics for a new Web site project. Write the topics next to the numbers below.

1.

2.

3.

4.

5.

ANS PROJECT 1-2

Think about each of the topics you brainstormed in Project 1-1. Sort and analyze your topic ideas as follows:

1. Rank these Web pages in order from your favorite topic to your least favorite topic.

    (Delete one topic now.)

2. Rank the four remaining topics again according to their depth. Some topics are very shallow and do not allow a great deal of content or information to be presented. Other topics are completely overwhelming, involving entirely too much information. Rank the most shallow topic with a 4, and the most in-depth or overwhelming topic with a 1.

    (Delete one topic now.)

3. Some topics are hard to write about. Creating a great Web site may require you to write a good deal. Rank the topics, with 1 being the easiest for you to write about and 3 being the hardest to write about.

    (Delete one topic now.)

4. Discuss your remaining two topics with peers or with your instructor and determine which would be the most suitable for a Web site project.

5. What is your final topic decision?

_____

SCANS PROJECT 1-3

1. Use a file management program to create folders for your Web site:
   A. Name the main folder **project**.
   B. Within the project folder, create a subfolder named **html**.
   C. Within the html folder, create a subfolder named **images**.

2. Use a text editor such as Notepad to create the welcome page for your site. Save the file as **index.html** in the html folder you created in step 1B.

3. Insert the basic structural HTML tags in the **index.html** file.

4. Insert an appropriate page title using the title tags.

5. Add a main heading for the page in the body section and format the heading using an appropriate heading tag.

6. List five possible subtopics of your main topic, using paragraph or break tags to format the list.

7. Format the list using font tags and the SIZE attribute.

8. Save changes and view your page in your browser. Make any necessary corrections in the text editor file.

9. Save changes again if necessary, close the Web page file, and exit the program.

SCANS WEB PROJECT

Search the Web and list at least five Web sites that discuss a topic the same as or similar to the one you selected in Project 1-2. Find as many good sources of information as you can. Record the URLs or Web addresses of each of the sites.

SCANS TEAMWORK PROJECT

Form a team and discuss your personal Web project with your teammates. Tell them about your plans for your Web site project. Ask them if they know of any other sources that might be helpful to you as you create this project. Ask them what types of Web page elements would be interesting to them as potential visitors to your Web site. Take notes of their comments, ideas, and suggestions.

CRITICAL _Thinking_

SCANS ACTIVITY 1-1

What Web site have you visited that had the greatest impact on you? What about it makes it so powerful? What elements make a great Web site—from your personal perspective? List the URL of the Web site you selected as having such an impact and explain why in a 250-word description.

FORMATTING AND LINKING WEB SITE PAGES

OBJECTIVES

Upon completion of this lesson, you should be able to:

- Explain how Web sites are structured.
- Center text.
- Add horizontal lines to a Web page.
- Change font face.
- Apply consistent look and feel to a Web site.
- Create hyperlinks on Web pages.
- Create a bulleted (unordered) list.
- Create a numbered (ordered) list.
- Create multiple pages for a Web site.

Estimated Time: 2 hours

VOCABULARY

Anchor tag

Broken links

Hierarchical structure

Linear structure

Navigation system

Random access structure

Web sites have been created on nearly every topic you can possibly imagine. They are invented by individuals, organizations, businesses, and even countries. They are created by salespeople, artists, advocates, teachers, students, doctors, lawyers, butchers, bakers, candlestick makers—in other words, people from every walk of life.

The reason there are so many Web sites is because they are so easy to create. All you need is access to a Web server, a text editor, and a little creativity, and you can produce an interesting Web site.

In this lesson, you create a Web site on the topic of graphics. Along the way, you learn how to format text using alignments and font faces, how to insert horizontal lines and lists, and how to link multiple Web pages using hyperlinks.

How Web Sites Are Structured

When two or more pages are linked together—on a common topic or for a common purpose—a Web site is created. Most Web sites use one (or parts) of three basic structures:

■ Linear structure

■ Random access structure

■ Hierarchical structure

A *linear structure* has users view pages one at a time, as shown in Figure 2-1. This structure is great for teaching people something new that requires step-by-step learning. A linear structure is recommended if information is best viewed one Web page at a time in a certain order, as in a presentation.

FIGURE 2-1
Diagram of a linear structure

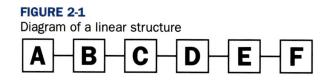

Another system, called a *random access structure*, allows Web site visitors to jump to any page on the Web site, as seen in Figure 2-2. This is a good organizational structure for sites that have just a few, interrelated pages. When the order in which the Web pages are viewed doesn't matter, then random order is a good organizational choice.

FIGURE 2-2
Diagram of a random access structure

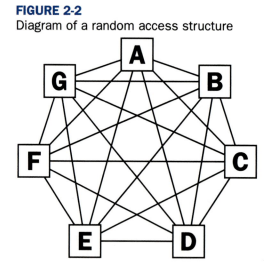

A third system, called a *hierarchical structure*, looks like a family tree with parents and children (and sometimes grandchildren), as shown in Figure 2-3. This is a great way to organize large amounts of information. The hierarchical structure uses categories and subcategories, like an outline someone might prepare prior to writing a paper.

FIGURE 2-3
Diagram of a hierarchical structure

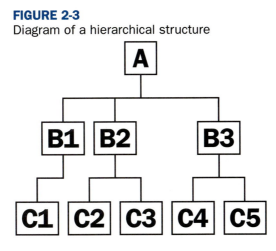

The Web site's content is the basis for selecting the organizational structure to use. For your Web site about graphics, a hierarchical structure makes a lot of sense at the beginning, but as you work on the site further, you will integrate elements of all three structures. Start by creating the first new page of this Web site.

S TEP-BY-STEP 2.1

1. Launch your text editor. For example, click the **Start** button on the Windows XP taskbar, click **All Programs**, click **Accessories**, and click **Notepad**.

2. Start your new Web page by entering the structural tags exactly as shown here.

```
<HTML>
<HEAD> <TITLE> </TITLE> </HEAD>
<BODY>
</BODY>
</HTML>
```

3. Now fill in the blanks! Enter the information shown in bold below about the Graphics Interchange Format (.gif) in the appropriate spots between your tags.

```
<HTML>
<HEAD> <TITLE>Graphic and Multimedia Formats </TITLE> </HEAD>
<BODY>
<H2> <P>Graphics Interchange Format</P> </H2>
<H2> <P>.gif</P> </H2>
<FONT SIZE="4">GIF files are popular for use on the World Wide Web. They
can contain up to 256 colors. They are used for cartoons, logos, graphics
with transparent areas, and animations.
</FONT>
</BODY>
</HTML>
```

STEP-BY-STEP 2.1 Continued

4. Click **File** on the menu bar, and then click **Save As**.

5. Navigate to the html folder you created in Lesson 1 and open it.

6. Enter the filename **gif.html**, and click the **Save** button.

7. Launch your Web browser. Click **File** on the menu bar, click **Open**, and then click the **Browse** button in the Open dialog box. Navigate to the html folder, click **gif.html**, and click the **Open** button. Click the **OK** button. Your Web page should look similar to Figure 2-4.

> **Did You Know?**
>
> Web sites sometimes use the same title between the <TITLE> tags on each page to remind visitors of the general topic of the site.

FIGURE 2-4
New Web page viewed in the browser

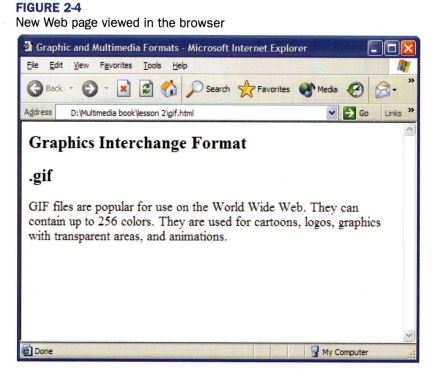

8. Minimize your browser. Leave the **gif.html** file open in the text editor to use in the next exercise.

Center Text

Web pages can be formatted, just like word processing documents. Formatting includes text design elements that add interest to Web pages. In the previous Step-by-Step exercise, you changed the size of the font. Font size is one aspect of formatting.

Text alignment is another aspect of formatting. As in a word processing document, you have three basic alignment options for text on a Web page: left aligned, centered, and right aligned. By default, HTML text is left-aligned, so all text lines up at the left margin of the Web page and forms a jagged edge on the right side of the page.

Centering is one of the easiest ways to add interest to a Web page. Centering uses one of the easiest to understand HTML tags, <CENTER> </CENTER>. Anything placed between these tags is balanced in the middle of a Web page, regardless of the size of the Web browser's window.

STEP-BY-STEP 2.2

1. In the **gif.html** file, enter the <CENTER> </CENTER> tags shown in bold below.

```
<HTML>
<HEAD> <TITLE>Graphic and Multimedia Formats </TITLE> </HEAD>
<BODY>
<CENTER> <H2> <P>Graphics Interchange Format</P> </H2> </CENTER>
<H2> <P>.gif</P> </H2>
<FONT SIZE="4">GIF files are popular for use on the World Wide Web. They
can contain up to 256 colors. They are used for cartoons, logos, graphics
with transparent areas, and animations.
</FONT>
</BODY>
</HTML>
```

2. Save your changes in the text editor.

3. View your page in your Web browser. It should look similar to Figure 2-5.

FIGURE 2-5
Center tags at work

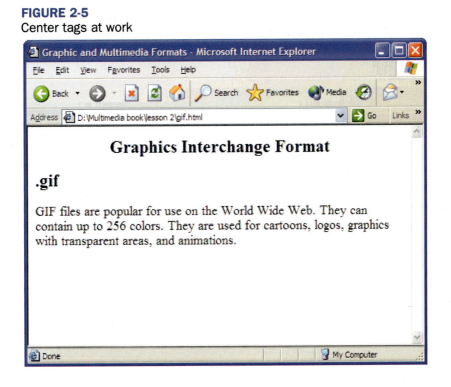

STEP-BY-STEP 2.2 Continued

4. Make any corrections that may be necessary in the text editor and save changes.

5. Leave the **gif.html** file open in the text editor to use in the next exercise.

> **Did You Know?**
>
> Learn as much you can about the graphics interchange format and other graphic formats. Read the content of the Web pages you create throughout this lesson. It will be valuable.

Add Horizontal Lines

Horizontal lines are easy to add. Lines, or *horizontal rules* as they are often called, create balance on a Web page. Horizontal lines help organize sections of text, which in turn makes it easier for Web site visitors to find the information they are looking for. Just a few simple lines can make a Web page much more pleasing to the eye.

Horizontal rules are created with the <HR> tag. This is one of the tags that does not need a closing tag. Place the tag where you want the rule to appear on the page.

STEP-BY-STEP 2.3

1. In the **gif.html** file, enter the following <HR> tags shown in bold below.

```
<HTML>
<HEAD> <TITLE>Graphic and Multimedia Formats </TITLE> </HEAD>
<BODY>
<CENTER> <H2> <P>Graphics Interchange Format</P> </H2> </CENTER>
<H2> <P>.gif</P> </H2>
<HR>
<FONT SIZE="4">GIF files are popular for use on the World Wide Web. They
can contain up to 256 colors. They are used for cartoons, logos, graphics
with transparent areas, and animations.
</FONT>
<HR>
</BODY>
</HTML>
```

2. Save changes in the text editor.

STEP-BY-STEP 2.3 Continued

3. View your page in your Web browser. It should look similar to Figure 2-6.

FIGURE 2-6
Horizontal rule tags at work

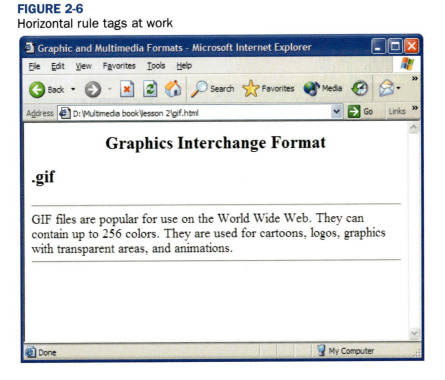

4. Make any corrections that may be necessary in the text editor and save changes.

5. Leave the **gif.html** file open in the text editor to use in the next exercise.

Change Font Face

Y ou have probably changed the font *face* in word processing documents or desktop publications. The font face, which is often simply called the *font*, is a set of characters in a specific design. Popular fonts include Arial, Helvetica, Times, Times New Roman, Script, Geneva, Century Gothic, and Tahoma.

Fonts are divided into two basic categories, *serif* and *sans serif*. Serif fonts, such as Georgia and Times New Roman, have tiny trailing edges on the strokes that make up each letter (see Figure 2-7). Serif fonts are easy to read and are often used for the main body of text on a page.

FIGURE 2-7
Serif and sans serif fonts

Georgia is a serif font

Arial is a sans serif font

Sans serif fonts (the word *sans* means "without") do not have trailing edges (Figure 2-7). Sans serif fonts are often used for headings, but may also be used for body text for a modern look.

The HTML tag combination <FONT FACE="*face*"> is used to change the font face. You can change the face to any font available to you. However, if the client computer that receives your Web page does not have the font you specify in its system, the page will not appear on the client computer in exactly the same way as you "ordered" it to via the tags you inserted. To prevent this problem, Web designers commonly list multiple fonts as alternatives, followed by either *serif* or *sans serif*, so the Web browser is directed to find a font that is at least similar to the one requested by the Web page. Examine the following tags:

```
<FONT SIZE="4" FACE="Georgia, Times New Roman, Times, serif"> </FONT>
```

This code tells the browser to display text in Georgia, if it is available. If Georgia is not available, the browser can use Times New Roman, Times, or the default serif font. Note that one tag, <FONT>, can have several attributes, such as SIZE and FACE.

S TEP-BY-STEP 2.4

1. In the **gif.html** file, enter the font attributes shown in bold below.

```
<HTML>
<HEAD> <TITLE>Graphic and Multimedia Formats </TITLE> </HEAD>
<BODY>
<CENTER> <H2> <P>Graphics Interchange Format</P> </H2> </CENTER>
<H2> <P>.gif</P> </H2>
<HR>
<FONT SIZE="4" FACE="Georgia, Times New Roman, Times, serif"> GIF files
are popular for use on the World Wide Web. They can contain up to
256 colors. They are used for cartoons, logos, graphics with transparent
areas, and animations.
</FONT>
<HR>
</BODY>
</HTML>
```

2. Save changes in the text editor.

STEP-BY-STEP 2.4 Continued

3. View your page in your Web browser. It should look similar to Figure 2-8.

FIGURE 2-8
Font face tags at work

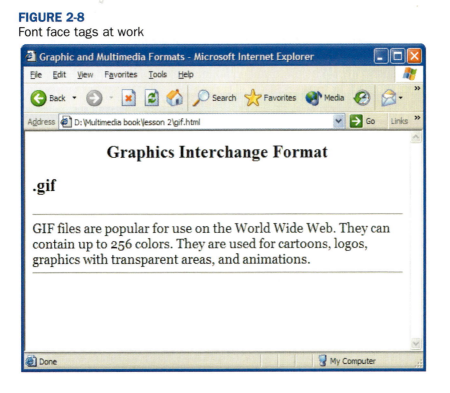

4. Make any corrections that may be necessary in the text editor and save changes.

5. You are finished with **gif.html** for now, but leave the file and the text editor open to use in the next exercise.

Apply a Consistent Look and Feel to Web Pages

One of the key aspects of Web design is to assure visitors that they are still on the same Web site no matter how many pages they visit. The "look and feel" of a Web site is important to maintain from page to page! This consistent look and feel can be accomplished with formatting, design elements, and even font face elements. If you change the look and feel dramatically from page to page, the Web site appears inconsistent and potentially confusing to visitors.

After you have experimented with and refined the look and feel of one page, you should apply the same look and feel to other pages on your Web site.

Extra for Experts

From your experience on the World Wide Web, can you think of sites that create a consistent look and feel from page to page? Think about this concept the next time you surf the Net.

STEP-BY-STEP 2.5

1. In the text editor, click **File** on the menu bar, and then click **Open**. In your html folder, click **index.html** and then click the **Open** button. This action automatically closes the gif.html file you had open. If you do not see the **index.html** file in the file list, click the **Files of type** list arrow and then click **All Files**. If you did not complete Lesson 1 or cannot find your **index.html** file, see your instructor.

2. Add the tags shown in bold below to your **index.html** file.

```
<HTML>
<HEAD> <TITLE>Graphic and Multimedia Formats </TITLE> </HEAD>
<BODY>
<CENTER> <H2> <P>Graphic and Multimedia Formats </P> </H2> </CENTER>
<HR>
<FONT SIZE="4" FACE="Georgia, Times New Roman, Times, serif">
Portable Network Graphic<BR>
Joint Photographic Experts Group <BR>
Graphics Interchange Format<BR>
Bitmap<BR>
Wireless Bitmap <BR>
Tagged Image File Format<BR>
Apple Macintosh PICT Format <BR> </FONT>
<HR>
</BODY>
</HTML>
```

3. Save changes in the text editor.

4. View the changes you have made with your Web browser. Your page should look similar to Figure 2-9.

FIGURE 2-9
Apply HTML design elements to index.html file

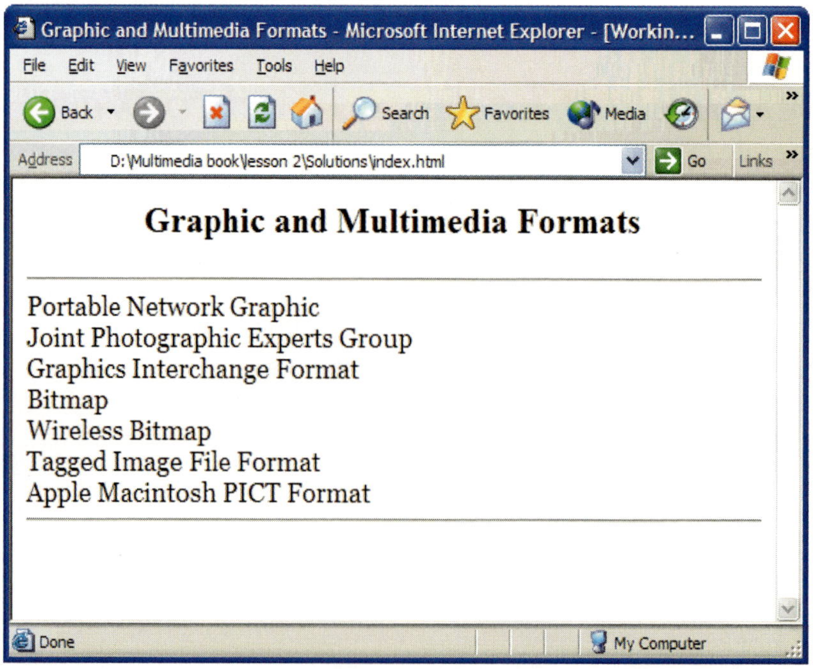

5. Leave the **index.html** file open in the text editor to use in the next exercise.

Create Hyperlinks on Web Pages

To this point, all you have created are two separate pages. You haven't really created a Web site yet, because until you link those pages together, they don't support each other or work together. To link pages, you use *hyperlinks*. As you probably know, you click a hyperlink (sometimes simply called a link) to open a different page in your browser window.

Hyperlinks are identified on a page by distinctive formatting. Usually, they appear in a color different from that of the surrounding text and are often underlined, as well.

In a good Web page design, you create links from the home or index page to all pages in the Web site. You should also create links *from* each page in the site back to the index page.

Create a Link from the Index Page to Other Pages

To insert a hyperlink on a Web page, you use an ***anchor tag*** <A>. The anchor tag requires a hypertext reference (HREF) and the name of a destination Web page file. For example:

```
<A HREF="gif.html"> Graphics Interchange Format </A> <BR>
```

The words that appear between the opening and closing anchor tags are visible to Web page visitors when they open the Web document and display hyperlink formatting. The rest of the information is hidden from view but jumps into action once the hyperlink has been clicked.

STEP-BY-STEP 2.6

1. In the **index.html** file, add the anchor tags shown in bold below.

```
<HTML>
<HEAD> <TITLE>Graphic and Multimedia Formats </TITLE> </HEAD>
<BODY>
<CENTER> <H2> <P>Graphic and Multimedia Formats </P> </H2> </CENTER>
<HR>
<FONT SIZE="4" FACE="Georgia, Times New Roman, Times, serif">
Portable Network Graphic<BR>
Joint Photographic Experts Group <BR>
<A HREF="gif.html"> Graphics Interchange Format </A> <BR>
Bitmap<BR>
Wireless Bitmap <BR>
Tagged Image File Format<BR>
Apple Macintosh PICT Format <BR> </FONT>
<HR>
</BODY>
</HTML>
```

2. Save changes in the text editor.

STEP-BY-STEP 2.6 Continued

3. View the changes you have made in your Web browser. Your hyperlink appears with an underline and in a different color, as shown in Figure 2-10. Try your hyperlink by clicking on it.

FIGURE 2-10
Anchor tags create hyperlinks

Graphic and Multimedia Formats - Microsoft Internet Explorer - [Workin...

File   Edit   View   Favorites   Tools   Help

Back ▾   ✕   ⟳   ⌂   Search   ⭐ Favorites   Media   ⌂   ✉ ▾

Address   D:\Multimedia book\lesson 2\Solutions\index.html   ✔ ➡ Go   Links »

Graphic and Multimedia Formats

Portable Network Graphic
Joint Photographic Experts Group
<u>Graphics Interchange Format</u>
Bitmap
Wireless Bitmap
Tagged Image File Format
Apple Macintosh PICT Format

Done   My Computer

4. If your link doesn't work, return to your text editor and make any necessary corrections. Save changes in the text editor.

5. Leave the **index.html** file open in the text editor to use in the next exercise.

Create a Link from a Web Page to the Index Page

After you have created a hyperlink from your index page to another page on your Web site, you need to create a link back to your index file. This is the beginning of what Web designers call a *navigation system*. Navigation systems allow users to find their way around a Web site without getting lost.

As you set up links on your pages, consider where they will be most useful to site visitors. Hyperlinks that return a viewer to a home page are often placed at the bottom of the page, to be handy when the viewer has finished reading the page. Many Web designers place hyperlinks in several locations on the page, so a viewer doesn't have to search for them.

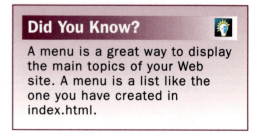

Did You Know?

A menu is a great way to display the main topics of your Web site. A menu is a list like the one you have created in index.html.

STEP-BY-STEP 2.7

1. Open the **gif.html** file in your text editor. (The index.html file automatically closes.)

2. Enter the anchor tags shown in bold below.

```
<HTML>
<HEAD> <TITLE>Graphic and Multimedia Formats </TITLE> </HEAD>
<BODY>
<CENTER> <H2> <P>Graphics Interchange Format</P> </H2> </CENTER>
<H2> <P>.gif</P> </H2>
<HR>
<FONT SIZE="4" FACE="Georgia, Times New Roman, Times, serif"> GIF files
are popular for use on the World Wide Web. They can contain up to
256 colors. They are used for cartoons, logos, graphics with transparent
areas, and animations. </FONT>
<HR>
<A HREF="index.html"> Menu </A>
</BODY>
</HTML>
```

3. Save changes in the text editor.

4. View your revised page in your Web browser. It should look similar to Figure 2-11.

> **Extra for Experts**
>
> Always test for **broken links**. A broken link is any link that doesn't go to the correct page. Test your links by trying them!

FIGURE 2-11
Hyperlink back to the main menu on the gif.html page

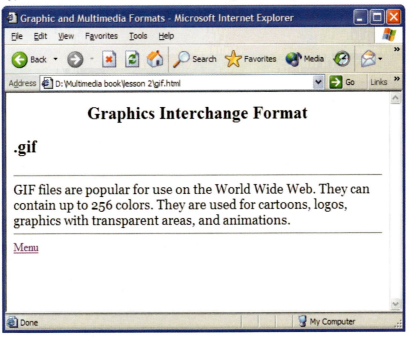

5. Make any corrections that may be necessary in the text editor and save changes.

6. Leave the **gif.html** file open in the text editor to use in the next exercise.

Create Lists on Web Pages

You can often improve the look and usefulness of Web page text by using lists. You can choose whether to create an ordered list that uses numbers or an unordered list that uses bullets.

When entering HTML code for a list, you precede each list item with the <LI> tag. The <LI> tag does not require a closing tag. The entire list is enclosed within the tags that indicate the type of list you are creating, ordered or unordered.

> **Did You Know?**
>
> Numbered lists imply an order, sequence, or level of importance. In other words, Web site visitors should proceed 1, 2, 3, 4, etc., through the items on the list. A bulleted list does not imply a specific order or level of importance.

Create a Bulleted (Unordered) List

Bullets are small dots or symbols used to draw attention to important items. Bullets are a great way to organize lists of information. To create a bulleted list, you use the unordered list <UL> </UL> tags. Insert the starting <UL> tag above the first list item, and the closing </UL> tag after the last list item. Each list item starts with the <LI> tag.

STEP-BY-STEP 2.8

1. Open the **index.html** file in the text editor.

2. Add the list tags shown in bold below to your **index.html** file.

```
<HTML>
<HEAD> <TITLE>Graphic and Multimedia Formats </TITLE> </HEAD>
<BODY>
<CENTER> <H2> <P>Graphic and Multimedia Formats </P> </H2> </CENTER>
<HR>
<FONT SIZE="4" FACE="Georgia, Times New Roman, Times, serif">
<UL>
<LI> Portable Network Graphic
<LI> Joint Photographic Experts Group
<LI> <A HREF="gif.html"> Graphics Interchange Format </A>
<LI> Bitmap
<LI> Wireless Bitmap
<LI> Tagged Image File Format
<LI> Apple Macintosh PICT Format
</UL>
</FONT>
<HR>
</BODY>
</HTML>
```

> **Did You Know?**
>
> When you use list tags, the break tags <BR> become unnecessary. You can leave them in or take them out as you choose. In this exercise, we have removed them. It is considered good form to remove unnecessary tags.

STEP-BY-STEP 2.8 Continued

3. Save changes in the text editor.

4. View the changes you have made in your Web browser. Your page should look similar to Figure 2-12.

FIGURE 2-12
Bulleted list tags at work

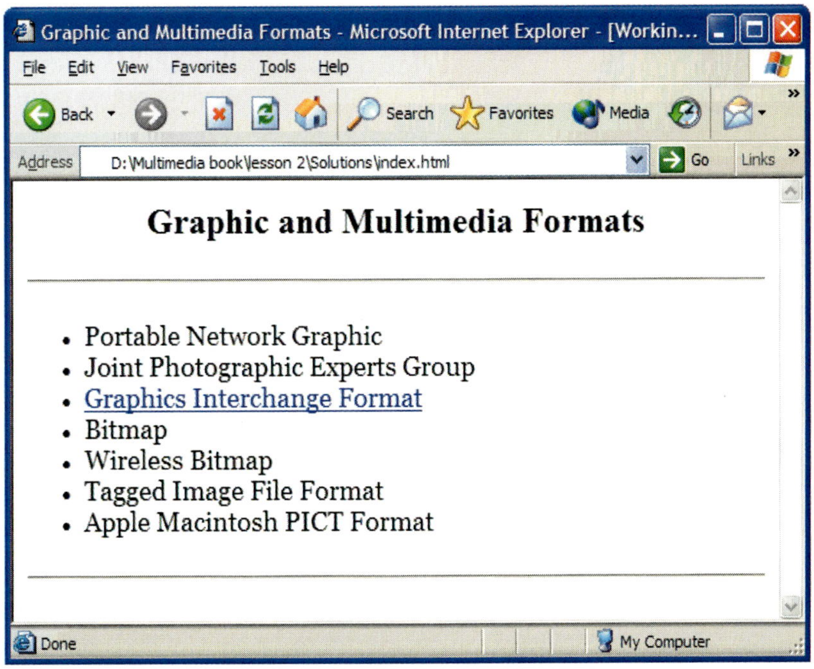

5. Leave the **index.html** file open in the text editor to use in the next exercise.

Create a Numbered Ordered List

Converting a bulleted list into a numbered list takes no time at all! A numbered list uses the ordered list tags <OL> </OL>. To change an unordered list to an ordered list, simply replace the letter *U* with the letter *O* in the HTML code. Make sure you leave the <LI> tags at the beginning of each item in the list.

STEP-BY-STEP 2.9

1. In the **index.html** file, change the list tags as shown in bold below.

```
<HTML>
<HEAD> <TITLE>Graphic and Multimedia Formats </TITLE> </HEAD>
<BODY>
<CENTER> <H2> <P>Graphic and Multimedia Formats </P> </H2> </CENTER>
<HR>
<FONT SIZE="4" FACE="Georgia, Times New Roman, Times, serif">
<OL>
<LI> Portable Network Graphic
<LI> Joint Photographic Experts Group
<LI> <A HREF="gif.html"> Graphics Interchange Format </A>
<LI> Bitmap
<LI> Wireless Bitmap
<LI> Tagged Image File Format
<LI> Apple Macintosh PICT Format
</OL>
</FONT>
<HR>
</BODY>
</HTML>
```

2. Save changes in the text editor.

3. View the changes you have made in your Web browser. The page should look similar to Figure 2-13.

FIGURE 2-13
Ordered list tags at work

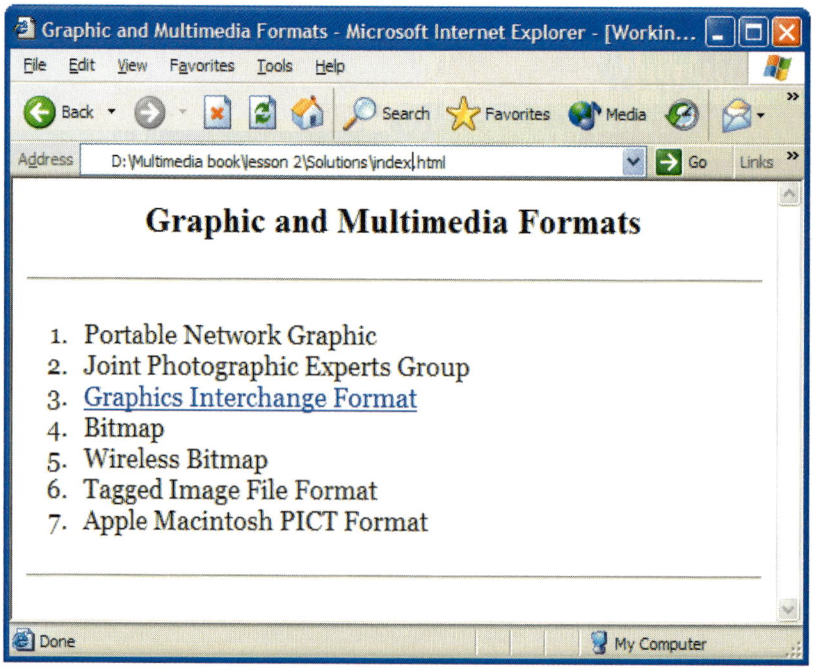

4. Leave the **index.html** file open in the text editor to use in the next exercise.

Add Multiple Pages to a Web Site

Now that you've done the hard work of crafting the look and feel of your Web site pages, it's time to create more content pages. Use the information provided in the Step-by-Step section below to create six new Web pages. After you create the new pages, you must link them to your index page.

Insert New Pages Using an Existing Page Design

Is there an easy way to create new pages with the same look and feel? Absolutely. Open the page you want to use as a model for the other pages and simply substitute the information, saving your files with all the appropriate formatting tags under a new name.

STEP-BY-STEP 2.10

1. Open the **gif.html** file in the text editor.

2. Substitute the information shown below in the appropriate places on your original gif.html Web page.

   Portable Network Graphic

   .png

   This format is often used for graphics on the World Wide Web. It can support up to 32-bit color as well as effects such as transparency. It is the native file format for Macromedia's Fireworks MX graphics program.

3. Save the file as **png.html** in your html folder.

4. View the page. It should look like Figure 2-14. Make any necessary corrections.

FIGURE 2-14
The png.html file

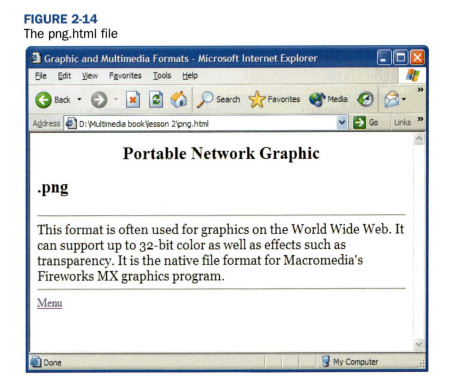

STEP-BY-STEP 2.10 Continued

5. In the text editor, substitute the information shown below into the appropriate places in the png.html Web page.

Joint Photographic Experts Group

.jpg or .jpeg

This format is used for photographs and other high-color images. It supports millions of colors and can be compressed. It does not support transparency.

Did You Know?

When you add new pages to a Web site, it's best to correct errors immediately to prevent the same mistakes from being passed along to the next page in the sequence. Stop problems early whenever possible.

6. Save the file as **jpeg.html** in your html folder.

7. View the page. It should look like Figure 2-15. Make any necessary corrections.

FIGURE 2-15
The jpeg.html file

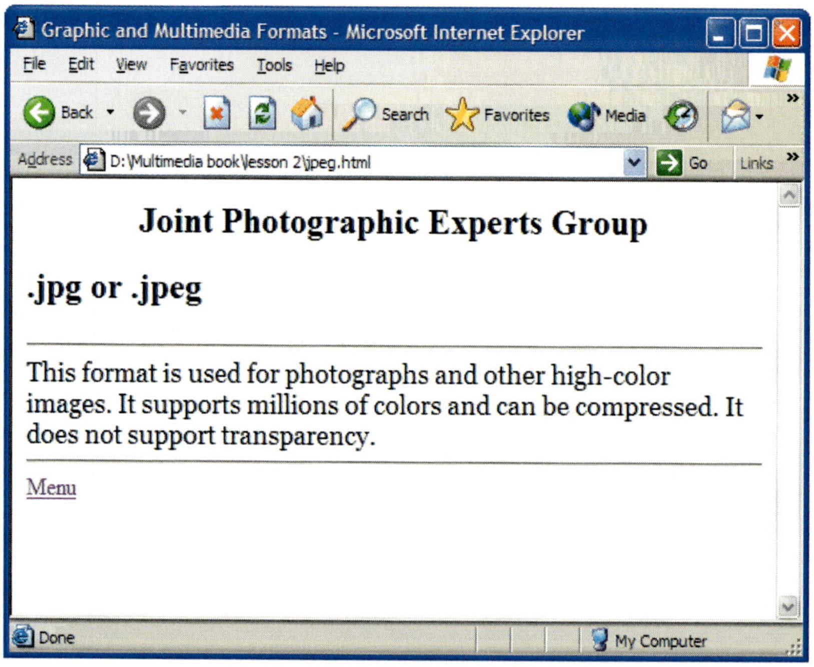

8. Substitute the information shown below in the appropriate places in the jpeg.html Web page.

Bitmap

.bmp

BMP is the Microsoft graphics file format and is used frequently for bitmap images.

9. Save the file as **bmp.html** in your html folder.

STEP-BY-STEP 2.10 Continued

10. View the page. It should look like Figure 2-16. Make any necessary corrections.

FIGURE 2-16
The bmp.html file

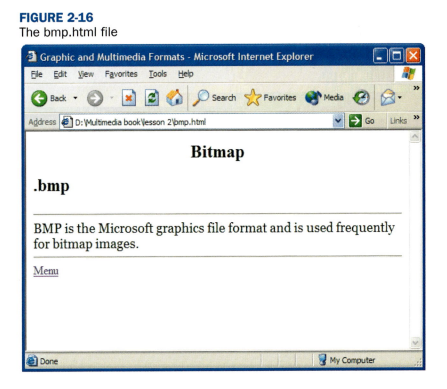

11. Substitute the information shown below in the appropriate places in the bmp.html Web page.

Wireless Bitmap

.wbmp

The Wireless Bitmap format is used for displayed images on Wireless Application Protocol (WAP) pages on mobile devices such as personal digital assistants (PDAs). It uses a 1-bit format, so can display only two colors, black and white.

12. Save the file as **wbmp.html** in your html folder.

STEP-BY-STEP 2.10 Continued

13. View the page. It should look like Figure 2-17. Make any necessary corrections.

FIGURE 2-17
The wbmp.html file

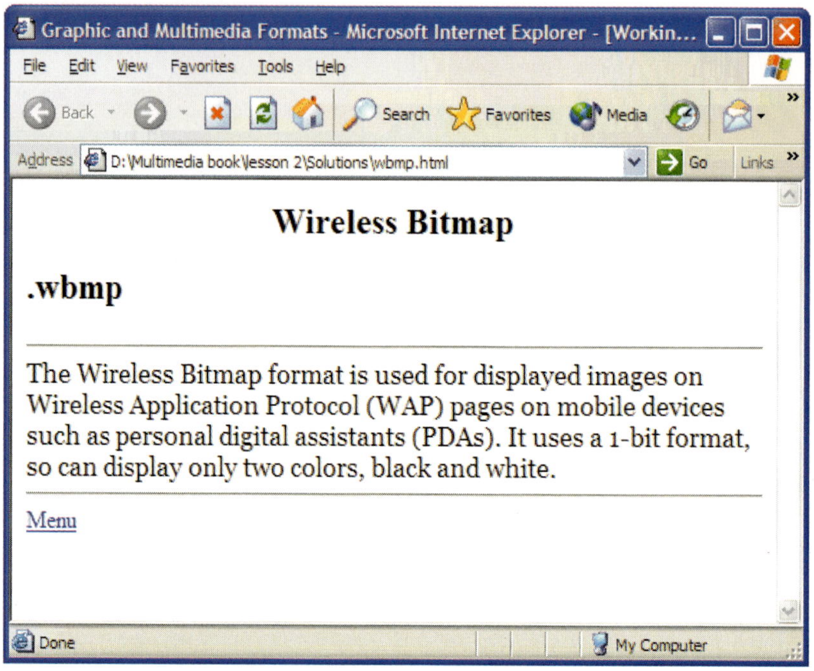

14. Substitute the information shown below in the appropriate places in the wbmp.html Web page.

Tagged Image File Format
.tif or .tiff
TIFF files are used for storing bitmap images. This format is commonly used in desktop publishing and other multimedia applications.

15. Save the file as **tiff.html** in your html folder.

STEP-BY-STEP 2.10 Continued

16. View the page. It should look like Figure 2-18. Make any necessary corrections.

FIGURE 2-18
The tiff.html file

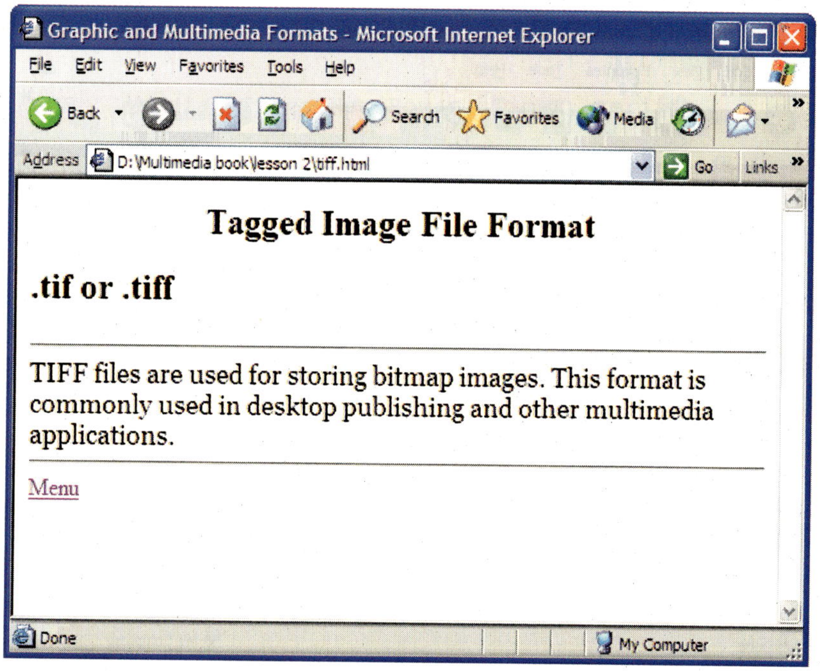

17. Substitute the information shown below in the appropriate places in the tiff.html Web page.
    PICT
    .pict
    PICT is the file format used by programs that run on Apple Macintosh computers.

18. Save the file as **pict.html** in your html folder.

Use Words to Specify Text Color

You can specify text color in either the body or font tag. In the <BODY> tag, use the TEXT attribute followed by = and a value assigned to the attribute. Follow the = sign with a one-word color description. In the example below, the value is RED. This value turns all the text on a Web page red unless the color is changed later by another color attribute and value.

```
<BODY TEXT=RED> </BODY>
```

Changing colors using only the body tag is a bit imprecise because it applies the same color to the entire page. When more precision is required, professionals use the COLOR attribute in the <FONT> tag to carefully specify the exact sections of text to change color. Examine the following tag with its attributes and values:

```
<FONT SIZE="4" COLOR=BLUE> </FONT>
```

S TEP-BY-STEP 3.1

1. Launch your text editor. Open the **index.html** file from your html folder. If you did not complete Lesson 2, see your instructor.

2. Enter the color attributes and values shown in bold below on your **index.html** page.

```
<HTML>
<HEAD> <TITLE>Graphic and Multimedia Formats </TITLE> </HEAD>
<BODY TEXT=RED>
<CENTER> <H2> <P>Graphic and Multimedia Formats </P> </H2> </CENTER>
<HR>
<FONT SIZE="4" COLOR=BLUE FACE="Georgia, Times New Roman, Times, serif">
<OL>
<LI> <A HREF="png.html">Portable Network Graphic </A>
<LI> <A HREF="jpeg.html">Joint Photographic Experts Group </A>
<LI> <A HREF="gif.html">Graphics Interchange Format </A>
<LI> <A HREF="bmp.html">Bitmap </A>
<LI> <A HREF="wbmp.html">Wireless Bitmap </A>
<LI> <A HREF="tiff.html">Tagged Image File Format </A>
<LI> <A HREF="pict.html">Apple Macintosh PICT Format </A>
</OL>
</FONT>
<HR>
</BODY>
</HTML>
```

STEP-BY-STEP 3.1 Continued

3. Save changes in the text editor. View the changes you made in your Web browser. Your page should look similar to Figure 3-1. If your hyperlinks are purple rather than blue, it is because you have used the links recently.

FIGURE 3-1
Color tags in the index.html file

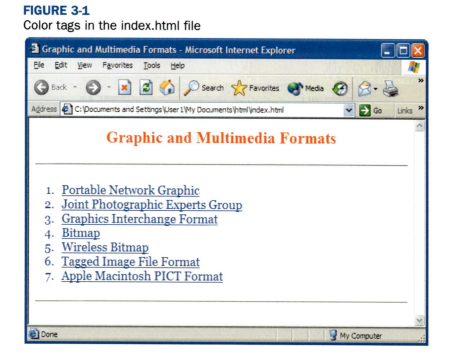

4. Now make the same changes to one of the content pages of your site to see how the colors work together on a page with a different format. Open the **gif.html** file from the html folder in the text editor and enter the new tags marked in bold below.

```
<HTML>
<HEAD> <TITLE>Graphic and Multimedia Formats </TITLE> </HEAD>
<BODY TEXT=RED>
<CENTER> <H2> <P>Graphics Interchange Format</P> </H2> </CENTER>
<H2> <P>.gif</P> </H2>
<HR>
<FONT SIZE="4" COLOR=BLUE FACE="Georgia, Times New Roman, Times, serif">
GIF files are popular for use on the World Wide Web. They can contain
up to 256 colors. They are used for cartoons, logos, graphics with
transparent areas, and animations. </FONT>
<HR>
<A HREF="index.html"> Menu </A>
</BODY>
</HTML>
```

Extra for Experts

In step 4's HTML code, FONT is the tag. The attributes for the <FONT> tag include SIZE and COLOR. The values for these attributes are the number 4 and the word BLUE. When using a number as a value, surround the value with quotation marks ("").

STEP-BY-STEP 3.1 Continued

5. Save changes in the text editor. View the changes in your Web browser. Your page should look similar to Figure 3-2.

FIGURE 3-2
Color tags in the gif.html file

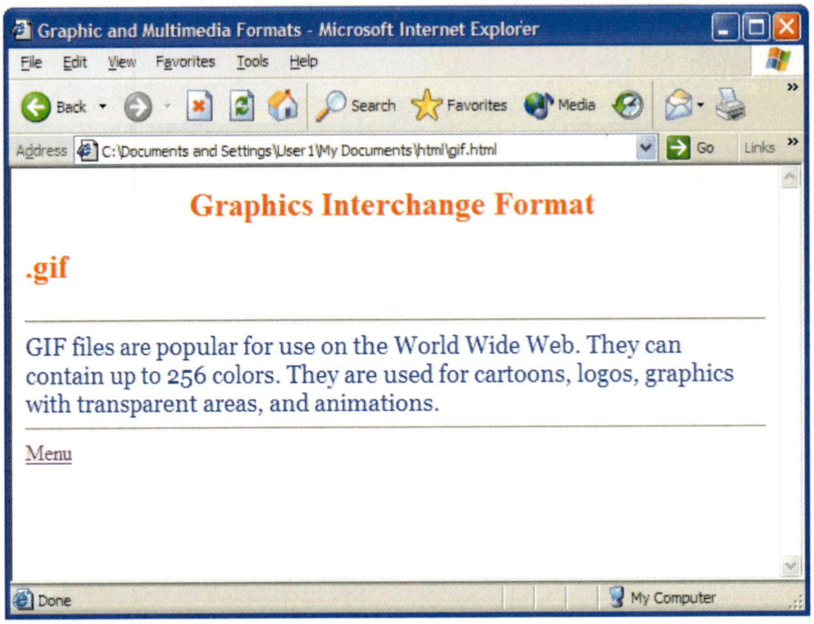

6. Make any necessary corrections to make your pages look the same as the figures.

7. Leave the **gif.html** file open in the text editor to use in the next exercise.

HTML tags should be *nested* when several tags apply to the same text or object. This means that sets of tags should be enclosed inside other sets. For example: <CENTER> <H2> <P> </P> </H2> </CENTER>. Note that the paragraph tags are nested within the <H2> tags, which are in turn nested within the center tags. If you enter your tags out of order like this—<H2> <P> <CENTER> </P> </H2> </CENTER>—your page may not look the way you expect.

Use Hexadecimal Values to Specify Color

Color values can be expressed by numbers as well as words. Numbers, however, are more precise. Color values can be carefully controlled to correspond with nearly every color in the rainbow using *hexadecimal* values. Hexadecimal is a numbering system based on 16 numbers, or a base-16 system. The hexadecimal characters are:

0, 1, 2, 3, 4, 5, 6, 7, 8, 9, A, B, C, D, E, and F

The standard hexadecimal values for the most common colors on the color wheel include:

White	="#FFFFFF"	Blue	="#0000FF"
Green	="#00FF00"	Red	="#FF0000"
Black	="#000000"	Yellow	="#FFFF00"

You can use hexadecimal values to change the color not only of text, but of other objects on a page, such as horizontal lines, graphic borders, and even the page background, as you learn later in this lesson. You do not have to experiment endlessly to come up with the correct combination of letters and numbers to define a particular color. Many Web sites offer tables of colors and their associated hexadecimal values to take the guesswork out of applying colors.

S TEP-BY-STEP 3.2

1. Open the **index.html** file in the text editor.

2. Enter the hexadecimal number values shown in bold below in your **index.html** file.

```
<HTML>
<HEAD> <TITLE>Graphic and Multimedia Formats </TITLE> </HEAD>
<BODY TEXT="#0000FF">
<CENTER> <H2> <P>Graphic and Multimedia Formats </P> </H2> </CENTER>
<HR>
<FONT SIZE="4" COLOR="#0000FF" FACE="Georgia, Times New Roman, Times,
serif">
<OL>
<LI> <A HREF="png.html">Portable Network Graphic </A>
<LI> <A HREF="jpeg.html">Joint Photographic Experts Group </A>
<LI> <A HREF="gif.html">Graphics Interchange Format </A>
<LI> <A HREF="bmp.html">Bitmap </A>
<LI> <A HREF="wbmp.html">Wireless Bitmap </A>
<LI> <A HREF="tiff.html">Tagged Image File Format </A>
<LI> <A HREF="pict.html">Apple Macintosh PICT Format </A>
</OL>
</FONT>
<HR>
</BODY>
</HTML>
```

STEP-BY-STEP 3.2 Continued

3. Save changes in the text editor. View your new page in your Web browser. It should look similar to Figure 3-3. (If your hyperlinks are purple rather than blue, it is because you have used the links recently.)

FIGURE 3-3
Hexadecimal color attributes displayed in the index.html file

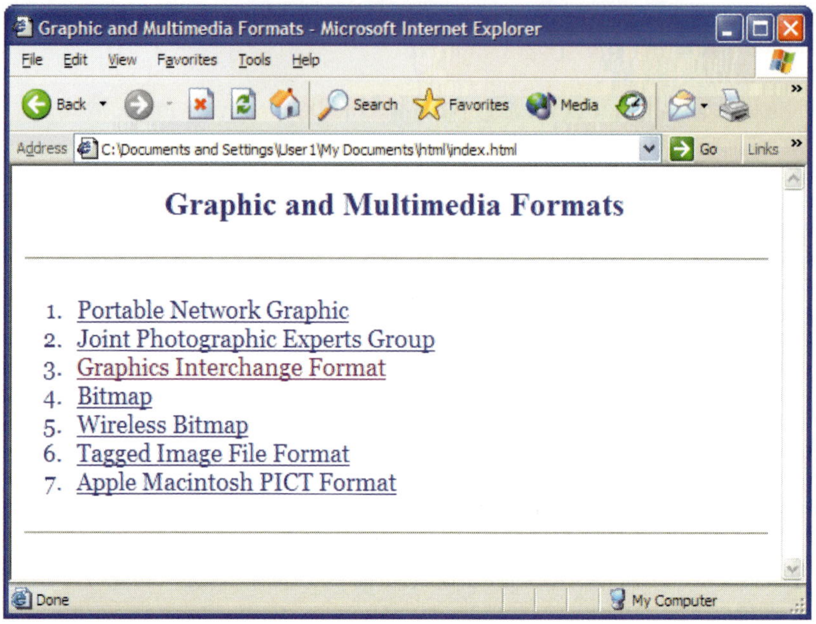

4. Now make the same changes in your gif.html file. Open the **gif.html** file and enter the hexadecimal number values shown in bold below.

```
<HTML>
<HEAD> <TITLE>Graphic and Multimedia Formats </TITLE> </HEAD>
<BODY TEXT="#0000FF">
<CENTER> <H2> <P>Graphics Interchange Format</P> </H2> </CENTER>
<H2> <P>.gif</P> </H2>
<HR>
<FONT SIZE="4" COLOR="#0000FF" FACE="Georgia, Times New Roman, Times,
serif"> GIF files are popular for use on the World Wide Web. They can
contain up to 256 colors. They are used for cartoons, logos, graphics
with transparent areas, and animations. </FONT>
<HR>
<A HREF="index.html"> Menu </A>
</BODY>
</HTML>
```

Did You Know?

Any combination of the numbers, 00, 33, 66, 99 and the letters CC and FF will produce colors that all browsers can display. For example, 003366, 99CCFF, and CC3399.

STEP-BY-STEP 3.2 Continued

5. Save changes in the text editor. View your new page in your Web browser. It should look similar to Figure 3-4.

FIGURE 3-4
Hexadecimal color attributes

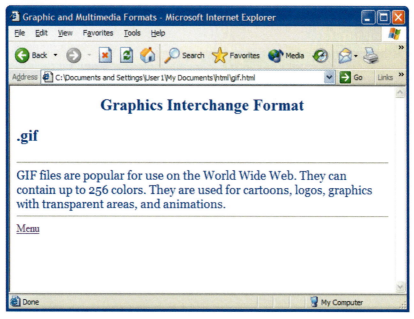

6. Make any corrections that may be necessary.

7. Leave the **gif.html** file open in the text editor to use in the next exercise.

Change Page Background Color

A simple attribute and value placed in the body tag can change the background color of a Web page. Use the BGCOLOR attribute in the <BODY> tag, and then use either a color word such as SILVER or a hexadecimal value for the color you want to use as the page background color.

Balancing colors is difficult on Web pages and usually requires some experimentation. You must be careful when you mix colors. For example, a dark background with dark text can make a page difficult to read.

When you attempt to balance several colors together on the same Web page, you are creating a *color scheme*. Color schemes for Web designs are often developed by artists who know what color combinations work well together. After a color scheme has been created, the same color scheme should then be applied to the entire Web site to provide consistency and an impressive look and feel.

STEP-BY-STEP 3.3

1. Open the **index.html** file in the text editor.

2. Enter the BGCOLOR attribute and hexadecimal value in the <BODY> tag as shown in bold below.

   ```
   <BODY TEXT="#0000FF" BGCOLOR="#66CCFF">
   ```

3. Save changes in the text editor. View your page in your Web browser. It should look similar to Figure 3-5.

   FIGURE 3-5
   Background color attributes in the index.html file

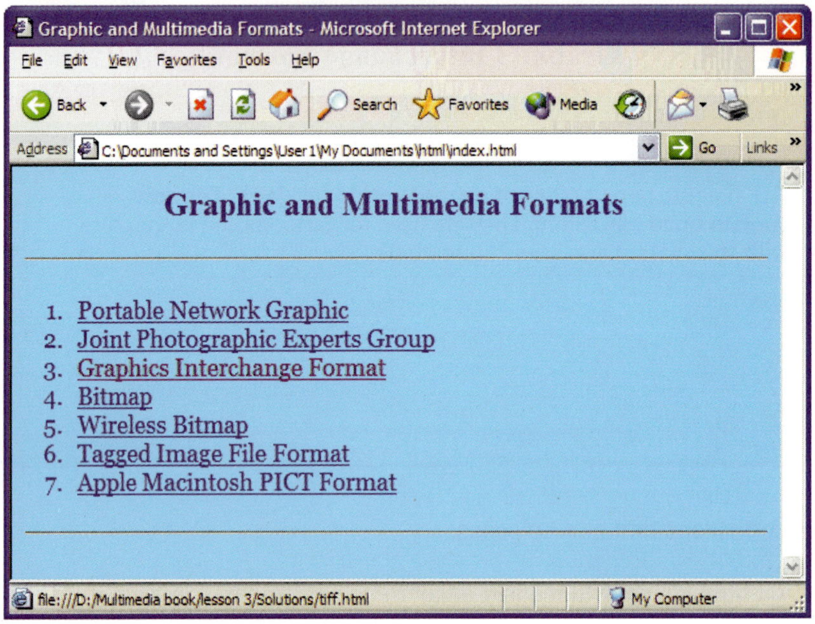

4. Open the **gif.html** file in the text editor.

5. Enter the background color attribute and value as shown in bold below.

   ```
   <BODY TEXT="#0000FF" BGCOLOR="#66CCFF">
   ```

STEP-BY-STEP 3.3 Continued

6. Save changes in the text editor. View your page in your Web browser. It should look similar to Figure 3-6.

FIGURE 3-6
Background color attributes in the gif.html file

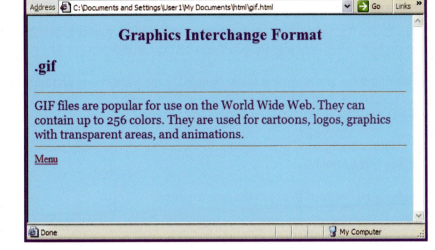

7. Make any corrections that may be necessary.

8. Leave the **gif.html** file open in the text editor to use in the next exercise.

Experiment with Web-Safe Colors

This is your chance to create a color scheme of your own. While there are literally millions of color options, some browsers can't display all these colors. To ensure consistency, Netscape devised 216 *Web-safe colors* as a standard that allows certain colors to be displayed in every Web browser. All these colors can be created with six pairs of hexadecimal numbers and letters, which are:

00, 33, 66, 99, CC, FF

You have already used several examples of Web-safe colors in the previous exercises; for example:

```
<BODY TEXT="#0000FF" BGCOLOR="#66CCFF">
```

Can you come up with better combinations of colors than we have? Give it a try. See if you can create a better color scheme.

STEP-BY-STEP 3.4

1. In the **gif.html** file, replace the hexadecimal number values in the <BODY> tag shown below with Web-safe colors using the following values: 00, 33, 66, 99, CC, and FF.

```
<BODY TEXT="#??????" BGCOLOR="#??????">
```

2. Replace the hexadecimal number values in the <FONT> tag shown below with Web-safe colors.

```
<FONT SIZE="4" COLOR="#??????" FACE="Georgia, Times New Roman, Times,
serif">
```

3. Save changes in the text editor. View your experimental colors in your browser, and then adjust the background and text colors until you are satisfied with the result.

4. Open the **index.html** file and make the same changes to the background and text colors.

5. Try again! Can you come up with an even better color scheme?

6. Change the colors of background and text back to those you applied in the previous exercise in both the **gif.html** and **index.html** files.

7. Leave the **index.html** file open to use in the next exercise.

Change Link Colors

There is one part of your color scheme that hasn't been adjusted, namely the link colors. You may have noticed that before you click on a hyperlink it appears in one color, and then it changes color after it has been selected. Web site designers control these colors by defining the LINK and VLINK attributes in the <BODY> tag. The LINK attribute controls the color of the link before it is selected, while the VLINK attribute controls the color of a visited link.

Before you can see these color changes, you may need to purge your history file so your browser won't think that you have visited a page previously. To purge history files in Internet Explorer, for example, click Internet Options on the Tools menu, and then click the Clear History button, as seen in Figure 3-7. Other browsers use similar commands to purge history files.

FIGURE 3-7
Clear History option

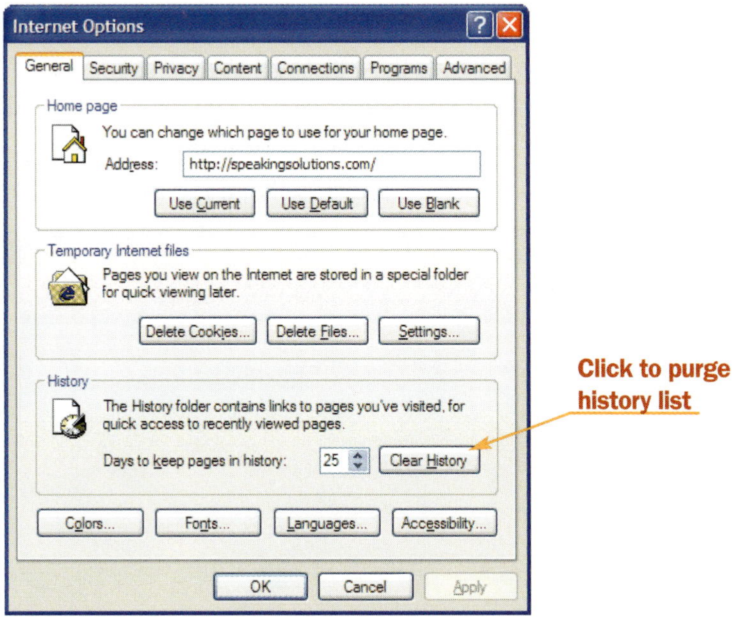

Click to purge
history list

STEP-BY-STEP 3.5

1. Open your Web browser, if necessary, and locate the command to clear recent pages visited. In Internet Explorer, for example, click **Tools** on the menu bar, click **Internet Options**, click the **Clear History** button, click **Yes** (or the button to confirm the deletion), and then click the **OK** button.

2. In the **index.html** file, add the LINK and VLINK hexadecimal number values in the <BODY> tag as shown in bold below.

```
<BODY TEXT="#0000FF" BGCOLOR="#66CCFF" LINK="#FF0000" VLINK="#FFFF00">
```

Did You Know?

Your Web browser stores or "caches" Web sites you have visited, so when you revisit those sites, the pages appear almost instantly. This system of *caching* reduces Internet traffic and Web page wait time.

STEP-BY-STEP 3.5 Continued

3. Save changes in the text editor. View the page in your browser to see the change in link color. Try several links and then return to the index.html page to see how the link color changed after you visited the pages. Your links should look similar to Figure 3-8 before and after they have been selected.

FIGURE 3-8
Link color tags at work in the index.html file

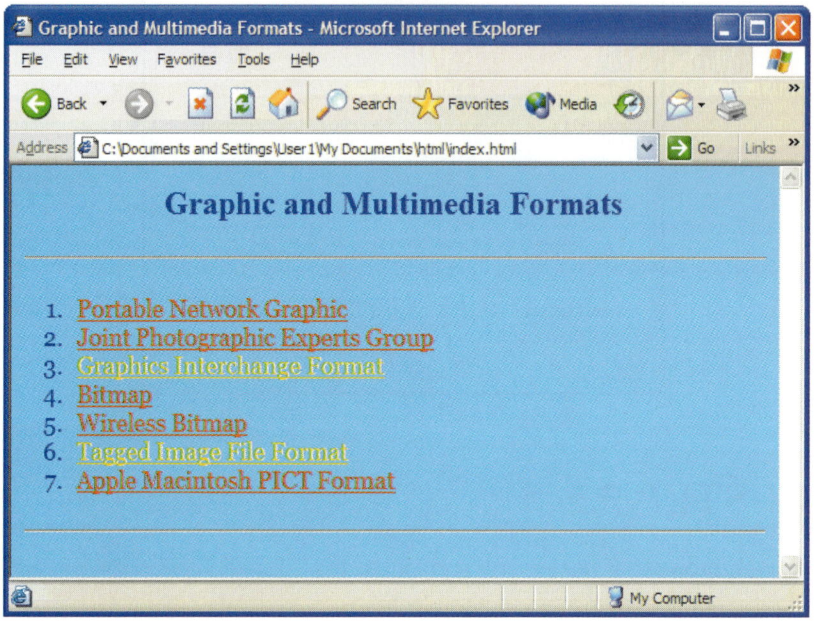

4. Make the same change to the **gif.html** file and view the page in your browser. Test the link on the page to see its color after you use it.

5. Make any corrections that may be necessary.

6. Leave the **gif.html** file open in the text editor to use in the next exercise.

> **Did You Know?**
>
> The **default color** for a hyperlink is blue. The visited link color is purple. Default colors are those colors chosen by the browser if the Web page designer does not specify alternative colors.

Acquire and Insert Graphics

There are two categories of Web graphics on the Net: those you can use, and those you can't. Those you can't use are copyrighted images, created by professionals and protected by the companies and organizations that own them. For example, the image of Mickey Mouse is owned and controlled by the Disney Corporation. The image of Mickey's ears is part of the company tradition, business plan, and profitability. Naturally, the company protects this image against illegal and unauthorized use by others.

But don't despair—not all images are copyright protected. In fact, if you use a search tool such as Yahoo or Google, you can find libraries of graphics available online for your use. Most online libraries provide information on how you can use their graphics. You may, for example, be allowed to download and use a graphic for a personal project or personal Web site, but not be allowed to publish the graphic on a commercial site. Some sites give you the option of purchasing graphics so you can use them however you want.

You are not limited to the Internet to acquire graphics suitable for your Web pages. You can also use graphics programs such as PhotoShop, Fireworks, or Illustrator to create your own graphics.

Once you have located the graphic files you want to use, you should copy them to the folder you have set up in your Web site to hold graphics, such as the images folder. This is both good organizational practice and a necessary step because the Web browser must "find" those graphics files within the Web site's folders, or the graphics cannot be displayed on the page.

Graphics are inserted on a Web page using the image tag, <IMG>. You must also use the search (SRC) attribute to define the image source, and a value that is the name of the graphics file you wish to display. However, between the " " marks, you must also include the path to the file. In the example below, the graphic file is stored in the images folder. The slash (/) separates the name of the images folder from the name of the colors.gif file.

```
<IMG SRC="images/colors.gif" WIDTH="94" HEIGHT="35">
```

You can make graphics as large or small as you need them to be with the help of the WIDTH and HEIGHT attributes, also used in the example shown above. The numbers define measurements in pixels. The word *pixel* is short for "picture element." A pixel is a small dot on a computer screen capable of displaying color. A single pixel in your computer's monitor would be very difficult to see without a magnifying glass.

STEP-BY-STEP 3.6

1. Launch a file management program such as Windows Explorer or My Computer.

2. Navigate to the data files folder for this lesson. Select all the files stored in the folder, click **Edit** on the menu bar, and then click **Copy**.

Important

You can also find the graphics files you need for this lesson on the Course Technology Web site. Use the URL www.course.com in your browser to open the site. Use the Search feature to locate the page for this book, *Multimedia BASICS*. Click the link to download student files and follow instructions. You can find the data files in the folder created automatically for the downloaded files.

STEP-BY-STEP 3.6 Continued

3. Navigate to your html folder. Open the **html** folder, and then open the **images** subfolder stored within the html folder. Click **Edit** on the menu bar, and then click **Paste**. The graphics files you need for this lesson are now available in your Web site's images folder, as shown in Figure 3-9. *Do not change the names of these files.*

FIGURE 3-9
Graphics files stored in images folder

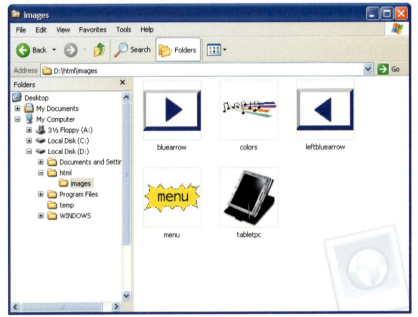

4. In the **gif.html** file in the text editor, add the image tag shown in bold below. Also add paragraph tags to create some space round the graphic and the paragraph.

```
<HTML>
<HEAD> <TITLE>Graphic and Multimedia
Formats </TITLE> </HEAD>
<BODY TEXT="#0000FF" BGCOLOR="#66CCFF"
LINK="#FF0000" VLINK="#FFFF00">


<CENTER> <H2> <P>Graphics Interchange
Format</P> </H2> </CENTER>
<H2> <P>.gif</P> </H2>
<HR>


<FONT SIZE="4" COLOR="#0000FF" FACE=
"Georgia, Times New Roman, Times, serif">


<P>
<IMG SRC="images/colors.gif" WIDTH="94" HEIGHT="35"> GIF files are
popular for use on the World Wide Web. They can contain up to
256 colors. They are used for cartoons, logos, graphics with
transparent areas, and animations.
```

Extra for Experts

The longer your pages, the more confusing the code can start to look. For this reason, spaces are added between various sections of code beginning with this Step-by-Step exercise. The spaces are not read by the Web browser and do not change the look of the page, but they make the HTML tags easier to read. You can add spaces as shown if you like.

STEP-BY-STEP 3.6 Continued

```
</P>

</FONT>

<HR>
<A HREF="index.html"> Menu </A>
</BODY>
</HTML>
```

5. Save changes in the text editor. View your image in your Web browser. It should look similar to Figure 3-10.

FIGURE 3-10
Graphic in the Web page

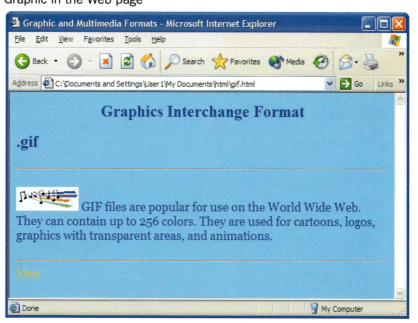

6. Make any corrections that may be necessary.

7. Leave the **gif.html** file open in the text editor to use in the next exercise.

Align Graphics

The graphic you just inserted in the Web page is an *inline graphic*. Inline graphics are displayed in relation to the line of text with which they are associated, with their bottoms aligned with the text baseline. The *baseline* is the bottom of letters that do not have *descenders*. Graphics can be aligned to the left or right of a line of text or so that

Extra for Experts

Unless you specify an alignment value, the graphic appears to the left of the text, lined up with the text baseline. The graphic extends above the line of text.

the graphic is centered vertically on a line of text. This means that the middle of the graphic aligns with the baseline of text. It does *not* mean that the graphic is centered between the left and right margins of the Web page.

STEP-BY-STEP 3.7

1. In the **gif.html** file, add the image tags, alignment values, and text shown in bold below.

```
<HTML>
<HEAD> <TITLE>Graphic and Multimedia Formats </TITLE> </HEAD>
<BODY TEXT="#0000FF" BGCOLOR="#66CCFF" LINK="#FF0000" VLINK="#FFFF00">

<CENTER> <H2> <P>Graphics Interchange Format</P> </H2> </CENTER>
<H2> <P>.gif</P> </H2>
<HR>

<FONT SIZE="4" COLOR="#0000FF" FACE="Georgia, Times New Roman, Times,
serif">

<P>
<IMG SRC="images/colors.gif" WIDTH="94" HEIGHT="35"> GIF files are
popular for use on the World Wide Web. They can contain up to
256 colors. They are used for cartoons, logos, graphics with transparent
areas, and animations.
</P>

<P>
<IMG SRC="images/bluearrow.gif" WIDTH="95" HEIGHT="66" ALIGN="MIDDLE">
GIF files are often used for buttons.
</P>

<P>
<IMG SRC="images/leftbluearrow.gif" WIDTH="93" HEIGHT="67" ALIGN="RIGHT">
You can align your graphic images to the left, right, or middle of the
line of text as shown in these examples.
</P>

</FONT>

<HR>
<A HREF="index.html"> Menu </A>
</BODY>
</HTML>
```

STEP-BY-STEP 3.7 Continued

2. Save changes in the text editor. View your new images in your Web browser. They should look similar to Figure 3-11. Observe the various inline alignment changes made in this section.

FIGURE 3-11
Inline graphics in the Web page

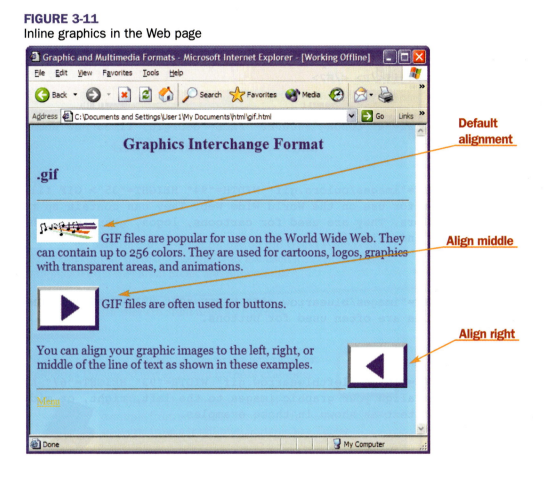

3. Make any corrections that may be necessary.

4. Leave the **gif.html** file open to use in the next exercise.

Insert an Animated GIF

GIF files are extremely versatile. For example, several GIF graphics can be combined to create simple animations, which are somewhat like cartoons, called *animated GIFs*. Use an animated GIF to provide visual interest on a page or to illustrate a process or product.

Insert an animated GIF the same way you insert any graphic. You can also specify an alignment for the GIF. You must display the page in a browser to see the animation work.

Change Graphic Borders

Hyperlinks are usually words displayed in a different color from surrounding text, are underlined, and may change in color after they have been selected, as you learned earlier in this lesson. But what about hyperlinks that are graphics? Graphics do not have underlines. Instead, a graphic has a thin color border to indicate that it is a hyperlink, as you can observe in Figure 3-13 in the previous section. This border changes color depending upon the LINK and VLINK values defined in the body tag, the same way text hyperlinks do.

You can change the size of a border or remove it altogether using the BORDER attribute, depending upon the look and feel you wish to convey on your page. You use a numerical value along with the attribute to determine the border width in pixels. The higher the value number is, the wider the border is. To remove the border altogether, set a width of 0.

STEP-BY-STEP 3.10

1. In the **gif.html** file, add the BORDER attribute and value as shown below:

```
</FONT>

<HR>

<A HREF="index.html"><IMG SRC="images/menu.gif" WIDTH="92" HEIGHT="51"
BORDER="10"></A>

</BODY>
</HTML>
```

2. Save changes in the text editor. View your change in your Web browser. The 10-pixel border should look similar to Figure 3-14.

FIGURE 3-14
A 10-pixel border in the gif.html file

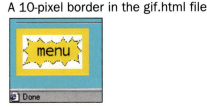

3. In the **gif.html** file in the text editor, change the size of your link border to 3.

```
BORDER="3"
```

STEP-BY-STEP 3.10 Continued

4. Save changes in the text editor. View the 3-pixel border, which should look similar to Figure 3-15.

FIGURE 3-15
A 3-pixel border in the gif.html file

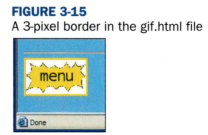

5. In the **gif.html** file, change the size of your link border to 0 to remove the border.

```
BORDER="0"
```

6. Save changes in the text editor. View the page in the browser. The graphic should have no border, as seen in Figure 3-16.

FIGURE 3-16
Border has been removed from graphic

7. Make any corrections that may be necessary.

8. Close your browser. Close the text editor.

SUMMARY

In this lesson, you learned:

■ You can change text color using either common color words or using hexadecimal values for more control over color.

■ The Web page background color can be modified using the BGCOLOR attribute.

■ Web-safe colors display correctly on any browser. Web-safe colors are created using combinations of 00, 33, 66, 99, CC, and FF.

■ Colors of hyperlinks can be changed using color values. Use the LINK attribute to change the color of an unvisited link, and VLINK to change the color of a visited link.

■ You can download graphics from the Internet and online graphic libraries. Insert graphics using the <IMG> tag and the SRC attribute. All graphics should be stored in a folder in the Web site file, such as the images folder.

- Graphics can be aligned to the left, right, and to the middle of a line of text.

- To add motion and visual interest to a Web page, insert animated graphics the same way you insert other graphics.

- You can turn a graphic into a hyperlink. To modify the look of the link, you can change the border width or remove the border altogether.

VOCABULARY *Review*

Define the following terms:

Animated GIF	Default color	Pixel
Attributes	Hexadecimal	Values
Caching	Inline graphic	Web-safe colors
Color scheme	Nested tags	

REVIEW *Questions*

TRUE / FALSE

Circle T if the statement is true or F if the statement is false.

T   F   1. Because all graphics on it are copyrighted, the Internet is one of the worst possible sources for graphics.

T   F   2. An attribute expands, refines, and clarifies what a tag is meant to display.

T   F   3. A value specifically defines an attribute.

T   F   4. The hexadecimal system is a 10-based numbering system that uses letters instead of numbers to represent values.

T   F   5. A reader-friendly color scheme involves mixing dark, rich-looking backgrounds with obscure and darkened text.

T   F   6. Color schemes are often developed by artists who know which color combinations work best.

T   F   7. There are 1,000 Web-safe colors.

T   F   8. Caching automatically places 10-pixel borders around animated GIFs.

T   F   9. You can purge your history file and fool your browser into thinking you have not visited a page previously.

T   F   10. The image of Mickey Mouse is copyrighted and protected against unauthorized use.

WRITTEN QUESTIONS

Write a brief answer to the following questions.

1. What are attributes and values and what is the difference between them?

2. How is an animated GIF different from a regular GIF file? What are some possible uses for animated GIFs?

3. Explain how to turn any GIF file into a hyperlink. What tags, attributes, and values would you use?

4. What are nested tags? Give an example of nested tags and tags that have not been nested properly.

5. What does "hexadecimal" refer to?

6. What are Web-safe colors and why are they important? How do you create Web-safe colors? How many Web-safe colors are there?

FILL IN THE BLANK

Complete the following sentences by writing the correct word or words in the blanks provided.

1. The hexadecimal color value for white = "#_____ "

2. The hexadecimal color value for green = "#_____ ".

3. The hexadecimal color value for black = "#_____ ".

4. The hexadecimal color value for blue = "#_____ ".

5. The hexadecimal color value for red = "#_____ ".

6. The hexadecimal color value for yellow = "#_____ ".

7. To add a page background color, insert the following attribute:
   <BODY _____ = "#FFFFFF">.

8. Insert an image into a Web page with the following tag
   <_____ SRC="images/picture.gif">.

9. Change the link color on a Web page by using the following attribute:
   <BODY _____ = "#FFFFFF">.

10. Change the visited link color on a Web page by using the following attribute:
    <BODY _____ = "#FFFFFF">.

PROJECTS

SCANS PROJECT 3-1

In the Step-by-Step exercises, we changed the color scheme only on the index.html and the gif.html files. We did this for a reason. It saves time to work with just a few pages on a Web site when experimenting on the color scheme. Only after you test and decide on the exact colors you want should you apply your refined color scheme to the rest of your Web pages.

Perfect the color scheme for your graphics Web site. Try various color combinations on the gif.html page. Choose the scheme you like best. Select colors that blend well and add to the overall look and feel of your site. Then, apply this color scheme to all the pages on the site.

SCANS PROJECT 3-2

Now that you have created a color scheme and applied it to your graphics Web site, what about your own personal Web site project? Choose a page from your Web site and start experimenting with a color scheme. After you have refined your color choices, apply these color choices to the remaining pages.

PROJECT 3-3

Note: *Finish the Teamwork project before completing this project. Completing that project before you continue with this exercise may save you time!*

It's time to search for graphics to use in your personal Web site project. Are there any graphics you can add? Search for appropriate graphics to use on your Web site pages. Find and download a different graphic for each page. Make sure each graphic fits the theme of your Web site and makes it more interesting. Insert a different graphic on every page. Be sure to download only those graphics that are free from copyright restrictions.

WEB PROJECT

Start this project by visiting some of your favorite Web sites. Make a table outlining the color schemes of at least five sites with interesting color schemes. List the primary background colors, the foreground colors (the colors used for text), and any accent colors for each site. Catalog in your table at least five sites with interesting color schemes.

TEAMWORK PROJECT

As a team, search the Web using several different search tools to locate copyright-free graphics. You may find the following search words useful:

Copyright free graphics (or, copyright-free graphics)

Animated GIF files

Graphics libraries

As a team, build a Web page with links to the various online resources you have found.

CRITICAL *Thinking*

ACTIVITY 3-1

Research the issue of copyright on the Web. Using online search tools, find sites that address different aspects of the copyright issue as it applies to the Internet. Then, prepare a 500-word summary that explains the different positions taken regarding copyright protections as they apply to the use of material found online.

WORKING IN A WEB SITE DESIGN PROGRAM

OBJECTIVES

Upon completion of this lesson, you should be able to:

- Explore the interface of your Web site design and management software.

- Define a new Web site.

- View the Web site in different modes.

- Add pages to a Web site.

- Format Web pages with your Web design software.

- Set up text and graphic links.

- Link pages in a linear structure.

Estimated Time: 2 hours

VOCABULARY

Code

Properties

Root level

WYSIWYG

As a result of the previous three lessons, you should understand how HTML tags are written and organized to produce interesting-looking Web pages. This is important background knowledge as you press forward in your Web site development experience. However, you probably have also learned what early Web site designers learned many years ago: Entering tags is tedious and time-consuming. There simply has to be a better way to get the job done!

Macromedia Dreamweaver and Microsoft FrontPage are software programs created to alleviate the time-consuming task of writing HTML tags. Each of these programs is a powerful Web page creation tool. These programs realize for Web site development what word processing programs accomplish for printed documents. When you use any Web design product, you save time and can focus more on the look and feel of your page rather than on the many different tags required to design Web pages.

If you don't have a Web site design program, you can still complete the exercises in this lesson by using the same text editor you used for the previous three lessons. No new tags are introduced in this lesson. Read each section and learn as much as you can about how a Web site design program works. Then use your text editor to create the text, links, and other elements for the new pages.

Explore Your Web Site Design Software

In contrast to the text editor you have been using, Web site design programs have a number of features to make it easy to create and organize Web sites. In this section, you explore your Web site design program's features.

The Web Site Design Window

All programs have a document window where you enter text and insert graphics and other Web page elements. Web site design programs usually also have a menu bar and toolbars or panels that give you quick access to commands and features. Figure 4-1 shows a typical Web site design screen. Your program's screen may have other elements such as a Views bar that allows you to perform different tasks on the Web site.

FIGURE 4-1
Dreamweaver MX screen

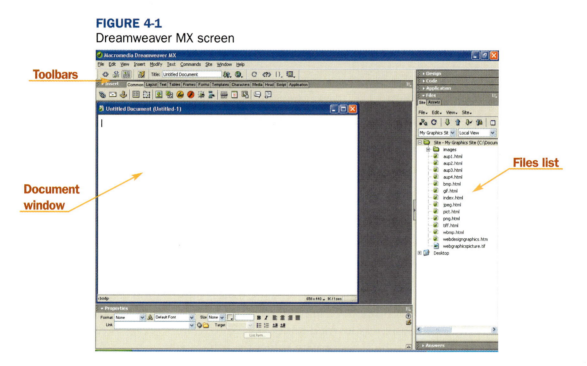

In addition to a document window where you enter the Web page content, most programs display a list of the files and folders in the current Web site. You can use this list to open pages, set up hyperlinks, or insert objects such as graphics.

STEP-BY-STEP 4.1

1. Launch your Web design software by clicking an icon on your desktop or by using the Windows Programs menu. For example, click the **Start** button on the Windows taskbar, click **All Programs**, open the folder that contains your program, and then click the program name on the submenu.

2. Your program may display a Web site you have worked on previously and/or display a new, untitled page. Take some time to become familiar with the program screen. Locate the menu bar, toolbars, and/or panels that contain tools and features for your program.

STEP-BY-STEP 4.1 Continued

3. Leave your Web site design program open to use in the next exercise.

Open an Existing Web Page

Even before you create or define a Web site, you can open any existing Web page in your Web site design program to view or edit it. Use a familiar command such as Open on the File menu to display a dialog box, navigate to the location of the Web page, select the page, and then click Open. Alternatively, you may be able to click an Open button on a toolbar to display an Open File dialog box.

Once you have opened a page, you can close it using the page's Close button or the Close command on the File menu.

Switch Between Code View and Design View

You can use a Web site design program's document window to construct a Web page much as you would create a document in a word processor. This default view is sometimes called the "What You See Is What You Get" or *WYSIWYG* view. Your program may call this the design or normal view. All programs also allow you to display the HTML code for the page you are creating. You can use this HTML or *code* view to check or correct page content, or you can choose to do all your work in this view if you are very familiar with HTML tags. Some programs allow you to display both design and code view in a single window, as shown in Figure 4-2, so you can see the code as you enter the text.

FIGURE 4-2
Some programs allow you to display both code and design views

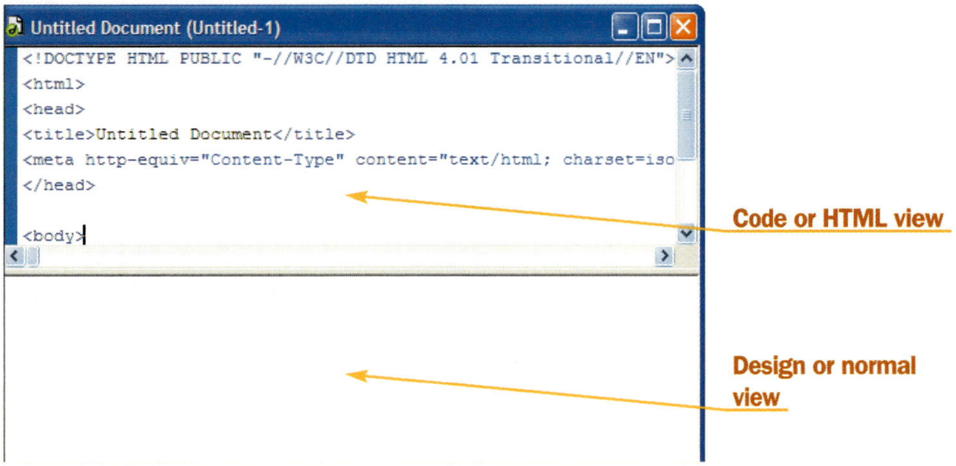

Code or HTML view

Design or normal view

To switch between design and code view, look for buttons such as Show Code View and Show Design View on a toolbar. In some programs, you can click HTML and Normal tabs at the bottom of the document window to switch between views.

S TEP-BY-STEP 4.2

1. In your Web site design program, click **File** on the menu bar, and then click **Open**. A dialog box opens to allow you to locate the file you want to open.

2. Navigate to your html folder, open the folder, and select the **gif.html** file. Click the **Open** button. Your page opens in the view that was used most recently and may look similar to Figure 4-3.

FIGURE 4-3
Web page in design or normal view

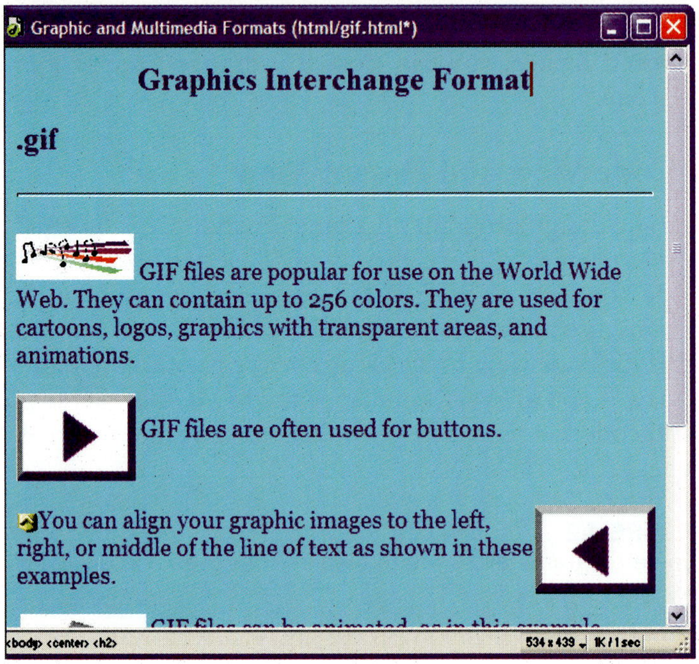

STEP-BY-STEP 4.2 Continued

3. If your page is not already displayed in code view, locate the button or tab that displays the page's HTML code. For example, click the **Show Code View** button on the Document toolbar or the **HTML** tab at the bottom of the document window. Your program displays the HTML code for the current page, as shown in Figure 4-4.

FIGURE 4-4
HTML tags in a Web site design program

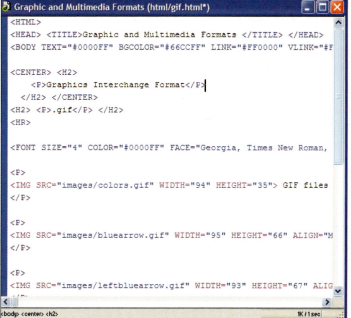

```
Graphic and Multimedia Formats (html/gif.html*)

<HTML>
<HEAD> <TITLE>Graphic and Multimedia Formats </TITLE> </HEAD>
<BODY TEXT="#0000FF" BGCOLOR="#66CCFF" LINK="#FF0000" VLINK="#F

<CENTER> <H2>
     <P>Graphics Interchange Format</P>
  </H2> </CENTER>
<H2> <P>.gif</P> </H2>
<HR>

<FONT SIZE="4" COLOR="#0000FF" FACE="Georgia, Times New Roman,

<P>
<IMG SRC="images/colors.gif" WIDTH="94" HEIGHT="35"> GIF files
</P>

<P>
<IMG SRC="images/bluearrow.gif" WIDTH="95" HEIGHT="66" ALIGN="M
</P>

<P>
<IMG SRC="images/leftbluearrow.gif" WIDTH="93" HEIGHT="67" ALIG

<body> <center> <h2>                                    1K / 1 sec
```

4. If your program allows you to display both design and code views at the same time, click the button to display this view. For example, click the **Show Code and Design Views** button on the Document toolbar.

5. Click the button or tab that restores design or normal view.

6. Close the **gif.html** page by clicking its Close button. Leave your Web site design program open to use in the next exercise.

Define a Web Site

Web site design programs take a lot of the effort out of managing a Web site. These programs keep track of all the various hypertext links from page to page, search for broken links, and allow you to visualize your site, whether it is a hierarchical, linear, or random access site.

The process of creating a new Web site differs by program. In some programs, you *define* a new Web site by establishing a *root level* folder in which to store your Web pages, subfolders, and images. You can use a new folder or an existing folder, such as the html folder you created in previous lessons. Give the site a name and indicate the path to the root level folder, and your site is defined. In other programs, you select a Web site type from a task pane or dialog box, enter a name for the Web folder that will hold all site files, and specify where to store the folder.

When you create a new Web site, your first task is usually to create a welcome page or home page that will be the first page displayed when a visitor accesses the site. Some programs automatically create a home page in a new Web site, while in other programs, you must create a new Web page and designate it as the home page. Many programs recognize a page with a name such as index.html as a home page.

You do not necessarily have to create all Web sites from scratch. If you have created pages in another program such as a text editor, you can use your Web site design program to open the entire site and work with it. To do so, you must define the folder that stores the pages as the root level folder or open the folder as a Web.

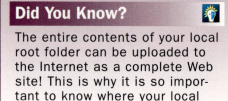

Did You Know?

The entire contents of your local root folder can be uploaded to the Internet as a complete Web site! This is why it is so important to know where your local root folder is located.

In the next exercise, you define a new Web site in your program using the html folder and files you created in earlier lessons. After you define the Web site, you can work with all pages of your site from within your Web site design program.

STEP-BY-STEP 4.3

1. In your Web site design program, issue the command to create a new Web site. For example, click **Site** on the menu bar, and then click **New Site**. Alternatively, click **File** on the menu bar, click **Open Web**, and then go to step 5.

STEP-BY-STEP 4.3 Continued

2. If your program displays a Site Definition dialog box, click the **Advanced** tab if necessary. In the Site Name box, enter **My Graphics Site** as the site name, as shown in Figure 4-5.

FIGURE 4-5
Give your site a name

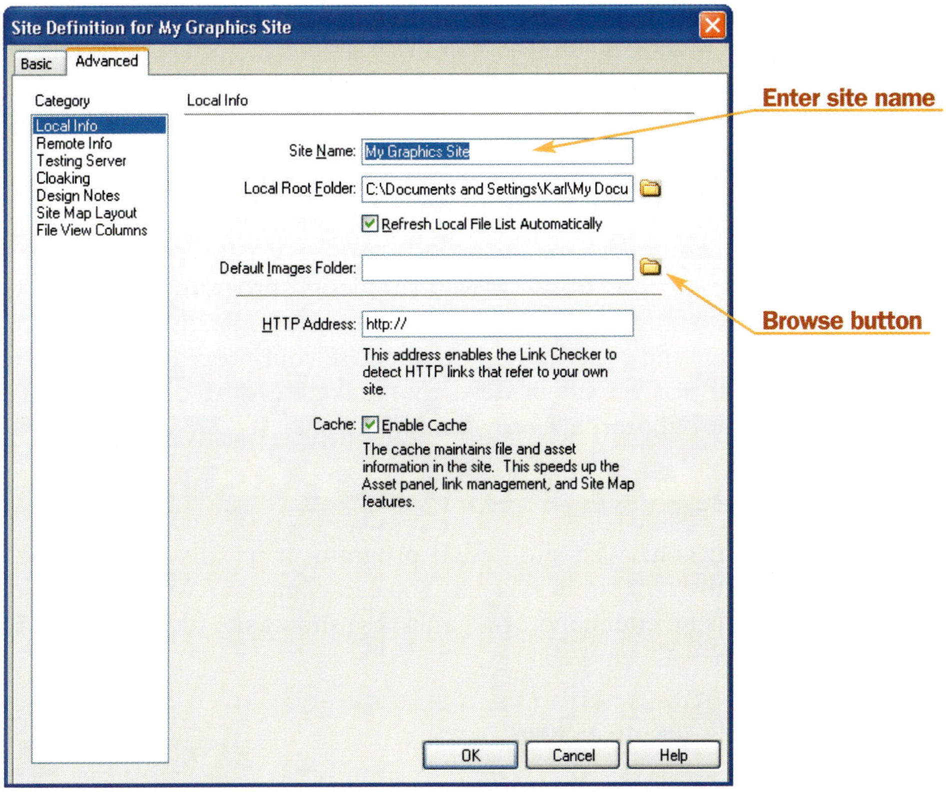

3. Click the **Browse** button to the right of the Local Root Folder box. The Choose Local Root Folder dialog box for the site opens. Navigate to your **html** folder and open it by double-clicking it. (The dialog box may automatically open to the html folder because you opened a page from the folder in a previous exercise.) You are now at the root level, and your dialog box should resemble Figure 4-6.

FIGURE 4-6
Root level of your Web site

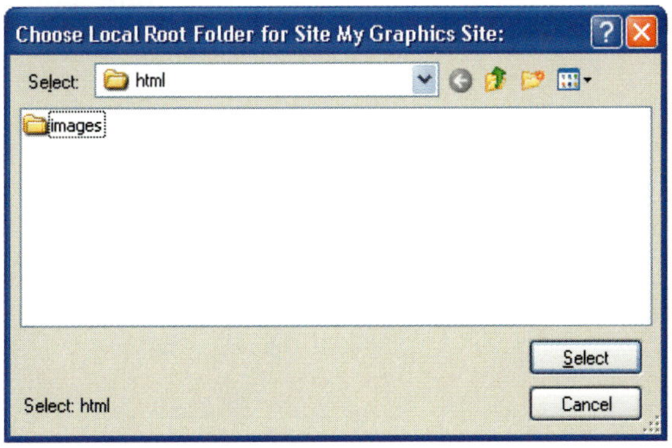

STEP-BY-STEP 4.3 Continued

4. Click the **Select** button. Click the **OK** button to close the Site Definition dialog box.

5. If your program displays a dialog box such as Open Web, use it to navigate to your **html** folder. Double-click the folder to open it, and then click the **Open** button. You may then see a message asking if your program can add content to the folder to manage it as a Web site. Click the **Yes** button.

6. Your graphics Web site is now open in your Web site design program. Close your Web site design program by clicking **File** on the menu bar, and then clicking **Exit**.

View a Web Site

One of the key reasons to use a Web site design program is the ease with which you can view and manage an entire Web site. As a Web site gets larger, it becomes increasingly difficult to account for each page and hyperlink on the site. Use your program's features to select the site you want to work on, display the site in views that make it easy to detect linking errors, and preview pages to see how they appear in a browser.

Open a Web Site

When you open your Web site design program, it usually displays the Web site that was active the last time the program was open. You can open your Web site if it doesn't automatically appear by using a menu command or a panel that shows site files. You may also be able to use a toolbar button such as Open Web.

View Related Pages in a Site

Most Web site design programs display a panel or list that shows the pages and folders in the current Web site. You can use this files list to perform a number of tasks: open pages in the site, rename pages, copy or delete pages, specify a page as the home page, and so on.

Hot Tip

Panels and lists can take up a lot of room on your screen. You can close panels or lists to make more room to work on your Web pages by deselecting them on a menu such as View or Window. You may also be able to hide panels using a show/hide button located at one side of a panel.

Most programs also allow you to see how the pages of a site relate to each other in various ways. For example, you can display a map view or hyperlink view that shows the home page in the site and all pages linked to it, as shown in Figure 4-7. This allows you to check that all pages in the site are linked properly. You can change the view of the site using menu commands, by clicking icons in a views bar, or by selecting a view from a drop-down list on a panel.

FIGURE 4-7
Site map in a Web site design program

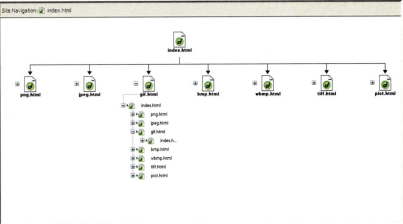

Notice in Figure 4-7 that some pages have small plus signs (+) next to the page icon in the map. The plus signs indicate that the page has other links on it. Click a plus sign to expand the map and see other links from that page. After you click a plus sign, it becomes a minus sign (–). Click the minus sign to collapse the map of interconnecting links.

Preview a Web Page in a Browser

Web site design programs allow you to easily preview your Web pages to see how they look in a browser. Click a button such as Preview in Browser on a toolbar and, if necessary, select the browser you want to use. Your browser opens to display the current page. You may also have a preview tab in the document window that allows you to see how a page looks in the browser without actually displaying it in the browser.

S TEP-BY-STEP 4.4

1. Launch your Web site design program. If your graphics Web site does not open automatically, open the Web site. For example, click **Site** on the menu bar, click **Edit Sites**, and select your site in the dialog box that opens. Alternatively, click **File** on the menu bar, click **Open Web**, and navigate to the location of the Web folder. Click the button that opens the site.

2. Make sure the panel or list that shows your site's files appears on the screen. If necessary, select the command to display the panel or list. You can find this command on the Window or View menu.

3. Change the view of your site's files to show how pages are linked. For example, click **Site** on the menu bar, and then click **Site Map**. Alternatively, click **View** on the menu bar, and then click **Hyperlinks**. The document window or the site panel changes to show links from the index.html page to other pages in the site, as shown in Figure 4-8. (Your view may differ significantly if you are using a program other than

STEP-BY-STEP 4.4 Continued

Dreamweaver.) Pages may be identified by their file-names or by their page titles. If your pages are identified by page title, all titles are the same. Right-click on a blank part of the display and deselect **Show Page Titles** from the shortcut menu to show filenames of the pages.

FIGURE 4-8
View the linked files in the site

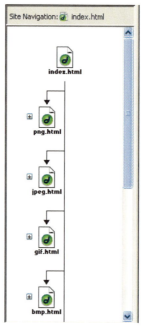

4. Click the plus sign (+) near any page in the map to expand the display and see links from that page to the home page. Click the minus sign (–) to collapse the display again.

5. Restore the local or page view: click **Local View** as shown in Figure 4-9, or click **View** on the menu bar and then click **Page**. The list of folders and files reappears.

FIGURE 4-9
Display the local view

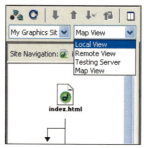

STEP-BY-STEP 4.4 Continued

6. In the file list, click the plus sign (+) to the left of the images folder. The images folder opens to display all the files stored in that folder. Click the minus sign (–) to collapse the folder again.

7. Double-click the **index.html** file in the file list to display the page in the document window.

8. Locate the toolbar button that allows you to preview your Web page in the browser and click the button. You may need to specify which browser to use for the preview.

9. Close the browser. Close the **index.html** page in the document window. Leave your Web site design program open to use in the next exercise.

Add Content to the Web Site

The real value of using a Web site design program becomes obvious when you start to add content to a site. You do not have to enter the codes required to display text or insert objects such as graphics or horizontal lines. Instead, you can simply enter your text in a document window and then use toolbar buttons, menu commands, or a properties panel to format the text and insert other objects. As mentioned earlier, most programs give you the choice of working in design view, which shows you approximately how the page appears in the browser, or in code view if you want to apply HTML codes yourself.

In this and future sections of this lesson, you create pages that give information on your site's policy for use. Almost every corporate, education, and government Web site has rules to protect the site and its visitors. These rules are often called *Terms of Use* or *Acceptable Use Policies (AUPs)*. AUPs outline the do's and don'ts of Web sites and the networks that support them. In fact, the Internet is just a network made up of thousands of smaller networks that all need to be protected from unauthorized use, hackers, viruses, and abuse.

Computer Ethics

Before you can use any network that connects to the Internet or develop Web sites professionally, you are required to adhere to the acceptable use policies of the sponsoring organization. As a Web site designer, you must be aware of AUPs because you may be asked to post your organization's Web site policies for all to read.

Acceptable use or terms of use policies outline the rights and responsibilities of users on networks and Web sites. There are three types of Web sites: public, subscription, and private. Public Web sites are familiar to everyone. Anyone who can enter the necessary URLs can go to these sites and search for information.

However, other Web sites are private. These are often called *intranets*, and they are reserved for specific groups of people. For example, a corporate intranet is available only to the employees of the company. Unauthorized visitors and competitors are prohibited from accessing private Web sites by passwords and login names. Intranets usually offer members of their groups e-mail services along with Web searching services.

Subscription Web sites are available only to those who pay a fee. For example, much of the information on America Online is available only to members who pay a monthly fee. Such sites often offer e-mail along with instant messaging and other services to their members.

Add a New Page to the Site

To add a new page to a Web site, use a command such as New on the File menu, or click a New toolbar button. You may need to choose the type of document you want to create from a list of page types. In some programs, you can use a box on a toolbar to enter the page title for the new page. In other programs, you change the page title when you save the page.

A new page does not become part of the Web site until you save it. Use a familiar command such as Save or Save As on the File menu to open a Save As dialog box where you can specify a name for the page and make sure it is saved in the current Web site.

S TEP-BY-STEP 4.5

1. In your graphics Web site, use the command to insert a new page. For example, click **File** on the menu bar, and then click **New**. If a dialog box or task pane opens, choose to create a basic HTML page or a blank page. A new untitled document opens in the document window.

2. Click the button or tab that displays the page in HTML code view. Look at the tags in the document window, similar to the ones shown in Figure 4-10. Do they look familiar? They include the basic structural tags you entered in Lesson 1.

FIGURE 4-10
New page in code view

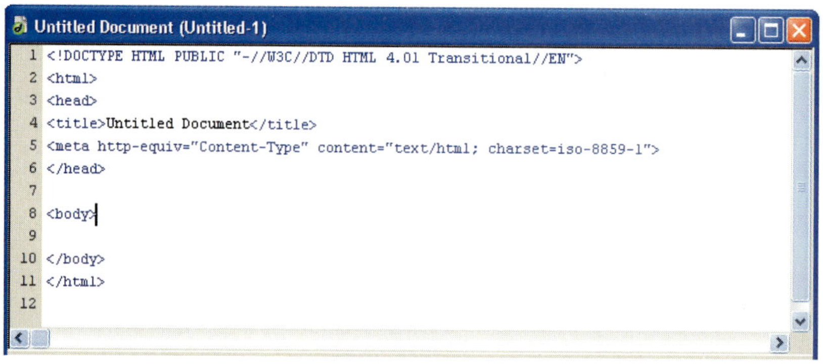

```
 Untitled Document (Untitled-1)
 1  <!DOCTYPE HTML PUBLIC "-//W3C//DTD HTML 4.01 Transitional//EN">
 2  <html>
 3  <head>
 4  <title>Untitled Document</title>
 5  <meta http-equiv="Content-Type" content="text/html; charset=iso-8859-1">
 6  </head>
 7
 8  <body>
 9
10  </body>
11  </html>
12
```

STEP-BY-STEP 4.5 Continued

3. Return to design or normal view. Click **File** on the menu bar, and then click **Save As**. Enter the file-name **aup1.html** as shown in Figure 4-11. If your program allows you to change the page title in the Save As dialog box, click the button to do so, enter **Acceptable Use** as the page title, and click the **OK** button. Click the **Save** button.

FIGURE 4-11
Save your file as aup1.html

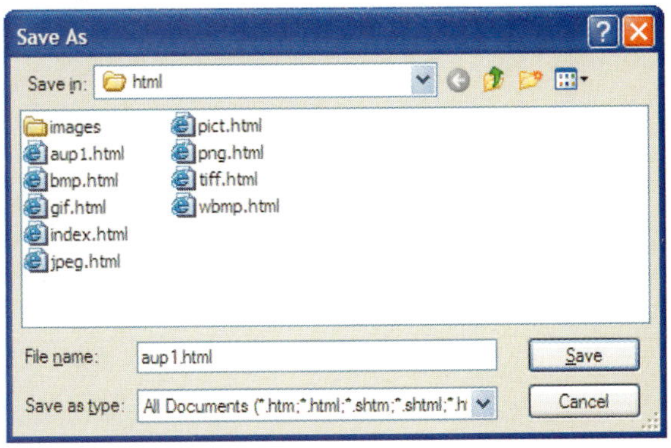

4. If you did not already change the page title, locate the title entry box above the document window (it may contain the text *Untitled Document*), enter **Acceptable Use**, and press **Enter**.

5. An insertion point should be blinking in the document window. Enter the text shown below, pressing **Enter** after each line.

Acceptable Use Policy

Page 1 of 4

6. If the insertion point is not below the text you just keyed, press **Enter**. Insert a horizontal rule: Click **Insert** on the menu bar, and then click **Horizontal Rule** or **Horizontal Line**. Click just to the right of the rule to deselect it, if necessary, and then press **Enter** to move the insertion point below the rule.

7. Enter the following text below the rule.

Access to this Web site is for official purposes only. You are specifically prohibited from using your access to this network for personal, non-official use. Users are also prohibited from using the network to publish or distribute libelous, slanderous, obscene, or inappropriate literature, graphics, or other offensive materials.

> **Extra for Experts**
>
> Most Web site design programs have spelling checkers. Look for a button on a toolbar or a command such as Spelling or Check Spelling on a Tools or Text menu.

STEP-BY-STEP 4.5 Continued

8. Press **Enter** after finishing the paragraph. Insert another horizontal rule. Deselect the rule if necessary and press **Enter**. Your page should look similar to Figure 4-12.

FIGURE 4-12
Enter the text and horizontal rule tags

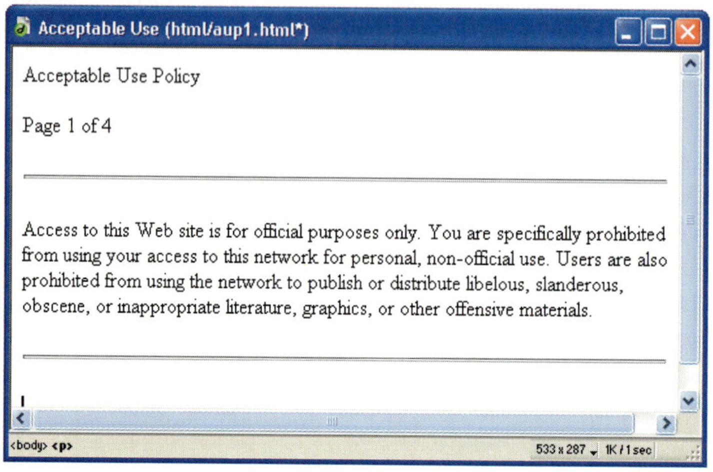

```
Acceptable Use (html/aup1.html*)                          [_][□][×]

Acceptable Use Policy

Page 1 of 4

_____

Access to this Web site is for official purposes only. You are specifically prohibited
from using your access to this network for personal, non-official use. Users are also
prohibited from using the network to publish or distribute libelous, slanderous,
obscene, or inappropriate literature, graphics, or other offensive materials.

_____

I
<
<body> <p>                                    533 x 287 ▾  1K / 1 sec
```

9. Display your page in code view. Does the code look familiar? When you have finished examining the code, switch back to design or normal view.

10. Save changes to the **aup1.html** page and leave it open to use in the next exercise.

Format Pages in a Web Site Design Program

When you created pages in a text editor, you entered HTML codes to format text. In a Web site design program, you can use buttons, menu commands, or tools on a panel to format text and other page elements.

The color of the text, the font, the text style, and the background colors are all considered to be *properties* of a Web page. Some programs group tools for changing such formats on a panel or in a dialog box. Your program, for example, may have a panel called the Property inspector that gives you access to many formatting options. In other programs, you can use Formatting toolbar buttons that may be familiar to you from word processing and other programs. If the panel or toolbars you need are not displayed on your screen, you can use commands on the View or Window menu to display them.

STEP-BY-STEP 4.6

1. In the **aup1.html** file, make sure your program displays the panel or toolbars necessary for you to format text. For example, click **Window** on the menu bar, and make sure **Properties** has a check mark in front of it. Alternatively, click **View** on the menu bar, click **Toolbars**, and make sure **Formatting** has a check mark in front of it.

2. Select all the text in the document window that you entered in the last exercise. (You can also select the horizontal rules.)

STEP-BY-STEP 4.6 Continued

3. Display your program's font list. For example, click the **Font** list arrow on the Property inspector or on the Formatting toolbar. Choose the **Georgia, Times New Roman, Times, serif** font option or simply the **Georgia** font.

4. Click in the heading *Acceptable Use Policy,* and then click the **Center** button on a panel or toolbar.

> **Did You Know?**
>
> As you learned in Lesson 2, it's always best to list several fonts (Georgia, Times New Roman, Times, serif) in case the Web browser viewing your page doesn't have your first or second choice.

5. With the insertion point still in the heading, display your program's styles list. For example, click the **Format** list arrow on the Property inspector or the **Style** list arrow on the Formatting toolbar. Click the **Heading 3** or level <H3> heading.

6. Select all the text on the page again. Display your program's text color palette. For example, click **Text Color** on the Property inspector or the **Font Color** list arrow on the Formatting toolbar. Choose a royal blue color. Deselect the text. Your page should look similar to Figure 4-13.

> **Note**
>
> Some programs allow you to enter a hexadecimal value for a color in a text box beside the text color button.

FIGURE 4-13
Formatted text

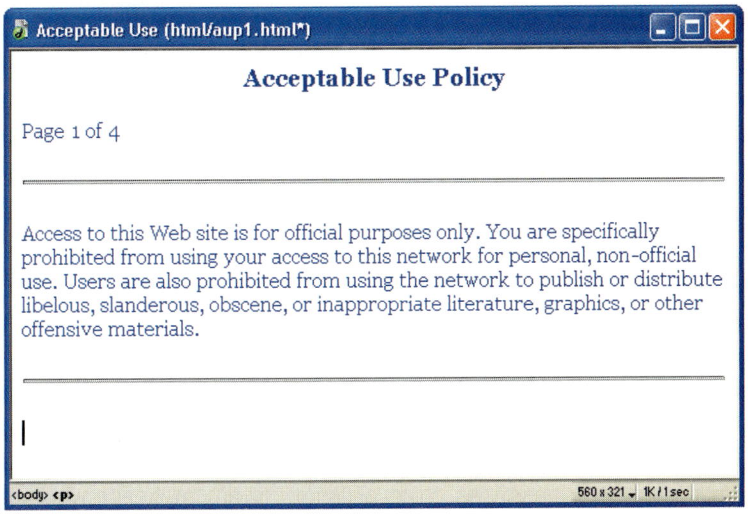

7. Save changes to the **aup1.html** page. Preview the page in the browser. Then close the browser.

8. Leave the **aup1.html** page open to use in the next exercise.

> **Extra for Experts**
>
> Switch to code view and scroll through the attributes and values in the BODY tag portion of your page. Do you see any familiar code that has been added to your Web page as a result of your format changes?

Create New Pages Based on Existing Pages

As when using a text editor, it is easy in a Web site design program to create multiple pages for a Web site based on an already formatted page. Use this process to maintain consistency among pages in a site and to save time.

You have several options for creating new pages from existing pages. You can select a page in the site's files list and use a toolbar button or shortcut menu command to copy it and then paste the copy. Right-click the copied page and click the Rename command to give the copy a new name. You can also use the Save As command on the File menu to save an existing page with a new name.

If you choose to use the Save As command, make sure you have saved all changes to your current page before issuing the command. Look at the page's title bar to see if you have unsaved changes. A page that has been changed since its last save displays an asterisk (*) after the page's name (such as aup1.html*).

In this exercise, you add three new pages to your site. The policies outlined in these three new pages often apply to intranets and subscription Web sites. As you read and work with them, notice that there are specific restrictions regarding password security, the use of e-mail, and the downloading of unlawful or copyrighted information.

S TEP-BY-STEP 4.7

1. With the **aup1.html** page open in your Web site design program, click **File** on the menu bar, and then click **Save As**. Enter the filename **aup2.html**. Do not change the page title. Click the **Save** button.

2. Change the text *Page 1 of 4* to **Page 2 of 4**. Then select the paragraph of text between the two horizontal rules and enter the following paragraph.

   Your username and network account is for your use only. You may not allow others to use your account. Your password is the primary way to protect your work, files, folders, and personal information. Guard it carefully and change it as necessary.

3. Save changes to **aup2.html**. Use the **Save As** command to create a new page and name it **aup3.html**.

4. Change the text *Page 2 of 4* to **Page 3 of 4**. Select the paragraph of text between the horizontal rules and enter the following paragraph.

   When using electronic mail or other Internet communications software, avoid propagating mass mailings, spam (unwanted messages or advertising), or any message with instructions to forward the communication to multiple addresses. You should also avoid any harassing communications and comply with requests to stop sending messages.

STEP-BY-STEP 4.7 Continued

5. Save changes to **aup3.html**. In the files list, right-click on **aup3.html** to display a shortcut menu, and then click **Copy**. Right-click in a blank area of the files list and click **Paste** to paste a copy of the page. Right-click the copy and click **Rename**. The filename is selected, as shown in Figure 4-14, so you can simply enter the new filename, **aup4.html** and press **Enter** to complete the renaming task.

FIGURE 4-14
Enter a new filename for the copied file

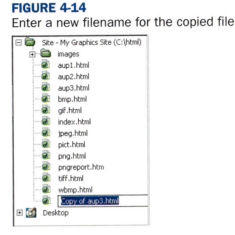

6. Close the **aup3.html** page, and double-click **aup4.html** in the files list to open it if necessary. Change the text *Page 3 of 4* to **Page 4 of 4**. Select the paragraph of text between the rules and enter the following paragraph.

Graphics, programs, databases, audio files, video files, and other works that are protected by copyright should not be acquired or distributed over this Web site without complying with the owner's licensing terms. Copyrighted information belongs to its owners and creators. Only lawful activities are allowed on the network.

7. Save changes and close the **aup4.html** page. Leave your graphics site and your Web site design program open to use in the next exercise.

Create a Navigation Structure in a Web Site Design Program

You will find it much easier to create a navigation structure in a Web site design program than by using a text editor. In a text editor, you must create hyperlinks using anchor tags that require you to enter the address of the page you want to link to. If you do not enter the path accurately, your link does not work correctly. In a Web site design program, you can use a dialog box to browse for the page you want to open. Moreover, most Web site design programs have features that check links to prevent link problems, such as broken links.

Set Up Text or Graphic Links

To create a link in a Web site design program, first select the text or graphic you want to use for the hyperlink. Then click a button such as Browse for File on a panel or Insert Hyperlink on a toolbar to open a dialog box such as the one shown in Figure 4-15.

FIGURE 4-15
Select the page to link to

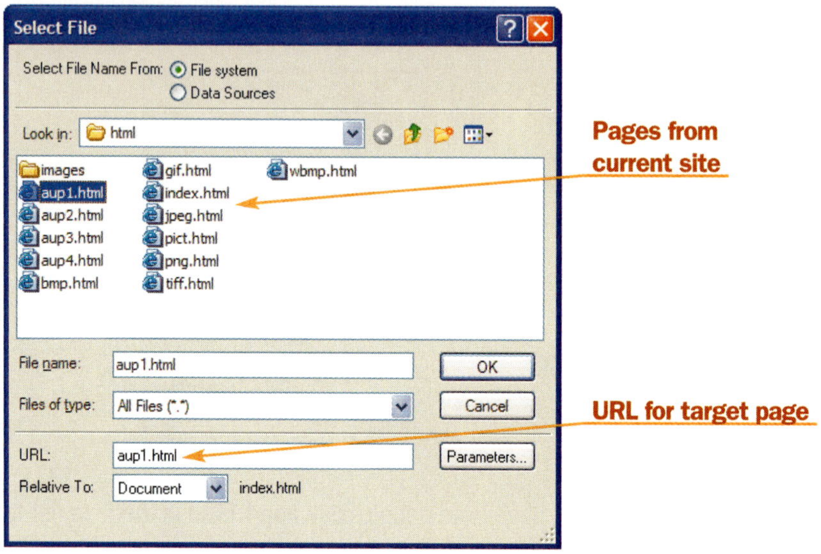

Pages from current site

URL for target page

The dialog box shows the files in the current Web site. Select the page you want to link to and click OK. You can also, if desired, enter the URL of a page outside the current site, such as the address of a page in another site, either on your local system or anywhere on the Internet.

If you select a page in the current site, the link's address consists only of the filename, such as aup1.html. Your program understands that this address indicates the page is in the same folder with the page on which you are inserting the link. This is called a *relative link*.

Extra for Experts

Some programs allow you to enter the full path for the hyperlink in a Link text box, so you do not have to browse for the target page. Your program may also allow you to point to a page in the files list to create the link, rather than use a dialog box.

If you want to link to a page outside the site, you must enter the entire URL, such as *http://www.course.com*, to tell the browser where on the Internet to find the page. This is called an *absolute link*.

STEP-BY-STEP 4.8

1. Open the **index.html** page in your Web site design program by double-clicking it in the files list.

2. Click at the bottom of the page, below the last horizontal rule. Enter the text **Our Use Policy**.

3. Select the text you just entered. Click the button in your program for setting up hyperlinks, such as the **Browse for File** button in the Property inspector or the **Insert Hyperlink** button on the Standard toolbar. A dialog box opens to allow you to choose a page to link to.

STEP-BY-STEP 4.8 Continued

4. In the dialog box, click the **aup1.html** file, and then click the **OK** button. Your page should look like Figure 4-16.

FIGURE 4-16
New link on index.html page

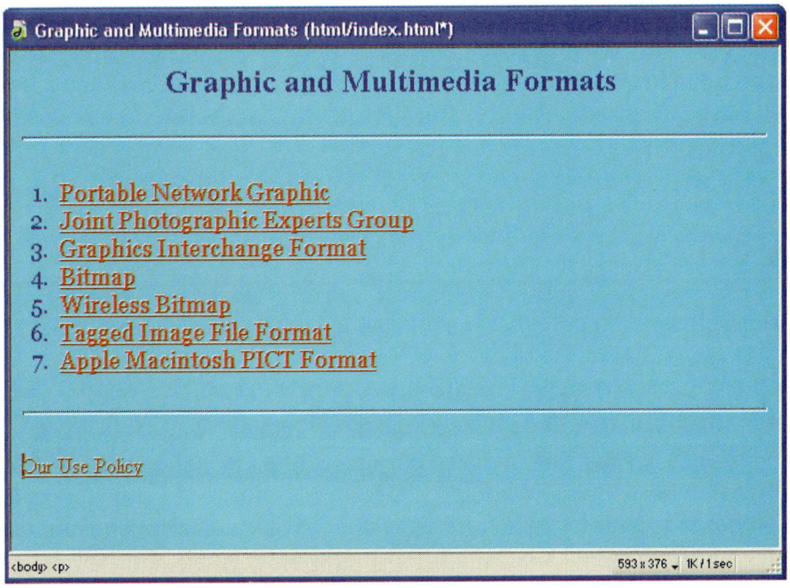

5. Now that you have linked the **aup1.html** page to the **index.html** page, it becomes part of your Web site. Display the site map or hyperlinks view for your site to see the new link between the two pages. If you do not see the **aup1.html** page, click on your program's Refresh button or save the **index.html** page.

6. Restore the regular page view. Preview the **index.html** page in the browser and try the new hyperlink. Notice that you do not have a link on the **aup1.html** page to return to the **index.html** page. You fix that problem later in this lesson.

7. Close your browser. Save changes to **index.html** if necessary and close the file.

8. Leave your graphics site and your Web site design program open to use in the next exercise.

Create a Linear Navigation Structure

It is frustrating for people to visit a Web site that is difficult to navigate; that is, to move from page to page in the site as they see fit. For example, in the previous exercise you created a hyperlink from the index.html page to the acceptable use policy page that is essentially a dead end. On reaching a dead end, a Web site visitor is more likely to move to a new Web site rather than explore the current Web site more thoroughly. You can avoid losing visitors by thinking carefully about your navigation structure and then setting up links that take visitors through the pages in the way you want them to proceed.

For topics such as an acceptable use policy, which consists of a number of pages you want visitors to read one after another, you can set up a linear structure. (Refer to Lesson 2 to review Web structures.) In a linear structure, you should include a link to the next page as well as to the previous page to make it easy for visitors to go back and forth among the pages. The first page in the linear section needs to have only a "next page" link, and the last page in the section needs to have both a "previous page" link and a link to the index page.

In the next exercise, you create links among the four Acceptable Use pages you created earlier in this lesson. You use graphics as the link objects.

You can insert any image on a page using a command such as Image or Picture on the Insert menu. Use the dialog box that opens after this command to locate the picture you want to use and open it. Some programs automatically store a new graphic in your site for you. In other programs, you store the image in the site the next time you save the page. Once a graphic is stored in your site's images folder, you can easily insert it on any page by simply dragging it from the images folder in the files list.

STEP-BY-STEP 4.9

1. Open the **aup1.html** file from the files list of your graphics site.

2. Click below the bottom horizontal rule. Issue the command to insert a graphic on the page. For example, click **Insert** on the menu bar, and then click **Image**. Alternatively, click **Insert** on the menu bar, click **Picture**, and then click **From File**. A dialog box opens to allow you to locate a graphic.

3. In the dialog box, navigate to the data files folder or the location where your downloaded files are stored. Open the folder for this lesson. Click the **rightarrow.gif** file and click the **OK** or **Insert** button.

4. Your program may inform you that the graphic file is outside the current root folder and ask if you want to copy the file to the root folder. If you see this message, click the **Yes** button. In the dialog box that opens, double-click the **images** folder to open it, and then click the **Save** button The graphic displays at the location of the insertion point, as shown in Figure 4-17.

FIGURE 4-17
Graphic added to the aup1.html page

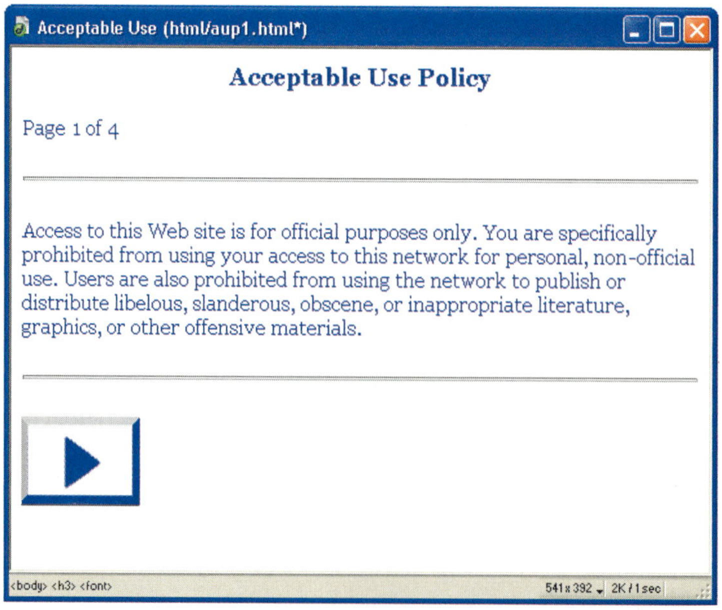

STEP-BY-STEP 4.9 Continued

5. Select the graphic and link it to the **aup2.html** page: Click the button in your program for setting up hyperlinks, such as the **Browse for Files** button or the **Insert Hyperlink** button. In the dialog box that opens, click **aup2.html**, and then click the **OK** button.

6. Save changes. If you have not already saved the graphic in your Web site, your program displays a dialog box such as Save Embedded Files. Click the **Change Folder** button, and then double-click the **images** folder to open it. Click the **OK** button twice. Close the **aup1.html** page.

7. Open the **aup2.html** file. Click at the bottom of the page below the horizontal rule. Issue the command to insert a graphic on the page, and insert the **leftarrow.gif** file as directed in step 3. If prompted, save the graphic in the images folder of your Web site as directed in step 4.

8. Using the same procedure as in step 5, link the **leftarrow.gif** graphic to the previous page in the linear section, **aup1.html**.

9. Click to the right of the **leftarrow.gif** graphic if necessary to display the blinking insertion point. Click the (+) to the left of the images folder in the files list to display all files in the folder. Click the **rightarrow.gif** file and drag the graphic to the right of the **leftarrow.gif** graphic. Your page should look similar to Figure 4-18.

FIGURE 4-18
Second graphic added to aup2.html page

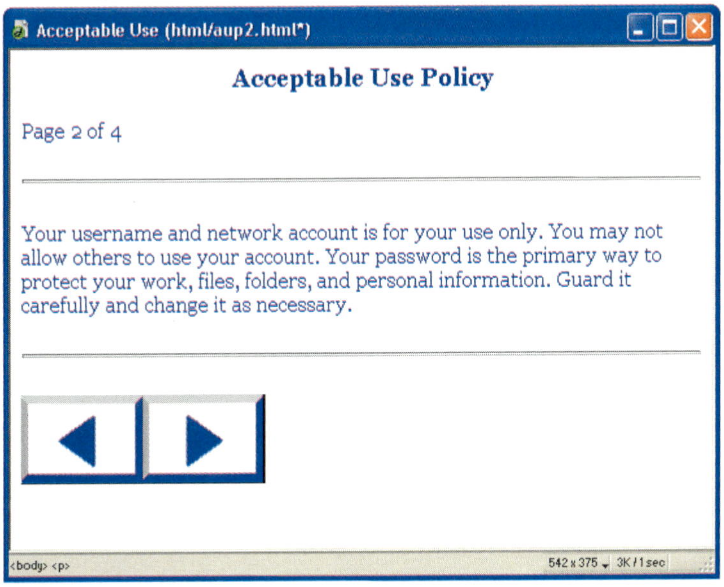

10. Link the **rightarrow.gif** graphic to the next page in the linear section, **aup3.html**. Save changes to **aup2.html**. If prompted, save the graphic to the images folder in your Web site. Close the page.

11. Open the **aup3.html** file. Click at the bottom of the page below the horizontal rule. Drag the **leftarrow.gif** graphic from the files list, and then drag the **rightarrow.gif** graphic next to it. Link the **leftarrow.gif** graphic to the previous page in the series, **aup2.html**. Link the **rightarrow.gif** graphic to the next page in the series, **aup4.html**.

STEP-BY-STEP 4.9 Continued

12. Save changes and close **aup3.html**. Leave your graphics site and your Web site design program open to use in the next exercise.

Complete the Navigation Structure

As mentioned earlier in this section, a good navigation structure controls how visitors to a site proceed through its pages. One of the most important tasks in setting up navigation is to provide links back to the beginning of the site. To complete the linear navigation structure for your site, you must therefore insert a link to allow visitors to return to the index page. This allows them to regain access to other pages in the site and prevents them from reaching a dead end.

STEP-BY-STEP 4.10

1. Open the **aup4.html** file in your graphics site.

2. Click at the bottom of the page below the horizontal rule and drag the **leftarrow.gif** graphic from the images folder onto the page. Link the graphic to the previous page in the series, **aup3.html**.

3. Drag the **menu.gif** graphic from the images folder and drop it to the right of the **leftarrow.gif** graphic, as seen in Figure 4-19.

FIGURE 4-19
Link back to index.html page

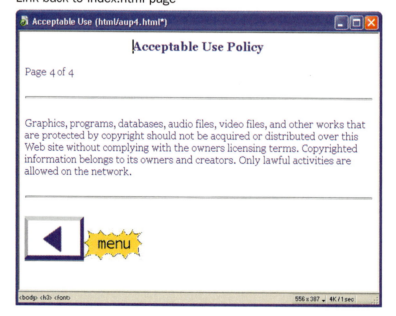

4. Link the **menu.gif** graphic to the **index.html** file.

STEP-BY-STEP 4.10 Continued

5. Save changes and close the **aup4.html** page. View the links you have set up in your program's map or hyperlinks view. Your site map may look similar to Figure 4-20.

FIGURE 4-20
View your linear links and pages

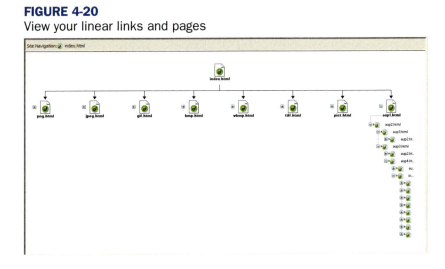

6. Return to your normal page view and open **index.html**. Preview in the browser the pages and links you have created in this lesson.

7. Close your browser. Close any open pages, and close your Web site design program.

Extra for Experts

As you choose the + signs in the map view this time, notice that you have created a linear section on this Web site that finally ends and links back to the index.html page, but only after users have visited every AUP page in a straight line, one after another in a linear fashion.

SUMMARY

In this lesson, you learned:

■ A Web site design program generally has a document window for entering text and panels and toolbars for working with the program's features.

■ You can switch between design view and code view in your Web site design program. Use toolbar buttons or tabs at the bottom of the document window to switch between views.

■ In some programs, you create a new Web site by defining the site at the root level. In any program, give the site a name, specify where to locate it, and then add content to it.

■ Web site design programs allow you to use a map or hyperlinks view to see how pages in the site are linked.

■ Enter text for a new page in the document window. You can enter a page title in the design view or when saving the page to your Web site.

■ Use your Web site design program's toolbars, menu commands, or panels to format page elements.

■ Create a navigation structure for a linear Web site using forward and previous links.

VOCABULARY *Review*

Define the following terms:

Code	Root level	WYSIWYG
Properties		

REVIEW *Questions*

TRUE / FALSE

Circle T if the statement is true or F if the statement is false.

T F **1.** Dreamweaver and FrontPage are two of the most popular software programs that help Web site development professionals create Web sites and Web pages.

T F **2.** Web page development software programs make entering tags even more tedious and time-consuming than using a program such as Notepad.

T F **3.** Web site design programs usually have a document window where you can create Web page content.

T F **4.** WYSIWYG refers to the code view in a Web site design program.

T F **5.** When you create a new Web site, you must usually give the site a name and specify its location.

T F **6.** The entire contents of a local root folder can be uploaded to the Internet as a complete Web site.

T F **7.** A new page does not become part of the Web site until you define it.

T F **8.** Acceptable Use Policies outline the do's and don'ts of a Web site and the networks that support them.

T F **9.** You don't need to worry whether visitors to your site can find their way back to the home page from a linear section.

T F **10.** Properties is another term used to describe WYSIWYG HTML code.

WRITTEN QUESTIONS

Write a brief answer to the following questions.

1. What does it mean to be able to navigate a Web site? Give examples.

2. What is a "dead end" in reference to hyperlinks on a Web site?

3. Why would you create previous and next hyperlinks in a linear section on a Web site?

4. How does a linear Web site differ from a hierarchical Web site?

5. What are AUPs, and why are they important on Web sites and networks?

FILL IN THE BLANK

Complete the following sentences by writing the correct word or words in the blanks provided.

1. In some programs, you must first _____ a new Web site by establishing the folder that holds its files.

2. Many programs recognize a page with a name such as index.html as a(n) _____ page.

3. To expand the view of a page's links, click the _____ sign for the page.

4. If you want to check the HTML tags used on a page, switch to _____ view.

5. A link to a page in the same folder of a Web site is called a(n) _____ link.

6. The color of text, the font, and the background color on a Web page are considered _____ of the page.

7. Web sites that are private in nature, for example, for employees only, are called _____.

8. _____ Web sites require that users pay a fee.

9. Visitors to a Web site wish to move around as they see fit. In other words, they wish to _____ the Web site through the use of hyperlinks.

10. The folder where all of your Web pages, subfolders, and images are stored is called the _____ level.

PROJECTS

PROJECT 4-1

In the project section of the previous lessons, you created a Web site project of your own design. Locate the root level of that project and import that Web site into your Web site design program. Do what is necessary to work with your Web site in your Web site design program. If you need assistance, review Step-by-Step 4.3.

PROJECT 4-2

Now that you have defined the root level of your Web site and imported your personal Web site project into your Web site design program, view various pages on the site in both HTML and WYSIWYG views. Also, use your Web site map view feature to view all the hyperlinks on your Web site. If you need assistance viewing your own Web site project, review Step-by-Step 4.4.

PROJECT 4-3

Your Web site needs an Acceptable Use Policy. Create two or more pages to hold the information you decide to use. You can borrow ideas, even pages, from the acceptable use section you created in this lesson.

WEB PROJECT

Create a product comparison table comparing the features of FrontPage and Dreamweaver. Visit the Web sites of the manufacturers of these products to prepare this table. Create your table in a word processing document, and start by listing 10 criteria you think are important features that should be offered by these programs. For example, you may believe that a program should offer both an HTML view that shows the code of a Web page and a WYSIWYG view that shows how the page might look in a browser. You may also list items such as "an easy way to create hyperlinks" or "an easy way to import graphics." Place your 10 important features in column A. Then, in columns B and C, indicate whether each feature is offered by the two Web development software programs. For example:

	Dreamweaver	FrontPage
1. HTML View	Yes or No	Yes or No
2. WYSIWYG View	Yes or No	Yes or No

3. Easy Way to Create Hyperlinks   Yes or No   Yes or No

4. Easy Way to Import Graphics   Yes or No   Yes or No

Brainstorm six more key features and add them below.

TEAMWORK PROJECT

As a team, search the Web and find one Acceptable Use Policy statement each from a corporate, government, and education Web site. These pages are often called "Terms of Use" agreements. Review these policies. As a team, analyze important statements from these terms of use or acceptable use pages that perhaps should be included in your acceptable use statements. Add at least one statement to your personal Web site project. Create a new page to contain this new statement.

CRITICAL *Thinking*

ACTIVITY 4-1

Ask yourself this question, "Why are Acceptable Use Policies or Terms of Use Agreements necessary on Web sites?" Prepare an essay of no fewer than 500 words explaining your thoughts on this question. Take a point–counterpoint position. In other words, look at both sides of the issue. In part of your essay, explain why Terms of Use or Acceptable Use Policies are essential, and in another part of your report, consider their usefulness and necessity in the online world.

POLISHING AND PUBLISHING YOUR WEB SITE

In previous lessons, you learned the nuts and bolts of Web site development: tags, links, fonts, graphics, files, folders, subfolders, roots, attributes, values, and software tools. As you progress in Web site design, you will become more familiar with other important concepts. In the book *Web Design BASICS*, authors Todd Stubbs and Karl Barksdale identify three essential elements: presentation design, interaction design, and information design.

Presentation design considers the look and feel of a site as discussed earlier in this unit. Presentation incorporates design elements such as background graphics, color schemes, and formatting features. The concept also includes testing, polishing, editing, and publishing a Web site. In this lesson, you perform a number of these tasks, including changing your Web site's presentation design, ensuring consistent design throughout the site, testing links on your site, and publishing it.

One aspect of *interaction design* considers how people move around or navigate a site. This is largely determined by the structure of the Web site. You are already familiar with the basic structures: hierarchical, linear, and random access. In previous lessons, you created a hierarchical Web site and added a linear section to it. In this lesson, you add a random access navigation system to improve the interaction possibilities of your site. Another important aspect of interaction design includes the testing of hyperlinks to make sure they *all* work properly, which you also do in this lesson.

Communication Skills

When you search the Internet for information to be included in something you produce, you must provide references to the sources you use in your resulting document, presentation, etc. Citing sources is easy, as explained in the following instructions adapted from the *Corporate View* series, which can be found online using the information from this citation:
Barksdale, Karl. "Corporate View: Corporate Communications Style Guide." *Corporate View*.
27 May 1998 <http://www.corpview.com/intranet/Mission-CriticalFunctions/
CorpCommunications/sgcite.htm>.

When you use others' material in your documents, you must give them credit for their work. It is unprofessional, usually illegal, and a serious breach of etiquette to use work that is not your own without providing citations. Different professions prefer somewhat different styles for documenting sources. However, some common denominators apply.

To cite an Internet resource, follow the same pattern you use to cite a print source. The eight key elements for citing resources are usually presented in this order:

1. Author's name.
2. Title of work.
3. Book title, publication, magazine, or title of Web page (as it appears in the title bar of your browser), underlined or italicized.
4. The page number (section number or identifying feature), if accessible.
5. The date the material was originally published.
6. The electronic address or URL in angle brackets: e.g., <http://www.mla.org>.
7. Begin the first line at the left margin and indent all the following lines in the citation.
8. Use periods, not commas, to separate parts of the citation.

Most documentation falls under these categories. You won't always be able to find *all* the information suggested, however. List as much as you can. Some examples follow.

Professional Web Page
The Nebraska Writer's Project. Ed. Ben Rand. Nebraska State University. 27 May 1998
<http://www.nstate.edu/writer/>.

Corporate Web Page
Barksdale, Karl. "Corporate View: Corporate Communications Style Guide." *Corporate View*.
27 May 1998 <http://www.corpview.com/intranet/Mission-CriticalFunctions/
CorpCommunications/sgcite.htm>.

Personal Web Page
Welsh, Shari. Web page. 1 July 1999 <http://www.handwritingsolutions.com>.

Online Magazine Article or Webzine
Rutter, Michael. *"Catching Lake Trout."* Outdoor Life. 1 May 1999
<http:// www.outdoorlife.com>.

Article in an Online Database
"Impressionism." *Britannica Online*. Vers. 99.1.1 May. Encyclopaedia Britannica. 29 May 1999
<http://www.eb.com:188>.

E-mail
Barksdale, Karl. *Amazon River Pollution Tests*. 22 May 1999
kbarksdale@handwritingsolutions.com.

An aspect of *information design* considers the information to include on your site and who can help you develop it. HTML deals only with the presentation of the information; no amount of HTML manipulation can make bad content into good content. In this lesson, you learn how content can be developed for your Web site using common word processing, spreadsheet, and presentation programs.

Change Page Background Properties

Professional Web site designers seldom use the background color attribute BGCOLOR to define the background of their Web site pages. Changing background colors is easy, but color doesn't provide any texture or richness to the presentation design. Instead, designers use graphics, sometimes only a few pixels in size, to create a background that guarantees a consistent look and feel when viewed in different browsers. Changing the background is an important aspect of *presentation design*.

The BACKGROUND attribute is used to apply a graphic background. It fits into the <BODY> tag as follows.

```
<BODY BACKGROUND="images/filename.gif">
```

In a Web site design program, of course, you do not need to insert the HTML code. You can use your program to locate and insert the graphic you want, and the program handles the coding for you. You specify the name of the graphic and its location in a dialog box such as Page Properties. In this dialog box, you may also be able to change other page properties such as page background color and colors for text and hyperlinks.

Extra for Experts

Background graphics are usually very small. GIF files are very popular for backgrounds because of their compact size. They can be created in a program such as Photoshop.

STEP-BY-STEP 5.1

1. Launch your Web site design program. If your graphics Web site does not open automatically, open the Web site. For example, click **Site** on the menu bar, click **Edit Sites**, and select your site in the dialog box that opens. Alternatively, click **File** on the menu bar, click **Open Web**, and navigate to the location of the Web folder. Click the button that opens the site.

2. Close the untitled page if your site displays one. Open the **index.html** page.

STEP-BY-STEP 5.1 Continued

3. Open the Page Properties dialog box in your program. For example, click **Modify** on the menu bar, and then click **Page Properties**. Alternatively, click **Format** on the menu bar, and then click **Background**. A Page Properties dialog box opens, similar to the one shown in Figure 5-1.

FIGURE 5-1
Page Properties dialog box

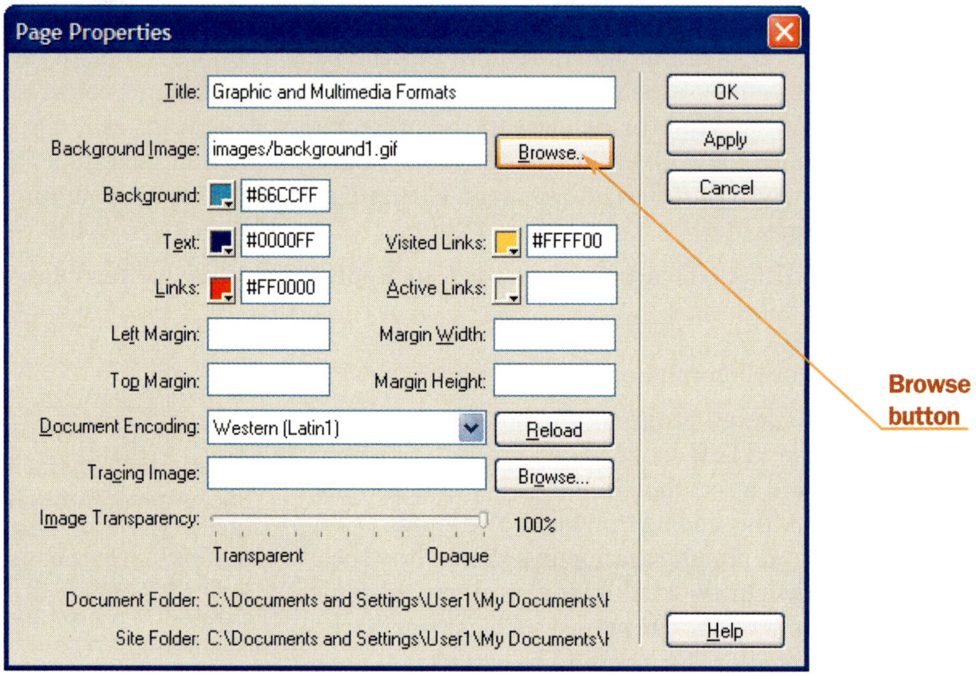

4. If necessary, click the check box to insert a background picture. Then click the **Browse** button to the right of the background image text box. A dialog box opens to allow you to locate the background image file.

5. Navigate to the data files folder or the location where your downloaded files are stored. Open the folder for this lesson. Click the **background1.gif** file, and then click the **OK** or **Open** button. If your program asks you to store the image in the current site, store it in the images folder as you learned in Lesson 4.

Hot Tip

If you know the path to the graphic you want to use, you can simply enter it in the text box to save time.

Extra for Experts

The graphic background1.gif creates a checkerboard effect. It was created in a graphics program using the gradient feature.

STEP-BY-STEP 5.1 Continued

6. In the Page Properties dialog box, the graphic name now appears in the background image text box. If you have an Apply button in this dialog box, you can click the button to see how the background looks on the page before you close the dialog box. Click the **OK** button to close the dialog box and apply the background. Your page should look similar to Figure 5-2.

FIGURE 5-2
New background on index.html page

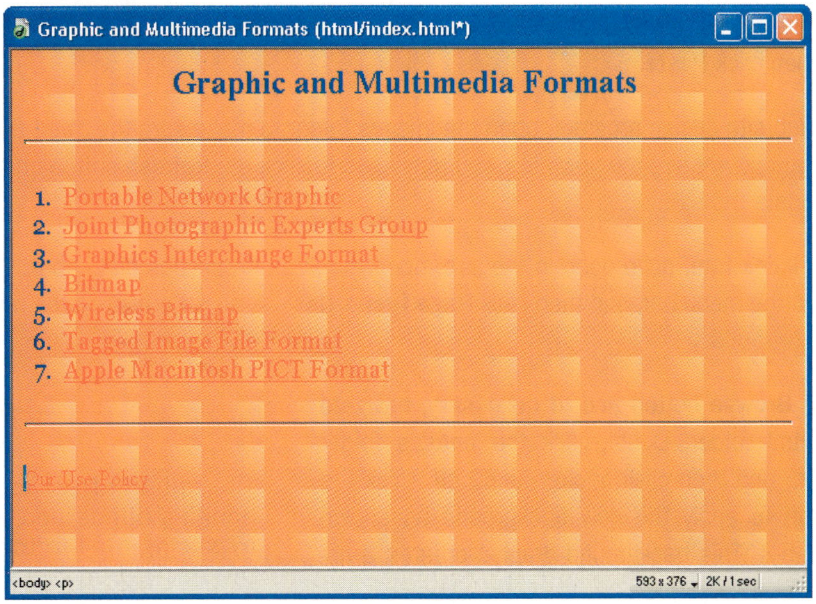

7. Save changes. If you are prompted to store the background file in the site, save it in the images folder as you learned in Lesson 4. Leave the **index.html** file open to use in the next exercise.

Experiment with Background Texture Properties

The background1.gif graphic used in the previous exercise created a checkerboard effect. However, the colors are somewhat overbearing and the background takes away from the presentation of the written text and makes it difficult to read. Web site designers must often do some experimenting to find a background that adds texture to a site's pages without overwhelming the text on the pages. This kind of experimentation is another part of *presentation design*. To change a background graphic, simply specify a new graphic file in the Page Properties dialog box.

> **Extra for Experts**
>
> The four background images used in this lesson were all created from the same original graphic. Each image was sliced from different portions of the original image to create the various textures seen in this lesson.

STEP-BY-STEP 5.2

1. To save time when experimenting with background graphics in this exercise, copy the graphics files you need to your images folder:

a. Using a file management program such as Windows Explorer or My Computer, navigate to the data files folder or the location where your downloaded files are stored. Open the folder for this lesson.

b. Select **background2.gif**, **background3.gif**, and **background4.gif** in the folder. Click **Edit** on the menu bar, and then click **Copy**.

c. Navigate to your html folder and open it. Open the images subfolder. Click **Edit** on the menu bar, and then click **Paste**.

2. In your Web site design program, open the images folder to make sure the three files you copied are there. If you do not see the new files, you may need to click the **Refresh** button on the Standard toolbar to update the site.

3. With the **index.html** page open in the site, open the Page Properties dialog box. For example, click **Modify** on the menu bar, and then click **Page Properties**. Or, click **Format** on the menu bar, and then click **Background**.

4. Click the **Browse** button and, if necessary, navigate to the html folder. Double-click the **images** folder to open it, and then click **background2.gif**. Click the **OK** button to apply the new background as shown in Figure 5-3. This background graphic creates a ribbon effect.

> ### Extra for Experts
>
> The ribbon effect looks like long hanging blinds and was created by slicing off the top portion of the background1.gif file.

FIGURE 5-3
New background in place on the page

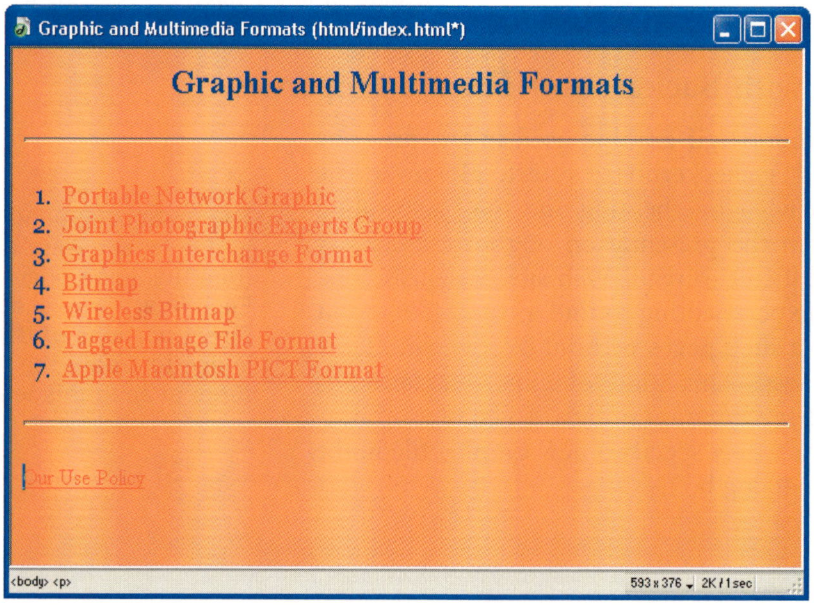

Graphic and Multimedia Formats (html/index.html*)

Graphic and Multimedia Formats

1. Portable Network Graphic
2. Joint Photographic Experts Group
3. Graphics Interchange Format
4. Bitmap
5. Wireless Bitmap
6. Tagged Image File Format
7. Apple Macintosh PICT Format

Our Use Policy

<body> <p>   593 x 376   2K / 1 sec

STEP-BY-STEP 5.2 Continued

5. Follow steps 3 and 4 to change the background using the **background3.gif** graphic. The result should look similar to Figure 5-4. This graphic creates a ribbed effect. Note that you can read the text much more easily with this background in place.

FIGURE 5-4
Background3.gif in place on the page

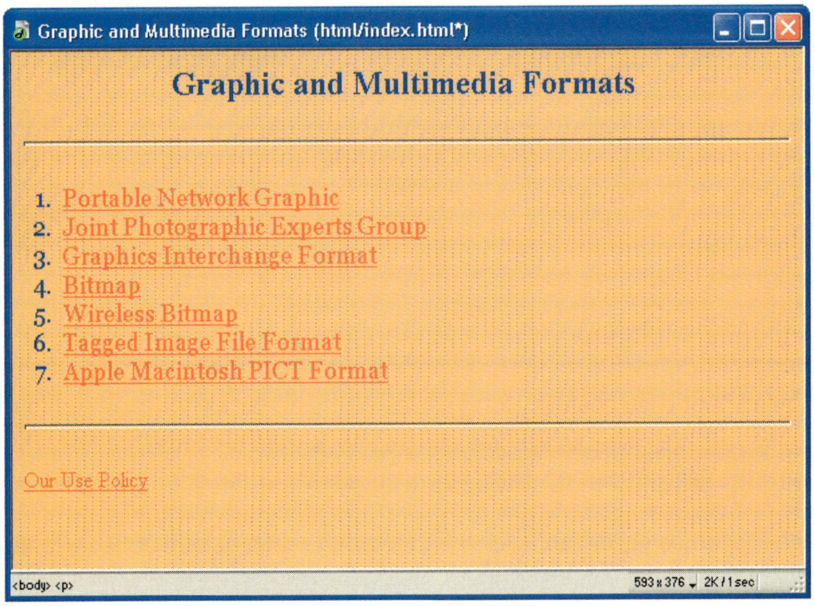

6. Follow steps 3 and 4 one more time to change the background using the **background4.gif** graphic. This graphic creates a glossy effect, as shown in Figure 5-5.

FIGURE 5-5
Background4.gif creates a glossy effect

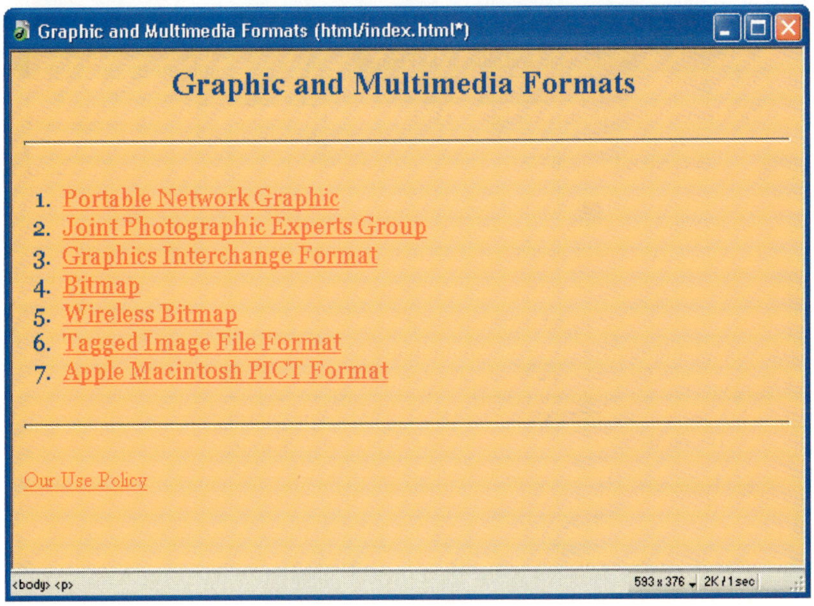

7. Save changes and leave the **index.html** page open to use in the next exercise.

Modify Page Properties Throughout a Site

Color and graphics are always important aspects of any Web site's *presentation design*. After you select a background graphic, you may need to modify your color scheme to complement your new background. Once you have settled on your background graphics and colors, you need to apply the scheme to all pages on your site. Does this sound like a lot of work? It can be. Some Web site design programs, however, make short work of such changes by allowing you to apply page properties from one page to another. If your program doesn't have such a feature, you will still find it much easier to use dialog boxes to apply formats to all pages in a site than to enter code on each page to do so.

Even if you have applied a graphic background to a page, it is a good idea to also specify a page color, in case your graphic does not load correctly for some reason. If it is necessary for the browser to display the background page color, your color scheme will still look approximately the same as with your graphic displayed.

STEP-BY-STEP 5.3

1. With the **index.html** page open in your graphics Web site, decide which of the four backgrounds you applied in the last exercise you like best and seems to work best with the text. Then apply that background using the Page Properties dialog box, if necessary. Leave the Page Properties dialog box open.

2. In the Page Properties dialog box, click the Background color palette or list and select a color similar to the color of the graphic you inserted, as shown in Figure 5-6. For example, use hexadecimal value FF9900 or FFCC00. In some programs, you may need to click **More Colors** on the list and then choose the desired color.

FIGURE 5-6
Change the background graphic and color

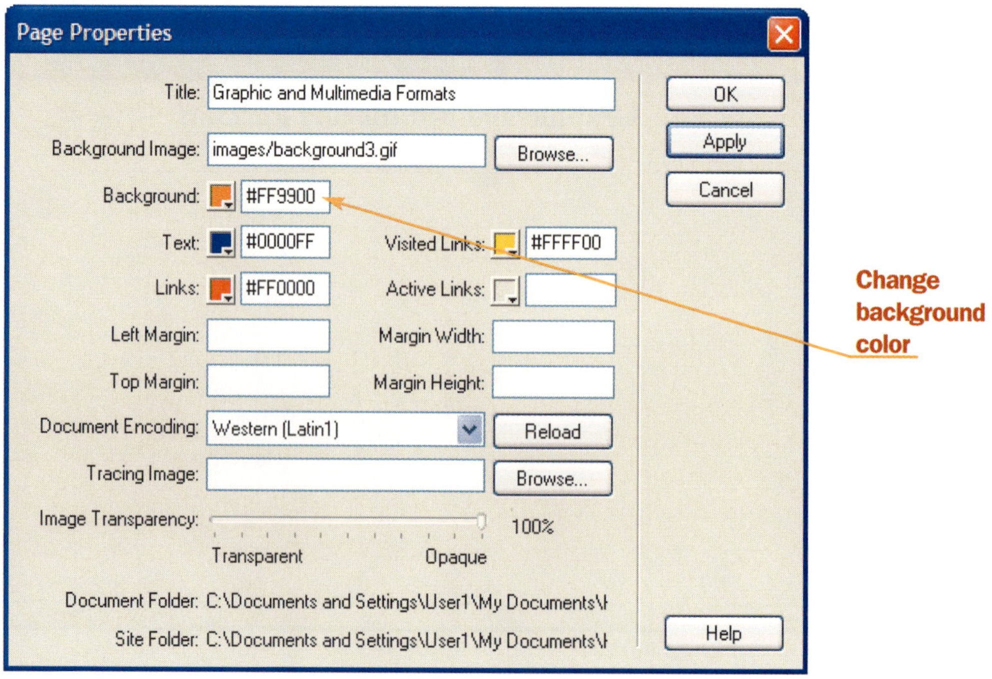

Change background color

STEP-BY-STEP 5.3 Continued

3. If desired, use the same procedure to change the color of text and links (including visited and active links). Use hexadecimal values that provide a strong contrast to the current background. Click the **OK** button when you have made your selections.

> **Hot Tip**
>
> In some programs, you can select a check box such as Get background information from another page and then select the index.html page to quickly apply the same formats to the current page.

4. Open each page on your Web site and add the same background graphic and color scheme combinations you have used for your **index.html** page. Each page should have the same background and the same color scheme. If you notice any other formats that need to be modified, such as headings styles, apply the correct formats.

5. You need to make another change to some pages in your site to ensure consistency. Currently, the **gif.html** page contains a graphic link to the **index.html** page, while other, similar pages use the *Menu* text link. Replace the text link on the following pages with the **menu.gif** graphic from the images folder, and link the graphic to the **index.html** page.

> **Extra for Experts**
>
> To save time, copy the graphic link on the gif.html page and then paste it on each page listed. This action pastes not only the graphic but the link to the index.html page, as well.

bmp.html

jpeg.html

pict.html

png.html

tiff.html

wbmp.html

6. Save and close all open pages. Leave your graphics Web site open to use in the next exercise.

Add a Random Navigation System

Web sites include navigation systems to make it easier for visitors to find the information they need quickly. Navigation is one critical aspect of *interaction design*. In previous lessons, you incorporated two of the three basic Web site structures: hierarchical and linear. In this section, you add a random access structure by inserting a list of links on each page that allows a visitor to jump to any page in the site.

You can use skills you learned in the last lesson to create either text or graphic links for a navigation structure. If you choose to use text links, you can help visitors differentiate among the links by inserting spaces or symbols such as | or ~ between them. These symbols also add visual interest to a page.

> **Note**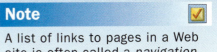
>
> A list of links to pages in a Web site is often called a *navigation bar* or *link bar*. Some programs allow you to insert a navigation bar that automatically links the pages in the navigation structure and also let you choose graphic buttons or text for the links.

STEP-BY-STEP 5.4

1. In your graphics Web site, open the **index.html** file.

2. Select the link text *Our Use Policy* at the bottom of the page and delete it.

3. Enter the text below to create links for the graphic Web pages located on your site. Your page should look similar to Figure 5-7 when you are finished. Your page background may vary if you chose an image other than background3.gif.

PNG I JPEG I GIF I BMP I WBMP I TIFF I PICT I Our Use Policy

<table>
<tr><td>

Did You Know?

The I symbol is called a vertical bar and can be inserted by pressing Shift and the key located on the backslash key just above the Enter key. If you're using speech recognition software, you can say "vertical bar" to create the symbol.

</td></tr>
</table>

FIGURE 5-7
Enter the names of the links you will create

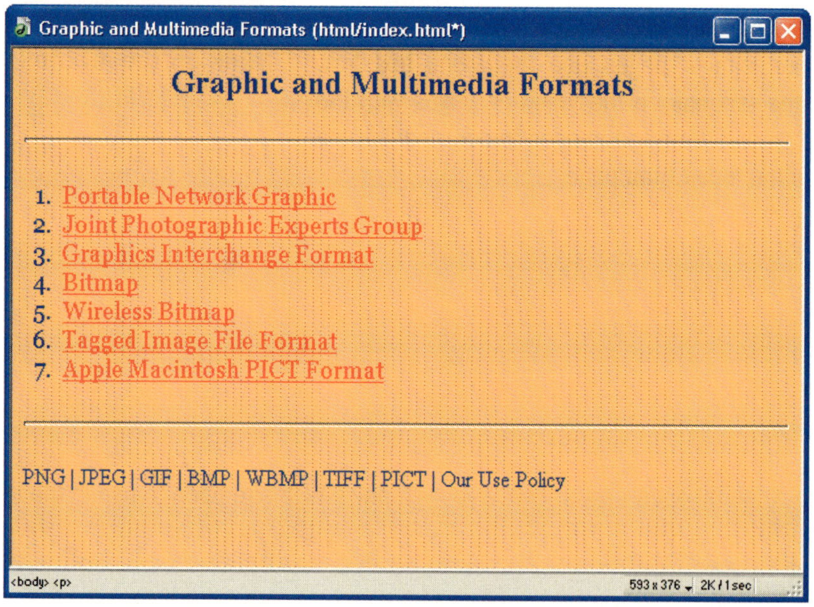

4. Select **PNG** in the navigation list. Use your program's hyperlink dialog box to create a link to the **png.html** file in the current Web site.

STEP-BY-STEP 5.4 Continued

5. Create hyperlinks for the remaining navigation bar entries to their corresponding files on your Web site as listed below. When you are finished, your page should look similar to Figure 5-8.

JPEG	to	jpeg.html
GIF	to	gif.html
BMP	to	bmp.html
WBMP	to	wbmp.html
TIFF	to	tiff.html
PICT	to	pict.html
Our Use Policy	to	aup1.html

FIGURE 5-8
Complete all the hyperlinks in your random access navigation system

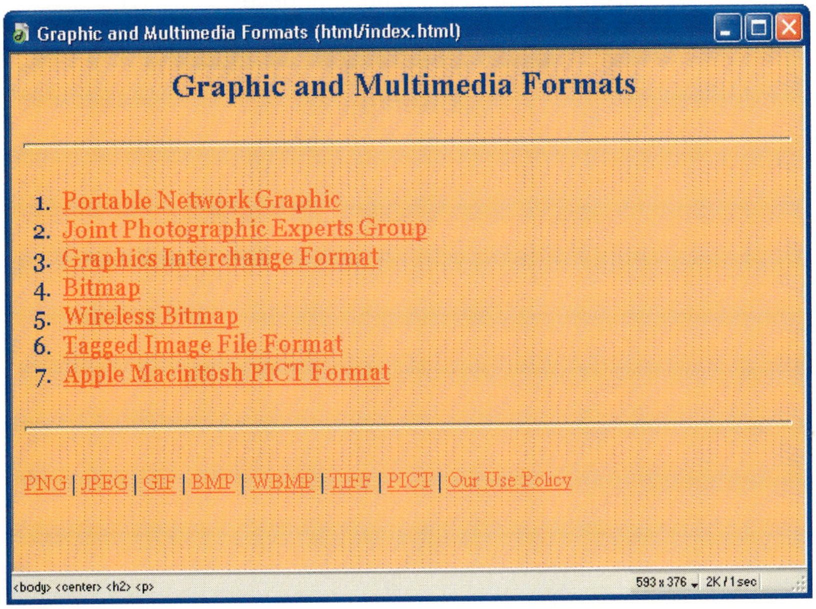

6. Save changes to the **index.html** page. Preview the page in the browser and test the links.

7. Close the browser. Leave the **index.html** page open to use in the next exercise.

Extra for Experts

Switch to code view to see how your program has added link codes to the page.

Ensure Navigation Consistency

A random access navigation system works only if each key page is linked to all the other key pages. Therefore, you must copy and paste all the navigation links from the site's index page to the other content or graphics pages on your Web site. To be truly random, the navigation system must be consistent from page to page, or the visitor gets lost or confused by the absence of this user-friendly interactive design.

When copying the links, keep in mind that you may not want the random navigation system on all pages in the site. For example, in a linear section of the site, visitors need to view pages in a specific order. So, it is necessary to maintain the linear navigation structure in that part of the site.

STEP-BY-STEP 5.5

1. With the **index.html** page open, select the entire list of navigation links at the bottom of the page.

2. Click **Edit** on the menu bar, and then click **Copy**.

3. Open the **bmp.html** page. Click to the left of the menu graphic and press **Enter** to insert a blank paragraph.

4. Click in the blank paragraph. Click **Edit** on the menu bar, and then click **Paste** to insert the copied navigation bar. Your navigation links should look like Figure 5-9.

> ### Did You Know?
> You can make sure you have selected all of the navigation code by checking the page in code view.

FIGURE 5-9
Paste the navigation system to the bmp.html page

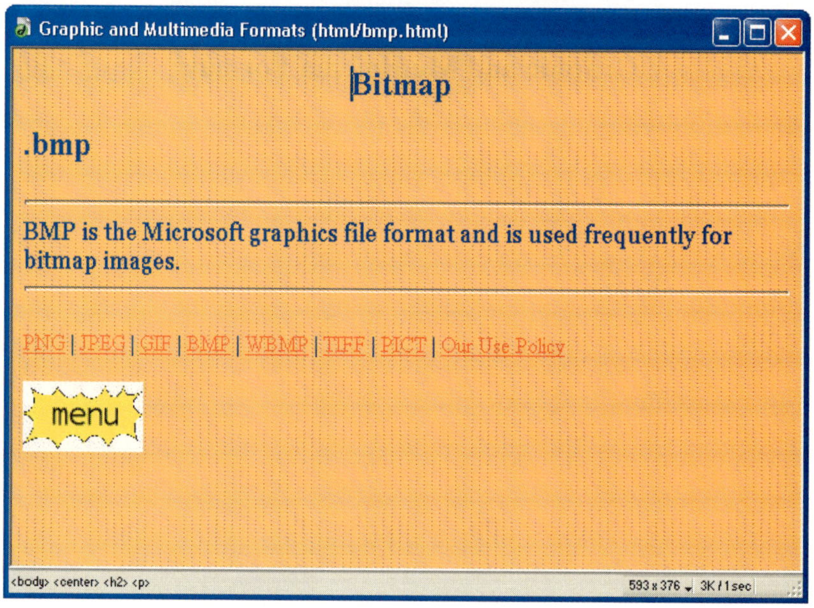

5. Save changes to the **bmp.html** page and close the page.

6. Open each of the pages listed below and repeat steps 3 and 4 to paste the navigation links. You do not have to re-copy the navigation bar each time, because it is still stored in the Clipboard. After inserting the navigation links, save and close each page.

   gif.html

   jpeg.html

   pict.html

   png.html

   tiff.html

   wbmp.html

7. Close all open pages, and leave the graphics Web site open to use in the next exercise.

Test Links and Page Properties

One of the most important parts of *interaction design* is to make sure all your hyperlinks work! Web site design programs such as Dreamweaver and FrontPage can tell you if you have any dead-end or "broken" links. A *broken link* is any link that goes nowhere or goes to the wrong place.

One way to test links in a site is to display the site map or hyperlinks view as you learned in Lesson 4. Depending on the program you're using, broken links are marked in red or by special symbols next to the link.

> **Extra for Experts**
>
> Most Web site design programs also have features such as Check Links Sitewide or Recalculate Hyperlinks that check links for you and identify linking problems so that you can correct them.

However, just because your software indicates that a link is working doesn't mean you're excused from checking the links yourself! A link may go to the wrong place, yet your software tells you it is working properly. To make sure all links are connecting pages they way they should, preview your site in the browser and test each link on each page.

Also, as you display each page to test your links, you can look for errors in your *presentation design*. As you test the links, review each page to make sure you have applied page properties consistently to each page on the site.

STEP-BY-STEP 5.6

1. Open the **index.html** page in your graphics Web site.

2. Display the site map or hyperlinks view for your site. Expand the view if possible to display the map in the full width of the screen. Click the plus signs for each page to see the links on that page. Your site map may resemble Figure 5-10.

> **Did You Know?**
>
> The lines between the files indicate that links connect each file to the index.html file. Notice how each page links to all the other key pages. However, the linear AUP section remains linear.

FIGURE 5-10
View the random access links on your Web site

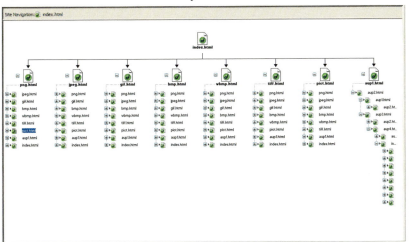

STEP-BY-STEP 5.6 Continued

3. When you have finished viewing the links, close the site map or hyperlinks view to return to your **index.html** file.

4. Check your links! Preview the page in your Web browser.

5. In your Web browser, locate the command to clear recently visited pages. In Internet Explorer, for example, click **Tools** on the menu bar, click **Internet Options**, click the **Clear History** button, click **Yes** to confirm the deletion, and then click the **OK** button. Click the **Refresh** button if necessary to restore the link colors.

6. Try each hyperlink in your new random access navigation system. As you try a link, it changes color, as shown in Figure 5-11. (The last link you visit may remain the original color.)

FIGURE 5-11
View links in browser

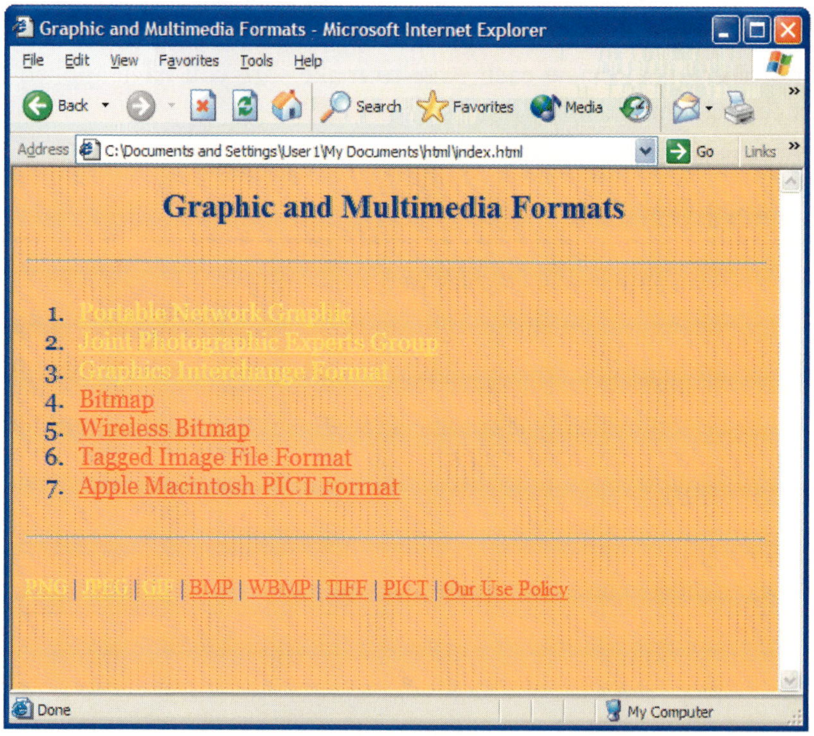

7. Return to your Web site design program by closing your browser. Correct any errors you may have found.

8. After you are convinced that all the links work properly, save and close all open pages. Leave your graphics Web site open to use in the next exercise.

Prepare to Publish a Site

Publishing a Web site is a major aspect of *presentation design*. **Publishing** simply means to place your site files and folders on a Web server so it can be accessed by a browser.

Publishing your Web site on the Internet isn't difficult, but it can vary quite a bit by program. Some programs require you to publish only to servers running special *extensions* (extensions are programs or scripts that perform specific tasks on the published pages). In other programs, you can publish to any server.

To prepare to publish a site, you must gather some information and sometimes configure your site for the specific publishing process you are going to use. One of your first tasks is to establish the URL of your site. You need to ask your instructor, system administrator, or Internet service provider to supply this information. This URL is your Web site address. You may include folder names and even filenames. For example:

www.handwritingsolutions.com

www.handwritingsolutions.com/html

www.handwritingsolutions.com/html/index.html

Your next task is to find out what protocol you need to use to transfer your site files to the Web server. Some standard protocols are *HTTP (Hypertext Transfer Protocol)* and *FTP (File Transfer Protocol)*. FTP has been used for decades and is older than the World Wide Web itself. It's a file transfer system that allows you to *put* files on an Internet server located somewhere on the World Wide Web. It also allows you to *get* files from a server on the Web and transfer them to your computer. The put operation is commonly called *uploading* and the get operation *downloading*.

After you have identified what protocol to use, you generally have to tell your Web site design program how to communicate with the Web server you are going to publish to. In some programs, you enter this information along with other site information. You specify the access protocol and the URL of the host Web server. This is commonly a name such as www.course.com, or it may be a number such as 159.62.35.12. You may also need to know the name of the folder or directory on that computer hosting your Web site in which your site files will be stored. Normally, FTP sites also require you to specify a login name and a password to protect the site from unauthorized use.

> ### Extra for Experts
>
> Some programs allow you to publish to a local server on your computer to test your site before uploading it to a Web server. This local server may have an address such as http://localhost. You can also publish any Web site to a location on your hard drive or network by supplying the correct path to the folder you want to publish in.

In the next two exercises, you prepare to publish your graphics site and then publish it. If you do not have access to a Web server to publish to, you can publish to a local address. See your instructor or your Web site design program's Help files for more information.

S TEP-BY-STEP 5.7

Publishing differs from program to program. Follow steps 1 to 3 to prepare for publishing in Dreamweaver. Follow steps 4 and 5 to prepare for publishing in FrontPage. If you are using a different Web site design program, consult your program's Help files for information on publishing.

1. In Dreamweaver, click **Site** on the menu bar, and then click **Edit Sites**. Make sure your site is selected in the Edit Sites dialog box, and then click the **Edit** button to open the Site Definition dialog box.

2. Click the **Advanced** tab, if necessary, and then click **Remote Info** in the Category list.

STEP-BY-STEP 5.7 Continued

3. Enter the information your instructor supplies for uploading your site to a server or local location. If you are going to upload using FTP, your information should look similar to that shown in Figure 5-12. Click the **OK** button when you are finished, and then click the **Done** button to close the Edit Sites dialog box.

FIGURE 5-12
Enter your publishing information

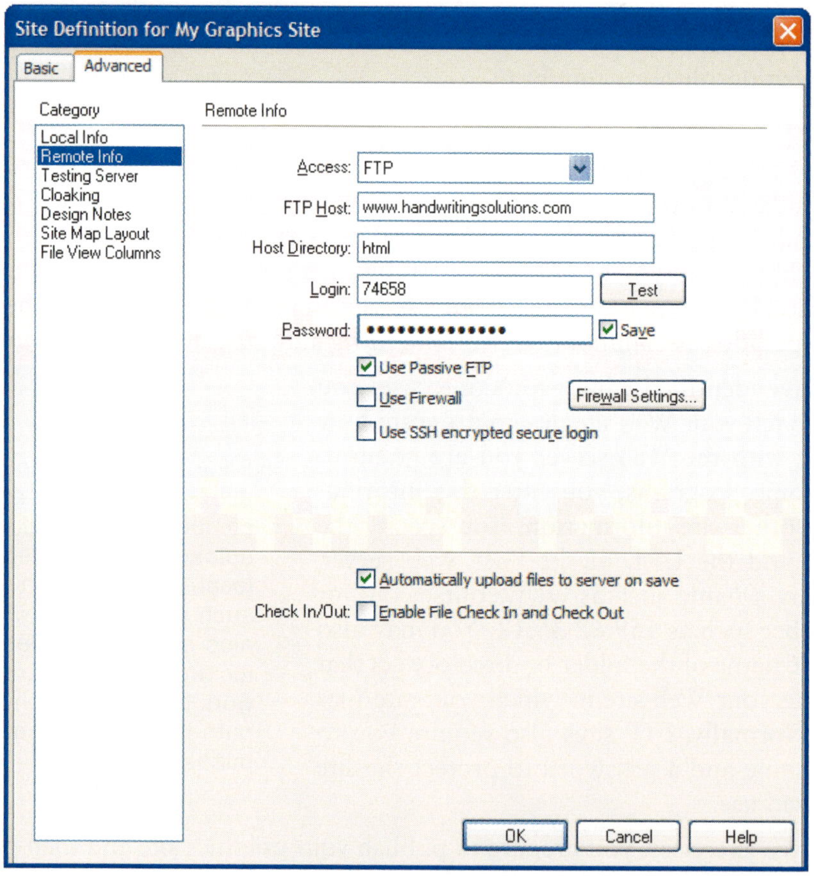

4. In FrontPage, click **File** on the menu bar, and then click **Publish Web**. Enter the publish destination your instructor supplies. Click the **OK** button.

5. If FrontPage asks to create a web at the location you specified, click the **OK** button.

6. Leave your graphics Web site and any displayed dialog boxes open to use in the next exercise.

Publish a Site

In the previous exercise, you prepared your Web site for publication. When you upload your site in its finished form, you are literally "publishing" your Web pages online. After your site is live—that is, uploaded—anyone in the world can view it if they know the Web address or URL.

To complete the publishing process, you need to actually transfer your Web site files and folders to the location you designated. Change the view or use a dialog box to see both your local files (those on your computer) and the remote site to which you intend to publish. Then click a button such as Put Files or Publish to start the transfer process. Your program shows you the progress of the transfer. After all files are transferred, you can see your files on both your local location and the remote location.

STEP-BY-STEP 5.8

1. If you are using Dreamweaver, click **Local View** in the Site panel to display the drop-down list, and then click **Remote View**. Click the **Expand/Collapse** button in the Site panel to see your local files (at the right side of the screen) and the location you are going to publish to (at the left side of the screen). If you are using FrontPage, the Publish Web dialog box should still be open, showing your local files on the left and the location you are going to publish to on the right. (If you don't see both locations, click the **Show** button to expand the Publish Web dialog box.)

2. Close any open folders in your local site files.

3. If necessary in your program, click the **Connect** button to connect to your remote site.

4. In Dreamweaver, select all your site's files and the images folder as shown in Figure 5-13. In FrontPage, all files should have a green check mark to indicate they are ready to publish.

FIGURE 5-13
Select the files you wish to publish online

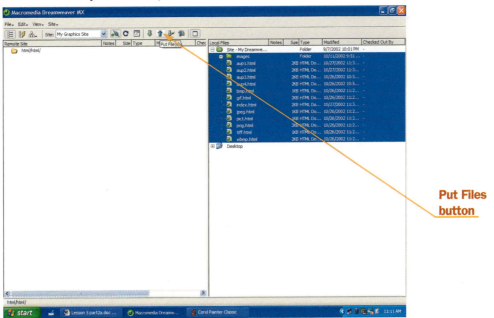

Put Files button

STEP-BY-STEP 5.8 Continued

5. Click the **Put Files** or the **Publish** button to upload all your selected files to your remote site. Click **Yes** if you are asked to include dependent files.

6. Your program may then display both your local and remote files (see Figure 5-14) or display a dialog box asking if you want to view your published site.

FIGURE 5-14
Local and remote sites are identical

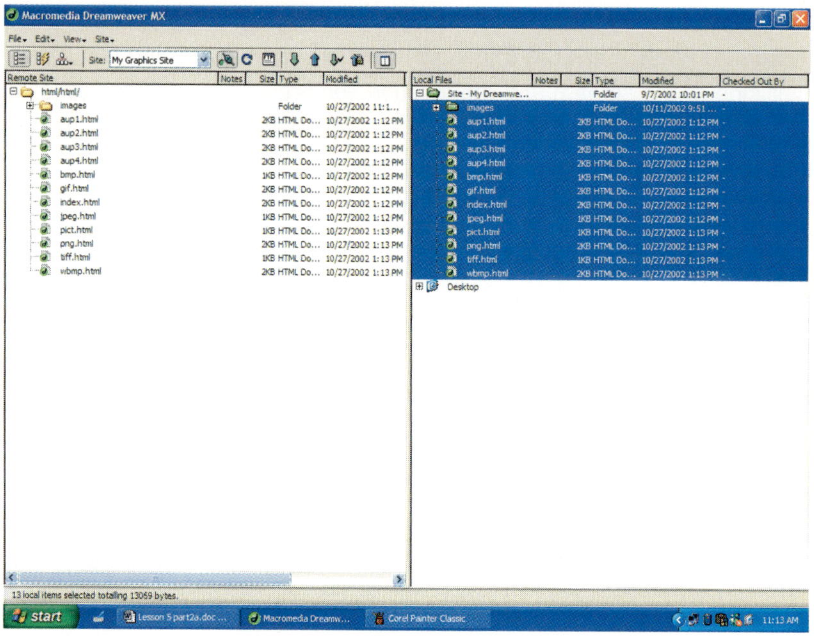

STEP-BY-STEP 5.8 Continued

7. Go online and try your Web site! Click the link your program supplies, or enter your URL in the browser's Address bar. Check all pages to see if everything uploaded properly. Figure 5-15 shows one page of the site in the browser.

FIGURE 5-15
View your site online by its URL

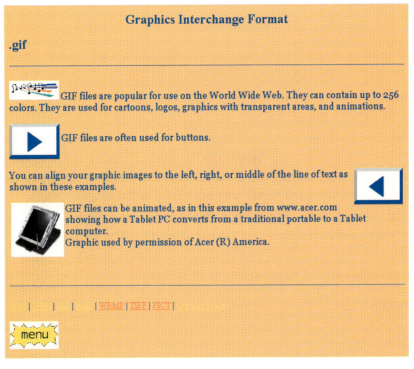

8. Close your browser. Return to design view in your Web site design program if necessary. Close any open pages in your graphics Web site if necessary and leave it open to use in the next exercise.

Team Collaboration with Other Applications

Many, if not most, of the people you work with on the job will not know much about HTML or Web site software such as Dreamweaver or FrontPage. However, with a little coaching and mentoring from you, they can still collaborate and add information to your Web site by using software packages they may already know, such as Microsoft Word or Corel WordPerfect, Microsoft PowerPoint, or even Microsoft Excel. Using other applications such as these allows you to add specific types of information such as charts and tables to a site, a key component of *information design.*

Create a Web Page in a Word Processing Application

Each of the major word processing programs has an option that allows users to convert a word processing document into a Web page. Some programs also provide a number of Web page formatting options such as themes and specific page designs to help you create a sophisticated-looking Web page.

Use a command such as Save as Web Page to give the file a name and save it in any location, such as your graphics Web site's HTML folder. Because you save the page in HTML format with an .htm or .html extension, you can then open the page in your Web site design program. From there, you can integrate the page into your site by formatting it to match other pages and creating hyperlinks to and from the new page.

STEP-BY-STEP 5.9

1. Open a word processing program such as Microsoft Word.

2. Enter the text shown below, which discusses the PNG graphics format. Press **Enter** twice at the end of each paragraph. When finished, your page should look similar to Figure 5-16.

   Special Report

   The Portable Network Graphic Format

   The portable network graphic format (PNG) was invented by an independent panel of graphics experts. Pronounced "ping," the format was designed to replace the older GIF format. It is considered an improvement over GIF file formats because it supports numerous colors, can be compressed, and does a better job of retaining the quality of the image.

   PNG files are often used for small graphics that require a lot of detail. In this situation, a GIF file would limit the number of colors that are possible. JPEG files often discard information to save space upon compression. PNG files retain more of the image quality.

   PNG files can also serve as an alternative to TIFF files.

FIGURE 5-16
Enter your text

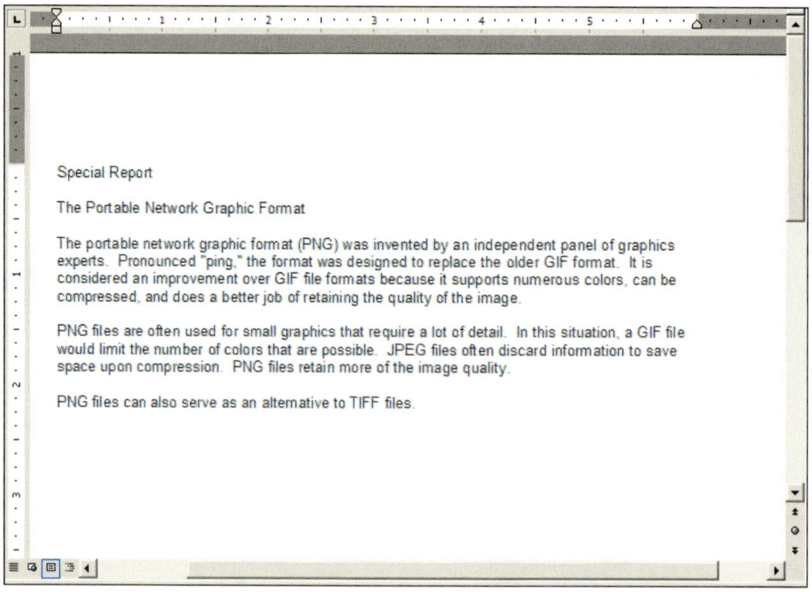

3. Issue the command to save your file as a Web page. For example, click **File** on the menu bar, and then click **Save as Web Page**.

4. In the Save As dialog box, navigate to your html folder. Enter the filename **pngreport.htm**. Click the **Save** button.

STEP-BY-STEP 5.9 Continued

5. Your word processing program may change the view of the document to a Web layout. Close the word-processing document and the word-processing program.

> **Note** ☑️
>
> Your word processing program may automatically select .htm as its default file extension instead of .html.

6. Open your Web site design program and verify that the **pngreport.htm** page has been stored in your graphics Web site in local view. If you do not see the page, you may need to click your program's **Refresh** button on the Standard toolbar.

7. Leave the Web site open to use in the next exercise.

Clean up Code in Word Processed Pages

Microsoft Word and other word processing programs generate code for both word processing and HTML files. The same file must work in the word processing application as well as on the Web. As a result, this dual-purpose file naturally contains a lot of unnecessary HTML code, as shown in Figure 5-17.

FIGURE 5-17
Word processor adds unnecessary code

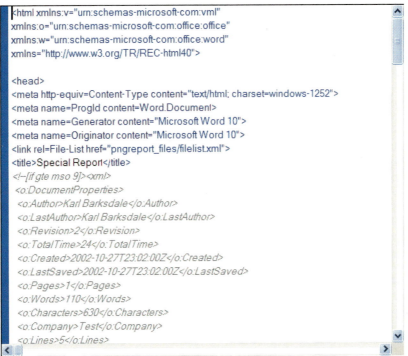

Some programs, such as Dreamweaver, have special features that delete all the unnecessary word processing code and leave a more pure HTML version of the file on your Web site. You can use this clean-up feature when importing a file into the site, or you can use a command such as Clean Up HTML or Clean Up Word HTML on the Commands menu to remove the unnecessary code after the page is part of the site.

If your program does not have a specific clean-up feature (FrontPage does not, for example), you can still clean up a word processed file in your program manually. Switch to HTML view and look for grayed-out sections of formatting code on the page. You can delete these sections, as your Web site design program doesn't need them.

STEP-BY-STEP 5.10

1. Open the **pngreport.htm** file in your Web site design program. Switch to code view and look at the extra and unnecessary code that the page contains.

2. If your program has a command to clean up HTML code, issue the command. For example, click **Commands** on the menu bar, and then click **Clean Up Word HTML**. The Clean Up Word HTML dialog box opens, as shown in Figure 5-18.

> **Important**
>
> If you are using FrontPage, your page may open in Word when you open it. Close the Word file and then, in FrontPage, right-click the page, click Open With, and then click FrontPage (frontpg.exe). This enables you to open the file automatically in FrontPage.

FIGURE 5-18
Clean Up Word HTML dialog box

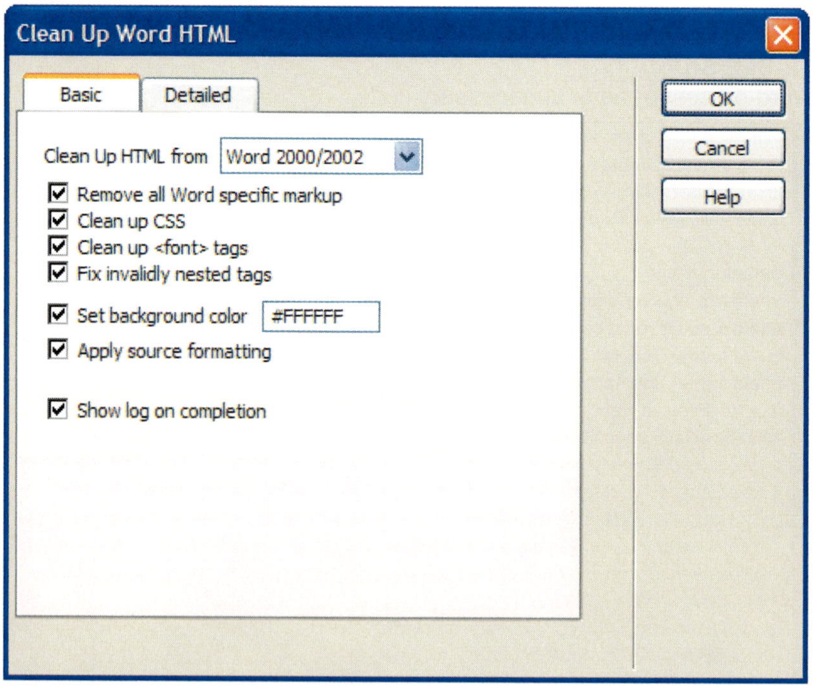

3. Make sure all check boxes on the Basic tab are selected, as indicated in Figure 5-18. Click the **OK** button. After completing the clean-up operation, your program displays a message box to let you know what it did. Click the **OK** button to close the message box.

STEP-BY-STEP 5.10 Continued

4. You should see the page still in code view, with many fewer HTML codes, as shown in Figure 5-19.

FIGURE 5-19
View the clean HTML code

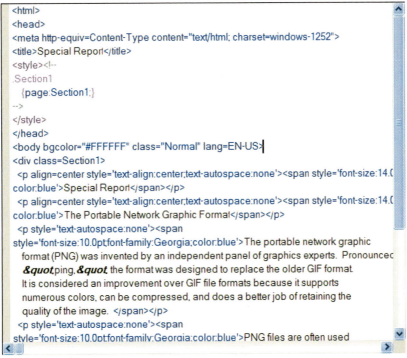

5. If your program does not have an automatic clean-up program, you may want to try your hand at cleaning out some of the unneeded code above and below the <title> and <style> tags in your code view. You may need to adjust spacing in design view afterwards.

6. Save changes to the **pngreport.htm** file. Now that your page is cleaned up, you can integrate it into your site. If desired, format the **pngreport.htm** page to be consistent with other pages in the site.

7. In design view, click at the end of the last paragraph on the page and press **Enter** to create a new paragraph. Enter **Return to PNG**. Link the text you just entered to the **png.htm** page. Save changes and close the page.

8. Open the **png.html** page. Click at the end of the paragraph between the horizontal rules and press **Shift + Enter** to insert a line break. Enter **More**. Link the word *More* to the **pngreport.htm** page.

9. Save changes and preview the **png.html** page in the browser. Test the link to the **pngreport.htm** page and the link from the **pngreport.htm** page back to **png.html**.

10. Close the browser and all open pages. Leave your graphics Web site open to use in the next exercise.

Create Web Pages with Other Applications

Other programs also generate HTML versions of their documents. For example, Microsoft PowerPoint and Excel both have options to save their files as Web pages. This ability to generate Web site content from applications makes it easy for team members to contribute specialized information to a site—an important aspect of *information design*.

Create PowerPoint Web Pages

PowerPoint is used to create linear presentations about a topic. When a presentation is saved as a series of Web pages, Web site visitors can go step-by-step, in a linear way, through a sequence of HTML pages, which look similar to the original PowerPoint presentation. In PowerPoint, you can add special effects such as sound, movie clips, and other graphics. These effects are then converted into files and saved in a folder that becomes part of the Web presentation. You can link to the PowerPoint show from your Web site.

If you have completed the Presentation Systems unit in this book already, you know that it is easy to save a PowerPoint presentation in HTML format. Click Save as Web Page on the File menu to open the Save As dialog box. Supply a name for the Web presentation, change the page title if necessary, and indicate where you want to store the presentation. Click the Save button to save the presentation in HTML format, or click the Publish button to make more detailed decisions about how the presentation will look and work in the browser.

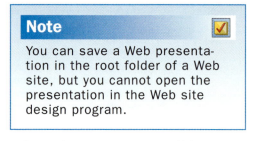

Note ✅

You can save a Web presentation in the root folder of a Web site, but you cannot open the presentation in the Web site design program.

Create Excel Web Pages

Microsoft Excel is a spreadsheet program used to organize and manipulate numerical data. Excel's worksheet data can also be converted into charts to represent data visually. You can save or publish both worksheet data and chart data as Web pages.

To save or publish an Excel worksheet as a Web page, use the Save as Web Page command on the File menu, just as in PowerPoint. You can choose whether to save the entire workbook, which may consist of more than one worksheet, or the current sheet only. When you choose the Sheet option, everything on the worksheet is saved to the Web page, including any charts or other objects on the sheet. If your worksheet has a chart on it, you can save or publish the chart only by selecting the chart first, then issuing the Save as Web Page command. You can then choose the Selection: Chart option in the Save As dialog box.

After you have entered a name and a page title, if desired, and specified the location where you want to save the Web page, click the Save button. Similarly to a PowerPoint presentation saved as a Web page, Excel also generates a folder to contain files required to display the

Extra for Experts 🏢

If you make the worksheet or chart interactive, visitors to your Web site can work with the data as if working in Excel to create formulas, change values, and so on.

Web page properly, as shown in Figure 5-20. For more control over Web page options, click the Publish button to open the Publish as Web Page dialog box. Here you can choose to publish only a range of cells, for example, or specify that the published Excel data be interactive.

FIGURE 5-20
Excel Web page saved in a Web site folder

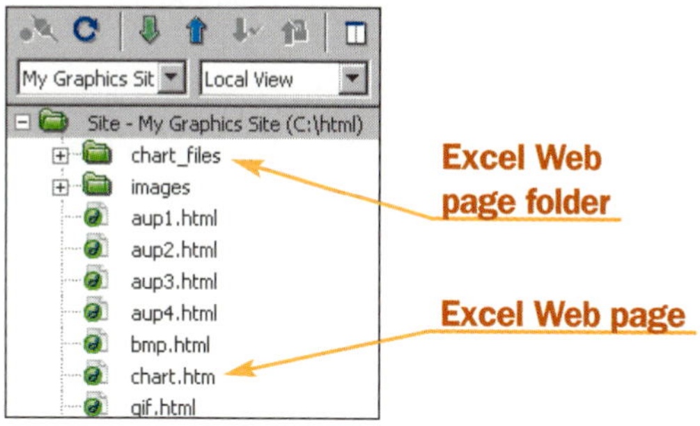

Similarly to a PowerPoint presentation, you can link an Excel Web page to an existing Web site. Create the links before publishing, or open the Excel Web page in your Web site design program to edit it.

This exercise gives you a quick overview of how to use PowerPoint and Excel to create additional content for your Web site. After you learn the basics of saving and integrating these files into your Web site, you can help instruct others on providing content to your Web site under your direction using PowerPoint or Excel.

S TEP-BY-STEP 5.11

1. Launch Microsoft PowerPoint and create a simple presentation on a subject related to your graphics Web site. For example, create a presentation that lists some Web sites you have found useful for downloading graphics, tells what kinds of graphics you can download at each site, and specifies the site's copyright requirements. You may want to insert links on your slides to useful Web sites.

2. Apply an appropriate design template. Illustrate the presentation as desired with clip art or animated graphics. Add special effects such as audio clips, as you learned in the Presentation Systems unit, and apply animations or slide transitions if you like.

3. After you are finished with your slide show, click **File** on the menu bar, and then click **Save as Web Page**. Change the page title if desired. Save the file with an appropriate name, and choose to store the presentation in your html folder. Click the **Save** button.

4. Close the presentation in PowerPoint. Close PowerPoint.

5. In your Web site program, open the **index.html** page. Below the navigation links, insert text that relates to your Web presentation, such as **Links to Graphics Sites**. Link this text to the presentation page in your html folder. Save changes to the **index.html** page.

6. Preview the **index.html** page in the browser, and click the link to take you to the PowerPoint presentation Web pages. Proceed through these pages, and then close the browser. Leave your Web site design program open.

STEP-BY-STEP 5.11 Continued

7. Launch Microsoft Excel and open **WS Step 5-11** from the data files folder. This worksheet provides data on hits (visits) to the graphics Web site for the previous year. You will publish only the chart as a Web page.

8. In the worksheet file, click the chart to select it. Click **File** on the menu bar, and then click **Save as Web page**. The Save As dialog box opens.

> **Extra for Experts**
>
> You can use the Edit with Microsoft PowerPoint command on Internet Explorer's File menu to open the presentation in PowerPoint and add a link to the index.html page to complete the navigation structure.

9. Click the **Selection: Chart** option. Click the **Change Title** button, and enter **Web Site Hits**. Click the **OK** button.

10. Enter the filename **chart.htm**, and navigate to your html folder from the Save in drop-down list. Click the **Save** button. Then close the Excel worksheet without saving changes and exit Excel.

11. In your Web site design program, open the **index.html** page if necessary. At the bottom of the page, enter text such as **Visits to This Site** and format the text to match other text on the page. Create a link from this text to the **chart.htm** page.

12. Open the **chart.htm** page. If desired, change the page background to the same graphic you are using throughout the site. Then click below the chart and enter text such as **Menu**, and link this text to the **index.html** page.

13. Save changes to both pages. Preview the **index.html** page in the browser. Click the link to the chart to view the Excel chart page. Note that the page title appears not only in the browser's title bar but as a title above the chart. Your page should look similar to Figure 5-21.

FIGURE 5-21
Chart.htm page in the browser

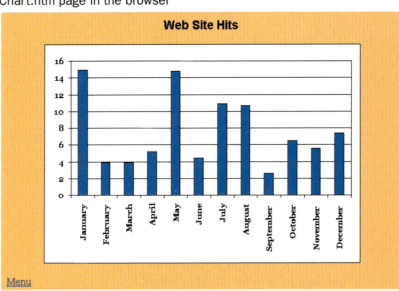

14. Close the browser and all open pages. Close your Web site design program.

SUMMARY

In this lesson, you learned:

- Presentation design, interaction design, and information design are three important concepts in Web site design.

- Use background graphics and change other Web page properties to add visual interest and texture to pages in a site.

- You should apply page properties consistently to Web pages on your Web site.

- Add a navigation bar to create a random access navigation system.

- You must test hyperlinks and make sure page properties are consistent before you publish a site.

- You can use protocols such as FTP to upload a Web site to an Internet Web server. Before you publish, you may need to supply the correct URL, login name, and password to access the Web server.

- Publishing a Web site on the Internet means transferring files and folders from your local Web site to the remote server.

- People with many different skills and backgrounds can collaborate to produce content for a Web site using word processing, spreadsheet, and presentation software.

VOCABULARY *Review*

Define the following terms:

Broken link	HTTP (Hypertext Transfer	Presentation design
Downloading	Protocol)	Publishing
FTP (File Transfer Protocol)	Information design	Uploading
	Interaction design	

REVIEW *Questions*

TRUE / FALSE

Circle T if the statement is true or F if the statement is false.

T   F   **1.** Information design is concerned with the look and feel of a Web site.

T   F   **2.** Interaction design is concerned with how users navigate a Web site.

T   F   **3.** You must test your interaction design by trying all of your hypertext links.

T   F   **4.** People with little or no HTML knowledge can't contribute content or information to a Web site.

T   F   **5.** You should always apply a random access navigation structure to all pages in a site.

T   F   **6.** Quotes from e-mailed messages don't need to be cited on a Web page.

T   F   **7.** Professional Web designers seldom use the BGCOLOR attribute to define a Web site's background.

T   F   **8.** The BACKGROUND attribute fits between the <HEAD> </HEAD> tags.

T   F   **9.** When you add a word processed page to a site, it does not open correctly until you clean up its HTML codes.

T   F **10.** Background graphics tend to be created with large JPEG or PNG files.

WRITTEN QUESTIONS

Write a brief answer to the following questions.

1. Describe presentation design.

2. Describe interaction design.

3. Describe information design.

4. Why is it important to provide citations for resources used from online sources?

5. What are the eight elements, in order, that should be included when citing sources?

FILL IN THE BLANK

Complete the following sentences by writing the correct word or words in the blanks provided

1. Color and graphics are important aspects of a Web site's _____ design.

2. The (|) symbol is called a(n) _____.

3. A(n) _____ access structure links every key page to every other key page with hypertext links.

4. A(n) _____ link leads to a dead end or goes to the wrong place.

5. URL is an acronym for Uniform _____ Locator.

6. FTP is an acronym for File _____ Protocol.

7. The put operation in FTP is also called _____.

8. The get operation in FTP is also called _____.

9. The PNG graphics file format is pronounced "_____."

10. _____ is a program created by Microsoft that can be used to create linear, multimedia Web presentations.

PROJECTS

 ## PROJECT 5-1

At some time in the future, you'll likely need the aid of people of various backgrounds and expertise to help you research Web page content. These people may not know much about HTML, but they probably know a great deal about their specialties. It's your job to teach them in this project how they can contribute to your Web site. Prepare this training by creating a linear Web presentation, using any tool at your disposal, that explains how to use word processing, presentation, or spreadsheet software to contribute valuable content to a Web site.

 ## PROJECT 5-2

Use your graphics software to create a background graphic for your personal Web site project, the project you began in Lesson 1. Apply this background graphic to each of the Web pages on your site to create a consistent look and feel for each page. Adjust the color scheme if necessary to enhance the background.

 ## PROJECT 5-3

Continue improving your personal Web project by adding a random access navigation system. Remember to apply your random navigation system to each key page on your Web site.

SCANS **WEB PROJECT**

Here is a project that requires teamwork. In Step-by-Step 5.9 you created a special report on the PNG graphics format. However, special reports must also be prepared for each of the following file formats:

GIF

BMP

WBMP

TIFF

PICT

Create a special report about each graphics format. Split up the work. Decide as a team who researches each of these individual formats. Then, hit the Net and search for information about the graphics file format(s) you have been assigned. As you conduct your research, be sure to keep track of the resources you use so they can be cited properly. If you forget how to create the citations, refer to the special feature in this lesson.

SCANS **TEAMWORK PROJECT**

In this final teamwork project, teach each other about the file formats researched in the Web project above. After all team members have taken a turn to teach, share your special report files. Integrate these reports into your graphics Web site project by creating links from the specific graphics format pages to these special reports.

CRITICAL *Thinking*

SCANS **ACTIVITY 5-1**

In this lesson, you touched briefly on three aspects of Web site design. Consider and discuss the following questions in a 500-word report. Which of the three aspects of design (presentation, interaction, and information) do you believe to be the most time-consuming? Which of these three aspects of design is the most important to start with as you begin a new Web site? Which aspect of design do you enjoy dealing with the most?

WEB SITE DEVELOPMENT

REVIEW *Questions*

TRUE / FALSE

Circle T if the statement is true or F if the statement is false.

T F **1.** Web sites are computers called servers that share information with Web clients.

T F **2.** A Web browser requests and displays Web pages.

T F **3.** The acronym http:// is known as a domain name.

T F **4.** The WYSIWYG view in programs such as Dreamweaver and FrontPage does not display HTML code, but shows how Web pages may appear in a Web browser.

T F **5.** When you use FTP to put files on your site, you are uploading or publishing a Web site.

T F **6.** A welcome page is usually the first page seen on a Web site by a visitor.

T F **7.** Bulleted or <UL> lists imply an order, sequence, or level of importance.

T F **8.** HTML tags should never be nested.

T F **9.** A hierarchical structure typically allows instant one-click access to any page on a Web site.

T F **10.** A proper navigation system allows visitors to find their way around a Web site without confusion.

MATCHING

Match the correct term in Column 1 to its description in Column 2.

Column 1 | **Column 2**

___ 1. www.course.com   A. An HTML structural or beginning tag.

___ 2. <BACKGROUND>   B. An example of an anchor tag.

___ 3. <A HREF> </A>   C. A file extension used for a Web graphic.

___ 4. <= "5">   D. A file extension used in naming a Web page.

___ 5. .gif   E. A critical thinking skill.

___ 6. <BODY>   F. An example of a Uniform Resource Locator.

___ 7. <OL>   G. A hexadecimal number.

___ 8. #FFFFFF   H. An example of an attribute.

___ 9. .html   I. A tag used to create a bulleted list.

___ 10. <UL>   J. A tag used to create a numbered list.

     K. An example of a value.

FILL IN THE BLANK

Complete the following sentences by writing the correct word or words in the blanks provided.

1. There are two major categories of fonts used on Web pages, serif and _____ serif.

2. _____ design examines the look and feel of the Web site.

3. Interaction design considers how people move around or _____ a Web site.

4. The colors, fonts, and background images selected for a Web page are all considered part of the page _____.

5. A(n) _____ link leads either to a dead end or to the wrong place on a Web site.

6. A(n) _____ is a private Web site reserved for a specific group, such as the employees of a company.

7. Terms of use policies are sometimes known as _____ use policies.

8. A color _____ is created when a Web site designer selects and balances the colors used on a Web site.

9. _____ colors include 216 colors identified by Netscape that all browsers can display successfully.

10. _____ graphics are displayed in relation to the line of text with which they are associated.

PROJECTS

PROJECT 1

Web sites are developed for all sorts of organizations. Most of us are aware of the many businesses that use the Internet to share information about their products and services. Schools and educational organizations offer sites to help students with their academic pursuits. Another category of Web sites is geared toward community service. These sites are usually designated by the .org top-level domain name. The .org designation is reserved for organizations. These include nonprofit groups as varied as environmental groups, churches, public safety groups, charitable societies, professional organizations, and health-related organizations. Often, these groups don't have a great deal of money to maintain a great-looking and informative Web site. Many of their Web pages are maintained by volunteers.

As a team, search for the Web sites of ten public service organizations. Try to find organizations active in your local area. You may come across a local chapter of the Red Cross or Red Crescent, organizations such as the United Way, a local food kitchen, or a church group involved in public service activities.

Rank your ten Web sites in terms of their presentation, interaction, and information design, and not according to the groups' charitable acts or goals. As a team, rank each of these sites from the highest (1) to the lowest (10). Present your findings in a report explaining the reasons for your rankings.

PROJECT 2

In this exercise, you plan a Web site for one of the public service organizations with a low-ranked Web site that you identified in the previous project. As a team, you must decide on an appropriate site structure; organization of material with lists; the location of graphics; use of horizontal rules; text color, fonts, styles, and alignments; background color or background graphic options; text and graphic links, link colors, and a system for testing links; how to prepare your project for online publication; the use of information created in Word or Excel; and how to present your information to the public service organization. In other words, you have a lot to do!

Follow these steps:

1. As a team, choose one of the lowest-ranked sites from the previous project. The whole team must agree on the site to revise.

2. Split up! Have each team member use 8.5-inch by 11-inch sheets of paper to prepare rough sketches detailing ideas on how the site can be improved.

3. Reunite your team. Review the sketches and design ideas that each team member has created.

4. Based on the designs that have been submitted by your team members, create a composite plan to redo this Web site.

5. Create a mock, local Web site for your team's choice of nonprofit or public service organization Web site and implement your design ideas.

6. If you feel confident enough in doing so, set up an appointment with local representatives of the organization you have chosen and present your ideas on how their site can be improved. You can demonstrate your local/mock Web site, create a PowerPoint shell, or print any sort of information you think is helpful to your clients. Of course, your presentation must be accompanied by an offer to help redo the site. Do you feel up to this task?

SIMULATION

As the marketing assistant for Swift River Travel, you have worked hard to define the image of your company. Now it's time for that work to go online.

JOB 1

Swift River Travel needs a Web site. You can use many of the same logos that you created in earlier units because it is important for a corporation to maintain a consistent look and feel between its Web site and the image portrayed through corporate business cards, stationery, brochures, and advertisements. You may need to convert some of the graphics into GIF or JPEG files for use online.

To begin this project, follow a development pattern similar to the one you used to help redesign the nonprofit or public service organization Web site in Project 2 above.

1. As a team, brainstorm to determine all the departments and sections needed on the corporate Web site. Take into consideration all the needs and concerns Swift River Travel must consider as it develops its online image. What sections and pages need to be developed?

2. Once again, split up! Have each team member independently develop a rough paper prototype of the proposed site. Prepare rough sketches detailing ideas on how the site should be organized. Should the site utilize a hierarchical, a random access, or a linear approach? What should the welcome screen look like?

3. Reunite your team. Review together the sketches and individual design ideas.

4. Based on the individual designs, create a composite plan for a Swift River Travel site.

5. Create a PowerPoint presentation to sell your company president on the ideas you have created for your Web site. Present this plan as a team, and provide your CEO with whatever information he or she needs to know all about Web site development to make a decision about funding your proposal.

JOB 2

The company president was impressed with your presentation about the new Web site. The CEO has authorized you to move ahead and develop a prototype of the new site.

1. Create a new Web site complete with an images folder, welcome page, and subordinate pages. Before you begin, take into account aspects of presentation, interaction, and information design as explained in Lesson 5.

2. Organize your folders and subfolders to support your site design—hierarchical, linear, or random—as discussed in Lessons 1 and 2.

3. Come up with a consistent look and feel for your Web site, format your pages accordingly, and link your Web pages together using a navigation system as explained in Lesson 2.

4. Add color, graphics, and even animation to your Web site as discussed in Lesson 3.

5. If you have access to Web site design and development software such as Dreamweaver or FrontPage, create your Web site using one of these tools. Otherwise, develop your Web site's pages using HTML tags in a text editor.

6. Polish and publish your Web site online as explained and discussed in Lesson 5.

JOB 3

In Project 1 at the beginning of this Unit Review, you and your team scrutinized ten Web sites, analyzing each in terms of its presentation, interaction, and information design. When you are on the job creating Web sites of your own, you too will be subjected to this type of scrutiny all the time. In fact, you should invite it! Constructive criticism of your work helps improve your skills.

After you have finished your team's Web site, invite others to visit it and watch carefully how they interact with it. Conduct focus groups and take feedback from the visitors as they view and critique your work. Some people may be hesitant to criticize the work you have done, so you must ask your participants direct questions to make them feel comfortable discussing your team's effort. Prepare these questions in advance so you are ready to talk with your participants. This process is a simple form of usability testing.

Take what you have learned from this experience and return to the drawing board. Revamp your site based upon what you've heard, making your team's site better, smarter, more informative, and more interactive—in other words, more usable to your audience.

INTEGRATED PROJECTS

SIMULATION

The Swift River Travel travel agency plans to expand its business to include guided adventure tours. Called Swift River Travel Adventures, the new division hopes to appeal to travelers interested in experiencing unusual activities in remote destinations. In preparation for the launch of the new business, the company is developing new marketing materials that incorporate multimedia solutions.

The following projects are set up to challenge your creativity and critical thinking skills. They provide suggestions instead of specific steps so you can develop your own ideas to explore the possibilities of multimedia applications. Each project requires the use of two or more multimedia programs such as graphics, animation, video, presentation systems, desktop publishing, or Web page development. Projects may also require use of supplementary programs such as word processors, text editors, spreadsheets, or databases. You may complete each project on your own or work in teams. For example, each team member could be responsible for completing the tasks associated with one program, and then the entire team could work together to integrate the results.

As you complete the projects, keep in mind everything you have learned about multimedia design and creation. Consider such factors as the audience and the message, as well as the basic principles of design and color. Think about whether a file will be printed or viewed on a computer screen and how that affects your work. At different stages, ask your classmates to review your work, and then use their suggestions to make improvements.

The following information is the company name, tagline, street address, telephone, fax, and Web site address that you should use when necessary in your documents and files:

Swift River Travel Adventures

"Seek Out the Unexpected"

56778 Gulf of Mexico Drive

Longboat Key, Florida 34228

Tel. (941) 555-5555

Fax (941) 555-5556

www.swiftriver.net

SCANS JOB 1

The company president wants a logo for the new Swift River Travel Adventures business to use on printed documents such as postcard mailers, brochures, and tour fact sheets. In this project, design and create the logo using a graphics program, and then use the logo to design and create a desktop publishing template and document.

1.   Use your graphics program to design and create the logo in a file saved with a descriptive name such as **Logo1**. You may start with an existing image, such as the logo created for Swift River Travel in the Graphics Unit Review, or you may start from scratch. Either way, you should include the company name or acronym and appropriate graphics elements. **Hint:** Adjust the size of the drawing area to just fit the graphic. That way, you will not export unnecessary blank space around the graphic. You may also want to change the background color from white to transparent if you have that option.

2.   When the logo is complete, optimize and export the file in a format suitable for use in printed documents, and save it with a descriptive name such as **Logo2**.

3.   Use your desktop publishing program to plan and create a template for a tour fact sheet. Swift River Travel uses fact sheets to print information about different tours to include in packets sent to potential customers. For example, a tour fact sheet may include a sample itinerary; information about the location, such as weather and sights; information about lodging; and so on. The publication should be a standard, letter-sized page with 1-inch margins, similar to letterhead stationery. It should include the logo graphics file as well as the company name, address, phone, fax, and Web site information either in the header or footer area, but the main body of the page should be blank so there is space for the customized tour fact information.

4. When the template file is complete, save it with a descriptive name such as **SRTFacts** and close it.

5. Use the Internet to research kayaking along the Maine Island Trail in Musgongus Bay, Maine. Try to locate information about the different islands, weather, water conditions, notable attractions, and camping facilities. You may also want to download a picture or two. Record the information in a word processing or text file and save the file with a descriptive name such as **Kayakinfo**, or write it on paper. If you download pictures, save them with descriptive names in a format suitable for printing. Don't forget to include source citations.

6. Use your desktop publishing program to create a new publication based on the fact sheet template and save it with a descriptive name such as **Kayak**.

7. Use the information you gathered about kayaking to create a customized fact sheet about a kayaking tour in Maine. Format and position the text and graphics appropriately on the page.

8. When the publication is complete, print it. Save and close all open files and programs.

JOB 2

The marketing director thinks that an animated version of the new logo would appeal to visitors to the Swift River Travel Web site. In this project, use your graphics program to modify the logo image for use in an animation program, and then use the result to create an animation file.

1. Start by planning how you want to animate the logo. For example, do you want to animate it as a whole, or do you want to animate individual parts? You could have the entire logo spin in place, or you could animate just the text. Use storyboarding to visualize and plan the animation.

2. Use your graphics program to save a copy of the original image that you can modify as necessary to prepare it for animation, or create a new image file to animate.

3. Save the file with a descriptive name, such as **Logo3**.

4. When the image is ready, optimize and export it in a format suitable for use in an animation, with a descriptive name such as **Logo4**. Alternatively, export it directly to your animation program or launch your animation program and import the file.

5. Use your animation program to animate the logo as you planned in step 1. **Hint:** Make sure the Stage is just large enough to hold the animation.

6. Test the animation to make sure it plays smoothly and optimize it as necessary. Play it for your classmates and incorporate their suggestions into the animation.

7. When the animation is complete, save the changes and close all open files and programs.

SCANS

JOB 3

After seeing the animated logo, the company president thinks it would be a good idea to use the static logo image as a link from the Swift River Travel home page to a page about the adventure tours, and then use the animated logo on the adventure tour page. To complete this project, you may use Web pages you created in the Web Site Development Unit Review, or you may create Web pages from scratch. Export the logo graphic from your graphics program and insert it on the home page. You also export the animation from your animation program and insert it on the adventure tour page. To complete the project, you link the two pages.

1. Use your Web site development program to create a home page for Swift River Travel, or open an existing home page. Save the home page with a descriptive name, such as **SRTindex**. On the home page, be sure to include text announcing the new guided adventure tours. Format the text so it stands out on the page. Also, add the page to the site navigation links.

2. Create a Web page for the guided adventure tours and save it with a descriptive name such as **SRTpage2**. Coordinate the page with the home page in terms of layout, formatting, and navigation links. List information about sample tours. For example, you may include the kayaking information you gathered in Job 1. You can use the Internet to find ideas about other adventure tours to include, such as backpacking in Alaska, or river rafting in South America. Consider inserting pictures on the Web page. Don't forget to include source citations.

3. Use your graphics program to optimize and export the original logo image in a format suitable for use on a Web page. Save the exported file with a descriptive name, such as **Weblogo**.

4. Use your Web site development program to insert the new logo file on the SRT home page, near the text announcing the new guided adventure tours.

5. Create a link from the logo image to the SRT adventure tours page. Test the links between the two pages.

6. Use your animation program to publish and optimize the animated logo file in a format suitable for use on a Web page. Save the published file with a descriptive name such as **Webanilogo**.

7. Use your Web site development program to insert the new animated logo file on the SRT adventure tours page.

8. Test the page and the links between the two pages.

9. When you are satisfied with the results, save and close all files and programs.

ANS JOB 4

Swift River Travel wants to create an automated, computer-based presentation about a guided SCUBA diving adventure tour to Aruba that it can run in its Longboat Key office. Visitors to the office who see the presentation may become interested in the tour. In this project, you research SCUBA diving in Aruba on the Internet and use the information to create the presentation. You also use both the logo image and the logo animation in the presentation.

1. Use the Internet to gather information about Aruba and SCUBA diving. Try to find out different places to dive as well as general information about the island, such as its location, currency, weather, and ocean conditions. You might also look up general information about diving, such as certification requirements. Record the information in a word processing or text file with a descriptive name, such as **Diveinfo**. Consider organizing the information as an outline to help you create the presentation. You may also want to download and save some pictures for the presentation. Don't forget to include source information.

2. Use your presentation program and the information about diving in Aruba to create a presentation of at least seven slides. Save it with a descriptive name such as **Divepres**. Alternatively, if you set up the dive information word processing file as an outline, import it into your presentation program to create the presentation file.

3. Format the presentation using an appealing design template, colors, and fonts. Insert graphics, such as the pictures you downloaded from the Internet. Apply slide transitions and animations as necessary, keeping in mind that the presentation will play on an unattended computer monitor in the travel agency office.

4. Test the presentation and show it to your classmates. Incorporate their suggestions in the presentation file.

5. Use your animation program to optimize and publish the animated logo file in a format suitable for use in a presentation. Publish the file with a descriptive name such as **Presanilogo**. **Hint:** You may want to change the background color of the Stage to coordinate with the design template you chose for your presentation.

6. Use your presentation program to insert the animation on the title slide. Set it to play automatically when the presentation starts.

7. Test the presentation and make changes and improvements as necessary.

8. Use your graphics program to optimize and export the original logo file in a format suitable for use in a presentation. Save the file with a descriptive name such as **Preslogo**.

9. Insert the logo on the presentation's slide master, so it is displayed on every slide in the presentation. Size and position the image for the best effect.

10. Test the presentation and make changes and improvements as necessary.

11. When you are satisfied with the results, save the file and close all open files and programs.

JOB 5

The presentation is such a success that the president wants it to reach a wider audience. In this project, you save the presentation as a Web site and then link it to the company's adventure travel Web page.

1. Use your presentation graphics program to save the diving presentation as a Web site. Give the Web site file a descriptive name, such as **Presweb**.

2. Test the presentation Web site, and set properties and make changes as necessary.

3. Use your Web site development program to incorporate the presentation Web site as part of the Swift River Travel Web site.

4. Set up links between the adventure travel tour page and the presentation Web site.

5. Test the links and make changes and improvements as necessary.

6. When you have finished, save and close all files and programs.

SCANS JOB 6

The first adventure tour returned and the guides brought back some video footage. In this project, you prepare the video and then insert it in the presentation. You then update the presentation Web site.

1. Use a video camera to record footage to illustrate an adventure tour. Make creative use of the area where you live or go to school. For example, you can shoot video that could be used to illustrate backpacking while you are walking through trees; video of a pond could appear to be any body of water. Alternatively, you may find some video clips on the Internet that are available with permission. You can also take "still" pictures with a digital camera to use as source clips.

2. Use your video program to edit and enhance the video for insertion in a presentation. Consider whether to incorporate titles or any special effects. If you use still photos, consider adding motion effects. Save the file with a descriptive name, such as **SRTvideo**. Export the file in a format you can use in a presentation, such as AVI.

3. Insert the video in the presentation about the diving tour, or create a new presentation about a different tour and insert the video in that.

4. Update the presentation Web site to include the changes, or, if you created a new presentation, save it as a new Web site and link it to the Swift River Travel home page.

5. Test the Web site and all links. Make changes as necessary.

6. When you are finished, save and close all open files and programs.

APPENDIX A

THE WINDOWS OPERATING SYSTEM

Microsoft Windows is the *operating system* that controls the way your computer works. An operating system is a software program that provides the instructions that allow you to communicate with your computer and all of its attached devices. Among other things, you use Windows to launch and exit programs, to find and open files, and to install new programs and hardware devices. This appendix covers some useful Windows features.

About Windows

There are different versions of Windows, but they all function in basically the same way. Information is displayed in *windows*, or rectangular areas, on your desktop. Some windows, called *folders*, are used to store files just like paper folders hold paper files in your desk drawer. When you open a folder window, it displays a list of all the files stored in that folder. Other windows, called program windows, are used to display a running program. There are also windows called *dialog boxes* that convey information between you and your computer.

Windows has a *graphical user interface* (GUI), which means you use easy-to-understand visual elements to communicate with your computer. Pictures called *icons* represent programs. Plain English commands are listed on easy-to-find *menus*. You can use a mouse or a keyboard or a combination of the two to make selections. One of the most convenient features of Windows is that it provides a common platform for all Windows programs. This means there are similarities in the way different programs look and function, so they are easier to learn and use.

The Windows Desktop

Depending on your version of Windows and the way your computer or network is set up, when you turn on your computer, you see either the Windows *desktop* or a *sign-in* screen. The Windows desktop is the main screen or workspace from which you can access all the tools you need to use your computer. The sign-in screen lists the names of all the people authorized to use the computer. From the sign-in screen, you click your name and then enter your password, if necessary, to display the desktop.

The default Windows XP desktop is shown in Figure A-1. Your desktop may look quite different because different versions of Windows have different default desktops, and your computer may be customized with different programs, different colors, and a different background. In any case, you should be able to locate the components described in Table A-1. You can also use *ScreenTips* to identify elements on your screen. ScreenTips are descriptions that appear when the mouse pointer rests on an item such as an icon or a *button*.

FIGURE A-1
Default Windows XP desktop

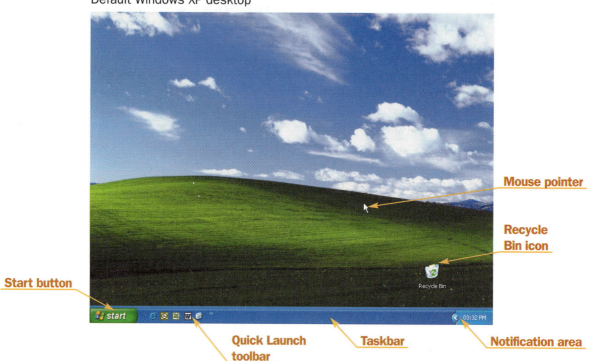

Mouse pointer

Recycle Bin icon

Start button

Quick Launch toolbar

Taskbar

Notification area

TABLE A-1
Desktop Components

COMPONENT NAME	DESCRIPTION
Start button	A button on the taskbar used to open the Start menu, from which you can access everything stored on your computer, including programs and files.
Taskbar	A row that usually appears at the bottom of the screen, used to display buttons and icons that provide quick access to common tasks. The taskbar displays the Start button, the Notification area, and buttons representing open programs and files. You can also opt to display toolbars such as Quick Launch on the taskbar.
Quick Launch toolbar	A list of icons representing commonly used programs. Click an icon to launch the program.
Recycle Bin icon	An icon representing the Recycle Bin folder, where deleted files and folders are stored until you remove them permanently.

TABLE A-1 (continued)

COMPONENT NAME	DESCRIPTION
Notification area	An area at the end of the taskbar used to display information about system components. Usually, the clock/calendar is displayed in the Notification area, as well as information about hardware devices such as printers and networks that are currently in use.
Mouse pointer	The mouse pointer indicates the current location of the mouse on your screen. It usually looks like an arrow, but the mouse pointer can change in shape depending on the current action. For example, it looks like an hourglass when the computer is busy processing a command.

Use the Mouse

You use your mouse and keyboard to make selections and issue commands in Windows. The mouse pointer represents the current location of the mouse on your screen. You move the mouse pointer by sliding the mouse on your desk or on a mouse pad. The four basic mouse actions are click, double-click, right-click, and click-and-drag.

■ *Click* means to press and release the left mouse button. This action is usually done to select an item, but sometimes is used to launch a program or open a window.

■ *Double-click* means to press and release the mouse button twice in rapid succession. Use this action to launch a program or open a window.

■ *Right-click* means to press and release the right mouse button. Right-click is used to open a shortcut menu of common commands.

■ *Click-and-drag* means to press and hold the left mouse button, and then slide the mouse to a different location. Click-and-drag is used for moving selected items.

Your mouse may also have a scroll wheel. Spin the wheel to shift the screen display up and down through the contents of a window.

> **Note** ☑
>
> If the taskbar is not displayed, your computer probably has been customized to hide it when it is not in use. This leaves more room to display data on the screen. Move the mouse pointer to the side of the screen where the taskbar is usually displayed (try the bottom first), and it should appear.

> **Note** ☑
>
> By default, mice are set up for right-handed users. If you are left handed, ask your instructor for information about seting up the mouse for your use.

Use the Keyboard

In addition to the standard text characters and numbers, most computer keyboards have special keys for quickly accessing computer features and commands. Table A-2 describes some common Windows keys.

TABLE A-2
Common Windows keys

KEY	DESCRIPTION
Modifier keys (Ctrl, Alt, Shift)	These keys are used in combination with other keys or mouse actions to select commands or perform actions. For example, pressing the Ctrl key and the *S* key at the same time usually saves the current file.
Directional keys	The directional keys include the up, down, left, and right arrows, as well as the Home, End, Page Up, and Page Down keys. These keys move the insertion point or selection box around the screen, or shift the display to show a different part of a window.
Enter key	The Enter key is used to execute a command or to start a new paragraph when you are keying text.
Escape key (Esc)	The Escape key is used to cancel a command.
Editing keys	The editing keys include Insert, Delete, and Backspace. They are used when you are keying data to control the way information is entered.
Function keys (F1–F12)	Usually found in a row above the standard keyboard keys, these keys are often assigned as shortcut keys for commands in programs. For example, F9 is often used to update information, and F2 is often used to repeat the most recent action.
Windows logo key	Usually located on either side of the spacebar, this key is used to open or close the Start menu, and in combination with other keys for other purposes.
Application key	Usually found to the right of the spacebar, this key is used in place of a right-click to open a shortcut menu of commands.

Launch a Program

Depending on how your computer is set up, there may be program icons displayed on the desktop or the taskbar. If so, click or double-click an icon to launch the program. If the program is not represented by a desktop icon, use the Start menu. The Start menu displays links to commonly used programs. Click the program name to launch the program. Figure A-2 shows both the Windows XP Start menu (on the left) and the Classic Windows Start menu (on the right).

FIGURE A-2
Windows XP Start menu and Classic Windows Start menu

To access any program installed on your computer, use the All Programs menu. Click the Start button to open the Start menu, and then click Programs or All Programs. A list of all programs installed on your computer is displayed, as shown in Figure A-3. Click the name of the program you want to launch. The program opens in a program window on the desktop.

Note ☑

If there is a right-pointing arrowhead next to a menu item, that means the item has a *submenu*. Click the item to open the submenu, and then click the program you want to launch. If there is an ellipse (…), it means the command opens a dialog box. If there is a shortcut key combination, press that combination to quickly select the command without using a menu.

FIGURE A-3
All Programs menu

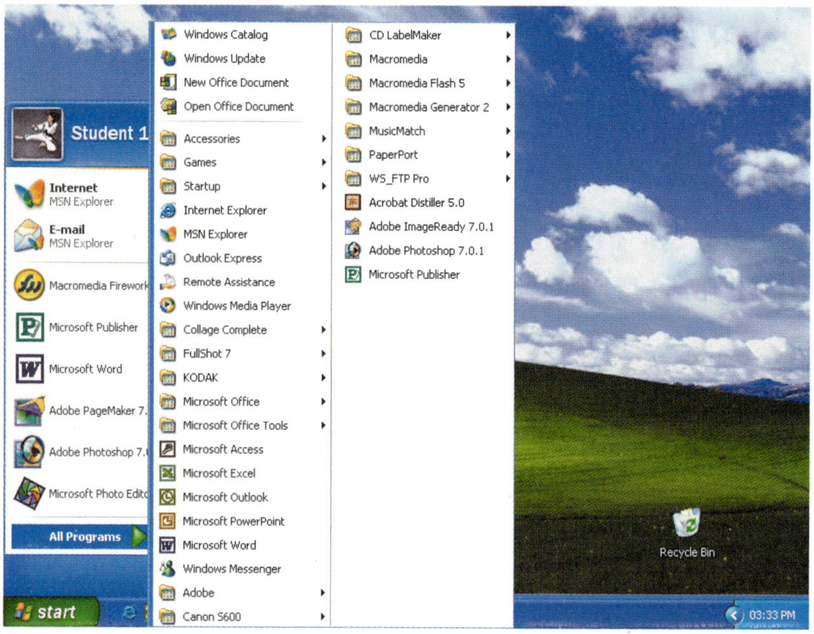

Most program windows have common elements, such as a title bar, a menu bar, and a toolbar. To exit a program, you can click the Program Close button, which is an X in the upper-right corner of the window, or you can click File on the menu bar, and then click Exit. A typical program window is shown in Figure A-4.

FIGURE A-4
Microsoft WordPad program window

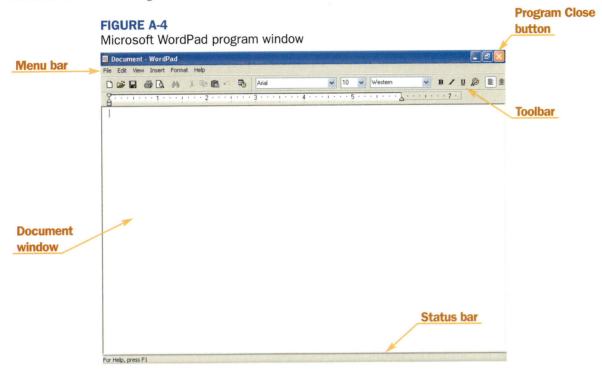

The Windows Filing System

One of the main functions of Windows is to help you keep the contents of your computer organized. Windows uses a multilevel filing system called Windows Explorer to keep track of *files* and *folders*. Files are the documents that store data, and folders are storage areas where you place files and other folders so you can find them easily.

Storage Devices

At the base of the filing system are the *disk drives* or other storage devices, which are the hardware devices on which the file and folder data is written electronically. Local storage devices are attached directly to your computer. Network storage devices may be attached anywhere on the network. You may have one or more of the following attached directly to your computer or to your network:

- Hard disk drive, which is fixed inside the computer case
- Floppy disk drive, which has a slot so you can insert and remove a disk
- CD or DVD drive, which has a drawer in which you can insert and remove a CD or DVD disk

Disk drives are named using letters. A floppy disk drive is always named drive A. If there is a second floppy disk drive, it is called drive B. The hard disk drive stored in your computer is usually called drive C. Additional drives are named using consecutive letters, so a CD drive may be drive D, a DVD drive may be drive E, and so on. You can usually add descriptive names or labels to the drive letter to help identify the storage device. To see a list of your *local* storage devices, click the Start button and then click My Computer on the Start menu. The My Computer window opens as shown in Figure A-5. Alternatively, double-click the My Computer icon on the Windows desktop. Remember, the contents of the My Computer window vary depending on the contents of your computer system.

Did You Know?

There are two basic types of CD drives: CD-ROM drives, which can read but not write information on a CD; and CD-RW drives, which can read and write information on a CD. To write information on a CD, you must have a CD-RW drive and CD-R or CD-RW discs. Some DVD drives can write information on DVDs, as well.

FIGURE A-5
My Computer window in Windows XP

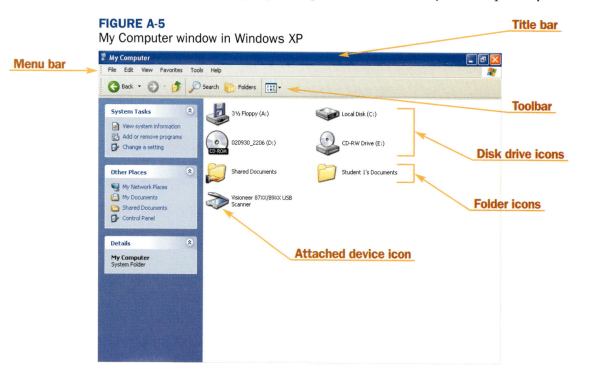

Folders

Files can be stored directly on a disk, but to keep things organized, you usually store them in folders, which are then stored in other folders, or on a disk. Windows comes with some default folders used for storing system information and data files. You can create new folders at any time. The default folders are usually listed on the Start menu or are represented by icons on the desktop. The following list describes some of the Windows default folders:

Note ☑

To see the network storage devices, click the Start button, and then click My Network Places on the Start menu to open the My Network Places window. Alternatively, double-click the Network Neighborhood icon on the Windows desktop.

- My Documents is the default storage location for data files.

- Shared Documents is used to store documents that can be opened by anyone on the network.

- My Computer displays the components of your computer system, such as disk drives and other attached devices.

- Control Panel provides access to your computer components so you can customize and control settings and options.

- Recycle Bin is used to store deleted files and folders until you choose to remove them permanently.

Navigate Through the Contents of Your Computer

To view the contents of a disk or folder, you open the window that displays the item, and then open the item itself. For example, to see the contents of a floppy disk in drive A, you click the Start button to open the Start menu and then click My Computer to open the My Computer window. In the My Computer window, you double-click the drive A icon to open the drive A window.

Most folder windows have similar characteristics, including a title bar, a menu bar, and possibly toolbars. The contents list is displayed in the main folder window. Some versions of Windows display additional information in the Explorer Bar pane along the left side of the window. You can change the contents of the Explorer Bar depending on what you are doing. By default, it displays the links bar, which lists links to common folders such as My Computer or My Documents. Click a link to open the folder.

You can change the Explorer Bar to display Folders if you want to navigate using a hierarchical tree diagram as shown in Figure A-6 (in versions of Windows prior to Windows XP, this feature is called Windows Explorer). Click the Folders button to display the hierarchical tree. Click an item in the tree to display its contents in the main folder window. Click a plus sign next to an item to expand the tree, or click a minus sign to collapse the tree.

FIGURE A-6
Folders Explorer Bar in Windows XP

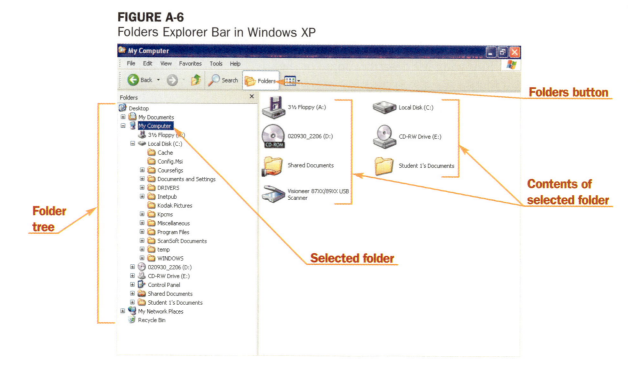

There may also be Back, Forward, and Up commands on the toolbar at the top of the window. Click Back or Forward to scroll through all of the windows you have opened recently, and click Up to open the folder in which the current folder is stored.

Change the Window Display

You can change the way items are displayed in a folder window. Click the Views button on the toolbar or the View command on the menu bar, and then click one of the following:

■ Thumbnails to display an icon or picture with the item name.

■ Tiles to display a smaller icon or picture with the item name, type, and size.

■ Icons to display a smaller icon or picture with the item name.

- List to list the items by name.

- Details to list the items including specific information such as name, type, size, and modification date, as shown in Figure A-7.

FIGURE A-7
Folder in Details view

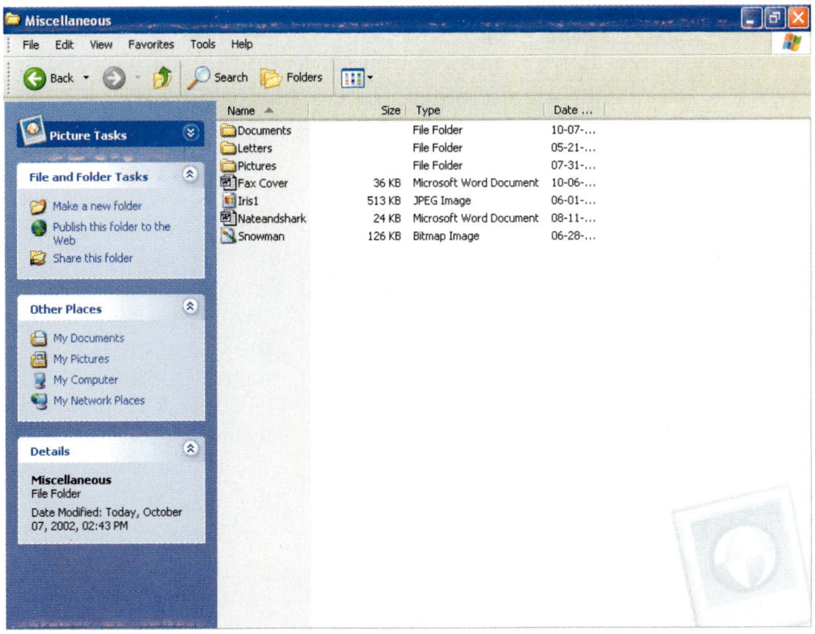

You can also change the sort order and grouping of the items in a folder window. Click View on the menu bar and then click Arrange Icons by. Click the sort order or grouping option you want to use.

> **Note**
>
> In some versions of Windows, folders containing picture files have a Filmstrip view option you can use to preview the images.

Work with Windows

As mentioned, information is displayed in windows on the Windows desktop. The two basic types of windows are program windows, used to display an open program, and folder windows, used to display lists of the contents of folders and storage devices. You can have more than one window open at a time, but only one can be active. The active window is the one in which you are currently working. All open windows have a button on the taskbar. To make a different window active, click its taskbar button. If there is not enough room on the taskbar to display buttons for each open window, Windows may group the buttons according to program and display one button for each group. When you click a group button, a menu of windows appears so you can click the specific window you want to make active.

Size and Position Windows

Windows open in the size and position they were in when you last used them. All windows have control buttons in the upper-right corner that you can use to change the window's size and position.

- Click the Maximize button to increase the size of a window to fill the entire desktop.

- Click the Minimize button to reduce a window so it is just a button on the taskbar.

- Click the Restore Down button to restore a maximized window to its previous size and position. The Restore Down button is available only in a maximized window.

- Click the Close button to close the window.

You can also drag a window by its title bar to move it to a different location on the desktop, and you can drag the borders of a window that is not maximized to change its size.

> **Note** ✅
>
> The current document or file may also have control buttons in the upper-right corner of the window. The program control icons are on the title bar, while the document control buttons are on the menu bar.

To arrange all open windows on the desktop, right-click a blank area of the taskbar and select one of the following commands:

- Cascade Windows to overlap the windows, showing only the title bars. The active window is on top, as shown in Figure A-8.

- Tile Windows Horizontally to arrange the windows across the width of the screen. You can see a portion of all windows. The title bar of the active window is brighter than the others.

- Tile Windows Vertically to stack the windows from the top to the bottom of the screen. You can see a portion of all windows, and the title bar of the active window is brighter than the others.

FIGURE A-8
Cascading windows

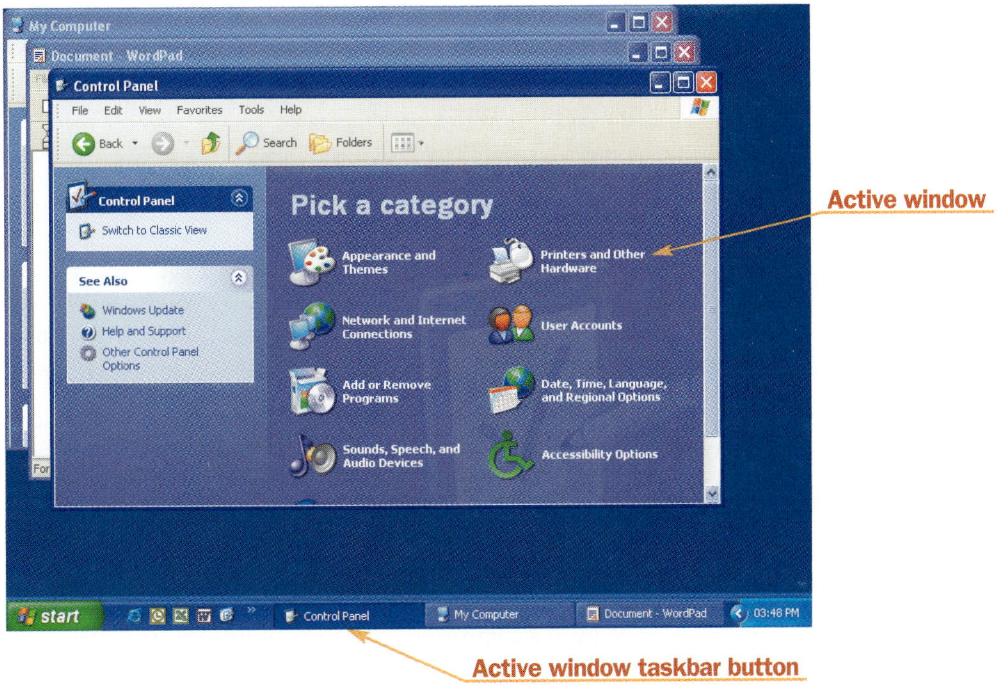

Install a Program

If you purchase a new program, you must install it on your computer so you can use it. Usually, you install a program from a CD-ROM. When you insert the CD-ROM in the CD-ROM drive, the installation usually begins automatically. You simply follow the instructions on the screen to install and set up the program. During the installation, you may have to enter information about your computer or about the program you are installing. For example, you may have to enter a key or code number and select the folder in which you want to store the program files. If the program does not start automatically, you can use the Add New Programs command in the Control Panel. If you use the Add New Programs command, you need to know the name of the installation or set-up file. Usually, it is setup.exe or install.exe.

Before you purchase a new program, read the package to make sure it is compatible with your computer system. The system requirements are usually listed on the back or side of the package. Most stores do not let you return opened software. To determine if a program is compatible, ask yourself the following questions:

- Does the program run on the version of Windows you have installed?

- Does your computer have enough memory to run the program?

- Does your computer have enough disk space to install the program?

Note

You may need to obtain permission from a system administrator or network administrator before installing a new program.

- Does the program require a particular hardware device or component, such as a video adapter card or monitor resolution?

You can locate information about your computer system in the System Properties dialog. To open the System Properties dialog box, right-click the My Computer icon and then click Properties, or open the Control Panel and either double-click the System icon, or click *See basic information about your computer*. In the System Properties dialog box, you can locate such information as the version of Windows running on your computer, the amount of memory you have installed, and the processor speed.

To find out how much disk space you have available, open My Computer, right-click on the icon for your hard drive, and click Properties.

Install a Hardware Device

*H*ardware *devices* are components that are connected to your computer system and controlled by your computer's microprocessor. Hardware devices can include your printer, modem, scanner, digital camera, video camera, microphone, speakers, keyboard, monitor, mouse, and disk drives.

> **Note** ☑
>
> You may need permission from a system administrator or network administrator to install a hardware device.

Before you can use a hardware device, you must install it on your computer. The first step in hardware installation is to connect the device to the computer. Some devices, such as internal modems, are attached to slots inside the computer, and other devices, such as printers, are attached by cables to ports on the outside of the computer. Still others, such as a wireless mouse, communicate via wireless connections such as infrared or satellite. Local devices are attached directly to your computer, and network devices are attached to the network. If a device installs inside the computer, you may want to consult a professional. If the device connects to a port outside the computer, you can install it yourself.

Next, you must install the correct device driver, which is a software program that provides the instructions that let the device communicate with Windows. Usually, the device driver comes on a floppy disk or CD-ROM with the device. Alternatively, you may be able to download it from the manufacturer's Web site. Windows comes with drivers for common hardware devices.

In most cases, when you plug the device into your computer, Windows detects it automatically and begins the installation procedure. Simply follow the instructions displayed on your screen to complete the installation and set-up. If the installation does not start automatically, you can use the Add New Hardware command in the Control Panel.

Use a Help Program

*W*indows and most Windows programs come with built-in help programs you can use to get information while you work. The Help program depends on the version of Windows you are using.

To start the Windows XP Help program, click the Start button to open the Start menu and then click Help and Support. The Help and Support Center screen is displayed, as shown in Figure A-9. You can click a link to go to a general topic page, from which you can click links to locate the specific information you need, or you can key a topic in the Search box and click the Go button. Windows displays a list of links to information about the topic.

FIGURE A-9
Windows XP Help and Support Center

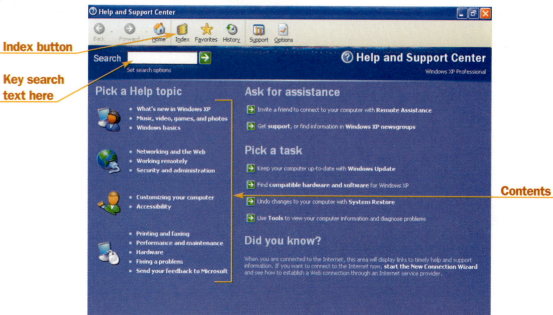

To start the Help program in a version of Windows prior to XP, click the Start button to open the Start menu and then click Help.

The program window has two panes. On the left you can select to use the Contents, Index, or Search tools. The specific help information is displayed on the right.

Note ✅

The Help programs that come with Windows programs all use a similar method for locating topics. You'll find that most offer a Contents page, an Index page, and a Search page in the left pane, and display the help information in the right pane.

■ Contents lists the major topics for which help is available. Click a book icon to display a list of subtopics, and then click a subtopic to display the information.

■ Index provides an alphabetical list of help topics. You can scroll through the list to find the topic you need, or you can key a topic in the keyword search box to jump to that topic. Click a topic in the list to display the information.

■ Search lets you search through all of the available help pages for a keyword. Key the word in the keyword search box, and then click the List Topics button to display a list of topics that contain that word. Click a topic in the list to display the information.

GLOSSARY

A

A/B roll A video-editing technique for combining multiple clips by switching back and forth between two source tape players.

Action item A reminder to do something related to a presentation. You can create action items while giving a presentation and then print them out or send them to Outlook as tasks.

Actions Compact programming code that defines interactivity.

ActionScript A popular scripting language resembling JavaScript.

Active Current, or in use.

Additive colors Colors that, when combined in full, value add up to white. Red, green, and blue are additive colors.

Adjustment handle A handle with a yellow dot that appears when particular AutoShapes are selected. Drag the handle to adjust the shape of the AutoShape object.

Align Position an object horizontally or vertically relative to the top, bottom, left, or right of the publication area.

Align left Format that lines words up straight against the left margin of the Web page and forms a jagged edge on the right side of the page.

Align right Format that lines words up straight against the right margin of the Web page and forms a jagged edge on the left side of the page.

All-over balance A type of balance in which objects are positioned using a grid-like design with focal points scattered throughout to direct the eye through the design.

Analog Data represented by physically measurable quantities. Analog video includes television broadcasts and VHS tapes.

Analogous colors Colors that are next to each other on the color wheel.

Analog-to-digital converter A device that converts data from analog (physical) to digital (computer) form.

Anchor tags Tags that create hypertext links. The anchor tag requires a hypertext reference attribute and then the name of a destination file as its value.

Animated GIF A specialized GIF file where two or more graphics cycle, creating animation effects.

Animation Graphics that display motion. Animations can include moving objects, blinking logos, flashing advertisements, product demonstrations, and tutorials.

Animation scheme A set of animations that control the appearance of an object on a slide. For example, you can have the slide title zoom in from the right, followed by the fading in of each item in a bulleted list.

ANSI (American National Standards Institute) A set of standard text-based characters that all computers can read and understand.

Ascenders The parts of characters that extend up above the main line of text.

ASCII (American Standard Code for Information Interchange) A set of standard text-based characters that all computers can read and understand.

Aspect ratio The relationship between an object's height and width. For example, an object that's twice as high as it is wide is said to have an aspect ratio of 2:1.

Attribute A definition or command added to an HTML tag that expands, refines, and clarifies what the tag is intended to do.

Audio effects Effects applied to audio tracks.

AUP (Acceptable Use Policy) Also called Terms of Use policies. Includes rules to protect Web sites and networks from unauthorized use, hackers, viruses, and abuse. The do's and don'ts of a Web site and the networks that support them.

AutoCorrect A list of common spelling errors and their corrected spellings. Microsoft Office programs use this list to automatically correct common errors as you type.

AutoRecover A Microsoft Office XP file that contains the changes made to a document, such as a PowerPoint presentation. The AutoRecover file is used to recover data not yet saved to a document, in the case of a sudden loss of power or system crash.

AutoShape A pre-drawn object, such as a banner, star, block arrow, etc. You create the shape simply by dragging to establish its location and size—the outline of the shape and any details are automatically drawn for you.

AVI Audio Video Interleave file format. The most common video file format used on the Windows platform.

B

Balance A basic principle of design that describes the visual weight of objects and the way they are arranged.

Bandwidth The rate at which a network or modem can transfer data.

Banner headline A headline that extends across the entire width of the page.

Baseline The bottom of a line of text.

Bevel An effect used to create the illusion of three-dimensionality by making the object appear to rise out of the drawing area.

Bindery A business that folds, binds, and trims publications. Usually part of a printing company's operations.

Binding Securing pages or sections of a book or booklet using stitching, staples, wire, plastic, tape, or glue.

Bitmap images Images represented by storing a value for each dot (pixel) in the image. (As opposed to vector images, which are created using mathematical formulas.)

Bleed Printing that extends to the edges of the paper.

Boundaries Nonprinting lines that mark the outer edges of objects such as text boxes and frames.

Bounding box A rectangular shape with selection handles displayed around a selected object.

Brightness A measurement of the amount of white or black added to a hue. Sometimes called *tint*. Also, a description of paper indicating how much light the paper reflects.

Broadcast A presentation transmitted live over the Internet/intranet, with accompanying live video and audio if desired, to audience participants who cannot be present in the audience locally. Viewers see the broadcast within their Web browser. In addition, the broadcast is recorded in a file that allows users to view the presentation at a later time if needed.

Broken link Hyperlink that leads to a dead end or that goes to the wrong place.

Bullet A symbol that precedes each item in a bulleted list. Typically, a bullet is a small circle, although it can be any graphic image.

Button An object in an animation or on a Web page that performs a specific task when a user clicks it with a mouse.

C

Caching A system where Web pages and their associated graphics are stored locally on a client computer to reduce Internet traffic and download wait time the next time the page is viewed.

Callout Text used to call attention to something else on the page. Usually connected by a line to the particular item.

Camera-ready Pages or artwork ready to be captured on film for reproduction.

Canvas In some programs, the term used to describe the drawing area.

Capture Acquiring video or images from an external source.

Capture card A card you can install in your computer that converts analog video to digital form for capture.

Cast coated paper Paper that has a finish similar to a glossy photograph.

CD-ROM Compact Disc–Read-Only Memory. A compact disc used to distribute data files.

Cell A part of a table, defined by the intersection of a column and a row within the table. Data is entered into each cell, where it can be formatted separately from other cells.

Chart A graphical representation of related numerical data, such as the sales revenues from three different regions of a large company or the number of various products shipped in a week.

Clip A video segment. A video is usually made up of a number of separate clips.

Clip art Pictures and other types of files that can be inserted into a document. Typically, clip art includes only drawn images and not photos, although lately the definition has been expanding to include both. Clip art images are typically copyright free, meaning that you can use them as much as you like, for any purpose, without worrying about paying a fee. PowerPoint comes with a collection of copyright-free clip art and photos, but you may be able to add to this collection with images you find on the Internet.

Clipboard A temporary storage area in the computer's memory, where data that has been cut or copied is stored until it is pasted into a new location.

CMY A color system or model used for printing that creates colors by blending different levels of cyan, magenta, and yellow.

CMYK A color system or model used for printing that creates colors by blending different levels of cyan, magenta, yellow, and black.

Code HTML tags are often called code.

Codec Short for **c**ompressor/**dec**ompressor. A codec is either hardware or software that converts an analog sound or video into a compressed digital format and then back again.

Color bar A linear palette that displays gradations in color ranging from red to violet.

Color depth The number of colors used in an image or on a screen.

Color palette A set of up to 256 colors that may be used in a file.

Color scheme Set of coordinated colors applied to all text, bullets, hyperlinks, shadows, fills, and the slide background. The color scheme is part of the *design template* in PowerPoint. Also, when colors are mixed and balanced for use throughout a Web site, contributing to a consistent look and feel.

Color system A system used to define standard colors, such as RGB (red, green, blue), which is used for computer monitors, or CMYK (cyan, magenta, yellow, black), which is used for printing. Sometimes called a color model.

Color wheel A circular palette that displays gradations in color ranging from red to violet.

Compatible Able to work together.

Complementary colors Colors that are opposite each other on the color wheel.

Composite A proof that includes all text, colors, graphics, and other objects on the same page.

Compress Shrink in size.

Compression Reducing the space required to store data by efficiently encoding the content.

Connection speed See *Bandwidth*.

Consistency The use of repetition to create a uniform and predictable design.

Content A group of special elements that can be placed on a slide, including clip art, graphic files, charts, tables, organization charts, and media files such as sound or video.

Contrast The degree of separation between the color values of different parts of the same publication. Also, a basic principle of design in which elements with opposite or complementary features are juxtaposed to create visual interest.

Cool colors The colors ranging from green to violet on the color wheel.

Coordinates Points on the drawing area used to position an object. The X coordinate positions the object horizontally and the Y coordinate positions the object vertically.

Crawling text Text that moves horizontally from one side of the screen to the other.

Crop To cut or remove portions of an image.

Crop marks Lines printed on a proof to indicate where the page should be cut down to size.

Cross dissolve A transition that fades one clip out and the next one in.

Custom show A collection of slides from a presentation. A custom show within a presentation displays only specific slides that relate to a particular audience.

D

Data series A row of data in the datasheet of a chart.

Datasheet A sheet of cells into which data is entered for a chart. Cells are formed on the datasheet by the intersection of columns and rows.

Default A standard setting or mode of operation.

Default colors The colors that are preset or predefined by the Web browser, before any changes are made by a Web designer.

Descenders   The parts of characters that extend below the baseline of text.

Design template   A collection of coordinated colors, backgrounds, text, and bullet styles that can be applied to selected slides in a single step.

Destination   The location to which you copy a file or paste a selection.

Device driver   A software program that enables a computer to communicate with a hardware device.

Diagram   A conceptual chart that's designed to show relationships. For example, an organization chart depicts the relationships between people in an organization.

Digital camera   A camera that takes pictures in digital format.

Digital data   Data represented in numerical form such as in a computer.

Digital video   Video data stored as a sequence of individual bitmapped images.

Digital video (DV) format   A digital format commonly used for digital cameras and digital video devices.

Discretionary hyphens   In some desktop publishing programs, hyphens that you insert manually.

Distort   To change the height or width of an object without retaining the original proportions.

Distribute   Adjust the space between objects in an image or publication.

Dithering   A process used to approximate colors that are not part of a file's color palette.

Domain name   Name by which Web site domains are known to Web visitors.

Dot leader   Dots repeated along the line preceding a tab stop.

Downloading   Copying files from one computer to another, usually from a network to a computer on the network. Also, the process of getting files from a remote server and placing them on a local hard drive.

Drawing area   The area within the document window in which you draw and edit images. Sometimes called the *canvas* or *stage*.

Drawing objects   Objects such as shapes that you draw in a document using the drawing tools. Usually, drawing objects are vectors.

Dropped capital   A decorative effect in which the first character in a paragraph is increased in size and inset or offset from the other lines in the paragraph.

Duplex printing   Printed on both sides of a sheet of paper.

DVD   Digital Video Disc, or sometimes, Digital Versatile Disc. The most commonly used video disc format.

E

Em dash   A special character that is roughly the width of a letter *M*. Usually used in place of two hyphens.

Embed   Place a copy of the fonts or sounds used in a presentation into the file so that the fonts or sounds are available on whatever computer it is played on. Embedding fonts and/or sounds makes files a bit larger. If fonts are not embedded, then they must be installed on the computer running the presentation, or Windows substitutes the closest looking font that is installed. If sound files are not embedded, they are linked, which means they must be copied to the new computer with the presentation, or they won't be found and can't be played. Also, to paste an object into a publication without maintaining a connection to the source file.

Emboss   An effect used to make an object appear to be inset into the drawing area. A raised emboss effect makes the object appear to rise out of the drawing area.

Emphasis   The use of color, lines, or shapes to highlight or focus attention on a particular aspect of an image.

En dash   A special character that is roughly half the width of an em dash. Usually used in place of the words *to* or *through*.

End title   A title that appears at the end of a video that usually includes the credits.

Executable file   A program file that can run on your computer.

Expandable text block   A text block that increases in width as characters are keyed so all characters fit on one line.

Export   Producing a video or still image file in a desired format or saving a file in a format that can be used by a different program.

F

Facing pages   A left-hand page and a right-hand page set to open opposite each other. Also called *mirrored pages* or *two-page spread*.

Field   A code representing a value that may change, such as a page number.

File format   The way data in a file is saved. Usually, a file format is associated with a particular program so that the program can read the data in the file.

Fill   The area inside a shape.

Finish   The characteristics of the surface of paper.

Fixed-width text block   A text block of a predetermined size in which text wraps from one line to the next.

Flip   To reverse an image horizontally or vertically.

Floating object   An object that can be sized and positioned anywhere on the page.

Font   A set of characters in a particular typeface, such as Times New Roman or Arial.

Font effects   Attributes applied to a character in a font set.

Font scheme   A collection of coordinated fonts.

Font size   The height of an uppercase letter in a font set measured in points.

Font style   The slant and weight of a character in a font set, i.e., attributes such as bold and italics that are applied to a font.

Footer   Information repeated at the bottom of every slide. Also, the area between the bottom margin and the bottom of the paper.

Formatting   Includes text design elements that add interest to Web pages.

Fps   Frames per second. The number of frames displayed during each second of a video or movie.

Frame   A placeholder object used to contain text or graphics. Also, a single image from the sequence of images that make up an animation or a video.

Frame inset   The margin between the edge of the frame and the text or graphics in the frame.

FTP   Short for File Transfer Protocol, ftp is a protocol (set of rules) that governs the transfer of files over the Internet.

G

Galleys   Printed proofs of publication pages.

GIF   Graphics Interchange Format. A format for storing images without losing quality that allows both static and animated image sequences. Gif images are limited to 256 colors and include the .gif extension in their names. They are popular for use on the World Wide Web and are used for cartoons, logos, graphics with transparent areas, and animations.

Glow   An effect that applies a highlight to an object. Glows apply a band of color around all edges, while inner glows apply a band of color inside the edges.

Grade   A rating used to categorize paper. There are seven basic grades: bond, uncoated book, coated book, text, cover, board, and specialty.

Gradient Color that shades gradually from a dark hue to a light hue.

Graphics Images that you use to enhance the appearance of a variety of projects, including drawings, photographs, cartoons, charts, and maps.

Graphics tablet A hardware device on which you write or draw with a stylus to input data into your computer.

Grayscale A color scheme that uses a range of blacks, whites, and grays.

Grid guides Nonprinting lines used to define columns and rows on pages in a publication and to assist in positioning and sizing objects.

Group Combine multiple objects into one unit.

Guides Nonprinting gridlines used to help align and position objects in a document.

Gutter The space between a margin and the binding, or between columns.

H

Halftone A reproduction of a photograph on paper.

Handles Small white circles that appear on the perimeter of a drawn object, such as a square or triangle, or a placeholder when that object/placeholder is selected. Drag the handles outward to make the object/placeholder bigger; drag them inward to make the object/placeholder smaller.

Hanging indent A paragraph in which the first line of text is closer to the left margin than the other lines in the paragraph. Sometimes also known as an *outdent*, a hanging indent is typically applied to a bulleted list to place the bullet (which is the first character on the first line) closer to the left margin, leaving the rest of the lines of text for that bulleted item farther away from the left margin and the bullet.

Hardware device A piece of hardware equipment, such as a printer or a modem, that is connected to a computer.

Header Information repeated at the top of every slide. Also, the area between the top margin and the top of the paper.

Hexadecimal code A standard alphanumeric value based on a combination of 16 letters and numbers (0, 1, 2, 3, 4, 5, 6, 7, 8, 9, A, B, C, D, E, and F) for identifying colors based on their components of red, green, and blue.

Hierarchical structure Web site structure that uses categories and subcategories, like a family tree with parents and children. A great way to organize large amounts of information.

Horizontal alignment The position of an object in relation to the left and right margins.

Horizontal rule A horizontal line inserted before or after a paragraph of text.

HSL color model Short for hue, saturation, luminance, the HSL color model defines a color based on its hue (color), saturation (the amount of gray in the color), and luminance (lightness or darkness of the hue). The HSL color model is sometimes also known as the HSB model, which stands for hue, saturation, and brightness.

HTML Short for HyperText Markup Language, HTML is a document description language that uses tags to mark up text. The tags describe how Web pages—their text, graphics, video, sound, animations, and so on—should be displayed by clients or browsers so the page elements can be properly viewed.

HTTP (Hypertext Transfer Protocol) A communication system used to transfer data over the World Wide Web between servers and clients.

Hue Color.

Hyperlink base A folder where objects linked from a presentation are assumed to be located. If the presentation is moved, you need only change the base's location to match the presentation's new location instead of editing each hyperlink in the presentation to point to the correct folder.

Hyphen　A character used to indicate the break in a word from the end of one line to the beginning of the next line.

Hyphenation zone　The area along the right margin in which words are hyphenated.

I

I-beam　The shape of the mouse pointer when you are working in a text-entering or text-editing mode.

IEEE 1394　An industry standard for connecting digital devices, including digital video cameras, to a computer. Also known as Firewire or iLink.

Import　Bringing graphics, video, or still images already on your computer into an animation or video-editing program. Also, opening a file created with one program in a different program.

Imposition　The placement and position of multiple pages printing on a single sheet of paper.

In point　The point at which to start copying from a source clip.

Indent　An extra amount of space between the left edge of a paragraph or bulleted list and the margin. PowerPoint does not support right indents.

Indents　Temporary margins set in a text box.

Information design　The aspect of Web site design that considers the information to be included on a Web site.

Inline graphic　A graphic displayed on the text baseline that can be aligned like any character of text.

In-line object　An object inserted like a character on a line of text.

Insertion edit　Adding content to a video by inserting it between existing clips.

Insertion point　A flashing vertical line that indicates where characters will be inserted in a text block.

Interaction design　The aspect of Web site design that considers how people move around or navigate a Web site.

Interactive　A feature that allows a viewer to respond to an animation by using buttons, links, menus, lists, and so on.

Intranets　Web sites that are private in nature are often called intranets and are reserved for specific groups of people. For example, a corporate intranet is available only to the employees of the company.

J

JavaScript　The most common scripting language in use.

JPEG　Joint Photographic Experts Group. An image compression method that trades off compression and image quality. This format is used for photographs and other high-color images. It supports millions of colors and can be compressed, but does not support transparency. Files in this format have the .jpg extension in their names.

Justified　An alignment option in which words are spaced so that the ends of lines are even with both the left and right margin.

K

Kerning　Spacing between specific pairs of characters.

Key term, Key word　Words selected as descriptive of the subject matter covered in a document, file, or Web page. Key words are often specified so a Web site can be indexed for a search engine.

Keyframe　A frame used to specify a change in an animation. Also, a frame compressed independently of other frames in a video.

Kiosk　A small, self-contained structure that provides information to passersby. Kiosks typically contain a computer and monitor. Some kiosks are interactive, allowing the user to select the information to view and occasionally provide information as well, such as preferences. Kiosks are popular in shopping malls, where they provide directions to specific stores or gather information on shopper preferences; in trade shows, where they display products for sale or provide information about a company; and at conferences, where they provide information on conference events.

Knock out In some programs, the term used to describe hiding an object as part of a special effect.

L

Landscape orientation (wide) A type of page orientation in which data is printed across the greatest dimension of the paper. For example, if you printed data in landscape orientation on 8.5-inch by 11-inch paper, the data would be printed across its 11-inch width.

Layer A transparent level on the Stage that can hold objects and enables objects to be manipulated separately from those on other layers.

Layout The arrangement of data on a slide.

Layout guides Nonprinting gridlines used on every page of a publication to ensure consistency throughout a document.

Leading The spacing between lines of text.

Legend Displays a symbol and a name for each of the *data series* in a chart.

Letterhead The text and graphics printed at the top or bottom of stationery, usually to identify a company name, address, and other contact information.

Linear gradient A gradient pattern in which the colors blend horizontally across an object.

Linear structure A Web site structure that has users view pages one at a time for step-by-step learning or if information is best viewed one Web page at a time in a certain order, as in a presentation.

Link Information that points to the location of sound files or other non-embedded objects used in a presentation. If sounds and objects are not embedded, they are linked. This means that these files must be copied to a similar location on a new computer if the presentation file is moved. Also, to paste an object in a publication maintaining a connection to the source file. When changes are made to the source file, the object can be updated.

Lobby page The opening Web page of a live broadcast. This is the page a user sees before the broadcast begins.

Logo A combination of text and graphics used as a symbol to represent a company or other organization.

Loop Replay a sound or movie file continually until stopped.

Loss A setting used to control compression by balancing file size with image quality.

M

Manual hyphens Hyphens that are inserted manually rather than automatically to control where a word breaks at the end of a line of text. In some programs, they are called *discretionary hyphens*.

Margins The area between the edges of the page and the objects in the document.

Mask An effect used to hide or accentuate a specific portion of an image.

Master page A model or template used to contain text and/or objects that appears on every page in the publication. In some programs, a publication can have more than one master page.

Masthead The banner headline displayed across the top of a newsletter. Also, a list of people involved in creating the publication.

MIDI A common sound file format. MIDI is short for Musical Instrument Digital Interface. A MIDI file contains data that represents individual notes on a musical scale, rather than entire waveforms.

Mirrored pages Facing pages or a two-page spread.

Mock-up A prototype, model, or sample of a publication.

Monochromatic A color scheme that uses black and one other color.

Motion path An animation effect in which an object on a slide moves along a defined path across the slide.

Motion path Path drawn on a guide layer to control path animation.

Movie In PowerPoint, both a video file and an animated GIF are considered "movies." In general, movies move independently of PowerPoint's animation feature. See also *Animation*.

MP3 A common sound file format. MP3 files record sound as digitized waveforms in a compressed format that results in a smaller file than a file recorded in WAV sound format.

MPEG Motion Pictures Expert Group. A file format and compression technique used for video discs such as DVDs and VCDs.

Music loop A short music sound clip, intended to be replayed continually (*looped*) to form a longer piece of music.

N

Native file format The default file format for a particular program.

Navigation system Allows users to find their way around a Web site.

Nested tags The universally recommended way to organize tags on a Web page, where the first tag used is the last tag closed and the most recent tag used is the first tag closed. For example, <B> <CENTER> </CENTER> </B>.

NTSC National Television Standards Committee. The format used for broadcast television in the United States.

O

Object An element of a slide, such as the title, subtitle, bulleted list, graphic, chart, or drawn rectangle, circle, and so on. Each object is individually selectable, so you can format it separately from the slide itself. Also, elements such as text boxes and graphics that are inserted or embedded in a publication file. Also, elements such as lines and shapes that comprise a drawing.

Onion skin A feature that enables you to view the contents of multiple frames onscreen at the same time.

Opacity A measurement of the level of transparency of color.

Opening title A title that appears at the beginning of a video that usually includes its name.

Optimize Prepare a file for export by selecting options to achieve the best combination of file size and quality. Also, to set options that best suit a particular purpose.

Orientation The way a document is printed across a sheet of paper. Portrait orientation—or tall—prints the document across the short side of a page, while landscape orientation—or wide—prints the document across the long side of the page. Also, the way text is positioned horizontally or vertically in a text block.

Out point The point at which to stop copying from a source clip.

Outdent An indent that pushes text towards the left margin. You typically use an outdent to move the first line of a bulleted item closer to the left margin so there's enough space for the text, and also so the bullet is more visible to readers and helps them navigate to important text.

Overlap A setting used when printing a large-sized publication on smaller, multiple sheets of paper. Overlap specifies how much of each sheet overlaps adjacent sheets to ensure that the content aligns correctly when the printed sheets are arranged. Sometimes called *tiling*.

Overlay edit Adding content to a video by over-writing portions of existing clips.

P

Page layout The organization used to design a page in a publication.

Page size The dimensions of the page on which a document is printed.

PAL Phase Alternation Line. The format used for broadcast television in Europe.

Pan The action of scrolling the drawing area to display a part that might otherwise be hidden outside the document window.

Panel Floating windows that contain commands, options, palettes, menus, and other features for quick reference while working in some programs.

Pantone Matching System A color system or model used to define spot color.

Paper size The dimensions of the paper on which a document is printed. Sometimes called *sheet size*.

Path animation Method of animating an object that requires the user to draw or create a path on a guide layer that the object follows.

Pattern A bitmap graphic used as a fill in some graphics programs. Also, a repetitive graphic design used in an image.

Picture frame A frame used as a placeholder for a graphics object.

Pixel A single tiny dot used as a unit of measure and to define images on a computer screen. Short for *picture element*. Also, a small dot of light capable of projecting colors on a computer monitor.

Placeholder The border that surrounds a title, subtitle, bulleted list, or numbered list. The place-holder is selected to format the text inside it.

Placeholder text Replaceable text, typically found in a presentation created by the AutoContent Wizard. Click the text to replace it with the real text that you want to use.

Playback rate The rate in frames per second at which the movie plays.

Playhead The vertical red marker in the Timeline that marks the progress of the animation when it is previewed in the animation program.

Plug-in A program component that loads into a Web browser.

PNG Portable Network Graphic. This format is often used for graphics on the World Wide Web. It can support up to 32-bit color as well as effects, such as transparency. It is the native file format for Macromedia's Fireworks MX graphics program. PNG files, like .gif files, do not lose image quality, but unlike .gif files, PNG files are not restricted to 256 colors. PNG files have the .png extension in their names.

Point A measurement for the height of text. One point is equal to 1/72nd of an inch.

Portrait orientation (tall) The most common page orientation, in which data is printed across the paper's smallest dimension. For example, if you print data in portrait orientation on 8.5-inch by 11-inch paper, the data prints across the 8.5-inch width.

PostScript A page description language used to define the way text and graphics are printed.

PostScript Printer Description file The file that stores the instructions for a PostScript printer.

Presentation design The aspect of Web site design that considers the look and feel of a Web site.

Presentation program A program designed to present information in a slide format for presentation on a computer monitor, television screen, or through a data projector onto a standard AV screen. Such presentations are used in classrooms, at training seminars and conferences, or in booths at trade shows, among other venues.

Primary colors The basic colors from which all other colors can be derived. Specifically, red, blue, and yellow.

Print properties Settings that control the way a file prints.

Printer's spreads Multiple pages laid out for printing on the same sheet so that, when the publication is bound, the pages are in the correct order.

Process color Cyan, magenta, yellow, and black, which are the colors of ink used in four-color printing.

Project file A file created to hold animation or video content.

Proof A printed copy of a publication used for checking the design, spelling, and layout.

Proofreader's marks Symbols written on a proof to inform a printer or editor of changes that should be made.

Properties Each page has certain properties, such as the color of the text, the font, and the background colors.

Proportion A basic principle of design that describes the size and location of an object in relation to other objects in an image.

Publication type An option in some desktop publishing programs that specifies the kind of document you are creating, such as a poster or booklet. Usually, when you select a publication type, the program automatically applies page layout settings designed specifically for that type.

Publish Make a publication available for reading, either in print or on the World Wide Web. Also, save a presentation in Web format so it can be displayed using a Web browser over the Internet/intranet. Also, upload Web site folders and pages from a local site to a Web server to make them available to anyone with a browser.

Q

QuickTime A cross-platform multimedia format that works on both Microsoft Windows and Apple Macintosh systems. One of the two most common formats along with AVI.

R

Radial balance A type of balance in which objects are distributed evenly around a focal point.

Radial gradient A gradient pattern in which the colors blend out from a center point.

Random access structure Web site structure that allows Web site visitors to jump to any page on a Web site. This is a good structure for sites with just a few interrelated pages.

Raster image Bitmap images.

Reader's spreads Multiple pages laid out for printing in consecutive order.

Reference point A point in an object used to identify an axis for rotation, reflection, and other transformations.

Reflect In some programs, the term used to describe the action of flipping or reversing an object.

Relative spaces Spaces that adjust in width only because of the font size, not the alignment or justification of the text.

Rendering video Converting text, transitions, still images, and segments of other video clips into a sequence of video frames.

Resolution The quality or sharpness of an image, usually measured in pixels per inch or pixels per centimeter. Sometimes resolution is written as an equation, such as: vertical dots per inch × horizontal dots per inch.

RGB color wheel RGB is short for red, green, and blue. The RGB color model mimics the way our eyes interpret color, so it is the color model used to display color on computer monitors, televisions, and similar devices. When equal amounts of red, green, and blue are mixed, the result is pure white. Mix equal amounts of any two of these colors to get the secondary colors yellow, cyan, and magenta. The RGB color model is used with documents and images for display on screens or the Web, but it is not appropriate for printed matter because printers use a different color model (CMYK) to blend inks and make colors.

Rolling text Text that scrolls vertically.

Rollover States defining the look or action of a control with relation to mouse actions. The four common rollover states are Up, Over, Down, and Hit.

Root level The root level is the folder where all your Web pages, subfolders, and images are stored. The root level is also the location of your index.html file.

Rotate To pivot an object around its center point.

Rotation handle A handle with a green dot that appears on a drawn object, picture, or clip art image when it's selected. Drag the rotation handle to rotate the object right or left.

Ruler guides Nonprinting gridlines used on a single page of a publication.

Rules Horizontal and vertical lines that print.

S

Sans serif fonts Fonts such as Arial and Helvetica that do not have trailing edges on character strokes. The word "sans" means *without*.

Saturation A measurement of the intensity of color.

Scale To change the size of an object. Also, the size of an object.

Scanner A hardware device used to transfer printed images or text into a computer file.

Scratch area An area outside the edges of a publication where text and graphics may be stored temporarily.

Screen An effect used to change the tint of a color.

Script A program that performs a specific task or carries out a specific action.

Search site A Web site that provides tools for locating other Web sites even if you don't know a specific address.

Secondary colors The colors created by mixing the primary colors. Orange, green, and violet are secondary colors.

Selection handles Small rectangles that are displayed around the edges of the current or selected object. They can usually be used to resize the object.

Separations Printed pages of the layout of each color in a publication.

Separator character The character that follows a number or bullet in a list.

Sepia A brown tint.

Serif fonts Fonts such as Georgia and Times New Roman that have little trailing edges on letters.

Service bureau A shop that specializes in print, photo, or slide processing.

Shadow An effect that creates the illusion of depth and dimension. Drop shadows add shading along two sides of the outer edge of an object. Inner shadows add shading along two inside edges.

Shapes Drawing objects that can be inserted in a document.

Sheet size Paper size.

Signature A group of pages printed on the same sheet of paper.

Sizing handles Small rectangles that are displayed around the edges of the current or selected object. They can usually be used to resize the object.

Skew To slant an object along its horizontal or vertical axis.

Slide A single screen of information within a presentation. A slide may contain text, graphics, charts, tables, and animations. The way the presentation moves from one slide to the next is called *transition*.

Slide master Controls most of the formatting of the slides in a presentation, such as the slide background, graphics, headers, footers, font, colors, and so on.

Smoothing The degree of sharpness allowed along edges in an image.

Source An image or video clip that provides content for the video you are producing. Also, the location from which you copy a file or object.

Spot color A process used primarily in printing in which a color is premixed to a color standard, such as the Pantone Matching System, and is not mixed during the printing process.

Stack Arrange objects in overlapping layers.

Stage In some programs, the term used to describe the drawing area. Also, the part of an animation program window where the content is composed and manipulated.

Standalone player A separate program that can play an animation.

Standoff The distance between an object and the text wrapped around it.

Stock Paper.

Story The text in a text box or article.

Streaming Watching part of a movie or listening to part of an audio file while downloading the rest.

Streaming rate The rate at which a movie or audio file can be downloaded to your computer.

Stroke The line used to draw an object.

Style A collection of saved formatting settings.

Stylus A pen-like device used with a graphics tablet and other touch-sensitive devices, including personal digital assistants.

Subscription Available to those who pay a fee.

Subtractive colors Colors that absorb light. Cyan, magenta, yellow, and black are subtractive colors.

SVCD An enhanced version of the VCD format that allows higher resolution and quality video to be stored on a standard CD.

Swatches Blocks of color displayed on a color palette.

Symbol Elements that may be used several times in an animation, such as buttons or other graphics, sound files, or even fonts. Symbols are stored in the library and manipulated in symbol-editing mode.

Symmetrical balance A type of balance in which a design is the same on both sides of a center axis, either horizontally or vertically.

T

Tab leaders Characters repeated along a line preceding a tab stop.

Table An organized collection of data entered into separate cells that are formed by the columns and rows of the table.

Table of contents A list of all headings in a publication. Usually, the table of contents also includes the page numbers on which the headings are printed.

Tabs Nonprinting characters used to align text at a single point.

Tags HTML commands surrounded by angle brackets <> that instruct a Web browser how to display an HTML document.

Template A file used to create other files. Templates store formatting and page layout settings as well as standard or sample text and graphics.

Terms of Use   See *AUP*.

Text block   An object used to contain lines of text in a graphics file.

Text box   An object used to contain text.

Text editor   An application that creates a simple text document, often used to create Web pages using HTML tags.

Text flow   The direction in which text is read—either left to right or right to left.

Text object   An object containing text that can be manipulated like a drawing object.

Texture   A pattern applied to a fill or stroke to make it look as if color is applied over a textured surface.

Three-point editing   Editing technique in which you mark the in and out point from a source and the in point on the destination.

Thumbnails   Small representations of larger graphic images. In PowerPoint, slides are shown on the Slides tab as very small thumbnails. Larger thumbnails are also used in Slide Sorter view. Clip art images in the Clip Organizer usually appear as thumbnails, as well.

TIFF   Tagged Image File Format. TIFF files are used for storing bitmap images. This format is commonly used in desktop publishing and other multimedia applications.

Tiling   Overlap.

Timeline   The part of the animation program window that organizes and controls an animation's content over time using layers and frames. Also, the window in a video-editing program where source clips, transitions, and audio files are arranged to create the video.

Timeline marker   A marker (like a bookmark) that allows you to quickly find a specific point in your video.

Tint   The brightness of a color.

Title   Text, shapes, logos, artwork, or other information added to video frames to provide additional information.

Title master   Controls the font, colors, graphics, and other formatting that appear on the title slides throughout a presentation.

Toggle   A feature or command that can be turned on or off. Also, the action of turning a feature or command on or off.

Tonal range   The distribution of pixels in a bitmap image.

Toolbox   An onscreen element used to display a collection of tools or buttons. In graphics programs, it usually displays the drawing and editing tools.

Tracking   The spacing between text characters.

Transform   Modify an object by either scaling, distorting, skewing, rotating, or flipping.

Transition   A method of displaying the next slide in a presentation. A transition may be quick, with the next slide simply popping on the screen, or it may be slower, with one slide dissolving into the next. Also, overlapping two animation or movie clips so one appears as the other disappears.

Transparency   A medium used for slides and overhead projectors. Also, the level of opacity of a color.

Trapping   A process used to avoid overlap and gaps between adjacent colors during the printing process.

Trigger   A custom animation option allowing you to coordinate the start of one effect on a slide by clicking another object on the slide.

TrueType fonts   Fonts that reproduce when printed the same as they appear on screen.

Truncate   To shorten or abbreviate.

TWAIN   The software language used by devices such as scanners and some digital cameras. It interprets data so that it can be read by a computer.

Tween   Calculation of an object's path from a specified beginning point to a specified ending point in an animation.

Two-page spread   A left-hand page and a right-hand page that open opposite each other. Also called *facing pages*.

U

Uploading   The process of putting files from a local hard drive on a remote server.

URL (Uniform Resource Locator)   Web address that supplies the complete path to a Web page.

V

Value   A specific definition, often in words or numbers, that defines an attribute. Also, the range from black to white in a hue.

Variety   A term used to describe the use of various elements of design to create visual interest in an image.

VCD   Video CD. A video disc format that uses standard CDs to store video.

Vector   A type of graphic in which the image is created using lines and curves defined by mathematical formulas.

Vector paths   The lines and curves that define a vector graphic.

Vertical alignment   The position of an object in relation to the top and bottom margin.

Video effects   Effects applied to video tracks to enhance the track.

View   The way a file is displayed on screen.

W

Warm color   The colors ranging from red to yellow on the color wheel.

Watermark   An object that is printed in the background. Usually, the brightness and contrast are adjusted so the object appears very faintly.

WAV   A sound file format supported by the Windows operating system. A WAV file records sound as a digitized waveform and is useful for short beeps, chirps, clicks, or voice narration rather than music, although it can be used for music. WAV files provide high-quality sound but can be quite large.

Waveform   Visual display of a sound's volume and frequency.

Web archive   A special format that includes not only a Web page's information, but its supporting files as well.

Web browser   A Web information viewer or interpreter that interprets HTML tags and displays Web pages according to the specified instructions.

Web clients   Software programs that talk to Web servers and display Web pages.

Web pages   Text documents consisting mostly of characters and HTML tags. Web pages may also contain graphics and display sounds or movies.

Web servers   Fast computers that store Web sites and Web pages to be shared with clients.

Web sites   Collections of Web pages in which two or more pages are linked.

Webcasting   Broadcasting a presentation over the Internet.

Web-safe colors   A 216-color palette defined by pairs of hexadecimal numbers, including 00, 33, 66, 99, CC, and FF. Websafe colors appear the same way on different computer systems, which make them suitable for use on Web pages.

Weight   Thickness. Used to measure strokes and lines as well as paper.

Welcome page   The first page someone sees when they visit a Web site.

White space   The blank space between visual elements in an image. It does not have to be white.

Wizard   An automated series of dialog boxes that prompts you through the steps necessary to complete a procedure.

Wrap   To flow text automatically from the end of one line to the beginning of the next. Also, to flow text around objects.

WYSIWYG ("What You See Is What You Get")   View of Web page code in the way it will look online.

Z

Zoom   The action of adjusting the magnification of a file by a percentage of its actual size. Also, the feature used for this purpose.

INDEX